Topical Contents

V. HISTORICISM AND INSTITUTIONALISM

VI. NEOCLASSICISM

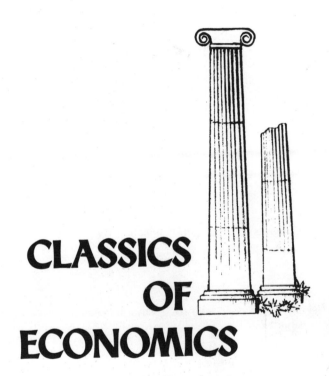

CLASSICS OF ECONOMICS

Edited by CHARLES W. NEEDY,
University of Hawaii

 MOORE PUBLISHING COMPANY, INC.
OAK PARK, ILLINOIS

Library of Congress Cataloging in Publication Data

Main entry under title:

Classics of economics.

    1. Economics—Addresses, essays, lectures.
2. Economics—History—Addresses, essays, lectures.
I. Needy, Charles W.
HB34.C52   330   80-15586
ISBN 0-935610-12-X

Classics of Economics, First Edition

Moore Publishing Company, Inc.
701 South Gunderson Avenue, Oak Park, Illinois 60304

VII. MODERN PERIOD

Chronological Contents

Preface

This book is an introduction to the history of economic thought. While instructors will surely agree that all of the following selections are classics, no one is expected to agree that they are *the* classics. I have attempted to include representative work of the most outstanding economists, but this effort has been somewhat moderated by the necessity of excluding work not commensurate with the abilities of the average student. It is our good fortune that there are classic papers by almost all of the luminaries in the economics profession that are well within the grasp of nonmathematical students.

So the readings will not belie the author's style or train of thought, I have endeavored to minimize deletions (denoted by three ellipsis points). Where this is not so, the repeated appearance of deletion marks can be explained by the author's profuse employment of textual references to excluded material. Accordingly, I have also shunned the too common practice of skipping through a book and picking up the most brilliant bits and pieces—which is to say that many anthologies compare too favorably with balls of string.

At the expense of narrowing the field of coverage, most readings have been chosen to show how the author develops and explains only one—or a few—of his best ideas. Consequently, I have included the famous exposition of the invisible hand by Smith; the principle of population by Malthus; Say's Law by Say; the Law of Comparative Advantage by Ricardo; the riddle of surplus value by Marx; the demand curve by Cournot; the marginal utility theory of value by Jevons, Menger, and Walras; the demand curve by Marshall; Pareto optimality by Pareto; monopolistic competition by Chamberlin; price discrimination by Robinson; the general theory of employment by Keynes; the role of mathematical economics by Samuelson; and monetary policy by Friedman. Of course, this is just a partial list of the many topics included, and many selections contain more than one important concept.

Beginning with mercantilism and ending with the modern period, this book is divided into seven sections, a categorical device which is generally consistent with that employed by standard textbooks in history of economic thought. The reader should note, however, that the division of authors into the "marginalism" and "neoclassicism" categories is highly arbitrary: all neoclassical economists were in some sense marginalists, too. The main purpose of this division is to roughly separate the twentieth century marginalist work from that of the nineteenth century, a design that is complicated by the fact that Marshall's *Principles* was first published in 1890. However, since his book dominated the early decades of the twentieth century, and since Marshall is regarded as not only the founder but also the most outstanding member of the neoclassical school, his work is categorized here under "neoclassicism."

I began and completed this anthology while teaching economics at the University of Hawaii. Although its organization and scope have been most heavily influenced by my classroom experience, the book has greatly benefitted from the comments of James Marsh (University of Hawaii), Ervin Zingler (University of Houston), William Kuhn (University of Nebraska), Jacob Oser, Harry Landreth, and Ingrid Rima (Temple University)—to all of whom I express my gratitude.

Because most of the following excerpts were taken from treatises many hundreds of pages long, every effort has been made to choose selections in a way that will provide students a feel for the original. Although I have only managed to take a slice from each of these great works, it is comforting to know that each slice is a center cut from which readers should at least be able to derive the flavor of the whole work. Accordingly, whereas there will surely be no general agreement as to what should have been excluded from this anthology, both instructors and students should be pleased with what has been included.

CHARLES W. NEEDY

I

Mercantilism and Physiocracy

Introduction. Adam Smith once described his predecessors as belonging to one of two systems of political economy—if the pre-Adamite economists are to be categorized according to their views on national wealth accumulation—which he called the "mercantile system" and the "system of agriculture." Following convention, we now refer to them as "mercantilism" and "physiocracy," respectively. It would be wrong to think of mercantilism as an integrated doctrine that was promoted by a united group of economists. Instead, the term describes diverse—and often conflicting—doctrines that were advocated throughout Europe by businessmen, politicians, and members of the clergy from the end of the 16th to the middle of the 18th centuries. Since most of this literature was written to win support for some particular piece of government legislation, and since the writers possessed no common body of analytical tools, it is not surprising that the "mercantilists" failed to produce a unified doctrine of economic thought.

Nevertheless, in retrospect we are able to identify the most prominent policy recommendations in mercantilist literature: strengthening of domestic industries by encouraging the importation of inexpensive raw materials, discouragement of exports, use of trade restrictions to create an inflow of money, and support of tariffs on imported finished goods. In essence, the mercantilists advocated a long-term favorable balance of trade. They realized that national wealth consists of much more than specie, but they believed that an inflow of specie was necessary to stimulate domestic production, from which wealth is derived. Their desire to promote industrial growth by encouraging international merchandising led Smith to label their doctrine the "mercantile system."

The mercantilist position is succinctly stated in the title of Mun's book, *England's Treasure by Forraign Trade: Or, the Ballance of our Forraign Trade is the Rule of our Treasure.* This work, now regarded the classic of English mercantilism, is actually a collection of papers written around 1630 and published posthumously by Mun's son more than thirty years later. Although its main ideas are not especially original, the book's prominence in mercantilist literature is best explained by its rich analytical detail and

1

the skillful manner in which it was written. Thomas Mun (1571-1641) was born in London, where his father was a wealthy mercer. In 1614 Mun became a member of the board of the East India Company and was quickly appointed to its commission on trade. The reigning economic doctrine of this period was bullionism, which held that a nation's wealth is best represented by the amount of bullion and coin in its possession. The English government was so supportive of this doctrine that it prohibited the exportation of specie and tried to control its merchants' activity in international trade. The East India Company came under strong attack from the bullionists, because it was importing far more than it was exporting to India. Hence, there was an outflow of bullion from England to India to make up the difference. Mun's book is essentially a defensive response to this criticism. In the following excerpt from his book (Chapters 4 through 6), Mun argued persuasively that the East India trade is profitable to England. He stated that imports from India fall into two main categories: (1) goods which are re-exported at considerable profit, leading to a net inflow of bullion, and (2) goods that would be more expensive if purchased elsewhere.

In sharp contrast to the disarrayed mercantilists, the physiocrats were a tightly knit group of men who formed the first school of economics. In fact, they even referred to themselves as the "Economists," a label that was changed to "Physiocrats" in 1768 by Dupont de Nemours. Quesnay was the leader of this group, and his devoted followers interpreted his work undeviatingly with a religious fervor. Whereas this school of economic thought demonstrated an unprecedented internal consistency, its unification was acquired at the cost of rigid adherence to ideas considered ridiculous even in their own day. Nevertheless, the physiocrats were the first group to make a clear distinction between moral philosophy and economics. From them Adam Smith received his notion of circularity in the process of production and distribution and his concept of wealth as a flow of consumable goods. Moreover, Smith regarded their system of thought as the finest that had yet been published in the field of economics, and he was especially pleased with their efforts to lower trade barriers and curtail government intervention in the marketplace.

Physiocracy may be best understood as a reaction to the mercantilist policies of protective trade barriers and favorable treatment of manufacturing industries. To pay for the excesses of the Versailles court, the French government relied most heavily upon a land tax that favored manufacturers at the expense of farmers. The French physiocrats simply wished to emulate England's success with land reform, which led them to advocate a single tax on rent and the removal of mercantilist barriers against the corn trade. With these goals in mind, they argued that only agriculture is capable of yielding a surplus in excess of production costs. Whereas trade and manufacturing are productive, their output is fully offset by factor costs, leaving these non-agricultural sectors barren or "sterile." Although such reasoning appears to confuse physical matter with economic value, the physiocrats were the first group to show that there is a body of economic laws existing independent of government legislation. Consequently, they were the founders of economic science.

François Quesnay (1694-1774), who was the court physician for both Madame de Pompadour and Louis XV, was not an advocate of economic doctrines until in his sixties. His strong influence on France's intellectual class is probably best explained by his reputation as a distinguished physician, his mature age, and his creative bent of mind. The main ideas in Quesnay's *Economic Table* are that money is simply a medium of exchange; that output flows through the economy to become factor income, which initiates another cycle of production and income distribution; and that trade can be reduced to barter. The *Economic Table*, which Quesnay wrote for King Louis XV, was considered in its time to be the finest product of the physiocrats. One of Quesnay's disciples even went so far as to say that mankind's three greatest inventions were money, writing, and the *Economic Table*. While it does graphically demonstrate the interdependence of three economic sectors, the table is in no way a general statement of physiocratic theory. Instead of explaining and defending this theory, Quesnay's work simply assumes it to be true, employing it as a base for his construction. Consequently, his table should be considered an addition to—not a summation of —the physiocratic creed.

After 200 years of debate, historians are only now reaching agreement on the curious history of the *Economic Table*. It appears that Quesnay produced the first "edition" in December 1758. It was probably given to one or a few disciples, but—although it may have been printed—no printed copy has been discovered. The second edition, which is the one most commonly referred to, was likely produced in early 1759. Although Quesnay said that he would have three copies of this edition printed, only two printed copies have been discovered. The third edition seems to have been printed in late 1759. It is believed that Quesnay had more copies made of the third than the second edition, although it is unlikely that any were sold to the public. Only two copies of this third edition are known to exist. It has been described by Dupont (one of the disciples) as "a very fine edition in quarto," and by historians Kuczynski and Meek as "the most comprehensive of the *Tableau* 'editions' which we know to have been worked out by Quesnay alone." Oddly, the third edition was discovered in 1905 but immediately lost. It was not rediscovered until sixty years later and was not made available to the English-speaking world until 1972.

1. England's Treasure by Forraign Trade*

THOMAS MUN

THE EXPORTATION OF OUR MONEYS IN TRADE OF MERCHANDIZE IS A MEANS TO ENCREASE OUR TREASURE

This position is so contrary to the common opinion, that it will require many and strong arguments to prove it before it can be accepted of the Multitude, who bitterly exclaim when they see any monies carried out of the Realm; affirming thereupon that wee have absolutely lost so much Treasure, and that this is an act directly against the long continued laws made and confirmed by the wisdom of this Kingdom in the High Court of Parliament, and that many places, nay *Spain* it self which is the Fountain of Mony, forbids the exportation thereof, some cases only excepted. To all which I might answer, that *Venice, Florence, Genoa*, the *Low Countreys* and divers other places permit it, their people applaud it, and find great benefit by it; but all this makes a noise and proves nothing, we must therefore come to those reasons which concern the business in question.

First, I will take that for granted which no man of judgment will deny, that we have no other means to get Treasure but by forraign trade, for Mines wee have none which do afford it, and how this mony is gotten in the managing of our said Trade I have already shewed, that it is done by making our commodities which are exported yearly to over ballance in value the forraign wares which we consume; so that it resteth only to

shew how our monyes may be added to our commodities, and being jointly exported may so much the more encrease our Treasure.

Wee have already supposed our yearly consumptions of forraign wares to be for the value of twenty hundred thousand pounds, and our exportations to exceed that two hundred thousand pounds, which sum wee have thereupon affirmed is brought to us in treasure to ballance the accompt. But now if we add three hundred thousand pounds more in ready mony unto our former exportations in wares, what profit can we have (will some men say) although by this means we should bring in so much ready mony more than wee did before, seeing that wee have carried out the like value.

To this the answer is, that when wee have prepared our exportations of wares, and sent out as much of every thing as wee can spare or vent abroad: It is not therefore said that then we should add our money thereunto to fetch in the more mony immediately, but rather first to enlarge our trade by enabling us to bring in more forraign wares, which being sent out again will in due time much encrease our Treasure.

For although in this manner wee do yearly multiply our importations to the maintenance of more Shipping and Mariners, improvement of His Majesties Customs and other benefits: yet our consumption of those forraign wares is no more than it was before; so that all

---

Source: Reprinted from the first English edition (London, 1664). The selection reprinted here originally appeared as chapters 4, 5 and 6. Margin notes deleted.

the said encrease of commodities brought in by the means of our ready mony sent out as is afore written, doth in the end become an exportation unto us of a far greater value than our said moneys were, which is proved by three several examples following.

1. For I suppose that 100000.l. being sent in our Shipping to the East Countreys, will buy there one hundred thousand quarters of wheat cleer aboard the Ships, which being after brought into England and housed, to export the same at the best time for vent thereof in Spain or Italy, it cannot yield less in those parts than two hundred thousand pounds to make the Merchant but a saver, yet by this reckning wee see the Kingdom hath doubled that Treasure.

2. Again this profit will be far greater when wee trade thus in remote Countreys, as for example, if wee send one hundred thousand pounds into the East-Indies to buy Pepper there; and bring it hither, and from hence send it for Italy or Turkey, it must yield seven hundred thousand pounds at least in those places, in regard of the excessive charge which the Merchant disburseth in those long voyages in Shipping, Wages, Victuals, Insurance, Interest, Customes, Imposts, and the like, all which notwithstanding the King and the Kingdom gets.

3. But where the voyages are short & the wares rich, which therefore will not employ much Shipping, the profit will be far less. As when another hundred thousand pounds shall be employed in Turkey in raw Silks, and brought hither to be after transported from hence into France, the Low Countreys, or Germany, the Merchant shall have good gain, although he sell it there but for one hundred and fifty thousand pounds: and thus take the voyages altogether in their Medium, the moneys exported will be returned unto us more than Trebled. But if any man will yet object, that these returns come to us in wares, and not really in mony as they were Issued out,

The answer is (keeping our first ground) that if our consumption of forraign wares be no more yearly than is already supposed, and that our exportations be so mightily encreased by this manner of Trading with ready money as is before declared: It is not then possible but that all the over-ballance or difference should return either in mony or in such wares as we must export again, which, as is already plainly shewed will be still a greater means to encrease our Treasure.

For it is in the stock of the Kingdom as in the estates of private men, who having store of wares, doe not therefore say that they will not venture out or trade with their mony (for this were ridiculous) but do also turn that into wares, whereby they multiply their Mony, and so by a continual and orderly change of one into the other grow rich, and when they please turn all their estates into Treasure; for they that have Wares cannot want mony.

Neither is it said that Mony is the Life of Trade, as if it could not subsist without the same; for we know that there was great trading by way of commutation or barter when there was little mony stirring in the world. The Italians and some other Nations have such remedies against this want, that it can neither decay nor hinder their trade, for they transfer bills of debt, and have Banks both publick and private, wherein they do assign their credits from one to another daily for very great sums with ease and satisfaction by writings only, whilst in the mean time the Mass of Treasure which gave foundation to these credits is employed in Forraign

Neither is it said that Mony is the Life of Trade, as if it could not subsist without the same; for we know that there was great trading by way of commutation or barter when there was little mony stirring in the world. The Italians and some other Nations have such remedies against this want, that it can neither decay nor hinder their trade, for they transfer bills of debt, and have Banks both publick and private, wherein they do assign their credits from one to another daily for very great sums with ease and satisfaction by writings only, whilst in the mean time the Mass of Treasure which gave foundation to these credits is employed in Forraign Trade as a Merchandize, and by the said means they have little other use of money in those countreys more than for their ordinary expences. It is not therefore the keeping of our money in the Kingdom, but the necessity and use of our wares in forraign Countries, and our want of their commodities that causeth the vent and consumption on all sides, which makes a quick and ample Trade. If wee were once poor, and now having gained some store of mony by trade with resolution to keep it still in the Realm; shall this cause other Nations to spend more of our commodities than formerly they have done, whereby we might say that our trade is Quickned and Enlarged? no verily, it will produce no such good effect: but rather according to the alteration of times by their true causes wee may expect the contrary; for all men do consent that plenty of mony in Kingdom doth make the native commodities dearer, which as it is to the profit of some private men in their revenues, so is it directly against the benefit of the Publique in the quantity of the trade; for as plenty of mony makes wares dearer, so dear wares decline their use and consumption, as hath been already plainly shewed in the last Chapter upon that particular of our cloth; And although this is a very hard lesson for some great landed men to learn, yet I am sure it is a true lesson for all the land to observe, lest when wee have gained some store of mony by trade, wee lose it again by not trading with our mony. I knew a Prince in *Italy* (of famous memory) *Ferdinando the first*, great Duke of *Tuscanie*, who being very rich in Treasure, endevoured therewith to enlarge his trade by issuing out to his Merchants great sums of money for very small profit; I my self had forty thousand crowns of him *gratis* for a whole year, although he knew that I would presently send it away in *Specie* for the parts of *Turkey* to be employed in wares for his Countries, he being well assured that in this course of trade it

would return again (according to the old saying) with a Duck in the mouth. This noble and industrious Prince by his care and diligence to countenance and favour Merchants in their affairs, did so encrease the practice thereof, that there is scarce a Nobleman or Gentleman in all his dominions that doth not Merchandize either by himself or in partnership with others, whereby within these thirty years the trade to his port of *Leghorn* is so much encreased, that of a poor little town (as I my self knew it) it is now become a fair and strong City, being one of the most famous places for trade in all Christendom. And yet it is worthy our observation, that the multitude of Ships and wares which come thither from *England*, and *Low Countreys*, and other places, have little or no means to make their returns from thence but only in ready mony, which they may and do carry away freely at all times, to the incredible advantage of the said great Duke of *Tuscanie* and his subjects, who are much enriched by the continual great concourse of Merchants from all the States of the neighbour Princes, bringing them plenty of mony daily to supply their wants of the said wares. And thus we see that the current of Merchandize which carries away their Treasure, becomes a flowing stream to fill them again in a greater measure with mony.

There is yet an objection or two as weak as all the rest: that is, if wee trade with our Mony wee shall issue out the less wares; as if a man should say, those Countreys which heretofore had occasion to consume our Cloth, Lead, Tin, Iron, Fish, and the like, shall now make use of our monies in the place of those necessaries, which were most absurd to affirm, or that the Merchant had not rather carry out wares by which there is ever some gains expected, than to export mony which is still but the same without any encrease.

But on the contrary there are many Countreys which may yield us very profitable trade for our mony, which otherwise afford us no trade at all, because they have no use of our wares, as namely the *East-Indies* for one in the first beginning thereof, although since by industry in our commerce with those Nations we have brought them into the use of much of our Lead, Cloth, Tin, and other things, which is a good addition to the former vent of our commodities.

Again, some men have alleged that those Countries which permit mony to be carried out, do it because they have few or no wares to trade withall: but wee have great store of commodities, and therefore their action ought not to be our example.

To this the answer is briefly, that if we have such a quantity of wares as doth fully provide us of all things needful from beyond the seas: why should we then doubt that our monys sent out in trade, must not necessarily come back again in treasure; together with the great gains which it may procure in such manner as is before set down? And on the other side, if those Nations which send out their monies do it because they have but few wares of their own, how come they then to have so much Treasure as we ever see in those places which suffer it freely to be exported at all times and by whomsoever? I answer, *Even by trading with their Moneys*; for by what other means can they get it, having no Mines of Gold or Silver?

Thus may we plainly see, that when this weighty business is duly considered in his end, as all our humane actions ought well to be weighed, it is found much contrary to that which most men esteem thereof, because they search no further than the beginning of the work, which mis-informs their judgments, and leads them into error: For if we only behold the actions of the husbandman in the seed-time when he casteth away much good corn into the ground, we will rather accompt him a mad man than a husbandman: but when we consider his labours in the harvest which is the end of his endeavours, we find the worth and plentiful encrease of his actions.

FORRAIGN TRADE IS THE ONLY MEANS TO IMPROVE THE PRICE OF OUR LANDS

It is a common saying, that plenty or scarcity of mony makes all things dear or good or cheap; and this mony is either gotten or lost in forraign trade by the over or underballancing of the same, as I have already shewed. It resteth now that I distinguish the seeming plenties of mony from that which is only substantial and able to perform the work: For there are divers ways and means whereby to procure plenty of mony into a Kingdom, which do not enrich but rather empoverish the same by the several inconveniences which ever accompany such alterations.

As first, if we melt down our plate into Coyn (which suits not with the Majesty of so great a Kingdom, except in cases of great extremity) it would cause Plenty of mony for a time, yet should we be nothing the richer, but rather this treasure being thus altered is made the more apt to be carried out of the Kingdom, if we exceed our means by excess in forraign wares, or maintain a war by Sea or Land, where we do not feed and cloath the Souldier and supply the armies with our own native provisions, by which disorders our treasure will soon be exhausted.

Again, if we think to bring in store of money by suffering forraign Coins to pass current at higher rates than their intrinsick value compared with our Standard, or by debasing or by enhancing our own moneys, all these have their several inconveniences and difficulties, (which hereafter I will declare) but admitting that by this means plenty of money might be brought into the Realm, yet should we be nothing the richer, neither can such treasure so gotten long remain with us. For if the stranger or the English Merchants bring in this money, it must be done upon a valuable consideration, either for wares carried out already, or after to be exported, which helps us nothing except the evil occasions of excess or war aforenamed be removed which do exhaust our treasure: for otherwise, what one man bringeth for gain, another man shall be forced to carry out for necessity; because there shall ever be a necessity to ballance our Accounts with strangers, although it should be done with loss upon the rate of the money, and Confiscation also if it be intercepted by the Law.

The conclusion of this business is briefly thus. That as the treasure which is brought into the Realm by the ballance of our forraign trade is that money which onely doth abide with us, and by which we are enriched: so by this plenty of money thus gotten (and no otherwise) do our Lands improve. For when the Merchant hath a good dispatch beyond the Seas for his Cloth and other wares, he doth presently return to buy up the greater quantity, which raiseth the price of our Woolls and other commodities, and consequently doth improve the Landlords Rents as the Leases expire daily: And also by this means money being gained, and brought more abundantly into the Kingdom, it doth enable many men to buy Lands, which will make them the dearer. But if our forraign trade come to a stop or declination by neglect at home or injuries abroad, whereby the Merchants are impoverished, and thereby the wares of the Realm less issued, then do all the said benefits cease, and our Lands fall of price daily.

THE SPANISH TREASURE CANNOT BE KEPT FROM OTHER KINGDOMS BY ANY PROHIBITION MADE IN SPAIN

All the Mines of Gold and Silver which are as yet discovered in the sundry places of the world, are not of so great value as those of the West-Indies which are in the possession of the King of Spain: who thereby is enabled not onely to keep in subjection many goodly States and Provinces in Italy and elsewhere, (which otherwise would soon fall from his obeisance) but also by a continual war taking his advantages doth still enlarge his Dominions, ambitiously aiming at a Monarchy by the power of his Moneys, which are the very sinews of his strength, that lies so far dispersed into so many Countreys, yet hereby united, and his wants supplied both for war and peace in a plentiful manner from all the parts of Christendom, which are therefore partakers of his treasure by a Necessity of Commerce; wherein the Spanish policy hath ever endeavoured to prevent all other Nations the most it could: For finding Spain to be too poor and barren to supply it self and the West-Indies with those varieties of forraign wares whereof they stand in need, they knew well that when their Native Commodities come short to this purpose, their Moneys must serve to make up the reckoning; whereupon they found an incredible advantage to adde the traffick of the East-Indies to the treasure of the West: for the last of these being employed in the first, they stored themselves infinitely with rich wares to barter with all the parts of Christendom for their Commodities, and so furnishing their own necessities, prevented others for carrying away their moneys: which in point of state they hold less dangerous to impart to the remote Indians, than to their neighbour Princes, lest it should too much enable them to resist (if not offend) their enemies. And this Spanish policy against others is the more remarkable, being done likewise so much to their own advantage; for every Ryal of Eight which they sent to the East-Indies brought home so much wares as saved them the disbursing of five Ryals of Eight here in Europe (at the least) to their Neighbours, especially in those times when that trade was only in their hands: but now this great profit is failed, and the mischief removed by the English, Dutch, and others which partake in those *East-India* trades as ample as the Spanish Subjects.

It is further to be considered, that besides the disability of the *Spaniards* by their native commodities to provide forraign wares for their necessities, (whereby they are forced to supply the want with mony) they have likewise that canker of war, which doth infinitely exhaust their treasure, and disperse it into Christendom even to their enemies, part by reprisal, but especially through a necessary maintenance of those armies which are composed of strangers, and lie so far remote, that they cannot feed, clothe, or otherwise provide them out of their own native means and provisions, but must receive this relief from other Nations: which kind of war is far different to that which a Prince maketh upon his own confines, or in his Navies by Sea, where the Souldier receiving money for his wages, must every day deliver it out again for his necessities, whereby the treasure remains still in the Kingdom, although it be exhausted from the King: But we see that the *Spaniard* (trusting in the power of his Treasure) undertakes wars in *Germany*, and in other remote places, which would soon begger the richest Kingdom in Christendom of all their mony; the want whereof would presently disorder and bring the armies to confusion, as it falleth out sometimes with *Spain* it self, who have the Fountain of mony, when either it is stopt in the passage by the force of their enemies, or drawn out faster than it flows by their own occasions; whereby also we often see that Gold and silver is so scant in *Spain*, that they are forced to use base copper money, to the great confusion of their Trade, and not without the undoing also of many of their own people.

But now that we have seen the occasions by which the Spanish treasure is dispersed into so many places of the world, let us likewise discover how and in what proportion each Countrey doth enjoy these Moneys, for we find that *Turkey* and divers other Nations have great plenty thereof, although they drive no trade with *Spain*, which seems to contradict the former reason, where we say that this treasure is obtained by a Necessity of Commerce. But to clear this point, we must know that all Nations (who have no Mines of their own) are enriched with Gold and Silver by one and the same means, which is already shewed to be the ballance of their forraign Trade: And this is not strictly tyed to be done in those Countries where the fountain of treasure is, but rather with such order and observations as are prescribed. For suppose *England* by trade with *Spain* may gain and bring home five hundred thousand Ryals of 8. yearly, if we lose as much by our trade in *Turkey*, and therefore carry the mony thither, it is not then the *English*, but the *Turks* which have got this treasure, although they have no trade with *Spain* from whence it was first brought. Again, if *England* having thus lost with *Turkey*, do notwithstanding gain twice as much by *France, Italy*, and other members of her general trade, then will there remain five hundred thousand Ryals of Eight cleer gains by the ballance of this trade: and this comparison holds between all other Nations, both for the manner of getting, and the proportion that is yearly gotten.

But if yet a question should be made, whether all Nations get treasure and Spain only lose it? I answer no; for some Countreys by war or by excess do lose that which they had gotten, as well as Spain by war and want of wares doth lose that which was its own.

2. Economic Table*

FRANÇOIS QUESNAY

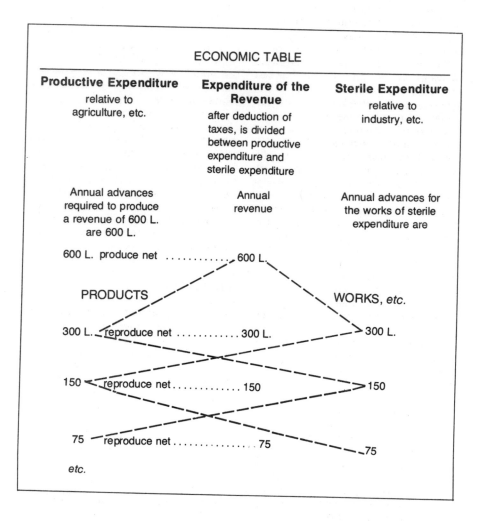

ECONOMIC TABLE

Productive Expenditure relative to agriculture, etc.	Expenditure of the Revenue after deduction of taxes, is divided between productive expenditure and sterile expenditure	Sterile Expenditure relative to industry, etc.
Annual advances required to produce a revenue of 600 L. are 600 L.	Annual revenue	Annual advances for the works of sterile expenditure are

600 L. produce net .... 600 L.

PRODUCTS   WORKS, *etc.*

300 L. reproduce net .... 300 L. → 300 L.

150 reproduce net .... 150 → 150

75 reproduce net .... 75 → 75

etc.

Source: Reprinted by permission of the publishers from *Quesnay's Tableau Économique,* edited by Marguerite Kuczynski and Ronald L. Meek (New York: Augustus M. Kelley, 1972). Copyright © 1972 Royal Economic Society. All footnotes deleted and the table, itself, shortened.

EXPLANATION OF THE *TABLEAU ÉCONOMIQUE*

Productive expenditure is employed in agriculture, grasslands, pastures, forests, mines, fishing, etc., in order to perpetuate wealth in the form of corn, drink, wood, livestock, raw materials for manufactured goods, etc.

Sterile expenditure is on manufactured commodities, house-room, clothing, interest on money, servants, commercial costs, foreign produce, etc.

The sale of the net product which the cultivator has generated in the previous year, by means of the *annual advances* of 600 livres employed in cultivation by the farmer, results in the payment to the proprietor of a *revenue* of 600 livres.

The *annual advances* of the sterile expenditure class, amounting to 300 livres, are employed for the capital and costs of trade, for the purchase of raw materials for manufactured goods, and for the subsistence and other needs of the artisan until he has completed and sold his work.

Of the *600 livres of revenue*, one-half is spent by the proprietor in purchasing bread, wine, meat, etc., from the productive expenditure class, and the other half in purchasing clothing, furnishings, utensils, etc., from the sterile expenditure class.

This expenditure may go more or less to one side or the other, according as the man who engages in it goes in more or less for luxury in the way of subsistence or for luxury in the way of ornamentation. We assume here a medium situation in which the reproductive expenditure renews the same revenue from year to year. But it is easy to estimate the changes which would take place in the annual reproduction of revenue, according as sterile expenditure or productive expenditure preponderated to a greater or lesser degree. It is easy to estimate them, I say, simply from the changes which would occur in the order of the *tableau*. Suppose, for example, that luxury in the way of or-

namentation increased by one-sixth in the case of the proprietor, by one-sixth in the case of the artisan, and by one-sixth in the case of the cultivator. Then the revenue reproduced, which is now 600 livres, would be reduced to 500 livres. Suppose, on the other hand, that an increase of the same degree took place in expenditure on the consumption or export of raw produce. Then the revenue reproduced would increase from 600 to 700 livres, and so on in progression. Thus it can be seen that an opulent nation which indulges in excessive luxury in the way of ornamentation can very quickly be overwhelmed by its sumptuousness.

The 300 livres of revenue which according to the order of the *tableau* have passed into the hands of the class of productive expenditure, return to this class its *advances* in the form of money. These advances reproduce 300 livres net, which represents the reproduction of part of the proprietor's revenue; and it is by means of the remainder of the distribution of the sums of money which are returned to this same class that the total revenue is reproduced each year. These 300 livres, I say, which are returned at the beginning of the process to the productive expenditure class, by means of the sale of the products which the proprietor buys from it, are spent by the farmer, one-half in the consumption of products provided by this class itself, and the other half in keeping itself in clothing, utensils, implements, etc., for which it makes payment to the sterile expenditure class. And the 300 livres are regenerated with the net product.

The 300 livres of the proprietor's revenue which have passed into the hands of the sterile expenditure class are spent by the artisan, as to one-half, in the purchase of products for his subsistence, for raw materials for his work, and for foreign trade, from the productive expenditure class; and the other half is distributed among the sterile expenditure class itself for its maintenance and for the restitution of its *advances*. This circulation and mutual distribution are continued in the same way by means of subdivisions down to the last penny of the sums of money which mutually pass from the hands of one expenditure class into those of the other.

Circulation brings 600 livres to the sterile expenditure class, from which 300 livres have to be kept back for the *annual advances*, which leaves 300 livres for wages. These wages are equal to the 300 livres which this class receives from the productive expenditure class, and the advances are equal to the 300 livres of revenue which pass into the hands of this same sterile expenditure class.

The products of the other class amount to 1200 livres, abstracting from taxes, tithes, and interest on the husbandman's advances, which will be considered separately in order not to complicate the order of expenditure too much. The 1200 livres' worth of product are disposed of as follows: The proprietor of the revenue buys 300 livres' worth of them. 300 livres' worth passes into the hands of the sterile expenditure class, of which one-half, amounting to 150 livres, is consumed for subsistence within this class, and the other half, amounting to 150 livres, is taken for external trade, which is included in this same class. Finally, 300 livres' worth are consumed within the productive expenditure class by the men who cause them to be generated; and 300 livres' worth are used for the feeding and maintenance of livestock. Thus of the 1200 livres' worth of product, 600 are consumed by this class, and its *advances* of 600 livres are returned to it in the form of money through the sales which it makes to the proprietor and to the sterile expenditure class. One-eighth of the total of this product enters into external trade, either as exports or as raw materials and subsistence for the country's workers who sell their goods to other nations. The sales of the merchant counterbalance the purchases of the commodities and

bullion which are obtained from abroad.

Such is the order of the distribution and consumption of raw produce as between the different classes of citizens; and such is the view which we ought to take of the use and extent of external trade in a flourishing agricultural nation.

Mutual sales from one expenditure class to the other distribute the revenue of 600 livres to both sides, giving 300 livres to each, in addition to the advances which are maintained intact. The proprietor subsists by means of the 600 livres which he spends. The 300 livres distributed to each expenditure class, together with the product of the taxes, the tithes, etc., which is added to them, can support one man in each: thus 600 livres of revenue together with the appurtenant sums can enable three heads of families to subsist. On this basis 600 millions of revenue can enable three million families to subsist, estimated at four persons of all ages per family.

The costs provided for by the *annual advances* of the productive expenditure class, which are also regenerated each year, and of which one-half is spent on the feeding of livestock and the other half in paying wages to the men engaged in the work carried on by this class, add 300 millions of expenditure to the total; and this, together with the share of the other products which are added to them, can enable another one million heads of families to subsist.

Thus these 900 millions, which, abstracting from taxes, tithes, and interest on the annual advances and original advances of the husbandman, would be annually regenerated from landed property, could enable 16 million people of all ages to subsist according to this order of circulation and distribution of the annual revenue.

By circulation is here meant the purchases at first hand, paid for by the revenue which is shared out among all classes of men, abstracting from trade, which multiplies sales and purchases without multiplying things, and which represents nothing but an addition to sterile expenditure.

The *wealth of the productive expenditure class*, in a nation where the proprietors of land regularly receive a revenue of 600 millions, can be worked out as follows:

A revenue of 600 millions for the proprietors presupposes an extra 300 millions for taxes; and 150 millions for tithes on the annual product, all charges included, which are levied on the tithable branches of cultivation. This makes a total of 1050 millions, including the revenue. Add to these the reproduction of 1050 millions of annual advances, and 110 millions of interest on these advances at 10 per cent, and the grand total becomes . . . 2,210,000,000 livres.

In a kingdom with many vineyards, forests, meadows, etc., only about two-thirds of these 2210 millions would be obtained by means of ploughing. Assuming a satisfactory state of affairs in which large-scale cultivation was being carried on with the aid of horses, this portion would require the employment of 333,334 ploughs at 120 *arpents* of land per plough; 333,334 men to drive them; and 40 million *arpents* of land.

With advances amounting to five or six milliards, it would be possible for this type of cultivation to be extended in France to more than 60 million *arpents*.

We are not speaking here of small-scale cultivation carried on with the aid of oxen, in which more than a million ploughs and about two million men would be required to work 40 million *arpents* of land, and which would bring in only two-fifths of the product yielded by large-scale cultivation. This small-scale cultivation, to which cultivators are reduced owing to their lack of the wealth necessary to make the original advances, and in which the land is largely employed merely to cover the costs, is carried on at the expense of landed property itself, and involves an excessive annual expenditure for the subsistence of the great numbers of men

engaged in this type of cultivation, which absorbs almost the whole of the product. This thankless type of cultivation, which reveals the poverty and ruin of those nations in which it predominates, has no connection with the order of the *tableau*, which is worked out on the basis of half the employment of a plough of land, where the annual advances are able, with the aid of the fund of original advances, to produce 100 per cent.

The full total of the original advances required for putting a plough of land under large-scale cultivation, for the first fund of expenditure on livestock, implements, seed, food, upkeep, wages, etc., in the course of two years' labour prior to the first harvest, is estimated at 10,000 livres. Thus the total for 333,334 ploughs is 3,333,340,000 livres. . . .

The interest on these advances ought to amount to 10 per cent at least, since the products of agriculture are subject to disastrous accidents which, over a period of ten years, destroy at least the value of one year's harvest. Moreover, these advances require a great deal of upkeep and renewal. Thus the total interest on the original advances required for setting up the husbandmen is . . . 333,322,000 livres.

Meadows, vineyards, ponds, forests, etc., do not require very great original advances on the part of the farmers. The value of these advances, including in them the original expenditure on plantations and other work carried out at the expense of the proprietors, can be reduced to 1,000,000,000 livres.

But vineyards and gardens require large annual advances which, taken together with those of the other branches, may on the average be included in the total of annual advances set out above.

The total annual reproduction of net product, of annual advances with the interest thereon, and of interest on the original advances, worked out in accordance with the order of the tableau, *is* . . . 2,543,322,000 livres.

The territory of France, given advances and markets, could produce as much as this and even a great deal more.

Of this sum of 2,543,322,000 livres, 525 millions constitutes that half of the reproduction of the annual advances which is employed in feeding livestock. There remains (if the whole of the taxes go back into circulation, and if they do not encroach upon the advances of the husbandmen) . . . 2,018,322,000 livres.

That makes **for men's expenditure,** *504,580,500 livres on the average for each million heads of families, or 562 livres for each individual head of family, which accidents reduce to about 530 livres.* On this basis a state is strong in taxable capacity and resources, and its people live in easy circumstances. . . .

We are speaking here of an opulent nation with a territory and advances which yield it annually and without any abatement a net product of 1050 millions. But all these items of wealth, which are successively maintained by this annual product, may be destroyed or lose their value if an agricultural nation falls into a state of decline, simply through the wasting away of the advances required for productive expenditure. This wasting away can make considerable headway in a short time for eight principal reasons:

1. A bad system of tax-assessment, which encroaches upon the cultivators' advances. *Noli me tangere*—that is the motto for these advances.

2. An extra burden of taxation due to the costs of collection.

3. An excess of luxury in the way of ornamentation.

4. Excessive expenditure on litigation.

5. A lack of external trade in the products of landed property.

6. A lack of freedom of internal trade in raw produce, and in cultivation.

7. The personal harassment of the inhabitants of the countryside.

8. Failure of the annual net product to return to the productive expenditure class.

II

Classicism

Introduction. The classical tradition was launched in 1776 by Adam Smith (1723-1790), an academician who spent most of his life in Scotland. Smith studied three years at the University of Glasgow, which he had entered at the young age of fourteen. He won a scholarship to attend the university at Oxford, where he spent the next six years. Smith then accepted an offer to become a lecturer on English literature and political economy at Edinburgh University, where he remained for only a short time. His alma mater in Glasgow offered him a professorship in logic and—within the year—a chair in moral philosophy. The latter position was one of the most prestigious positions at the university, where he worked intensely for thirteen years. In 1759 Smith published the *Theory of Moral Sentiments*, a book on ethics that attracted public attention and spread his reputation as a philosopher. This led in turn to his being invited to tutor the Duke of Buccleuch, an aristocratic youth from Scotland. It was during this boring—though very lucrative—two and one-half years with the duke that Smith began writing his magnum opus, *Wealth of Nations*.

Surprisingly, his *Theory of Moral Sentiments* was much more highly regarded by contemporary opinion than his second book, the full title for which is *An Inquiry into the Nature and Causes of the Wealth of Nations*. Even so, *Wealth of Nations* had forceful impact on public opinion in Smith's day and is now regarded by many as the greatest work in the field of economics. It raised issues which dominated economic thought for the next seventy-five years and which remain highly relevant even to this day.

Wealth of Nations has arrived at the fate of most classics, being much talked about and little read. No doubt students are intimidated by its sheer bulk, which runs to well over 700 pages and far exceeds the combined length of all readings in this text. Obviously, whereas the following excerpts are highlights in Smith's book, they are only representative of a work that is vast in scope. The three selections are taken from the fifth edition, which was the last published before Smith's death. The first excerpt is the book's three-page introduction, chosen because it concisely states the manner in which Smith breaks with the economic doctrines that had preceded him. Whereas the real source of a nation's wealth had been thought by the bullionists to be gold, by the mercantilists to be manufacturing, and by the physiocrats to be agriculture, Adam Smith identifies the source to be annual labor. Hence, the very first sentence of his book contends that "the annual labour of every nation is the fund which originally supplies it with all the necessaries and conveniencies of life. . . ."

The second excerpt is book 1, chapter 10, part 1, which economic historian Mark Blaug has judged to be "perhaps the best single piece of economic analysis in the Wealth of Nations. . . ." Although it is titled "Inequalities Arising from the Nature of the Employments Themselves," Smith was not simply concerned with explaining inequalities. He also explained that, although competition cannot be expected to equalize wages, it does tend to equalize the sum of pecuniary and nonpecuniary advantages enjoyed by different workers in various occupations. Accordingly, Smith argued that in a competitive market a relatively high wage must be paid to offset one or more of five factors: (1) the work is very unpleasant, (2) the needed skill is very difficult or expensive to acquire, (3) the job is seasonal or in some other way unreliable, (4) the job is risky since the worker must win and sustain the trust of his employer, and (5) the work is risky due to the improbability of success.

The thread that ties Wealth of Nations together is the concept of the "invisible hand," the book's major theme. Its description occurs in book 4, chapter 2, which is reprinted below. Here we find the famous statement that when an individual favors domestic products over foreign imports "he intends only his own gain, and he is in this, as in many other cases, led by an invisible hand to promote an end which was no part of his intention." Also appearing in this section—and equally famous—is Smith's declaration that "what is prudence in the conduct of every private family, can scarce be folly in that of a great kingdom. If a foreign country can supply us with a commodity cheaper than we ourselves can make it, better buy it of them. . . ." It is in this short chapter that the world is first clearly told that the pricing mechanism in a competitive environment will tend to harmonize the interests of individuals with those of society as a whole.

Smith's Wealth of Nations made a strong impression on Thomas Robert Malthus (1766-1834), who was outstanding as a student of theology and mathematics at Cambridge and distinguished as a parish minister for the Church of England. Malthus wrote much in the field of economics, and his publications include "Observations on the Effects of the Corn Laws" (1814), "Nature and Progress of Rent" (1815), and "Measure of Value" (1823). His Principles of Political Economy Considered with a View to Their Practical Applications (1820) is considered by many today to be as good as—if not better than—the work of David Ricardo. Even so, students of economics still associate Malthus with his very first publication, a thin booklet that appeared anonymously in 1798. Although its exact title is An

Essay on the Principles of Population as It Affects the Future Improvement of Society, with Remarks on the Speculations of Mr. Godwin, M. Condorcet and Other Writers, it is understandable that scholars simply refer to it as the *Essay on Population*. This pamphlet was such a bombshell in the literary world that Malthus was forced to identify himself as author. Moreover, he produced a revised, second edition in 1803 that was four times as long as the first. Before Malthus's death, the booklet appeared in four more editions, although they are little different from the second. The work appearing below is extracted from the eighth edition.

As is suggested in its full title, Malthus's *Essay* is a reaction to the idealistic, utopian visions of Godwin and Condorcet. These two philosophers had predicted that mankind would eventually attain a state of perfection and immortality. They had argued that this would be made possible by man's further development of his intellectual ability. Finding their arguments unrealistic, Malthus argued extensively on the subject with his father, who was so impressed with his son's ideas that he persuaded him to put them on paper. The resulting *Essay* was so successful that, of course, it drew much criticism. This prompted Malthus to leave England to find empirical support for his ideas on the Continent. This empirical research, along with the more carefully structured arguments, are the basis of the second edition. The central theme is that world population must ultimately outstrip the world food supply, since population increases at a geometrical rate (*i.e.*, 2, 4, 8, 16) whereas food increases at an arithmetical rate (*i.e.*, 2, 3, 4, 5). The population explosion is retarded by positive checks, which increase the death rate, and by preventative checks, which reduce the birth rate. In his second edition, Malthus added "moral restraint" as one of the preventative checks. By "moral restraint" he meant continence before marriage in combination with the delay of marriage. Unfortunately, this addition made his theory untestable: critics who identified a country that displayed a rising living standard were still unable to refute the theory, since Malthus could counter that they had simply found evidence of moral restraint. Quite understandably, readers who were shocked by Malthus's *Essay* found little comfort in the fact that his theory was untestable or that the world population had never grown at anything near the maximum biological rate.

The *Essay* is generally credited for implying the Law of Diminishing Returns. If this law is actually implied by Malthus—and not simply inferred by his readers—the implication is not made without confusion. Within the context of the *Essay*, this law would require Malthus to show diminishing returns to the variable input (*i.e.*, labor) given a fixed input (*i.e.*, land) and a fixed technology. However, Malthus did not hold technology constant, arguing instead that it will advance, but at a rate insufficient to offset the population growth. Although it is feasible that diminishing returns could occur with investment in technology, it is not inevitable and it is not related to the static Law of Diminishing Returns. The confusion on this issue will be apparent in the following excerpts. Sections 1 and 2 of part 1 are reproduced completely, since they present the entire Malthusian theory. In addition, excerpts have been taken from section 1 of part 2, which discusses society's responsibility in practicing moral restraint. Despite its weaknesses, Malthus's *Essay* is one of the best known classics in any field. Probably the greatest testimonial to its importance are the acknowledgements by Charles Darwin and Alfred Wallace, the co-discoverers of the theory of evolution, of their indebtedness to Malthus.

One of Malthus's contemporaries on the Continent was Jean-Baptiste Say (1767-1832), whose Protestant family had been exiled from France until their return to that country in the middle of the eighteenth century. Say was so impressed by Smith's *Wealth of Nations*, which had been available in a French edition as early as 1779, that he undertook the task of systematizing Smith's work. This resulted in his finest work, *A treatise on Political Economy* (1803), which organizes economics into the classic categories of production, distribution, and consumption. This division was subsequently adopted as a convenient format by textbook writers for many decades. Moreover, his *Treatise* is still highly regarded for its introduction of badly needed definitions (i.e., "entrepreneur") into the literature. Clearly written and tightly organized, it became the first popular economics book that was published on the European continent. Although the book was translated into several languages, the major foreign demand for it was in the United States, where the American edition was used as a textbook throughout the first half of the nineteenth century.

Say lived through the turbulent times of the Napoleonic era, two French revolutions, and the Restoration of the Bourbons. At various times he served his country as a journalist, soldier, politician, businessman, professor of economics, and writer. Say even served briefly on the Tribunate with Napolean's government. He was forced to resign from this position when his *Treatise* appeared in 1803, since his book—shamefully liberal for the times—disagreed with government policy on many important issues. At this time he became a cotton-spinning manufacturer, and he remained in this profession until he was employed as a college professor ten years later. In his last few years, Say founded the French classical school, a liberal and optimistic group that was highly influential throughout most of the nineteenth century. He is best remembered today, of course, for Say's Law, which asserts that general overproduction is impossible, because "supply creates its own demand." His finest exposition of this concept occurs in chapter 15, reprinted here. This chapter demonstrates Say's intent to avoid the fallacy of composition: that what is true of the part must be true for the whole. Although an excess production of one good may occur (relative to all other goods), Say argued that all goods together cannot be produced in relative excess.

About 1811 Malthus began his correspondence with David Ricardo (1772-1823), an Englishman who was already an eminent scholar (although never an academician). In his youth, Ricardo had been disowned by his father when he abandoned the Jewish faith, embraced Christianity, and married a Quaker. Although he was only twenty-one at the time, Ricardo prospered on his own, accumulating a substantial fortune on the stock exchange before his twenty-fifth birthday. This wealth enabled him to devote considerable time to pursuing scientific interests, and when he was twenty-seven he became captivated by Smith's *Wealth of Nations*. Approximately ten years later he produced his first publication, "The High Price of Bullion, a Proof of the Depreciation of Bank Notes," which received much attention in the London newspapers. During the Napoleonic wars, Ricardo was a financier for the British government. When only forty-two, he retired from the business community altogether to work full-time on his book, *Principles of Political Economy and Taxation*. His rough draft of this work was published three years later, in 1817, but Ricardo's reputation as the finest economist of his day had been established before the book's release. Whereas Say had founded the French classical school, Ricardo founded the English classical school. Ricardo agreed to publish his unfinished manuscript, because friends urged him to get it into print. It may also be true, of course, that he simply got tired of looking at the unfinished draft. In any event, he passed up opportunities to systematize the book in its second and third editions, which came out before his death in 1823.

Of all the classic treatises in the field of economics, the most difficult to read is probably Ricardo's *Principles*. There are two main reasons for this obscurity: First, the book is so ill organized that many paragraphs actually appear to be misplaced—and very probably are. Lacking Say's gift with the written word, the brilliant but modest Ricardo was graceless both as a speaker and a writer. He found it so painful to put his thoughts on paper that, in 1816, he wrote Malthus, ". . . I find the greatest difficulty to avoid confusion in the most simple of my statements." Second, the book is a masterpiece of abstraction, which has led more than one historian to label Ricardo the "Newton of economics." As a pioneer in the use of abstract theoretical models, Ricardo—more than anyone else—is responsible for economists having to bear the label, "armchair philosophers."

The first edition of Ricardo's *Principles* totalled 750 copies, and that small volume took several months to print (at the rate of one sheet a day). Chapter 7 of the *Principles* has been chosen for this collection, because it contains Ricardo's most longlasting contribution to economics—the Law of Comparative Advantage. It is in this section, one of the more readable chapters in the treatise, that Ricardo persuasively argues the merits of unrestricted international trade. He also explains how international payments are self-balancing under a system of free exchange rates and how wage rates and prices are self-adjusting under a system of exchange that is tied to a gold standard. It should also be noted that chapter 7 displays Ricardo's brilliant use of comparative statistics, a characteristic of the entire book.

In 1848 the synthesis of Smith's *Wealth of Nations* with the work of Malthus, Ricardo, and Senior was accomplished in John Stuart Mill's *Principles of Political Economy*. In the same way that Say's *Treatise* had served as the world's economics textbook for the first half of the nineteenth century, Mill's *Principles* was the authoritative text during the last half of that century. It lost part of the market to Jevon's *Principles* in 1871 and was eventually displaced at the turn of the century by Marshall's *Principles* (which will be discussed later under the heading "Neoclassicism"). John Stuart Mill (1806-1873) was the son of James Mill, an economist of some renown who personally provided his son with an intensive education beginning at a very early age. The younger Mill studied Greek when he was three and was reading extensively in Greek and Latin—as well as solving algebra and geometry problems—by the age of ten. When he was only thirteen, at the request of his father, he made a comparative analysis of the works of Smith and Ricardo. This precocious youngster began contributing articles to newspapers at the age of sixteen and then continued to be a prolific writer throughout his entire life.

Mill achieved fame in his thirty-seventh year with the publication of his brilliant book, *System of Logic*, which is today regarded a classic in its field. Because of the success of this book, it was easy for him to find a publisher for his *Essays on Some Unsettled Questions of Political Economy* the next year, 1844. (Before the release of *System of Logic*, his *Essays* had been rejected by the publishers.) The year 1848 marked the appearance of Mill's *Principles of Political Economy*, which—at over 1,000 pages—was even longer than Smith's *Wealth of Nations*. One can begin to appreciate Mill's intellectual force and energy by noting that he wrote this enormous book in only a year and a half—during free time away from his full-time job! His *Principles* covered as wide an area as Smith's *Wealth of Nations*, exhibited a clear writing style comparable to that in Say's *Treatise*, and primarily reflected the economic doctrines of Ricardo's *Principles*.

The work by Ricardo and Mill that has stood up the best over time and which is most easily recognized in the guise of modern terminology is undoubtedly the theory of international trade. To Ricardo's Law of Comparative Advantage, Mill added the Equation of International Demand; both of these concepts were later encompassed by the Hecksher-Ohlin theory, which explains trade on the basis of a nation's relative factor endowments. Mill reviewed the theory of comparative advantage in chapter

17 of his *Principles*. He introduced his theory of reciprocal demand and the Equation of International Demand in chapter 18, titled "Of International Values," most of which is excerpted here. The reader should compare this selection with that from Ricardo to see how Mill has extended the Ricardian analysis of international trade.

3. An Inquiry into the Nature and Causes of the Wealth of Nations*

ADAM SMITH

INTRODUCTION AND PLAN OF THE WORK

The annual labour of every nation is the fund which originally supplies it with all the necessaries and conveniencies of life which it annually consumes, and which consist always either in the immediate produce of that labour, or in what is purchased with that produce from other nations.

According therefore, as this produce, or what is purchased with it, bears a greater or smaller proportion to the number of those who are to consume it, the nation will be better or worse supplied with all the necessaries and conveniencies for which it has occasion.

But this proportion must in every nation be regulated by two different circumstances; first, by the skill, dexterity, and judgment with which its labour is generally applied; and, secondly, by the proportion between the number of those who are employed in useful labour, and that of those who are not so employed. Whatever be the soil, climate, or extent of territory of any particular nation, the abundance or scantiness of its annual supply must, in that particular situation, depend upon those two circumstances.

The abundance or scantiness of this supply too seems to depend more upon the former of those two circumstances than upon the latter. Among the savage nations of hunters and fishers, every individual who is able to work, is more or less employed in useful labour, and endeavours to provide, as well as he can, the necessaries and conveniencies of life, for himself, or such of his family or tribe as are either too old, or too young, or too infirm to go a hunting and fishing. Such nations, however, are so miserably poor, that from mere want, they are frequently reduced, or, at least, think themselves reduced, to the necessity sometimes of directly destroying, and sometimes of abandoning their infants, their old people, and those afflicted with lingering diseases, to perish with hunger, or to be devoured by wild beasts. Among civilized and thriving nations, on the contrary, though a great number of people do not labour at all, many of whom consume the produce of ten times, frequently of a hundred times more labour than the greater part of those who work; yet the produce of the whole labour of the society is so great, that all are often abundantly supplied, and a workman, even of the lowest and poorest order, if he is

*Source: Reprinted from the 5th edition, 1789. The selection reprinted here originally appeared as the introduction and chapters 2 and 10. Footnotes and margin notes deleted.

frugal and industrious, may enjoy a greater share of the necessaries and conveniencies of life than it is possible for any savage to acquire.

The causes of this improvement, in the productive powers of labour, and the order, according to which its produce is naturally distributed among the different ranks and conditions of men in the society, make the subject of the First Book of this Inquiry.

Whatever be the actual state of the skill, dexterity, and judgment with which labour is applied in any nation, the abundance or scantiness of its annual supply must depend, during the continuance of that state, upon the proportion between the number of those who are annually employed in useful labour, and that of those who are not so employed. The number of useful and productive labourers, it will hereafter appear, is every where in proportion to the quantity of capital stock which is employed in setting them to work, and to the particular way in which it is so employed. The Second Book, therefore, treats of the nature of capital stock, of the manner in which it is gradually accumulated, and of the different quantities of labour which it puts into motion, according to the different ways in which it is employed.

Nations tolerably well advanced as to skill, dexterity, and judgment, in the application of labour, have followed very different plans in the general conduct or direction of it; and those plans have not all been equally favourable to the greatness of its produce. The policy of some nations has given extraordinary encouragement to the industry of the country; that of others to the industry of towns. Scarce any nation has dealt equally and impartially with every sort of industry. Since the downfall of the Roman empire, the policy of Europe has been more favourable to arts, manufactures, and commerce, the industry of towns; than to agriculture, the industry of the country. The circumstances which seem to have introduced and established this policy are explained in the Third Book.

Though those different plans were, perhaps, first introduced by the private interests and prejudices of particular orders of men, without any regard to, or foresight of, their consequences upon the general welfare of the society; yet they have given occasion to very different theories of political economy; of which some magnify the importance of that industry which is carried on in towns, others of that which is carried on in the country. Those theories have had a considerable influence, not only upon the opinions of men of learning, but upon the public conduct of princes and sovereign states. I have endeavoured, in the Fourth Book, to explain, as fully and distinctly as I can, those different theories, and the principal effects which they have produced in different ages and nations.

To explain in what has consisted the revenue of the great body of the people, or what has been the nature of those funds, which, in different ages and nations, have supplied their annual consumption, is the object of these Four first Books. The Fifth and last Book treats of the revenue of the sovereign, or commonwealth. In this book I have endeavoured to show; first, what are the necessary expenses of the sovereign, or commonwealth; which of those expenses ought to be defrayed by the general contribution of the whole society; and which of them, by that of some particular part only, or of some particular members of it: secondly, what are the different methods in which the whole society may be made to contribute towards defraying the expenses incumbent on the whole society, and what are the principal advantages and inconveniencies of each of those methods: and, thirdly and lastly, what are the reasons and causes which have induced almost all modern governments to mortgage some part of this revenue, or to contract debts, and what have been the effects of those debts upon the real wealth, the annual produce of the land and labour of the society. . . .

OF RESTRAINTS UPON THE IMPORTATION FROM FOREIGN COUNTRIES OF SUCH GOODS AS CAN BE PRODUCED AT HOME

By restraining, either by high duties, or by absolute prohibitions, the importation of such goods from foreign countries as can be produced at home, the monopoly of the home market is more or less secured to the domestic industry employed in producing them. Thus the prohibition of importing either live cattle or salt provisions from foreign countries secures to the graziers of Great Britain the monopoly of the home market for butcher's meat. The high duties upon the importation of corn, which in times of moderate plenty amount to a prohibition, give a like advantage to the growers of that commodity. The prohibition of the importation of foreign woollens is equally favourable to the woollen manufacturers. The silk manufacture, though altogether employed upon foreign materials, has lately obtained the same advantage. The linen manufacture has not yet obtained it, but is making great strides towards it. Many other sorts of manufacturers have, in the same manner, obtained in Great Britain, either altogether, or very nearly a monopoly against their countrymen. The variety of goods of which the importation into Great Britain is prohibited, either absolutely, or under certain circumstances, greatly exceeds what can easily be suspected by those who are not well acquainted with the laws of the customs.

That this monopoly of the home-market frequently gives great encouragement to that particular species of industry which enjoys it, and frequently turns towards that employment a greater share of both the labour and stock of the society than would otherwise have gone to it, cannot be doubted. But whether it tends either to increase the general industry of the society, or to give it the most advantageous direction, is not, perhaps, altogether so evident.

The general industry of the society never can exceed what the capital of the society can employ. As the number of workmen that can be kept in employment by any particular person must bear a certain proportion to his capital, so the number of those that can be continually employed by all the members of a great society, must bear a certain proportion to the whole capital of that society, and never can exceed that proportion. No regulation of commerce can increase the quantity of industry in any society beyond what its capital can maintain. It can only divert a part of it into a direction into which it might not otherwise have gone; and it is by no means certain that this artificial direction is likely to be more advantageous to the society than that into which it would have gone of its own accord.

Every individual is continually exerting himself to find out the most advantageous employment for whatever capital he can command. It is his own advantage, indeed, and not that of the society, which he has in view. But the study of his own advantage naturally, or rather necessarily leads him to prefer that employment which is most advantageous to the society.

First, every individual endeavours to employ his capital as near home as he can, and consequently as much as he can in the support of domestic industry; provided always that he can thereby obtain the ordinary, or not a great deal less than the ordinary profits of stock.

Thus, upon equal or nearly equal profits, every wholesale merchant naturally prefers the home-trade to the foreign trade of consumption, and the foreign trade of consumption to the carrying trade. In the home-trade his capital is never so long out of his sight as it frequently is in the foreign trade of consumption. He can know better the character and situation of the persons whom he trusts, and if he should happen to be deceived, he knows better the laws of the country from which he must seek redress. In the carrying trade, the capital of the merchant is, as it were, divided between two foreign countries, and no part of it is ever necessarily brought home, or placed under his own immediate view and command. The capital which an Amsterdam merchant employs in carrying corn from Konnigsberg to Lisbon, and fruit and wine from Lisbon to Konnigsberg, must generally be the one-half of it at Konnigsberg and the other half at Lisbon. No part of it need ever come to Amsterdam. The natural residence of such a merchant should either be at Konnigsberg or Lisbon, and it can only be some very particular circumstances which can make him prefer the residence of Amsterdam. The uneasiness, however, which he feels at being separated so far from his capital, generally determines him to bring part both of the Konnigsberg goods which he destines for the market of Lisbon, and of the Lisbon goods which he destines for that of Konnigsberg, to Amsterdam: and though this necessarily subjects him to a double charge of loading and unloading, as well as to the payment of some duties and customs, yet for the sake of having some part of his capital always under his own view and command, he willingly submits to this extraordinary charge; and it is in this manner that every country which has any considerable share of the carrying trade, becomes always the emporium, or general market, for the goods of all the different countries whose trade it carries on. The merchant, in order to save a second loading and unloading, endeavours always to sell in the home-market as much of the goods of all those different countries as he can, and thus, so far as he can, to convert his carrying trade into a foreign trade of consumption. A merchant, in the same manner, who is engaged in the foreign trade of consumption, when he collects goods for foreign markets, will always be glad, upon equal or nearly equal profits, to sell as great a part of them at home as he can. He saves himself the risk and trouble of exportation, when, so far as he can, he thus converts his foreign trade of consumption into a home-trade. Home is in this manner the center, if I may say so, round which the capitals of the inhabitants of every country are continually circulating, and towards which they are always tending, though by particular causes they may sometimes be driven off and repelled from it towards more distant employments. But a capital employed in the home-trade, it has already been shown, necessarily puts into motion a greater quantity of domestic industry, and gives revenue and employment to a greater number of the inhabitants of the country, than an equal capital employed in the foreign trade of consumption: and one employed in the foreign trade of consumption has the same advantage over an equal capital employed in the carrying trade. Upon equal, or only nearly equal profits, therefore, every individual naturally inclines to employ his capital in the manner in which it is likely to afford the greatest support to domestic industry, and to give revenue and employment to the greatest number of people of his own country.

Secondly, every individual who employs his capital in the support of domestic industry, necessarily endeavours so to direct that industry, that its produce may be of the greatest possible value.

The produce of industry is what it adds to the subject or materials upon which it is employed. In proportion as the value of this produce is great or small, so will likewise be the profits of the employer. But it is only for the sake of profit that any man employs a capital in the support of industry; and he will always, therefore, endeavour to employ it in the support of that industry of which the produce is likely to be of the greatest value, or to exchange for the greatest quantity either of money or of other goods.

But the annual revenue of every society is always precisely equal to the exchangeable value of the whole annual produce of its industry, or rather is precisely the same thing with that exchangeable value. As every individual, therefore, endeavours as much as he can both to employ his capital in the support of domestic industry, and so to direct that industry that its produce may be of the greatest value; every individual necessarily labours to render the annual revenue of the society as great as he can. He generally, indeed, neither intends to promote the public interest, nor knows how much he is promoting it. By preferring the support of domestic to that of foreign industry, he intends only his own security; and by directing that industry in such a manner as its produce may be of the greatest value, he intends only his own gain, and he is in this, as in many other cases, led by an invisible hand to promote an end which was no part of his intention. Nor is it always the worse for the society that it was no part of it. By pursuing his own interest he frequently promotes that of the society more effectually than when he really intends to promote it. I have never known much good done by those who affected to trade for the public good. It is an affectation, indeed, not very common among merchants, and very few words need be employed in dissuading them from it.

What is the species of domestic industry which his capital can employ, and of which the produce is likely to be of the greatest value, every individual, it is evident, can, in his local situation, judge much better than any statesman or lawgiver can do for him. The statesman, who should attempt to direct private people in what manner they ought to employ their capitals, would not only load himself with a most unnecessary attention, but assume an authority which could safely be trusted, not only to no single person, but to no council or senate whatever, and which would nowhere be so dangerous as in the hands of a man who had folly and presumption enough to fancy himself fit to exercise it.

To give the monopoly of the home-market to the produce of domestic industry, in any particular art or manufacture, is in some measure to direct private people in what manner they ought to employ their capitals, and must, in almost all cases, be either a useless or a hurtful regulation. If the produce of domestic can be brought there as cheap as that of foreign industry, the regulation is evidently useless. If it cannot, it must generally be hurtful. It is the maxim of every prudent master of a family, never to attempt to make at home what it will cost him more to make than to buy. The taylor does not attempt to make his own shoes, but buys them of the shoemaker. The shoemaker does not attempt to make his own clothes, but employs a taylor. The farmer attempts to make neither the one nor the other, but employs those different artificers. All of them find it for their interest to employ their whole industry in a way in which they have some advantage over their neighbours, and to purchase with a part of its produce, or what is the same thing, with the price of a part of it, whatever else they have occasion for.

What is prudence in the conduct of every private family, can scarce be folly in that of a great kingdom. If a foreign country can supply us with a commodity cheaper than we ourselves can make it, better buy it of them with some part of the produce of our own industry, employed in a way in which we have some advantage. The general industry of the country, being always in proportion to the capital which employs it, will not thereby be diminished, no more than that of the above-mentioned artificers; but only left to find out the way in which it can be employed with the greatest advantage. It is certainly not employed to the greatest advantage, when it is thus directed towards an object which it can buy cheaper than it can make. The value of its annual produce is certainly more or less diminished, when it is thus turned away from producing commodities evidently of more value than the commodity which it is directed to produce. According to the supposition, that commodity could be purchased from foreign countries cheaper than it can be made at home. It could, therefore, have been purchased with a part only of the commodities, or, what is the same thing, with a part only of the price of the commodities, which the industry employed by an equal capital would have produced at home, had it been left to follow its natural course. The industry of the country, therefore, is thus turned away from a more, to a less advantageous employment, and the exchangeable value of its annual produce, instead of being increased, according to the intention of the lawgiver, must necessarily be diminished by every such regulation.

By means of such regulations, indeed, a particular manufacture may sometimes be acquired sooner than it could have been otherwise, and after a certain time may be made at home as cheap or cheaper than in the foreign country. But though the industry of the society may be thus carried with advantage into a particular channel sooner than it could have been otherwise, it will by no means follow that the sum total, either of its industry, or of its revenue, can ever be augmented by any such regulation. The industry of the society can augment only in proportion as its capital augments, and its capital can augment only in proportion to what can be gradually saved out of its revenue. But the immediate effect of every such regulation is to diminish its revenue, and what diminishes its revenue is certainly not very likely to augment its capital faster than it would have augmented of

its own accord, had both capital and industry been left to find out their natural employments.

Though for want of such regulations the society should never acquire the proposed manufacture, it would not, upon that account, necessarily be the poorer in any one period of its duration. In every period of its duration its whole capital and industry might still have been employed, though upon different objects, in the manner that was most advantageous at the time. In every period its revenue might have been the greatest which its capital could afford, and both capital and revenue might have been augmented with the greatest possible rapidity.

The natural advantages which one country has over another in producing particular commodities are sometimes so great, that it is acknowledged by all the world to be in vain to struggle with them. By means of glasses, hotbeds, and hotwalls, very good grapes can be raised in Scotland, and very good wine too can be made of them at about thirty times the expense for which at least equally good can be brought from foreign countries. Would it be a reasonable law to prohibit the importation of all foreign wines, merely to encourage the making of claret and burgundy in Scotland? But if there would be a manifest absurdity in turning towards any employment, thirty times more of the capital and industry of the country, than would be necessary to purchase from foreign countries an equal quantity of the commodities wanted, there must be an absurdity, though not altogether so glaring, yet exactly of the same kind, in turning towards any such employment a thirtieth, or even a three hundredth part more of either. Whether the advantages which one country has over another, be natural or acquired, is in this respect of no consequence. As long as the one country has those advantages, and the other wants them, it will always be more advantageous for the latter, rather to buy of the former than to make. It is an acquired advantage only, which one artificer has over his neighbour, who exercises another trade; and yet they both find it more advantageous to buy of one another, than to make what does not belong to their particular trades.

Merchants and manufacturers are the people who derive the greatest advantage from this monopoly of the home-market. The prohibition of the importation of foreign cattle, and of salt provisions, together with the high duties upon foreign corn, which in times of moderate plenty amount to a prohibition, are not near so advantageous to the graziers and farmers of Great Britain, as other regulations of the same kind are to its merchants and manufacturers. Manufactures, those of the finer kind especially, are more easily transported from one country to another than corn or cattle. It is in the fetching and carrying manufactures, accordingly, that foreign trade is chiefly employed. In manufactures, a very small advantage will enable foreigners to undersell our own workmen, even in the home market. It will require a very great one to enable them to do so in the rude produce of the soil. If the free importation of foreign manufactures were permitted, several of the home manufactures would probably suffer, and some of them, perhaps, go to ruin altogether, and a considerable part of the stock and industry at present employed in them, would be forced to find out some other employment. But the freest importation of the rude produce of the soil could have no such effect upon the agriculture of the country.

If the importation of foreign cattle, for example, were made ever so free, so few could be imported, that the grazing trade of Great Britain could be little affected by it. Live cattle are, perhaps, the only commodity of which the transportation is more expensive by sea than by land. By land they carry themselves to market. By sea, not only the cattle, but their food and their water too, must be carried at no small expense and incon-

veniency. The short sea between Ireland and Great Britain, indeed, renders the importation of Irish cattle more easy. But though the free importation of them, which was lately permitted only for a limited time, were rendered perpetual, it could have no considerable effect upon the interest of the graziers of Great Britain. Those parts of Great Britain which border upon the Irish sea are all grazing countries. Irish cattle could never be imported for their use, but must be drove through those very extensive countries, at no small expense and inconveniency, before they could arrive at their proper market. Fat cattle could not be drove so far. Lean cattle, therefore, only could be imported, and such importation could interfere, not with the interest of the feeding or fattening countries, to which, by reducing the price of lean cattle, it would rather be advantageous, but with that of the breeding countries only. The small number of Irish cattle imported since their importation was permitted, together with the good price at which lean cattle still continue to sell, seem to demonstrate that even the breeding countries of Great Britain are never likely to be much affected by the free importation of Irish cattle. The common people of Ireland, indeed, are said to have sometimes opposed with violence the exportation of their cattle. But if the exporters had found any great advantage in continuing the trade, they could easily, when the law was on their side, have conquered this mobbish opposition.

Feeding and fattening countries, besides, must always be highly improved, whereas breeding countries are generally uncultivated. The high price of lean cattle, by augmenting the value of uncultivated land, is like a bounty against improvement. To any country which was highly improved throughout, it would be more advantageous to import its lean cattle than to breed them. The province of Holland, accordingly, is said to follow this maxim at present. The mountains of Scotland, Wales and

Northumberland, indeed, are countries not capable of much improvement, and seem destined by nature to be the breeding countries of Great Britain. The freest importation of foreign cattle could have no other effect than to hinder those breeding countries from taking advantage of the increasing population and improvement of the rest of the kingdom, from raising their price to an exorbitant height, and from laying a real tax upon all the more improved and cultivated parts of the country.

The freest importation of salt provisions, in the same manner, could have as little effect upon the interest of the graziers of Great Britain as that of live cattle. Salt provisions are not only a very bulky commodity, but when compared with fresh meat, they are a commodity both of worse quality, and as they cost more labour and expense, of higher price. They could never, therefore, come into competition with the fresh meat, though they might with the salt provisions of the country. They might be used for victualling ships for distant voyages, and such like uses, but could never make any considerable part of the food of the people. The small quantity of salt provisions imported from Ireland since their importation was rendered free, is an experimental proof that our graziers have nothing to apprehend from it. It does not appear that the price of butcher's-meat has ever been sensibly affected by it.

Even the free importation of foreign corn could very little affect the interest of the farmers of Great Britain. Corn is a much more bulky commodity than butcher's-meat. A pound of wheat at a penny is as dear as a pound of butcher's-meat at fourpence. The small quantity of foreign corn imported even in times of the greatest scarcity, may satisfy our farmers that they can have nothing to fear from the freest importation. The average quantity imported one year with another, amounts only, according to the very well informed author of the tracts upon the corn trade, to twenty-three thousand seven hundred and twenty-eight quarters of all sorts of grain, and does not exceed the five hundredth and seventy-one part of the annual consumption. But as the bounty upon corn occasions a greater exportation in years of plenty, so it must of consequence occasion a greater importation in years of scarcity, than in the actual state of tillage would otherwise take place. By means of it, the plenty of one year does not compensate the scarcity of another, and as the average quantity exported is necessarily augmented by it, so must likewise, in the actual state of tillage, the average quantity imported. If there were no bounty, as less corn would be exported, so it is probable that, one year with another, less would be imported than at present. The corn merchants, the fetchers and carriers of corn between Great Britain and foreign countries, would have much less employment, and might suffer considerably; but the country gentlemen and farmers could suffer very little. It is in the corn merchants accordingly, rather than in the country gentlemen and farmers, that I have observed the greatest anxiety for the renewal and continuation of the bounty.

Country gentlemen and farmers are, to their great honour, of all people, the least subject to the wretched spirit of monopoly. The undertaker of a great manufactory is sometimes alarmed if another work of the same kind is established within twenty miles of him. The Dutch undertaker of the woollen manufacture at Abbeville stipulated, that no work of the same kind should be established within thirty leagues of that city. Farmers and country gentlemen, on the contrary, are generally disposed rather to promote than to obstruct the cultivation and improvement of their neighbours farms and estates. They have no secrets, such as those of the greater part of manufacturers, but are generally rather fond of communicating to their neighbours, and of extending as far as possible any new practice which they have found to be advantageous. *Pius Questus,* says old Cato, *stabilissimus-que, minimeque invidiosus; minimeque male cogitantes sunt, qui in eo studio occupati sunt.* Country gentlemen and farmers, dispersed in different parts of the country, cannot so easily combine as merchants and manufacturers, who being collected into towns, and accustomed to that exclusive corporation spirit which prevails in them, naturally endeavour to obtain against all their countrymen, the same exclusive privilege which they generally possess against the inhabitants of their respective towns. They accordingly seem to have been the original inventors of those restraints upon the importation of foreign goods, which secure to them the monopoly of the home market. It was probably in imitation of them, and to put themselves upon a level with those who, they found, were disposed to oppress them, that the country gentlemen and·farmers of Great Britain so far forgot the generosity which is natural to their station, as to demand the exclusive privilege of supplying their countrymen with corn and butcher's-meat. They did not perhaps take time to consider, how much less their interest could be affected by the freedom of trade, than that of the people whose example they followed.

To prohibit by a perpetual law the importation of foreign corn and cattle, is in reality to enact, that the population and industry of the country shall at no time exceed what the rude produce of its own soil can maintain.

There seem, however, to be two cases in which it will generally be advantageous to lay some burden upon foreign, for the encouragement of domestic industry.

The first is, when some particular sort of industry is necessary for the defence of the country. The defence of Great Britain, for example, depends very much upon the number of its sailors and shipping. The act of navigation, therefore, very properly endeavours to give the sailors and shipping of Great Britain the monopoly of the trade of their own country, in some cases, by absolute prohibitions, and in others by heavy burdens upon the shipping of foreign countries. The following are the principal dispositions of this act.

First, all ships, of which the owners, masters, and three-fourths of the mariners are not British subjects, are prohibited, upon pain of forfeiting ship and cargo, from trading to the British settlements and plantations, or from being employed in the coasting trade of Great Britain.

Secondly, a great variety of the most bulky articles of importation can be brought into Great Britain only, either in such ships as are above described, or in ships of the country where those goods are produced, and of which the owners, masters, and three-fourths of the mariners, are of that particular country; and when imported even in ships of this latter kind, they are subject to double aliens duty. If imported in ships of any other country, the penalty is forfeiture of ship and goods. When this act was made, the Dutch were, what they still are, the great carriers of Europe, and by this regulation they were entirely excluded from being the carriers to Great Britain, or from importing to us the goods of any other European country.

Thirdly, a great variety of the most bulky articles of importation are prohibited from being imported, even in British ships, from any country but that in which they are produced; under pain of forfeiting ship and cargo. This regulation too was probably intended against the Dutch. Holland was then, as now, the great emporium for all European goods, and by this regulation, British ships were hindered from loading in Holland the goods of any other European country.

Fourthly, salt fish of all kinds, whale-fins, whale-bone, oil, and blubber, not caught by and cured on board British vessels, when imported into Great Britain, are subjected to double aliens duty. The Dutch, as they are still the principal, were then the only fishers in Europe that attempted to supply foreign nations with fish. By this regulation, a very heavy burden was laid upon their supplying Great Britain.

When the act of navigation was

made, though England and Holland were not actually at war, the most violent animosity subsisted between the two nations. It had begun during the government of the long parliament, which first framed this act, and it broke out soon after in the Dutch wars during that of the Protector and of Charles the Second. It is not impossible, therefore, that some of the regulations of this famous act may have proceeded from national animosity. They are as wise, however, as if they had all been dictated by the most deliberate wisdom. National animosity at that particular time aimed at the very same object which the most deliberate wisdom would have recommended, the diminution of the naval power of Holland, the only naval power which could endanger the security of England.

The act of navigation is not favourable to foreign commerce, or to the growth of that opulence which can arise from it. The interest of a nation in its commercial relations to foreign nations is, like that of a merchant with regard to the different people with whom he deals, to buy as cheap and to sell as dear as possible. But it will be most likely to buy cheap, when by the most perfect freedom of trade it encourages all nations to bring to it the goods which it has occasion to purchase; and, for the same reason, it will be most likely to sell dear, when its markets are thus filled with the greatest number of buyers. The act of navigation, it is true, lays no burden upon foreign ships that come to export the produce of British industry. Even the ancient aliens duty, which used to be paid upon all goods exported as well as imported, has, by several subsequent acts, been taken off from the greater part of the articles of exportation. But if foreigners, either by prohibitions or high duties, are hindered from coming to sell, they cannot always afford to come to buy; because coming without a cargo, they must lose the freight from their own country to Great Britain. By diminishing the number of sellers, therefore, we necessarily diminish that of buyers, and are thus likely not only to buy foreign goods dearer, but to sell our own cheaper, than if there was a more perfect freedom of trade. As defence, however, is of much more importance than opulence, the act of navigation is, perhaps, the wisest of all the commercial regulations of England.

The second case, in which it will generally be advantageous to lay some burden upon foreign for the encouragement of domestic industry, is, when some tax is imposed at home upon the produce of the latter. In this case, it seems reasonable that an equal tax should be imposed upon the like produce of the former. This would not give the monopoly of the home market to domestic industry, nor turn towards a particular employment a greater share of the stock and labour of the country, than what would naturally go to it. It would only hinder any part of what would naturally go to it from being turned away by the tax, into a less natural direction, and would leave the competition between foreign and domestic industry, after the tax, as nearly as possible upon the same footing as before it. In Great Britain, when any such tax is laid upon the produce of domestic industry, it is usual at the same time, in order to stop the clamorous complaints of our merchants and manufacturers, that they will be undersold at home, to lay a much heavier duty upon the importation of all foreign goods of the same kind.

This second limitation of the freedom of trade according to some people should, upon some occasions, be extended much farther than to the precise foreign commodities which could come into competition with those which had been taxed at home. When the necessaries of life have been taxed in any country, it becomes proper, they pretend, to tax not only the like necessaries of life imported from other countries, but all sorts of foreign goods which can come into competition with any thing that is the produce of domestic industry. Subsistence, they say, becomes necessarily dearer in consequence of such taxes; and the price of labour must always rise with the price of the labourers subsistence. Every commodity, therefore, which is the produce of domestic industry, though not immediately taxed itself, becomes dearer in consequence of such taxes, because the labour which produces it becomes so. Such taxes, therefore, are really equivalent, they say, to a tax upon every particular commodity produced at home. In order to put domestic upon the same footing with foreign industry, therefore, it becomes necessary, they think, to lay some duty upon every foreign commodity, equal to this enhancement of the price of the home commodities with which it can come into competition.

Whether taxes upon the necessaries of life, such as those in Great Britain upon soap, salt, leather, candles, &c. necessarily raise the price of labour, and consequently that of all other commodities, I shall consider hereafter, when I come to treat of taxes. Supposing, however, in the mean time, that they have this effect, and they have it undoubtedly, this general enhancement of the price of all commodities, in consequence of that of labour, is a case which differs in the two following respects from that of a particular commodity, of which the price was enhanced by a particular tax immediately imposed upon it.

First, it might always be known with great exactness how far the price of such a commodity could be enhanced by such a tax: but how far the general enhancement of the price of labour might affect that of every different commodity about which labour was employed, could never be known with any tolerable exactness. It would be impossible, therefore, to proportion with any tolerable exactness the tax upon every foreign, to this enhancement of the price of every home commodity.

Secondly, taxes upon the necessaries of life have nearly the same effect upon the circumstances of the people as a poor soil and a bad climate. Provisions are thereby rendered dearer in the same manner as if it required extraordinary labour and expense to raise them. As in the natural scarcity arising from soil and climate, it would be absurd to direct the people in what manner they ought to employ their capitals and industry, so is it likewise in the artificial scarcity arising from such taxes. To be left to accommodate, as well as they could, their industry to their situation, and to find out those employments in which, notwithstanding their unfavourable circumstances, they might have some advantage either in the home or in the foreign market, is what in both cases would evidently be most for their advantage. To lay a new tax upon them, because they are already overburdened with taxes, and because they already pay too dear for the necessaries of life, to make them likewise pay too dear for the greater part of other commodities, is certainly a most absurd way of making amends.

Such taxes, when they have grown up to a certain height, are a curse equal to the barrenness of the earth and the inclemency of the heavens; and yet it is in the richest and most industrious countries that they have been most generally imposed. No other countries could support so great a disorder. As the strongest bodies only can live and enjoy health, under an unwholesome regimen; so the nations only, that in every sort of industry have the greatest natural and acquired advantages, can subsist and prosper under such taxes. Holland is the country in Europe in which they abound most, and which from peculiar circumstances continues to prosper, not by means of them, as has been most absurdly supposed, but in spite of them.

As there are two cases in which it will generally be advantageous to lay some burden upon foreign, for the encouragement of domestic industry; so there are two others in which it may sometimes be a matter of deliberation; in the one, how far it is proper to continue the free importation of certain foreign goods; and in the other, how far, or in what manner, it may be proper to restore that free importation after it has been for some time interrupted.

The case in which it may sometimes be a matter of deliberation how far it is proper to continue the free importation of certain foreign goods, is, when some foreign nation restrains by high duties or prohibitions the importation of some of our manufactures into their country. Revenge in this case naturally dictates retaliation, and that we should impose the like duties and prohibitions upon the importation of some or all of their manufactures into ours. Nations accordingly seldom fail to retaliate in this manner. The French have been particularly forward to favour their own manufactures by restraining the importation of such foreign goods as could come into competition with them. In this consisted a great part of the policy of Mr. Colbert, who, notwithstanding his great abilities, seems in this case to have been imposed upon by the sophistry of merchants and manufacturers, who are always demanding a monopoly against their countrymen. It is at present the opinion of the most intelligent men in France that his operations of this kind have not been beneficial to his country. That minister, by the tariff of 1667, imposed very high duties upon a great number of foreign manufactures. Upon his refusing to moderate them in favour of the Dutch, they in 1671 prohibited the importation of the wines, brandies and manufactures of France. The war of 1672 seems to have been in part occasioned by this commercial dispute. The peace of Nimeguen put an end to it in 1678, by moderating some of those duties in favour of the Dutch, who in consequence took off their prohibition. It was about the same time that the French and English began mutually to oppress each other's industry, by the like duties and prohibitions, of which the French, however, seem to have set the first example. The spirit of hostility which has subsisted between the two nations ever since, has hitherto hindered them from being moderated on

either side. In 1697 the English prohibited the importation of bonelace, the manufacture of Flanders. The government of that country, at that time under the dominion of Spain, prohibited in return the importation of English woollens. In 1700, the prohibition of importing bonelace into England, was taken off upon condition that the importation of English woollens into Flanders should be put on the same footing as before.

There may be good policy in retaliations of this kind, when there is a probability that they will procure the repeal of the high duties or prohibitions complained of. The recovery of a great foreign market will generally more than compensate the transitory inconveniency of paying dearer during a short time for some sorts of goods. To judge whether such retaliations are likely to produce such an effect, does not, perhaps, belong so much to the science of a legislator, whose deliberations ought to be governed by general principles which are always the same, as to the skill of that insidious and crafty animal, vulgarly called a statesman or politican, whose councils are directed by the momentary fluctuations of affairs. When there is no probability that any such repeal can be procured, it seems a bad method of compensating the injury done to certain classes of our people, to do another injury ourselves, not only to those classes, but to almost all the other classes of them. When our neighbours prohibit some manufacture of ours, we generally prohibit, not only the same, for that alone would seldom affect them considerably, but some other manufacture of theirs. This may no doubt give encouragement to some particular class of workmen among ourselves, and by excluding some of their rivals, may enable them to raise their price in the home-market. Those workmen, however, who suffered by our neighbours' prohibition will not be benefited by ours. On the contrary, they and almost all the other classes of our citizens will thereby be obliged to pay dearer than before for certain goods. Every such law, therefore, imposes a real tax upon the whole country, not in favour of that particular class of workmen who were injured by our neighbours' prohibition, but of some other class.

The case in which it may sometimes be a matter of deliberation, how far, or in what manner, it is proper to restore the free importation of foreign goods, after it has been for some time interrupted, is, when particular manufactures, by means of high duties or prohibitions upon all foreign goods which can come into competition with them, have been so far extended as to employ a great multitude of hands. Humanity may in this case require that the freedom of trade should be restored only by slow gradations, and with a good deal of reserve and circumspection. Were those high duties and prohibitions taken away all at once, cheaper foreign goods of the same kind might be poured so fast into the home market, as to deprive all at once many thousands of our people of their ordinary employment and means of subsistence. The disorder which this would occasion might no doubt be very considerable. It would in all probability, however, be much less than is commonly imagined, for the two following reasons:

First, all those manufactures, of which any part is commonly exported to other European countries without a bounty, could be very little affected by the freest importation of foreign goods. Such manufactures must be sold as cheap abroad as any other foreign goods of the same quality and kind, and consequently must be sold cheaper at home. They would still, therefore, keep possession of the home market, and though a capricious man of fashion might sometimes prefer foreign wares, merely because they were foreign, to cheaper and better goods of the same kind that were made at home, this folly could, from the nature of things, extend to so few, that it could make no sensible impression upon the general employ-ment of the people. But a great part of all the different branches of our woollen manufacture, of our tanned leather, and of our hard-ware, are annually exported to other European countries without any bounty, and these are the manufactures which employ the greatest number of hands. The silk, perhaps, is the manufacture which would suffer the most by this freedom of trade, and after it the linen, though the latter much less than the former.

Secondly, though a great number of people should, by thus restoring the freedom of trade, be thrown all at once out of their ordinary employment and common method of subsistence, it would by no means follow that they would thereby be deprived either of employment or subsistence. By the reduction of the army and navy at the end of the late war, more than a hundred thousand soldiers and seamen, a number equal to what is employed in the greatest manufactures, were all at once thrown out of their ordinary employment; but, though they no doubt suffered some inconveniency, they were not thereby deprived of all employment and subsistence. The greater part of the seamen, it is probable, gradually betook themselves to the merchant-service as they could find occasion, and in the meantime both they and the soldiers were absorbed in the great mass of the people, and employed in a great variety of occupations. Not only no great convulsion, but no sensible disorder arose from so great a change in the situation of more than a hundred thousand men, all accustomed to the use of arms, and many of them to rapine and plunder. The number of vagrants was scarce any-where sensibly increased by it in any occupation, so far as I have been able to learn, except in that of seamen in the merchant-service. But if we compare together the habits of a soldier and of any sort of manufacturer, we shall find that those of the latter do not tend so much to disqualify him from being employed in a new trade, as those of the former from being employed in any. The manufacturer has always been accustomed to look for his subsistence from his labour only: the soldier to expect it from his pay. Application and industry have been familiar to the one; idleness and dissipation to the other. But it is surely much easier to change the direction of industry from one sort of labour to another, than to turn idleness and dissipation to any. To the greater part of manufactures besides, it has already been observed, there are other collateral manufactures of so similar a nature, that a workman can easily transfer his industry from one of them to another. The greater part of such workmen too are occasionally employed in country labour. The stock which employed them in a particular manufacture before, will still remain in the country to employ an equal number of people in some other way. The capital of the country remaining the same, the demand for labour will likewise be the same, or very nearly the same, though it may be exerted in different places and for different occupations. Soldiers and seamen, indeed, when discharged from the king's service, are at liberty to exercise any trade, within any town or place of Great Britain or Ireland. Let the same natural liberty of exercising what species of industry they please, be restored to all his majesty's subjects, in the same manner as to soldiers and seamen; that is, break down the exclusive privileges of corporations, and repeal the statute of apprenticeship, both which are real encroachments upon natural liberty, and add to these the repeal of the law of settlements, so that a poor workman, when thrown out of employment either in one trade or in one place, may seek for it in another trade or in another place, without the fear either of a prosecution or of a removal, and neither the public nor the individuals will suffer much more from the occasional disbanding some particular classes of manufacturers, than from that of soldiers. Our manufacturers have

no doubt great merit with their country, but they cannot have more than those who defend it with their blood, nor deserve to be treated with more delicacy.

To expect, indeed, that the freedom of trade should ever be entirely restored in Great Britain, is as absurd as to expect that an Oceana or Utopia should ever be established in it. Not only the prejudices of the public, but what is much more unconquerable, the private interests of many individuals, irresistibly oppose it. Were the officers of the army to oppose with the same zeal and unanimity any reduction in the number of forces, with which master manufacturers set themselves against every law that is likely to increase the number of their rivals in the home market; were the former to animate their soldiers, in the same manner as the latter enflame their workmen, to attack with violence and outrage the proposers of any such regulation; to attempt to reduce the army would be as dangerous as it has now become to attempt to diminish in any respect the monopoly which our manufacturers have obtained against us. This monopoly has so much increased the number of some particular tribes of them, that, like an overgrown standing army, they have become formidable to the government, and upon many occasions intimidate the legislature. The member of parliament who supports every proposal for strengthening this monopoly, is sure to acquire not only the reputation of understanding trade, but great popularity and influence with an order of men whose numbers and wealth render them of great importance. If he opposes them, on the contrary, and still more if he has authority enough to be able to thwart them, neither the most acknowledged probity, nor the highest rank, nor the greatest public services, can protect him from the most infamous abuse and detraction, from personal insults, nor sometimes from real danger, arising from the insolent outrage of furious and disappointed monopolists.

The undertaker of a great manufacture, who, by the home markets being suddenly laid open to the competition of foreigners, should be obliged to abandon his trade, would no doubt suffer very considerably. That part of his capital which had usually been employed in purchasing materials and in paying his workmen, might, without much difficulty, perhaps, find another employment. But that part of it which was fixed in workhouses, and in the instruments of trade, could scarce be disposed of without considerable loss. The equitable regard, therefore, to his interest requires that changes of this kind should never be introduced suddenly, but slowly, gradually, and after a very long warning. The legislature, were it possible that its deliberations could be always directed, not by the clamorous importunity of partial interests, but by an extensive view of the general good, ought upon this very account, perhaps, to be particularly careful neither to establish any new monopolies of this kind, nor to extend further those which are already established. Every such regulation introduces some degree of real disorder into the constitution of the state, which it will be difficult afterwards to cure without occasioning another disorder.

How far it may be proper to impose taxes upon the importation of foreign goods, in order, not to prevent their importation, but to raise a revenue for government, I shall consider hereafter when I come to treat of taxes. Taxes imposed with a view to prevent, or even to diminish importation, are evidently as destructive of the revenue of the customs as of the freedom of trade. . . .

OF WAGES AND PROFIT IN THE DIFFERENT EMPLOYMENTS OF LABOUR AND STOCK

The whole of the advantages and disadvantages of the different employments of labour and stock must, in the same neighbourhood, be either perfectly equal or continually tending to equality.

If in the same neighbourhood, there was any employment evidently either more or less advantageous than the rest, so many people would crowd into it in the one case, and so many would desert it in the other, that its advantages would soon return to the level of other employments. This at least would be the case in a society where things were left to follow their natural course, where there was perfect liberty, and where every man was perfectly free both to choose what occupation he thought proper, and to change it as often as he thought proper. Every man's interest would prompt him to seek the advantageous, and to shun the disadvantageous employment.

Pecuniary wages and profit, indeed, are every-where in Europe extremely different according to the different employments of labour and stock. But this difference arises partly from certain circumstances in the employments themselves, which, either really, or at least in the imaginations of men, make up for a small pecuniary gain in some, and counter-balance a great one in others; and partly from the policy of Europe, which no-where leaves things at perfect liberty. . . .

PART I: INEQUALITIES ARISING FROM THE NATURE OF THE EMPLOYMENTS THEMSELVES

The five following are the principal circumstances which, so far as I have been able to observe, make up for a small pecuniary gain in some employments, and counter-balance a great one in others: first, the agreeableness or disagreeableness of the employments themselves; secondly, the easiness and cheapness, or the difficulty and expense of learning them; thirdly, the constancy or inconstancy of employment in them; fourthly, the small or great trust which must be reposed in those who exercise them; and fifthly, the probability or improbability of success in them.

● First, the wages of labour vary with the ease or hardship, the cleanliness or

dirtiness, the honourableness or dishon-
ourableness of the employment. Thus in
most places, take the year round, a
journeyman taylor earns less than a
journeyman weaver. His work is much
easier. A journeyman weaver earns less
than a journeyman smith. His work is
not always easier, but it is much clean-
lier. A journeyman blacksmith, though
an artificer, seldom earns so much in
twelve hours as a collier, who is only a
labourer, does in eight. His work is not
quite so dirty, is less dangerous, and is
carried on in day-light, and above
ground. Honour makes a great part of
the reward of all honourable professions. In point of pecuniary gain, all
things considered, they are generally
under-recompensed, as I shall endeavour to show by and by. Disgrace
has the contrary effect. The trade of a
butcher is a brutal and an odious business; but it is in most places more profitable than the greater part of common
trades. The most detestable of all
employments, that of public execution-
er, is, in proportion to the quantity of
work done, better paid than any common trade whatever.

Hunting and fishing, the most important employments of mankind in the
rude state of society, become in its advanced state their most agreeable
amusements, and they pursue for pleasure what they once followed from
necessity. In the advanced state of society, therefore, they are all very poor
people who follow as a trade, what
other people pursue as a pastime.
Fishermen have been so since the time
of Theocritus. A poacher is every-where
a very poor man in Great Britain. In
countries where the rigour of the law
suffers no poachers, the licensed hunter
is not in a much better condition. The
natural taste for those employments
makes more people follow them than
can live comfortably by them, and the
produce of their labour, in proportion to
its quantity, comes always too cheap to
market to afford anything but the most
scanty subsistence to the labourers. *

Disagreeableness and disgrace affect
the profits of stock in the same manner
as the wages of labour. The keeper of an
inn or tavern, who is never master of his
own house, and who is exposed to the
brutality of every drunkard, exercises
neither a very agreeable nor a very creditable business. But there is scarce any
common trade in which a small stock
yields so great a profit.

● Secondly, the wages of labour vary
with the easiness and cheapness, or the
difficulty and expense of learning the
business.

When any expensive machine is
erected, the extraordinary work to be
performed by it before it is worn out, it
must be expected, will replace the capital laid out upon it, with at least the ordinary profits. A man educated at the
expense of much labour and time to any
of those employments which require extraordinary dexterity and skill, may be
compared to one of those expensive
machines. The work which he learns to
perform, it must be expected, over and
above the usual wages of common
labour, will replace to him the whole
expense of his education, with at least
the ordinary profits of an equally valuable capital. It must do this too in a reasonable time, regard being had to the
very uncertain duration of human life,
in the same manner as to the more certain duration of the machine.

The difference between the wages of
skilled labour and those of common
labour, is founded upon this principle.

The policy of Europe considers the
labour of all mechanics, artificers, and
manufacturers, as skilled labour; and
that of all country labourers as common
labour. It seems to suppose that of the
former to be of a more nice and delicate
nature than that of the latter. It is so
perhaps in some cases; but in the
greater part it is quite otherwise, as I
shall endeavour to shew by and by. The
laws and customs of Europe, therefore,
in order to qualify any person for exercising the one species of labour, impose
the necessity of an apprenticeship,

though with different degrees of rigour in different places. They leave the other free and open to every body. During the continuance of the apprenticeship, the whole labour of the apprentice belongs to his master. In the mean time he must, in many cases, be maintained by his parents or relations, and in almost all cases must be cloathed by them. Some money too is commonly given to the master for teaching him his trade. They who cannot give money, give time, or become bound for more than the usual number of years; a consideration which, though it is not always advantageous to the master, on account of the usual idleness of apprentices, is always disadvantageous to the apprentice. In country labour, on the contrary, the labourer, while he is employed about the easier, learns the more difficult parts of his business, and his own labour maintains him through all the different stages of his employment. It is reasonable, therefore, that in Europe the wages of mechanics, artificers, and manufacturers, should be somewhat higher than those of common labourers. They are so accordingly, and their superior gains make them in most places be considered as a superior rank of people. This superiority, however, is generally very small; the daily or weekly earnings of journeymen in the more common sorts of manufactures, such as those of plain linen and woollen cloth, computed at an average, are, in most places, very little more than the day wages of common labourers. Their employment, indeed, is more steady and uniform, and the superiority of their earnings, taking the whole year together, may be somewhat greater. It seems evidently, however, to be no greater than what is sufficient to compensate the superior expense of their education.

Education in the ingenious arts and in the liberal professions, is still more tedious and expensive. The pecuniary recompence, therefore, of painters and sculptors, of lawyers and physicians, ought to be much more liberal: and it is so accordingly.

The profits of stock seem to be very little affected by the easiness or difficulty of learning the trade in which it is employed. All the different ways in which stock is commonly employed in great towns seem, in reality, to be almost equally easy and equally difficult to learn. One branch either of foreign or domestic trade, cannot well be a much more intricate business than another.

• Thirdly, the wages of labour in different occupations vary with the constancy or inconstancy of employment.

Employment is much more constant in some trades than in others. In the greater part of manufactures, a journeyman may be pretty sure of employment almost every day in the year that he is able to work. A mason or bricklayer, on the contrary, can work neither in hard frost nor in foul weather, and his employment at all other times depends upon the occasional calls of his customers. He is liable, in consequence, to be frequently without any. What he earns, therefore, while he is employed, must not only maintain him while he is idle, but make him some compensation for those anxious and desponding moments which the thought of so precarious a situation must sometimes occasion. Where the computed earnings of the greater part of manufacturers, accordingly, are nearly upon a level with the day wages of common labourers, those of masons and bricklayers are generally from one half more to double those wages. Where common labourers earn four and five shillings a week, masons and bricklayers frequently earn seven and eight; where the former earn six, the latter often earn nine and ten, and where the former earn nine and ten, as in London, the latter commonly earn fifteen and eighteen. No species of skilled labour, however, seems more easy to learn than that of masons and bricklayers. Chairmen in London, during the summer season, are said sometimes to be employed as bricklayers. The high wages of those workmen, therefore, are not so much the recompence of their skill, as the compensation for the inconstancy of their employment.

A house carpenter seems to exercise rather a nicer and more ingenious trade than a mason. In most places, however, for it is not universally so, his day-wages are somewhat lower. His employment, though it depends much, does not depend so entirely upon the occasional calls of his customers; and it is not liable to be interrupted by the weather.

When the trades which generally afford constant employment, happen in a particular place not to do so, the wages of the workmen always rise a good deal above their ordinary proportion to those of common labour. In London almost all journeymen artificers are liable to be called upon and dismissed by their masters from day to day, and from week to week, in the same manner as day-labourers in other places. The lowest order of artificers, journeymen taylors, accordingly, earn their half a crown a day, though eighteen pence may be reckoned the wages of common labour. In small towns and country villages, the wages of journeymen taylors frequently scarce equal those of common labour; but in London they are often many weeks without employment, particularly during the summer.

When the inconstancy of employment is combined with the hardship, disagreeableness, and dirtiness of the work, it sometimes raises the wages of the most common labour above those of the most skilful artificers. A collier working by the piece is supposed, at Newcastle, to earn commonly about double, and in many parts of Scotland about three times the wages of common labour. His high wages arise altogether from the hardship, disagreeableness, and dirtiness of his work. His employment may, upon most occasions, be as constant as he pleases. The coal-heavers in London exercise a trade which in hardship, dirtiness, and disagreeableness, almost equals that of colliers; and

from the unavoidable irregularity in the arrivals of coal-ships, the employment of the greater part of them is necessarily very inconstant. If colliers, therefore, commonly earn double and triple the wages of common labour, it ought not to seem unreasonable that coal-heavers should sometimes earn four and five times those wages. In the enquiry made into their condition a few years ago, it was found that at the rate at which they were then paid, they could earn from six to ten shillings a day. Six shillings are about four times the wages of common labour in London, and in every particular trade, the lowest common earnings may always be considered as those of the far greater number. How extravagant so-ever those earnings may appear, if they were more than sufficient to compensate all the disagreeable circumstances of the business, there would soon be so great a number of competitors as, in a trade which has no exclusive privilege, would quickly reduce them to a lower rate.

The constancy or inconstancy of employment cannot affect the ordinary profits of stock in any particular trade. Whether the stock is or is not constantly employed depends, not upon the trade, but the trader.

● *Fourthly, the wages of labour vary according to the small or great trust which must be reposed in the workmen.*

The wages of goldsmiths and jewelers are every-where superior to those of many other workmen, not only of equal, but of much superior ingenuity; on account of the precious materials with which they are intrusted.

We trust our health to the physician; our fortune and sometimes our life and reputation to the lawyer and attorney. Such confidence could not safely be reposed in people of a very mean or low condition. Their reward must be such, therefore, as may give them that rank in the society which so important a trust requires. The long time and the great expense which must be laid out in their education, when combined with this circumstance, necessarily enhance still further the price of their labour.

When a person employs only his own stock in trade, there is no trust; and the credit which he may get from other people, depends, not upon the nature of his trade, but upon their opinion of his fortune, probity, and prudence. The different rates of profit, therefore, in the different branches of trade, cannot arise from the different degrees of trust reposed in the traders.

● *Fifthly, the wages of labour in different employments vary according to the probability or improbability of success in them.*

The probability that any particular person shall ever be qualified for the employment to which he is educated, is very different in different occupations. In the greater part of mechanic trades, success is almost certain; but very uncertain in the liberal professions. Put your son apprentice to a shoemaker, there is little doubt of his learning to make a pair of shoes: But send him to study the law, it is at least twenty to one if ever he makes such proficiency as will enable him to live by the business. In a perfectly fair lottery, those who draw the prizes ought to gain all that is lost by those who draw the blanks. In a profession where twenty fail for one that succeeds, that one ought to gain all that should have been gained by the unsuccessful twenty. The counsellor at law who, perhaps, at near forty years of age, begins to make something by his profession, ought to receive the retribution, not only of his own so tedious and expensive education, but of that of more than twenty others who are never likely to make any thing by it. How extravagant soever the fees of counsellors at law may sometimes appear, their real retribution is never equal to this. Compute in any particular place, what is likely to be annually spent, by all the different workmen in any common trade, such as that of shoemakers or weavers, and you will find that the former sum will generally exceed the latter. But make the same computation with regard to all the counsellors and students of law, in all the different inns of court, and you will find that their annual gains bear but a very small proportion to their annual expense, even though you rate the former as high, and the latter as low, as can well be done. The lottery of the law, therefore, is very far from being a perfectly fair lottery; and that, as well as many other liberal and honourable professions, is, in point of pecuniary gain, evidently under-recompenced.

Those professions keep their level, however, with other occupations, and, notwithstanding these discouragements, all the most generous and liberal spirits are eager to crowd into them. Two different causes contribute to recommend them. First, the desire of the reputation which attends upon superior excellence in any of them; and, secondly, the natural confidence which every man has more or less, not only in his own abilities, but in his own good fortune.

To excel in any profession, in which but few arrive at mediocrity, is the most decisive mark of what is called genius or superior talents. The public admiration which attends upon such distinguished abilities, makes always a part of their reward; a greater or smaller in proportion as it is higher or lower in degree. It makes a considerable part of that reward in the profession of physic; a still greater perhaps in that of law; in poetry and philosophy it makes almost the whole.

There are some very agreeable and beautiful talents of which the possession commands a certain sort of admiration; but of which the exercise for the sake of gain is considered, whether from reason or prejudice, as a sort of public prostitution. The pecuniary recompence, therefore, of those who exercise them in this manner, must be sufficient, not only to pay for the time, labour, and expense of acquiring the talents, but for the discredit which attends the employment of them as the means of subsistence. The exorbitant rewards of players, opera-singers, opera-dancers, &c. are founded upon those two principles; the rarity and beauty of the talents, and the discredit of employing them in this manner. It seems absurd at first sight that we should despise their persons, and yet reward their talents with the most profuse liberality. While we do the one, however, we must of necessity do the other. Should the public opinion or prejudice ever alter with regard to such occupations, their pecuniary recompence would quickly diminish. More people would apply to them, and the competition would quickly reduce the price of their labour. Such talents, though far from being common, are by no means so rare as is imagined. Many people possess them in great perfection, who disdain to make this use of them; and many more are capable of acquiring them, if any thing could be made honourably by them.

The over-weening conceit which the greater part of men have of their own abilities, is an ancient evil remarked by the philosophers and moralists of all ages. Their absurd presumption in their own good fortune, has been less taken notice of. It is, however, if possible, still more universal. There is no man living who, when in tolerable health and spirits, has not some share of it. The chance of gain is by every man more or less over-valued, and the chance of loss is by most men under-valued, and by scarce any man, who is in tolerable health and spirits, valued more than it is worth.

That the chance of gain is naturally over-valued, we may learn from the universal success of lotteries. The world neither ever saw, nor ever will see, a perfectly fair lottery; or one in which the whole gain compensated the whole loss; because the undertaker could make nothing by it. In the state lotteries the tickets are really not worth the price which is paid by the original subscribers, and yet commonly sell in the market for twenty, thirty, and sometimes forty per cent advance. The vain hope of gaining some of the great prizes is the sole cause of this demand. The soberest people scarce look upon it as a folly to pay a small sum for the chance of gaining ten or twenty thousand pounds; though they know that even that small sum is perhaps twenty or thirty per cent more than the chance is worth. In a lottery in which no prize exceeded twenty pounds, though in other respects it approached much nearer to a perfectly fair one than the common state lotteries, there would not be the same demand for tickets. In order to have a better chance for some of the great prizes, some people purchase several tickets, and others, small shares in a still greater number. There is not, however, a more certain proposition in mathematics, than that the more tickets you adventure upon, the more likely you are to be a loser. Adventure upon all the tickets in the lottery, and you lose for certain; and the greater the number of your tickets the nearer you approach to this certainty.

That the chance of loss is frequently undervalued, and scarce ever valued more than it is worth, we may learn from the very moderate profit of insurers. In order to make insurance, either from fire or sea-risk, a trade at all, the common premium must be sufficient to compensate the common losses, to pay the expense of management, and to afford such a profit as might have been drawn from an equal capital employed in any common trade. The person who pays no more than this, evidently pays no more than the real value of the risk, or the lowest price at which he can reasonably expect to insure it. But though many people have made a little money by insurance, very few have made a great fortune; and from this consideration alone, it seems evident enough, that the ordinary balance of profit and loss is not more advantageous in this, than in other common trades by which so many people make fortunes. Moderate, however, as the premium of insurance commonly is, many people despise the risk too much to care to pay it. Taking the whole kingdom at an average, nineteen houses in twenty, or rather, perhaps, ninety-nine in a hundred, are not insured from fire. Sea risk is more alarming to the greater part of people, and the proportion of ships insured to those not insured is much greater. Many sail, however, at all seasons, and even in time of war, without any insurance. This may sometimes perhaps be done without any imprudence. When a great company, or even a great merchant, has twenty or thirty ships at sea, they may, as it were, insure one another. The premium saved upon them all, may more than compensate such losses as they are likely to meet with in the common course of chances. The neglect of insurance upon shipping, however, in the same manner as upon houses, is, in most cases, the effect of no such nice calculation, but of mere thoughtless rashness and presumptuous contempt of the risk.

The contempt of risk and the presumptuous hope of success, are in no period of life more active than at the age at which young people choose their professions. How little the fear of misfortune is then capable of balancing the hope of good luck, appears still more evidently in the readiness of the common people to enlist as soldiers, or to go to sea, than in the eagerness of those of better fashion to enter into what are called the liberal professions.

What a common soldier may lose is obvious enough. Without regarding the danger, however, young volunteers never enlist so readily as at the beginning of a new war; and though they have scarce any chance of preferment, they figure to themselves, in their youthful fancies, a thousand occasions of acquiring honour and distinction which never occur. These romantic hopes make the whole price of their blood. Their pay is less than that of common labourers, and in actual service their fatigues are much greater.

The lottery of the sea is not altogether so disadvantageous as that of the army. The son of a creditable labourer or artificer may frequently go to sea with his father's consent; but if he enlists as a soldier, it is always without it. Other people see some chance of his making something by the one trade: nobody but himself sees any of his making any thing by the other. The great admiral is less the object of public admiration than the great general, and the highest success in the sea service promises a less brilliant fortune and reputation than equal success in the land. The same difference runs through all the inferior degrees of preferment in both. By the rules of precedency a captain in the navy ranks with a colonel in the army: but he does not rank with him in the common estimation. As the great prizes in the lottery are less, the smaller ones must be more numerous. Common sailors, therefore, more frequently get some fortune and preferment than common soldiers; and the hope of those prizes is what principally recommends the trade. Though their skill and dexterity are much superior that of almost any artificers, and though their whole life is one continual scene of hardship and danger, yet for all this dexterity and skill, for all those hardships and dangers, while they remain in the condition of common sailors, they receive scarce any other recompence but the pleasure of exercising the one and of surmounting the other. Their wages are not greater than those of common labourers at the port which regulates the rate of seamen's wages. As they are continually going from port to port, the monthly pay of those who sail from all the different ports of Great Britain, is more nearly upon a level than that of any other workmen in those different places; and the rate of the port to and from which the greatest number sail, that is the port of London, regulates that of all the rest. At London the wages of the greater part of the different classes of workmen are about double those of the same classes at Edinburgh. But the sailors who sail from the port of London seldom earn above three or four shillings a month more than those who sail from the port of Leith, and the difference is frequently not so great. In time of peace, and in the merchant service, the London price is from a guinea to about seven-and-twenty shillings the calendar month. A common labourer in London, at the rate of nine or ten shillings a week, may earn in the calendar month from forty to five-and-forty shillings. The sailor, indeed, over and above his pay, is supplied with provisions. Their value, however, may not perhaps always exceed the difference between his pay and that of the common labourer; and though it sometimes should, the excess will not be clear gain to the sailor, because he cannot share it with his wife and family, whom he must maintain out of his wages at home.

The dangers and hair-breadth escapes of a life of adventures, instead of disheartening young people, seem frequently to recommend a trade to them. A tender mother, among the inferior ranks of people, is often afraid to send her son to school at a sea-port town, lest the sight of the ships and the conversation and adventures of the sailors should entice him to go to sea. The distant prospect of hazards, from which we can hope to extricate ourselves by courage and address, is not disagreeable to us, and does not raise the wages of labour in any employment. It is otherwise with those in which courage and address can be of no avail. In trades which are known to be very unwholesome, the wages of labour are always remarkably high. Unwholesomeness is a species of disagreeableness, and its effects upon the wages of labour are to be ranked under that general head.

In all the different employments of stock, the ordinary rate of profit varies more or less with the certainty or uncertainty of the returns. These are in general less uncertain in the inland than in the foreign trade, and in some branches of foreign trade than in others; in the trade to North America, for example, than in that to Jamaica. The ordinary rate of profit always rises more or less with the risk. It does not, however, seem to rise in proportion to it, or so as to compensate it completely. Bankruptcies are most frequent in the most hazardous trades. The most hazardous of all trades, that of a smuggler, though when the adventure succeeds it is likewise the most profitable, is the infallible road to bankruptcy. The presumptuous hope of success seems to act here as upon all other occasions, and to entice so many adventurers into those hazardous trades, that their competition reduces the profit below what is sufficient to compensate the risk. To compensate it completely, the common returns ought, over and above the ordinary profits of stock, not only to make up for all occasional losses, but to afford a surplus profit to the adventurers of the same nature with the profit of insurers. But if the common returns were sufficient for all this, bankruptcies would not be more frequent in these than in other trades.

Of the five circumstances, therefore, which vary the wages of labour, two only affect the profits of stock; the agreeableness or disagreeableness of the business, and the risk or security with which it is attended. In point of agreeableness or disagreeableness, there is little or no difference in the far greater part of the different employments of stock; but a great deal in those of labour; and the ordinary profit of stock, though it rises with the risk, does not always seem to rise in proportion to it. It should follow from all this, that, in the same society or neighbourhood, the average and ordinary rates of profit in the different employments of stock should be more nearly upon a level than the pecuniary wages of the different sorts of labour. They are so accordingly. The difference between the earnings of a common labourer and those of a well employed lawyer or physician, is evidently much greater than that between the ordinary profits in any two different branches of trade. The apparent difference, besides, in the profits of different trades, is generally a deception arising from our not always distinguishing what ought to be considered as wages, from what ought to be considered as profit.

Apothecaries profit is become a bye-word, denoting something uncommonly extravagant. This great apparent profit, however, is frequently no more than the reasonable wages of labour. The skill of an apothecary is a much nicer and more delicate matter than that of any artificer whatever; and the trust which is reposed in him is of much greater importance. He is the physician of the poor in all cases, and of the rich when the distress or danger is not very great. His reward, therefore, ought to be suitable to his skill and his trust, and it arises generally from the price at which he sells his drugs. But the whole drugs which the best employed apothecary, in a large market town, will sell in a year, may not perhaps cost him above thirty or forty pounds. Though he should sell them, therefore, for three or four hundred, or at a thousand per cent profit, this may frequently be no more than the reasonable wages of his labour charged, in the only way in which he can charge them, upon the price of his drugs. The greater part of the apparent profit is real wages disguised in the garb of profit.

In a small sea-port town, a little grocer will make forty or fifty per cent upon a stock of a single hundred pounds, while a considerable wholesale merchant in the same place will scarce make eight or ten per cent upon a stock of ten thousand. The trade of the grocer may be necessary for the conveniency of the inhabitants, and the narrowness of the market may not admit the employment of a larger capital in the business. The man, however, must not only live by his trade, but live by it suitably to the qualifications which it requires. Besides possessing a little capi-tal, he must be able to read, write, and account, and must be a tolerable judge too of, perhaps, fifty or sixty different sorts of goods, their prices, qualities, and the markets where they are to be had cheapest. He must have all the knowledge, in short, that is necessary for a great merchant, which nothing hinders him from becoming but the want of a sufficient capital. Thirty or forty pounds a year cannot be considered as too great a recompence for the labour of a person so accomplished. Deduct this from the seemingly great profits of his capital, and little more will remain, perhaps, than the ordinary profits of stock. The greater part of the apparent profit is, in this case too, real wages.

The difference between the apparent profit of the retail and that of the wholesale trade, is much less in the capital than in small towns and country villages. Where ten thousand pounds can be employed in the grocery trade, the wages of the grocer's labour make but a very trifling addition to the real profits of so great a stock. The apparent profits of the wealthy retailer, therefore, are there more nearly upon a level with those of the wholesale merchant. It is upon this account that goods sold by retail are generally as cheap and frequently much cheaper in the capital than in small towns and country villages. Grocery goods, for example, are generally much cheaper; bread and butcher's meat frequently as cheap. It costs no more to bring grocery goods to the great town than to the country village; but it costs a great deal more to bring corn and cattle, as the greater part of them must be brought from a much greater distance. The prime cost of grocery goods, therefore, being the same in both places, they are cheapest where the least profit is charged upon them. The prime cost of bread and butcher's meat is greater in the great town than in the country village; and though the profit is less, therefore they are not always cheaper there, but often equally cheap. In such articles as bread and butcher's meat, the same cause, which diminishes apparent profit, increases prime cost. The extent of the market, by giving employment to greater stocks, diminishes apparent profit; but by requiring supplies from a greater distance, it increases prime cost. This diminution of the one and increase of the other seem, in most cases, nearly to counter-balance one another; which is probably the reason that, though the prices of corn and cattle are commonly very different in different parts of the kingdom, those of bread and butcher's meat are generally very nearly the same through the greater part of it.

Though the profits of stock both in the wholesale and retail trade are generally less in the capital than in small towns and country villages, yet great fortunes are frequently acquired from small beginnings in the former, and scarce ever in the latter. In small towns and country villages, on account of the narrowness of the market, trade cannot always be extended as stock extends. In such places, therefore, though the rate of a particular person's profits may be very high, the sum or amount of them can never be very great, nor consequently that of his annual accumulation. In great towns, on the contrary, trade can be extended as stock increases, and the credit of a frugal and thriving man increases much faster than his stock. His trade is extended in proportion to the amount of both, and the sum or amount of his profits is in proportion to the extent of his trade, and his annual accumulation in proportion to the amount of his profits. It seldom happens, however, that great fortunes are made even in great towns by any one regular, established, and well-known branch of business, but in consequence of a long life of industry, frugality, and attention. Sudden fortunes, indeed, are sometimes made in such places by what is called the trade of speculation. The speculative merchant exercises no one regular, established, or well known branch of business. He is a corn merchant this year,

and a wine merchant the next, and a sugar, tobacco, or tea merchant the year after. He enters into every trade when he foresees that it is likely to be more than commonly profitable, and he quits it when he foresees that its profits are likely to return to the level of other trades. His profits and losses, therefore, can bear no regular proportion to those of any one established and well-known branch of business. A bold adventurer may sometimes acquire a considerable fortune by two or three successful speculations; but is just as likely to lose one by two or three unsuccessful ones. This trade can be carried on no where but in great towns. It is only in places of the most extensive commerce and correspondence that the intelligence requisite for it can be had.

The five circumstances above mentioned, though they occasion considerable inequalities in the wages of labour and profits of stock, occasion none in the whole of the advantages and disadvantages, real or imaginary, of the different employments of either. The nature of those circumstances is such, that they make up for a small pecuniary gain in some, and counter-balance a great one in others.

In order, however, that this equality may take place in the whole of their advantages or disadvantages, three things are requisite even where there is the most perfect freedom. First, the employments must be well known and long established in the neighbourhood; secondly, they must be in their ordinary, or what may be called their natural state; and thirdly, they must be the sole or principal employments of those who occupy them.

● *First, this equality can take place only in those employments which are well known, and have been long established in the neighbourhood.*

Where all other circumstances are equal, wages are generally higher in new than in old trades. When a projector attempts to establish a new manufacture, he must at first entice his workmen from other employments by higher wages than they can either earn in their own trades, or than the nature of his work would otherwise require, and a considerable time must pass away before he can venture to reduce them to the common level. Manufactures for which the demand arises altogether from fashion and fancy, are continually changing, and seldom last long enough to be considered as old established manufactures. Those, on the contrary, for which the demand arises chiefly from use or necessity, are less liable to change, and the same form or fabric may continue in demand for whole centuries together. The wages of labour, therefore, are likely to be higher in manufactures of the former, than in those of the latter kind. Birmingham deals chiefly in manufactures of the former kind; Sheffield in those of the latter; and the wages of labour in those two different places, are said to be suitable to this difference in the nature of their manufactures.

The establishment of any new manufacture, of any new branch of commerce, or of any new practice in agriculture, is always a speculation, from which the projector promises himself extraordinary profits. These profits sometimes are very great, and sometimes, more frequently, perhaps, they are quite otherwise; but in general they bear no regular proportion to those of other old trades in the neighbourhood. If the project succeeds, they are commonly at first very high. When the trade or practice becomes thoroughly established and well known, the competition reduces them to the level of other trades.

• *Secondly, this equality in the whole of the advantages and disadvantages of the different employments of labour and stock, can take place only in the ordinary, or what may be called the natural state of those employments.*

The demand for almost every different species of labour is sometimes greater and sometimes less than usual. In the one case the advantages of the employment rise above, in the other they fall below the common level. The demand for country labour is greater at haytime and harvest, than during the greater part of the year; and wages rise with the demand. In time of war, when forty or fifty thousand sailors are forced from the merchant service into that of the king, the demand for sailors to merchant ships necessarily rises with their scarcity, and their wages upon such occasions commonly rise from a guinea and seven-and-twenty shillings, to forty shillings and three pounds a month. In a decaying manufacture, on the contrary, many workmen, rather than quit their old trade, are contented with smaller wages than would otherwise be suitable to the nature of their employment.

The profits of stock vary with the price of the commodities in which it is employed. As the price of any commodity rises above the ordinary or average rate, the profits of at least some part of the stock that is employed in bringing it to market, rise above their proper level, and as it falls they sink below it. All commodities are more or less liable to variations of price, but some are much more so than others. In all commodities which are produced by human industry, the quantity of industry annually employed is necessarily regulated by the annual demand, in such a manner that the average annual produce may, as nearly as possible, be equal to the average annual consumption. In some employments, it has already been observed, the same quantity of industry will always produce the same, or very nearly the same quantity of commodities. In the linen or woollen manufactures, for example, the same number of hands will annually work up very nearly the same quantity of linen and woollen cloth. The variations in the market price of such commodities, therefore, can arise only from some accidental variation in the demand. A public mourning raises the price of black cloth. But as the demand for most sorts of plain linen and woollen cloth is pretty uniform, so is likewise the price. But there are other employments in which the same quantity of industry will not always produce the same quantity of commodities. The same quantity of industry, for example, will, in different years, produce very different quantities of corn, wine, hops, sugar tobacco, &c. The price of such commodities, therefore, varies not only with the variations of demand, but with the much greater and more frequent variations of quantity, and is consequently extremely fluctuating. But the profit of some of the dealers must necessarily fluctuate with the price of the commodities. The operations of the speculative merchant are principally employed about such commodities. He endeavours to buy them up when he foresees that their price is likely to rise, and to sell them when it is likely to fall.

• *Thirdly, this equality in the whole of the advantages and disadvantages of the different employments of labour and stock, can take place only in such as are the sole or principal employments of those who occupy them.*

When a person derives his subsistence from one employment, which does not occupy the greater part of his time; in the intervals of his leisure he is often willing to work at another for less wages than would otherwise suit the nature of the employment.

There still subsists in many parts of Scotland a set of people called Cotters or Cottagers, though they were more frequent some years ago than they are now. They are a sort of out-servants of the landlords and farmers. The usual reward which they receive from their masters is a house, a small garden for pot herbs, as much grass as will feed a cow, and, perhaps, an acre or two of bad arable land. When their master has occasion for their labour, he gives them, besides, two pecks of oatmeal a week, worth about sixteen pence sterling. During a great part of the year he has little or no occasion for their labour, and the cultivation of their own little possession is not sufficient to occupy the time which is left at their own disposal. When such occupiers were more numerous than they are at present, they are said to have been willing to give their spare time for a very small recompence to any body, and to have wrought for less wages than other labourers. In ancient times they seem to have been common all over Europe. In countries ill cultivated and worse inhabited, the greater part of the landlords and farmers could not otherwise provide themselves with the extraordinary number of hands, which country labour requires at certain seasons. The daily or weekly recompence which such labourers occasionally received from their masters, was evidently not the whole price of their labour. Their small tenement made a considerable part of it. This daily or weekly recompence, however, seems to have been considered as the whole of it, by many writers who have collected the prices of labour and provisions in ancient times, and who have taken pleasure in representing both as wonderfully low.

The produce of such labour comes frequently cheaper to market than would otherwise be suitable to its nature. Stockings in many parts of Scotland are knit much cheaper than they can any-where be wrought upon the loom. They are the work of servants and labourers, who derive the principal part of their subsistence from some other employment. More than a thousand pair of Shetland stockings are annually imported into Leith, of which the price is from five pence to seven pence a pair. At Learwick, the small capital of the Shetland islands, ten pence a day, I have been assured, is a common price of common labour. In the same islands they knit worsted stockings to the value of a guinea a pair and upwards.

The spinning of linen yarn is carried on in Scotland nearly in the same way as the knitting of stockings, by servants who are chiefly hired for other purposes. They earn but a very scanty subsistence, who endeavour to get their whole livelihood by either of those trades. In most parts of Scotland she is a good spinner who can earn twenty pence a week.

In opulent countries the market is generally so extensive that any one trade is sufficient to employ the whole labour and stock of those who occupy it. Instances of people's living by one employment, and at the same time deriving some little advantage from another, occur chiefly in poor countries. The following instance, however, of something of the same kind is to be found in the capital of a very rich one. There is no city in Europe, I believe, in which house-rent is dearer than in London, and yet I know no capital in which a furnished apartment can be hired so cheap. Lodging is not only much cheaper in London than in Paris; it is much cheaper than in Edinburgh of the same degree of goodness; and what may seem extraordinary, the dearness of house-rent is the cause of the cheapness of lodging. The dearness of house-rent in London arises, not only from those causes which render it dear in all great capitals, the dearness of labour, the dearness of all the materials of building,

which must generally be brought from a great distance, and above all the dearness of ground-rent, every landlord acting the part of a monopolist, and frequently exacting a higher rent for a single acre of bad land in a town, that can be had for a hundred of the best in the country; but it arises in part from the peculiar manners and customs of the people which oblige every master of a family to hire a whole house from top to bottom. A dwelling-house in England means every thing that is contained under the same roof. In France, Scotland, and many other parts of Europe, it frequently means no more than a single story. A tradesman in London is obliged to hire a whole house in that part of the town where his customers live. His shop is upon the ground-floor, and he and his family sleep in the garret; and he endeavours to pay a part of his house-rent by letting the two middle stories to lodgers. He expects to maintain his family by his trade, and not by his lodgers. Whereas, at Paris and Edinburgh, the people who let lodgings have commonly no other means of subsistence; and the price of the lodging must pay, not only the rent of the house, but the whole expense of the family.

4. An Essay on the Principle of Population*

THOMAS ROBERT MALTHUS

PART ONE: OF THE CHECKS TO POPULATION IN THE LESS CIVILISED PARTS OF THE WORLD AND IN PAST TIMES

I. STATEMENT OF THE SUBJECT. RATIOS OF THE INCREASE OF POPULATION AND FOOD

In an inquiry concerning the improvement of society, the mode of conducting

the subject which naturally presents itself, is—

1. To investigate the causes that have hitherto impeded the progress of mankind towards happiness; and,
2. To examine the probability of the total or partial removal of these causes in future.

To enter fully into this question, and to enumerate all the causes that have

*Source: Excerpted from the 8th edition (London: Reeves and Turner, 1878).

hitherto influenced human improvement, would be much beyond the power of an individual. The principal object of the present essay is to examine the effects of one great cause intimately united with the very nature of man; which, though it has been constantly and powerfully operating since the commencement of society, has been little noticed by the writers who have treated this subject. The facts which establish the existence of this cause have, indeed, been repeatedly stated and acknowledged; but its natural and necessary effects have been almost totally overlooked; though probably among these effects may be reckoned a very considerable portion of that vice and misery, and of that unequal distribution of the bounties of nature, which it has been the unceasing object of the enlightened philanthropist in all ages to correct.

The cause to which I allude, is the constant tendency in all animated life to increase beyond the nourishment prepared for it.

It is observed by Dr. [Benjamin] Franklin, that there is no bound to the prolific nature of plants or animals but what is made by their crowding and interfering with each other's means of subsistence. Were the face of the earth, he says, vacant of other plants, it might be gradually sowed and overspread with one kind only, as, for instance, with fennel: and were it empty of other inhabitants, it might in a few ages be replenished from one nation only, as, for instance, with Englishmen.

This is incontrovertibly true. Throughout the animal and vegetable kingdoms Nature has scattered the seeds of life abroad with the most profuse and liberal hand; but has been comparatively sparing in the room and the nourishment necessary to rear them. The germs of existence contained in this earth, if they could freely develop themselves, would fill millions of worlds in the course of a few thousand years. Necessity, that imperious, all-pervading law of nature, restrains them within the prescribed bounds. The race of plants and the race of animals shrink under this great restrictive law; and man cannot by any efforts of reason escape from it.

In plants and irrational animals, the view of the subject is simple. They are all impelled by a powerful instinct to the increase of their species, and this instinct is interrupted by no doubts about providing for their offspring. Wherever, therefore, there is liberty, the power of increase is exerted, and the superabundant effects are repressed afterwards by want of room and nourishment.

The effects of this check on man are more complicated. Impelled to the increase of his species by an equally powerful instinct, reason interrupts his career, and asks him whether he may not bring beings into the world for whom he cannot provide the means of support. If he attend to this natural suggestion, the restriction too frequently produces vice. If he hear it not, the human race will be constantly endeavouring to increase beyond the means of subsistence, But as, by that law of our nature which makes food necessary to the life of man, population can never actually increase beyond the lowest nourishment capable of supporting it, a strong check on population, from the difficulty of acquiring food, must be constantly in operation. This difficulty must fall somewhere, and must necessarily be severely felt in some or other of the various forms of misery, or the fear of misery, by a large portion of mankind.

That population has this constant tendency to increase beyond the means of subsistence, and that it is kept to its necessary level by these causes, will sufficiently appear from a review of the different states of society in which man has existed. But, before we proceed to this review, the subject will perhaps be seen in a clearer light, if we endeavour to ascertain what would be the natural increase of population, if left to exert itself with perfect freedom; and what might be expected to be the rate of increase in the productions of the earth, under the most favourable circumstances of human industry.

It will be allowed that no country has hitherto been known, where the manners were so pure and simple, and the means of subsistence so abundant, that no check whatever has existed to early marriages from the difficulty of providing for a family, and that no waste of the human species has been occasioned by vicious customs, by towns, by unhealthy occupations, or too severe labour. Consequently in no state that we have yet known, has the power of population been left to exert itself with perfect freedom.

Whether the law of marriage be instituted or not, the dictate of nature and virtue seems to be an early attachment to one woman; and where there were no impediments of any kind in the way of a union to which such an attachment would lead, and no causes of depopulation afterwards, the increase of the human species would be evidently much greater than any increase which has been hitherto known.

In the northern states of America, where the means of subsistence have been more ample, the manners of the people more pure, and the checks to early marriages fewer, than in any of the modern states of Europe, the population has been found to double itself, for above a century and a half successively, in less than twenty-five years. Yet, even during these periods, in some of the towns, the deaths exceeded the births, a circumstance which clearly proves that in those parts of the country which supplied this deficiency, the increase must have been much more rapid than the general average.

In the back settlements, where the sole employment is agriculture, and vicious customs and unwholesome occupations are little known, the population has been found to double itself in fifteen years. Even this extraordinary rate of increase is probably short of the utmost

power of population. Very severe labour is requisite to clear a fresh country; such situations are not in general considered as particularly healthy; and the inhabitants, probably, are occasionally subject to the incursions of the Indians, which may destroy some lives, or at any rate diminish the fruits of industry.

According to a table of Euler, calculated on a mortality of 1 in 36, if the births be to the deaths in the proportion of 3 to 1, the period of doubling will be only twelve years and four-fifths. And this proportion is not only a possible supposition, but has actually occurred for short periods in more countries than one.

Sir William Petty supposes a doubling possible in so short a time as ten years.

But, to be perfectly sure that we are far within the truth, we will take the slowest of these rates of increase, a rate in which all concurring testimonies agree, and which has been repeatedly ascertained to be from procreation only.

It may safely be pronounced, therefore, that population, when unchecked, goes on doubling itself every twenty-five years, or increases in a geometrical ratio.

The rate according to which the productions of the earth may be supposed to increase, will not be so easy to determine. Of this, however, we may be perfectly certain, that the ratio of their increase in a limited territory must be of a totally different nature from the ratio of the increase of population. A thousand millions are just as easily doubled every twenty-five years by the power of population as a thousand. But the food to support the increase from the greater number will by no means be obtained with the same facility. Man is necessarily confined in room. When acre has been added to acre till all the fertile land is occupied, the yearly increase of food must depend upon the melioration of the land already in possession. This is a fund, which, from the nature of all soils, instead of increasing, must be gradually diminishing. But population, could it be supplied with food, would go on with unexhausted vigour; and the increase of one period would furnish the power of a greater increase the next, and this without any limit.

From the accounts we have of China and Japan, it may be fairly doubted, whether the best directed efforts of human industry could double the produce of these countries even once in any number of years. There are many parts of the globe, indeed, hitherto uncultivated and almost unoccupied; but the right of exterminating, or driving into a corner where they must starve, even the inhabitants of these thinly peopled regions, will be questioned in a moral view. The process of improving their minds and directing their industry would necessarily be slow; and during this time, as population would regularly keep pace with the increasing produce, it would rarely happen that a great degree of knowledge and industry would have to operate at once upon rich unappropriated soil. Even where this might take place, as it does sometimes in new colonies, a geometrical ratio increases with such extraordinary rapidity, that the advantage could not last long. If the United States of America continue increasing, which they certainly will do, though not with the same rapidity as formerly, the Indians will be driven farther and farther back into the country, till the whole race is ultimately exterminated, and the territory is incapable of further extension.

These observations are, in a degree, applicable to all the parts of the earth where the soil is imperfectly cultivated. To exterminate the inhabitants of the greatest part of Asia and Africa, is a thought that could not be admitted for a moment. To civilise and direct the industry of the various tribes of Tartars and Negroes, would certainly be a work of considerable time, and of variable and uncertain success.

Europe is by no means so fully peopled as it might be. In Europe there is the fairest chance that human industry may receive its best direction. The science of agriculture has been much studied in England and Scotland; and there is still a great portion of uncultivated land in these countries. Let us consider at what rate the produce of this island (Great Britain) might be supposed to increase under circumstances the most favourable to improvement.

If it be allowed that by the best possible policy, and great encouragements to agriculture, the average produce of the island could be doubled in the first twenty-five years, it will be allowing, probably, a greater increase than could with reason be expected.

In the next twenty-five years, it is impossible to suppose that the produce could be quadrupled. It would be contrary to all our knowledge of the properties of land. The improvement of the barren parts would be a work of time and labour; and it must be evident to those who have the slightest acquaintance with agricultural subjects, that in proportion as cultivation extended, the additions that could yearly be made to the former average produce must be gradually and regularly diminishing. That we may be the better able to compare the increase of population and food, let us make a supposition, which, without pretending to accuracy, is clearly more favourable to the power of production in the earth than any experience we have had of its qualities will warrant.

Let us suppose that the yearly additions which might be made to the former average produce, instead of decreasing, which they certainly would do, were to remain the same; and that the produce of this island might be increased every twenty-five years, by a quantity equal to what it at present produces. The most enthusiastic speculator cannot suppose a greater increase than this. In a few centuries it would make every acre of land in the island like a garden.

If this supposition be applied to the

whole earth, and if it be allowed that the subsistence for man which the earth affords might be increased every twenty-five years by a quantity equal to what it at present produces, this will be supposing a rate of increase much greater than we can imagine that any possible exertions of mankind could make it.

It may be fairly pronounced, therefore, that, considering the present average state of the earth, the means of subsistence, under circumstances the most favourable to human industry, could not possibly be made to increase faster than in an arithmetical ratio.

The necessary effects of these two different rates of increase, when brought together, will be very striking. Let us call the population of this island eleven millions; and suppose the present produce equal to the easy support of such a number. In the first twenty-five years the population would be twenty-two millions, and the food being also doubled, the means of subsistence would be equal to this increase. In the next twenty-five years, the population would be forty-four millions, and the means of subsistence only equal to the support of thirty-three millions. In the next period the population would be eighty-eight millions, and the means of subsistence just equal to the support of half that number. And, at the conclusion of the first century, the population would be a hundred and seventy-six millions, and the means of subsistence only equal to the support of fifty-five millions, leaving a population of a hundred and twenty-one millions totally unprovided for.

Taking the whole earth, instead of this island, emigration would of course be excluded; and, supposing the present population equal to a thousand millions, the human species would increase as the numbers, 1, 2, 4, 8, 16, 32, 64, 128, 256; and subsistence as 1, 2, 3, 4, 5, 6, 7, 8, 9. In two centuries the population would be to the means of subsistence as 256 to 9; in three centuries as 4096 to 13, and in two

thousand years the difference would be almost incalculable.

In this supposition no limits whatever are placed to the produce of the earth. It may increase for ever, and be greater than any assignable quantity; yet still the power of population being in every period so much superior, the increase of the human species can only be kept down to the level of the means of subsistence by the constant operation of the strong law of necessity, acting as a check upon the greater power.

II. OF THE GENERAL CHECKS TO POPULATION, AND THE MODE OF THEIR OPERATION

The ultimate check to population appears then to be a want of food, arising necessarily from the different ratios according to which population and food increase. But this ultimate check is never the immediate check, except in cases of actual famine.

The immediate check may be stated to consist in all those customs, and all those diseases, which seem to be generated by a scarcity of the means of subsistence; and all those causes, independent of this scarcity, whether of a moral or physical nature, which tend prematurely to weaken and destroy the human frame.

These checks to population, which are constantly operating with more or less force in every society, and keep down the number to the level of the means of subsistence, may be classed under two general heads—the preventive and the positive checks.

The preventive check, as far as it is voluntary, is peculiar to man, and arises from that distinctive superiority in his reasoning faculties which enables him to calculate distant consequences. The checks to the indefinite increase of plants and irrational animals are all either positive or, if preventive, involuntary. But man cannot look around him, and see the distress which frequently presses upon those who have large families; he cannot contemplate his present possessions or earnings, which he now nearly consumes himself, and calculate the amount of each share, when with very little addition they must be divided, perhaps, among seven or eight, without feeling a doubt whether, if he follow the bent of his inclinations, he may be able to support the offspring which he will probably bring into the world. In a state of equality, if such can exist, this would be the simple question. In the present state of society other considerations occur. Will he not lower his rank in life, and be obliged to give up in great measure his former habits? Does any mode of employment present itself by which he may reasonably hope to maintain a family? Will he not at any rate subject himself to greater difficulties, and more severe labour, than in his single state? Will he not be unable to transmit to his children the same advantages of education and improvement that he had himself possessed? Does he even feel secure that, should he have a large family, his utmost exertions can save them from rags and squalid poverty, and their consequent degradation in the community? And may he not be reduced to the grating necessity of forfeiting his independence, and of being obliged to the sparing hand of charity for support?

These considerations are calculated to prevent, and certainly do prevent, a great number of persons in all civilised nations from pursuing the dictate of nature in an early attachment to one woman.

If this restraint do not produce vice, it is undoubtedly the least evil that can arise from the principle of population. Considered as a restraint on a strong natural inclination, it must be allowed to produce a certain degree of temporary unhappiness; but evidently slight, compared with the evils which result from any of the other checks to population; and merely of the same nature as many other sacrifices of temporary to permanent gratification, which it is the business of a moral agent continually to make.

When this restraint produces vice, the evils which follow are but too conspicuous. A promiscuous intercourse to such a degree as to prevent the birth of children, seems to lower, in the most marked manner, the dignity of human nature. It cannot be without its effect on men, and nothing can be more obvious than its tendency to degrade the female character, and to destroy all its most amiable and distinguishing characteristics. Add to which, that among those unfortunate females with which all great towns abound, more real distress and aggravated misery are, perhaps, to be found, than in any other department of human life.

When a general corruption of morals, with regard to the sex, pervades all the classes of society, its effects must necessarily be to poison the springs of domestic happiness, to weaken conjugal and parental affection, and to lessen the united exertions and ardour of parents in the care and education of their children;—effects which cannot take place without a decided diminution of the general happiness and virtue of society; particularly as the necessity of art in the accomplishment and conduct of intrigues, and in the concealment of their consequences, necessarily leads to many other vices.

The positive checks to population are extremely various, and include every cause, whether arising from vice or misery, which in any degree contribute to shorten the natural duration of human life. Under this head, therefore, may be enumerated all unwholesome occupations, severe labour and exposure to the seasons, extreme poverty, bad nursing of children, large towns, excesses of all kinds, the whole train of common diseases and epidemics, wars, plague, and famine.

On examining these obstacles to the increase of population which are classed under the heads of preventive and positive checks, it will appear that they are all resolvable into moral restraint, vice, and misery.

Of the preventive checks, the restraint from marriage which is not followed by irregular gratifications may properly be termed moral restraint.

Promiscuous intercourse, unnatural passions, violations of the marriage bed, and improper arts to conceal the consequences of irregular connections, are preventive checks that clearly come under the head of vice.

Of the positive checks, those which appear to arise unavoidably from the laws of nature, may be called exclusively misery; and those which we obviously bring upon ourselves, such as wars, excesses, and many others which it would be in our power to avoid, are of a mixed nature. They are brought upon us by vice, and their consequences are misery.

The sum of all these preventive and positive checks, taken together, forms the immediate check to population; and it is evident that, in every country where the whole of the procreative power cannot be called into action, the preventive and the positive checks must vary inversely as each other; that is, in countries either naturally unhealthy, or subject to a great mortality, from whatever cause it may arise, the preventive check will prevail very little. In those countries, on the contrary, which are naturally healthy, and where the preventive check is found to prevail with considerable force, the positive check will prevail very little, or the mortality be very small.

In every country some of these checks are, with more or less force, in constant operation; yet, notwithstanding their general prevalence, there are few states in which there is not a constant effort in the population to increase beyond the means of subsistence. This constant effort as constantly tends to subject the lower classes of society to distress, and to prevent any great permanent melioration of their condition.

These effects, in the present state of society, seem to be produced in the following manner. We will suppose the means of subsistence in any country just equal to the easy support of its inhabitants. The constant effort towards population, which is found to act even in the most vicious societies, increases the number of people before the means of subsistence are increased. The food, therefore, which before supported eleven millions, must now be divided among eleven millions and a half. The poor consequently must live much worse, and many of them be reduced to severe distress. The number of labourers also being above the proportion of work in the market, the price of labour must tend to fall, while the price of provisions would at the same time tend to rise. The labourer therefore must do more work to earn the same as he did before. During this season of distress, the discouragements to marriage and the difficulty of rearing a family are so great, that the progress of population is retarded. In the meantime, the cheapness of labour, the plenty of labourers, and the necessity of an increased industry among them, encourage cultivators to employ more labour upon their land, to turn up fresh soil, and to manure and improve more completely what is already in tillage, till ultimately the means of subsistence may become in the same proportion to the population as at the period from which we set out. The situation of the labourer being then again tolerably comfortable, the restraints to population are in some degree loosened; and, after a short period, the same retrograde and progressive movements with respect to happiness are repeated.

This sort of oscillation will not probably be obvious to common view; and it may be difficult even for the most attentive observer to calculate its periods. Yet that, in the generality of old states, some alternation of this kind does exist, though in a much less marked, and in a much more irregular manner, than I have described it, no reflecting man, who considers the subject deeply, can well doubt.

One principal reason why this oscillation has been less remarked, and less decidedly confirmed by experience than might naturally be expected, is, that the histories of mankind which we possess are, in general, histories only of the higher classes. We have not many accounts that can be depended upon, of the manners and customs of that part of mankind where these retrograde and progressive movements chiefly take place. A satisfactory history of this kind, of one people and of one period, would require the constant and minute attention of many observing minds in local and general remarks on the state of the lower classes of society, and the causes that influenced it; and, to draw accurate inferences upon this subject, a succession of such historians for some centuries would be necessary. This branch of statistical knowledge has, of late years, been attended to in some countries, and we may promise ourselves a clearer insight into the internal structure of human society from the progress of these inquiries. But the science may be said yet to be in its infancy, and many of the objects on which it would be desirable to have information, have been either omitted or not stated with sufficient accuracy. Among these, perhaps, may be reckoned the proportion of the number of adults to the number of marriages; the extent to which vicious customs have prevailed in consequence of the restraints upon matrimony; the comparative mortality among the children of the most distressed part of the community, and of those who live rather more at their ease; the variations in the real price of labour; the observable differences in the state of the lower classes of society, with respect to ease and happiness, at different times during a certain period; and very accurate registers of births, deaths, and marriages, which are of the utmost importance in this subject.

A faithful history, including such particulars, would tend greatly to elucidate the manner in which the constant check upon population acts; and would prob-

ably prove the existence of the retrograde and progressive movements that have been mentioned; though the times of their vibration must necessarily be rendered irregular from the operation of many interrupting causes; such as, the introduction or failure of certain manufactures; a greater or less prevalent spirit of agricultural enterprise; years of plenty, or years of scarcity; wars, sickly seasons, poor-laws, emigrations and other causes of a similar nature.

A circumstance which has, perhaps, more than any other, contributed to conceal this oscillation from common view, is the difference between the nominal and real price of labour. It very rarely happens that the nominal price of labour universally falls; but we well know that it frequently remains the same, while the nominal price of provisions has been gradually rising. This, indeed, will generally be the case, if the increase of manufactures and commerce be sufficient to employ the new labourers that are thrown into the market, and to prevent the increased supply from lowering the money price. But an increased number of labourers receiving the same money wages will necessarily, by their competition, increase the money price of corn. This is, in fact, a real fall in the price of labour; and, during this period, the condition of the lower classes of the community must be gradually growing worse. But the farmers and capitalists are growing rich from the real cheapness of labour. Their increasing capitals enable them to employ a greater number of men; and, as the population had probably suffered some check from the greater difficulty of supporting a family, the demand for labour, after a certain period, would be great in proportion to the supply, and its price would of course rise, if left to find its natural level; and thus the wages of labour, and consequently the condition of the lower classes of society, might have progressive and retrograde movements, though the price of labour might never nominally fall.

In savage life, where there is no regular price of labour, it is little to be doubted that similar oscillations take place. When population has increased nearly to the utmost limits of the food, all the preventive and the positive checks will naturally operate with increased force. Vicious habits with respect to the sex will be more general, the exposing of children more frequent, and both the probability and fatality of wars and epidemics will be considerably greater; and these causes will probably continue their operation till the population is sunk below the level of the food; and then the return to comparative plenty will again produce an increase, and, after a certain period, its further progress will again be checked by the same causes.

But without attempting to establish these progressive and retrograde movements in different countries, which would evidently require more minute histories than we possess, and which the progress of civilisation naturally tends to counteract, the following propositions are intended to be proved:—

1. Population is necessarily limited by the means of subsistence.

2. Population invariably increases where the means of subsistence increase, unless prevented by some very powerful and obvious checks.

3. These checks, and the checks which repress the superior power of population, and keep its effects on a level with the means of subsistence, are all resolvable into moral restraint, vice, and misery. . . .

PART TWO: OF OUR FUTURE PROSPECTS RESPECTING THE REMOVAL OR MITIGATION OF THE EVILS ARISING FROM THE PRINCIPLE OF POPULATION

I. OF MORAL RESTRAINT, AND OUR OBLIGATION TO PRACTISE THIS VIRTUE

As it appears that in the actual state of every society which has come within our review the natural progress of population has been constantly and powerfully checked, and as it seems evident that no improved form of government, no plans of emigration, no benevolent institutions, and no degree or direction of national industry can prevent the continued action of a great check to population in some form or other, it follows that we must submit to it as an inevitable law of nature; and the only inquiry that remains is how it may take place with the least possible prejudice to the virtue and happiness of human society.

All the immediate checks to population which have been observed to prevail in the same and different countries seem to be resolvable into moral restraint, vice, and misery; and if our choice be confined to these three, we cannot long hesitate in our decision respecting which it would be most eligible to encourage.

In the first edition of this essay I observed that as from the laws of nature it appeared that some check to population must exist, it was better that this check should arise from a foresight of the difficulties attending a family and the fear of dependent poverty than from the actual presence of want and sickness. This idea will admit of being pursued farther; and I am inclined to think that from the prevailing opinions respecting population, which undoubtedly originated in barbarous ages, and have been continued and circulated by that part of every community which may be supposed to be interested in their support, we have been prevented from attending to the clear dictates of reason and nature on this subject.

Natural and moral evil seem to be the instruments employed by the Deity in admonishing us to avoid any mode of conduct which is not suited to our being, and will consequently injure our happiness. If we are intemperate in eating and drinking, our health is disordered; if we indulge the transports of anger, we seldom fail to commit acts of which we afterwards repent; if we multiply too fast, we die miserably of poverty and contagious diseases. The laws of nature in all these cases are similar and uniform. They indicate to us that we have followed these impulses too far, so as to trench upon some other law, which equally demands attention. The uneasiness we feel from repletion, the injuries that we inflict on ourselves or others in anger, and the inconveniences we suffer on the approach of poverty, are all admonitions to us to regulate these impulses better; and if we heed not this admonition, we justly incur the penalty of our disobedience, and our sufferings operate as a warning to others. . . .

After the desire of food, the most powerful and general of our desires is the passion between the sexes, taken in an enlarged sense. Of the happiness spread over human life by this passion very few are unconscious. Virtuous love, exalted by friendship, seems to be that sort of mixture of sensual and intellectual enjoyment particularly suited to the nature of man, and most powerfully calculated to awaken the sympathies of the soul, and produce the most exquisite gratifications. Perhaps there is scarcely a man who has once experienced the genuine delight of virtuous love, however great his intellectual pleasures may have been, who does not look back to that period as the sunny spot in his whole life, where his imagination loves most to bask, which he recollects and contemplates with the fondest regret, and which he would wish to live over again.

It has been said by Mr. [William] Godwin, in order to show the evident inferiority of the pleasures of sense, "Strip the commerce of the sexes of all its attendant circumstances, and it would be generally despised." He might as well say to a man who admires trees, Strip them of their spreading branches and lovely foliage, and what beauty can you see in a bare pole? But it was the tree with the branches and foliage, and not without them, that excited admiration. It is "the symmetry of person, the

vivacity, the voluptuous softness of temper, the affectionate kindness of feeling, the imagination, and the wit" of a woman, as Mr. Godwin says, which excites the passion of love and not the mere distinction of her being a female.

It is a very great mistake to suppose that the passion between the sexes only operates and influences human conduct when the immediate gratification of it is in contemplation. The formation and steady pursuit of some particular plan of life has been justly considered as one of the most permanent sources of happiness; but I am inclined to believe that there are not many of these plans formed which are not connected in a considerable degree with the prospect of the gratification of this passion, and with the support of children arising from it. The evening meal, the warm house, and the comfortable fireside would lose half their interest if we were to exclude the idea of some object of affection with whom they were to be shared.

We have also great reason to believe that the passion between the sexes has the most powerful tendency to soften and meliorate the human character, and keep it more alive to all the kindlier emotions of benevolence and pity. Observations on savage life have generally tended to prove that nations in which this passion appeared to be less vivid, were distinguished by a ferocious and malignant spirit, and particularly by tyranny and cruelty to the sex. If indeed this bond of conjugal affection were considerably weakened, it seems probable either that the man would make use of his superior physical strength, and turn his wife into a slave, as among the generality of savages, or at best that every little inequality of temper, which must necessarily occur between two persons, would produce a total alienation of affection; and this could hardly take place without a diminution of parental fondness and care, which would have the most fatal effect on the happiness of society.

5. Of the Demand or Market for Products*

JEAN-BAPTISTE SAY

It is common to hear adventurers in the different channels of industry assert, that their difficulty lies not in the production, but in the disposal of commodities; that products would always be abundant, if there were but a ready demand, or market for them. When the demand for their commodities is slow, difficult, and productive of little advantage, they pronounce money to be scarce; the grand object of their desire is, a consumption brisk enough to quicken sales and keep up prices. But ask them what peculiar causes and circumstances facilitate the demand for their products, and you will soon perceive that most of them have extremely vague notions of these matters; that their observation of facts is imperfect, and their explanation still more so; that they treat doubtful points as matter of certainty, often pray for what is directly opposite to their interests, and importunately solicit from authority a protection of the most mischievous tendency.

To enable us to form clear and correct practical notions in regard to markets for the products of industry, we must carefully analyse the best established and most certain facts, and apply to them the inferences we have already deduced from a similar way of proceeding; and thus perhaps we may arrive at new and important truths, that may serve to enlighten the views of the agents of industry, and to give confidence to the measures of governments anxious to afford them encouragement.

A man who applies his labour to the investing of objects with value by the creation of utility of some sort, can not expect such a value to be appreciated and paid for, unless where other men have the means of purchasing it. Now, of what do these means consist? Of other values of other products, likewise the fruits of industry, capital, and land. Which leads us to a conclusion that may at first sight appear paradoxical, namely, that it is production which opens a demand for products.

Should a tradesman say, "I do not want other products for my woollens, I want money," there could be little difficulty in convincing him that his customers could not pay him in money, without having first procured it by the sale of some other commodities of their own. "Yonder farmer," he may be told, will buy your woollens, if his crops be good, and will buy more or less according to their abundance or scantiness; he can buy none at all, if his crops fail altogether. Neither can you buy his wool nor his corn yourself, unless you contrive to get woollens or some other article to buy withal. You say, you only want money; I say, you want other commodities, and not money. For what, in point of fact, do you want the money? Is it not for the purchase of raw materials or stock for your trade, or victuals for your support?[1] Wherefore, it is products that you want, and not money. The silver coin you will have received on the sale of your own products, and given in the purchase of those of other people, will the next moment execute the same of-

---

*Source: Reprinted from the first American edition of Jean-Baptiste Say, A Treatise on Political Economy, or the Production, Distribution, and Consumption of Wealth, chapter 15 (reprinted in 1880 by Claxton, Rensen & Haffelfinger in Philadelphia). Footnotes renumbered.

fice between other contracting parties, and so from one to another to infinity; just as a public vehicle successively transports objects one after another. If you can not find a ready sale for your commodity, will you say, it is merely for want of a vehicle to transport it? For, after all, money is but the agent of the transfer of values. Its whole utility has consisted in conveying to your hands the value of the commodities, which your customer has sold, for the purpose of buying again from you; and the very next purchase you make, it will again convey to a third person the value of the products you may have sold to others. So that you will have bought, and every body must buy, the objects of want or desire, each with the value of his respective products transformed into money for the moment only. Otherwise, how could it be possible that there should now be bought and sold in France five or six times as many commodities, as in the miserable reign of Charles VI.? Is it not obvious, that five or six times as many commodities must have been produced, and that they must have served to purchase one or the other?

Thus, to say that sales are dull, owing to the scarcity of money, is to mistake the means for the cause; an error that proceeds from the circumstance, that almost all produce is in the first instance exchanged for money, before it is ultimately converted into other produce: and the commodity, which recurs so repeatedly in use, appears to vulgar apprehensions the most important of commodities, and the end and object of all transactions, whereas it is only the medium. Sales cannot be said to be dull because money is scarce, but because other products are so. There is always money enough to conduct the circulation and mutual interchange of other values, when those values really exist. Should the increase of traffic require more money to facilitate it, the want is easily supplied, and is a strong indication of prosperity—a proof that a great abundance of values has been created, which it is wished to exchange for other values. In such cases, merchants know well enough how to find substitutes for the product serving as the medium of

exchange or money:[2] and money itself soon pours in, for this reason, that all produce naturally gravitates to that place where it is most in demand. It is a good sign when the business is too great for the money; just in the same way as it is a good sign when the goods are too plentiful for the warehouses.

When a superabundant article can find no vent, the scarcity of money has so little to do with the obstruction of its sale, that the sellers would gladly receive its value in goods for their own consumption at the current price of the day: they would not ask for money, or have any occasion for that product, since the only use they could make of it would be to convert it forthwith into articles of their own consumption.[3]

This observation is applicable to all cases, where there is a supply of commodities or of services in the market. They will universally find the most extensive demand in those places, where the most of values are produced; because in no other places are the sole means of purchase created, that is, values. Money performs but a momentary function in this double exchange; and when the transaction is finally closed, it will always be found, that one kind of commodity has been exchanged for another.

It is worth while to remark, that a product is no sooner created, than it, from that instant, affords a market for other products to the full extent of its own value. When the producer has put the finishing hand to his product, he is most anxious to sell it immediately, lest its value should diminish in his hands. Nor is he less anxious to dispose of the money he may get for it; for the value of money is also perishable. But the only way of getting rid of money is in the purchase of some product or other. Thus, the mere circumstance of the creation of one product immediately opens a vent for other products.

For this reason, a good harvest is favourable, not only to the agriculturist, but likewise to the dealers in all commodities generally. The greater the crop, the larger are the purchases of the growers. A bad harvest, on the contrary, hurts the sale of commodities at large. And so it is also with the products of manufacture and commerce. The success of one branch of commerce supplies more ample means of purchase, and consequently opens a market for the products of all the other branches; on the other hand, the stagnation of one channel of manufacture, or of commerce, is felt in all the rest.

But it may be asked, if this be so, how does it happen, that there is at times so great a glut of commodities in the market, and so much difficulty in finding a vent for them? Why cannot one of these superabundant commodities be exchanged for another? I answer that the glut of a particular commodity arises from its having outrun the total demand for it in one or two ways; either because it has been produced in excessive abundance, or because the production of other commodities has fallen short.

It is because the production of some commodities has declined, that other commodities are superabundant. To use a more hackneyed phrase, people have bought less, because they have made less profit:[4] and they have made less profit for one or two causes; either they have found difficulties in the employment of their productive means, or these means have themselves been deficient.

It is observable, moreover, that precisely at the same time that one commodity makes a loss, another commodity is making excessive profit.[5] And, since such profits must operate as a powerful stimulus to the cultivation of that particular kind of products, there must needs be some violent means, or some extraordinary cause, a political or natural convulsion, or the avarice or ignorance of authority, to perpetuate this scarcity on the one hand, and consequent glut on the other. No sooner is the cause of this political disease removed, than the means of production feel a natural impulse towards the va-

cant channels, the replenishment of which restores activity to all the others. One kind of production would seldom outstrip every other, and its products be disproportionately cheapened, were production left entirely free.[6]

Should a producer imagine, that many other classes, yielding no material products, are his customers and consumers equally with the classes that raise themselves a product of their own; as, for example, public functionaries, physicians, lawyers, churchmen, &c., and thence infer, that there is a class of demand other than that of the actual producers, he would but expose the shallowness and superficiality of his ideas. A priest goes to a shop to buy a gown or a surplice; he takes the value, that is to make the purchase, in the form of money. Whence had he that money? From some tax-gatherer who has taken it from a tax-payer. But whence did this latter derive it? From the value he has himself produced. This value, first produced by the tax-payer, and afterwards turned into money, and given to the priest for his salary, has enabled him to make the purchase. The priest stands in the place of the producer, who might himself have laid the value of his product on his own account, in the purchase, perhaps, not of a gown or surplice, but of some other more serviceable product. The consumption of the particular product, the gown or surplice, has but supplanted that of some other product. It is quite impossible that the purchase of one product can be affected, otherwise than by the value of another.[7]

From this important truth may be deduced the following important conclusions:—

1. That, in every community the more numerous are the producers, and the more various their productions, the more prompt, numerous, and extensive are the markets for those productions; and, by a natural consequence, the more profitable are they to the producers; for price rises with the demand. But this advantage is to

be derived from real production alone, and not from a forced circulation of products; for a value once created is not augmented in its passage from one hand to another, nor by being seized and expended by the government, instead of by an individual. The man, that lives upon the productions of other people, originates no demand for those productions; he merely puts himself in the place of the producer, to the great injury of production, as we shall presently see.

2. That each individual is interested in the general prosperity of all, and that the success of one branch of industry promotes that of all the others. In fact, whatever profession or line of business a man may devote himself to, he is the better paid and the more readily finds employment, in proportion as he sees others thriving equally around him. A man of talent, that scarcely vegetates in a retrograde state of society, would find a thousand ways of turning his faculties to account in a thriving community that could afford to employ and reward his ability. A merchant established in a rich and populous town, sells to a much larger amount than one who sets up in a poor district, with a population sunk in indolence and apathy. What could an active manufacturer, or an intelligent merchant, do in a small deserted and semi-barbarous town in a remote corner of Poland or Westphalia? Though in no fear of a competitor, he could sell but little, because little was produced; whilst at Paris, Amsterdam, or London, in spite of the competition of a hundred dealers in his own line, he might do business on the largest scale. The reason is obvious: he is surrounded with people who produce largely in an infinity of ways, and who make purchases, each with his respective products, that is to say, with the money arising from the sale of what he may have produced.

This is the true source of the gains made by the towns' people out of the country people, and again by the latter out of the former; both of them have wherewith to buy more largely, the more amply they themselves produce. A city, standing in the centre of a rich surrounding country, feels no want of rich and numerous customers and, on the other hand, the vicinity of an opulent city gives additional value to the produce of the country. The division of na-

tions into agricultural, manufacturing, and commercial, is idle enough. For the success of a people in agriculture is a stimulus to its manufacturing and commercial prosperity; and the flourishing condition of its manufacture and commerce reflects a benefit upon its agriculture also.[8]

The position of a nation, in respect of its neighbours, is analogous to the relation of one of its provinces to the others, or of the country to the town; it has an interest in their prosperity, being sure to profit by their opulence. The government of the United States, therefore, acted most wisely, in their attempt, about the year 1802, to civilize their savage neighbours, the Creek Indians. The design was to introduce habits of industry amongst them, and make them producers capable of carrying on a barter trade with the States of the Union; for there is nothing to be got by dealing with a people that have nothing to pay. It is useful and honourable to mankind, that one nation among so many should conduct itself uniformly upon liberal principles. The brilliant results of this enlightened policy will demonstrate, that the systems and theories really destructive and fallacious, are the exclusive and jealous maxims acted upon by the old European governments, and by them most impudently styled *practical truths*, for no other reason, as it would seem, than because they have the misfortune to put them in practice. The United States will have the honour of proving experimentally, that true policy goes hand-in-hand with moderation ahd humanity.[9]

3. From this fruitful principle, we may draw this further conclusion, that it is no injury to the internal or national industry and production to buy and import commodities from abroad; for nothing can be bought from strangers, except with native products, which find a vent in this external traffic. Should it be objected, that this foreign produce may have been bought with specie, I answer, specie is not always a native. product, but must have been bought itself with the products of native industry; so that, whether the foreign articles be paid for in specie or in home products, the vent for national industry is the same in both cases.[10]

4. The same principle leads to the conclusion, that the encouragement of mere consumption is no benefit to commerce;

for the difficulty lies in supplying the means, not in stimulating the desire of consumption; and we have seen that production alone, furnishes those means. Thus, it is the aim of good government to stimulate production, of bad government to encourage consumption.

For the same reason that the creation of a new product is the opening of a new market for other products, the consumption or destruction of a product is the stoppage of a vent for them. This is no evil where the end of the product has been answered by its destruction, which end is the satisfying of some human want, or the creation of some new product designed for such a satisfaction. Indeed, if the nation be in a thriving condition, the gross national re-production exceeds the gross consumption. The consumed products have fulfilled their office, as it is natural and fitting they should. The consumption, however, has opened no new market, but just the reverse![11]

Having once arrived at the clear conviction, that the general demand for products is brisk in proportion to the activity of production, we need not trouble ourselves much to inquire towards what channel of industry production may be most advantageously directed. The products created give rise to various degrees of demand, according to the wants, the manners, the comparative capital, industry, and natural resources of each country; the article most in request, owing to the competition of buyers, yields the best interest of money to the capitalist, the largest profits to the adventurer, and the best wages to the labourer; and the agency of their respective services is naturally attracted by these advantages towards those particular channels.

In a community, city, province, or nation, that produces abundantly, and adds every moment to the sum of its products, almost all the branches of commerce, manufacture, and generally of industry, yield handsome profits, because the demand is great, and because there is always a large quantity of products in the market, ready to bid for new productive services. And, *vice versâ*, wherever, by reason of the blunders of the nation or its government, production is stationary, or does not keep pace with consumption, the demand gradually declines, the value of the prod-

uct is less than the charges of its production; no productive exertion is properly rewarded; profits and wages decrease; the employment of capital becomes less advantageous and more hazardous; it is consumed piecemeal, not through extravagance, but through necessity, and because the sources of profit are dried up.[12] The labouring classes experience a want of work; families before in tolerable circumstances are more cramped and confined; and those before in difficulties are left altogether destitute. Depopulation, misery, and returning barbarism, occupy the place of abundance and happiness.

Such are the concomitants of declining production, which are only to be remedied by frugality, intelligence, activity, and freedom.

NOTES

1. Even when money is obtained with a view to hoard or bury it, the ultimate object is always to employ it in a purchase of some kind. The heir of the lucky finder uses it in that way, if the miser do not; for money, as money, has no other use than to buy with.

2. By bills at sight, or after date, banknotes, running-credits, write-offs, &c. as at London and Amsterdam.

3. I speak here of their aggregate consumption, whether unproductive and designed to satisfy the personal wants of themselves and their families, or expended in the sustenance of reproductive industry. The woollen or cotton manufacturer operates a two-fold consumption of wool and cotton: 1. For his personal wear. 2. For the supply of his manufacture; but, be the purpose of his consumption what it may, whether personal gratification or reproduction, he must needs buy what he consumes with what he produces.

4. Individual profits must, in every description of production, from the general merchant to the common artisan, be derived from the participation in the values produced. The ratio of that participation will form the subject of Book II., *infrà*.

5. The reader may easily apply these maxims to any time or country he is acquainted with. We have had a striking instance in France during the years 1811,

1812, and 1813; when the high prices of colonial produce of wheat, and other articles, went hand-in-hand with the low price of many others that could find no advantageous market.

6. These considerations have hitherto been almost wholly overlooked, though forming the basis of correct conclusions in matters of commerce, and of its regulation by the national authority. The right course where it has, by good luck been pursued, appears to have been selected by accident, or, at most, by a confused idea of its propriety, without either self-conviction, or the ability to convince other people.

Sismondi, who seems not to have very well understood the principles laid down in this and the three first chapters of Book II. of this work, instances the immense quantity of manufactured products with which England has of late inundated the markets of other nations, as a proof, that it is impossible for industry to be too productive. *(Nouv. Prin.* liv. iv. c. 4.) But the glut thus occasioned proves nothing more than the feebleness of production in those countries that have been thus glutted with English manufactures. Did Brazil produce wherewithal to purchase the English goods exported thither, those goods would not glut her market. Were England to admit the import of the products of the United States, she would find a better market for her own in those States. The English government, by the exorbitance of its taxation upon import and consumption, virtually interdicts to its subjects many kinds of importation, thus obliging the merchant to offer to foreign countries a higher price for those articles, whose import is practicable, as sugar, coffee, gold, silver, &c. for the price of the precious metals to them is enhanced by the low price of their commodities, which accounts for the ruinous returns of their commerce.

I would not be understood to maintain in this chapter, that one product can not be raised in too great abundance, in relation to all others; but merely that nothing is more favourable to the demand of one product, than the supply of another; that the import of English manufactures into Brazil would cease to be excessive and be rapidly absorbed, did Brazil produce on her side returns sufficiently ample; to which end it would be necessary that the legislative bodies of either country should consent, the one to free production, the other to free importation. In Brazil every thing is grasped by monopoly, and property

is not exempt from the invasion of the government. In England, the heavy duties are a serious obstruction to the foreign commerce of the nation, inasmuch as they circumscribe the choice of returns. I happen myself to know of a most valuable and scientific collection of natural history, which could not be imported from Brazil into England by reason of the exorbitant duties. . . .

7. The capitalist, in spending the interest of his capital, spends his portion of the products raised by the employment of that capital. The general rules that regulate the ratio he receives will be investigated in Book II., *infrà.* Should he ever spend the principal, still he consumes products only; for capital consists of products, devoted indeed to reproductive, but susceptible of unproductive consumption; to which it is in fact consigned whenever it is wasted or dilapidated.

8. A productive establishment on a large scale is sure to animate the industry of the whole neighbourhood. ''In Mexico,'' says Humboldt,

the best cultivated tract, and that which brings to the recollection of the traveller the most beautiful part of French scenery, is the level country extending from Salamanca as far as Silao, Guanaxuato, and Villa de Leon, and encircling the richest mines of the known world. Wherever the veins of precious metal have been discovered and worked, even in the most desert part of the Cordilleras, and in the most barren and insulated spots, the working of the mines, instead of interrupting the business of superficial cultivation, has given it more than usual activity. The opening of a considerable vein is sure to be followed by the immediate erection of a town; farming concerns are established in the vicinity; and the spot so lately insulated in the midst of wild and desert mountains, is soon brought into contact with the tracts before in tillage.

Essai pol. sur. la Nouv. Espagne.

9. It is only by the recent advances of political economy, that these most important truths have been made manifest, not to vulgar apprehension alone, but even to the most distinguished and enlightened observers. We read in Voltaire that

such is the lot of humanity, that the patriotic desire for one's country's grandeur, is but a wish for the humiliation of one's neighbours;—that it is clearly impossible for one country to gain, except by the loss of another.

(Dict. Phil. Art. Patrie.) By a continuation of

the same false reasoning, he goes on to declare, that a thorough citizen of the world cannot wish his country to be greater or less, richer or poorer. It is true, that he would not desire her to extend the limits of her dominion, because, in so doing, she might endanger her own well-being; but he will desire her to progress in wealth, for her progressive prosperity promotes that of all other nations.

10. This effect has been sensibly experienced in Brazil of late years. The large imports of European commodities, which the freedom of navigation directed to the markets of Brazil, has been so favourable to its native productions and commerce, that Brazilian products never found so good a sale. So there is an instance of a national benefit arising from importation. By the way it might have perhaps been better for Brazil if the prices of her products and the profits of her producers had risen more slowly and gradually; for exorbitant prices never lead to the establishment of a permanent commercial intercourse; it is better to gain by the multiplication of one's own products than by their increased price.

11. If the barren consumption of a product be of itself adverse to re-production, and a diminution *pro tanto* of the existing demand or vent for produce, how shall we designate that degree of insanity, which would induce a government deliberately to burn and destroy the imports of foreign products, and thus to annihilate the sole advantage accruing from unproductive consumption, that is to say the gratification of the wants of the consumer?

12. Consumption of this kind gives no encouragement to future production, but devours products already in existence. No additional demand can be created until there be new products raised. There is only an exchange of one product for another. Neither can one branch of industry suffer without affecting the rest.

6. On Foreign Trade*

DAVID RICARDO

No extension of foreign trade will immediately increase the amount of value in a country, although it will very powerfully contribute to increase the mass of commodities, and therefore the sum of enjoyments. As the value of all foreign goods is measured by the quantity of the produce of our land and labour, which is given in exchange for them, we should have no greater value, if by the discovery of new markets, we obtained double the quantity of foreign goods in exchange for a given quantity of our's. If by the purchase of English goods to the amount of 1000*l.*, a merchant can obtain a quantity of foreign goods, which he can sell in the English market for 1200*l.*, he will obtain 20 per cent. profit by such an employment of his capital; but neither his gains, nor the value of the commodities imported, will be increased or diminished by the greater or smaller quantity of foreign goods obtained. Whether, for example, he imports twenty-five or fifty pipes of wine, his interest can be no way affected, if at one time the twenty-five pipes, and at another the fifty pipes, equally sell for 1200*l.* In either case his profit will be limited to 200*l.*, or 20 per cent. on his capital; and in either case the same value will be imported into England. If the fifty pipes sold for more than 1200*l.*, the profits of this individual merchant would exceed the general rate of profits, and capital would naturally

*Source: Reprinted from the third edition (London, 1821) of David Ricardo, On the Principles of Political Economy and Taxation, chapter 7. Some footnotes deleted.

flow into this advantageous trade, till the fall of the price of wine had brought every thing to the former level.

It has indeed been contended, that the great profits which are sometimes made by particular merchants in foreign trade, will elevate the general rate of profits in the country, and that the abstraction of capital from other employments, to partake of the new and beneficial foreign commerce, will raise prices generally, and thereby increase profits. It has been said, by high authority, that less capital being necessarily devoted to the growth of corn, to the manufacture of cloth, hats, shoes, &c. while the demand continues the same, the price of these commodities will be so increased, that the farmer, hatter, clothier, and shoemaker, will have an increase of profits, as well as the foreign merchant.[1]

They who hold this argument agree with me, that the profits of different employments have a tendency to conform to one another; to advance and recede together. Our variance consists in this: They contend, that the equality of profits will be brought about by the general rise of profits; and I am of opinion, that the profits of the favoured trade will speedily subside to the general level.

For, first, I deny that less capital will necessarily be devoted to the growth of corn, to the manufacture of cloth, hats, shoes, &c. unless the demand for these commodities be diminished; and if so, their price will not rise. In the purchase of foreign commodities, either the same, a larger, or a less portion of the produce of the land and labour of England will be employed. If the same portion be so employed, then will the same demand exist for cloth, shoes, corn, and hats, as before, and the same portion of capital will be devoted to their production. If, in consequence of the price of foreign commodities being cheaper, a less portion of the annual produce of the land and labour of England is employed in the purchase of foreign commodities,

more will remain for the purchase of other things. If there be a greater demand for hats, shoes, corn, &c. than before, which there may be, the consumers of foreign commodities having an additional portion of their revenue disposable, the capital is also disposable with which the greater value of foreign commodities was before purchased; so that with the increased demand for corn, shoes, &c. there exists also the means of procuring an increased supply, and therefore neither prices nor profits can permanently rise. If more of the produce of the land and labour of England be employed in the purchase of foreign commodities, less can be employed in the purchase of other things, and therefore fewer hats, shoes, &c. will be required. At the same time that capital is liberated from the production of shoes, hats, &c. more must be employed in manufacturing those commodities with which foreign commodities are purchased; and consequently in all cases the demand for foreign and home commodities together, as far as regards value, is limited by the revenue and capital of the country. If one increases, the other must diminish. If the quantity of wine, imported in exchange for the same quantity of English commodities, be doubled, the people of England can either consume double the quantity of wine that they did before, or the same quantity of wine and a greater quantity of English commodities. If my revenue had been 1000*l.*, with which I purchased annually one pipe of wine for 100*l.* and a certain quantity of English commodities for 900*l.*; when wine fell to 50*l.* per pipe, I might lay out the 50*l.* saved, either in the purchase of an additional pipe of wine, or in the purchase of more English commodities. If I bought more wine, and every wine-drinker did the same, the foreign trade would not be in the least disturbed; the same quantity of English commodities would be exported in exchange for wine, and we should receive double the quantity, though not double the value of wine. But if I, and others, contented ourselves with the same quantity of wine as before, fewer English commodities would be exported, and the wine-drinkers might either consume the commodities which were before exported, or any others for which they had an inclination. The capital required for their production would be supplied by the capital liberated from the foreign trade.

There are two ways in which capital may be accumulated: it may be saved either in consequence of increased revenue, or of diminished consumption. If my profits are raised from 1000*l.* to 12000*l.* while my expenditure continues the same, I accumulate annually 200*l.* more than I did before. If I save 200*l.* out of my expenditure, while my profits continue the same, the same effect will be produced; 200*l.* per annum will be added to my capital. The merchant who imported wine after profits had been raised from 20 per cent. to 40 per cent., instead of purchasing his English goods for 1000*l.* must purchase them for 857*l.* 2*s.* 10*d.*, still selling the wine which he imports in return for those goods for 1200*l.*, or, if he continued to purchase his English goods for 1000*l.* must raise the price of his wine to 1400*l.*; he would thus obtain 40 instead of 20 per cent. profit on his capital; but if, in consequence of the cheapness of all the commodities on which his revenue was expended, he and all other consumers could save the value of 200*l.* out of every 1000*l.* they before expended, they would more effectually add to the real wealth of the country; in one case, the savings would be made in consequence of an increase of revenue, in the other, in consequence of diminished expenditure.

If, by the introduction of machinery, the generality of the commodities on which revenue was expended fell 20 per cent. in value, I should be enabled to save as effectually as if my revenue had been raised 20 per cent.; but in one case the rate of profits is stationary, in the other it is raised 20 per cent.—If, by the introduction of cheap foreign goods, I can save 20 per cent. from my expenditure, the effect will be precisely the same as if machinery had lowered the expense of their production, but profits would not be raised.

It is not, therefore, in consequence of the extension of the market that the rate of profit is raised, although such extension may be equally efficacious in increasing the mass of commodities, and may thereby enable us to augment the funds destined for the maintenance of labour, and the materials on which labour may be employed. It is quite as important to the happiness of mankind, that our enjoyments should be increased by the better distribution of labour, by each country producing those commodities for which by its situation, its climate, and its other natural or artificial advantages, it is adapted, and by their exchanging them for the commodities of other countries, as that they should be augmented by a rise in the rate of profits.

It has been my endeavour to shew throughout this work, that the rate of profits can never be increased but by a fall in wages, and that there can be no permanent fall of wages but in consequence of a fall of the necessaries on which wages are expended. If, therefore, by the extension of foreign trade, or by improvements in machinery, the food and necessaries of the labourer can be brought to market at a reduced price, profits will rise. If, instead of growing our own corn, or manufacturing the clothing and other necessaries of the labourer, we discover a new market from which we can supply ourselves with these commodities at a cheaper price, wages will fall and profits rise; but if the commodities obtained at a cheaper rate, by the extension of foreign commerce, or by the improvement of machinery, be exclusively the commodities consumed by the rich, no alteration will take place in the rate of profits. The rate of wages would not be affected, although wine, velvets, silks, and other expensive commodities should fall 50 per cent., and consequently profits would continue unaltered.

Foreign trade, then, though highly beneficial to a country, as it increases the amount and variety of the objects on which revenue may be expended, and affords, by the abundance and cheapness of commodities, incentives to saving, and to the accumulation of capital, has no tendency to raise the profits of stock, unless the commodities imported be of that description on which the wages of labour are expended.

The remarks which have been made respecting foreign trade, apply equally to home trade. The rate of profits is never increased by a better distribution of labour, by the invention of machinery, by the establishment of roads and canals, or by any means of abridging labour either in the manufacture or in the conveyance of goods. These are causes which operate on price, and never fail to be highly beneficial to consumers; since they enable them with the same labour, or with the value of the produce of the same labour, to obtain in exchange a greater quantity of the commodity to which the improvement is applied; but they have no effect whatever on profit. On the other hand, every diminution in the wages of labour raises profits, but produces no effect on the price of commodities. One is advantageous to all classes, for all classes are consumers; the other is beneficial only to producers; they gain more, but every thing remains at its former price. In the first case they get the same as before; but every thing on which their gains are expended, is diminished in exchangeable value.

The same rule which regulates the relative value of commodities in one country, does not regulate the relative value of the commodities exchanged between two or more countries.

Under a system of perfectly free commerce, each country naturally devotes its capital and labour to such employments as are most beneficial to each. This pursuit of individual advantage is admirably connected with the universal good of the whole. By stimulating industry, by rewarding ingenuity, and by using most efficaciously the peculiar powers bestowed by nature, it distributes labour most effectively and most economically: while, by increasing the general mass of productions, it diffuses general benefit, and binds together by one common tie of interest and intercourse, the universal society of nations throughout the civilized world. It is this principle which determines that wine shall be made in France and Portugal, that corn shall be grown in America and Poland, and that hardware and other goods shall be manufactured in England.

In one and the same country, profits are, generally speaking, always on the same level; or differ only as the employment of capital may be more or less secure and agreeable. It is not so between different countries. If the profits of capital employed in Yorkshire, should exceed those of capital employed in London, capital would speedily move from London to Yorkshire, and an equality of profits would be effected; but if in consequence of the diminished rate of production in the lands of England, from the increase of capital and population, wages should rise, and profits fall, it would not follow that capital and population would necessarily move from England to Holland, or Spain, or Russia, where profits might be higher.

If Portugal had no commercial connexion with other countries, instead of employing a great part of her capital and industry in the production of wines, with which she purchases for her own use the cloth and hardware of other countries, she would be obliged to devote a part of that capital to the manufacture of those commodities, which she would thus obtain probably inferior in quality as well as quantity.

The quantity of wine which she shall give in exchange for the cloth of England, is not determined by the respective quantities of labour devoted to the production of each, as it would be, if both commodities were manufactured in England, or both in Portugal.

England may be so circumstanced, that to produce the cloth may require the labour of 100 men for one year; and if she attempted to make the wine, it might require the labour of 120 men for the same time. England would therefore find it her interest to import wine, and to purchase it by the exportation of cloth.

To produce the wine in Portugal, might require only the labour of 80 men for one year, and to produce the cloth in the same country, might require the labour of 90 men for the same time. It would therefore be advantageous for her to export wine in exchange for cloth. This exchange might even take place, notwithstanding that the commodity imported by Portugal could be produced there with less labour than in England. Though she could make the cloth with the labour of 90 men, she would import it from a country where it required the labour of 100 men to produce it, because it would be advantageous to her rather to employ her capital in the production of wine, for which she would obtain more cloth from England, than she could produce by diverting a portion of her capital from the cultivation of vines to the manufacture of cloth.

Thus England would give the produce of the labour of 100 men, for the produce of the labour of 80. Such an exchange could not take place between the individuals of the same country. The labour of 100 Englishmen cannot be given for that of 80 Englishmen, but the produce of the labour of 100 Englishmen may be given for the produce of the labour of 80 Portuguese, 60 Russians, or 120 East Indians. The difference in this respect, between a single country and many, is easily accounted for, by considering the difficulty with which capital moves from one country to another, to seek a more profitable employment, and the activity with which it invariably passes from one province to another in the same country.[2]

It would undoubtedly be advantageous to the capitalists of England, and to the consumers in both countries, that under such circumstances, the wine and the cloth should both be made in Portugal, and therefore that the capital and labour of England employed in making cloth, should be removed to Portugal for that purpose. In that case, the relative value of these commodities would be regulated by the same principle, as if one were the produce of Yorkshire, and the other of London: and in every other case, if capital freely flowed towards those countries where it could be most profitably employed, there could be no difference in the rate of profit, and no other difference in the real or labour price of commodities, than the additional quantity of labour required to convey them to the various markets where they were to be sold.

Experience, however, shews, that the fancied or real insecurity of capital, when not under the immediate control of its owner, together with the natural disinclination which every man has to quit the country of his birth and connexions, and intrust himself with all his habits fixed, to a strange government and new laws, check the emigration of capital. These feelings, which I should be sorry to see weakened, induce most men of property to be satisfied with a low rate of profits in their own country, rather than seek a more advantageous employment for their wealth in foreign nations.

Gold and silver having been chosen for the general medium of circulation, they are, by the competition of commerce, distributed in such proportions amongst the different countries of the world, as to accommodate themselves to the natural traffic which would take place if no such metals existed, and the trade between countries were purely a trade of barter.

Thus, cloth cannot be imported into Portugal, unless it sell there for more gold than it cost in the country from which it was imported; and wine cannot be imported into England, unless it will sell for more there than it cost in Portugal. If the trade were purely a trade of barter, it could only continue whilst England could make cloth so cheap as to obtain a greater quantity of wine with a given quantity of labour, by manufacturing cloth than by growing vines; and also whilst the industry of Portugal were attended by the reverse effects. Now suppose England to discover a process for making wine, so that it should become her interest rather to grow it than import it; she would naturally divert a portion of her capital from the foreign trade to the home trade; she would cease to manufacture cloth for exportation, and would grow wine for herself. The money price of these commodities would be regulated accordingly; wine would fall here while cloth continued at its former price, and in Portugal no alteration would take place in the price of either commodity. Cloth would continue for some time to be exported from this country, because its price would continue to be higher in Portugal than here; but money instead of wine would be given in exchange for it, till the accumulation of money here, and its diminution abroad, should so operate on the relative value of cloth in the two countries, that it would cease to be profitable to exyort it. If the improvement in making wine were of a very important description, it might become profitable for the two countries to exchange employments; for England to make all the wine, and Portugal all the cloth consumed by them; but this could be effected only by a new distribution of the precious metals, which should raise the price of cloth in England, and lower it in Portugal. The relative price of wine would fall in England in consequence of

the real advantage from the improvement of its manufacture; that is to say, its natural price would fall; the relative price of cloth would rise there from the accumulation of money.

Thus, suppose before the improvement in making wine in England, the price of wine here were 50*l*. per pipe, and the price of a certain quantity of cloth were 45*l*., whilst in Portugal the price of the same quantity of wine was 45*l*., and that of the same quantity of cloth 50*l*.; wine would be exported from Portugal with a profit of 5*l*. and cloth from England with a profit of the same amount.

Suppose that, after the improvement, wine falls to 45*l*. in England, the cloth continuing at the same price. Every transaction in commerce is an independent transaction. Whilst a merchant can buy cloth in England for 45*l*. and sell it with the usual profit in Portugal, he will continue to export it from England. His business is simply to purchase English cloth, and to pay for it by a bill of exchange, which he purchases with Portuguese money. It is to him of no importance what becomes of this money: he has discharged his debt by the remittance of the bill. His transaction is undoubtedly regulated by the terms on which he can obtain this bill, but they are known to him at the time; and the causes which may influence the market price of bills, or the rate of exchange, is no consideration of his.

If the markets be favourable for the exportation of wine from Portugal to England, the exporter of the wine will be a seller of a bill, which will be purchased either by the importer of the cloth, or by the person who sold him his bill; and thus without the necessity of money passing from either country, the exporters in each country will be paid for their goods. Without having any direct transaction with each other, the money paid in Portugal by the importer of cloth will be paid to the Portuguese exporter of wine; and in England by the negotiation of the same bill, the exporter of the cloth will be authorized to receive its value from the importer of wine.

But if the prices of wine were such that no wine could be exported to England, the importer of cloth would equally purchase a bill; but the price of that bill would be higher, from the knowledge which the seller of it would possess, that there was no counter bill in the market by which he could ultimately settle the transactions between the two countries; he might know that the gold or silver money which he received in exchange for his bill, must be actually exported to his correspondent in England, to enable him to pay the demand which he had authorized to be made upon him, and he might therefore charge in the price of his bill all the expenses to be incurred, together with his fair and usual profit.

If then this premium for a bill on England should be equal to the profit on importing cloth, the importation would of course cease; but if the premium on the bill were only 2 per cent., if to be enabled to pay a debt in England of 100*l.*, 102*l.* should be paid in Portugal, whilst cloth which cost 45*l.* would sell for 50*l.*, cloth would be imported, bills would be bought, and money would be exported, till the diminution of money in Portugal, and its accumulation in England, had produced such a state of prices as would make it no longer profitable to continue these transactions.

But the diminution of money in one country, and its increase in another, do not operate on the price of one commodity only, but on the prices of all, and therefore the price of wine and cloth will be both raised in England, and both lowered in Portugal. The price of cloth, from being 45*l.* in one country and 50*l.* in the other, would probably fall to 49*l.* or 48*l.* in Portugal, and rise to 46*l.* or 47*l.* in England, and not afford a sufficient profit after paying a premium for a bill to induce any merchant to import that commodity.

It is thus that the money of each country is apportioned to it in such quantities only as may be necessary to regulate a profitable trade of barter. England exported cloth in exchange for wine, because, by so doing, her industry was rendered more productive to her; she had more cloth and wine than if she had manufactured both for herself; and Portugal imported cloth and exported wine, because the industry of Portugal could be more beneficially employed for both countries in producing wine. Let there be more difficulty in England in producing cloth, or in Portugal in producing wine, or let there be more facility in England in producing wine, or in Portugal in producing cloth, and the trade must immediately cease.

No change whatever takes place in the circumstances of Portugal; but England finds that she can employ her labour more productively in the manufacture of wine, and instantly the trade of barter between the two countries changes. Not only is the exportation of wine from Portugal stopped, but a new distribution of the precious metals takes place, and her importation of cloth is also prevented.

Both countries would probably find it their interest to make their own wine and their own cloth; but this singular result would take place: in England, though wine would be cheaper, cloth would be elevated in price, more would be paid for it by the consumer; while in Portugal the consumers, both of cloth and of wine, would be able to purchase those commodities cheaper. In the country where the improvement was made, prices would be enhanced; in that where no change had taken place, but where they had been deprived of a profitable branch of foreign trade, prices would fall.

This, however, is only a seeming advantage to Portugal, for the quantity of cloth and wine together produced in that country would be diminished, while the quantity produced in England would be increased. Money would in some degree have changed its value in the two countries, it would be lowered in England and raised in Portugal. Estimated in money, the whole revenue of Portugal would be diminished; estimated in the same medium, the whole revenue of England would be increased.

Thus then it appears, that the improvement of a manufacture in any country tends to alter the distribution of the precious metals amongst the nations of the world: it tends to increase the quantity of commodities, at the same time that it raises general prices in the country where the improvement takes place.

To simplify the question, I have been supposing the trade between two countries to be confined to two commodities—to wine and cloth; but it is well known that many and various articles enter into the list of exports and imports. By the abstraction of money from one country, and the accumulation of it in another, all commodities are affected in price, and consequently encouragement is given to the exportation of many more commodities besides money, which will therefore prevent so great an effect from taking place on the value of money in the two countries as might otherwise be expected.

Beside the improvements in arts and machinery, there are various other causes which are constantly operating on the natural course of trade, and which interfere with the equilibrium, and the relative value of money. Bounties on exportation or importation, new taxes on commodities, sometimes by their direct, and at other times by their indirect operation, disturb the natural trade of barter, and produce a consequent necessity of importing or exporting money, in order that prices may be accommodated to the natural course of commerce; and this effect is produced not only in the country where the disturbing cause takes place, but, in a greater or less degree, in every country of the commercial world.

This will in some measure account for the different value of money in different countries; it will explain to us why the prices of home commodities, and those of great bulk, though of comparatively small value, are, independently of other causes, higher in those countries where manufactures flourish. Of two countries having precisely the same population, and the same quantity of land of equal fertility in cultivation, with the same knowledge too of agriculture, the prices of raw produce will be highest in that where the greater skill, and the better machinery is used in the manufacture of exportable commodities. The rate of profits will probably differ but little; for wages, or the real reward of the labourer, may be the same in both; but those wages, as well as raw produce, will be rated higher in money in that country, into which, from the advantages attending their skill and machinery, an abundance of money is imported in exchange for their goods.

Of these two countries, if one had the advantage in the manufacture of goods of one quality, and the other in the manufacture of goods of another quality, there would be no decided influx of the precious metals into either; but if the advantage very heavily preponderated in favour of either, that effect would be inevitable.

In the former part of this work, we have assumed, for the purpose of argument, that money always continued of the same value; we are now endeavouring to shew that besides the ordinary variations in the value of money, and those which are common to the whole commercial world, there are also partial variations to which money is subject in particular countries; and in fact, that the value of money is never the same in any two countries, depending as it does on relative taxation, on manufacturing skill, on the advantages of climate, natural productions, and many other causes.

Although, however, money is subject to such perpetual variations, and consequently the prices of the commodities which are common to most countries, are also subject to considerable difference, yet no effect will be produced on the rate of profits, either from the influx or efflux of money. Capital will not be increased, because the circulating medium is augmented. If the rent paid by the farmer to his landlord, and the wages to his labourers, be 20 per cent. higher in one country than another, and if at the same time the nominal value of the farmer's capital be 20 per cent. more, he will receive precisely the same rate of profits, although he should sell his raw produce 20 per cent. higher.

Profits, it cannot be too often repeated, depend on wages; not on nominal, but real wages; not on the number of pounds that may be annually paid to the labourer, but on the number of days' work, necessary to obtain those pounds. Wages may therefore be precisely the same in two countries; they may bear too the same proportion to rent, and to the whole produce obtained from the land, although in one of those countries the labourer should receive ten shillings per week, and in the other twelve.

In the early states of society, when manufactures have made little progress, and the produce of all countries is nearly similar, consisting of the bulky and most useful commodities, the value of money in different countries will be chiefly regulated by their distance from the mines which supply the precious metals; but as the arts and improvements of society advance, and different nations excel in particular manufactures, although distance will still enter into the calculation, the value of the precious metals will be chiefly regulated by the superiority of those manufactures.

Suppose all nations to produce corn, cattle, and coarse clothing only, and that it was by the exportation of such commodities that gold could be obtained from the countries which produced them, or from those who held them in subjection; gold would naturally be of greater exchangeable value in Poland than in England, on account of the greater expense of sending such a bulky commodity as corn the more distant voyage, and also the greater expense attending the conveying of gold to Poland.

This difference in the value of gold, or which is the same thing, this difference in the price of corn in the two countries, would exist, although the facilities of producing corn in England should far exceed those of Poland, from the greater fertility of the land, and the superiority in the skill and implements of the labourer.

If however Poland should be the first to improve her manufactures, if she should succeed in making a commodity which was generally desirable, including great value in little bulk, or if she should be exclusively blessed with some natural production, generally desirable, and not possessed by other countries, she would obtain an additional quantity of gold in exchange for this commodity, which would operate on the price of her corn, cattle, and coarse clothing. The disadvantage of distance would probably be more than compensated by the advantage of having an exportable commodity of great value, and money would be permanently of lower value in Poland than in England. If, on the contrary, the advantage of skill and machinery were possessed by England, another reason would be added to that which before existed, why gold should be less valuable in England than in Poland, and why corn, cattle, and clothing, should be at a higher price in the former country.

These I believe to be the only two causes which regulate the comparative value of money in the different countries of the world; for although taxation occasions a disturbance of the equilibrium of money, it does so by depriving the country in which it is imposed of some of the advantages attending skill, industry, and climate.

It has been my endeavour carefully to distinguish between a low value of money, and a high value of corn, or any other commodity with which money may be compared. These have been generally considered as meaning the same thing; but it is evident, that when corn rises from five to ten shillings a bushel, it may be owing either to a fall in the value of money, or to a rise in the value of corn. Thus we have seen, that from the necessity of having recourse successively to land of a worse and worse quality, in order to feed an increasing population, corn must rise in relative value to other things. If therefore money continue permanently of the same value, corn will exchange for more of such money, that is to say, it will rise in price. The same rise in the price of corn will be produced by such improvement of machinery in manufactures, as shall enable us to manufacture commodities with peculiar advantages: for the influx of money will be the consequence; it will fall in value, and therefore exchange for less corn. But the effects resulting from a high price of corn when produced by the rise in the value of corn, and when caused by a fall in the value of money, are totally different. In both cases the money price of wages will rise, but if it be in consequence of the fall in the value of money, not only wages and corn, but all other commodities will rise. If the manufacturer has more to pay for wages, he will receive more for his manufactured goods, and the rate of profits will remain unaffected. But when the rise in the price of corn is the effect of the difficulty of production, profits will fall; for the manufacturer will be obliged to pay more wages, and will not be enabled to remunerate himself by raising the price of his manufactured commodity.

Any improvement in the facility of working the mines, by which the precious metals may be produced with a less quantity of labour, will sink the value of money generally. It will then exchange for fewer commodities in all countries; but when any particular country excels in manufactures, so as to occasion an influx of money towards it, the value of money will be lower, and the prices of corn and labour will be relatively higher in that country, than in any other.

This higher value of money will not be indicated by the exchange; bills may continue to be negotiated at par, although the prices of corn and labour should be 10, 20, or 30 per cent. higher in one country than another. Under the circumstances supposed, such a difference of prices is the natural order of things, and the exchange can only be at par, when a sufficient quantity of money is introduced into the country excelling in manufactures, so as to raise the price of its corn and labour. If foreign countries should prohibit the exportation of money, and could successfully enforce obedience to such a law, they might indeed prevent the rise in the prices of the corn and labour of the manufacturing country; for such rise can only take place after the influx of the precious metals, supposing paper money not to be used; but they could not prevent the exchange from being very unfavourable to them. If England were the manufacturing country, and it were possible to prevent the importation of money, the exchange with France, Holland, and Spain, might be 5, 10, or 20 per cent. against those countries.

Whenever the current of money is forcibly stopped, and when money is prevented from settling at its just level, there are no limits to the possible variations of the exchange. The effects are similar to those which follow, when a paper money, not exchangeable for specie at the will of the holder, is forced into circulation. Such a currency is necessarily confined to the country where it is issued: it cannot, when too abundant, diffuse itself generally amongst other countries. The level of circulation is destroyed, and the exchange will inevitably be unfavourable to the country where it is excessive in quantity: just so would be the effects of a metallic circulation, if by forcible means, by laws which could not be evaded, money should be detained in a country, when the stream of trade gave it an impetus towards other countries.

When each country has precisely the quantity of money which it ought to have, money will not indeed be of the same value in each, for with respect to many commodities it may differ 5, 10, or even 20 per cent., but the exchange will be at par. One hundred pounds in England, or the silver which is in 100*l*., will purchase a bill of 100*l*., or an equal quantity of silver in France, Spain, or Holland.

In speaking of the exchange and the comparative value of money in different countries, we must not in the least refer to the value of money estimated in commodities, in either country. The exchange is never ascertained by estimating the comparative value of money in corn, cloth, or any commodity whatever, but by estimating the value of the currency of one country, in the currency of another.

It may also be ascertained by comparing it with some standard common to both countries. If a bill on England for 100*l*. will purchase the same quantity of goods in France or Spain, that a bill on Hamburgh for the same sum will do, the exchange between Hamburgh and England is at par; but if a bill on England for 130*l*., will purchase no more than a bill on Hamburgh for 100*l*., the exchange is 30 per cent. against England.

In England 100*l*. may purchase a bill, or the right of receiving 101*l*. in Holland, 102*l*. in France, and 105*l*. in Spain. The exchange with England is, in that case, said to be 1 per cent. against Holland, 2 per cent. against France, and 5 per cent. against Spain. It indicates that the level of currency is higher than it should be in those countries, and the comparative value of their currencies, and that of England, would be immediately restored to par, by abstracting from theirs, or by adding to that of England.

Those who maintained that our currency was depreciated during the last ten years, when the exchange varied from 20 to 30 per cent. against this country, have never contended, as they have been accused of doing, that money could not be more valuable in one country than another, as compared with various commodities; but they did contend, that 130*l*. could not be detained in England, unless it was depreciated, when it was of no more value, estimated in the money of Hamburgh, or of Holland, than the bullion in 100*l*.

By sending 130*l*. good English pounds sterling to Hamburgh, even at an expense of 5*l*., I should be possessed there of 125*l*.; what then could make me consent to give 130*l*. for a bill which would give me 100*l*. in Hamburgh, but that my pounds were not good pounds sterling?—they were deteriorated, were degraded in intrinsic value below the pounds sterling of Hamburgh, and if actually sent there, at an expense of 5*l*., would sell only for 100*l*. With metallic pounds sterling, it is not denied that my 130*l*. would procure me 125*l*. in Hamburgh, but with paper pounds sterling I can only obtain 100*l*.; and yet it was maintained that 130*l*. in paper, was of equal value with 130*l*. in silver or gold.

Some indeed more reasonably maintained, that 130*l*. in paper was not of equal value with 130*l*. in metallic money; but they said that it was the metallic money which had changed its value, and not the paper money. They wished to confine the meaning of the word depreciation to an actual fall of value, and not to a comparative difference between the value of money, and the standard by which by law it is regulated. One hundred pounds of English money was formerly of equal value with, and could purchase 100*l*. of Hamburgh money: in any other country a bill of 100*l*. on England, or on Hamburgh, could purchase precisely the same quantity of commodities. To obtain the same things, I was lately obliged to give 130*l*. English money, when Hamburgh could obtain them for 100*l*. Hamburgh money. If English money was of the same value then as before, Hamburgh money must have risen in value. But where is the proof of this? How is it to be ascertained whether English money has fallen, or Hamburgh money has risen? there is no standard by which this can be determined. It is a plea which admits of no proof, and can neither be positively affirmed, nor positively contradicted. The nations of the world must have been early convinced, that there was no standard of value in nature, to which they might unerringly refer, and therefore chose a medium, which on the whole appeared to them less variable than any other commodity.

To this standard we must conform till the law is changed, and till some other commodity is discovered, by the use of which we shall obtain a more perfect standard, than that which we have established. While gold is exclusively the standard in this country, money will be depreciated, when a pound sterling is not of equal value with 5 dwts. and 3 grs. of standard gold, and that, whether gold rises or falls in general value.

NOTES

1. See Adam Smith, book 1, chapter 9.
2. It will appear then, that a country possessing very considerable advantages in machinery and skill, and which may therefore be enabled to manufacture commodities with much less labour than her neighbours, may, in return for such commodities, import a portion of the corn required for its consumption, even if its land were more fertile, and corn could be grown with less labour than in the country from which it was imported. Two men can both make shoes and hats, and one is superior to the other in both employments; but in making hats, he can only exceed his competitor by one-fifth or 20 per cent., and in making shoes he can excel him by one-third or 33 per cent.;—will it not be for the interest of both, that the superior man should employ himself exclusively in making shoes, and the inferior man in making hats?

7. Of International Values*

JOHN STUART MILL

1. The values of imported commodities depend on the terms of international interchange. The values of commodities produced at the same place, or in places sufficiently adjacent for capital to move freely between them—let us say, for simplicity, of commodities produced in the same country—depend (temporary fluctuations apart) upon their cost of production. But the value of commodity brought from a distant place, especially from a foreign country, does not depend on its cost of production in the place from whence it comes. On what, then, does it depend? The value of a thing in any place, depends on the cost of its acquisition in that place; which in the case of an imported article, means the cost of production of the thing which is exported to pay for it.

Since all trade is in reality barter, money being a mere instrument for exchanging things against one another, we will, for simplicity, begin by supposing the international trade to be in form,

*Source: Reprinted from the seventh edition (Longmans, 1871) of John Stuart Mill, Principles of Political Economy, with Some of Their Applications to Social Philosophy, book 3, Chapter 18. Some footnotes deleted.

what it always is in reality, an actual trucking of one commodity against another. As far as we have hitherto proceeded, we have found all the laws of interchange to be essentially the same, whether money is used or not; money never governing, but always obeying, those general laws.

If, then, England imports wine from Spain, giving for every pipe of wine a bale of cloth, the exchange value of a pipe of wine in England will not depend upon what the production of the wine may have cost in Spain, but upon what the production of the cloth has cost in England. Though the wine may have cost in Spain the equivalent of only ten days' labour, yet, if the cloth costs in England twenty days' labour, the wine, when brought to England, will exchange for the produce of twenty days' English labour, *plus* the cost of carriage; including the usual profit on the importer's capital, during the time it is locked up, and withheld from other employment.

The value, then, in any country, of a foreign commodity, depends on the quantity of home produce which must be given to the foreign country in exchange for it. In other words, the values of foreign commodities depend on the terms of international exchange. What, then, do these depend upon? What is it, which, in the case supposed, causes a pipe of wine from Spain to be exchanged with England for exactly that quantity of cloth? We have seen that it is not their cost of production. If the cloth and the wine were both made in Spain, they would exchange at their cost of production in Spain; if they were both made in England, they would exchange at their cost of production in England: but all the cloth being made in England, and all the wine in Spain, they are in circumstances to which we have already determined that the law of cost of production is not applicable. We must accordingly, as we have done before in a similar embarrassment, fall back upon an antecedent law, that of supply and demand: and in this we

shall again find the solution of our difficulty.

I have discussed this question in a separate Essay, already once referred to; and a quotation of part of the exposition then given, will be the best introduction to my present view of the subject. I must give notice that we are now in the region of the most complicated questions which political economy affords; that the subject is one which cannot possibly be made elementary; and that a more continuous effort of attention than has yet been required, will be necessary to follow the series of deductions. The thread, however, which we are about to take in hand, is in itself very simple and manageable; the only difficulty is in following it through the windings and entanglements of complex international transactions.

2. The terms of international interchange depend on the Equation of International Demand.

When the trade is established between the two countries, the two commodities will exchange for each other at the same rate of interchange in both countries—bating the cost of carriage, of which, for the present, it will be more convenient to omit the consideration. Supposing, therefore, for the sake of argument, that the carriage of the commodities from one country to the other could be effected without labour and without cost, no sooner would the trade be opened than the value of the two commodities, estimated in each other, would come to a level in both countries.

Suppose that 10 yards of broadcloth cost in England as much labour as 15 yards of linen, and in Germany as much as 20.

In common with most of my predecessors, I find it advisable, in these intricate investigations, to give distinctness and fixity to the conception by numerical examples. These examples must sometimes, as in the present case, by purely supposititious. I should have preferred real ones; but all that is essential is, that the numbers should be such as admit of being easily followed through the subsequent combinations into which they enter.

This supposition then being made, it would be the interest of England to import linen from Germany, and of Germany to import cloth from England.

When each country produced both commodities for itself, 10 yards of cloth exchanged for 15 yards of linen in England, and for 20 in Germany. They will now exchange for the same number of yards of linen in both. For what number? If for 15 yards, England will be just as she was, and Germany will gain all. If for 20 yards, Germany will be as before, and England will derive the whole of the benefit. If for any number intermediate between 15 and 20, the advantage will be shared between the two countries. If, for example, 10 yards of cloth exchange for 18 of linen, England will gain an advantage of 3 yards on every 15, Germany will save 2 out of every 20. The problem is, what are the causes which determine the proportion in which the cloth of England and the linen of Germany will exchange for each other.

As exchange value, in this case as in every other, is proverbially fluctuating, it does not matter what we suppose it to be when we begin: we shall soon see whether there be any fixed point about which it oscillates, which it has a tendency always to approach to, and to remain at. Let us suppose, then, that by the effect of what Adam Smith calls the higgling of the market, 10 yards of cloth in both countries, exchange for 17 yards of linen.

The demand for a commodity, that is, the quantity of it which can find a purchaser, varies as we have before remarked, according to the price. In Germany the price of 10 yards of cloth is now 17 yards of linen, or whatever quantity of money is equivalent in Germany to 17 yards of linen. Now, that being the price, there is some particular number of yards of cloth, which will be in demand, or will find purchasers, at that price. There is some given quantity of cloth, more than which could not be disposed of at that price; less than which, at that price, would not fully satisfy the demand. Let us suppose this quantity to be 1000 times 10 yards.

Let us now turn our attention to England. There, the price of 17 yards of linen is 10 yards of cloth, or whatever quantity of money is equivalent in England to 10 yards of cloth. There is some particular number of yards of linen which, at that price, will

exactly satisfy the demand, and no more. Let us suppose that this number is 1000 times 17 yards.

As 17 yards of linen are to 10 yards of cloth, so are 1000 times 17 yards to 1000 times 10 yards. At the existing exchange value, the linen which England requires will exactly pay for the quantity of cloth which, on the same terms of interchange, Germany requires. The demand on each side is precisely sufficient to carry off the supply on the other. The conditions required by the principle of demand and supply are fulfilled, and the two commodities will continue to be interchanged, as we supposed them to be, in the ratio of 17 yards of linen for 10 yards of cloth.

But our suppositions might have been different. Suppose that, at the assumed rate of interchange, England has been disposed to consume no greater quantity of linen than 800 times 17 yards: it is evident that, at the rate supposed, this would not have sufficed to pay for the 1000 times 10 yards of cloth which we have supposed Germany to require at the assumed value. Germany would be able to procure no more than 800 times 10 yards at that price. To procure the remaining 200, which she would have no means of doing but by bidding higher for them, she would offer more than 17 yards of linen in exchange for 10 yards of cloth: let us suppose her to offer 18. At this price, perhaps, England would be inclined to purchase a greater quantity of linen. She would consume, possibly, at that price, 900 times 18 yards. On the other hand, cloth having risen in price, the demand of Germany for it would probably have diminished. If, instead of 1000 times 10 yards, she is now contented with 900 times 10 yards, these will exactly pay for the 900 times 18 yards of linen which England is willing to take at the altered price: the demand on each side will again exactly suffice to take off the corresponding supply; and 10 yards for 18 will be the rate at which, in both countries, cloth will exchange for linen.

The converse of all this would have happened, if, instead of 800 times 17 yards, we had supposed that England, at the rate of 10 for 17, would have taken 1200 times 17 yards of linen. In this case, it is England whose demand is not fully supplied; it is England who, by bidding for more linen, will alter the rate of interchange to her own disadvantage; and 10 yards of cloth will fall, in both countries, below the value of 17 yards of linen. By this fall of cloth, or what is the same thing, this rise of linen, the demand of Germany for cloth will increase, and the demand of England for linen will diminish, till the rate of interchange has so adjusted itself that the cloth and the linen will exactly pay for one another; and when once this point is attained, values will remain without further alteration.

It may be considered, therefore, as established, that when two countries trade together in two commodities, the exchange value of these commodities relatively to each other will adjust itself to the inclinations and circumstances of the consumers on both sides, in such manner that the quantities required by each country, of the articles which it imports from its neighbour, shall be exactly sufficient to pay for one another. As the inclinations and circumstances of consumers cannot be reduced to any rule, so neither can the proportions in which the two commodities will be interchanged. We know that the limits within which the variation is confined, are the ratio between their costs of production in the one country, and the ratio between their costs of production in the other. Ten yards of cloth cannot exchange for more than 20 yards of linen, nor for less than 15. But they may exchange for any intermediate number. The ratios, therefore, in which the advantage of the trade may be divided between the two nations, are various. The circumstances on which the proportionate share of each country more remotely depends, admit only of a very general indication.

It is even possible to conceive an extreme case, in which the whole of the advantage resulting from the interchange would be reaped by one party, the other country gaining nothing at all. There is no absurdity in the hypothesis that, of some given commodity, a certain quantity is all that is wanted at any price; and that, when that quantity is obtained, no fall in the exchange value would induce other consumers to come forward, or those who are already supplied, to take more. Let us suppose that this is the case in Germany with cloth. Before her trade with England commenced, when 10 yards of cloth cost her as much labour as 20 yards of linen, she nevertheless consumed as much cloth as she wanted under any circumstances, and,

if she could obtain it at the rate of 10 yards of cloth for 15 of linen, she would not consume more. Let this fixed quantity be 1000 times 10 yards. At the rate, however, of 10 for 20, England would want more linen than would be equivalent to this quantity of cloth. She would consequently, offer a higher value for linen; or, what is the same thing, she would offer her cloth at a cheaper rate. But, as by no lowering of the value could she prevail on Germany to take a greater quantity of cloth, there would be no limit to the rise of linen or fall of cloth, until the demand of England for linen was reduced by the rise of its value, to the quantity which 1000 times 10 yards of cloth would purchase. It might be, that to produce this diminution of the demand a less fall would not suffice than that which would make 10 yards of cloth exchange for 15 of linen. Germany would then gain the whole of the advantage, and England would be exactly as she was before the trade commenced. It would be for the interest, however, of Germany herself to keep her linen a little below the value at which it could be produced in England, in order to keep herself from being supplanted by the home producer. England, therefore, would always benefit in some degree by the existence of the trade, though it might be a very trifling one.

In this statement, I conceive, is contained the first elementary principle of International Values. I have, as is indispensable in such abstract and hypothetical cases, supposed the circumstances to be much less complex than they really are: in the first place, by suppressing the cost of carriage; next, by supposing that there are only two countries trading together; and lastly, that they trade only in two commodities. To render the exposition of the principle complete, it is necessary to restore the various circumstances thus temporarily left out to simplify the argument. Those who are accustomed to any kind of scientific investigation will probably see, without formal proof, that the introduction of these circumstances cannot alter the theory of the subject. Trade among any number of countries, and in any number of commodities, must take place on the same essential principles as trade between two countries and in two commodities. Introducing a greater number of agents precisely similar, cannot change the law of their action, no more than putting additional weights into the two scales of a balance alters the law of gravitation. It alters nothing but the numerical results. . . .

6. The preceding theory not complete. Thus far had the theory of international values been carried in the first and second editions of this work. But intelligent criticisms (chiefly those of my friend Mr. William Thornton), and subsequent further investigation, have shown that the doctrine stated in the preceding pages, though correct as far as it goes, is not yet the complete theory of the subject matter.

It has been shown that the exports and imports between the two countries (or, if we suppose more than two, between each country and the world) must in the aggregate pay for each other, and must therefore be exchanged for one another at such values as will be compatible with the equation of international demand. That this, however, does not furnish the complete law of the phenomenon, appears from the following consideration: that several different rates of international value may all equally fulfil the conditions of this law.

The supposition was, that England could produce 10 yards of cloth with the same labour as 15 of linen, and Germany with the same labour as 20 of linen; that a trade was opened between the two countries; that England thenceforth confined her production to cloth, and Germany to linen; and, that if 10 yards of cloth should thenceforth exchange for 17 of linen, England and Germany would exactly supply each other's demand: that, for instance, if England wanted at that price 17,000 yards of linen, Germany would want exactly the 10,000 yards of cloth, which, at that price, England would be required to give for the linen. Under these suppositions it appeared, that 10

cloth for 17 linen, would be, in point of fact, the international values.

But it is quite possible that some other rate, such as 10 cloth for 18 linen, might also fulfil the conditions of the equation of international demand. Suppose that at this last rate, England would want more linen than at the rate of 10 for 17, but not in the ratio of the cheapness; that she would not want the 18,000 which she could now buy with 10,000 yards of cloth, but would be content with 17,500, for which she would pay (at the new rate of 10 for 18) 9722 yards of cloth. Germany, again, having to pay dearer for cloth than when it could be bought at 10 for 17, would probably reduce her consumption to an amount below 10,000 yards, perhaps to the very same number, 9722. Under these conditions the Equation of International Demand would still exist. Thus, the rate of 10 for 17, and that of 10 for 18, would equally satisfy the Equation of Demand: and many other rates of interchange might satisfy it in like manner. It is conceivable that the conditions might be equally satisfied by every numerical rate which could be supposed. There is still therefore a portion of indeterminateness in the rate at which the international values would adjust themselves; showing that the whole of the influencing circumstances cannot yet have been taken into account.

7. International values depend not solely on the quantities demanded, but also on the means of production available in each country for the supply of foreign markets. It will be found that to supply this deficiency, we must take into consideration not only, as we have already done, the quantities demanded in each country, of the imported commodities; but also the extent of the means of supplying that demand, which are set at liberty in each country by the change in the direction of its industry.

To illustrate this point it will be necessary to choose more convenient numbers than those which we have hitherto employed. Let it be supposed that in England 100 yards of cloth, previously to the trade, exchanged for 100 of linen, but that in Germany 100 of cloth exchanged for 200 of linen. When the trade was opened, England would supply cloth to Germany, Germany linen to England, at an exchange value which would depend partly on the element already discussed, viz. the comparative degree in which, in the two countries, increased cheapness operates in increasing the demand; and partly on some other element not yet taken into account. In order to isolate this unknown element, it will be necessary to make some definite and invariable supposition in regard to the known element. Let us therefore assume, that the influence of cheapness on demand conforms to some simple law, common to both countries and to both commodities. As the simplest and most convenient, let us suppose that in both countries any given increase of cheapness produces an exactly proportional increase of consumption: or, in other words, that the value expended in the commodity, the cost incurred for the sake of obtaining it, is always the same, whether that cost affords a greater or a smaller quantity of the commodity.

Let us now suppose that England, previously to the trade, required a million of yards of linen, which were worth at the English cost of production, a million yards of cloth. By turning all the labour and capital with which that linen was produced, to the production of cloth, she would produce for exportation a million yards of cloth. Suppose that this is the exact quantity which Germany is accustomed to consume. England can dispose of all this cloth in Germany at the German price; she must consent indeed to take a little less until she has driven the German producer from the market, but as soon as this is effected, she can sell her million of cloth for two millions of linen; being the

quantity that the German clothiers are enabled to make, by transferring their whole labour and capital from cloth to linen. Thus England would gain the whole benefit of the trade, and Germany nothing. This would be perfectly consistent with the equation of international demand: since England (according to the hypothesis in the preceding paragraph) now requires two millions of linen (being able to get them at the same cost at which she previously obtained only one), while the prices in Germany not being altered, Germany requires as before exactly a million of cloth, and can obtain it by employing the labour and capital set at liberty from the production of cloth, in producing the two millions of linen required by England.

Thus far we have supposed that the additional cloth which England could make, by transferring to cloth the whole of the capital previously employed in making linen, was exactly sufficient to supply the whole of Germany's existing demand. But suppose next that it is more than sufficient. Suppose that while England could make with her liberated capital a million yards of cloth for exportation, the cloth which Germany had heretofore required was 800,000 yards only, equivalent at the German cost of production to 1,600,000 yards of linen. England therefore could not dispose of a whole million of cloth in Germany at the German prices. Yet she wants, whether cheap or dear (by our supposition), as much linen as can be bought for a million of cloth: and since this can only be obtained from Germany, or by the more expensive process of production at home, the holders of the million of cloth will be forced by each other's competition to offer it to Germany on any terms (short of the English cost of production) which will induce Germany to take the whole. What terms these would be, the supposition we have made enables us exactly to define. The 800,000 yards of cloth which Germany consumed, cost her the equivalent of 1,600,000 linen, and that invariable cost is what she is willing to expend in cloth, whether the quantity it obtains for her be more or less. England therefore, to induce Germany to take a million of cloth, must offer it for 1,600,000 of linen. The international values will thus be 100 cloth for 160 linen, intermediate between the ratio of the costs of production in England and that of the costs of production in Germany: and the two countries will divide the benefit of the trade, England gaining in the aggregate 600,000 yards of linen, and Germany being richer by 200,000 additional yards of cloth.

Let us now stretch the last supposition still farther, and suppose that the cloth previously consumed by Germany was not only less than the million yards which England is enabled to furnish by discontinuing her production of linen, but less in the full proportion of England's advantage in the production, that is, that Germany only required half a million. In this case, by ceasing altogether to produce cloth, Germany can add a million, but a million only, to her production of linen, and this million, being the equivalent of what the half million previously cost her, is all that she can be induced by any degree of cheapness to expend in cloth. England will be forced by her own competition to give a whole million of cloth for this million of linen, just as she was forced in the preceding case to give it for 1,600,000. But England could have produced at the same cost a million yards of linen for herself. England therefore derives, in this case, no advantage from the international trade. Germany gains the whole; obtaining a million of cloth instead of half a million, at what the half million previously cost her. Germany, in short, is in this third case, exactly in the same situation as England was in the first case; which may easily be verified by reversing the figures.

As the general result of the three cases, it may be laid down as a theorem, that under the supposition we have made of a demand exactly in proportion to the cheapness, the law of international value will be as follows:—

> The whole of the cloth which England can make with the capital previously devoted to linen, will exchange for the whole of the linen which Germany can make with the capital previously devoted to cloth.

Or, still more generally,

> The whole of the commodities which the two countries can respectively make for exportation, with the labour and capital thrown out of employment by importation, will exchange against one another.

This law, and the three different possibilities arising from it in respect to the division of the advantage, may be conveniently generalized by means of algebraical symbols, as follows:—

> Let the quantity of cloth which England can make with the labour and capital withdrawn from the production of linen, be $= n$.
>
> Let the cloth previously required by Germany (at the German cost of production) be $= m$.
>
> Then n of cloth will always exchange for exactly $2m$ of linen.
>
> Consequently if $n = m$, the whole advantage will be on the side of England.
>
> If $n = 2m$, the whole advantage will be on the side of Germany.
>
> If n be greater than m, but less than $2m$, the two countries will share the advantage; England getting $2m$ of linen where she before got only n; Germany getting n of cloth where she before got only m.
>
> It is almost superfluous to observe that the figure 2 stands where it does, only because it is the figure which expresses the advantage of Germany over England in linen as estimated in cloth, and (what is the same thing) of England over Germany in cloth as estimated in linen. If we had supposed that in Germany, before the trade, 100 of cloth exchanged for 1000 instead of 200 of linen, then n (after the trade commenced) would have exchanged for $10m$ instead of $2m$. If instead of 1000 or 200 we had supposed only 150, n would have exchanged for only $3/2m$. If (in fine) the cost value of cloth (as estimated in linen) in Germany, exceeds the cost

value similarly estimated in England, in the ratio of p to q, then will n, after the opening of the trade, exchange for $p/q\ m$.[1]

8. The practical result is little affected by this additional element. We have now arrived at what seems a law of International Values, of great simplicity and generality. But we have done so by setting out from a purely arbitrary hypothesis respecting the relation between demand and cheapness. We have assumed their relation to be fixed, though it is essentially variable. We have supposed that every increase of cheapness produces an exactly proportional extension of demand; in other words, that the same invariable value is laid out in a commodity whether it be cheap or dear; and the law which we have investigated holds good only on this hypothesis, or some other practically equivalent to it. Let us now, therefore, combine the two variable elements of the question, the variations of each of which we have considered separately. Let us suppose the relation between demand and cheapness to vary, and to become such as would prevent the rule of interchange laid down in the last theorem from satisfying the conditions of the Equation of International Demand. Let it be supposed, for instance, that the demand of England for linen is exactly proportional to the cheapness, but that of Germany for cloth, not proportional. To revert to the second of our three cases, the case in which England by discontinuing the production of linen could produce for exportation a million yards of cloth, and Germany by ceasing to produce cloth could produce an additional 1,600,000 yards of linen. If the one of these quantities exactly exchanged for the other, the demand of England would on our present supposition be exactly satisfied, for she requires all the linen which can be got for a million yards of cloth: but Germany perhaps, though she required 800,000 cloth at a cost equivalent to 1,600,000 linen, yet when she can get a million of cloth at the same cost, may not require

the whole million; or may require more than a million. First, let her not require so much; but only as much as she can now buy for 1,500,000 linen. England will still offer a million for these 1,500,000; but even this may not induce Germany to take so much as a million; and if England continues to expend exactly the same aggregate cost on linen whatever be the price, she will have to submit to take for her million of cloth any quantity of linen (not less than a million) which may be requisite to induce Germany to take a million of cloth. Suppose this to be 1,400,000 yards. England has now reaped from the trade a gain not of 600,000 but only of 400,000 yards; while Germany, besides having obtained an extra 200,000 yards of cloth, has obtained it with only seven-eighths of the labour and capital which she previously expended in supplying herself with cloth, and may expend the remainder in increasing her own consumption of linen, or of any other commodity.

Suppose on the contrary that Germany, at the rate of a million cloth for 1,600,000 linen, requires more than a million yards of cloth. England having only a million which she can give without trenching upon the quantity she previously reserved for herself, Germany must bid for the extra cloth at a higher rate than 160 for 100, until she reaches a rate (say 170 for 100) which will either bring down her own demand for cloth to the limit of a million, or else tempt England to part with some of the cloth she previously consumed at home.

Let us next suppose that the proportionality of demand to cheapness, instead of holding good in one country but not in the other, does not hold good in either country, and that the deviation is of the same kind in both; that, for instance, neither of the two increases its demand in a degree equivalent to the increase of cheapness. On this supposition, at the rate of one million cloth for 1,600,000 linen, England will not want so much as 1,600,000 linen, nor Germany so much as a million cloth; and if they fall short of that amount in exactly the same degree: if England only wants linen to the amount of nine-tenths of 1,600,000 (1,440,000), and Germany only nine hundred thousand of cloth, the interchange will continue to take place at the same rate. And so if England wants a tenth more than 1,600,000, and Germany a tenth more than a million. This coincidence (which, it is to be observed, supposes demand to extend cheapness in a corresponding, but not in an equal degree[2]) evidently could not exist unless by mere accident: and in any other case, the equation of international demand would require a different adjustment of international values.

The only general law, then, which can be laid down, is this. The values at which a country exchanges its produce with foreign countries depend on two things: first, on the amount and extensibility of their demand for its commodities, compared with its demand for theirs; and secondly, on the capital which it has to spare, from the production of domestic commodities for its own consumption. The more the foreign demand for its commodities exceeds its demand for foreign commodities, and the less capital it can spare to produce for foreign markets, compared with what foreigners spare to produce for its markets, the more favourable to it will be the terms of interchange: that is, the more it will obtain of foreign commodities in return for a given quantity of its own.

But these two influencing circumstances are in reality reducible to one: for the capital which a country has to spare from the production of domestic commodities for its own use, is in proportion to its own demand for foreign commodities: whatever proportion of its collective income it expends in purchases from abroad, that same proportion of its capital is left without a home market for its productions. The new element, therefore, which for the sake of scientific correctness we have introduced into the theory of international values, does not seem to make any very material difference in the practical result. It still appears, that the countries which carry on their foreign trade on the most advantageous terms, are those whose commodities are most in demand by foreign countries, and which have themselves the least demand for foreign commodities. From which, among other consequences, it follows, that the richest countries, *cæteris paribus*, gain the least by a given amount of foreign commerce: since, having a greater demand for commodities generally, they are likely to have a greater demand for foreign commodities, and thus modify the terms of interchange to their own disadvantage. Their aggregate gains by foreign trade, doubtless, are generally greater than those of poorer countries, since they carry on a greater amount of such trade, and gain the benefit of cheapness on a larger consumption: but their gain is less on each individual article consumed.

NOTES

1. It may be asked, why we have supposed the number n to have as its extreme limits, m and $2m$ (or $p/q\ m$)? why may not n be less than m, or greater than $2m$; and if so, what will be the result?

This we shall now examine, and when we do so it will appear that n is always, practically speaking, confined within these limits.

Suppose, for example, that n is less than m; or, reverting to our former figures, that the million yards of cloth, which England can make, will not satisfy the whole of Germany's pre-existing demand; that demand being (let us suppose) for 1,200,000 yards. It would then, at first sight, appear that England would supply Germany with cloth up to the extent of a million; that Germany would continue to supply herself with the remaining 200,000 by home production: that this portion of the supply would regulate the price of the whole; that England therefore would be able permanently to sell her million of cloth at the German cost of production (viz. for two millions of linen) and would gain the whole advantage of the trade, Germany being no better off than before.

That such, however, would not be the practical result, will soon be evident. The residuary demand of Germany for 200,000 yards of cloth furnishes a resource to England for purposes of foreign trade of which it is still her interest to avail herself; and though she has no more labour and capital which she can withdraw from linen for the production of this extra quantity of cloth, there must be some other commodities in which Germany has a relative advantage over her (though perhaps not so great as in linen): these she will now import, instead of producing, and the labour and capital formerly employed in producing them will be transferred to cloth, until the required amount is made up. If this transfer just makes up the 200,000 and no more, this augmented n will

now be equal to m; England will sell the whole 1,200,000 at the German values; and will still gain the whole advantage of the trade. But if the transfer makes up more than the 200,000, England will have more cloth than 1,200,000 yards to offer; n will become greater than m, and England must part with enough of the advantage to induce Germany to take the surplus. Thus the case which seemed at first sight to be beyond the limits, is transformed practically into a case either coinciding with one of the limits or between them. And so with every other case which can be supposed.

2. The increase of demand from 800,000 to 900,000, and that from a million to 1,440,000, are neither equal in themselves, nor bear an equal proportion to the increase of cheapness. Germany's demand for cloth has increased one-eighth, while the cheapness is increased one-fourth. England's demand for linen is increased 44 per cent, while the cheapness is increased 60 per cent.

III

Criticism of Classicism

Introduction. Probably the finest intellect ever devoted to socialism was Karl Marx (1818-1883), born and raised in Germany. Although his parents were of Jewish origin, they were converted to Christianity when their son was still a young child. At the age of seventeen, Marx enrolled at the University of Bonn. It was his desire at that time to follow his father into the legal profession. However, the very next year he transferred to the University of Berlin, where he studied history, philosophy, and fine arts. It was during his time in Bonn that Marx first encountered the dialectical concept in the Hegelian philosophy—a concept that was to later have great influence on his own work. In 1841 he received a Doctor of Philosophy degree at the university in Jena. Unable to find an academic post because of his radical views and his membership in the Young Hegelians, Marx did freelance writing until he landed a job as a newspaper editor the following year. This position was short-lived, however, since his editorials were so inflammatory that the newspaper was suppressed by the Prussian government.

Marx married Jenny von Westphalen and took her to Paris, which was a gathering place for radical socialists in 1844. It was in Paris that he became editor of the *Franco-German Year Books*, which would have been more properly called the *Year Book* since only one issue was published. Although this job was also transitory, it did introduce him to Frederick Engels, a contributor to the year book who became Marx's lifelong friend. Among the many other radical thinkers that Marx met in Paris was the famous anarchist Pierre Joseph Proudhon, author of a book subtitled *The Philosophy of Poverty*. Playing upon this subtitle, Marx later attacked Proudhons's ideas with his book, *The Poverty of Philosophy* (1847). Proudhon had proposed that the working class be transformed into property owners through the creation of corporate organizations. The purpose of Marx's book was to distance socialism from anarchism. Marx remained in France for only one year, because the French government forced him to leave the country in 1845.

Marx left Paris for Belgium, where he and Engels were approached in Brussels by leaders of the League of the Just, a group of working-class radicals from many different countries. At that same time the rest of the group was holding a convention in London. In Brussels, Marx and Engels were asked to write a declaration of principles, because this underground organization was now wanting to announce its beliefs to the public at large. The two men drew up the famous *Communist Manifesto*, which was built around a proposition that—in Engels' words—was "to do for history what Darwin's theory has done for biology. . . ." The proposition states that the history of mankind is a history of struggle between the exploiting and exploited classes, but mankind is now developed to a stage where it will free itself from exploitation and all class distinctions. Under the influence of Marx and Engels, the League of the Just changed their name to the Communist League. It was because the 1848 Belgian revolution was producing much social unrest that this radical group then dared to come out into public view. Nevertheless, the revolution so frightened the government that it forced the entire group to leave Belguim, limiting Marx's stay there to three years.

Marx returned to Germany, where he took part in the German revolution and edited a newspaper that lasted about eighteen months. Immediately following the revolution, he was pressured by the German government to leave the country. Returning to Paris, he was again expelled from France after a very brief stay. The unwelcome fugitive moved to England in 1850, finally putting down roots in London, his home for the rest of his life. Throughout the 1850s Marx and his family lived at a subsistence level in London's slums. Fortunately, he received some financial support from Engels, who was working for his wealthy father in England's textile industry. During this period Marx did some free-lance writing but mainly spent his time studying works of the classical economists. He also did extensive reading in the government's "blue books," reports of investigating committees on working conditions in various industries. In 1859 he published his *Critique of Political Economy*, and in 1864 he helped organize the International Workingmen's Association, which later fell apart due to infighting among its leaders.

The first volume of Marx's magnum opus, *Capital*, appeared in a German edition in 1867. The first English translation was not published until 1886. The second and third volumes of *Capital* were published posthumously and were edited by Engels. Marx had left notes for a fourth volume, but that material was organized by Karl Kautsky into a book entitled *Theories of Surplus Value*. Frequently referred to as the "Bible of Socialism," *Capital* is a monumental work encompassing sociology, history, philosophy and economics. Although it has had no significant impact on the structure of modern theories of value and distribution, and although it has failed to fine tune classical theory in general, it has been a source of inspiration to working-class movements in every part of the world. Because of this powerful influence, Marx is still remembered in places where the name of every classical economist has been long forgotten. The selections reprinted here are taken from parts 2 and 3 of volume 1 of *Capital*. Marx's famous riddle of surplus value is introduced to the reader in chapter 4 of part 2. This excerpt is followed by his solution to the riddle in chapters 6 and 7, where Marx distinguished between "labor" and "labor power" and identified what he believed to be "unpaid labor."

8. Capital*

KARL HEINRICH MARX

THE GENERAL FORMULA FOR CAPITAL

The circulation of commodities is the starting-point of capital. The production of commodities, their circulation, and that more developed form of their circulation called commerce, these form the historical ground-work from which it rises. The modern history of capital dates from the creation in the 16th century of a world-embracing commerce and a world-embracing market.

If we abstract from the material substance of the circulation of commodities, that is, from the exchange of the various use-values, and consider only the economic forms produced by this process of circulation, we find its final result to be money: this final product of the circulation of commodities is the first form in which capital appears.

As a matter of history, capital, as opposed to landed property, invariably takes the form at first of money; it appears as moneyed wealth, as the capital of the merchant and of the usurer. But we have no need to refer to the origin of capital in order to discover that the first form of appearance of capital is money.

We can see it daily under our very eyes. All new capital, to commence with, comes on the stage, that is, on the market, whether of commodities, labour, or money, even in our days, in the shape of money that by a definite process has to be transformed into capital.

The first distinction we notice between money that is money only, and money that is capital, is nothing more than a difference in their form of circulation.

The simplest form of the circulation of commodities is C—M—C, the transformation of commodities into money, and the change of the money back again into commodities; or selling in order to buy. But alongside of this form we find another specifically different form: M—C—M, the transformation of money into commodities, and the change of commodities back again into money; or buying in order to sell. Money that circulates in the latter manner is thereby transformed into, becomes capital, and is already potentially capital.

Now let us examine the circuit M—C—M a little closer. It consists, like the other, of two antithetical phases. In the first phase, M—C, or the purchase,

---

Source: Reprinted from the English edition (London: Swan Sonnenschein, Lowry & Company) 1887, translated from the third German edition. The selection reprinted here originally appeared as part 2, chapters 4, 6 and 7. Footnotes deleted.

the money is changed into a commodity. In the second phase, C—M, or the sale, the commodity is changed back again into money. The combination of these two phases constitutes the single movement whereby money is exchanged for a commodity, and the same commodity is again exchanged for money; whereby a commodity is bought in order to be sold, or, neglecting the distinction in form between buying and selling, whereby a commodity is bought with money, and then money is bought with a commodity. The result, in which the phases of the process vanish, is the exchange of money for money, M—M. If I purchase 2,000 lbs. of cotton for £100, and resell the 2,000 lbs. of cotton for £110, I have, in fact, exchanged £100 for £110, money for money.

Now it is evident that the circuit M—C—M would be absurd and without meaning if the intention were to exchange by this means two equal sums of money, £100 for £100. The miser's plan would be far simpler and surer; he sticks to his £100 instead of exposing it to the dangers of circulation. And yet, whether the merchant who has paid £100 for his cotton sells it for £110, or lets it go for £100, or even £50, his money has, at all events, gone through a characteristic and original movement, quite different in kind from that which it goes through in the hands of the peasant who sells corn, and with the money thus set free buys clothes. We have therefore to examine first the distinguishing characteristics of the forms of the circuits M—C—M and C—M—C, and in doing this the real difference that underlies the mere difference of form will reveal itself.

Let us see, in the first place, what the two forms have in common.

Both circuits are resolvable into the same two antithetical phases, C—M, a sale, and M—C, a purchase. In each of these phases the same material elements—a commodity, and money, and the same economic dramatis per-

sonae, a buyer and a seller—confront one another. Each circuit is the unity of the same two antithetical phases, and in each case this unity is brought about by the intervention of three contracting parties, of whom one only sells, another only buys, while the third both buys and sells.

What, however, first and foremost distinguishes the circuit C—M—C from the circuit M—C—M, is the inverted order of succession of the two phases. The simple circulation of commodities begins with a sale and ends with a purchase, while the circulation of money as capital begins with a purchase and ends with a sale. In the one case both the starting-point and the goal are commodities, in the other they are money. In the first form the movement is brought about by the intervention of money, in the second by that of a commodity.

In the circulation C—M—C, the money is in the end converted into a commodity, that serves as a use-value; it is spent once for all. In the inverted form, M—C—M, on the contrary, the buyer lays out money in order that, as a seller, he may recover money. By the purchase of his commodity he throws money into circulation, in order to withdraw it again by the sale of the same commodity. He lets the money go, but only with the sly intention of getting it back again. The money, therefore, is not spent, it is merely advanced.

In the circuit C—M—C, the same piece of money changes its place twice. The seller gets it from the buyer and pays it away to another seller. The complete circulation, which begins with the receipt, concludes with the payment, of money for commodities. It is the very contrary in the circuit M—C—M. Here it is not the piece of money that changes its place twice, but the commodity. The buyer takes it from the hands of the seller and passes it into the hands of another buyer. Just as in the simple circulation of commodities the double change of place of the same piece of money effects its passage from one hand into another, so here the double change of place of the same commodity brings about the reflux of the money to its point of departure.

Such reflux is not dependent on the commodity being sold for more than was paid for it. This circumstance influences only the amount of the money that comes back. The reflux itself takes place, so soon as the purchased commodity is resold, in other words, so soon as the circuit M—C—M is completed. We have here, therefore, a palpable difference between the circulation of money as capital, and its circulation as mere money.

The circuit C—M—C comes completely to an end, so soon as the money brought in by the sale of one commodity is abstracted again by the purchase of another.

If, nevertheless, there follows a reflux of money to its starting-point, this can only happen through a renewal or repetition of the operation. If I sell a quarter of corn for £3, and with this £3 buy clothes, the money, so far as I am concerned, is spent and done with. It belongs to the clothes merchant. If I now sell a second quarter of corn, money indeed flows back to me, not however as a sequel to the first transaction, but in consequence of its repetition. The money again leaves me, so soon as I complete this second transaction by a fresh purchase. Therefore, in the circuit C—M—C, the expenditure of money has nothing to do with its reflux. On the other hand, in M—C—M, the reflux of the money is conditioned by the very mode of its expenditure. Without this reflux, the operation fails, or the process is interrupted and incomplete, owing to the absence of its complementary and final phase, the sale.

The circuit C—M—C starts with one commodity, and finishes with another, which falls out of circulation and into consumption. Consumption, the satisfaction of wants, in one word, use-

value, is its end and aim. The circuit M—C—M, on the contrary, commences with money and ends with money. Its leading motive, and the goal that attracts it, is therefore mere exchange-value.

In the simple circulation of commodities, the two extremes of the circuit have the same economic form. They are both commodities, and commodities of equal value. But they are also use-values differing in their qualities, as, for example, corn and clothes. The exchange of products, of the different materials in which the labour of society is embodied, forms here the basis of the movement. It is otherwise in the circulation M—C—M, which at first sign appears purposeless, because tautological. Both extremes have the same economic form. They are both money, and therefore are not qualitatively different use-values; for money is but the converted form of commodities, in which their particular use-values vanish. To exchange £100 for cotton, and then this same cotton again for £100, is merely a roundabout way of exchanging money for money, the same for the same, and appears to be an operation just as purposeless as it is absurd. One sum of money is distinguishable from another only by its amount. The character and tendency of the process M—C—M, is therefore not due to any qualitative difference between its extremes, both being money, but solely to their quantitative difference. More money is withdrawn from circulation at the finish than was thrown into it at the start. The cotton that was bought for £100 is perhaps resold for £100 + £10 or £110. The exact form of this process is therefore M—C—M, where M' = M + ΔM = the original sum advanced, plus an increment. This increment or excess over the original sum advanced, plus an increment. This increment or excess over the original value I call "surplus-value." The value originally advanced, therefore, not only remains intact while in circulation, but adds to itself a surplus-value or expands itself. It is this movement that converts it into capital.

Of course, it is also possible, that in C—M—C, the two extremes C-–C, say corn and clothes, may represent different quantities of value. The farmer may sell his corn above its value, or may buy the clothes at less than their value. He may, on the other hand, "be done" by the clothes merchant. Yet, in the form of circulation now under consideration, such differences in value are purely accidental. The fact that the corn and the clothes are equivalents, does not deprive the process of all meaning, as it does in M—C—M. The equivalence of their values is rather a necessary condition to its normal course.

The repetition or renewal of the act of selling in order to buy, is kept within bounds by the very object it aims at, namely, consumption or the satisfaction of definite wants, an aim that lies altogether outside the sphere of circulation. But when we buy in order to sell, we, on the contrary, begin and end with the same thing, money, exchange-value; and thereby the movement becomes interminable. No doubt, M becomes M + ΔM, £100 become £110. But when viewed in their qualitative aspect alone, £110 are the same as £100, namely money; and considered quantitatively, £110 is, like £100, a sum of definite and limited value. If now, the £110 be spent as money, they cease to play their part. They are no longer capital. Withdrawn from circulation, they become petrified into a hoard, and though they remained in that state till doomsday, not a single farthing would accrue to them. If, then, the expansion of value is once aimed at, there is just the same inducement to augment the value of the £110 as that of the £100; for both are but limited expressions for exchange-value, and therefore both have the same vocation to approach, by quantitative increase, as near as possible to absolute wealth. Momentarily,

indeed, the value originally advanced, the £100 is distinguishable from the surplus-value of £10 that is annexed to it during circulation; but the distinction vanishes immediately. At the end of the process, we do not receive with one hand the original £100, and with the other, the surplus-value of £10. We simply get a value of £110, which is in exactly the same condition and fitness for commencing the expanding process, as the original £100 was. Money ends the movement only to begin it again. Therefore, the final result of every separate circuit, in which a purchase and consequent sale are completed, forms of itself the starting-point of a new circuit. The simple circulation of commodities—selling in order to buy—is a means of carrying out a purpose unconnected with circulation, namely, the appropriation of use-values, the satisfaction of wants. The circulation of money as capital is, on the contrary, an end in itself, for the expansion of value takes place only within this constantly renewed movement. The circulation of capital has therefore no limits.

As the conscious representative of this movement, the possessor of money becomes a capitalist. His person, or rather his pocket, is the point from which the money starts and to which it returns. The expansion of value, which is the objective basis or main-spring of the circulation M—C—M, becomes his subjective aim, and it is only in so far as the appropriation of ever more and more wealth in the abstract becomes the sole motive of his operations, that he functions as a capitalist, that is, as capital personified and endowed with consciousness and a will. Use-values must therefore never be looked upon as the real aim of the capitalist; neither must the profit on any single transaction. The restless never-ending process of profit-making alone is what he aims at. This boundless greed after riches, this passionate chase after exchange-value, is common to the capitalist and the miser;

but while the miser is merely a capitalist gone mad, the capitalist is a rational miser. The never-ending augmentation of exchange-value, which the miser strives after, by seeking to save his money from circulation, is attained by the more acute capitalist, by constantly throwing it afresh into circulation.

The independent form, i.e., the money-form, which the value of commodities assumes in the case of simple circulation, serves only one purpose, namely, their exchange, and vanishes in the final result of the movement. On the other hand, in the circulation M—C—M, both the money and the commodity represent only different modes of existence of value itself, the money its general mode, and the commodity its particular, or, so to say, disguised mode. It is constantly changing from one form to the other without thereby becoming lost, and thus assumes an automatically active character. If now we take in turn each of the two different forms which self-expanding value successively assumes in the course of its life, we then arrive at these two propositions: Capital is money: Capital is commodities. In truth, however, value is here the active factor in a process, in which, while constantly assuming the form in turn of money and commodities, it at the same time changes in magnitude, differentiates itself by throwing off surplus-value from itself; the original value, in other words, expands spontaneously. For the movement, in the course of which it adds surplus-value, is its own movement, its expansion, therefore, is automatic expansion. Because it is value, it has acquired the occult quality of being able to add value to itself. It brings forth living offspring, or, at the least, lays golden eggs.

Value, therefore, being the active factor in such a process, and assuming at one time the form of money, at another that of commodities, but through all these changes preserving itself and expanding, it requires some independent form, by means of which its identity may at any time be established. And this form it possesses only in the shape of money. It is under the form of money that value begins and ends, and begins again, every act of its own spontaneous generation. It began by being £100, it is now £110, and so on. But the money itself is only one of the two forms of value. Unless it takes the form of some commodity, it does not become capital. There is here no antagonism, as in the case of hoarding, between the money and commodities. The capitalist knows that all commodities, however scurvy they may look, or however badly they may smell, are in faith and in truth money, inwardly circumcised Jews, and what is more, a wonderful means whereby out of money to make more money.

In simple circulation, C—M—C, the value of commodities attained at the most a form independent of their use-values, i.e., the form of money; but that same value now in the circulation M—C—M, or the circulation of capital, suddenly presents itself as an independent substance, endowed with a motion of its own, passing through a life-process of its own, in which money and commodities are mere forms which it assumes and casts off in turn. Nay, more: instead of simply representing the relations of commodities, it enters now, so to say, into private relations with itself. It differentiates itself as original value from itself as surplus-value; as the father differentiates himself from himself quâ the son, yet both are one and of one age: for only by the surplus-value of £10 does the £100 originally advanced become capital, and so soon as this takes place, so soon as the son and by the son, the father, is begotten, so soon does their difference vanish, and they again become one, £110.

Value therefore now becomes value in process, money in process, and, as such, capital. It comes out of circulation, enters into it again, preserves and multiplies itself within its circuit, comes back out of it with expanded bulk, and begins the same round ever afresh. M—M', money which begets money, such is the description of Capital from the mouths of its first interpreters, the Mercantilists.

Buying in order to sell, or, more accurately, buying in order to sell dearer, M—C—M', appears certainly to be a form peculiar to one kind of capital alone, namely, merchants' capital. But industrial capital too is money, that is changed into commodities, and by the sale of these commodities, is reconverted into more money. The events that take place outside the sphere of circulation, in the interval between the buying and selling, do not affect the form of this movement. Lastly, in the case of interest-bearing capital, the circulation M—C—M' appears abridged. We have its result without the intermediate stage, in the form M—M', "en style lapidaire" so to say, money that is worth more money, value that is greater than itself.

M—C—M' is therefore in reality the general formula of capital as it appears prima facie within the sphere of circulation. . . .

THE BUYING AND SELLING OF LABOUR-POWER

The change of value that occurs in the case of money intended to be converted into capital, cannot take place in the money itself, since in its function of means of purchase and of payment, it does no more than realise the price of the commodity it buys or pays for; and, as hard cash, it is value petrified, never varying. Just as little can it originate in the second act of circulation, the re-sale of the commodity, which does no more than transform the article from its bodily form back again into its money-form. The change must, therefore, take place in the commodity bought by the first act, M—C, but not in its value, for equivalents are exchanged, and the commodity is paid for at its full value.

We are, therefore, forced to the conclusion that the change originates in the use-value, as such, of the commodity, i.e., in its consumption. In order to be able to extract value from the consumption of a commodity, our friend, Moneybags, must be so lucky as to find, within the sphere of circulation, in the market, a commodity, whose use-value possesses the peculiar property of being a source of value, whose actual consumption, therefore, is itself an embodiment of labour, possesses the peculiar property of being a source of value, whose actual consumption, therefore, is itself an embodiment of labour, and, consequently, a creation of value. The possessor of money does find on the market such a special commodity in capacity for labour or labour-power.

By labour-power or capacity for labour is to be understood the aggregate of those mental and physical capabilities existing in a human being, which he exercises whenever he produces a use-value of any description.

But in order that our owner of money may be able to find labour-power offered for sale as a commodity, various conditions must first be fulfilled. The exchange of commodities of itself implies no other relations of dependence than those which result from its own nature. On this assumption, labour-power can appear upon the market as a commodity, only if, and so far as, its possessor, the individual whose labour-power it is, offers it for sale, or sells it, as a commodity. In order that he may be able to do this, he must have it at his disposal, must be the untrammelled owner of his capacity for labour, i.e., of his person. He and the owner of money meet in the market, and deal with each other as on the basis of equal rights, with this difference alone, that one is buyer, the other seller; both, therefore, equal in the eyes of the law. The continuance of this relation demands that the owner of the labour-power should sell it only for a definite period, for if he were to sell it rump and stump, once for all, he would be selling himself, converting himself from a free man into a slave, from an owner of a commodity into a commodity. He must constantly look upon his labour-power as his own property, his own commodity, and this he can only do by placing it at the disposal of the buyer temporarily, for a definite period of time. By this means alone can he avoid renouncing his rights of ownership over it.

The second essential condition to the owner of money finding labour-power in the market as a commodity is this— that the labourer instead of being in the position to sell commodities in which his labour is incorporated, must be obliged to offer for sale as a commodity that very labour-power, which exists only in his living self.

In order that a man may be able to sell commodities other than labour-power, he must of course have the means of production, as raw material, implements, &c. No boots can be made without leather. He requires also the means of subsistence. Nobody—not even "a musician of the future"—can live upon future products, or upon use-values in an unfinished state; and ever since the first moment of his appearance on the world's stage, man always has been, and must still be a consumer, both before and while he is producing. In a society where all products assume the form of commodities, these commodities must be sold after they have been produced, it is only after their sale that they can serve in satisfying the requirements of their producer. The time necessary for their sale is superadded to that necessary for their production.

For the conversion of his money into capital, therefore, the owner of money must meet in the market with the free labourer, free in the double sense, that as a free man he can dispose of his labour-power as his own commodity, and that on the other hand he has no other commodity for sale, is short of everything necessary for the realisation of his labour-power.

The question why this free labourer confronts him in the market, has no interest for the owner of money, who regards the labour-market as a branch of the general market for commodities. And for the present it interests us just as little. We cling to the fact theoretically, as he does practically. One thing, however, is clear—Nature does not produce on the one side owners of money or commodities, and on the other men possessing nothing but their own labour-power. This relation has no natural basis, neither is its social basis one that is common to all historical periods. It is clearly the result of a past historical development, the product of many economic revolutions, of the extinction of a whole series of older forms of social production.

So, too, the economic categories, already discussed by us, bear the stamp of history. Definite historical conditions are necessary that a product may become a commodity. It must not be produced as the immediate means of subsistence of the producer himself. Had we gone further, and inquired under what circumstances all, or even the majority of products take the form of commodities, we should have found that this can only happen with production of a very specific kind, capitalist production. Such an inquiry, however, would have been foreign to the analysis of commodities. Production and circulation of commodities can take place, although the great mass of the objects produced are intended for the immediate requirements of their producers, are not turned into commodities, and consequently social production is not yet by a long way dominated in its length and breadth by exchange-value. The appearance of products as commodities pre-supposes such a development of the social division of labour, that the separation of use-value from exchange-value, a separation which first begins with barter, must already have been completed. But such a degree of development is common to many forms of society, which in other respects present the most varying historical features. On the other hand, if we consider money, its existence implies a definite stage in the exchange of commodities. The particular functions of money which it performs, either as the mere equivalent of commodities, or as means of circulation, or means of payment, as hoard or as universal money, point, according to the extent and relative preponderance of the one function or the other, to very different stages in the process of social production. Yet we know by experience that a circulation of commodities relatively primitive, suffices for the production of all these forms. Otherwise with capital. The historical conditions of its existence are by no means given with the mere circulation of money and commodities. It can spring into life, only when the owner of the means of production and subsistence meets in the market with the free labourer selling his labour-power. And this one historical condition comprises a world's history. Capital, therefore, announces from its first appearance a new epoch in the process of social production.

We must now examine closely this peculiar commodity, labour-power. Like all others it has a value. How is that value determined?

The value of labour-power is determined, as in the case of every other commodity, by the labour-time necessary for the production, and consequently also the reproduction, of this special article. So far as it has value, it represents no more than a definite quantity of the average labour of society incorporated in it. Labour-power exists only as a capacity, or power of the living individual. Its production consequently pre-supposes his existence. Given the individual, the production of labour-power consists in his reproduction of himself or his maintenance. For his maintenance he requires a given quantity of the means of subsistence. Therefore the labour-time requisite for

the production of labour-power reduces itself to that necessary for the production of those means of subsistence; in other words, the value of labour-power is the value of the means of subsistence necessary for the maintenance of the labourer. Labour-power, however, becomes a reality only by its exercise; it sets itself in action only by working. But thereby a definite quantity of human muscle, nerve, brain, &c., is wasted, and these require to be restored. This increased expenditure demands a larger income. If the owner of labour-power works to-day, to-morrow he must again be able to repeat the same process in the same conditions as regards health and strength. His means of subsistence must therefore be sufficient to maintain him in his normal state as a labouring individual. His natural wants, such as food, clothing, fuel, and housing, vary according to the climatic and other physical conditions of his country. On the other hand, the number and extent of his so-called necessary wants, as also the modes of satisfying them, are themselves the product of historical development, and depend therefore to a great extent on the degree of civilisation of a country, more particularly on the conditions under which, and consequently on the habits and degree of comfort in which, the class of free labourers has been formed. In contradistinction therefore to the case of other commodities, there enters into the determination of the value of labour-power a historical and moral element. Nevertheless, in a given country, at a given period, the average quantity of the means of subsistence necessary for the labourer is practically known.

The owner of labour-power is mortal. If then his appearance in the market is to be continuous, and the continuous conversion of money into capital assumes this, the seller of labour-power must perpetuate himself, "in the way that every living individual perpetuates himself, by procreation." The labour-power withdrawn from the market by wear and tear and death, must be continually replaced by, at the very least, an equal amount of fresh labour-power. Hence the sum of the means of subsistence necessary for the production of labour-power must include the means necessary for the labourer's substitutes, *i.e.*, his children, in order that this race of peculiar commodity-owners may perpetuate its appearance in the market.

In order to modify the human organism, so that it may acquire skill and handiness in a given branch of industry, and become labour-power of a special kind, a special education or training is requisite, and this, on its part, costs an equivalent in commodities of a greater or less amount. This amount varies according to the more or less complicated character of the labour-power. The expenses of this education (excessively small in the case of ordinary labour-power), enter pro tanto into the total value spent in its production.

The value of labour-power resolves itself into the value of a definite quantity of the means of subsistence. It therefore varies with the value of these means or with the quantity of labour requisite for their production.

Some of the means of subsistence, such as food and fuel, are consumed daily, and a fresh supply must be provided daily. Others such as clothes and furniture last for longer periods and require to be replaced only at longer intervals. One article must be bought or paid for daily, another weekly, another quarterly, and so on. But in whatever way the sum total of these outlays may be spread over the year, they must be covered by the average income, taking one day with another. . . . Suppose that in this mass of commodities requisite for the average day there are embodied 6 hours of social labour, then there is incorporated daily in labour-power half a day's average social labour, in other words, half a day's labour is requisite for the daily production of labour-power. This quantity of labour forms the value of a day's labour-power or the

value of the labour-power daily reproduced. If half a day's average social labour is incorporated in three shillings, then three shillings is the price corresponding to the value of a day's labour-power. If its owner therefore offers it for sale at three shillings a day, its selling price is equal to its value, and according to our supposition, our friend Moneybags, who is intent upon converting his three shillings into capital, pays this value.

The minimum limit of the value of labour-power is determined by the value of the commodities, without the daily supply of which the labourer cannot renew his vital energy, consequently by the value of those means of subsistence that are physically indispensable. If the price of labour-power fall to this minimum, it falls below its value, since under such circumstances it can be maintained and developed only in a crippled state. But the value of every commodity is determined by the labour-time requisite to turn it out so as to be of normal quality.

It is a very cheap sort of sentimentality which declares this method of determining the value of labour-power, a method prescribed by the very nature of the case, to be a brutal method, and which wails with Rossi that,

> To comprehend capacity for labour (puissance de travail) at the same time that we make abstraction from the means of subsistence of the labourers during the process of production, is to comprehend a phantom (être de raison). When we speak of labour, or capacity for labour, we speak at the same time of the labourer and his means of subsistence, of labourer and wages.

When we speak of capacity for labour, we do not speak of labour, any more than when we speak of capacity for digestion, we speak of digestion. The latter process requires something more than a good stomach. When we speak of capacity for labour, we do not abstract from the necessary means of subsistence. On the contrary, their value is expressed in its value. If his capacity for labour remains unsold, the labourer derives no benefit from it, but rather he will feel it to be a cruel nature-imposed necessity that this capacity has cost for its production a definite amount of the means of subsistence and that it will continue to do so for its reproduction. He will then agree with Sismondi: "that capacity for labour . . . is nothing unless it is sold."

One consequence of the peculiar nature of labour-power as a commodity is, that its use-value does not, on the conclusion of the contract between the buyer and seller, immediately pass into the hands of the former. Its value, like that of every other commodity, is already fixed before it goes into circulation, since a definite quantity of social labour has been spent upon it; but its use-value consists in the subsequent exercise of its force. The alienation of labour-power and its actual appropriation by the buyer, its employment as a use-value, are separated by an interval of time. But in those cases in which the formal alienation by sale of the use-value of a commodity, is not simultaneous with its actual delivery to the buyer, the money of the latter usually functions as means of payment. In every country in which the capitalist mode of production reigns, it is the custom not to pay for labour-power before it has been exercised for the period fixed by the contract, as for example, the end of each week. In all cases, therefore, the use-value of the labour-power is advanced to the capitalist: the labourer allows the buyer to consume it before he receives payment of the price; he everywhere gives credit to the capitalist. That this credit is no mere fiction, is shown not only by the occasional loss of wages on the bankruptcy of the capitalist, but also by a series of more enduring consequences. Nevertheless, whether money serves as a means of purchase or as a means of payment, this makes no alteration in the nature of the exchange of commodities. The price of

the labour-power is fixed by the contract, although it is not realised till later, like the rent of a house. The labour-power is sold, although it is only paid for at a later period. It will, therefore, be useful, for a clear comprehension of the relation of the parties, to assume provisionally, that the possessor of labour-power, on the occasion of each sale, immediately receives the price stipulated to be paid for it.

We now know how the value paid by the purchaser to the possessor of this peculiar commodity, labour-power, is determined. The use-value which the former gets in exchange, manifests itself only in the actual usufruct, in the consumption of the labour-power. The money-owner buys everything necessary for this purpose, such as raw material, in the market, and pays for it at its full value. The consumption of labour-power is at one and the same time the production of commodities and of surplus-value. The consumption of labour-power is completed, as in the case of every other commodity, outside the limits of the market or of the sphere of circulation. Accompanied by Mr. Moneybags and by the possessor of labour-power, we therefore take leave for a time of this noisy sphere, where everything takes place on the surface and in view of all men, and follow them both into the hidden abode of production, on whose threshold there stares us in the face "No admittance except on business." Here we shall see, not only how capital produces, but how capital is produced. We shall at least force the secret of profit making.

This sphere that we are deserting, within whose boundaries the sale and purchase of labour-power goes on, is in fact a very Eden of the innate rights of man. There alone rule Freedom, Equality, Property and Bentham. Freedom, because both buyer and seller of a commodity, say of labour-power, are constrained only by their own free will. They contract as free agents, and the agreement they come to, is but the form in which they give legal expression to their common will. Equality, because each enters into relation with the other, as with a simple owner of commodities, and they exchange equivalent for equivalent. Property, because each disposes only of what is his own. And Bentham, because each looks only to himself. The only force that brings them together and puts them in relation with each other, is the selfishness, the gain and the private interests of each. Each looks to himself only, and no one troubles himself about the rest, and just because they do so, do they all, in accordance with the pre-established harmony of things, or under the auspices of an all-shrewd providence, work together to their mutual advantage, for the common weal and in the interest of all.

On leaving this sphere of simple circulation or of exchange of commodities, which furnishes the "Free-trader Vulgaris" with his views and ideas, and with the standard by which he judges a society based on capital and wages, we think we can perceive a change in the physiognomy of our dramatis personæ. He, who before was the money-owner, now strides in front as capitalist; the possessor of labour-power follows as his labourer. The one with an air of importance, smirking, intent on business; the other, timid and holding back, like one who is bringing his own hide to market and has nothing to expect but—a hiding.

THE LABOUR-PROCESS AND THE PROCESS OF PRODUCING SURPLUS-VALUE

SECTION 1. THE LABOUR-PROCESS OR THE PRODUCTION OF USE-VALUES

The capitalist buys labour-power in order to use it; and labour-power in use is labour itself. The purchaser of labour-power consumes it by setting the seller of it to work. By working, the latter becomes actually, what before he only was potentially, labour-power in action, a labourer. In order that his labour may re-appear in a commodity, he must, before all things, expend it on something useful, on something capable of satisfying a want of some sort. Hence, what the capitalist sets the labourer to produce, is a particular use-value, a specified article. The fact that the production of use-values, or goods, is carried on under the control of a capitalist and on his behalf, does not alter the general character of that production. We shall, therefore, in the first place, have to consider the labour-process independently of the particular form it assumes under given social conditions.

Labour is, in the first place, a process in which both man and Nature participate, and in which man of his own accord starts, regulates, and controls the material re-actions between himself and Nature. He opposes himself to Nature as one of her own forces, setting in motion arms and legs, head and hands, the natural forces of his body, in order to appropriate Nature's productions in a form adapted to his own wants. By thus acting on the external world and changing it, he at the same time changes his own nature. He develops his slumbering powers and compels them to act in obedience to his sway. We are not now dealing with those primitive instinctive forms of labour that remind us of the mere animal. An immeasurable interval of time separates the state of things in which a man brings his labour-power to market for sale as a commodity, from that state in which human labour was still in its first instinctive stage. We presuppose labour in a form that stamps it as exclusively human. A spider conducts operations that resemble those of a weaver, and a bee puts to shame many an architect in the construction of her cells. But what distinguishes the worst architect from the best of bees is this, that the architect raises his structure in imagination before he erects it in reality. At the end of every labour-process, we get a result that already existed in the imagination of the labourer at its commencement. He not only effects a change of form in the material on which he works, but he also realises a purpose of his own that gives the law to his modus operandi, and to which he must subordinate his will. And this subordination is no mere momentary act. Besides the exertion of the bodily organs, the process demands that, during the whole operation, the workman's will be steadily in consonance with his purpose. This means close attention. The less he is attracted by the nature of the work, and the mode in which it is carried on, and the less, therefore, he enjoys it as something which gives play to his bodily and mental powers, the more close his attention is forced to be.

The elementary factors of the labour-process are (1) the personal activity of man, i.e., work itself, (2) the subject of that work, and (3) its instruments.

The soil (and this, economically speaking, includes water) in the virgin state in which it supplies man with necessaries or the means of subsistence ready to hand, exists independently of him, and is the universal subject of human labour. All those things which labour merely separates from immediate connexion with their environment, are subjects of labour spontaneously provided by Nature. Such are fish which we catch and take from their element, water, timber which we fell in the virgin forest, and ores which we extract from their veins. If, on the other hand, the subject of labour has, so to say, been filtered through previous labour, we call it raw material; such is ore already extracted and ready for washing. All raw material is the subject of labour, but not every subject of labour is raw material: it can only become so, after it has undergone some alteration by means of labour.

An instrument of labour is a thing, or a complex of things, which the labourer interposes between himself and the subject of his labour, and which serves as the conductor of his activity. He makes use of the mechanical, physical, and chemical properties of some substances in order to make other substances subservient to his aims. Leaving out of consideration such ready-made means of subsistence as fruits, in gathering which a man's own limbs serve as the instruments of his labour, the first thing of which the labourer possesses himself is not the subject of labour but its instrument. Thus Nature becomes one of the organs of his activity, one that he annexes to his own bodily organs, adding stature to himself in spite of the Bible. As the earth is his original larder, so too it is his original tool house. It supplies him, for instance, with stones for throwing, grinding, pressing, cutting, &c. The earth itself is an instrument of labour, but when used as such in agriculture implies a whole series of other instruments and a comparatively high development of labour. No sooner does labour undergo the least development, than it requires specially prepared instruments. Thus in the oldest caves we find stone implements and weapons. In the earliest period of human history domesticated animals, i.e., animals which have been bred for the purpose, and have undergone modifications by means of labour, play the chief part as instruments of labour along with specially prepared stones, wood, bones, and shells. The use and fabrication of instruments of labour, although existing in the germ among certain species of animals, is specifically characteristic of the human labour-process, and Franklin therefore defines man as a tool-making animal. Relics of bygone instruments of labour possess the same importance for the investigation of extinct economic forms of society, as do fossil bones for the determination of extinct species of animals. It is not the articles made, but how they are made, and by what instruments, that enables us to distinguish different economic epochs. Instruments of labour not only supply a standard of the degree of development to which human labour has attained, but they are also indicators of the social conditions under which that labour is carried on. Among the instruments of labour, those of a mechanical nature, which, taken as a whole, we may call the bone and muscles of production, offer much more decided characteristics of a given epoch of production, than those which, like pipes, tubs, baskets, jars, &c., serve only to hold the materials for labour, which latter class, we may in a general way, call the vascular system of production. The latter first begins to play an important part in the chemical industries.

In a wider sense we may include among the instruments of labour, in addition to those things that are used for directly transferring labour to its subject, and which therefore, in one way or another, serve as conductors of activity, all such objects as are necessary for carrying on the labour-process. These do not enter directly into the process, but without them it is either impossible for it to take place at all, or possible only to a partial extent. Once more we find the earth to be a universal instrument of this sort, for it furnishes a locus standi to the labourer and a field of employment for his activity. Among instruments that are the result of previous labour and also belong to this class, we find workshops, canals, roads, and so forth.

In the labour-process, therefore, man's activity, with the help of the instruments of labour, effects an alteration, designed from the commencement, in the material worked upon. The process disappears in the product; the latter is a use-value, Nature's material adapted by a change of form to the wants of man. Labour has incorporated itself with its subject: the former is materialised, the latter transformed. That which in the labourer appeared as movement, now appears in the product as a fixed quality without motion. The blacksmith forges and the product is a forging.

If we examine the whole process from the point of view of its result, the prod-uct, it is plain that both the instruments and the subject of labour, are means of production, and that the labour itself is productive labour.

Though a use-value, in the form of a product, issues from the labour-process, yet other use-values, products of previous labour, enter into it as means of production. The same use-value is both the product of a previous process, and a means of production in a latter process. Products are therefore not only results, but also essential conditions of labour.

With the exception of the extractive industries, in which the material for labour is provided immediately by Nature, such as mining, hunting, fishing, and agriculture (so far as the latter is confined to breaking up virgin soil), all branches of industry manipulate raw material, objects already filtered through labour, already products of labour. Such is seed in agriculture. Animals and plants, which we are accustomed to consider as products of Nature, are in their present form, not only products of, say last year's labour, but the result of a gradual transformation, continued through many generations, under man's superintendence, and by means of his labour. But in the great majority of cases, instruments of labour show even to the most superficial observer, traces of the labour of past ages.

Raw material may either form the principal substance of a product, or it may enter into its formation only as an accessory. An accessory may be consumed by the instruments of labour, as coal under a boiler, oil by a wheel, hay by draft-horses, or it may be mixed with the raw material in order to produce some modification thereof, as chlorine into unbleached linen, coal with iron, dye-stuff with wool, or again, it may help to carry on the work itself, as in the case of the materials used for heating and lighting workshops. The distinction between principal substance and accessory vanishes in the true chemical industries, because there none of the raw material re-appears, in its original composition, in the substance of the product.

Every object possesses various properties, and is thus capable of being applied to different uses. One and the same product may therefore serve as raw material in very different processes. Corn, for example, is a raw material for millers, starch-manufacturers, distillers, and cattle-breeders. It also enters as raw material into its own production in the shape of seed; coal, too, is at the same time the product of, and a means of production in, coal-mining.

Again, a particular product may be used in one and the same process, both as an instrument of labour and as raw material. Take, for instance, the fattening of cattle, where the animal is the raw material, and at the same time an instrument for the production of manure.

A product, though ready for immediate consumption, may yet serve as raw material for a further product, as grapes when they become the raw material for wine. On the other hand, labour may give us its product in such a form, that we can use it only as raw material, as is the case with cotton, thread, and yarn. Such a raw material, though itself a product, may have to go through a whole series of different processes: in each of these in turn, it serves, with constantly varying form, as raw material, until the last process of the series leaves it a perfect product, ready for individual consumption, or for use as an instrument of labour.

Hence we see, that whether a use-value is to be regarded as raw material, as instrument of labour, or as product, this is determined entirely by its function in the labour-process, by the position it there occupies: as this varies, so does its character.

Whenever therefore a product enters as a means of production into a new labour-process, it thereby loses its character of product, and becomes a mere factor in the process. A spinner treats spindles only as implements for spinning, and flax only as the material that he spins. Of course it is impossible to spin without material and spindles; and therefore the existence of these things as products, at the commencement of the spinning operation, must be presumed: but in the process itself, the fact that they are products of previous labour, is a matter of utter indifference; just as in the digestive process, it is of no importance whatever, that bread is the produce of the previous labour of the farmer, the miller, and the baker. On the contrary, it is generally by their imperfections as products, that the means of production in any process assert themselves in their character of products. A blunt knife or weak thread forcibly remind us of Mr. A., the cutler, or Mr. B., the spinner. In the finished product the labour by means of which it has acquired its useful qualities is not palpable, has apparently vanished.

A machine which does not serve the purposes of labour, is useless. In addition, it falls a prey to the destructive influence of natural forces. Iron rusts and wood rots. Yarn with which we neither weave nor knit, is cotton wasted. Living labour must seize upon these things and rouse them from their death-sleep, change them from mere possible use-values into real and effective ones. Bathed in the fire of labour, appropriated as part and parcel of labour's organism, and, as it were, made alive for the performance of their functions in the process, they are in truth consumed, but consumed with a purpose, as elementary constituents of new use-values, of new products, ever ready as means of subsistence for individual consumption, or as means of production for some new labour-process.

If then, on the one hand, finished products are not only results, but also necessary conditions, of the labour-process, on the other hand, their assumption into that process, their contact with living labour, is the sole means by which they can be made to retain their character of use-values, and be utilised.

Labour uses up its material factors, its subject and its instruments, consumes them, and is therefore a process of consumption. Such productive consumption is distinguished from individual consumption by this, that the latter uses up products, as means of subsistence for the living individual; the former, as means whereby alone, labour, the labour-power of the living individual, is enabled to act. The product, therefore, of individual consumption, is the consumer himself, the result of productive consumption, is a product distinct from the consumer.

In so far then, as its instruments and subjects are themselves products, labour consumes products in order to create products, or in other words, consumes one set of products by turning them into means of production for another set. But, just as in the beginning, the only participators in the labour-process were man and the earth, which latter exists independently of man, so even now we still employ in the process many means of production, provided directly by Nature, that do not represent any combination of natural substances with human labour.

The labour-process, resolved as above into its simple elementary factors, is human action with a view to the production of use-values, appropriation of natural substances to human requirements: it is the necessary condition for effecting exchange of matter between man and Nature; it is the everlasting Nature-imposed condition of human existence, and therefore is independent of every social phase of that existence, or rather, is common to every such phase. It was, therefore, not necessary to represent our labourer in connexion with other labourers; man and his labour on one side, Nature and its materials on the other, sufficed. As the taste of the porridge does not tell you who grew the oats, no more does this simple process

tell you of itself what are the social conditions under which it is taking place, whether under the slave-owner's brutal lash, or the anxious eye of the capitalist, whether Cincinnatus carries it on in tilling his modest farm or a savage in killing wild animals with stones.

Let us now return to our would-be capitalist. We left him just after he had purchased, in the open market, all the necessary factors of the labour-process; its objective factors, the means of production, as well as its subjective factor, labour-power. With the keen eye of an expert, he has selected the means of production and the kind of labour-power best adapted to his particular trade, be it spinning, bootmaking, or any other kind. He then proceeds to consume the commodity, the labour-power that he has just bought, by causing the labourer, the impersonation of that labour-power, to consume the means of production by his labour. The general character of the labour-process is evidently not changed by the fact, that the labourer works for the capitalist instead of for himself; moreover, the particular methods and operations employed in bootmaking or spinning are not immediately changed by the intervention of the capitalist. He must begin by taking the labour-power as he finds it in the market, and consequently be satisfied with labour of such a kind as would be found in the period immediately preceding the rise of capitalists. Changes in the methods of production by the subordination of labour to capital, can take place only at a later period, and therefore will have to be treated of in a later chapter.

The labour-process, turned into the process by which the capitalist consumes labour-power, exhibits two characteristic phenomena. First, the labourer works under the control of the capitalist to whom his labour belongs; the capitalist taking good care that the work is done in a proper manner, and that the means of production are used with intelligence, so that there is no unnecessary waste of raw material, and no wear and tear of the implements beyond what is necessarily caused by the work.

Secondly, the product is the property of the capitalist and not that of the labourer, its immediate producer. Suppose that a capitalist pays for a day's labour-power at its value; then the right to use that power for a day belongs to him, just as much as the right to use any other commodity, such as a horse that he has hired for the day. To the purchaser of a commodity belongs its use, and the seller of labour-power, by giving his labour, does no more, in reality, than part with the use-value that he has sold. From the instant he steps into the workshop, the use-value of his labour-power, and therefore also its use, which is labour, belongs to the capitalist. By the purchase of labour-power, the capitalist incorporates labour, as a living ferment, with the lifeless constituents of the product. From his point of view, the labour-process is nothing more than the consumption of the commodity purchased, i.e., of labour-power; but this consumption cannot be effected except by supplying the labour-power with the means of production. The labour-process is a process between things that the capitalist has purchased, things that have become his property. The product of this process belongs, therefore, to him, just as much as does the wine which is the product of a process of fermentation completed in his cellar.

SECTION 2. THE PRODUCTION OF SURPLUS-VALUE

The product appropriated by the capitalist is a use-value, as yarn, for example, or boots. But, although boots are, in one sense, the basis of all social progress, and our capitalist is a decided "progressist," yet he does not manufacture boots for their own sake. Use-value is, by no means, the thing qu'on aime pour lui-même in the production of commodities. Use-values are only produced by capitalists, because, and in so far as, they are the material substratum, the depositories of exchange-value. Our capitalist has two objects in view: in the first place, he wants to produce a use-value that has a value in exchange, that is to say, an article destined to be sold, a commodity; and secondly, he desires to produce a commodity whose value shall be greater than the sum of the values of the commodities used in its production, that is, of the means of production and the labour-power, that he purchased with his good money in the open market. His aim is to produce not only a use-value, but a commodity also; not only use-value, but value; not only value, but as the same time surplus-value.

It must be borne in mind, that we are now dealing with the production of commodities, and that, up to this point, we have only considered one aspect of the process. Just as commodities are, at the same time, use-values and values, so the process of producing them must be a labour-process, and at the same time, a process of creating value.

Let us now examine production as a creation of value.

We know that the value of each commodity is determined by the quantity of labour expended on and materialised in it, by the working-time necessary, under given social conditions, for its production. This rule also holds good in the case of the product that accrued to our capitalist, as the result of the labour-process carried on for him. Assuming this product to be 10 lbs. of yarn, our first step is to calculate the quantity of labour realised in it.

For spinning the yarn, raw material is required; suppose in this case 10 lbs. of cotton. We have no need at present to investigate the value of this cotton, for our capitalist has, we will assume, bought it at its full value, say of ten shillings. In this price the labour required for the production of the cotton is already expressed in terms of the average labour of society. We will further assume that the wear and tear of the spindle, which, for our present purpose, may represent all other instruments of labour employed, amounts to the value of 2s. If, then, twenty-four hours' labour, or two working-days, are required to produce the quantity of gold represented by twelve shillings, we have here, to begin with, two days' labour already incorporated in the yarn.

We must not let ourselves be misled by the circumstance that the cotton has taken a new shape while the substance of the spindle has to a certain extent been used up. By the general law of value, if the value of 40 lbs. of yarn = the value of 40 lbs. of cotton + the value of a whole spindle, *i.e.*, if the same working-time is required to produce the commodities on either side of this equation, then 10 lbs. of yarn are an equivalent for 10 lbs. of cotton, together with one-fourth of a spindle. In the case we are considering the same working-time is materialised in the 10 lbs. of yarn on the one hand, and in the 10 lbs. of cotton and the fraction of a spindle on the other. Therefore, whether value appears in cotton, in a spindle, or in yarn, makes no difference in the amount of that value. The spindle and cotton, instead of resting quietly side by side, join together in the process, their forms are altered, and they are turned into yarn; but their value is no more affected by this fact than it would be if they had been simply exchanged for their equivalent in yarn.

The labour required for the production of the cotton, the raw material of the yarn, is part of the labour necessary to produce the yarn, and is therefore contained in the yarn. The same applies to the labour embodied in the spindle, without whose wear and tear the cotton could not be spun.

Hence, in determining the value of the yarn, or the labour-time required for its production, all the special processes carried on at various times and in different places, which were necessary, first to produce the cotton and the wasted portion of the spindle, and then with the cotton and spindle to spin the yarn, may together be looked on as different and successive phases of one and the same process. The whole of the labour in the yarn is past labour; and it is a matter of no importance that the operations necessary for the production of its constituent elements were carried on at times which, referred to the present, are more remote than the final operation of spinning. If a definite quantity of labour, say thirty days, is requisite to build a house, the total amount of labour incorporated in it is not altered by the fact that the work of the last day is done twenty-nine days later than that of the first. Therefore the labour contained in the raw material and the instruments of labour can be treated just as if it were labour expended in an earlier stage of the spinning process, before the labour of actual spinning commenced.

The values of the means of production, *i.e.*, the cotton and the spindle, which values are expressed in the price of twelve shillings, are therefore constituent parts of the value of the yarn, or, in other words, of the value of the product.

Two conditions must nevertheless be fulfilled. First, the cotton and spindle must concur in the production of a use-value; they must in the present case become yarn. Value is independent of the particular use-value by which it is borne, but it must be embodied in a use-value of some kind. Secondly, the time occupied in the labour of production must not exceed the time really necessary under the given social conditions of the case. Therefore, if no more than 1 lb. of cotton be requisite to spin 1 lb. of yarn, care must be taken that no more than this weight of cotton is consumed in the production of 1 lb. of yarn; and similarly with regard to the spindle. Though the capitalist have a hobby, and use a gold instead of a steel spindle, yet the only labour that counts for anything in the value of the yarn is that which would be required to produce a steel spindle, because no more is necessary under the given social conditions.

We now know what portion of the value of the yarn is owing to the cotton and the spindle. It amounts to twelve shillings or the value of two days' work. The next point for our consideration is, what portion of the value of the yarn is added to the cotton by the labour of the spinner.

We have now to consider this labour under a very different aspect from that which it had during the labour-process; there, we viewed it solely as that particular kind of human activity which changes cotton into yarn; there, the more the labour was suited to the work, the better the yarn, other circumstances remaining the same. The labour of the spinner was then viewed as specifically different from other kinds of productive labour, different on the one hand in its special aim, viz., spinning, different, on the other hand, in the special character of its operations, in the special nature of its means of production and in the special use-value of its product. For the operation of spinning, cotton and spindles are a necessity, but for making rifled cannon they would be of no use whatever. Here, on the contrary, where we consider the labour of the spinner only so far as it is value-creating, i.e., a source of value, his labour differs in no respect from the labour of the man who bores cannon, or (what here more nearly concerns us), from the labour of the cotton-planter and spindle-maker incorporated in the means of production. It is solely by reason of this identity, that cotton planting, spindle making and spinning, are capable of forming the component parts, differing only quantitatively from each other, of one whole, namely, the value of the yarn. Here, we have nothing more to do with the quality, the nature and the specific character of the labour, but merely with its quantity. And this simply requires to be calculated. We proceed upon the assumption that spinning is simple, unskilled labour, the average labour of a

given state of society. Hereafter we shall see that the contrary assumption would make no difference.

While the labourer is at work, his labour constantly undergoes a transformation: from being motion, it becomes an object without motion; from being the labourer working, it becomes the thing produced. At the end of one hour's spinning, that act is represented by a definite quantity of yarn; in other words, a definite quantity of labour, namely that of one hour, has become embodied in the cotton. We say labour, i.e., the expenditure of his vital force by the spinner, and not spinning labour, because the special work of spinning counts here, only so far as it is the expenditure of labour-power in general, and not in so far as it is the specific work of the spinner.

In the process we are now considering it is of extreme importance, that no more time be consumed in the work of transforming the cotton into yarn than is necessary under the given social conditions. If under normal, i.e., average social conditions of production, a pounds of cotton ought to be made into b pounds of yarn by one hour's labour, then a day's labour does not count as 12 hours' labour unless 12 a pounds of cotton have been made into 12 b pounds of yarn; for in the creation of value, the time that is socially necessary alone counts.

Not only the labour, but also the raw material and the product now appear in quite a new light, very different from that in which we viewed them in the labour-process pure and simple. The raw material serves now merely as an absorbent of a definite quantity of labour. By this absorption it is in fact changed into yarn, because it is spun, because labour-power in the form of spinning is added to it; but the product, the yarn, is now nothing more than a measure of the labour absorbed by the cotton. If in one hour $1\frac{2}{3}$ lbs. of cotton can be spun into $1\frac{2}{3}$ lbs. of yarn, then 10 lbs. of yarn indicate the absorption of 6 hours' labour. Definite quantities of product, these quantities being determined by experience, now represent nothing but definite quantities of labour, definite masses of crystallised labour-time. They are nothing more than the materialisation of so many hours or so many days of social labour.

We are here no more concerned about the facts, that the labour is the specific work of spinning, that its subject is cotton and its product yarn, than we are about the fact that the subject itself is already a product and therefore raw material. If the spinner, instead of spinning, were working in a coal mine, the subject of his labour, the coal, would be supplied by Nature; nevertheless, a definite quantity of extracted coal, a hundredweight for example, would represent a definite quantity of absorbed labour.

We assumed, on the occasion of its sale, that the value of a day's labour-power is three shillings, and that six hours' labour is incorporated in that sum; and consequently that this amount of labour is requisite to produce the necessaries of life daily required on an average by the labourer. If now our spinner by working for one hour, can convert 1⅔ lbs. of cotton into 1⅔ lbs. of yarn, it follows that in six hours he will convert 10 lbs. of cotton into 10 lbs. of yarn. Hence, during the spinning process, the cotton absorbs six hours' labour. The same quantity of labour is also embodied in a piece of gold of the value of three shillings. Consequently by the mere labour of spinning, a value of three shillings is added to the cotton.

Let us now consider the total value of the product, the 10 lbs. of yarn. Two and a half days' labour has been embodied in it, of which two days were contained in the cotton and in the substance of the spindle worn away, and half a day was absorbed during the process of spinning. This two and a half days' labour is also represented by a piece of gold of the value of fifteen shillings. Hence, fifteen shillings is an adequate price for the 10 lbs. of yarn, or the price of one pound is eighteen-pence.

Our capitalist stares in astonishment. The value of the product is exactly equal to the value of the capital advanced. The value so advanced has not expanded, no surplus-value has been created, and consequently money has not been converted into capital. The price of the yarn is fifteen shillings, and fifteen shillings were spent in the open market upon the constituent elements of the product, or, what amounts to the same thing, upon the factors of the labour-process; ten shillings were paid for the cotton, two shillings for the substance of the spindle worn away, and three shillings for the labour-power. The swollen value of the yarn is of no avail, for it is merely the sum of the values formerly existing in the cotton, the spindle, and the labour-power: out of such a simple addition of existing values, no surplus-value can possibly arise. These separate values are now all concentrated in one thing; but so they were also in the sum of fifteen shillings, before it was split up into three parts, by the purchase of the commodities.

There is in reality nothing very strange in this result. The value of one pound of yarn being eighteenpence, if our capitalist buys 10 lbs. of yarn in the market, he must pay fifteen shillings for them. It is clear that, whether a man buys his house ready built, or gets it built for him, in neither case will the mode of acquisition increase the amount of money laid out on the house.

Our capitalist, who is at home in his vulgar economy, exclaims: "Oh! but I advanced my money for the express purpose of making more money." The way to Hell is paved with good intentions, and he might just as easily have intended to make money, without producing at all. He threatens all sorts of things. He won't be caught napping again. In future he will buy the commodities in the market, instead of manufacturing them himself. But if all his brother capitalists were to do the same, where would he find his commodities in the market? And his money he cannot eat. He tries persuasion.

Consider my abstinence; I might have played ducks and drakes with the 15 shillings; but instead of that I consumed it productively, and made yarn with it.

Very well, and by way of reward he is now in possession of good yarn instead of a bad conscience; and as for playing the part of a miser, it would never do for him to relapse into such bad ways as that; we have seen before to what results such asceticism leads. Besides, where nothing is, the king has lost his rights; whatever may be the merit of his abstinence, there is nothing wherewith specially to remunerate it, because the value of the product is merely the sum of the values of the commodities that were thrown into the process of production. Let him therefore console himself with the reflection that virtue is its own reward. But no, he becomes importunate. He says: "The yarn is of no use to me: I produced it for sale." In that case let him sell it, or, still better, let him for the future produce only things for satisfying his personal wants, a remedy that his physician MacCulloch has already prescribed as infallible against an epidemic of over-production. He now gets obstinate. "Can the labourer," he asks,

merely with his arms and legs, produce commodities out of nothing? Did I not supply him with the materials, by means of which, and in which alone, his labour could be embodied? And as the greater part of society consists of such ne'er-do-wells, have I not rendered society incalculable service by my instruments of production, my cotton and my spindle, and not only society, but the labourer also, whom in addition I have provided with the necessaries of life? And am I to be allowed nothing in return for all this service?

Well, but has not the labourer rendered him the equivalent service of changing his cotton and spindle into yarn? Moreover, there is here no question of

service. A service is nothing more than the useful effect of a use-value, be it of a commodity, or be it of labour. But here we are dealing with exchange-value. The capitalist paid to the labourer a value of 3 shillings, and the labourer gave him back an exact equivalent in the value of 3 shillings, added by him to the cotton: he gave him value for value. Our friend, up to this time so purse-proud, suddenly assumes the modest demeanour of his own workman, and exclaims:

Have I myself not worked? Have I not performed the labour of superintendence and of overlooking the spinner? And does not this labour, too, create value?

His overlooker and his manager try to hide their smiles. Meanwhile, after a hearty laugh, he re-assumes his usual mien. Though he chanted to us the whole creed of the economists, in reality, he says, he would not give a brass farthing for it. He leaves this and all such like subterfuges and juggling tricks to the professors of Political Economy, who are paid for it. He himself is a practical man; and though he does not always consider what he says outside his business, yet in his business he knows what he is about.

Let us examine the matter more closely. The value of a day's labour-power amounts to 3 shillings, because on our assumption half a day's labour is embodied in that quantity of labour-power, i.e., because the means of subsistence that are daily required for the production of labour-power, cost half a day's labour. But the past labour that is embodied in the labour-power, and the living labour that it can call into action; the daily cost of maintaining it, and its daily expenditure in work, are two totally different things. The former determines the exchange-value of the labour-power, the latter is its use-value. The fact that half a day's labour is necessary to keep the labourer alive during 24 hours, does not in any way prevent him from working a whole day. Therefore, the value of labour-power, and the value which that labour-power creates in the labour-process, are two entirely different magnitudes; and this difference of the two values was what the capitalist had in view, when he was purchasing the labour-power. The useful qualities that labour-power possesses, and by virtue of which it makes yarn or boots, were to him nothing more than a conditio sine qua non; for in order to create value, labour must be expended in a useful manner. What really influenced him was the specific use-value which this commodity possesses of being a *source not only of value, but of more value than it has itself*. This is the special service that the capitalist expects from labour-power, and in this transaction he acts in accordance with the "eternal laws" of the exchange of commodities. The seller of labour-power, like the seller of any other commodity, realises its exchange-value, and parts with its use-value. He cannot take the one without giving the other. The use-value of labour-power, or in other words, labour, belongs just as little to its seller, as the use-value of oil after it has been sold belongs to the dealer who has sold it. The owner of the money has paid the value of a day's labour-power; his, therefore, is the use of it for a day, a day's labour belongs to him. The circumstance, that on the one hand the daily sustenance of labour-power costs only half a day's labour, while on the other hand the very same labour-power can work during a whole day, that consequently the value which its use during one day creates, is double what he pays for that use, this circumstance is, without doubt, a piece of good luck for the buyer, but by no means an injury to the seller.

Our capitalist foresaw this state of things, and that was the cause of his laughter. The labourer therefore finds, in the workshop, the means of production necessary for working, not only during six, but during twelve hours. Just as during the six hours' process our 10 lbs. of cotton absorbed six hours' labour, and

became 10 lbs. of yarn, so now, 20 lbs. of cotton will absorb 12 hours' labour and be changed into 20 lbs. of yarn. Let us now examine the product of this prolonged process. There is now materialised in this 20 lbs. of yarn the labour of five days, of which four days are due to the cotton and the lost steel of the spindle, the remaining day having been absorbed by the cotton during the spinning process. Expressed in gold, the labour of five days is thirty shillings. This is therefore the price of the 20 lbs. of yarn, giving, as before, eighteenpence as the price of a pound. But the sum of the values of the commodities that entered into the process amounts to 27 shillings. The value of the yarn is 30 shillings. Therefore the value of the product is $1\frac{1}{9}$ greater than the value advanced for its production; 27 shillings have been transformed into 30 shillings; a surplus-value of 3 shillings has been created. The trick has at last succeeded; money has been converted into capital.

Every condition of the problem is satisfied, while the laws that regulate the exchange of commodities, have been in no way violated. Equivalent has been exchanged for equivalent. For the capitalist as buyer paid for each commodity, for the cotton, the spindle and the labour-power, its full value. He then did what is done by every purchaser of commodities; he consumed their use-value. The consumption of the labour-power, which was also the process of producing commodities, resulted in 20 lbs. of yarn, having a value of 30 shillings. The capitalist, formerly a buyer, now returns to market as a seller, of commodities. He sells his yarn at eighteenpence a pound, which is its exact value. Yet for all that he withdraws 3 shillings more from circulation than he originally threw into it. This metamorphosis, this conversion of money into capital, takes place both within the sphere of circulation and also outside it; within the circulation, because conditioned by the purchase of the labour-power in the market; outside the circulation, because what is done within it is only a stepping-stone to the production of surplus-value, a process which is entirely confined to the sphere of production. Thus "tout est pour le mieux dans le meilleur des mondes possibles."

By turning his money into commodities that serve as the material elements of a new product, and as factors in the labour-process, by incorporating living labour with their dead substance, the capitalist at the same time converts value, i.e., past, materialised, and dead labour into capital, into value big with value, a live monster that is fruitful and multiplies.

If we now compare the two processes of producing value and of creating surplus-value, we see that the latter is nothing but the continuation of the former beyond a definite point. If on the one hand the process be not carried beyond the point, where the value paid by the capitalist for the labour-power is replaced by an exact equivalent, it is simply a process of producing value; if, on the other hand, it be continued beyond that point, it becomes a process of creating surplus-value.

If we proceed further, and compare the process of producing value with the labour-process, pure and simple, we find that the latter consists of the useful labour, the work, that produces use-values. Here we contemplate the labour as producing a particular article; we view it under its qualitative aspect alone, with regard to its end and aim. But viewed as a value-creating process, the same labour-process presents itself under its quantitative aspect alone. Here it is a question merely of the time occupied by the labourer in doing the work; of the period during which the labour-power is usefully expended. Here, the commodities that take part in the process, do not count any longer as necessary adjuncts of labour-power in the production of a definite, useful object. They count merely as depositories of so much absorbed or materialised labour; that labour, whether previously embodied in the means of production, or incorporated in them for the first time during the process by the action of labour-power, counts in either case only according to its duration; it amounts to so many hours or days as the case may be.

Moreover, only so much of the time spent in the production of any article is counted, as, under the given social conditions, is necessary. The consequences of this are various. In the first place, it becomes necessary that the labour should be carried on under normal conditions. If a self-acting mule is the implement in general use for spinning, it would be absurd to supply the spinner with a distaff and spinning wheel. The cotton too must not be such rubbish as to cause extra waste in being worked, but must be of suitable quality. Otherwise the spinner would be found to spend more time in producing a pound of yarn than is socially necessary, in which case the excess of time would create neither value nor money. But whether the material factors of the process are of normal quality or not, depends not upon the labourer, but entirely upon the capitalist. Then again, the labour-power itself must be of average efficacy. In the trade in which it is being employed, it must possess the average skill, handiness and quickness prevalent in that trade, and our capitalist took good care to buy labour-power of such normal goodness. This power must be applied with the average amount of exertion and with the usual degree of intensity; and the capitalist is as careful to see that this is done, as that his workmen are not idle for a single moment. He has bought the use of the labour-power for a definite period, and he insists upon his rights. He has no intention of being robbed. Lastly, and for this purpose our friend has a penal code of his own, all wasteful consumption of raw material or instruments of labour is strictly forbidden, because what is so wasted, represents labour superfluously expended, labour that does not count in the product or enter into its value.

We now see, that the difference between labour, considered on the one hand as producing utilities, and on the other hand, as creating value, a difference which we discovered by our analysis of a commodity, resolves itself into a distinction between two aspects of the process of production.

The process of production, considered on the one hand as the unity of the labour-process and the process of creating value, is production of commodities; considered on the other hand as the unity of the labour-process and the process of producing surplus-value, it is the capitalist process of production, or capitalist production of commodities.

We stated, on a previous page, that in the creation of surplus-value it does not in the least matter, whether the labour appropriated by the capitalist be simple unskilled labour of average quality or more complicated skilled labour. All labour of a higher or more complicated character than average labour is expenditure of labour-power of a more costly kind, labour-power whose production has cost more time and labour, and which therefore has a higher value, than unskilled or simple labour-power. This power being of higher value, its consumption is labour of a higher class, labour that creates in equal times proportionally higher values than unskilled labour does. Whatever difference in skill there may be between the labour of a spinner and that of a jeweller, the portion of his labour by which the jeweller merely replaces the value of his own labour-power, does not in any way differ in quality from the additional portion by which he creates surplus-value. In the making of jewellery, just as in spinning, the surplus-value results only from a quantitative excess of labour, from a lengthening-out of one and the same labour-process, in the one case, of the process of making jewels, in the other of the process of making yarn.

But on the other hand, in every process of creating value, the reduction of skilled labour to average social labour, e.g., one day of skilled to six days of unskilled labour, is unavoidable. We therefore save ourselves a superfluous operation, and simplify our analysis, by the assumption, that the labour of the workman employed by the capitalist is unskilled average labour.

IV

Marginalism

Introduction. In 1838 the French classical tradition, which had been founded upon the work of Say and his followers, was given new direction by Cournot's *Researches into the Mathematical Principles of the Theory of Wealth*. Historian Mark Blaug describes this work as the most original and boldly conceived book in the history of economic theory. Moreover, Joseph Schumpeter credits Cournot with being the first "... to visualize the general interdependence of all economic quantities and the necessity of representing this cosmos by a system of equations," although Cournot was essentially a master of partial-equilibrium analysis. Antoine-Augustin Cournot (1801-1877), in addition to being the founder of mathematical economics, was also a prominent teacher, philosopher, and administrator. During his lifetime the works which brought him public acclaim were concerned with epistemology and probability theory—not economics. Cournot's *Theory of Wealth* failed to receive world recognition until two years after his death, at which time Jevons gave him the credit he had long deserved. A remarkable intellect, Cournot was the first economist to define and draw a demand function. He was also the first to prove that profit maximization requires that marginal revenue equal marginal cost. His accomplishments may be better appreciated if we recall that during the middle of the nineteenth century the non-mathematical, "literary" economists were having great difficulty in specifying the function that was later to be known as "Marshall's" demand curve. At this same time, Cournot not only specified the demand function, he also developed the first theoretical models for both monopoly and oligopoly! Reprinted in this section is his famous Chapter 4, in which the first published demand curve appears.

The year 1871 produced not one but two great classics: Jevons's *The Theory of Political Economy* and Menger's *Principles of Economics*. Only three years later Walras published his *Elements of Pure Economics*. All three of these works rejected the labor theory of value, which they displaced with their formulations of the marginal-utility theory of value. The almost simultaneous appearance of these three books had led many historians to speak of the marginal "revolution," although it must be noted that the labor theory of value was not dislodged from the minds of most economists until twenty years later. The surprising similarity of the works by Jevons, Menger and Walras explains the general practice of linking their names together. Hence, they are commonly referred to as the "triumvirate" or the "subjective value trio." Remarkably, the three authors wrote their books and conceived their theories completely independently of each other, and it was not until 1886 that Walras made note of parallel features in the three books. It remains a mystery to this day to explain the almost simultaneous appearance of three independently conceived works of such a similar nature. Although these three men were not the first discoverers of marginal utility, they were the first to achieve so much with the concept and are, for this reason, regarded the three main founders of marginalism.

William Stanley Jevons (1835-1882) was born in Liverpool and educated at University College in London. Because of his outstanding work in chemistry at the university, he was given a job as assayer at the new gold mint in Sydney, Australia, when he was only eighteen years old. It was during his stay in Australia that Jevons developed an interest in reading books on economics. His novel approach to economics was already well formed at the early age of twenty-seven, at which time he presented a paper, "Notice of a General Mathematical Theory of Political Economy," to the British Association for the Advancement of Science. When he was thirty-one years old, he began teaching political economy at Owens College. Nine years later he accepted a teaching position at his alma mater, where he worked only four more years. Because of his introverted nature, research interests, and active participation at scholarly meetings, Jevons was often ill prepared for his classroom lectures. Sadly, his brilliant career as a scholar was cut short when he drowned at a bathing resort at the age of forty-six.

Jevons's main accomplishments include the specification of the Law of Diminishing Marginal Utility, which—unlike other economists of that century—he based on the physiological principle that a repeated stimulus effects a diminishing response within a given period of time. This topic is taken up in the third chapter of his treatise, *The Theory of Political Economy*. Excerpts from that chapter, titled "The Theory of Utility," are presented here. The reader should note that "marginal utility" (or, more accurately, "differential utility") is in Jevons's words the "final degree of utility." Similarly, the "Law of Diminishing Marginal Utility" is described by his statement that "the degree of utility varies with the quantity of commodity, and ultimately decreases as that quantity increases." The same excerpt from chapter 3 may also be observed to contain Jevons's introduction of the term "disutility," which has outlived another of his coined terms: "discommodity." Diminishing marginal utility is more fully explained in his "Theory of Exchange" (chapter 4). Our selections from this chapter include his solution to the famous diamond-water paradox by means of an "equation of exchange."

Carl Menger (1840-1921), the founder of the Austrian school of economic thought, was born in Galicia, which later became a part of Poland. He was a student at the Universities of Vienna and Prague and he earned his Ph.D. degree at the University of Cracow. It was during his career as a government economist (in the late 1860s and early 1870s) that he produced his greatest work, *Principles of Economics*, in 1871. Two years later he became a professor at the University of Vienna, where he remained almost continually for the next thirty years. When Menger's book went out of print, he failed to bring out a second edition. Furthermore, there was no English translation of the book for seventy years. It is not surprising, then, that his sphere of influence was limited mainly to Austria and that his impact on economic theory was primarily produced by his devoted students. For example, although Menger had clearly described the concept of marginal utility, the first economist to use the term "marginal utility" was one of Menger's students, F. von Wieser. Our selection from "The Theory of Value" (chapter 3 of Menger's *Principles*) contains his solution to the diamond-water paradox, which the reader should compare with the answer given by Jevons. Such a comparison will show that Menger—unlike Jevons—neither bases his concept of marginal utility on mathematics nor on philosophic principles. The absence of mathematics makes Menger easier to read, and the lack of a hedonistic philosophy frees his work from the many attacks that have been made against hedonism.

The names of Jevons and Menger are normally associated with the name of Léon Walras (1834-1910), the third "codiscoverer" of marginal utility analysis. Actually, this association does not speak highly enough of Walras, a scholar whom Schumpeter deemed to be the greatest economist in history. Walras was born and reared in France, where he twice failed the entrance exam to École Polytechnique. After being admitted to the École des Mines, he remained in that school for less than a year, since engineering proved to be incompatible with his Bohemian spirit. During the next few years he wrote and published several novels, none of which were successful. At the age of twenty-three Walras decided to follow his father's footsteps into the economics profession, but twelve years passed before he won his first teaching position at the Academy of Lausanne in Switzerland. He remained at this Academy until 1892, at which time he was succeeded by Vilfredo Pareto. Walras was essentially self-taught; his only formal training in economic theory was given to him by his father. This lack of institutional preparation may explain why he was never offered a teaching position in his homeland. Walras had been teaching only four years when he published the first half of his greatest work, *Elements of Pure Economics or the Theory of Social Wealth* (1874). The second half of the book was published three years later. Like Jevons's *Theory*, Walras's *Elements* makes heavy use of differential calculus and places marginal utility (*i.e.*, Jevons's "final degree of utility" and Walras's "rareté") at the center of the analysis.

Walras's description of "rareté" as the cause of value (a claim made by his father in 1831) is given in chapter 10, which appears here. It should be noted that Walras's greatest contribution is his creation of the first mathematical formulation of a general equilibrium model (which, unfortunately, is too difficult and lengthy to permit inclusion here). Also excerpted is his brief description of the workings of a competitive market and his statement of primary concern with the value of normal goods (chapter 5).

The last economist known to have made an independent discovery of marginal analysis is John Bates Clark (1847-1938), the master of American marginalism who was primarily responsible for the growth of this analytical tool in the United States. Although Clark was very influential over Americans and many foreign economists, he never quite succeeded in establishing a school of thought. For one thing, there never was a "core" of disciples for Clark as there had been for Ricardo and Marshall. Moreover, the extent of Clark's influence cannot be accurately estimated, since the economics profession was being influenced by other marginalists at the same time. Nonetheless, Clark is still considered to be a member of a separate school called marginalism, although—as Schumpeter has pointed out—marginalism would be more properly called a tool of analysis than a school of thought. In Schumpeter's words, the marginal principle "can no more serve to characterize a school of economics than the use of the calculus can serve to characterize a scientific school or group in mathematics or physics."

Clark was born in Rhode Island and educated at Brown University and Amherst, from which he was graduated at the age of twenty-five. Upon leaving Amherst he went to Germany, where he spent three years studying under Roscher and Knies, now regarded the founders of the German Historical School. Although this experience in Germany may well explain Clark's critical attitude toward the classical school and his involvement with social issues, he remained a theoretician and showed no interest in becoming a historian. When he returned to the United States, Clark taught at Carleton College (where his best student was Thorstein Veblen), Smith College, and Amherst. In 1895 he joined the faculty of Columbia University, with which he was associated until he retired in 1923. Clark's three outstanding works are The Philosophy of Wealth (1885), The Distribution of Wealth (1899), and Essentials of Economic Theory (1907).

Although Clark had many predecessors in the marginalist school, he is regarded an outstanding contributor because of his innovative approach to a theory of distribution based upon marginal productivity analysis (which, quite naturally, led him to also discover the concept of marginal utility). This contribution is most clearly presented in Clark's best work, The Distribution of Wealth. The intent of this book, as Clark states in the opening sentence, is ". . . to show that the distribution of the income of society is controlled by a natural law, and that this law, if it worked without friction, would give to every agent of production the amount of wealth which that agent creates." Hence, the book was designed to clear up the confusion surrounding the marginal productivity theory of factor demand. This confusion is evident, for example, in the work of Böhm-Bawerk, who argued that paying all workers a wage determined by the product of the marginal labor unit would cause the intramarginal workers to be exploited (assuming diminishing returns to labor). The intramarginal workers, he argued, are exploited when they receive anything less than their contribution to total product. Clark's lucid response to this argument is most clearly and concisely stated in chapters 12 and 13, which—except for the margin notes and one footnote—are reprinted here in their entirety.

9. Researches into the Mathematical Principles of the Theory of Wealth*

ANTOINE-AUGUSTIN COURNOT

OF THE LAW OF DEMAND

To lay the foundations of the theory of exchangeable values, we shall not accompany most speculative writers back to the cradle of the human race; we shall undertake to explain neither the origin of property nor that of exchange or division of labour. All this doubtless belongs to the history of mankind, but it has no influence on a theory which could only become applicable at a very advanced state of civilization, at a period when (to use the language of mathematicians) the influence of the *initial* conditions is entirely gone.

We shall invoke but a single axiom, or, if you prefer, make but a single hypothesis, *i.e.* that each one seeks to derive the greatest possible value from his goods or his labour. But to deduce the rational consequences of this principle, we shall endeavour to establish better than has been the case the elements of the data which observation alone can furnish. Unfortunately, this fundamental point is one which theorists, almost with one accord, have presented to us, we will not say falsely, but in a manner which is really meaningless.

It has been said almost unanimously that "the price of goods is in the inverse ratio of the quantity offered, and in the direct ratio of the quantity demanded." It has never been considered that the statistics necessary for accurate numerical estimation might be lacking, whether of the quantity offered or of the quantity demanded, and that this might prevent deducing from this principle general consequences capable of useful

Source: Reprinted from the American edition (MacMillan Company, 1897), translated by Nathaniel Bacan from the 1838 French edition. The selection reprinted here originally appeared as chapters 4, 5 and 7. Footnotes deleted, and equations renumbered.

application. But wherein does the principle itself consist? Does it mean that in case a double quantity of any article is offered for sale, the price will fall one-half? Then it should be more simply expressed, and it should only be said that the price is in the inverse ratio of the quantity offered. But the principle thus made intelligible would be false; for, in general, that 100 units of an article have been sold at 20 francs is no reason that 200 units would sell at 10 francs in the same lapse of time and under the same circumstances. Sometimes less would be marketed; often much more.

Furthermore, what is meant by the quantity demanded? Undoubtedly it is not that which is actually marketed at the demand of buyers, for then the generally absurd consequence would result from the pretended principle, that the more of an article is marketed the dearer it is. If by demand only a vague desire of possession of the article is understood, without reference to the *limited price* which every buyer supposes in his demand, there is scarcely an article for which the demand cannot be considered indefinite; but if the price is to be considered at which each buyer is willing to buy, and the price at which each seller is willing to sell, what becomes of the pretended principle? It is not, we repeat, an erroneous proposition—it is a proposition devoid of meaning. Consequently all those who have united to proclaim it have likewise united to make no use of it. Let us try to adhere to less sterile principles.

The cheaper an article is, the greater ordinarily is the demand for it. The sales or the demand (for to us these two words are synonymous, and we do not see for what reason theory need take account of any demand which does not result in a sale)—the sales or the demand generally, we say, increases when the price decreases.

We add the word *generally* as a corrective; there are, in fact, some objects of whim and luxury which are only desirable on account of their rarity and of the high price which is the consequence thereof. If any one should succeed in carrying out cheaply the crystallization of carbon, and in producing for one franc the diamond which to-day is worth a thousand, it would not be astonishing if diamonds should cease to be used in sets of jewellery, and should disappear as articles of commerce. In this case a great fall in price would almost annihilate the demand. But objects of this nature play so unimportant a part in social economy that it is not necessary to bear in mind the restriction of which we speak.

The demand might be in the inverse ratio of the price; ordinarily it increases or decreases in much more rapid proportion—an observation especially applicable to most manufactured products. On the contrary, at other times the variation of the demand is less rapid; which appears (a very singular thing) to be equally applicable both to the most necessary things and to the most superfluous. The price of violins or of astronomical telescopes might fall one-half and yet probably the demand would not double; for this demand is fixed by the number of those who cultivate the art or science to which these instruments belong; who have the disposition requisite and the leisure to cultivate them and the means to pay teachers and to meet the other necessary expenses, in consequence of which the price of the instruments is only a secondary question. On the contrary, firewood, which is one of the most useful articles, could probably double in price, from the progress of clearing land or increase in population, long before the annual consumption of fuel would be halved; as a large number of consumers are disposed to cut down other expenses rather than get along without firewood.

Let us admit therefore that the sales or the annual demand D is, for each article, a particular function $F(p)$ of the price p of such article. To know the form of this function would be to know what we call *the law of demand or of sales*. It depends evidently on the kind of utility of the article, on the nature of the services it can render or the enjoyments it can procure, on the habits and customs of the people, on the average wealth, and on the scale on which wealth is distributed.

Since so many moral causes capable of neither enumeration nor measurement affect the law of demand, it is plain that we should no more expect this law to be expressible by an algebraic formula than the law of mortality, and all the laws whose determination enters into the field of statistics, or what is called social arithmetic. Observation must therefore be depended on for furnishing the means of drawing up between proper limits a table of the corresponding values of D and p; after which, by the well-known methods of interpolation or by graphic processes, an empiric formula or a curve can be made to represent the function in question; and the solution of problems can be pushed as far as numerical applications.

But even if this object were unattainable (on account of the difficulty of obtaining observations of sufficient number and accuracy, and also on account of the progressive variations which the law of demand must undergo in a country which has not yet reached a practically stationary condition), it would be nevertheless not improper to introduce the unknown law of demand into analytical combinations, by means of an indeterminate symbol; for it is well known that one of the most important functions of analysis consists precisely in assigning determinate relations between quantities to which numerical values and even algebraic forms are absolutely unassignable.

Unknown functions may none the less possess properties or general characteristics which are known; as, for instance, to be indefinitely increasing or decreasing, or periodical, or only real between certain limits. Nevertheless such data, however imperfect they may

seem, by reason of their very generality and by means of analytical symbols, may lead up to relations equally general which would have been difficult to discover without this help. Thus without knowing the law of decrease of the capillary forces, and starting solely from the principle that these forces are inappreciable at appreciable distances, mathematicians have demonstrated the general laws of the phenomena of capillarity, and these laws have been confirmed by observation.

On the other hand, by showing what determinate relations exist between unknown quantities, analysis reduces these unknown quantities to the smallest possible number, and guides the observer to the best observations for discovering their values. It reduces and coordinates statistical documents; and it diminishes the labour of statisticians at the same time that it throws light on them.

For instance, it is impossible *a priori* to assign an algebraic form to the law of mortality; it is equally impossible to formulate the function expressing the subdivision of population by ages in a stationary population; but these two functions are connected by so simple a relation, that, as soon as statistics have permitted the construction of a table of mortality, it will be possible, without recourse to new observations, to deduce from this table one expressing the proportion of the various ages in the midst of a stationary population, or even of a population for which the annual excess of deaths over births is known.

Who doubts that in the field of social economy there is a mass of figures thus mutually connected by assignable relations, by means of which the easiest to determine empirically might be chosen, so as to deduce all the others from it by means of theory?

We will assume that the function $F(p)$, which expresses the law of demand or of the market, is a *continuous* function, *i.e.* a function which does not pass suddenly from one value to another, but which takes in passing all intermediate values. It might be otherwise if the number of consumers were very limited: thus in a certain household the same quantity of firewood will possibly be used whether wood costs 10 francs or 15 francs the stere, and the consumption may suddenly be diminished if the price of the stere rises above the latter figure. But the wider the market extends, and the more the combinations of needs, of fortunes, or even of caprices, are varied among consumers, the closer the function $F(p)$ will come to varying with p in a continuous manner. However little may be the variation of p, there will be some consumers so placed that the slight rise or fall of the article will affect their consumptions, and will lead them to deprive themselves in some way or to reduce their manufacturing output, or to substitute something else for the article that has grown dearer, as, for instance, coal for wood or anthracite for soft coal. Thus the "exchange" is a thermometer which shows by very slight variations of rates the fleeting variations in the estimate of the chances which affect government bonds, variations which are not a sufficient motive for buying or selling to most of those who have their fortunes invested in such bonds.

If the function $F(p)$ is continuous, it will have the property common to all functions of this nature, and on which so many important applications of mathematical analysis are based: *the variations of the demand will be sensibly proportional to the variations in price so long as these last are small fractions of the original price.* Moreover, these variations will be of opposite signs, *i.e.* an increase in price will correspond with a diminution of the demand.

Suppose that in a country like France the consumption of sugar is 100 million kilograms when the price is 2 francs a kilogram, and that it has been observed to drop to 99 millions when the price reached 2 francs 10 centimes. Without

considerable error, the consumption which would correspond to a price of 2 francs 20 centimes can be valued at 98 millions, and the consumption corresponding to a price of 1 franc 90 centimes at 101 millions. It is plain how much this principle, which is only the mathematical consequence of the continuity of functions, can facilitate applications of theory, either by simplifying analytical expressions of the laws which govern the movement of values, or in reducing the number of data to be borrowed from experience, if the theory becomes sufficiently developed to lend itself to numerical determinations.

Let us not forget that, strictly speaking, the principle just enunciated admits of exceptions, because a continuous function may have interruptions of continuity in some points of its course; but just as friction wears down roughnesses and softens outlines, so the wear of commerce tends to suppress these exceptional cases, at the same time that commercial machinery moderates variations in prices and tends to maintain them between limits which facilitate the application of theory.

To define with accuracy the quantity D, or the function $F(p)$ which is the expression of it, we have supposed that D represented the quantity sold *annually* throughout the extent of the country or of the market under consideration. In fact, the year is the natural unit of time, especially for researches having any connection with social economy. All the wants of mankind are reproduced during this term, and all the resources which mankind obtains from nature and by labour. Nevertheless, the price of an article may vary notably in the course of a year, and, strictly speaking, the law of demand may also vary in the same interval, if the country experiences a movement of progress or decadence. For greater accuracy, therefore, in the expression $F(p)$, p must be held to denote the annual average price, and the curve which represents function F to be in itself an average of all the curves which would represent this function at different times of the year. But this extreme accuracy is only necessary in case it is proposed to go on to numerical applications, and it is superfluous for researches which only seek to obtain a general expression of average results, independent of periodical oscillations.

Since the function $F(p)$ is continuous, the function $pF(p)$, which expresses the total value of the quantity annually sold, must be continuous also. This function would equal zero if p equals zero, since the consumption of any article remains finite even on the hypothesis that it is absolutely free; or, in other words, it is theoretically always possible to assign the symbol p a value so small that the product $pF(p)$ will vary imperceptibly from zero. The function $pF(p)$ disappears also when p becomes infinite, or, in other words, theoretically a value can always be assigned to p so great that the demand for the article and the production of it would cease. Since the function $pF(p)$ at first increases, and then decreases as p increases, there is therefore a value of p which makes this function a maximum, and which is given by the equation,

(1) $F(p) + pF'(p) = o$,

in which F', according to Lagrange's notation, denotes the differential coefficient of function F.

If we lay out the curve *anb* (Fig. I), of which the abscissas *oq* and the ordinates *qn* represent the variables p and D, the root of equation (1) will be the abscissa of the point *n* from which the triangle *ont*, formed by the tangent *nt* and the radius vector *on*, is isosceles, so that we have $oq = qt$.

We may admit that it is impossible to determine the function $F(p)$ empirically for each article, but it is by no means the case that the same obstacles prevent the approximate determination of the value of p which satisfies equation (1) or which renders the product $pF(p)$ a maximum. The construction of a table, where these values could be found,

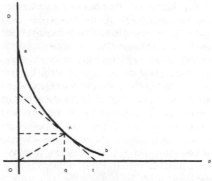

Fig. 1.

would be the work best calculated for preparing for the practical and rigorous solution of questions relating to the theory of wealth.

But even if it were impossible to obtain from statistics the value of p which should render the product $pF(p)$ a maximum, it would be easy to learn, at least for all articles to which the attempt has been made to extend commercial statistics, whether current prices are above or below this value. Suppose that when the price becomes $p + \Delta p$, the annual consumption as shown by statistics, such as customhouse records, becomes $D - \Delta D$. According as

$$\frac{\Delta D}{\Delta p} < \text{ or } > \frac{D}{p},$$

the increase in price, Δp, will increase or diminish the product $pF(p)$; and, consequently, it will be known whether the two values p and $p + \Delta p$ (assuming Δp to be a small fraction of p) fall above or below the value which makes the product under consideration a maximum.

Commercial statistics should therefore be required to separate articles of high economic importance into two categories, according as their current prices are above or below the value which makes a maximum of $pF(p)$. We shall see that many economic problems have different solutions, according as the article in question belongs to one or the other of these two categories.

We know by the theory of maxima and minima that equation (1) is satisfied as well by the values of p which render $pF(p)$ a minimum as by those which render this product a maximum. The argument used at the beginning of the preceding article shows, indeed, that the function $pF(p)$ necessarily has a maximum, but it might have several and pass through minimum values between. A root of equation (1) corresponds to a maximum or a minimum according as

$$2F'(p) + pF''(p) < \text{or} > 0,$$

or, substituting for p its value and considering the essentially negative sign of $F'(p)$,

$$2[F'(p)]^2 - F(p) \times F''(p) > \text{or} < 0.$$

In consequence, whenever $F''(p)$ is negative, or when the curve $D = F(p)$ turns its concave side to the axis of the abscissas, it is impossible that there should be a minimum, nor more than one maximum. In the contrary case, the existence of several maxima or minima is not proved to be impossible.

But if we cease considering the question from an exclusively abstract standpoint, it will be instantly recognized how improbable it is that the function $pF(p)$ should pass through several intermediate maxima and minima inside of the limits between which the value of p can vary; and as it is unnecessary to consider maxima which fall beyond these limits, if any such exist, all problems are the same as if the function $pF(p)$ only admitted a single maximum. The essential question is always whether, for the extent of the limits of oscillation of p, the function $pF(p)$ is increasing or decreasing for increasing values of p.

Any demonstration ought to proceed from the simple to the complex: the simplest hypothesis for the purpose of investigating by what laws prices are fixed, is that of monopoly, taking this word in its most absolute meaning, which supposes that the production of an article is in one man's hands. This hypothesis is not purely fictitious: it is realized in certain cases; and, moreover, when we have studied it, we can analyze more accurately the effects of competition of producers.

10. The Theory of Political Economy*

WILLIAM STANLEY JEVONS

THE THEORY OF UTILITY

UTILITY IS NOT AN INTRINSIC QUALITY

My principal work now lies in tracing out the exact nature and conditions of utility. It seems strange indeed that economists have not bestowed more minute attention on a subject which doubtless furnishes the true key to the problem of economics.

In the first place, utility, though a quality of things, is *no inherent quality*. It is better described as *a circumstance of things* arising out of their relation to man's requirements. As Senior most accurately says, "Utility denotes no intrinsic quality in the things which we call useful; it merely expresses their relations to the pains and pleasures of mankind." We can never, therefore, say ab-

*Source: Reprinted from the third edition (London: Macmillan and Co., Ltd., 1888). The selection reprinted here originally appeared as chapters 3 and 4.

solutely that some objects have utility and others have not. The ore lying in the mine, the diamond escaping the eye of the searcher, the wheat lying unreaped, the fruit ungathered for want of consumers, have no utility at all. The most wholesome and necessary kinds of food are useless unless there are hands to collect and mouths to eat them sooner or later. Nor, when we consider the matter closely, can we say that all portions of the same commodity possess equal utility. Water, for instance, may be roughly described as the most useful of all substances. A quart of water per day has the high utility of saving a person from dying in a most distressing manner. Several gallons a day may possess much utility for such purposes as cooking and washing; but after an adequate supply is secured for these uses, any additional quantity is a matter of comparative indifference. All that we can say, then, is that water, up to a certain quantity, is indispensable; that further quantities will have various degrees of utility; but that beyond a certain quantity the utility sinks gradually to zero; it may even become negative, that is to say, further supplies of the same substance may become inconvenient and hurtful.

Exactly the same considerations apply more or less clearly to every other article. A pound of bread per day supplied to a person saves him from starvation, and has the highest conceivable utility. A second pound per day has also no slight utility; it keeps him in a state of comparative plenty, though it be not altogether indispensable. A third pound would begin to be superfluous. It is clear, then, that *utility is not proportional to commodity:* the very same articles vary in utility according as we already possess more or less of the same article. The like may be said of other things. One suit of clothes per annum is necessary, a second convenient, a third desirable, a fourth not unacceptable, but we sooner or later reach a point at which further supplies are not desired

with any perceptible force unless it be for subsequent use.

LAW OF THE VARIATION OF UTILITY

Let us now investigate this subject a little more closely. Utility must be considered as measured by, or even as actually identical with, the addition made to a person's happiness. It is a convenient name for the aggregate of the favorable balance of feeling produced,—the sum of the pleasure created and the pain prevented. We must now carefully discriminate between the *total utility* arising from any commodity and the utility attaching to any particular portion of it. Thus the total utility of the food we eat consists in maintaining life, and may be considered as infinitely great; but if we were to subtract a tenth part from what we eat daily, our loss would be but slight. We should certainly not lose a tenth part of the whole utility of food to us. It might be doubtful whether we should suffer any harm at all.

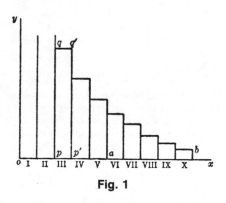

Fig. 1

Let us imagine the whole quantity of food which a person consumes on an average during twenty-four hours to be divided into ten equal parts. If his food be reduced by the last part, he will suffer but little; if a second tenth part be deficient, he will feel the want distinctly; the subtraction of the third tenth part will be decidedly injurious; with every subsequent subtraction of a tenth part his sufferings will be more and more serious, until at length he will be upon the verge of starvation. Now, if we call each of the tenth parts *an increment*, the meaning of these facts is, that each increment of food is less necessary, or possesses less utility, than the previous one. To explain this variation of utility we may make use of space representations, which I have found convenient in illustrating the laws of economics in my college lectures during fifteen years past.

Let the line *ox* be used as a measure of the quantity of food, and let it be divided into ten equal parts to correspond to the ten portions of food mentioned above. Upon these equal lines are constructed rectangles and the area of each rectangle may be assumed to represent the utility of the increment of food corresponding to its base. Thus the utility of the last increment is small, being proportional to the small rectangle on *x*. As we approach towards *o*, each increment bears a larger rectangle, that standing upon III being the largest complete rectangle. The utility of the next increment, II, is undefined, as also that of I, since these portions of food would be indispensable to life, and their utility, therefore, infinitely great.

We can now form a clear notion of the utility of the whole food, or of any part of it, for we have only to add together the proper rectangles. The utility of the first half of the food will be the sum of the rectangles standing on the line *oa*; that of the second half will be represented by the sum of the smaller rectangles between *a* and *b*. The total utility of the food will be the whole sum of the rectangles, and will be infinitely great.

The comparative utility of the several portions is, however, the most important. Utility may be treated as *a quantity of two dimensions*, one dimension consisting in the quantity of the commodity, and another in the intensity of the effect produced upon the consumer. Now the quantity of the commodity is measured on the horizontal line *ox*, and the intensity of utility will be measured by the length of the upright lines, or *ordinates*. The intensity of utility of the third increment is measured either by *pq*, or *p'q'*, and its utility is the product of the units in *pp'* multiplied by those in *pq*.

But the division of the food into ten equal parts is an arbitrary supposition. If we had taken twenty or a hundred or more equal parts, the same general principle would hold true, namely, that each small portion would be less useful and necessary than the last. The law may be considered to hold true theoretically, however small the increments are made; and in this way we shall at last reach a figure which is undistinguishable from a continuous curve. The notion of infinitely small quantities of food may seem absurd as regards the consumption of one individual; but when we consider the consumption of a nation as a whole, the consumption may well be conceived to increase or diminish by quantities which are, practically speaking, infinitely small compared with the whole consumption. The laws which we are about to trace out are to be conceived as theoretically true of the individual; they can only be practically verified as regards the aggregate transactions, productions, and consumptions of a large body of people. But the laws of the aggregate depend of course upon the laws applying to individual cases.

The law of the variation of the degree of utility of food may thus be represented by a continuous curve *pbq*, and the perpendicular height of each point at the curve above the line *ox* represents the degree of utility of the commodity when a certain amount has been consumed. [*See Figure 2.*]

Thus, when the quantity *oa* has been consumed, the degree of utility corresponds to the length of the line *ab*; for if we take a very little more food, *aa'*, its utility will be the product of *aa'* and *ab* very nearly, and more nearly the less is the magnitude of *aa'*. The degree of utility is thus properly measured by the height of a very narrow rectangle corre-

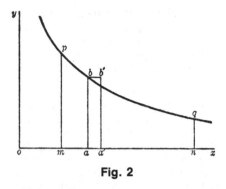

Fig. 2

sponding to a very small quantity of food, which theoretically ought to be infinitely small.

TOTAL UTILITY AND DEGREE OF UTILITY

We are now in a position to appreciate perfectly the difference between the *total utility* of any commodity and the *degree of utility* of the commodity at any point. These are, in fact, quantities of altogether different kinds, the first being represented by an area, and the second by a line. We must consider how we may express these notions in appropriate mathematical language.

Let x signify, as is usual in mathematical books, the quantity which varies independently—in this case the quantity of commodity. Let u denote the *whole utility* proceeding from the consumption of x. Then u will be, an mathematicians say, *a function of x;* that is, it will vary in some continuous and regular, but probably unknown, manner, when x is made to vary. Our great object at present, however, is to express the *degree of utility*.

Mathematicians employ the sign Δ prefixed to a sign of quantity, such as x, to signify that a quantity of the same nature as x, but small in proportion to x, is taken into consideration. Thus Δx means a small portion of x, and $x + \Delta x$ is therefore a quantity a little greater than x. Now when x is a quantity of commodity, the utility of $x + \Delta x$ will be more than that of x as a general rule. Let the whole utility of $x + \Delta x$ be denoted by $u + \Delta u$; then it is obvious that the increment of utility Δu belongs to the increment of commodity Δx; and if, for the sake of argument, we suppose the degree of utility uniform over the whole of Δx, which is nearly true, owing to its smallness, we shall find the corresponding degree of utility by dividing Δu by Δx.

We find these considerations fully illustrated by the last figure, in which oa represents x, and ab is the degree of utility at the point a. Now, if we increase x by the small quantity aa', or Δx, the utility is increased by the small rectangle $abb'a'$, or Δu; and since a rectangle is the product of its sides, we find that the length of the line ab, the degree of utility, is represented by the fraction $\Delta u/\Delta x$.

As already explained, however, the utility of a commodity may be considered to vary with perfect continuity, so that we commit a small error in assuming it to be uniform over the whole increment Δx. To avoid this, we must imagine Δx to be reduced to an infinitely small size, Δu decreasing with it. The smaller the quantities are the more nearly we shall have a correct expression for ab, the degree of utility at the point a. Thus the *limit* of this fraction $\Delta u/\Delta x$, or, as it is commonly expressed, du/dx, is the degree of utility corresponding to the quantity of commodity x. *The degree of utility is,* in mathematical language, *the differential coefficient of u considered as a function of x,* and will itself be another function of x.

We shall seldom need to consider the degree of utility except as regards the last increment which has been consumed, or, which comes to the same thing, the next increment which is about to be consumed. I shall therefore commonly use the expression *final degree of utility,* as meaning the degree of utility of the last addition, or the next possible addition of a very small, or infinitely small, quantity to the existing stock. In ordinary circumstances, too, the final degree of utility will not be great compared with what it might be. Only in famine or other extreme circumstances do we approach the higher degrees of utility. Accordingly we can often treat the lower portions of the curves of variations *(pbq)* which concern ordinary commercial transactions, while we leave out of sight the portions beyond *p* or *q*. It is also evident that we may know the degree of utility at any point while ignorant of the total utility, that is, the area of the whole curve. To be able to estimate the total enjoyment of a person would be an interesting thing, but it would not be really so important as to be able to estimate the additions and subtractions to his enjoyment which circumstances occasion. In the same way a very wealthy person may be quite unable to form any accurate statement of his aggregate wealth, but he may nevertheless have exact accounts of income and expenditure, that is, of additions and subtractions.

VARIATION OF THE FINAL DEGREE OF UTILITY

The final degree of utility is that function upon which the theory of economics will be found to turn. Economists, generally speaking, have failed to discriminate between this function and the total utility, and from this confusion has arisen much perplexity. Many commodities which are most useful to us are esteemed and desired but little. We cannot live without water, and yet in ordinary circumstances we set no value on it. Why is this? Simply because we usually have so much of it that its final degree of utility is reduced nearly to zero. We enjoy every day the almost infinite utility of water, but then we do not need to consume more than we have. Let the supply run short by drought, and we begin to feel the higher degrees of utility, of which we think but little at other times.

The variation of the function expressing the final degree of utility is the all-important point in economic problems. We may state, as a general law, that *the degree of utility varies with the quantity of commodity, and ultimately decreases as that quantity increases.* No commodity can be named which we continue to desire with the same force, whatever be the quantity already in use or possession. All our appetites are capable of *satisfaction* or *satiety* sooner or later, in fact, both these words mean, etymologically, that we have had *enough*, so that more is of no use to us. It does not follow, indeed, that the degree of utility will always sink to zero. This may be the case with some things, especially the simple animal requirements, such as food, water, air, etc. But the more refined and intellectual our needs become, the less are they capable of satiety. To the desire for articles of taste, science, or curiosity, when once excited, there is hardly a limit.

DISUTILITY AND DISCOMMODITY

A few words will suffice to suggest that as utility corresponds to the production of pleasure, or, at least, a favorable alteration in the balance of pleasure and pain, so negative utility will consist in the production of pain, or the unfavorable alteration of the balance. In reality we must be almost as often concerned with the one as with the other; nevertheless, economists have not employed any distinct technical terms to express that production of pain which accompanies so many actions of life. They have fixed their attention on the more agreeable aspect of the matter. It will be allowable, however, to appropriate the good English word *discommodity*, to signify any substance or action which is the opposite of *commodity*, that is to say, *anything which we desire to get rid of*, like ashes or sewage. Discommodity is, indeed, properly an abstract form signifying inconvenience, or disadvantage; but as the noun *commodities* has been used in the English language for four hundred years at least as a concrete term, so we may now convert discommodity into a concrete term, and speak of *discommodities* as substances or things which possess the quality of causing inconvenience or harm. For the abstract notion, the opposite or negative of utility, we may invent the term *disutility*, which will mean something different from inutility, or the absence of utility. It is obvious that utility passes through inutility before changing into disutility, these notions being related as +, O, and −.

DISTRIBUTION OF COMMODITY IN DIFFERENT USES

The principles of utility may be illustrated by considering the mode in which we distribute a commodity when it is capable of several uses. There are articles which may be employed for many distinct purposes: thus, barley may be used either to make beer, spirits, bread, or to feed cattle; sugar may be used to eat, or for producing alcohol; timber may be used in construction, or as fuel; iron and other metals may be applied to many different purposes. Imagine, then, a community in the possession of a certain stock of barley; what principles will regulate their mode of consuming it? Or, as we have not yet reached the subject of exchange, imagine an isolated family, or even an individual, possessing an adequate stock, and using some in one way and some in another. The theory of utility gives, theoretically speaking, a complete solution of the question.

Let s be the whole stock of some commodity, and let it be capable of two distinct uses. Then we may represent the two quantities appropriated to these uses by x_1 and y_1, it being a condition that $x_1 + y_1 = s$. The person may be conceived as successively expending small quantities of the commodity; now it is the inevitable tendency of human nature to choose that course which appears to offer the greatest advantage at the moment. Hence, when the person remains satisfied with the distribution he has made, it follows that no alteration would yield him more pleasure, which amounts to saying that an increment of commodity would yield exactly as much utility in one use as in another. Let Δu_1, Δu_2 be the increments of utility which might arise respectively from consuming an increment of commodity in the two different ways. When the distribution is completed, we ought to have $\Delta u_1 = \Delta u_2$; or at the limit we have the equation

$$\frac{du_1}{dx} = \frac{du_2}{dy},$$

which is true when x, y are respectively equal to x_1, y_1. We must, in other words, have the *final degrees of utility* in the two uses equal.

The same reasoning which applies to uses of the same commodity will evidently apply to any two uses, and hence to all uses simultaneously, so that we obtain a series of equations less numerous by a unit than the number of ways of using the commodity. The general result is that commodity, if consumed by a perfectly wise being, must be consumed with a maximum production of utility.

We should often find these equations to fail. Even when x is equal to 99/100 of the stock, its degree of utility might still exceed the utility attaching to the remaining 1/100 part in either of the other uses. This would mean that it was preferable to give the whole commodity to the first use. Such a case might perhaps be said to be not the exception but the rule; for whenever a commodity is capable of only one use, the circumstance is theoretically represented by saying that the final degree of utility in this employment always exceeds that in any other employment.

Under peculiar circumstances great changes may take place in the consumption of a commodity. In a time of scarcity the utility of barley as food might rise so high as to exceed altogether its utility, even as regards the smallest quantity, in producing alcoholic liquors; its consumption in the latter way would then cease. In a besieged town the employment of articles becomes revolutionized. Things of great utility in other respects are ruthlessly applied to strange purposes. In Paris a vast stock of horses was eaten, not so much because they were useless in other ways, as because they were needed more strongly as food. A certain stock of horses had, indeed, to be retained as a necessary aid to locomotion, so that the equation of the degrees of utility never wholly failed.

THEORY OF EXCHANGE

POPULAR USE OF THE TERM VALUE

In the popular use of the word value no less than three distinct though connected meanings seem to be confused together. These may be described as

(1) Value in use;
(2) Esteem, or urgency of desire;
(3) Ratio of exchange.

Adam Smith, in the familiar passage already referred to distinguished between the first and the third meanings. He said,

The word value, it is to be observed, has two different meanings, and sometimes expresses the power of purchasing other goods which the possession of that object conveys. The one may be called "value in use"; the other "value in exchange." The things which have the greatest value in use have frequently little or no value in exchange; and, on the contrary those which have the greatest value in exchange have frequently little or no value in use. Nothing is more useful than water: but it will purchase scarce anything; scarce anything can be had in exchange for it. A diamond, on the contrary, has scarce any value in use; but a very great quantity of other goods may frequently be had in exchange for it.[1]

It is sufficiently plain that, when Smith speaks of water as being highly useful and yet devoid of purchasing power, he means *water in abundance*, that is to say, water so abundantly supplied that it has exerted its full useful effect, or its *total utility*. Water, when it becomes very scarce, as in a dry desert, acquires exceedingly great purchasing power. Thus Smith evidently means by value in use, *the total utility of a substance of which the degree of utility has sunk very low, because the want of such substance has been well nigh satisfied*. By purchasing power he clearly means the ratio of exchange for other commodities. But here he fails to point out that the quantity of goods received in exchange depends just as much upon the nature of the goods received, as on the nature of those given for them. In exchange for a diamond we can get a great quantity of iron, or corn, or paving-stones, or other commodity of which there is abundance; but we can get very few rubies, sapphires, or other precious stones. Silver is of high purchasing power compared with zinc, or lead, or iron, but of small purchasing power compared with gold, platinum, or iridium. Yet we might well say in any case that diamond and silver are things of high value. Thus I am led to think that the word value is often used in reality to mean *intensity of desire or esteem for a thing*. A silver ornament is a beautiful object apart from all ideas of traffic; it may thus be valued or esteemed simply because it suits the taste and fancy of its owner, and is the only one possessed. Even Robinson Crusoe must have looked upon each of his possessions with varying esteem and desire for more, although he was incapable of exchanging with any other person. Now, in this sense value seems to be identical with the final degree of utility of a commodity, as defined in a previous page; it is measured by the intensity of the pleasure or benefit which would be obtained from a new increment of the same commodity. No doubt there is a close connection between value in this meaning, and value as ratio of exchange. Nothing can have a high purchasing power unless it be highly esteemed in itself; but it may be highly esteemed apart from all comparison with other things; and, though highly esteemed, it may have a low purchasing power, because those things against which it is measured are still more esteemed.

Thus I come to the conclusion that, in the use of the word value, three distinct meanings are habitually confused together, and require to be thus distinguished—

(1) Value in use = total utility;
(2) Esteem = final degree of utility;
(3) Purchasing power = ratio of exchange.

It is not to be expected that we could profitably discuss such matters as economic doctrines, while the fundamental ideas of the subject are thus jumbled up together in one ambiguous word. The only thorough remedy consists in substituting for the dangerous name *value* that one of the three stated meanings which is intended in each case. In this work, therefore, I shall discontinue the use of the word value altogether, and when, as will be most often the case in the remainder of the book, I need to refer to the third meaning, often called by economists *exchange* or *exchangeable value*, I shall substitute the wholly unequivocal expression *Ratio of Exchange*, specifying at the same time what are the *two articles* exchanged. When we speak of the ratio of exchange of pig-iron and gold, there can be no possible doubt that we intend to refer to the ratio of the number of units of the one commodity to the number of units of the other commodity for which it exchanges, the units being arbitrary concrete magnitudes, but the ratio an abstract number.

When I proposed, in the first edition of this book, to use Ratio of Exchange instead of the word value, the expression had been so little, if at all, employed by English economists, that it amounted to an innovation. J. S. Mill, indeed, in his chapters on Value, speaks once and again of things exchanging for each other "in the ratio of their cost of production"; but he always omits to say distinctly that exchange value is itself a matter of ratio. As to Ricardo, Malthus, Adam Smith, and other great English

economists, although they usually discourse at some length upon the meanings of the word value, I am not aware that they ever explicitly apply the name *ratio* to exchange or exchangeable value. Yet ratio is unquestionably the correct scientific term, and the only term which is strictly and entirely correct.

It is interesting, therefore, to find that, although overlooked by English economists, the expression had been used by two or more of the truly scientific French economists, namely, Le Trosne and Condillac. Le Trosne carefully defines value in the following terms:

La valeur consiste dans le rapport d'échange qui se trouve entre telle chose et telle autre, entre telle mesure d'une production et telle mesure des autres.

Condillac apparently adopts the words of Le Trosne, saying of value: "Qu'elle consiste dans le rapport d'échange entre telle chose et telle autre." Such economical works as those of Baudeau, Le Trosne, and Condillac were almost wholly unknown to English readers until attention was drawn to them by Mr. H. D. Macleod and Professor Adamson; but I shall endeavour for the future to make proper use of them.

DIMENSION OF VALUE

There is no difficulty in seeing that, when we use the word Value in the sense of ratio of exchange, its dimension will be simply zero. Value will be expressed, like angular magnitude and other ratios in general, by abstract number. Angular magnitude is measured by the ratio of a line to a line, the ratio of the arc subtended by the angle to the radius of the circle. So value in this sense is a ratio of the quantity of one commodity to the quantity of some other commodity exchanged for it. If we compare the commodities simply as physical quantities, we have the dimensions M divided by M, or MM^{-1}, or M^0. Exactly the same result would be obtained if, instead of taking the mere

Popular Expression of Meaning	Scientific Expression	Dimensions
(1) Value in use	Total Utility	MU
(2) Esteem, or Urgency of Desire for more	Final Degree of Utility	U
(3) Purchasing Power	Ratio of Exchange ...	M^0

physical quantities, we were to compare their utilities, for we should then have MU divided by MU or M^0U^0, which, as it really means *unity*, is identical in meaning with M^0.

When we use the word value in the sense of esteem, or urgency of desire, the feeling with which Oliver Twist must have regarded a few more mouthfuls when he "asked for more," the meaning of the word, as already explained, is identical with *degree of utility*, of which the dimension is U. Lastly, the *value in use* of Adam Smith, or the *total utility*, is the integral of .U.dM, and has the dimensions MU. We may thus tabulate our results concerning the ambiguous uses of the word *value*—

THE LAW OF INDIFFERENCE

When a commodity is perfectly uniform or homogeneous in quality, any portion may be indifferently used in place of an equal portion: hence, in the same market, and at the same moment, all portions must be exchanged at the same ratio. There can be no reason why a person should treat exactly similar things differently, and the slightest excess in what is demanded for one over the other will cause him to take the latter instead of the former. In nicely balanced exchanges it is a very minute scruple which turns the scale and governs the choice. A minute difference of quality in a commodity may thus give rise to preference, and cause the ratio of exchange to differ. But where no difference exists at all, or where no difference is known to exist, there can be no ground for preference whatever. If, in selling a quantity of perfectly equal and uniform barrels of flour, a merchant arbitrarily fixed different prices on them, a purchaser would of course select the cheaper ones; and where there was ab-

solutely no difference in the thing purchased, even an excess of a penny in the price of a thing worth a thousand pounds would be a valid ground of choice. Hence follows what is undoubtedly true, with proper explanations, that *in the same open market, at any one moment, there cannot be two prices for the same kind of article.* Such differences as may practically occur arise from extraneous circumstances, such as the defective credit of the purchasers, their imperfect knowledge of the market, and so on.

The principle above expressed is a general law of the utmost importance in Economics, and I propose to call it *The Law of Indifference*, meaning that, when two objects or commodities are subject to no important difference as regards the purpose in view, they will either of them be taken instead of the other with perfect indifference by a purchaser. Every such act of indifferent choice gives rise to an equation of degrees of utility, so that in this principle of indifference we have one of the central pivots of the theory.

Though the price of the same commodity must be uniform at any one moment, it may vary from moment to moment, and must be conceived as in a state of continual change. Theoretically speaking, it would not usually be possible to buy two portions of the same commodity *successively* at the same ratio of exchange, because, no sooner would the first portion have been bought than the conditions of utility would be altered. When exchanges are made on a large scale, this result will be verified in practice. If a wealthy person invested £100,000 in the funds in the morning, it is hardly likely that the operation could be repeated in the afternoon at the same price. In any market, if a person goes on buying largely, he will ultimately raise the price against himself. Thus it is apparent that extensive purchases would best be made gradually, so as to secure the advantage of a lower price upon the earlier portions. In theory this effect of exchange upon the ratio of exchange must be conceived to exist in some degree, however small may be the purchases made. Strictly speaking, the ratio of exchange at any moment is that of dy to dx, of an infinitely small quantity of one commodity to the infinitely small quantity of another which is given for it. The ratio of exchange is really a differential coefficient. The quantity of any article purchased is a function of the price at which it is purchased, and the ratio of exchange expresses the rate at which the quantity of the article increases compared with what is given for it.

We must carefully distinguish, at the same time, between the Statics and Dynamics of this subject. The real condition of industry is one of perpetual motion and change. Commodities are being continually manufactured and exchanged and consumed. If we wished to have a complete solution of the problem in all its natural complexity, we should have to treat it as a problem of motion—a problem of dynamics. But it would surely be absurd to attempt the more difficult question when the more easy one is yet so imperfectly within our power. It is only as a purely statical problem that I can venture to treat the action of exchange. Holders of commodities will be regarded not as continuously passing on these commodities in streams of trade, but as possessing certain fixed amounts which they exchange until they come to equilibrium. It is much more easy to determine the point at which a pendulum will come to rest than to calculate the velocity at which it will move when displaced from that point of rest. Just so, it is a far more easy task to lay down the conditions under which trade is completed and interchange ceases, than to attempt to as-

certain at what rate trade will go on when equilibrium is not attained.

The difference will present itself in this form: dynamically we could not treat the ratio of exchange otherwise than as the ratio of dy and dx, infinitesimal quantities of commodity. Our equations would then be regarded as differential equations, which would have to be integrated. But in the statical view of the question we can substitute the ratio of the finite quantities y and x. Thus, from the self-evident principle, stated earlier, that there cannot, in the same market, at the same moment, be two different prices for the same uniform commodity, it follows that *the last increments in an act of exchange must be exchanged in the same ratio as the whole quantities exchanged.* Suppose that two commodities are bartered in the ratio of x for y; then every m^{th} part of x is given for the mth part of y, and it does not matter for which of the mth parts. No part of the commodity can be treated differently from any other part. We may carry this division to an indefinite extent by imagining m to be constantly increased, so that, at the limit, even an infinitely small part of x must be exchanged for an infinitely small part of y, in the same ratio as the whole quantities. This result we may express by stating that the increments concerned in the process of exchange must obey the equation.

$$\frac{dy}{dx} = \frac{y}{x}.$$

The use which we shall make of this equation will be seen in the next section.

THE THEORY OF EXCHANGE

The keystone of the whole Theory of Exchange, and of the principal problems of Economics, lies in this proposition— *The ratio of exchange of any two commodities will be the reciprocal of the ratio of the final degrees of utility of the quantities of commodity available for consumption after the exchange is com-*

pleted. When the reader has reflected a little upon the meaning of this proposition, he will see, I think, that it is necessarily true, if the principles of human nature have been correctly represented in previous pages.

Imagine that there is one trading body possessing only corn, and another possessing only beef. It is certain that, under these circumstances, a portion of the corn may be given in exchange for a portion of the beef with a considerable increase of utility. How are we to determine at what point the exchange will cease to be beneficial? This question must involve both the ratio of exchange and the degrees of utility. Suppose, for a moment, that the ratio of exchange is approximately that of ten pounds of corn for one pound of beef: then if, to the trading body which possesses corn, ten pounds of corn are less useful than one of beef, that body will desire to carry the exchange further. Should the other body possessing beef find one pound less useful than ten pounds of corn, this body will also be desirous to continue the exchange. Exchange will thus go on until each party has obtained all the benefit that is possible, and loss of utility would result if more were exchanged. Both parties, then, rest in satisfaction and equilibrium, and the degrees of utility have come to their level, as it were.

This point of equilibrium will be known by the criterion, that an infinitely small amount of commodity exchanged in addition, at the same rate, will bring neither gain nor loss of utility. In other words, if increments of commodities be exchanged at the established ratio, their utilities will be equal for both parties. Thus, if ten pounds of corn were of exactly the same utility as one pound of beef, there would be neither harm nor good in further exchange at this ratio.

It is hardly possible to represent this theory completely by means of a diagram, but [Figure 3] may, perhaps, render it clearer. Suppose the line *pqr* to be a small portion of the curve of utility of

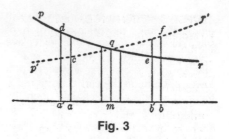

Fig. 3

one commodity, while the broken line *p'qr'* is the like curve of another commodity which has been reversed and superposed on the other. Owing to this reversal, the quantities of the first commodity are measured along the base line from *a* towards *b*, whereas those of the second must be measured in the opposite direction. Let units of both commodities be represented by equal lengths: then the little line of *a'a* indicates an increase of the first commodity, and a decrease of the second. Assume the ratio of exchange to be that of unit for unit, or 1 to 1: then, by receiving the commodity *a'a* the person will gain the utility *ad*, and lose the utility *a'c*; or he will make a net gain of the utility corresponding to the mixtilinear figure *cd*. He will, therefore, wish to extend the exchange. If he were to go up to the point *b'*, and were still proceeding, he would, by the next small exchange, receive the utility *be*, and part with *b'f*; or he would have a net loss of *ef*. He would, therefore, have gone too far; and it is pretty obvious that the point of intersection, *q*, defines the place where he would stop with the greatest advantage. It is there that a net gain is converted into a net loss, or rather where, for an infinitely small quantity, there is neither gain nor loss. To represent an infinitely small quantity, or even an exceedingly small quantity, on a diagram is, of course, impossible; but on either side of the line *mq* I have represented the utilities of a small quantity of commodity more or less, and it is apparent that the net gain or loss upon the exchange of these quantities would be trifling.

SYMBOLIC STATEMENT OF THE THEORY

To represent this process of reasoning in symbols, let Δx denote a small increment of corn, and Δy a small increment of beef exchanged for it. Now our Law of Indifference comes into play. As both the corn and the beef are homogeneous commodities, no parts can be exchanged at a different ratio from other parts in the same market: hence, if x be the whole quantity of corn given for y the whole quantity of beef received, Δy must have the same ratio to Δx as y to x; we have then,

$$\frac{\Delta y}{\Delta x} = \frac{y}{x}, \text{ or } \Delta y = \frac{y}{x}\Delta x.$$

In a state of equilibrium, the utilities of these increments must be equal in the case of each party, in order that neither more nor less exchange would be desirable. Now the increment of beef, Δy, is $\frac{y}{x}$ times as great as the increment of corn, Δx, so that, in order that their utilities shall be equal, the degree of utility of beef must be $\frac{x}{y}$ times as great as the degree of utility of corn. Thus we arrive at the principle that *the degrees of utility of commodities exchanged will be in the inverse proportion of the magnitudes of the increments exchanged.*

Let us now suppose that the first body, A, originally possessed the quantity a of corn, and that the second body, B, possessed the quantity b of beef. As the exchange consists in giving x of corn for y of beef, the state of things after exchange will be as follows:—

A holds $a - x$ of corn, and y of beef,
B holds x of corn, and $b - y$ of beef.

Let $\phi_1(a - x)$ denote the final degree of utility of corn to A, and $\phi_2 x$ the corresponding function for B. Also let $\psi_1 y$ denote A's final degree of utility for beef, and $\psi_2(b - y)$ B's similar function. Then, as explained previously A will not be satisfied unless the following equation holds true:—

$$\phi_1(a - x) \cdot dx = \psi_1 y \cdot dy;$$

$$\text{or } \frac{\phi_1(a - x)}{\psi_1 y} = \frac{dy}{dx}.$$

Hence, substituting for the second member by the equation given previously we have

$$\frac{\phi_1(a - x)}{\psi_1 y} = \frac{y}{x}.$$

What holds true of A will also hold true of B, *mutatis mutandis.* He must also derive exactly equal utility from the final increments, otherwise it will be for his interest to exchange either more or less, and he will disturb the conditions of exchange. Accordingly the following equation must hold true:

$$\psi_2(b - y) \cdot dy = \phi_2 x \cdot dx;$$

or, substituting as before,

$$\frac{\phi_2 x}{\psi_2(b - y)} = \frac{y}{x}.$$

We arrive, then, at the conclusion, that whenever two commodities are exchanged for each other, and *more or less can be given or received in infinitely small quantities*, the quantities exchanged satisfy two equations, which may be thus stated in a concise form—

$$\frac{\phi_1(a - x)}{\psi_1 y} = \frac{y}{x} = \frac{\phi_2 x}{\psi_2(b - y)};$$

The two equations are sufficient to determine the results of exchange; for there are only two unknown quantities concerned, namely, x and y, the quantities given and received. . . .

THE ORIGIN OF VALUE

[*Paragraph omitted.*] I have pointed out the excessive ambiguity of the word Value, and the apparent impossibility of using it safely. When intended to express the mere fact of certain articles exchanging in a particular ratio, I have proposed to substitute the unequivocal expression—*ratio of exchange*. But I am inclined to believe that a ratio is not the meaning which most persons attach to the word Value. There is a certain sense of esteem or desirableness, which we may have with regard to a thing apart from any distinct consciousness of the ratio in which it would exchange for other things. I may suggest that this distinct feeling of value is probably identical with the final degree of utility. While Adam Smith's often-quoted *value in use* is the total utility of a commodity to us, the *value in exchange* is defined by the *terminal utility*, the remaining desire which we or others have for possessing more.

There remains the question of labour as an element of value. Economists have not been wanting who put forward labour as the *cause of value*, asserting that all objects derive their value from the fact that labour has been expended on them; and it is thus implied, if not stated, that value will be proportional to labour. This is a doctrine which cannot stand for a moment, being directly opposed to facts. Ricardo disposes of such an opinion when he says:

> There are some commodities, the value of which is determined by their scarcity alone. No labour can increase the quantity of such goods, and therefore their value cannot be lowered by an increased supply. Some rare statues and pictures, scarce books and coins, wines of a peculiar quality, which can be made only from grapes grown on a particular soil, of which there is a very limited quantity, are all of this description. Their value is wholly independent of the quantity of labour originally necessary to produce them, and varies with the varying wealth and inclinations of those who are desirous to possess them.[2]

The mere fact that there are many things, such as rare ancient books, coins, antiquities, etc., which have high values, and which are absolutely incapable of production now, disperses the notion that value depends on labour. Even those things which are producible in any quantity by labour seldom exchange exactly at the corresponding values. The market price of corn, cotton, iron, and most other things is, in the prevalent theories of value, allowed to fluctuate above or below its natural or cost value. There may, again, be any discrepancy between the quantity of labour spent upon an object and the value ultimately attaching to it. A great undertaking like the Great Western Railway, or the Thames Tunnel, may embody a vast amount of labour, but its value depends entirely upon the number of persons who find it useful. If no use could be found for the *Great Eastern* steamship, its value would be *nil*, except for the utility of some of its materials. On the other hand, a successful undertaking, which happens to possess great utility, may have a value, for a time at least, far exceeding what has been spent upon it, as in the case of the [first] Atlantic Cable. The fact is, that *labour once spent has no influence on the future value of any article:* it is gone and lost for ever. In commerce bygones are for ever bygones; and we are always starting clear at each moment, judging the values of things with a view to future utility. Industry is essentially prospective, not retrospective; and seldom does the result of any undertaking exactly coincide with the first intentions of its promoters.

But though labour is never the cause of value, it is in a large proportion of cases the determining circumstance, and in the following way:—*Value depends solely on the final degree of utility. How can we vary this degree of utility?—By having more or less of the commodity to consume. And how shall we get more or less of it?—By spending more or less labour in obtaining a supply.* According to this view, then, there are two steps between labour and value. Labour affects supply, and supply affects the degree of utility, which governs value, or the ratio of exchange. In order that there may be no possible mistake about this all-important series of relations, I will re-state it in a tabular form, as follows:—

Cost of production determines supply;
Supply determines final degree of utility;
Final degree of utility determines value.

But it is easy to go too far in considering labour as the regulator of value; it is equally to be remembered that labour is itself of unequal value. Ricardo, by a violent assumption, founded his theory of value on quantities of labour considered as one uniform thing. He was aware that labour differs infinitely in quality and efficiency, so that each kind is more or less scarce, and is consequently paid at a higher or lower rate of wages. He regarded these differences as disturbing circumstances which would have to be allowed for; but his theory rests on the assumed equality of labour. This theory rests on a wholly different ground. I hold labour to be *essentially variable, so that its value must be determined by the value of the produce, not the value of the produce by that of the labour.* I hold it to be impossible to compare à *priori* the productive powers of a navvy, a carpenter, an iron-puddler, a schoolmaster, and a barrister. Accordingly, it will be found that not one of my equations represents a comparison between one man's labour and another's. The equation, if there is one at all, is between the same person in two or more different occupations. The subject is one in which complicated action and reaction takes place, and which we must defer until after we have described, in the next chapter, the Theory of Labour.

NOTES

1. *Wealth of Nations*, book 1, chap. 4, near the end.
2. *On the Principles of Political Economy and Taxation,* 3rd ed., 1821, p. 2.

11. The Theory of Value*

CARL MENGER

If we summarize what has been said, we obtain the following principles as the result of our investigation thus far:

1) The importance that goods have for us and which we call value is merely imputed. Basically, only satisfactions have importance for us, because the maintenance of our lives and well-being depend on them. But we logically impute this importance to the goods on whose availability we are conscious of being dependent for these satisfactions.

2) The magnitudes of importance that different satisfactions of concrete needs (the separate acts of satisfaction that can be realized by means of individual goods) have for us are unequal, and their measure lies in the degree of their importance for the maintenance of our lives and welfare.

3) The magnitudes of the importance of our satisfactions that are imputed to goods—that is, the magnitudes of their values—are therefore also unequal, and their measure lies in the degree of importance that the satisfactions dependent on the goods in question have for us.

4) In each particular case, of all the satisfactions assured by the whole available quantity of a good, only those that have the least importance to an economizing individual are dependent on command of a given portion of the whole quantity.

5) The value of a particular good or of a given portion of the whole quantity of a good at the disposal of an economizing

*Source: From Carl Menger, *Principles of Economics*, trans. Bert F. Hoselitz and James Dingwall (Glencoe, Ill.: The Free Press, 1950), chapter 3, pp. 139-51. Copyright © 1950 by The Institute for Humane Studies, Inc. Reprinted by permission. Footnotes renumbered or deleted.

individual is thus for him equal to the importance of the least important of the satisfactions assured by the whole available quantity and achieved with any equal portion. For it is with respect to these least important satisfactions that the economizing individual concerned is dependent on the availability of the particular good, or given quantity of a good.

Thus, in our investigation to this point, we have traced the differences in the value of goods back to their ultimate causes, and have also, at the same time, found the ultimate, and original, measure by which the values of all goods are judged by men.

If what has been said is correctly understood, there can be no difficulty in solving any problem involving the explanation of the causes determining the differences between the values of two or more concrete goods or quantities of goods.

If we ask, for example, why a pound of drinking water has no value whatsoever to us under ordinary circumstances, while a minute fraction of a pound of gold or diamonds generally exhibits a very high value, the answer is as follows: Diamonds and gold are so rare that all the diamonds available to mankind could be kept in a chest and all the gold in a single large room, as a simple calculation will show. Drinking water, on the other hand, is found in such large quantities on the earth that a reservoir can hardly be imagined large enough to hold it all. Accordingly, men are able to satisfy only the most important needs that gold and diamonds serve to satisfy, while they are usually in a position not only to satisfy their needs for drinking water fully but, in addition, also to let large quantities of it escape unused, since they are unable to use up the whole available quantity. Under ordinary circumstances, therefore, no human need would have to remain unsatisfied if men were unable to command some particular quantity of drinking water. With gold and diamonds, on the other hand, even the least significant

satisfactions assured by the total quantity available still have a relatively high importance on economizing men. Thus concrete quantities of drinking water usually have *no* value to economizing men but concrete quantities of gold and diamonds a *high* value.

All this holds only for the ordinary circumstances of life, when drinking water is available to us in copious quantities and gold and diamonds in very small quantities. In the desert, however, where the life of a traveller is often dependent on a drink of water, it can by all means be imagined that more important satisfactions depend, for an individual, on a pound of water than on even a pound of gold. In such a case, the value of a pound of water would consequently be greater, for the individual concerned, than the value of a pound of gold. And experience teaches us that such a relationship, or one that is similar, actually develops where the economic situation is as I have just described.

THE INFLUENCE OF DIFFERENCES IN THE QUALITY OF GOODS ON THEIR VALUE.

Human needs can often be satisfied by goods of different types and still more frequently by goods that differ, not as to type, but as to kind. Where we deal with given complexes of human needs, on the one side, and with the quantities of goods available for their satisfaction, on the other side . . . , the needs do not, therefore, always stand opposite quantities of homogeneous goods, but often opposite goods of different types, and still more frequently opposite goods of different kinds.

For greater simplicity of exposition I have, until now, omitted consideration of the differences between goods, and have, in the preceding sections, considered only cases in which quantities of completely homogeneous goods stand opposite needs of a specific type (stressing particularly the way in which their importance decreases in accordance with the degree of completeness of the satisfaction already attained). In this way, I was able to give greater emphasis to the influence that differences in the available quantities exercise on the value of goods.

The cases that now remain to be taken into consideration are those in which given human needs may be satisfied by goods of different types or kinds and in which, therefore, given human requirements stand opposite available quantities of goods of which separate portions are qualitatively different.

In this connection, it should first be noted that differences between goods, whether they be differences of type or of kind, cannot affect the value of the different units of a given supply if the satisfaction of human needs is in no way affected by these differences. Goods that satisfy human needs in an identical fashion are for this very reason regarded as completely homogeneous from an economic point of view, even though they may belong to different types or kinds on the basis of external appearance.

If the differences, as to type or kind, between two goods are to be responsible for differences in their value, it is necessary that they also have different capacities to satisfy human needs. In other words, it is necessary that they have what we call, from an economic point of view, differences in *quality*. An examination of the influence that differences in quality exercise on the value of particular goods is therefore the subject of the following investigation.

From an economic standpoint, the qualitative differences between goods may be of two kinds. Human needs may be satisfied either in a *quantitatively* or in a *qualitatively* different manner by means of equal quantities of qualitatively different goods. With a given quantity of beech-wood, for instance, the human need for warmth may be satisfied in a *quantitatively* more intensive manner than with the same quantity of fir. But two equal quantities of

foodstuffs of equal food value may satisfy the need for food in *qualitatively* different fashions, since the consumption of one dish may, for example, provide enjoyment while the other may provide either no enjoyment or only an inferior one. With goods of the first category, the inferior quality can be fully compensated for by a larger quantity, but with goods of the second category this is not possible. Fir, alder, or pine can replace beech-wood for heating purposes, and if coal of inferior carbon content, oak bark of inferior tannin content, and the ordinary labor services of tardy or less efficient day-laborers are only available to economizing men in sufficiently large quantities, they can generally replace the more highly qualified goods perfectly. But even if unpalatable foods or beverages, dark and wet rooms, the services of mediocre physicians, etc., are available in the largest quantities, they can never satisfy our needs as well, *qualitatively*, as the corresponding more highly qualified goods.

When economizing individuals appraise the value of a good, it is purely a question, as we have seen, of estimating the importance of satisfaction of those needs with respect to which they are dependent on command of the good. . . . The quantity of a good that will bring about a given satisfaction is, however, only a secondary factor in valuation. For if smaller quantities of a more highly qualified good will satisfy a human need in the same (that is, in a quantitatively and qualitatively identical) manner as larger quantities of a less qualified good, it is evident that the smaller quantities of the more highly qualified good will have the same value to economizing men as the larger quantities of the less qualified good. Thus equal quantities of goods having different qualities of the first kind will display values that are unequal in the proportion indicated. If, for example, in determining the value of oak bark we take account exclusively of its tannin content, and seven hundred-weight of one grade has the same effectiveness as eight hundred-weight of another grade, it will also have the same value as the latter quantity to the artisans using the bark. Merely reducing these goods to quantities of equal economic effectiveness (a procedure actually employed in the economic activities of men in all such cases) thus completely removes the difficulty in determining the value of given quantities of different qualities (so far as their effectiveness is merely quantitatively different). In this way, the more complicated case under consideration is reduced to the simple relationship explained earlier. . . .

The question of the influence of different qualities on the values of particular goods is more complicated when the qualitative differences between the goods cause needs to be satisfied in qualitatively different ways. There can be no doubt, after what has been said about the general principle of value determination . . . , that it is the importance of the needs that would remain unsatisfied if we did not have command of a particular good of not only the general type but also the specific quality corresponding to these needs that is, in this case too, the factor determining its value. The difficulty I am discussing here does not, therefore, lie in the general principle of value determination being inapplicable to these goods, but rather in the determination of the particular satisfaction that depends on a particular concrete good when a whole group of needs stands opposite goods whose various units are capable of satisfying these needs in qualitatively different ways. In other words, it lies in the practical application of the general principle of value determination to human economic activity. The solution to this problem arises from the following considerations.

Economizing individuals do not use the quantities of goods available to them without regard to differences in quality when these exist. A farmer who

has grain of different grades at his disposal does not, for example, use the worst grade for seeding, grain of medium quality as cattle feed, and the best for food and the production of beverages. Nor does he use the grains of different grades indiscriminately for one purpose or another. Rather, with a view to his requirements, he employs the best grade for seeding, the best that remains for food and beverages, and the grain of poorest quality for fattening cattle.

With goods whose units are homogeneous, the total available quantity of a good stands opposite the whole set of concrete needs that can be satisfied by means of it. But in cases where the different units of a good satisfy human needs in qualitatively different ways, the total available quantity of a good no longer stands opposite whole set of needs; each available quantity of specific quality instead stands opposite corresponding specific needs of the economizing individuals.

If, with respect to a given consumption purpose, a good of a certain quality cannot be replaced at all by goods of any other quality, the principle of value determination previously demonstrated . . . applies fully and directly to particular quantities of that good. Thus the value of any particular unit of such a good is equal to the importance of the least important satisfaction that is provided for by the total available quantity of this precise quality of good, since it is with respect to this satisfaction that we are actually dependent on command of the particular unit of this quality.

But human needs can be satisfied by means of goods of different qualifications, although in qualitatively different ways. If goods of one quality can be replaced by goods of another quality, though not with the same effectiveness, the value of a unit of the goods of superior quality is equal to the importance of the least important satisfaction that is provided for by the goods of superior quality minus a value quota[1] that is greater: (1) the smaller the value of the goods of inferior quality by which the particular need in question can also be satisfied, and (2) the smaller the difference to men between the importance of satisfying the particular need with the superior good and the importance of satisfying it with the inferior one.

Thus we arrive at the result that, even in cases in which a complex of needs stands opposite a quantity of goods of different qualities, satisfactions of given intensities always depend on each partial quantity or on each concrete unit of these goods. Hence, in all the cases discussed, the principle of value determination that I formulated above maintains its full applicability.

THE SUBJECTIVE CHARACTER OF THE MEASURE OF VALUE. LABOR AND VALUE. ERROR.

When I discussed the nature of value, I observed that value is nothing inherent in goods and that it is not a property of goods. But neither is value an independent thing. There is no reason why a good may not have value to one economizing individual but no value to another individual under different circumstances. The measure of value is entirely subjective in nature, and for this reason a good can have great value to one economizing individual, little value to another, and no value at all to a third, depending upon the differences in their requirements and available amounts. What one person disdains or values lightly is appreciated by another, and what one person abandons is often picked up by another. While one economizing individual esteems equally a given amount of one good and a greater amount of another good, we frequently observe just the opposite evaluations with another economizing individual.

Hence not only the nature but also the measure of value is subjective. Goods always have value to certain economizing individuals and this value

is also determined only by these individuals.

The value an economizing individual attributes to a good is equal to the importance of the particular satisfaction that depends on his command of the good. There is no necessary and direct connection between the value of a good and whether, or in what quantities, labor and other goods of higher order were applied to its production. A non-economic good (a quantity of timber in a virgin forest, for example) does not attain value for men if large quantities of labor or other economic goods were applied to its production. Whether a diamond was found accidentally or was obtained from a diamond pit with the employment of a thousand days of labor is completely irrelevant for its value. In general, no one in practical life asks for the history of the origin of a good in estimating its value, but considers solely the services that the good will render him and which he would have to forgo if he did not have it at his command. Goods on which much labor has been expended often have no value, while others, on which little or no labor was expended, have a very high value. Goods on which much labor was expended and others on which little or no labor was expended are often of equal value to economizing men. The quantities of labor or of other means of production applied to its production cannot, therefore, be the determining factor in the value of a good. Comparison of the value of a good with the value of the means of production employed in its production does, of course, show whether and to what extent its production, an act of past human activity, was appropriate or economic. But the quantities of goods employed in the production of a good have neither a necessary nor a directly determining influence on its value.

Equally untenable is the opinion that the determining factor in the value of goods is the quantity of labor or other means of production that are necessary for their *reproduction*. A large number of goods cannot be reproduced (antiques, and paintings by old masters, for instance) and thus, in a number of cases, we can observe value but no possibility of reproduction. For this reason, any factor connected with reproduction cannot be the determining principle of value in general. Experience, moreover, shows that the value of the means of production necessary for the reproduction of many goods (old-fashioned clothes and obsolete machines, for instance) is sometimes considerably higher and sometimes lower than the value of the products themselves.

The determining factor in the value of a good, then, is neither the quantity of labor or other goods necessary for its production nor the quantity necessary for its reproduction, but rather the magnitude of importance of those satisfactions with respect to which we are conscious of being dependent on command of the good. This principle of value determination is universally valid, and no exception to it can be found in human economy.

The importance of a satisfaction to us is not the result of an arbitrary decision, but rather is measured by the importance, which is not arbitrary, that the satisfaction has for our lives or for our well-being. The relative degrees of importance of different satisfactions and of successive acts of satisfaction are nevertheless matters of judgment on the part of economizing men, and for this reason, their knowledge of these degrees of importance is, in some instances, subject to error.

We saw earlier that the satisfactions on which their lives depend have the highest importance to men, that the satisfactions following next in importance are those on which their well-being depends, and that satisfactions on which a higher degree of well-being depends (with equal intensity a longer enduring satisfaction, and with the same duration a more intensive one) have a higher importance to men than those on

which a lower degree of their well-being is dependent.

But what has been said by no means excludes the possibility that stupid men may, as a result of their defective knowledge, sometimes estimate the importance of various satisfactions in a manner contrary to their real importance. Even individuals whose economic activity is conducted rationally, and who therefore certainly endeavor to recognize the true importance of satisfactions in order to gain an accurate foundation for their economic activity, are subject to error. Error is inseparable from all human knowledge.

Men are especially prone to let themselves be misled into overestimating the importance of satisfactions that give intense momentary pleasure but contribute only fleetingly to their well-being, and so into underestimating the importance of satisfactions on which a less intensive but longer enduring well-being depends. In other words, men often esteem passing, intense enjoyments more highly than their permanent welfare, and sometimes even more than their lives.

If men are thus already often in error with respect to their knowledge of the subjective factor of value determination, when it is merely a question of appraising their own states of mind, they are even more likely to err when it is a question of their perception of the objective factor of value determination, especially when it is a question of their knowledge of the magnitudes of the quantities available to them and of the different qualities of goods.

For these reasons alone it is clear why the determination of the value of particular goods is beset with manifold errors in economic life. But in addition to value fluctuations that arise from changes in human needs, from changes in the quantities of goods available to men, and from changes in the physical properties of goods, we can also observe fluctuations in the values of goods that are caused simply by *changes in* the *knowledge* men have of the importance of goods for their lives and welfare.

THE PRINCIPLE DETERMINING THE VALUE OF GOODS OF HIGHER ORDER.

Among the most egregious of the fundamental errors that have had the most far-reaching consequences in the previous development of our science is the argument that goods attain value for us because goods were employed in their production that had value to us. Later, when I come to the discussion of the prices of goods of higher order, I shall show the specific causes that were responsible for this error and for its becoming the foundation of the accepted theory of prices (in a form hedged about with all sorts of special provisions, of course). Here I want to state, above all, that this argument is so strictly opposed to all experience . . . that it would have to be rejected even if it provided a *formally* correct solution to the problem of establishing a principle explaining the value of goods.

But even this last purpose cannot be achieved by the argument in question, since it offers an explanation only for the value of goods we may designate as "products" but not for the value of all other goods, which appear as original factors of production. It does not explain the value of goods directly provided by nature, especially the services of land. It does not explain the value of labor services. Nor does it even, as we shall see later, explain the value of the services of capital. For the value of all these goods cannot be explained by the argument that goods derive their value from the value of the goods expended in their production. Indeed, it makes their value completely incomprehensible.

This argument, therefore, provides neither a formally correct solution nor one that conforms with the facts of reality, to the problem of discovering a universally valid explanation of the value of goods. On the one hand, it is in contradiction with experience; and on the other hand, it is patently inapplicable wherever we have to deal with goods that are not the product of the combination of goods of higher order. The value of goods of lower order cannot, therefore, be determined by the value of the goods of higher order that were employed in their production. On the contrary, it is evident that the value of goods of higher order is always and without exception determined by the prospective value of the goods of lower order in whose production they serve.[2] The existence of our *requirements* for goods of higher order is dependent upon the goods they serve to produce having expected economic character . . . and hence expected *value*. In securing our requirements for the satisfaction of our needs, we do not need command of goods that are suitable for the production of goods of lower order that have no expected value (since we have no requirements for them). We therefore have the principle that the value of goods of higher order is dependent upon the expected value of the goods of lower order they serve to produce. Hence goods of higher order can attain value, or retain it once they have it, only if, or as long as, they serve to produce goods that we expect to have value for us. If this fact is established, it is clear also that the value of goods of higher order cannot be the *determining* factor in the prospective value of the corresponding goods of lower order. Nor can the value of the goods of higher order already expended in producing a good of lower order be the determining factor in its present value. On the contrary, the value of goods of higher order is, in all cases, regulated by the prospective value of the goods of lower order to whose production they have been or will be assigned by economizing men.

The prospective value of goods of lower order is often—and thus must be carefully observed—very different from the value that similar goods have in the present. For this reason, the value of the goods of higher order by means of which we shall have command of goods of lower order at some future time . . . is by no means measured by the current value of similar goods of lower order, but rather by the prospective value of the goods of lower order in whose production they serve.

Suppose, for example, that we have the saltpetre, sulphur, charcoal, specialized labor services, appliances, etc., necessary for the production of a certain quantity of gunpowder, and that thus, by means of these goods, we shall have this quantity of gunpowder at our command in three months time. It is clear that the value this gunpowder is expected to have for us in three months time need not necessarily be equal to, but may be greater or less than, the value of an identical quantity of gunpowder at the present time. Hence also, the magnitude of the value of the above goods of higher order is measured, not by the value of gunpowder at present, but by the prospective value of their product at the end of the production period. Cases can even be imagined in which a good of lower or first order is completely valueless at present (ice in winter, for example), while simultaneously available corresponding goods of higher order that assure quantities of the good of lower order for a future time period (all the materials and implements necessary for the production of artificial ice, for example) have value with respect to this future time period—and vice versa.

Hence there is no necessary connection between the value of goods of lower or first order in the present and the value of currently available goods of higher order serving for the production of such goods. On the contrary, it is evident that the former derive their value from the relationship between requirements and available quantities in the present, while the latter derive their value from the prospective relationship between the requirements and the quantities that will be available at the future points in time when the products created by means of the goods of higher order will become available. If the prospective future value of a good of lower order rises, other things remaining equal, the value of the goods of higher order whose possession assures us future command of the good of lower order rises also. But the rise or fall of the value of a good of lower order available in the present has no necessary causal connection with the rise or fall of the value of currently available corresponding goods of higher order.

Hence the principle that the value of goods of higher order is governed, not by the value of corresponding goods of lower order of the present, but rather by the prospective value of the product, is the universally valid principle of the determination of the value of goods of higher order.

NOTES

1. *"Werthquote."* Menger presents the argument underlying this proposition at length on pages 163 to 165. But an explanatory note may perhaps be helpful due to the brevity and peculiar form of the present passage. Assume that the least important satisfaction rendered by a unit of the superior good has an importance of 5 in Use A, that the least important satisfaction rendered by a unit of the inferior good in Use B has an importance of 2, and that a unit of the inferior good would render a satisfaction with an importance of 3 if it were to replace a unit of the superior good in Use A. Menger contends that the use-value of a unit of a superior good that can be replaced by an inferior good is equal, not to the importance of the least important satisfaction actually rendered by a unit of the superior good, but to the importance of the satisfactions dependent on continued command of that unit. In the present instance, if command of a unit of the superior good is lost and a unit of the inferior good is moved from Use B to Use A to take its place, the satisfactions lost to the consumer are: (1) a satisfaction in Use B with an

importance of 2, which is lost because one less unit of the inferior good is employed in Use B, and (2) a satisfaction in Use A with an importance of 2 (the difference between the 5 units lost because one unit less of the superior good is employed in Use A and the 3 units gained because of the employment of a unit of the inferior good in its place). The use-value of a unit of the superior good is

therefore 4, the sum of these two items. The "value quota" mentioned by Menger in the text is the difference between the least important satisfaction that the superior good would render in Use A and its use-value calculated in this way. The "value-quota" in this example is thus 5 minus 4, or 1.—TR.

2. The remainder of this paragraph is a footnote in the original.—TR.

12. Elements of Pure Economics*

LÉON WALRAS

THE MARKET AND COMPETITION. PROBLEM OF EXCHANGE OF TWO COMMODITIES FOR EACH OTHER

In our general introductory survey we defined social wealth as the sum total of all things, material or immaterial, that are scarce, i.e. that are both useful and limited in quantity. We proved that all scarce things and nothing else have value and are exchangeable. Here we shall proceed differently. Starting with a definition of social wealth as the sum total of all things, material or immaterial, which are valuable and exchangeable, we shall prove that all valuable and exchangeable things, to the exclusion of everything else, are useful and at the same time limited in quantity. Up to this point we reasoned from cause to effect, but now we shall reason from effect to cause. It is clear that once the close connection between scarcity and value in exchange has been demonstrated, we may reason in whichever direction we please. I think, however, that in a systematic study of any general phenomenon like value in exchange, an inquiry into its nature should precede the investigation of its origin.

Value in exchange is a property, which certain things possess, of not being given or taken freely, but of being bought and sold, that is, of being received and conveyed in return for other things in definite quantitative proportions. The buyer of a thing is the seller of that which he gives in exchange. The seller of a thing is the buyer of that which he takes in exchange. In other words, every exchange of one thing for another is made up of a double purchase and a double sale.

Things that are valuable and exchangeable are also known as commodities. The market is a place where commodities are exchanged. Thus the phenomenon of value in exchange manifests itself in the market, and we must go to the market to study value in exchange.

Value in exchange, when left to itself, arises spontaneously in the market as the result of competition. As buyers, traders make their demands by outbidding each other. As sellers, traders make their offers by underbidding each other. The coming together of buyers and sellers then results in giving commodities certain values in exchange,

*Source: From Léon Walras, Elements of Pure Economics or the Theory of Social Wealth (Homewood, Ill.: Richard D. Irwin, Inc., 1954), lessons 5 and 10, pp. 83-86, 143-49. Translated by William Jaffé from the 1926 French definitive version of the 4th edition. Footnotes deleted.

sometimes rising, sometimes falling, sometimes stationary. The more perfectly competition functions, the more rigorous is the manner of arriving at value in exchange. The markets which are best organized from the competitive standpoint are those in which purchases and sales are made by auction, through the instrumentality of stockbrokers, commercial brokers or criers acting as agents who centralize transactions in such a way that the terms of every exchange are openly announced and an opportunity is given to sellers to lower their prices and to buyers to raise their bids. This is the way business is done in the stock exchange, commercial markets, grain markets, fish markets, etc. Besides these markets, there are others, such as the fruit, vegetable and poultry markets, where competition, though not so well organized, functions fairly effectively and satisfactorily. City streets with their stores and shops of all kinds— baker's, butcher's, grocer's, tailor's, shoemaker's, etc.—are markets where competition, though poorly organized, nevertheless operates quite adequately. Unquestionably competition is also the primary force in setting the value of the doctor's and the lawyer's consultations, of the musician's and the singer's recitals, etc. In fact, the whole world may be looked upon as a vast general market made up of diverse special markets where social wealth is bought and sold. Our task then is to discover the laws to which these purchases and sales tend to conform automatically. To this end, we shall suppose that the market is perfectly competitive, just as in pure mechanics we suppose, to start with, that machines are perfectly frictionless.

We shall see, now, how competition works in a well-organized market. Let us go into the stock exchange of a large investment centre like Paris or London. What is bought and sold in such places are titles to property in shares of very important kinds of social wealth, such as fractions of State and municipal loans or shares of railways, canals, metallur-

gical plants, etc. Our first impression on entering such an exchange is that of confused uproar and chaotic movement. Once, however, we are informed of what is going on, this clamour and bustle become perfectly comprehensible.

Let us take, for example, trading in 3 per cent French Rentes on the Paris Stock Exchange and confine our attention to these operations alone.

The three per cents, as they are called, are quoted at 60 francs. At this price, brokers who have received some orders to sell at 60 francs and other orders [authorizing them to sell] at less than 60 francs, will offer a certain quantity of 3 per cent Rentes, that is, a certain number of certificates each yielding 3 francs annually payable by the French State. We shall apply the term *effective offer* to any offer made, in this way, of a definite amount of a commodity at a definite price. *Per contra*, the brokers who have received some orders to buy at 60 francs and others [authorizing them to buy] at more than 60 francs will demand a certain quantity of 3 per cent Rentes, when 60 francs is quoted. We shall apply the term *effective demand* to any such demand for a definite amount of a commodity at a definite price.

We have now to make three suppositions according as the demand is *equal to, greater than,* or *less than* the offer.

First Supposition. The quantity demanded at 60 francs is equal to the quantity offered at this same price. Each broker, on either the buying or the selling side, finds another broker with an exactly equivalent counter-proposal to sell or to buy. Exchange takes place. The rate of 60 francs is maintained. The market is in a *stationary state* or in *equilibrium*.

Second Supposition. The brokers with orders to buy can no longer find brokers with orders to sell. This is a clear indication that the quantity of three per cents demanded at 60 francs is greater than the quantity offered at that price. Theoretically, trading should come to a halt. Brokers who have orders to buy at 60 francs 05 centimes *or who have orders to buy at higher prices* make bids at 60 francs 05 centimes. They raise the market price.

Two results follow from this bidding: first, those buyers who would have bought at 60 francs but who refuse to buy at 60 francs 05 centimes, withdraw; second, those sellers who are willing to sell at 60 francs 05 centimes but who previously refused to sell at 60 francs, come forward. These buyers and sellers will now give orders to this effect to their brokers if they have not already done so. Then, in consequence of a two-sided movement, the difference between effective demand and effective offer is reduced. If equality between effective offer and effective demand is restored, the *rise in price* ceases. Otherwise, the price continues to go up from 60 francs 05 centimes to 60 francs 10 centimes, and from 60 francs 10 centimes to 60 francs 15 centimes until offer equals demand. A new stationary state is thus found at a higher price.

Third Supposition. Brokers with orders to sell can no longer find brokers with orders to buy. This is a clear indication that the quantity of three per cents offered at 60 francs is greater than the quantity demanded at that price. Trading stops. Brokers who have orders to sell at 59 francs 95 centimes *or who have orders to sell at lower prices* make offers at 59 francs 95 centimes. They lower the price.

Two results follow: first, the withdrawal of those who would have sold at 60 francs but who refuse to sell at 59 francs 95 centimes; second, the advent of those who are willing to buy at 59 francs 95 centimes but who previously refused to buy at 60 francs. The difference between offer and demand is reduced. The price *falls*, if it has to, from 59 francs 95 centimes to 59 francs 90 centimes and from 59 francs 90 centimes to 59 francs 85 centimes until equality between offer and demand is restored. Thus a new equilibrium is found at a lower price.

Suppose now, that at the same time that this sort of trading is going on in 3 per cent French Rentes, similar trading is taking place in the securities of other governments, English, Italian, Spanish, Turkish and Egyptian, and in stocks and bonds issued by railways, ports, canals, mines, gas works, other factories, banks, credit institutions, etc.; suppose that all this trading proceeds by conventional shifts in price of 5 centimes, 25 centimes, 1 franc 25 centimes, 5 francs, or 25 francs, according to the value of the securities; and suppose that besides *cash* transactions there are *future* transactions, some *firm* and others *optional*, then the tumult of the stock market resolves itself into a veritable symphony in which each player plays his part.

We shall study value in exchange as it arises under such competitive conditions. Economists, generally speaking, have fallen all too frequently into the error of studying value in exchange under unusual circumstances. They are always talking about diamonds, Raphael's paintings, and concert recitals given by famous singers. De Quincey, whom John Stuart Mill quotes, imagines two men "on Lake Superior in a steam boat." One owns "a musical snuffbox"; the other, who is "making his way to an unsettled region 800 miles ahead of civilization," suddenly realizes that "in the hour of leaving London" he had forgotten to buy one of these instruments possessing "a magic power . . . which lulls your agitations of mind"; and, "when the last knell of the clock has sounded, which summons you to buy now or to forfeit for ever," he buys the musical snuff-box from his fellow-passenger for 60 guineas. Of course, our theory should cover all such special cases. The general laws of the market should apply to the diamond market, the market for Raphael's paintings and to the market for tenors and sopranos. These laws should even apply to a market like the one Mr. De Quincey imagines, in which there is a single buyer, a single seller, one commodity and only one minute in which to make the exchange. But logic demands that we consider general before special cases, and not the other way round. What physicist would deliberately pick cloudy weather for astronomical observations instead of taking advantage of a cloudless night? . . .

RARETÉ, THE CAUSE OF VALUE IN EXCHANGE

In the last analysis, the utility curves and the quantities possessed constitute the necessary and sufficient data for the establishment of current or equilibrium prices. From these data we proceed, first of all, to the mathematical derivation of individual and aggregate demand curves in view of the fact that each party to an exchange seeks the greatest possible satisfaction of his wants. And then, from the individual or aggregate demand curves, we derive mathematically the current equilibrium prices since there can be only one price in the market, namely the price at which total effective demand equals total effective offer, that is to say, since each trader must give up quantities which stand in a definite ratio to the quantities received and vice versa.

Thus: *The exchange of two commodities for each other in a perfectly competitive market is an operation by which all holders of either one, or of both, of the two commodities can obtain the greatest possible satisfaction of their wants consistent with the condition that the two commodities are bought and sold at one and the same rate of exchange throughout the market.*

The main object of the theory of social wealth is to generalize this proposition by showing, first, that it applies to the exchange of several commodities for one another as well as to the exchange of two commodities for each other, and secondly, that, under perfect competition, it applies to production as well as to exchange. The main object of the theory of production of social wealth is to show how the principle of organization of agriculture, industry and commerce can be deduced as a logical consequence of the above proposition. We may say, therefore, that this proposition embraces the whole of pure and applied economics.

If we let v_a and v_b be values in exchange of commodities (A) and (B) such that the ratios between them constitute the current equilibrium prices, and if we let $r_{a,1}$, $r_{b,1}$, $r_{a,2}$, $r_{b,2}$, $r_{a,3}$, $r_{b,3}$ . . . be the *raretés* of these commodities, i.e. the intensities of the last wants satisfied for holders (1), (2), (3) . . . after the exchange, then by virtue of the theorem of maximum satisfaction we have

$$\frac{r_{a,1}}{r_{b,1}} = p_a \qquad \text{and} \qquad \frac{r_{b,1}}{r_{a,1}} = p_b$$

for holder (1);

$$\frac{r_{a,2}}{r_{b,2}} \quad p_a \qquad \text{and} \qquad \frac{r_{b,2}}{r_{a,2}} \quad p_b$$

for holder (2);

$$\frac{r_{a,3}}{r_{b,3}} = p_a \qquad \text{and} \qquad \frac{r_{b,3}}{r_{a,3}} = p_b$$

for holder (3); and so on. It follows, then, that

$$p_a = \frac{r_{a,1}}{r_{b,1}} = \frac{r_{a,2}}{r_{b,2}} = \frac{r_{a,3}}{r_{b,3}} = \dots$$

and

$$p_b = \frac{r_{b,1}}{r_{a,1}} = \frac{r_{b,2}}{r_{a,2}} = \frac{r_{b,3}}{r_{a,3}} = \dots,$$

which can be rewritten as follows:

$$v_a : v_b$$
$$: : r_{a,1} : r_{b,1}$$
$$: : r_{a,2} : r_{b,2}$$
$$: : r_{a,3} : r_{b,3}$$
$$: : \dots \dots$$

It should be observed that if any of these commodities are of such a nature that they can be consumed in whole units only and their utility curves are discontinuous, then some of the terms in the above table of *raretés* will have to be proportional terms specially underlined, to indicate . . . that they are close approximations of the arithmetical mean of the intensities of the last wants satisfied and of the first wants unsatisfied.

It is also possible that one of the two terms may be missing in one or more of the ratios of the *raretés*. For example, it may happen that at the price p_a holder (2) does not want any of (A) at all. Then there would be no *rareté* of (A) for holder (2) because no want would be satisfied by (A) so far as he was concerned. Consequently the term $r_{a, 2}$ would have to be replaced by $p_a r_{b, 2}$ which would be greater than $\alpha_{r, 2}$ or the intensity of the first want which holder (2) has for (A). It may also happen that at the price p_a holder (3), for example, demands all the (A) he can get unconditionally at whatever price he must pay, in other words, he may offer all he possesses of (B). Then there would be no *rareté* of (B) for holder (3), because no want would be satisfied by (B) so far as he was concerned. Then the term $r_{b, 3}$ would have to be replaced by $p_b r_{a, 3}$ which would be greater than $\beta_{r, 3}$ or the intensity of the first want which holder (3) has for (B). We could introduce the convention of putting the terms $p_a r_{b, 2}$ and $p_b r_{a, 3}$ in parentheses as they are entered in the above tables. This would be tantamount to defining *rareté* as the intensity of the last want which *is* or which *might have been* satisfied.

Subject to these two reservations, we may formulate the following proposition:

Current prices or equilibrium prices are equal to the ratios of the raretés. In other words:

Values in exchange are proportional to the raretés.

As regards the exchange of two commodities for each other, we have now reached the goal we set ourselves when we began our study of the mathematical theory of exchange. We undertook at that point, to deduce *rareté* from value in exchange, instead of deducing value in exchange from scarcity. . . . In fact, the *rareté* defined . . . as the intensity of the last want satisfied is

precisely the same thing as the *scarcity* we had defined earlier . . . in terms of the twin conditions of utility and limitation in quantity. There could not possibly be a last want satisfied if there were no want, that is to say, if a commodity had neither extensive nor intensive utility, or if it were *useless*. Moreover, the intensity of the last want satisfied would be zero if a commodity which possessed a utility curve were so plentiful that its quantity exceeded its extensive utility, as would be the case, for example, if it were unlimited in quantity. Thus the *rareté* we have been discussing in the last lessons turns out to be synonymous with the *scarcity* [also 'rareté' in French] we mentioned earlier. There is only this difference: *rareté* is taken to be a measurable magnitude which is not only inevitably associated with value in exchange but is also, of necessity, proportionate to this value, in the same way that weight is related to mass. If, therefore, it is certain that *rareté* and value in exchange are two concomitant and proportional phenomena, it is equally certain that *rareté* is the cause of value in exchange.

Value in exchange, like weight, is a *relative* phenomenon; while *rareté*, like mass, is an absolute phenomenon. If, of the two commodities, (A) and (B), one of them became useless, or, though useful, became unlimited in quantity, that commodity would no longer be scarce and would cease to have value in exchange. Under these circumstances, the other commodity too would lose its value in exchange, but it would not stop being scarce; it would only be more or less scarce and have a determinate *rareté* for each of the holders of the commodity.

I say for each of the holders of this commodity—and I wish to emphasize this point—because there is no such thing as *the rareté* of commodity (A) or *the rareté* of commodity (B), or as the ratio of the *rareté* of (A) to the *rareté* of (B) or of the *rareté* of (B) to the *rareté* of (A); there are no other *raretés* than the *raretés* of (A) or (B) for holders (1), (2), (3) . . . of these commodities, and it is only for these holders that there are ratios of *raretés* of (A) to *raretés* of (B) or of *raretés* of (B) to those of (A). *Rareté* is *personal* or *subjective*; value in exchange is *real* or *objective*. It is only with respect to a given individual that we can define *rareté* in terms of *effective utility* and *quantity possessed* in a manner strictly analogous to the definition of *velocity* in terms of *distance passed over* and *the time taken to pass over it*, so that *rareté* defined as *the derivative of effective utility with respect to the quantity possessed* corresponds exactly to *velocity* defined as *the derivative of distance passed over to the time taken to pass over it*.

If we were looking for something that we might call *the rareté* of commodity (A) or of commodity (B), we should have to take the *average rareté*, which would be the arithmetical average of the *raretés* of each of these commodities for all parties to the exchange after the exchange was completed. This conception of an *average rareté* is no more far-fetched than that of an average height or an average life span in a given country. For certain purposes it may even be more useful. These average *raretés* would themselves be proportional to the [corresponding] values in exchange.

The theorist has the right to assume that the underlying price determinants are invariant over the period he has chosen to use in his formulation of the law of equilibrium prices. But, once this formulation has been completed, it is his duty to remember that the forces that underlie prices are by their nature variable, and consequently he must formulate the law of the variation of equilibrium prices. This now remains to be done. Fortunately, the second formulation follows immediately from the first, for the forces underlying the establishment of prices are the very forces that underlie the variation of prices, viz. the utilities and the quantities possessed of the commodities considered. These forces are, therefore, the primary causes and conditions of the variation of prices.

If we suppose that in the same market where (A) and (B) were previously traded at the above-mentioned current prices, $\frac{1}{\mu}$ of (A) in terms of (B) and μ of (B) in terms of (A), the trading now takes place at different current prices, $\frac{1}{\mu}$ of (A) in terms of (B) and μ' of (B) in terms of (A), then we may posit that this change in price is the result of one, or more, of the following four causes:

1. A change in the utility of commodity (A).
2. A change in the quantity of commodity (A) possessed by one or more holders.
3. A change in the utility of commodity (B).
4. A change in the quantity of commodity (B) possessed by one or more holders.

These circumstances, which are absolute, could be determined under ideal conditions. In practice, of course, this determination may prove to be more or less difficult; but there is no reason to regard it as impossible in theory. By putting questions to each and every individual about the elements that enter into the making of his individual demand curve, the problem might be solved by direct investigation. A case may conceivably arise, where one of the causes of a change in price impresses the investigators as the primary cause in one sense or another. For example, if we suppose a rise in price from μ to μ' to coincide with the discovery of a remarkable new property in commodity (B) or with a catastrophe destroying part of the supply of this commodity, we could not possibly avoid associating one or the other of these events with the rise in price. Such inescapable inferences are not beyond the sounds of possibility. By their aid the primary causes and conditions of variations in prices are often determined.

Let us suppose that equilibrium is established and that the several parties to the exchange possess whatever quantities of (A) and (B) are necessary to yield them maximum satisfactions at the reciprocal prices $\frac{1}{\mu}$ of (A) in terms of (B) and μ of (B) in terms of (A). This condition of maximum satisfaction is fulfilled as long as prices are equal to the ratios of the *raretés*, and it ceases the moment this equality is destroyed. Let us inquire, then, how variations in utility and in the quantity possessed disturb the condition of maximum satisfaction and let us investigate the consequences of such a disturbance.

Variations in utility may occur in very different ways: there may be an increase in intensive utility and a decrease in extensive utility or vice versa, and so on. We must, therefore, take care how we enunciate general propositions in this respect. For example, we shall restrict our use of the expressions *increase in utility* and *decrease in utility* to shifts in the want curve which entail an increase or decrease in *rareté*, i.e. in the intensity of the last want satisfied after the completion of exchange. With this in mind, let us suppose an increase in the utility of (B), or in other words, a shift in the want curve of (B) resulting in an increase in the *rareté* of (B) for certain parties. These individuals will no longer derive maximum satisfaction [by maintaining the *status quo*]. Hence, they will find it to their advantage to demand (B) by offering some of their (A) at the current reciprocal prices $\frac{1}{\mu}$ and μ. Inasmuch as the offer was equal to the demand for each of the two commodities at the prices 1 and μ [before the increase in the utility of (B) for some of the traders], there will now be an excess of demand over offer in the case of (B) and an excess of offer over demand in the case of (A) at these same prices, and hence a rise in p_b *and a in fall in p_a. It follows also that the other traders* [for whom the utility of (B) had not increased] will no longer derive maximum satisfaction [from the previously determined quantities of (A) and

(B) which they consume]. They will find it, therefore, to their advantage, when the price of (B) becomes greater than μ and the price of (A) less than 1, to offer some of their (B) and to demand (A) in exchange. Equilibrium will be re-established when the demand and offer of the two commodities are equated at a new price of (B) higher than μ and at a new price of (A) lower than $\frac{1}{\mu}$ Thus an increase in the utility of (B) for some of our individuals will finally result in a rise in the price of (B).

If there had been a decrease in the utility of (B), it would obviously entail a fall in the price of (B).

A glance at the want curves is sufficient to show that an increase or decrease in the quantity possessed will result in a decrease or an increase in *rareté*. Moreover, we have just seen that price decreases or increases as *rareté* decreases or increases. Consequently, the effect of changes in the quantity possessed is exactly the opposite of the effect of changes in utility. We may now enunciate the law we have been looking for in the following terms.

Given two commodities in a market in a state of equilibrium, if, all other things being equal, the utility of one of these two commodities increases or decreases for one or more parties, the value of this commodity in relation to the value of the other commodity, i.e. its price, will increase or decrease.

If, all other things being equal, the quantity of one of the two commodities in the hands of one or more holders increases or decreases, the price of this commodity will decrease or increase.

We should point out, however, before going any further, that although a change in prices necessarily implies a change in the forces underlying these prices, it does not follow that stability of prices necessarily implies stability of the forces behind them. Indeed we may also enunciate, without further demonstration, the following double proposition:

Given two commodities, if both the utility and the quantity of one of these two commodities in the hands of one or more traders or holders vary in such a way that their raretés *remain unchanged, then the value of this commodity in relation to the value of the other commodity, i.e. its price, will not change.*

If the utility and the quantity of both commodities in the hands of one or more parties or holders vary in such a way that the ratios of their raretés *remain unchanged, then the prices of the two commodities will not change.*

13. The Distribution of Wealth*

JOHN BATES CLARK

FINAL PRODUCTIVITY THE REGULATOR OF BOTH WAGES AND INTEREST

Instead of the plantation in our late illustration, we will think at once of the world, with its innumerable industries and its complete outfit of agents and appliances. It is, of course, isolated, since neither products, workers nor instruments can migrate to it or from it; and the rate of wages that it affords must be determined entirely within itself.

We can now derive an advantage from the imaginary process of supplying the labor for this community, unit by unit, provided that we can do this without getting the impression that the action of the law of final productivity depends on it. This is only one way of illustrating the action of that law. The actual and practical test of the productive power of one unit of labor is made, if one unit only is taken out of a complete force and if the ensuing reduction of the product is noted. This test we have already applied. It is for the sake of having a more complete view of the action of the law of final productivity that we now build up a working force, unit by unit, leaving capital unchanged in amount, though changing in its forms with the arrival of each new unit of labor. We will let a thousand workers constitute each increment of labor, and let farmers, carpenters, smiths, weavers, printers, etc., be represented in it in carefully adjusted proportions. Every occupation must have its representatives, and the comparative number of them must be fixed according to a law that it will soon be our duty to study. All that we now need to know about this law is, that it so apportions labor among the different groups and sub-groups that the productive power of labor is brought to a certain uniformity in the various occupations. Common and adaptable labor is made to produce as much in one sub-group as in another.

Give, now, to this isolated community a hundred million dollars' worth of capital, and introduce gradually a corresponding force of workers. Put a thousand laborers into the rich environment that these conditions afford, and their product *per capita* will be enormous. Their work will be aided by capital to the extent of a hundred thousand dollars per man. This sum will

---

*Source: Reprinted from John Bates Clark, *The Distribution of Wealth, A Theory of Wages, Interest and Profits,* chapters 12 and 13 (New York: The Macmillan Company, 1902). Margin notes and one footnote deleted.

take such forms as the workers can best use, and a profusion of the available tools, machines, materials, etc., will be at every laborer's hand. If we were to try to imagine the forms of productive wealth that such a condition would require, we should bring before the mind a picture of automatic machinery, of electrical motors and of power obtained from cataracts, tides and waves. We should see chemical wonders performed in the preparing of materials, the creating of soil and the like. We should place the worker in the position of a lordly director of natural forces so great and so varied that they would seem more like occult powers of the air than like tools of mundane trades. All this, however, is only a picture of what would be slowly and remotely approached, if capital were quietly to outgrow population and were to reveal its power of taking the forms that the needs of the relatively few workers would require. Something like this is the goal of natural economic tendencies.

Add, now, a second thousand workers to the force; and, with the appliances at their service changed in form—as they must be—to adapt them to the uses of the larger number of men, the output per man will be smaller than before. This second increment of labor has at its disposal capital amounting to only half a hundred thousand dollars per man; and this it has taken from the men who were formerly using it. In using capital, the new force of workers goes share in share with the force that was already in the field. Where one of the original workers had an elaborate machine, he now has a cheaper and less efficient one; and the new workers by his side also have machines of the cheaper variety. This reduction in the efficiency of the instrument that the original worker used must be taken into account, in estimating how much the new worker can add to the product of industry. His presence has cheapened the instruments used by the first set of workers and has taken something from their effi-

ciency. His own share of the original capital, as it is made over to him by the workers formerly in his immediate part of the field, consists also in the cheaper and less efficient instruments. For two reasons, therefore, he brings into existence less wealth than did one of the first division of laborers.

All over the field the hundred million dollars has, as it were, stretched itself out to meet the needs of a double force of workers. Of some kinds of tools there are now twice as many as before; but they are all less costly and less efficient. Cheaper buildings and more of them, is the rule. Railroads have more curves and grades, less durable bridges and, in general, less substantial plants. There are two sailing vessels, where there was formerly one steamer; and there are two wooden ships, where there was one of steel. The capital of the community, without changing in amount, has taken a form that is more extended than its earlier one—the instruments are everywhere multiplied and cheapened.

We must be careful as to the arithmetic of the change. The product that can be attributed to this second increment of labor is, of course, not all that it creates *by the aid of the capital that the earlier division of workers has surrendered to it;* it is only what its presence adds to the product previously created. With a thousand workers using the whole capital, the product was four units of value; with two thousand, it is four plus; and the plus quantity, whatever it is, measures the product that is attributable to the second increment of labor only. There is a minus quantity to be taken into account in calculating the product that is attributable to the final unit of labor. If we take, first, all that it creates by the aid of the capital that is surrendered to it, and then deduct what is taken from the product of the earlier workers and their capital by reason of the share of capital that they surrender to the new workers, we shall have the net addition that the new workers make to the product of industry.

With the vast capital utilized, the product that the new unit of labor adds to the product that could have been had without it will be very great, though it will be less than was created by the first unit. Every man in the new working force produces enough to rival a fortunate gold hunter. Add increment after increment of labor, till the force is decupled; and the product that is due to the last of the additions is still great. Continue to add to the force till it numbers a hundred thousand, having still the hundred million dollars' worth of capital, but in changed form. The workers are then about as well equipped as are those of the United States at the present day. The last increment of labor may be supposed to add to the product that the society would have realized without its aid about as much as a working force of the same size, in this country, could separately create, by adding itself to the force already employed.

If, now, this hundredth increment of labor is the last one that the isolated society contains, we have the law of wages. We have set the population working till no reserve exists from which we can get more. The last composite unit of labor—the final division of a thousand men—has created its own distinguishable product. This is less than the product that was attributable to any of the earlier divisions; but, now that this section of the laboring force is in the field, no division is effectively worth any more than is this one. If any earlier section of the working force were to demand more than the last one produces, the employer could discharge it and put into its place the last section of men. What he would lose by the departure of any body of a thousand men, is measured by the product that was brought into existence by the last body that was set working.

Each unit of labor, then, is worth to its employer what the last unit produces. When the force is complete, no one body of a thousand men can withdraw without lessening the product of the whole society by the same amount that we have attributed to the one that we last set working. The effective value of any unit of labor is always what the whole society with all its capital produces, minus what it would produce if that unit were to be taken away. This sets the universal standard of pay. A unit of labor consists, in the supposed case, of a thousand men, and the product of it is the natural pay of a thousand men. If the men are equal, a thousandth part of this amount is the natural pay of any one of them.

We are seeking, of course, a static standard of wages; but the process that gradually builds up a force of laborers from a thousand to a hundred thousand, and causes capital to modify its forms as the increase of the force goes on, is not a static process. It is a dynamic operation which brings the working force up to its static complement. From the time that the force is complete, however, we leave it unchanged: we let the static condition thus attained continue forever. The importance of going through the illustrative dynamic process, and making up the permanent force unit by unit, lies in the clear view that this gives of the product that can be attributed to the "final" unit.

Actually, no unit is last in time. The hundred thousand men, with the hundred million dollars' worth of capital, work on year after year, and no one division of a thousand can be singled out as constituting the particular division whose product fixes wages. Any one such body of men is always worth to its employers what the final division would produce, if we were to set them working in such an order of succession as, for illustration, we have described. That the men will get this amount, is insured by employers' competition. The final division of a thousand men has in its hands a certain potential product, when it offers its service to employers. If one set of *entrepreneurs* will not give them the value of it, another will, provided that competition is perfect. With an ideally complete and free competitive system, each unit of labor can get exactly what a final unit produces. With an imperfect competition, it still *tends* to get that amount. The final product of labor sets a standard for the pay of labor; and actual wages tend toward it, with variations.

We have noted the fact that an *entrepreneur's* net profit is an incentive to competition. Such a profit is mercantile, and means that employers are selling their products for more than they are paying out in wages and interest—that the price of the goods exceeds the cost of the elements that compose them. We noted the fact that "natural price," as defined by economists, is really a wages-and-interest price; for it equals the sum of these two outlays. A profit-giving price exceeds that sum, but the competition that tends to annihilate the profit cuts it off at both ends. By bidding against each other in selling goods, employers make the prices smaller; and by bidding against each other in hiring labor and capital, they make wages and interest larger. There is a profit on labor, so long as the men in a working force are paid less than the final one produces; but competition tends to annihilate that profit and to make the pay of labor equal to the product of the final unit of it.

As has again and again been said, we have constructed an ideal society in which disturbing facts are omitted, and we have so far described none of the obstacles that pure law encounters in real life. We have made no estimate of the amount of deviation from the final productivity standard that the pay of workmen actually reveals. All such studies have a place in the dynamic division of our work. As real as gravitation is the force that draws the actual pay of men *toward* a standard that is set by the final productivity law. This law is universal and permanent: everywhere it will outlive the local and changeful influences that modify its operation. We are to get what we produce—such is the

dominant rule of life; and what we are able to produce by means of labor, is determined by what a final unit of mere labor can add to the product that can be created without its aid. *Final productivity governs wages.* We may now summarize the conclusions that we have thus far reached, concerning the natural standard of wages, in the following series of propositions:—

1) Labor, like commodities, is subject to a law of marginal appraisal. The rate that the market puts on the final unit of the supply of each of them, it puts on the entire supply. As the last unit of consumers' goods is a price-making one, so the last unit of labor is the one that fixes wages.

2) The term *final* does not designate a particular unit that can be identified and separated from others. There is not, for example, in the elevators of the United States a special lot of wheat that is in a strategic position and has a price-making power that other wheat does not possess. Any unit whatever of this commodity is final in the economic sense; inasmuch as, by its presence, it brings the supply to its present actual magnitude. Similarly, the *final, marginal* or *last* unit of labor does not consist of particular men. It is especially necessary to guard against the idea that the final men, whose products fix the general rate of wages, are those who would naturally be employed last, because they are the poorest. We have been careful to say that it is units of labor, as such, that are the basis of the law of wages; and a body of men must be of the average quality of ordinary laborers, if it is to constitute such a unit.

3) In presenting the law of final utility, it is customary to arrange the units of a commodity in an imaginary series, to present them one at a time and to ascertain how important each one is to the consumer. Yet commodities never come to the market in such an order. The whole present supply of a commodity is offering in the market; but the price that it is bringing is fixed by the importance that would attach to the final unit, *if the supply were offered in such a series of units.*

In like manner, we may find it useful, in presenting the law by which wages are fixed, to go through an imaginary operation of setting men at work, one man at a time or one company of men at a time, and thus to find what importance the market places on the last one. This reveals the operation of a law of diminishing productivity; and whether we take a single man or a body of men as the unit of labor, *any unit can get, as pay, what the last one would produce, if the force were set working in this way.*

4) The standard of wages thus attained is a static one. So long as the labor and the capital continue unchanged in amount, and produce the same things, by the same processes and under an unchanging form of organization, wages will continue at the rate that this test establishes. Setting men at work in succession is a bit of imaginary dynamics, but what it reveals is a *static law.*

Let the number of units of labor be measured, in the following figure, along the line AD. Let them be set working in a series, in connection with a fixed amount of capital. The product of the first unit of labor, as aided by all the capital, is measured by the line AB. What the second unit of labor adds to this product is the amount expressed by A'B'. The third unit enlarges the output by the amount A''B'', the next by A'''B''', the next by A''''B'''' and the last by DC. DC measures the effective productivity of any unit of labor in the series and fixes the general rate of pay.

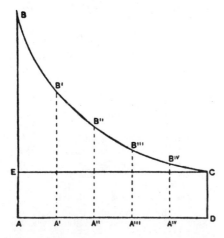

If the first unit of labor claims more than the amount DC, employers will let it withdraw, and will substitute for it the last unit. What they lose by the withdrawal of any one unit in the entire force is the amount DC.

A fact of great importance now appears. We may reverse the application of this law, and by so doing get a law of interest. Let the labor be the element that is unchanged in amount, and let capital be the one that is supplied in a succession of increments.

AB is now the product gained by using one increment of capital in connection with the whole working force. A'B' is the additional product that is created by a second increment of capital. A''B'' is the product of the third increment and DC is the amount produced by the last. This amount, DC, fixes the rate of interest. No one of the series of units of capital can secure for its owner more than the last one produces. If the owner of the first increment asks more than this for the use of it, the *entrepreneur* will relinquish this bit of capital and will put the last unit in its place. What he will lose, in the way of product, is measured by the amount DC, the direct product of the final increment of capital. This expresses the *effective* product of every increment, since it is the amount that would be lost if any one of the series were withdrawn.

All that we have said about the change that must take place in the forms of capital, when the amount of it is fixed and the working force is increasing, applies here, where these conditions are reversed. The steady increase of the capital, if the amount of the labor be fixed, compels a similar change of forms. With one unit of capital and ten units of labor, the instruments will be simple and cheap. Hand tools will generally prevail; and buildings, roadways, bridges, vehicles, etc., will be of a makeshift kind, which will, at a small cost for each instrument, enable the men in some way to work. With two units of capital, a better type of instruments begins to prevail. Every increase in the amount of the capital shows itself primarily in transmuting poor appliances into better ones. There are, indeed, more tools, and there is more raw material; but the striking fact is that all the tools, etc., are costlier and more efficient. With the addition of the tenth unit of capital, the condition may be thought of as approximating that of our own country at the present day. There is much costly machinery, many durable buildings, a good supply of large ships, efficient railroads, etc.

At the cost of what may be a tedious repetition, we have now described the series of changes that an increasing capital undergoes, because this is what is actually taking place. Capital is the element that is outgrowing labor. We may take the world that exists instead of an imaginary one, as our illustration. As the accumulation of capital actually goes on, it shows itself more and more in qualitative changes of existing instruments. Society pulls down its barns and builds others, better as well as larger; it carries its mercantile buildings farther into the air, and makes them fireproof and durable; it substitutes steel ships for wooden ones and steamers for sailing craft; it takes the curves and grades out of its railroads, and makes bridges and viaducts of the kind that defies time and strain; it bores tunnels through mountain ranges to avoid climbing over them and cuts canals across isthmuses to shorten the voyages of ships. As capital grows very abundant, there are made longer tunnels and canals; and they have, as their purpose, the avoiding of climbs that are easier and voyages that are shorter than were those that were avoided by the earlier engineering works. They thus represent a greater outlay incurred for a smaller gain. Society also makes all its machinery as nearly automatic as it can, so that one laborer's guidance shall keep much machinery in successful motion. Everywhere there are taking place such adaptations of capital as fit a large amount of it to the needs of a relatively small amount of labor.

The changes that have to be made in the forms of the capital, as the amount of it increases, reveal a reason for the decline in the rate of its earnings. The rudest hatchet that can be made may vastly increase the owner's power to get firewood. It may wear out in a year; but in that period it may save enough of time, that would otherwise have been devoted to a slow and painful mode of wood gathering, to enable the owner to make six new hatchets. Though he will probably not use the liberated time for this particular purpose, whatever he does secure by it represents an interest of 500 per cent on the capital invested in this first and most productive tool. A second tool may liberate labor enough to replace itself only five times. The owner will actually replace it once, and will employ the time that could give him four duplicates of it in making other things for his own use; but the fruit of the spare time that the second tool makes available is now 400 per cent of the cost of the tool, as computed in terms of unaided labor.

Tools are, of course, employed in the order of their productivity, so far as men judge their several powers of production correctly. It soon ceases to be possible to add to a working equipment anything that produces a multiple of its own cost in a year, and the interest on the final increment of capital becomes a fraction of that capital itself. This fraction steadily diminishes, as the productive fund grows larger, and as improvement in the quality of tools, etc., becomes one form of investment for the growing accumulations. The difference between the cost of a rude and poor hatchet and that of a better one represents an increment of capital; but it has less power to reproduce itself, in amount, than had the investment that was made in the original tool.

As accumulation proceeds, there are always made costlier machines, representing more capital; and the product that comes from using them is a smaller fraction of their cost. The straightening of the curves in railroads is one of the ways in which capital may find investment. This may cost as much as the first making of the corresponding parts of the road themselves; but it does not liberate as much labor, in proportion to its cost, as did the building of the old and crooked road. The boring of a long tunnel, to avoid a short climb over the mountains, does not result in as large earnings for the capital that is thus invested as did the making of a short tunnel to avoid a higher climb. Everywhere do the forms of the capital show differences in earning power; and the owners choose first the most productive forms, and later the less productive. To this fact is due the present low rate of interest. We are utilizing the opportunities for investment that stand late in the series and are low in the scale of productivity.

We have said that no increment of capital can get for its owner more than the last increment produces. We may state this in another way by saying that no form of capital can claim and get for its owners in a year a larger fraction of its cost than the least productive form produces. Under modern conditions, if the man who lends "money" for the procuring of a highly necessary tool demands the whole amount that is secured through the use of it, the *entrepreneur*, who is the borrower, will refuse the money and will use, for the procuring of the tool which is so much needed, the money that formerly went into the tool that was last and least important on the list. In terms of more primitive life, if the man who performs the labor of making a very necessary tool demands the whole product that it creates, the *entrepreneur* will decline to utilize this tool-making labor and will divert to the making of the needed instrument that labor which has been used for the making of the least important part of his working equipment. Cap-

ital is, it thus appears, completely transmutable in form. Society can quit making one kind of instrument and make another. Capital-goods are, then, interchangeable; and while this is so, no increment of capital can ever secure for its owner more than the final increment produces.

It is, of course, true that labor also has to change its forms, as capital accumulates. The man who watches a complicated machine is going through a set of movements very different from those executed by a man working with a hand tool. Every time that we change the form of the capital, we change, by that very fact, the character of the labor. Mutual adaptation in form is the general rule for these two producing agents. Change the merely quantitative ratio of one of them to the other, and you make it necessary to transform both of them in character. As with ten units of capital for ten units of labor there will be one grade of instruments and certain kinds of work performed in connection with them, so with eleven units of capital for ten units of labor there will be somewhat different kinds of instruments and different modes of working. This double transformation must, moreover, theoretically extend through the whole mass of capital and the whole process of labor. Everywhere there are to be seen new and improved kinds of capital-goods and new modes of using them.

With this qualification, we may represent the law of interest by the process of building up, increment by increment, the fund of social capital and measuring the product produced by each unit of it. In this imaginary process we have revealed a true law of varying productivity. As we have said, the addition to the product caused by the last unit of capital fixes the rate of interest. Every unit of capital can secure for its owner what the last unit produces, and it can secure no more. The principle of final productivity, in short, acts in two ways, affording a theory of wages and of interest.

THE PRODUCTS OF LABOR AND CAPITAL, AS MEASURED BY THE FORMULA FOR RENT

It has been customary to define rent as the income derived from land. In attempting to solve problems of distribution, furthermore, it has been customary to eliminate from the earnings of society the element of ground rent, and then to try to find principles that will account for the division of what remains. That ground rent is entirely unlike wages, interest or *entrepreneurs'* profit, has been the most prevalent theory. According to this view, the income from land is a differential gain fixed by a law of its own, which does not apply elsewhere. The rent of a particular piece of ground is measured by comparing its product with that which can be had from the poorest piece that is utilized by the application of the same amount of labor and capital. When, by this independent reckoning, the part of the income of society that is derived from land has been disposed of, it is thought that one step has been taken in the direction of solving the really difficult problems of distribution. Wages, interest and net profits, it is believed, can be accounted for the more readily when the product of land has been put out of sight.

It has become obvious, however, that wages are fixed by the final productivity of the labor that is used in connection with a fixed amount of total capital; and in computing that total capital, we make confusion, if we do not take all kinds of capital-goods into account. It is the whole fund of productive wealth, in every form that such wealth takes, which constitutes the complex agency that coöperates with labor. When the amount of productive wealth in its entirety remains fixed and the quantity of labor increases, the law of diminishing returns that we have stated operates. The final unit of the agent, labor,—cooperating, as it does, with land and every other instrument,—produces less

and less, as the units of labor become more numerous; and thus the standard of wages falls. When the increase in the working force ceases, the rate of wages remains fixed.

It may be alleged that the same result will be reached by assuming that capital in artificial forms remains fixed in amount, while the working force grows larger. Land, it may be claimed, is fixed in amount by nature; and, if we can measure the productive wealth that exists in the shape of buildings, tools, materials and the like, and keep that also unchanged in amount, we shall have the condition that we have described. The total amount of productive wealth will then be a fixed quantity; and we can let the labor increase, unit by unit, testing its final productivity as we have done.

This method of statement would tell the truth about the decline in the productivity of labor, but it would not assign that effect to its true cause. What the labor combines itself with is not merely the artificial capital: it is that *and the land,* as they are combined in one and make a general labor-aiding agency. As the working population has grown larger, some of it has betaken itself to hitherto rentless ground—the enlargement of the laboring force has pressed outward the margin of utilization of land. During the same period of growth, moreover, new labor has constantly added itself to the force that has tilled good land. More and more intensively has land everywhere been cultivated and otherwise used. The artificial capital, as such, has received, as it were, only its own fraction of the increasing force of labor. It has aided the land, and together they have received all of the new workers. Wages fall because such capital and land together cannot make the tenth unit of labor as productive as they made the first.

It is, therefore, the whole economic environment of the growing population that has to be considered, if the cause of the decline in the final productivity of labor is to be understood. Land and artificial goods are blended in an intimate mixture; and the last unit of labor produces what this whole composite agent enables it to produce. There are only two generic members in the combination by which the rate of wages is determined. Indeed, as we have noticed, the variations in the comparative amounts of these two agents, labor and all capital, determine both wages and interest.

No controversy need arise over the question of mere nomenclature. It is necessary to find some term to designate the whole permanent fund of productive wealth, and the natural name for it is capital.[1] It is also necessary to have a term for all kinds of concrete goods in which this permanent fund consists; and we shall call these things, including land, capital-goods. As our analysis of the process of distribution proceeds, we shall hope to justify this nomenclature by its fruits. In any case, it is important to note that it is the quantity of labor, on the one hand, and that of all productive wealth, on the other, that fix the natural or static standards of wages and interest.

Ground rent we shall study as the earnings of one kind of capital-goods—as merely a part of interest. We are now able to see that wages and interest, though they are determined by the law of final productivity, are also capable of being measured exactly as ground rent has been measured. That is to say, the Ricardian formula, which describes what is earned by a piece of land, may be used to describe what is earned by the whole fund of social capital: all interest may be made to take the form of a differential gain, or a surplus. Again, the Ricardian formula may be employed to describe the earnings of the whole force of social labor; for wages, in their entirety, are a differential gain. It is one of the most striking of economic facts that the income of all labor, on the one hand, and that of all

capital, on the other, should be thus entirely akin to ground rent. They are the two generic rents, if by that term we mean differential products; and the earnings of land constitute a fraction of one of them.

Let us now simplify the law of ground rent, by disregarding the auxiliary capital that, in advanced agricultural states, is applied in large quantities to land. Let the ground that we use as an illustration be worked by labor that is practically empty-handed. Every laborer brings with him a simple tool, but the interest on the capital that the tool represents is so small a part of what the man earns in a year that it may be disregarded. We have, then, only two producing agents to deal with, and they are the land—which now embodies all the capital that needs to be considered—and labor. The neglect of auxiliary capital affects no principle that we are studying; for what we have to prove could be established as completely, though less clearly, if we made our illustration more complex by taking all kinds of capital into account. The differential gain of labor as applied unaided to fertile land, offers the clearest illustration of the different incomes that can be measured by the Ricardian formula. It is the type of all the rents.[2]

Labor, as thus applied to land, is subject to a law of diminishing returns. Put one man on a quarter section of land, containing prairie and forest, and he will get a rich return. Two laborers on the same ground will get less per man; three will get still less; and, if you enlarge the force to ten, it may be that the last man will get wages only. We must, however, be very careful to make sure of the reason why the tenth man gets only his wages. If the men are hired by the owner of the land at the prevalent rate of wages, what has happened is that the force has been enlarged till the last man produces only what is paid to him. In this case, as was said in the tenth chapter, wages fix the intensive margin of cultivation of this land. The rate that we must pay to the men decides for us how many of them we can employ on our farm. If, however, our farm is isolated and the workers are a society by themselves, and if there are ten of them to be employed, we shall set them all working and pay to each of them as much as the last one produces. Here it is the product of the marginal labor that fixes the rate of wages, as we noted in the chapter referred to; and here, also, the situation illustrates the true law of rent.[3]

All the earlier men in the series create surplus products, over and above the amount created by the last man. They get only what the last one produces, and the farmer-landlord gets the remainder. What goes to the owner of the land is the sum of a series of remainders that are made by taking, in each case, the product that is attributable to one of the earlier men as a minuend and the product that is imputable to the last man as a subtrahend.

Call the product that the single worker creates, when he has the whole field to himself, P^{1st}. Call the additional product that the second man is able to bring into existence P^{2d}, etc.; call the enlargement in the output made by the last man P^{10th}.

$P^{1st} - P^{10th}$ = surplus created by the first worker.

$P^{2d} - P^{10th}$ = surplus created by the second worker.

$P^{9th} - P^{10th}$ = surplus created by the ninth worker.

If we complete the series of such subtractions and add the nine remainders, the sum of them all will be the rent of the piece of land. This is the amount that the owner can keep, from the total created by the different workers aided by the land.

The sum of $P^{1st} + P^{2d} + P^{3d}$, etc., to and including P^{10th}, is the whole product of the field and the labor that is spent on it. It is the sum of all the minuends in the foregoing series, with the product of the final man added to it. $10 \times P^{10th}$ equals the total subtrahend;

and the total rent of the field is the difference between these amounts. It is, in other words, the whole product minus ten times the product of the tenth and last unit of labor.

Let us, again, measure the number of laborers by the line AD, and the product of successive increments of labor by AB, A'B', etc. If we give to these lines an appreciable width, so that a series of them will fill the entire figure, ABCD, that area will measure the product of all the labor and all the capital in our illustrative agricultural community. The capital is virtually all in the form of land; and we are now able to attribute to the land that part of the product which, in effect, it creates.

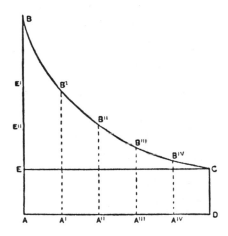

The last unit of labor creates the amount of product that is expressed by DC; and, accordingly, each unit of labor is effectively worth just that amount to the employing farmer, and each unit gets that amount as its wages. AECD measures total wages, and EBC measures the entire rent of the land. This amount we have spoken of as composed of a series of surpluses, or differential products, and we have measured them in each case by subtracting from what we have called the product of one of the earlier increments of labor the product of the last increment. AB minus DC gives such a surplus, and it is a part of the rent. It looks, at a careless view, as though land had the capacity to cut off and claim for itself a part of the product of labor—that is, the surplus part of the product of all the earlier increments of *labor* appears to be the *rent* of the *land*.

In reality, this surplus is the fruit of the aid that the land affords, and is attributable to the land only. A correct conception of the nature of any rent makes it a concrete addition which one producing agent is able to make to the product that is attributable to another producing agent. Land makes its own addition to the product of each unit of labor except the last one. When there was available only a piece of land, with no labor to till it, the product was *nil*. When one unit of labor combined itself with the land, the product was AB; and in this form of statement we impute the whole product to the labor. A second unit of labor now comes, unaided by capital, into the field and adds itself, empty-handed, to the working force. Whatever it produces, it brings into existence by adding to what the field yielded to one man's cultivation. The product thus created by an addition to labor, with no addition to capital, is A'B'. The difference between AB and A'B', which is the line E'B, measures the surplus that a man can produce when he has the whole field to aid him above what he can create when he is unaided. The last man adds labor and no land to the productive combination; while the first man had land, and the addition that the land itself made to the bare product of labor constitutes the differential quantity which is the rent of the land. The science of rent is a science of economic causation, which traces products to their sources. The rent getter is a product creator.

The third man, also empty-handed, creates the amount A''B''; and E'B + E''E' measures the contribution that the land has thus far made to the joint product of land and labor. Extending the

vertical lines and giving to them width enough to make them fill the area of the entire figure, we have AECD as the product of all the labor, when it is taken unit by unit and made to work virtually unaided. ABCD is what it creates as it is aided by the land, and EBC is the amount that the land contributes to the product of the combination. This measures the difference between the product of ten units of aided labor and ten units of unaided labor.

We can now make the really important application of the principle of diminishing returns, which fixes both marginal productivity and rent. This is the application that is actually making everywhere in the business world. The isolated farm, with its whole capital in land, is an illustration only; while the real field for labor, to which the farm corresponds, is the world, with its whole circle of industries and its complex equipment of capital.

For a fixed area of land read, now, a fixed fund of permanent social capital. It is at this moment an exact sum; and it will, as it were, prolong the conditions of this moment, remaining at exactly its present size. The artificial instruments are, of course, perishing and renewing; but, if there is no need of changing the form of the capital, a wornout instrument will be replaced by another that is exactly like it. A hoe will replace a hoe, and a ship will succeed a ship; and the new instruments of production will be exact duplicates of the old. This would be clear in a completely static condition. We are, however, to introduce labor, increment by increment, into this general field of industry; and this, of course, compels such a change in the forms of the capital as we have already described. The amount of the capital remaining fixed, the instruments become more numerous and cheaper, as the force of labor enlarges.

Labor, applied to the whole fund of capital, in land and all other instruments, is now subject to the law of diminishing returns. The first unit produces the amount AB, the second produces the amount A'B', the third creates the quantity A''B'' and the last the quantity DC. This last amount sets the rate of wages, and the area AECD measures the amount of wages. It leaves the amount expressed by the area EBC as the rent of the fund of social capital. All interest is thus a surplus, entirely akin to the rent of land, as that is expressed by the Ricardian formula: it is a concrete product, attributable to the agent that claims it as an income.

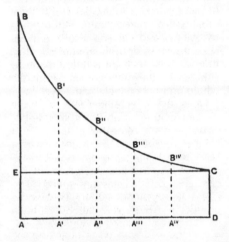

This rent is, moreover, made up of a series of genuine differential gains. It is not like the rent of the farm, in our former illustration, which, as we found, really depends on the rate of wages that prevails elsewhere. The rent of the whole fund of social capital is the sum of a series of differences between certain products and a final, or standard, product. True differentials lie between different products, and not between products and wages. The line DC, which sets the rate of wages, expresses primarily the product of the last unit of labor. We have set all the men in the society working, we have measured the amount created by the last addition to the force, and we have measured the surplus that each earlier unit of labor

creates above this amount. The surplus is, in each case, a true differential product; since it is not merely a remainder that is left after paying wages, but is a difference between one product and another. It is the difference between the product of aided labor and that of the labor that is virtually unaided, and the sum of all these differences is the rent of the social fund of capital.

Reverse now the situation. Let labor be the fixed element and let social capital enlarge, changing its forms of course, in the enlarging.

ABCD is the total product. AB is the product of the first unit of capital, A'B' the product of the second, A''B'' that of the third and DC that of the last. A unit of capital, adding itself with no new labor to the productive combination, enlarges the product by the amount DC. So much can be attributed to any unit of capital, separately considered. The effective importance of every one of the units of capital is the same. While capital-goods are not interchangeable, true capital is completely so; and all parts of it are, therefore, on a plane in their earning capacity. A merchant, a manufacturer or a farmer, if he can offer good security, can hire all the "money" that he needs at the rate that the least necessary sum which he invests in his business will earn for him. Does this imply an exploitation of the earlier units of capital? Does the borrower of these sums rob the lender?

If the final unit of capital produces the amount DC, it will get that amount as interest; and certainly no other unit can get any more. AECD will be the total amount of interest, and EBC will be a surplus; but it will be a surplus that is causally attributable to labor, and to labor only. The difference between the product that is solely due to capital and that which is due to capital and another agent in combination is the effect of the presence and the work of that other agent.

If we were to apply the term *rent* to all such surpluses, we should say that

EBC is the rent of the force of laborers that is at work in connection with capital. This amount is made up of a series of differential products. Apparently AB − DC is the difference between the product of the first unit of capital and that of the last, A'B' − DC is the difference between the product of the second unit of capital and that of the last, etc. *The rent of the labor,* if we use that expression, is the sum of the surplus products connected with the earlier units of capital but not attributable to them as a cause. The laborers seem to get a part of what the earlier units of capital produce; whereas, in reality, this is the difference between what capital and labor jointly produce and what capital alone contributes to the product of the combination. EBC is, therefore, the amount that is imputable to labor only.

One law governs wages and interest—the law of final productivity. By one mode of statement of the law (Figure 1), we get wages as an amount directly determined by this principle: it is the area AECD of our diagram. Arithmetically stated, the earnings of all labor equal the product of the final unit of labor multiplied by the number of the units. In Figure 1, in which wages are thus determined, interest is a surplus that is of the nature of rent. By another mode of stating the law (Figure 2), we get interest as the amount that is positively fixed by the final productivity law, and wages are now the surplus that is akin to rent. These amounts together make up the whole static income of society.

Profit has no place in such static conditions. The two incomes that are permanent and independent of dynamic changes are the products, respectively, of labor and of capital. Each of them is directly determined by the final productivity law, and each is also a remainder—a surplus or a differential quantity. In one use of terms, it is a rent made by subtracting the other income from the whole product of social industry.

Does such a remainder ever go to the persons who naturally get it, merely because it is a remainder and is not claimed by others? In Figure 1, where EBC, representing interest, is a surplus governed by the law of rent, does the capitalist get this amount merely because labor cannot get it? The whole product is ABCD, and labor can have

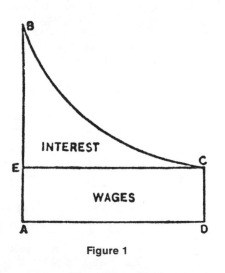

Figure 1

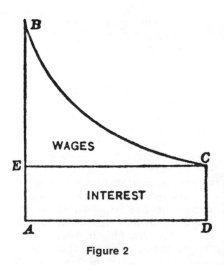

Figure 2

only AECD. If there is no profit, capital must get the remainder. Do the capitalists, then, come into the possession of this income merely because it is thus left for them by the laborers?

This point is of much consequence. The question at issue is nothing less than whether any static income is determined residually. Clearly it is never so determined. No static income is what it is merely because the deducting of another income from the social product leaves a certain remainder. Any income that is nothing but a remainder must go to the *entrepreneur*. Because EBC, in Figure 1, is not claimed by labor, it is left in the hands of the *entrepreneur*. Thus far it is a residuum. It is, moreover, important that this amount should thus be left in the employer's hands, for by this means he is made able to pay the interest that the capitalist will claim; but there is in the mere fact that he has this sum nothing that makes it necessary for him to pay it to the capitalist. What the owners of capital can force *entrepreneurs* to pay them, is determined by the final productivity of capital. Employers of capital must pay for the final increment of it just what that increment produces, and they must pay for all other increments at the same rate. If this necessity takes from them the whole amount, EBC, which labor leaves in their hands, then EBC goes to the capitalist. It does so, however, only because the capitalist can claim and get it, by the direct action of the final productivity law. What the capitalist can get under this principle is expressed by Figure 2. AECD is here the amount of interest, as directly and positively fixed. This amount must pass, in any case, from the *entrepreneurs* to the capitalists.

The *entrepreneur*, then, after paying wages, as indicated by AECD in Figure 1, has left in his hands EBC, out of which he can pay interest. What he must pay as interest, is AECD in Figure 2. If the area EBC in Figure 1 were larger than AECD in Figure 2, there

would be a remainder left for the *entrepreneur*. This would be a pure profit, the only kind of income that is ever residually determined.

It is clear, on the face of the facts, that the two static incomes—those, namely, of the laborer and of the capitalist—are paid to them by the *entrepreneur*, who receives and sells the product of their joint industry. In the cotton mill, it is the hirer of capital and of labor who puts the goods on the market and from the proceeds pays the workmen and the owners of capital. If he pays first to the capitalists what the final productivity law, as applied to capital, calls for, he has a remainder out of which he must pay wages; and now it is the final productivity law that decides what he must pay as wages. If there is anything left on his hands after the two payments are made, it is a profit; and the terms *profit* and *residual income* are thus synonymous.

This truth we may demonstrate by using our diagrams in a reversed order. In Figure 2 *AECD* is interest, as directly determined, and *EBC* is the remainder, which is left in the *entrepreneur's* hands for the payment of wages. What the *entrepreneur* must pay to the workmen is AECD of Figure 1. If that is less than ECD of Figure 2, there is a residuum, or profit, for the *entrepreneur*. Static conditions, however, exclude such a profit by making these two areas equal.

We have, then, established the following propositions:—

1) Wages and interest are both determined by the law of final productivity.

2) When, in an illustrative case, one of these incomes is so determined, the other appears to be a residuum.

3) As a residuum, such an income would be left in the *entrepreneurs'* hands; but it is actually taken from them by a further action of the final productivity law.

4) *Entrepreneurs'* profit and residual income are synonymous terms.[4] The static conditions assumed in the present study preclude the existence of such *entrepeneurs'* gains.

NOTES

1. It will be seen that this is not calling land capital. When land is referred to, it will be called by its ordinary name. There is a constant necessity for referring to the total fund of permanent productive wealth that is embodied in land and in artificial instruments. When this is thought of, in practical life, as "money invested in business," it is designated by the term capital; and in this work it will be so called. The objection to calling land one variety of capital-goods vanishes, if it is admissible to call all productive wealth, "in the abstract," capital. Any objection that may arise to this usage is less serious than is the objection to using through a long discussion such a phrase as "permanent fund of productive wealth," or some equivalent and equally inconvenient expression. The nomenclature that we adopt guards not only against confounding land with this fund, but against confounding any other instrument, as concretely regarded, with it. In this, at least, it is a strict constructionist nomenclature.

2. These are (1) the rent of all capital, (2) that of all labor, (3) that of particular capital-goods, and (4) that of particular laborers.

3. The law of rent, as commonly stated, has the defect that is illustrated by the former of these cases, where it is applied to the reward for labor. The farmer who figures in the current statement of the law hires his men at the wages that prevail in the various industries that are carried on about him; and, when he finds that more men will not produce their wages, he quits enlarging his force. Each of the earlier men creates a surplus above his wages. When we are considering the rent of a limited piece of land devoted to one use, the scientific way to calculate the rent is to use as the subtrahend wages, rather than the final product of labor; since it is wages that fix final product. If what we want is a genuine differential product, we must isolate our working society, count the laborers, set them all at work and let the last produce what he can. There will then be a difference between what each of the earlier men produces and this final or standard product. This is, in each case, a true differential product. It is measured by comparing, not products created for the farmer and wages paid by him, but one product with another product.

4. The above theses appear sharply to contradict the theory of wages advanced by the late . . . Francis A. Walker, in which wages are called the residual share in distribution. It is an aid in removing causes of confusion from the discussion, and in giving to the theory of this eminent economist what is due to it, to notice the fact that his study was essentially a study of a subject in economic dynamics. If the total product of industry becomes larger than it has been, and if interest, rent and profit do not become any greater than they were, wages must absorb the whole increase. In this view, the residuum may be regarded as a remainder that is left when the former product of the whole industry is subtracted from the present product. Such a view of the power of labor to get all the increase that dynamic changes create would be consistent with the view that, in the merely static adjustment that takes place at all times, wages are determined directly by the law of final productivity, as are other shares of the total product. We might claim that the progress which makes industry, as a whole, more productive makes labor, separately considered, more so, but leaves the productivity of other agents unchanged. Laborers would then, in each static adjustment that takes place, force *entrepreneurs* to give them their product, just as capitalists would do. Statically, wages would be determined directly; while dynamically they would consist partly in a residuum, made by deducting the former product of industry, as a whole, from the present product.

In our view, progress in methods of production makes both labor and capital more productive; and the fruits of progress are thus shared by the two agents, according to the degrees of specific productivity that the progress gives to them. Labor, then, does not get the whole difference between the former product of industry and the present product. What we are trying to make clear is that, in a merely static adjustment of shares in distribution, both wages and interest must be determined directly, and not residually. After paying interest, the *entrepreneur* has wages left in his hands; but he is forced to pay it to labor *because it is the product of labor*. In making his bargain, the worker has the benefit of free competition. He is virtually selling his forthcoming product, and can resort to another employer, if the present one refuses to give him the full value of it. The capitalist, in making this contract for the payment of interest, is in the same way selling a product, and can exact the value of it. Without this power, neither laborers nor capitalists could get their shares from the *entrepreneur's* hands. For an early statement of the principles presented in this chapter, the reader is referred to an article by the present writer, in the *Quarterly Journal of Economics,* for April, 1891, on "Distribution as Determined by a Law of Rent."

V

Historicism and Institutionalism

Introduction. The most important forerunner of the Historical School is probably Friedrich List (1789-1846). He was born and reared in Würtemberg, one of many principalities that were to be eventually united into Germany. While teaching at the University of Tübingen, List became president of an association of businessmen dedicated to the economic and political unification of Germany. At that time trade among the many German states was impeded by customs houses and high internal customs dues. Foreign manufactured goods, however, were charged very low customs dues. It is not surprising, then, that List and his association agitated for the elimination of the internal tariffs, the commercial unification of all German states, and the imposition of selective protective tariffs on foreign manufactured goods. List not only championed these causes in print but he also wrote and promoted a petition advocating the needed reforms. Sadly, his "unauthorized" political activity angered the king, and List was sentenced to ten months in prison. After serving a few months of the sentence, List was released when he agreed to renounce his citizenship as a Würtemberger and leave the country.

List travelled to America, where he became a successful publisher and businessman in Pennsylvania and Maryland. In 1832 he was sent to Leipzig as consul for the United States, and he remained in Europe the rest of his life. List wrote extensively and exercised considerable influence on the trade policies of many countries. He criticized Adam Smith's theory of free trade as being valid for a whole world of single individuals but not for a world of nationalities. Free trade between two nations, he argued, is mutually advantageous only if both countries have developed industrially to approximately the same level. List's focus on nationality is especially apparent in the title of his greatest work in economics, *The National System of Political Economy*. This focus is also evident in our two selections from the book: extracts from the author's preface and "Private Economy and National Economy" (chapter 14). In both of these excerpts List promoted the famous infant-industry argument. Students should note the way in which List supported his views with concrete examples and a historical approach.

Because he was concerned with the application of theory and not with its construction, List contributed nothing to the theory itself.

The central figures of the Institutional School are Veblen, Mitchell, and Commons. Each of these men took a different approach to criticizing orthodox economic theory: Veblen relied heavily on sociology, Mitchell on statistics, and Commons on legal institutions. What they shared in common, however, was their distaste for the casual empiricism of other economists, highly abstract economic models, and the unnecessary segregation of economics from the other social sciences. Although these men were successful in exposing the weakness of the assumptions underlying conventional theory, the institutionalist movement died out in the 1930s, because they were unable to come up with a better alternative to the theory which they criticized. Even so, the contributions of these three scholars have been long lasting, and Schumpeter has classified "economic sociology"—along with economic theory, history, and statistics—as one of the four basic fields of economics.

Thorstein Veblen (1857-1929) is better described a social scientist than an economist, since his expertise also included sociology, anthropology, and philosophy. In many ways this man was a failure: he had two unhappy marriages; he was introspective with no gift for getting along with people; he moved from one teaching position to another; he was disliked by his undergraduate students and criticized by most of his colleagues; he never rose above the level of assistant professor; and he was never successful financially. Worst of all, as a married man he had numerous affairs with "other" women, a scandalous situation in his day. Yet the man was simply brilliant. He has been described by John Kenneth Galbraith as "the nearest thing in the United States to an academic legend—the equivalent of that of Scott Fitzgerald in fiction or of the Barrymores in the theater. . . ."

Veblen was born and reared on a farm in Wisconsin. At the age of twenty he enrolled at Carleton College, where he had the good fortune of studying under John Bates Clark. Veblen's creativity and wild imagination were already showing themselves: he wrote a tongue-in-cheek essay that classified people according to the shape of their noses and delivered a speech in favor of cannibalism. Veblen went on to study philosophy at Johns Hopkins (for less than one term) and at Yale, from which he received his Ph.D. degree. After receiving his doctorate, however, he spent seven apparently idle years back on the family farm. Unable to find a teaching position in all this time, he finally resumed his studies in 1891 by doing graduate work in the economics department at Cornell University. There he made a favorable impression on Laurence Laughlin, who took Veblen with him to the University of Chicago on a teaching fellowship. Veblen was eventually promoted to the rank of assistant professor and the role of editor for the new *Journal of Political Economy*. He later taught at other schools, including Stanford, the University of Missouri, and the New School for Social Research.

Veblen is known for his contrasts of "business enterprise" with the "machine process," of "pecuniary employments" with "industrial employments," and of "service-ability" with "vendibility." He was a master of words, being especially clever at coining new terms. This skill is especially evident in the fourth chapter of *The Theory of the Leisure Class*. That chapter, titled "Conspicuous Consumption," displays Veblen's employment of language to surprise the reader with an almost perverse use of words. Like the rest of the book, this chapter is a put-down of the rich. It demonstrates the effect of wealth on behavior in a way that no other economist had envisioned.

Wesley Clair Mitchell (1874-1948) was one of Veblen's students at the University of Chicago, and it was Mitchell who became the leader of the American Institutional School when Veblen died. Upon the completion of his schooling, Mitchell worked briefly at the Census Bureau. He secured teaching positions at the University of Chicago, the University of California, and Columbia University (where he spent most of his teaching career). During the First World War, he worked as head of the War Industries Board. It took Mitchell three years of concentrated effort to write his most famous work, *Business Cycles* (1913), which is about 600 pages long. The first part of this book summarizes the theories of business cycles, which were most prominent in 1912. Part 2 of *Business Cycles* contains a wealth of statistics taken from business annals up through the year 1911. Although the survey in part 1 and the statistics in part 2 are now long outdated, it must be remembered that Mitchell's primary contribution to economics is this pioneering employment of statistical data. Even so, it is part 3 that will be of major interest to us now, because it is here that we find Mitchell's realistic description of the various stages of a business cycle. Included here is the fourth chapter from part 3. It contains his account of how "crisis breeds depression" and how "depression breeds prosperity." The reader should observe how—in the same way that Veblen emphasizes "pecuniary employments" at the expense of "industrial employments"—Mitchell finds more importance in the money-making process than the industrial process.

As with Veblen and Mitchell, John Rogers Commons (1862-1945) added little to the common body of economic theory. Instead, his contribution was his success in changing the way politicians and legislators viewed the government's role in the marketplace. In those pre-Depression days, economists favored individualism and a "hands-off policy" for government. In that political climate, Commons appeared to be an alarmist when he warned of the growing dangers of monopoly power. He proposed setting up "administrative commissions" to regulate a wide range of economic activity, including job safety, labor laws, minimum wages, employment of women and children, and job security. These commissions were initiated in Wisconsin, where the state government had a close working relationship with the University of Wisconsin (with which Commons was primarily associated during his teaching career). The other states were to eventually pattern their commissions after those developed in Wisconsin.

Commons was born in Ohio and educated at Oberlin College. His graduate work was completed at Johns Hopkins, where he was greatly influenced by Richard Ely's approach to economics. Ely integrated economics with ethics and sociology, a combination that shows up in Commons's preoccupation with the relationship between collective and individual actions. After graduation, Commons taught at Wesleyan College, Oberlin College, the University of Indiana, and Syracuse University. He lost his job at Syracuse in 1899 when a few rich patrons of the university became angered by his defense of labor unions and the common worker. He then worked for the United States Industrial Commission for five years until, in 1904, Richard Ely secured an academic post for him at the University of Wisconsin. In 1924 Commons wrote *The Legal Foundations of Capitalism,* which integrated legal and economic analysis in an innovative fashion. The ideas that he expressed in this book were more clearly formulated ten years later in his finest work, *Institutional Economics*. It is from this second book that our reading is taken. Appearing as section 2 of chapter 2, it was intended to be an outline for the remainder of the book. Students should note Commons's well-known distinction among bargaining transactions, managerial transactions, and rationing transactions—all three of which he brings together in a more comprehensive unit called the "Going Concern."

14. The National System of Political Economy*

FRIEDRICH LIST

EXTRACTS FROM PREFACE TO FIRST EDITION

More than thirty-three years have elapsed since I first entertained doubts as to the truth of the prevailing theory of political economy, and endeavoured to investigate (what appeared to me) its er-

rors and their fundamental causes. My avocation (as Professor) gave me the motive to undertake that task—the opposition which it was my fate to meet with forcibly impelled me to pursue it further.

My German contemporaries will remember to what a low ebb the well-

---

*Source: Reprinted from the 1885 English edition (London: Longmans, Green, and Company), translated from the German by Sampson S. Lloyd. The selection reprinted here originally appeared as the preface and chapter 14. Footnotes deleted.

being of Germany had sunk in 1818. I prepared myself by studying works on political economy. I made myself as fully acquainted as others with what had been thought and written on that subject. But I was not satisfied with teaching young men that science in its present form; I desired also to teach them by what economical policy the welfare, the culture, and the power of Germany might be promoted. The popular theory inculcated the principle of freedom of trade. That principle appeared to me to be accordant with common sense, and also to be proved by experience, when I considered the results of the abolition of the internal provincial tariffs in France, and of the union of the three kingdoms under one government in Great Britain. But the wonderfully favourable effects of Napoleon's Continental system, and the destructive results of its abolition, were events too recent for me to overlook; they seemed to me to be directly contradictory of what I previously observed. And in endeavouring to ascertain on what that contradiction was founded, the idea struck me that *the theory was quite true, but only so in case all nations would reciprocally follow the principles of free trade, just as those provinces had done*. This led me to consider the nature of *nationality*. I perceived that the popular theory took no account of *nations*, but simply of the entire human race on the one hand, or of single individuals on the other. I saw clearly that free competition between two nations which are highly civilised can only be mutually beneficial in case both of them are in a nearly equal position of industrial development, and that any nation which owing to misfortunes is behind others in industry, commerce, and navigation, while she nevertheless possesses the mental and material means for developing those acquisitions, must first of all strengthen her own individual powers, in order to fit herself to enter into free competition with more advanced nations. In a word,

I perceived the distinction between *cosmopolitical* and *political* economy. I felt that Germany must abolish her internal tariffs, and by the adoption of a common uniform commercial policy towards foreigners, strive to attain to the same degree of commercial and industrial development to which other nations have attained by means of their commercial policy.

In 1819 all Germany teemed with schemes and projects for new political institutions. Rulers and subjects, nobles and plebeians, officers of State and men of learning, were all occupied with them. Germany was like an estate which had been ravaged by war, whose former owners on resuming possession of it are about to arrange it afresh. Some wanted to restore everything exactly as it had been, down to every petty detail; others to have everything on a new plan and with entirely modern implements; while some, who paid regard both to common sense and to experience, desired to follow a middle course, which might accommodate the claims of the past with the necessities of the present. Everywhere were contradiction and conflict of opinion, everywhere leagues and associations for the promotion of patriotic objects. The constitution of the Diet itself was new, framed in a hurry, and regarded by the most enlightened and thoughtful diplomatists as merely an embryo from which a more perfect state of things might be hoped for in the future. One of its articles (the 19th) expressly left the door open for the establishment of a *national commercial system*. This article appeared to me to provide a basis on which the future industrial and commercial prosperity of the German Fatherland might rest, and hence the idea arose of establishing a league of German merchants and manufacturers for the abolition of our internal tariffs and the adoption of a common commercial policy for the whole of Germany. How this league took root, and led to united action between the noble-minded and enlightened rulers of

Bavaria and W·urtemberg, and later to the establishment of the German Zollverein, is well known.

As adviser of this German commercial league, I had a difficult position. All the scientifically educated Government employés, all the newspaper editors, all the writers on political economy, had been trained up in the cosmopolitical school, and regarded every kind of protective duty as a theoretical abomination. They were aided by the interests of England, and by those of the dealers in English goods in the ports and commercial cities of Germany. It is notorious what a powerful means of controlling public opinion abroad, is possessed by the English Ministry in their "secret service money"; and they are not accustomed to be niggardly where it can be useful to their commercial interests. An innumerable army of correspondents and leader-writers, from Hamburg and Bremen, from Leipzig and Frankfort, appeared in the field to condemn the unreasonable desires of the German manufacturers for a uniform protective duty, and to abuse their adviser in harsh and scornful terms; such as, that he was ignorant of the first principles of political economy as held by the most scientific authorities, or else had not brains enough to comprehend them. The work of these advocates of the interests of England was rendered all the easier by the fact that the popular theory and the opinions of German learned men were on their side.

The contest was clearly being fought with unequal weapons. On one side a theory thoroughly elaborated and uncontradicted, a compact school, a powerful party which had advocates in every legislature and learned society, but above all the great motive power—money. On the other side poverty and want, internal divisions, differences of opinion, and absolute lack of a theoretical basis.

In the course of the daily controversy which I had to conduct, I was led to perceive the distinction between the *theory of values* and the *theory of the powers of production,* and beneath the false line of argument which the popular school has raised out of the term *capital.* I learned to know the difference between *manufacturing power* and *agricultural power.* I hence discovered the basis of the fallacy of the arguments of the school, that it urges reasons which are only justly applicable to free trade in agricultural products, as grounds on which to justify free trade in manufactured goods. I began to learn to appreciate more thoroughly the principle of the division of labour, and to perceive how far it is applicable to the circumstances of *entire nations.* At a later period I travelled through Austria, North Germany, Hungary, Switzerland, France, and England, everywhere seeking instruction from observation of the actual condition of those countries as well as from written works. When afterwards I visited the United States, I cast all books aside—they would only have tended to mislead me. The best work on political economy which one can read in that modern land is actual life. There one may see wildernesses grow into rich and mighty States; and progress which requires centuries in Europe, goes on there before one's eyes, viz. that from the condition of the mere hunter to the rearing of cattle—from that to agriculture, and from the latter to manufactures and commerce. There one may see how rents increase by degrees from nothing to important revenues. There the simple peasant knows practically far better than the most acute savants of the old world how agriculture and rents can be improved; he endeavours to attract *manufacturers and artificers* to his vicinity. Nowhere so well as there can one learn the importance of means of transport, and their effect on the mental and material life of the people.

That book of actual life, I have earnestly and diligently studied, and compared with the results of my previous studies, experience, and reflections.

And the result has been (as I hope) the propounding of a system which, however defective it may as yet appear, is not founded on bottomless cosmopolitanism, but on the nature of things, on the lessons of history, and on the requirements of the nations. It offers the means of placing theory in accord with practice, and makes political economy comprehensible by every educated mind, by which previously, owing to its scholastic bombast, its contradictions, and its utterly false terminology, the sound sense of mankind had been bewildered.

I would indicate, as the distinguishing characteristic of my system, *nationality*. On the nature of *nationality,* as the intermediate interest between those of *individualism* and of *entire humanity,* my whole structure is based. I hesitated for some time whether I should not term mine the *natural* system of political economy, but was dissuaded from so doing by the remark of a friend, that under that title superficial readers might suppose my book to be a mere revival of the physiocratic system.

I have been accused by the popular school, of merely seeking to revive the (so-called) "mercantile" system. But those who read my book will see that I have adopted in my theory merely the valuable parts of that much-decried system, whilst I have rejected what is false in it; that I have advocated those valuable parts on totally different grounds from those urged by the (so-called) mercantile school, namely on the grounds of history and of nature; also that I have refuted for the first time from those sources the arguments urged a thousand times by the cosmopolitical school, and have exposed for the first time the false train of reasoning which it bases on a bottomless cosmopolitanism, on the use of terms of double meaning, and on illogical arguments.

If I appear to condemn in too strong language the opinions and the works of individual authors or of entire schools, I have not done so from any personal arrogance. But as I hold that the views which I have controverted are injurious to the public welfare, it is necessary to contradict them energetically. And authors of celebrity do more harm by their errors than those of less repute, therefore they must be refuted in more energetic terms.

To candid and thoughtful critics I would remark (as respects tautology and recapitulation), that everyone who has studied political economy knows how in that science all individual items are interwoven in manifold ways, and that it is far better to repeat the same thing ten times over, than to leave one single point in obscurity. I have not followed the prevailing fashion of citing a multitude of quotations. But I may say that I have read a hundred-fold more writings than those from which I have quoted.

In writing this preface I am humbly conscious that much fault may be found with my work; nay, that I myself might even now do much of it better. But my sole encouragement lies in the thought, that nevertheless much will be found in my book that is new and true, and also somewhat that may serve especially to benefit my German Fatherland.

PRIVATE ECONOMY AND NATIONAL ECONOMY

... in the present chapter we have now to demonstrate how the popular school has concealed its misunderstanding of the national interests and of the effects of national union of powers, by confounding the principles of private economy with those of national economy.

"What is prudence in the conduct of every private family," says Adam Smith, "can scarce be folly in that of a great kingdom." Every individual in pursuing his own interests necessarily promotes thereby also the interests of the community. It is evident that every individual, inasmuch as he knows his own local circumstances best and pays most attention to his occupation, is far better able to judge than the statesman or legislator how his capital can most profitably be invested. He who would venture to give advice to the people how to invest their capital would not merely take upon himself a useless task, but would also assume to himself an authority which belongs solely to the producer, and which can be entrusted to those persons least of all who consider themselves equal to so difficult a task. Adam Smith concludes from this:

Restrictions on trade imposed on the behalf of the internal industry of a country, are mere folly; every nation, like every individual, ought to buy articles where they can be procured the cheapest; in order to attain to the highest degree of national prosperity, we have simply to follow the maxim of letting things alone (laisser faire et laisser aller).

Smith and Say compare a nation which seeks to promote its industry by protective duties, to a tailor who wants to make his own boots, and to a bootmaker who would impose a toll on those who enter his door, in order to promote his prosperity. As in all errors of the popular school, so also in this one does Thomas Cooper go to extremes in his book which is directed against the American system of protection. "Political economy," he alleges,

is almost synonymous with the private economy of all individuals; *politics* are no essential ingredient of *political economy*; it is folly to suppose that the community is something quite different from the individuals of whom it is composed. Every individual knows best how to invest his labour and his capital. The wealth of the community is nothing else than the aggregate of the wealth of all its individual members; and if every individual can provide best for himself, that nation must be the richest in which every individual is most left to himself.

The adherents of the American system of protection had opposed themselves to this argument, which had formerly been adduced by importing merchants in favour of free trade; the American navigation laws had greatly increased the carrying trade, the foreign commerce, and fisheries of the United States; and for the mere protection of their mercantile marine millions had been annually expended on their fleet; according to his theory those laws and this expense also would be as reprehensible as protective duties. "In any case," exclaims Mr. Cooper, "no commerce by sea is worth a naval war; the merchants may be left to protect themselves."

Thus the popular school, which had begun by ignoring the principles of nationality and national interests, finally comes to the point of altogether denying their existence, and of leaving individuals to defend them as they may solely by their own individual powers.

How? Is the wisdom of private economy, also wisdom in national economy? Is it in the nature of individuals to take into consideration the wants of future centuries, as those concern the nature of the nation and the State? Let us consider only the first beginning of an American town; every individual left to himself would care merely for his own wants, or at the most for those of his nearest successors, whereas all individuals united in one community provide for the convenience and the wants of the most distant generations; they subject the present generation for this object to privations and sacrifices which no reasonable person could expect from individuals. Can the individual further take into consideration in promoting his private economy, the defence of the country, public security, and the thousand other objects which can only be attained by the aid of the whole community? Does not the State require individuals to limit their private liberty according to what these objects require? Does it not even require that they should sacrifice for these some part of their earnings, of their mental and bodily labour, nay, even their own life? We must first root out, as Cooper does, the very ideas of "State" and "nation" before this opinion can be entertained.

No; that may be wisdom in national

economy which would be folly in private economy, and vice versa; and owing to the very simple reason, that a tailor is no nation and a nation no tailor, that one family is something very different from a community of millions of families, that one house is something very different from a large national territory. Nor does the individual merely by understanding his own interests best, and by striving to further them, if left to his own devices, always further the interests of the community. We ask those who occupy the benches of justice, whether they do not frequently have to send individuals to the tread-mill on account of their excess of inventive power, and of their all too great industry. Robbers, thieves, smugglers, and cheats know their own local and personal circumstances and conditions extremely well, and pay the most active attention to their business; but it by no means follows therefrom, that society is in the best condition where such individuals are least restrained in the exercise of their private industry.

In a thousand cases the power of the State is compelled to impose restrictions on private industry. It prevents the ship-owner from taking on board slaves on the west coast of Africa, and taking them over to America. It imposes regulations as to the building of steamers and the rules of navigation at sea, in order that passengers and sailors may not be sacrificed to the avarice and caprice of the captains. In England certain rules have recently been enacted with regard to shipbuilding, because an infernal union between assurance companies and shipowners has been brought to light, whereby yearly thousands of human lives and millions in value were sacrificed to the avarice of a few persons. In North America millers are bound under a penalty to pack into each cask not less than 198 lbs. of good flour, and for all market goods market inspectors are appointed, although in no other country is individual liberty more highly prized.

Everywhere does the State consider it to be its duty to guard the public against danger and loss, as in the sale of necessaries of life, so also in the sale of medicines, &c.

But the cases which we have mentioned (the school will reply) concern unlawful damages to property and to the person, not the honourable exchange of useful objects, not the harmless and useful industry of private individuals; to impose restrictions on these latter the State has no right whatever. Of course not, so long as they remain harmless and useful; that which, however, is harmless and useful in itself, in general commerce with the world, can become dangerous and injurious in national internal commerce, and vice versa. In time of peace, and considered from a cosmopolitan point of view, privateering is an injurious profession; in time of war, Governments favour it. The deliberate killing of a human being is a crime in time of peace, in war it becomes a duty. Trading in gunpowder, lead, and arms in time of peace is allowed; but whoever provides the enemy with them in time of war, is punished as a traitor.

For similar reasons the State is not merely justified in imposing, but bound to impose, certain regulations and restrictions on commerce (which is in itself harmless) for the best interests of the nation. By prohibitions and protective duties it does not give directions to individuals how to employ their productive powers and capital (as the popular school sophistically alleges); it does not tell the one, "You must invest your money in the building of a ship, or in the erection of a manufactory"; or the other, "You must be a naval captain or a civil engineer"; it leaves it to the judgment of every individual how and where to invest his capital, or to what vocation he will devote himself. It merely says,

It is to the advantage of our nation that we manufacture these or the other goods ourselves; but as by free competition with foreign countries we can never obtain possession of this advantage, we have imposed restrictions on that competition, so far as in our opinion is necessary, to give those among us who invest their capital in these new branches of industry, and those who devote their bodily and mental powers to them, the requisite guarantees that they shall not lose their capital and shall not miss their vocation in life; and further to stimulate foreigners to come over to our side with their productive powers.

In this manner, it does not in the least degree restrain private industry; on the contrary, it secures to the personal, natural, and moneyed powers of the nation a greater and wider field of activity. It does not thereby do something which its individual citizens could understand better and do better than it; on the contrary, it does something which the individuals, even if they understood it, would not be able to do for themselves.

The allegation of the school, that the system of protection occasions unjust and anti-economical encroachments by the power of the State against the employment of the capital and industry of private individuals, appears in the least favourable light if we consider that it is the *foreign* commercial regulations which allow such encroachments on *our* private industry to take place, and that only by the aid of the system of protection are we enabled to counteract those injurious operations of the foreign commercial policy. If the English shut out our corn from their markets, what else are they doing than compelling our agriculturists to grow so much less corn than they would have sent out to England under systems of free importation? If they put such heavy duties on our wool, our wines, or our timber, that our export trade to England wholly or in great measure ceases, what else is thereby effected than that the power of the English nation restricts proportionately our branches of production? In these cases a direction is evidently given by *foreign legislation* to *our* capital and *our* personal productive powers, which but for the regulations made by it

they would scarcely have followed. It follows from this, that were we to disown giving, by means of *our* own legislation, a direction to our own national industry in accordance with our own national interests, we could not prevent foreign nations from regulating our national industry after a fashion which corresponds with their own real or presumed advantage, and which in any case operates disadvantageously to the development of our own productive powers. But can it possibly be wiser on our part, and more to the advantage of those who nationally belong to us, for us to allow our private industry to be regulated by a foreign national Legislature, in accordance with foreign national interests, rather than regulate it by means of our own Legislature and in accordance with our own interests? Does the German or American agriculturist feel himself less restricted if he has to study every year the English Acts of Parliament, in order to ascertain whether that body deems it advantageous to encourage or to impose restrictions on his production of corn or wool, than if his own Legislature imposes certain restrictions on him in respect of foreign manufactured goods, but at the same time insures him a market for all his products, of which he can never again be deprived by foreign legislation?

If the school maintains that protective duties secure to the home manufacturers a monopoly to the disadvantage of the home consumers, in so doing it makes use of a weak argument. For as every individual in the nation is free to share in the profits of the home market which is thus secured to native industry, this is in no respect a private monopoly, but a privilege, secured to all those who belong to our nation, as against those who nationally belong to foreign nations, and which is the more righteous and just inasmuch as those who nationally belong to foreign nations possess themselves the very same monopoly, and those who belong to us are merely thereby put on the same footing with them. It is neither a privilege to the exclusive advantage of the producers, nor to the exclusive disadvantage of the consumers; for if the producers at first obtain higher prices, they run great risks, and have to contend against those considerable losses and sacrifices which are always connected with all beginnings in manufacturing industry. But the consumers have ample security that these extraordinary profits shall not reach unreasonable limits, or become perpetual, by means of the competition at home which follows later on, and which, as a rule, always lowers prices further than the level at which they had steadily ranged under the free competition of the foreigner. If the agriculturists, who are the most important consumers to the manufacturers, must also pay higher prices, this disadvantage will be amply repaid to them by increased demands for agricultural products, and by increased prices obtained for the latter.

It is a further sophism, arrived at by confounding the theory of mere values with that of the powers of production, when the popular school infers from the doctrine,

> that the wealth of the nation is merely the aggregate of the wealth of all individuals in it, and that the private interest of every individual is better able than all State regulations to incite to production and accumulation of wealth,

the conclusion that the national industry would prosper best if only every individual were left undisturbed in the occupation of accumulating wealth. That doctrine can be conceded without the conclusion resulting from it at which the school desires thus to arrive; for the point in question is not (as we have shown in a previous chapter) that of immediately increasing by commercial restrictions the amount of *the values of exchange* in the nation, but of increasing *the amount of its productive powers*. But that the aggregate of the productive powers of the nation is not synonymous with the aggregate of the productive powers of all individuals, each consid-

ered separately—that the total amount of these powers depends chiefly on social and political conditions, but especially on the degree in which the nation has rendered effectual the division of labour and the confederation of the powers of production within itself—we believe we have sufficiently demonstrated in the preceding chapters.

This system everywhere takes into its consideration only individuals who are in free unrestrained intercourse among themselves, and who are contented if we leave everyone to pursue his own private interests according to his own private natural inclination. This is evidently not a system of national economy, but a system of the private economy of the human race, as that would constitute itself were there no interference on the part of any Government, were there no wars, no hostile foreign tariff restrictions. Nowhere do the advocates of that system care to point out by what means those nations which are now prosperous have raised themselves to that stage of power and prosperity which we see them maintain, and from what causes others have lost that degree of prosperity and power which they formerly maintained. We can only learn from it how in private industry, natural ability, labour and capital, are combined in order to bring into exchange valuable products, and in what manner these latter are distributed among the human race and consumed by it. But what means are to be adopted in order to bring the natural powers belonging to any individual nation into activity and value, to raise a poor and weak nation to prosperity and power, cannot be gathered from it, because the school totally ignoring politics, ignores the special conditions of the nation, and concerns itself merely about the prosperity of the whole human race. Wherever international commerce is in question, the native individual is throughout simply pitted against the foreign individual; examples from the private dealings of separate merchants are throughout the only ones adduced—goods are spoken of in general terms (without considering whether the question is one of raw products or of manufactured articles)— in order to prove that it is equally for the benefit of the nation whether its exports and imports consist of money, of raw materials, or of manufactured goods, and whether or not they balance one another. If we, for example, terrified at the commercial crises which prevail in the United States of North America like native epidemics, consult this theory as to the means of averting or diminishing them, it leaves us utterly without comfort or instruction; nay, it is indeed impossible for us to investigate these phenomena scientifically, because, under the penalty of being taken for muddleheads and ignoramuses, we must not even utter the term "balance of trade," while this term is, notwithstanding, made use of in all legislative assemblies, in all bureaux of administration, on every exchange. For the sake of the welfare of humanity, the belief is inculcated on us that exports always balance themselves spontaneously by imports; notwithstanding that we read in public accounts how the Bank of England comes to the assistance of the nature of things; notwithstanding that corn laws exist, which make it somewhat difficult for the agriculturist of those countries which deal with England to pay with his own produce for the manufactured goods which he consumes.

The school recognises no distinction between nations which have attained a higher degree of economical development, and those which occupy a lower stage. Everywhere it seeks to exclude the action of the power of the State; everywhere, according to it, will the individual be so much better able to produce, the less the power of the State concerns itself for him. In fact, according to this doctrine savage nations ought to be the most productive and wealthy of the earth, for nowhere is the individual left more to himself than in the savage state, nowhere is the action of the power of the State less perceptible.

Statistics and history, however, teach, on the contrary, that the necessity for the intervention of legislative power and administration is everywhere more apparent, the further the economy of the nation is developed. As individual liberty is in general a good thing so long only as it does not run counter to the interests of society, so is it reasonable to hold that private industry can only lay claim to unrestricted action so long as the latter consists with the well-being of the nation. But whenever the enterprise and activity of individuals does not suffice for this purpose, or in any case where these might become injurious to the nation, there does private industry rightly require support from the whole power of the nation, there ought it for the sake of its own interests to submit to legal restrictions.

If the school represents the free competition of all producers as the most effectual means for promoting the prosperity of the human race, it is quite right from the point of view which it assumes. On the hypothesis of a universal union, every restriction on the honest exchange of goods between various countries seems unreasonable and injurious. But so long as other nations subordinate the interests of the human race as a whole to their national interests, it is folly to speak of free competition among the individuals of various nations. The arguments of the school in favour of free competition are thus only applicable to the exchange between those who belong to one and the same nation. Every great nation, therefore, must endeavour to form an aggregate within itself, which will enter into commercial intercourse with other similar aggregates so far only as that intercourse is suitable to the interests of its own special community. These interests of the community are, however, infinitely different from the private interests of all the separate individuals of the nation, if each individual is to be regarded as existing for himself alone and not in the character of a member of the national community, if we regard (as Smith and Say do) individuals as mere producers and consumers, not citizens of states or members of nations; for as such, mere individuals do not concern themselves for the prosperity of future generations—they deem it foolish (as Mr. Cooper really demonstrates to us) to make certain and present sacrifices in order to endeavour to obtain a benefit which is as yet uncertain and lying in the vast field of the future (if even it possess any value at all); they care but little for the continuance of the nation—they would expose the ships of their merchants to become the prey of every bold pirate—they trouble themselves but little about the power, the honour, or the glory of the nation, at the most they can persuade themselves to make some material sacrifices for the education of their children, and to give them the opportunity of learning a trade, provided always that after the lapse of a few years the learners are placed in a position to earn their own bread.

Indeed, according to the prevailing theory, so analogous is national economy to private economy that J. B. Say, where (exceptionally) he allows that internal industry may be protected by the State, makes it a condition of so doing, that every probability must exist that after the lapse of a *few years* it will attain independence, just as a shoemaker's apprentice is allowed only a few years' time in order to perfect himself so far in his trade as to do without parental assistance.

15. Conspicuous Consumption*

THORSTEIN VEBLEN

In what has been said of the evolution of the vicarious leisure class and its differentiation from the general body of the working classes, reference has been made to a further division of labour,—that between different servant classes. One portion of the servant class, chiefly those persons whose occupation is vicarious leisure, come to undertake a new, subsidiary range of duties—the vicarious consumption of goods. The most obvious form in which this consumption occurs is seen in the wearing of liveries and the occupation of spacious servants' quarters. Another, scarcely less obtrusive or less effective form of vicarious consumption, and a much more widely prevalent one, is the consumption of food, clothing, dwelling, and furniture by the lady and the rest of the domestic establishment.

But already at a point in economic evolution far antedating the emergence of the lady, specialised consumption of goods as an evidence of pecuniary strength had begun to work out in a more or less elaborate system. The beginning of a differentiation in consumption even antedates the appearance of anything that can fairly be called pecuniary strength. It is traceable back to the initial phase of predatory culture, and there is even a suggestion that an incipient differentiation in this respect lies back of the beginnings of the predatory life. This most primitive differentia-

*Source: Reprinted from Thorstein Veblen, The Theory of the Leisure Class, chapter 4 (Macmillan Company, 1899).

tion in the consumption of goods is like the later differentiation with which we are all so intimately familiar, in that it is largely of a ceremonial character, but unlike the latter it does not rest on a difference in accumulated wealth. The utility of consumption as an evidence of wealth is to be classed as a derivative growth. It is an adaptation to a new end, by a selective process, of a distinction previously existing and well established in men's habits of thought.

In the earlier phases of the predatory culture the only economic differentiation is a broad distinction between an honourable superior class made up of the able-bodied men on the one side, and a base inferior class of labouring women on the other. According to the ideal scheme of life in force at that time it is the office of the men to consume what the women produce. Such consumption as falls to the women is merely incidental to their work; it is a means to their continued labour, and not a consumption directed to their own comfort and fulness of life. Unproductive consumption of goods is honourable, primarily as a mark of prowess and a perquisite of human dignity; secondarily it becomes substantially honourable in itself, especially the consumption of the more desirable things. The consumption of choice articles of food, and frequently also of rare articles of adornment, becomes tabu to the women and children; and if there is a base (servile) class of men, the tabu holds also for them. With a further advance in culture this tabu may change into simple custom of a more or less rigorous character; but whatever be the theoretical basis of the distinction which is maintained, whether it be a tabu or a larger conventionality, the features of the conventional scheme of consumption do not change easily. When the quasi-peaceable stage of industry is reached, with its fundamental institution of chattel slavery, the general principle, more or less rigorously applied, is that the base, industrious class should consume only what may be necessary to their subsistence. In the nature of things, luxuries and the comforts of life belong to the leisure class. Under the tabu, certain victuals, and more particularly certain beverages, are strictly reserved for the use of the superior class.

The ceremonial differentiation of the dietary is best seen in the use of intoxicating beverages and narcotics. If these articles of consumption are costly, they are felt to be noble and honorific. Therefore the base classes, primarily the women, practise an enforced continence with respect to these stimulants, except in countries where they are obtainable at a very low cost. From archaic times down through all the length of the patriarchal régime it has been the office of the women to prepare and administer these luxuries, and it has been the perquisite of the men of gentle birth and breeding to consume them. Drunkenness and the other pathological consequences of the free use of stimulants therefore tend in their turn to become honorific, as being a mark, at the second remove, of the superior status of those who are able to afford the indulgence. Infirmities induced by over-indulgence are among some peoples freely recognised as manly attributes. It has even happened that the name for certain diseased conditions of the body arising from such an origin has passed into everyday speech as a synonym for "noble" or "gentle." It is only at a relatively early stage of culture that the symptoms of expensive vice are conventionally accepted as marks of a superior status, and so tend to become virtues and command the deference of the community; but the reputability that attaches to certain expensive vices long retains so much of its force as to appreciably lessen the disapprobation visited upon the men of the wealthy or noble class for any excessive indulgence. The same invidious distinction adds force to the current disapproval of any indulgence of this kind on the part of women, minors, and inferiors. This invidious traditional distinction has not lost its force even among the more advanced peoples of to-day. Where the example set by the leisure class retains its imperative force in the regulation of the conventionalities, it is observable that the women still in great measure practise the same traditional continence with regard to stimulants.

This characterisation of the greater continence in the use of stimulants practised by the women of the reputable classes may seem an excessive refinement of logic at the expense of common sense. But facts within easy reach of any one who cares to know them go to say that the greater abstinence of women is in some part due to an imperative conventionality; and this conventionality is, in a general way, strongest where the patriarchal tradition—the tradition that the woman is a chattel—has retained its hold in greatest vigour. In a sense which has been greatly qualified in scope and rigour, but which has by no means lost its meaning even yet, this tradition says that the woman, being a chattel, should consume only what is necessary to her sustenance,—except so far as her further consumption contributes to the comfort or the good repute of her master. The consumption of luxuries, in the true sense, is a consumption directed to the comfort of the consumer himself, and is, therefore, a mark of the master. Any such consumption by others can take place only on a basis of sufferance. In communities where the popular habits of thought have been profoundly shaped by the patriarchal tradition we may accordingly look for survivals of the tabu on luxuries at least to the extent of a conventional deprecation of their use by the unfree and dependent class. This is more particularly true as regards certain luxuries, the use of which by the dependent class would detract sensibly from the comfort or pleasure of their masters, or which are held to be of doubtful legitimacy on other grounds. In the apprehension of the great conservative middle class of

Western civilisation the use of these various stimulants is obnoxious to at least one, if not both, of these objections; and it is a fact too significant to be passed over that it is precisely among these middle classes of the Germanic culture, with their strong surviving sense of the patriarchal proprieties, that the women are to the greatest extent subject to a qualified tabu on narcotics and alcoholic beverages. With many qualifications—with more qualifications as the patriarchal tradition has gradually weakened—the general rule is felt to be right and binding that women should consume only for the benefit of their masters. The objection of course presents itself that expenditure on women's dress and household paraphernalia is an obvious exception to this rule; but it will appear in the sequel that this exception is much more obvious than substantial.

During the earlier stages of economic development, consumption of goods without stint, especially consumption of the better grades of goods,—ideally all consumption in excess of the subsistence minimum,—pertains normally to the leisure class. This restriction tends to disappear, at least formally, after the later peaceable stage has been reached, with private ownership of goods and an industrial system based on wage labour or on the petty household economy. But during the earlier quasi-peaceable stage, when so many of the traditions through which the institution of a leisure class has affected the economic life of later times were taking form and consistency, this principle has had the force of a conventional law. It has served as the norm to which consumption has tended to conform, and any appreciable departure from it is to be regarded as an aberrant form, sure to be eliminated sooner or later in the further course of development.

The quasi-peaceable gentleman of leisure, then, not only consumes of the staff of life beyond the minimum required for subsistence and physical efficiency, but his consumption also undergoes a specialisation as regards the quality of the goods consumed. He consumes freely and of the best, in food, drink, narcotics, shelter, services, ornaments, apparel, weapons and accoutrements, amusements, amulets, and idols or divinities. In the process of gradual amelioration which takes place in the articles of his consumption, the motive principle and the proximate aim of innovation is no doubt the higher efficiency of the improved and more elaborate products for personal comfort and well-being. But that does not remain the sole purpose of their consumption. The canon of reputability is at hand and seizes upon such innovations as are, according to its standard, fit to survive. Since the consumption of these more excellent goods is an evidence of wealth, it becomes honorific; and conversely, the failure to consume in due quantity and quality becomes a mark of inferiority and demerit.

This growth of punctilious discrimination as to qualitative excellence in eating, drinking, etc., presently affects not only the manner of life, but also the training and intellectual activity of the gentleman of leisure. He is no longer simply the successful, aggressive male,—the man of strength, resource, and intrepidity. In order to avoid stultification he must also cultivate his tastes, for it now becomes incumbent on him to discriminate with some nicety between the noble and the ignoble in consumable goods. He becomes a connoisseur in creditable viands of various degrees of merit, in manly beverages and trinkets, in seemly apparel and architecture, in weapons, games, dances, and the narcotics. This cultivation of the aesthetic faculty requires time and application, and the demands made upon the gentleman in this direction therefore tend to change his life of leisure into a more or less arduous application to the business of learning how to live a life of ostensible leisure in a becoming way. Closely related to the requirement that the gentleman must consume freely and of the right kind of goods, there is the requirement that he must know how to consume them in a seemly manner. His life of leisure must be conducted in due form. Hence arise good manners in the way pointed out in an earlier chapter. High-bred manners and ways of living are items of conformity to the norm of conspicuous leisure and conspicuous consumption.

Conspicuous consumption of valuable goods is a means of reputability to the gentleman of leisure. As wealth accumulates on his hands, his own unaided effort will not avail to sufficiently put his opulence in evidence by this method. The aid of friends and competitors is therefore brought in by resorting to the giving of valuable presents and expensive feasts and entertainments. Presents and feasts had probably another origin than that of naïve ostentation, but they acquired their utility for this purpose very early, and they have retained that character to the present; so that their utility in this respect has now long been the substantial ground on which these usages rest. Costly entertainments, such as the potlatch or the ball, are peculiarly adapted to serve this end. The competitor with whom the entertainer wishes to institute a comparison is, by this method, made to serve as a means to the end. He consumes vicariously for his host at the same time that he is a witness to the consumption of that excess of good things which his host is unable to dispose of singlehanded, and he is also made to witness his host's facility in etiquette.

In the giving of costly entertainments other motives, of a more genial kind, are of course also present. The custom of festive gatherings probably originated in motives of conviviality and religion; these motives are also present in the later development, but they do not continue to be the sole motives. The latterday leisure-class festivities and entertainments may continue in some slight degree to serve the religious need and in a higher degree the needs of recreation and conviviality, but they also serve an invidious purpose; and they serve it none the less effectually for having a colourable non-invidious ground in these more avowable motives. But the economic effect of these social amenities is not therefore lessened, either in the vicarious consumption of goods or in the exhibition of difficult and costly achievements in etiquette.

As wealth accumulates, the leisure class develops further in function and structure, and there arises a differentiation within the class. There is a more or less elaborate system of rank and grades. This differentiation is furthered by the inheritance of wealth and the consequent inheritance of gentility. With the inheritance of gentility goes the inheritance of obligatory leisure; and gentility of a sufficient potency to entail a life of leisure may be inherited without the complement of wealth required to maintain a dignified leisure. Gentle blood may be transmitted without goods enough to afford a reputably free consumption at one's ease. Hence results a class of impecunious gentlemen of leisure, incidentally referred to already. These half-caste gentlemen of leisure fall into a system of hierarchical gradations. Those who stand near the higher and the highest grades of the wealthy leisure class, in point of birth, or in point of wealth, or both, outrank the remoter-born and the pecuniarily weaker. These lower grades, especially the impecunious, or marginal, gentlemen of leisure, affiliate themselves by a system of dependence or fealty to the great ones; by so doing they gain an increment of repute, or of the means with which to lead a life of leisure, from their patron. They become his courtiers or retainers, servants; and being fed and countenanced by their patron they are indices of his rank and vicarious consumers of his superfluous wealth. Many of these affiliated gentlemen of leisure are at the same time lesser men of substance in their own right; so that some

of them are scarcely at all, others only partially, to be rated as vicarious consumers. So many of them, however, as make up the retainers and hangers-on of the patron may be classed as vicarious consumers without qualification. Many of these again, and also many of the other aristocracy of less degree, have in turn attached to their persons a more or less comprehensive group of vicarious consumers in the persons of their wives and children, their servants, retainers, etc.

Throughout this graduated scheme of vicarious leisure and vicarious consumption the rule holds that these offices must be performed in some such manner, or under some such circumstance or insignia, as shall point plainly to the master to whom this leisure or consumption pertains, and to whom therefore the resulting increment of good repute of right inures. The consumption and leisure executed by these persons for their master or patron represents an investment on his part with a view to an increase of good fame. As regards feasts and largesses this is obvious enough, and the imputation of repute to the host or patron here takes place immediately, on the ground of common notoriety. Where leisure and consumption is performed vicariously by henchmen and retainers, imputation of the resulting repute to the patron is effected by their residing near his person so that it may be plain to all men from what source they draw. As the group whose good esteem is to be secured in this way grows larger, more patent means are required to indicate the imputation of merit for the leisure performed, and to this end uniforms, badges, and liveries come into vogue. The wearing of uniforms or liveries implies a considerable degree of dependence, and may even be said to be a mark of servitude, real or ostensible. The wearers of uniforms and liveries may be roughly divided into two classes—the free and the servile, or the noble and the ignoble. The services performed by them are likewise divisible into noble and ignoble. Of course the distinction is not observed with strict consistency in practice; the less debasing of the base services and the less honorific of the noble functions are not infrequently merged in the same person. But the general distinction is not on that account to be overlooked. What may add some perplexity is the fact that this fundamental distinction between noble and ignoble, which rests on the nature of the ostensible service performed, is traversed by a secondary distinction into honorific and humiliating, resting on the rank of the person for whom the service is performed or whose livery is worn. So, those offices which are by right the proper employment of the leisure class are noble; such are government, fighting, hunting, the care of arms and accoutrements, and the like,—in short, those which may be classed as ostensibly predatory employments. On the other hand, those employments which properly fall to the industrious class are ignoble; such as handicraft or other productive labour, menial services, and the like. But a base service performed for a person of very high degree may become a very honorific office; as for instance the office of a Maid of Honour or of a Lady in Waiting to the Queen, or the King's Master of the Horse or his Keeper of the Hounds. The two offices last named suggest a principle of some general bearing. Whenever, as in these cases, the menial service in question has to do directly with the primary leisure employments of fighting and hunting, it easily acquires a reflected honorific character. In this way great honour may come to attach to an employment which in its own nature belongs to the baser sort.

In the later development of peaceable industry, the usage of employing an idle corps of uniformed men-at-arms gradually lapses. Vicarious consumption by dependents bearing the insignia of their patron or master narrows down to a corps of liveried menials. In a heightened degree, therefore, the livery comes to be a badge of servitude, or rather of servility. Something of a honorific character always attached to the livery of the armed retainer, but this honorific character disappears when the livery becomes the exclusive badge of the menial. The livery becomes obnoxious to nearly all who are required to wear it. We are yet so little removed from a state of effective slavery as still to be fully sensitive to the sting of any imputation of servility. This antipathy asserts itself even in the case of the liveries or uniforms which some corporations prescribe as the distinctive dress of their employees. In this country the aversion even goes the length of discrediting—in a mild and uncertain way—those government employments, military and civil, which require the wearing of a livery or uniform.

With the disappearance of servitude, the number of vicarious consumers attached to any one gentleman tends, on the whole, to decrease. The like is of course true, and perhaps in a still higher degree, of the number of dependents who perform vicarious leisure for him. In a general way, though not wholly nor consistently, these two groups coincide. The dependent who was first delegated for these duties was the wife, or the chief wife; and, as would be expected, in the later development of the institution, when the number of persons by whom these duties are customarily performed gradually narrows, the wife remains the last. In the higher grades of society a large volume of both these kinds of service is required; and here the wife is of course still assisted in the work by a more or less numerous corps of menials. But as we descend the social scale, the point is presently reached where the duties of vicarious leisure and consumption devolve upon the wife alone. In the communities of the Western culture, this point is at present found among the lower middle class.

And here occurs a curious inversion. It is a fact of common observation that in this lower middle class there is no pretence of leisure on the part of the head of the household. Through force of circumstances it has fallen into disuse. But the middle-class wife still carries on the business of vicarious leisure, for the good name of the household and its master. In descending the social scale in any modern industrial community, the primary fact—the conspicuous leisure of the master of the household—disappears at a relatively high point. The head of the middle-class household has been reduced by economic circumstances to turn his hand to gaining a livelihood by occupations which often partake largely of the character of industry, as in the case of the ordinary business man of to-day. But the derivative fact—the vicarious leisure and consumption rendered by the wife, and the auxiliary vicarious performance of leisure by menials—remains in vogue as a conventionality which the demands of reputability will not suffer to be slighted. It is by no means an uncommon spectacle to find a man applying himself to work with the utmost assiduity, in order that his wife may in due form render for him that degree of vicarious leisure which the common sense of the time demands.

The leisure rendered by the wife in such cases is, of course, not a simple manifestation of idleness or indolence. It almost invariably occurs disguised under some form of work or household duties or social amenities, which prove on analysis to serve little or no ulterior end beyond showing that she does not and need not occupy herself with anything that is gainful or that is of substantial use. As has already been noticed under the head of manners, the greater part of the customary round of domestic cares to which the middle-class housewife gives her time and effort is of this character. Not that the results of her attention to household matters, of a decorative and mundificatory character, are not pleasing to the sense of men trained in middle-class proprieties; but the taste to which these effects of household adornment and tidiness appeal is a taste which has been formed under the selective guidance of a canon of propriety that demands just these evidences of wasted effort. The effects are pleasing to us chiefly because we have been taught to find them pleasing. There goes into these domestic duties much solicitude for a proper combination of form and colour, and for other ends that are to be classed as aesthetic in the proper sense of the term; and it is not denied that effects having some substantial aesthetic value are sometimes attained. Pretty much all that is here insisted on is that, as regards these amenities of life, the housewife's efforts are under the guidance of traditions that have been shaped by the law of conspicuously wasteful expenditure of time and substance. If beauty or comfort is achieved,—and it is a more or less fortuitous circumstance if they are,—they must be achieved by means and methods that commend themselves to the great economic law of wasted effort. The more reputable, "presentable" portion of middle-class household paraphernalia are, on the one hand, items of conspicuous consumption, and on the other hand, apparatus for putting in evidence the vicarious leisure rendered by the housewife.

The requirement of vicarious consumption at the hands of the wife continues in force even at a lower point in the pecuniary scale than the requirement of vicarious leisure. At a point below which little if any pretence of wasted effort, in ceremonial cleanness and the like, is observable, and where there is assuredly no conscious attempt at ostensible leisure, decency still requires the wife to consume some goods conspicuously for the reputability of the household and its head. So that, as the latter-day outcome of this evolution of an archaic institution, the wife, who was at the outset the drudge and chattel of the man, both in fact and in theory,—the producer of goods for him to consume,—has become the ceremonial consumer of goods which he produces. But she still quite unmistakably remains his chattel in theory; for the habitual rendering of vicarious leisure and consumption is the abiding mark of the unfree servant.

This vicarious consumption practised by the household of the middle and lower classes can not be counted as a direct expression of the leisure-class scheme of life, since the household of this pecuniary grade does not belong within the leisure class. It is rather that the leisure-class scheme of life here comes to an expression at the second remove. The leisure class stands at the head of the social structure in point of reputability; and its manner of life and its standards of worth therefore afford the norm of reputability for the community. The observance of these standards, in some degree of approximation, becomes incumbent upon all classes lower in the scale. In modern civilized communities the lines of demarcation between social classes have grown vague and transient, and wherever this happens the norm of reputability imposed by the upper class extends its coercive influence with but slight hindrance down through the social structure to the lowest strata. The result is that the members of each stratum accept as their ideal of decency the scheme of life in vogue in the next higher stratum, and bend their energies to live up to that ideal. On pain of forfeiting their good name and their self-respect in case of failure, they must conform to the accepted code, at least in appearance.

The basis on which good repute in any highly organised industrial community ultimately rests is pecuniary strength; and the means of showing pecuniary strength, and so of gaining or retaining a good name, are leisure and a conspicuous consumption of goods. Accordingly, both of these methods are in vogue as far down the scale as it remains possible; and in the lower strata in which the two methods are employed, both offices are in great part delegated to the wife and children of the household. Lower still, where any degree of leisure, even ostensible, has become impracticable for the wife, the conspicuous consumption of goods remains and is carried on by the wife and children. The man of the household also can do something in this direction, and, indeed, he commonly does; but with a still lower descent into the levels of indigence—along the margin of the slums—the man, and presently also the children, virtually cease to consume valuable goods for appearances, and the woman remains virtually the sole exponent of the household's pecuniary decency. No class of society, not even the most abjectly poor, foregoes all customary conspicuous consumption. The last items of this category of consumption are not given up except under stress of the direst necessity. Very much of squalor and discomfort will be endured before the last trinket or the last pretence of pecuniary decency is put away. There is no class and no country that has yielded so abjectly before the pressure of physical want as to deny themselves all gratification of this higher or spiritual need.

From the foregoing survey of the growth of conspicuous leisure and consumption, it appears that the utility of both alike for the purposes of reputability lies in the element of waste that is common to both. In the one case it is a waste of time and effort, in the other it is a waste of goods. Both are methods of demonstrating the possession of wealth, and the two are conventionally accepted as equivalents. The choice between them is a question of advertising expediency simply, except so far as it may be affected by other standards of propriety, springing from a different source. On grounds of expediency the preference may be given to the one or the other at different stages of the economic development. The question is, which of the two methods will most effectively reach the persons whose convictions it is desired to affect. Usage has answered this question in different ways under different circumstances.

So long as the community or social group is small enough and compact enough to be effectually reached by common notoriety alone,—that is to say, so long as the human environment to which the individual is required to adapt himself in respect of reputability is comprised within his sphere of personal acquaintance and neighbourhood gossip,—so long the one method is about as effective as the other. Each will therefore serve about equally well during the earlier stages of social growth. But when the differentiation has gone farther and it becomes necessary to reach a wider human environment, consumption begins to hold over leisure as an ordinary means of decency. This is especially true during the later, peaceable economic stage. The means of communication and the mobility of the population now expose the individual to the observation of many persons who have no other means of judging of his reputability than the display of goods (and perhaps of breeding) which he is able to make while he is under their direct observation.

The modern organisation of industry works in the same direction also by another line. The exigencies of the modern industrial system frequently place individuals and households in juxtaposition between whom there is little contact in any other sense than that of juxtaposition. One's neighbours, mechanically speaking, often are socially not one's neighbours, or even acquaintances; and still their transient good opinion has a high degree of utility. The only practicable means of impressing one's pecuniary ability on these unsympathetic observers of one's everyday life is an unremitting demonstration of ability to pay. In the modern community there is also a more frequent attendance at large gatherings of people to whom one's everyday life is unknown; in such places as churches, theatres, ballrooms, hotels, parks, shops, and the like. In order to impress these transient observers, and to retain one's self-complacency under their observation, the signature of one's pecuniary strength should be written in characters which he who runs may read. It is evident, therefore, that the present trend of the development is in the direction of heightening the utility of conspicuous consumption as compared with leisure.

It is also noticeable that the serviceability of consumption as a means of repute, as well as the insistence on it as an element of decency, is at its best in those portions of the community where the human contact of the individual is widest and the mobility of the population is greatest. Conspicuous consumption claims a relatively larger portion of the income of the urban than of the rural population, and the claim is also more imperative. The result is that, in order to keep up a decent appearance, the former habitually live hand-to-mouth to a greater extent than the latter. So it comes, for instance, that the American farmer and his wife and daughters are notoriously less modish in their dress, as well as less urbane in their manners, than the city artisan's family with an equal income. It is not that the city population is by nature much more eager for the peculiar complacency that comes of a conspicuous consumption, nor has the rural population less regard for pecuniary decency. But the provocation to this line of evidence, as well as its transient effectiveness, are more decided in the city. This method is therefore more readily resorted to, and in the struggle to outdo one another the city population push their normal standard of conspicuous consumption to a higher point, with the result that a relatively greater expenditure in this direction is required to indicate a given degree of pecuniary decency in the city. The requirement of conformity to this higher conventional standard becomes mandatory. The standard of decency is higher, class for class, and this requirement of decent appearance must be lived up to on pain of losing caste.

Consumption becomes a larger element in the standard of living in the city than in the country. Among the country population its place is to some extent taken by savings and home comforts known through the medium of neighbourhood gossip sufficiently to serve the like general purpose of pecuniary repute. These home comforts and the leisure indulged in—where the indulgence is found—are of course also in great part to be classed as items of conspicuous consumption; and much the same is to be said of the savings. The smaller amount of the savings laid by by the artisan class is no doubt due, in some measure, to the fact that in the case of the artisan the savings are a less effective means of advertisement, relative to the environment in which he is placed, than are the savings of the people living on farms and in the small villages. Among the latter, everybody's affairs, especially everybody's pecuniary status, are known to everybody else. Considered by itself simply—taken in the first degree—this added provocation to which the artisan and the urban labouring classes are exposed may not very seriously decrease the amount of savings; but in its cumulative action, through raising the standard of decent expenditure, its deterrent effect on the tendency to save cannot but be very great.

A felicitous illustration of the manner in which this canon of reputability works out its results is seen in the practice of dram-drinking, "treating," and smoking in public places, which is customary among the labourers and handicraftsmen of the towns, and among the lower middle class of the urban population generally. Journeymen printers may be named as a class among whom this form of conspicuous consumption has a great vogue, and among whom it carries with it certain well-marked consequences that are often deprecated. The peculiar habits of the class in this respect are commonly set down to some kind of an ill-defined moral deficiency with which this class is credited, or to a morally deleterious influence which their occupation is supposed to exert, in some unascertainable way, upon the men employed in it. The state of the case for the men who work in the composition and press rooms of the common run of printing-houses may be summed up as follows. Skill acquired in any printing-house or any city is easily turned to account in almost any other house or city; that is to say, the inertia due to special training is slight. Also, this occupation requires more than the average of intelligence and general information, and the men employed in it are therefore ordinarily more ready than many others to take advantage of any slight variation in the demand for their labour from one place to another. The inertia due to the home feeling is consequently also slight. At the same time the wages in the trade are high enough to make movement from place to place relatively easy. The result is a great mobility of the labour employed in printing; perhaps greater than in any other equally well-defined and considerable body of workmen. These men are constantly thrown in contact with new groups of acquaintances, with whom the relations established are transient or ephemeral, but whose good opinion is valued none the less for the time being. The human proclivity to ostentation, reënforced by sentiments of goodfellowship, leads them to spend freely in those directions which will best serve these needs. Here as elsewhere prescription seizes upon the custom as soon as it gains a vogue, and incorporates it in the accredited standard of decency. The next step is to make this standard of decency the point of departure for a new move in advance in the same direction,—for there is no merit in simple spiritless conformity to a standard of dissipation that is lived up to as a matter of course by every one in the trade.

The greater prevalence of dissipation among printers than among the average of workmen is accordingly attributable, at least in some measure, to the greater ease of movement and the more transient character of acquaintance and human contact in this trade. But the substantial ground of this high requirement in dissipation is in the last analysis no other than that same propensity for a manifestation of dominance and pecuniary decency which makes the French peasant-proprietor parsimonious and frugal, and induces the American millionaire to found colleges, hospitals and museums. If the canon of conspicuous consumption were not offset to a considerable extent by other features of human nature, alien to it, any saving should logically be impossible for a population situated as the artisan and labouring classes of the cities are at present, however high their wages or their income might be.

But there are other standards of repute and other, more or less imperative, canons of conduct, besides wealth and its manifestation, and some of these come in to accentuate or to qualify the broad, fundamental canon of conspicuous waste. Under the simple test of effectiveness for advertising, we should expect to find leisure and the conspicuous consumption of goods dividing the field of pecuniary emulation pretty evenly between them at the outset. Leisure might then be expected gradually to yield ground and tend to obsolescence as the economic development goes forward, and the community increases in size; while the conspicuous consumption of goods should gradually gain in importance, both absolutely and relatively, until it had absorbed all the available product, leaving nothing over beyond a bare livelihood. But the actual course of development has been somewhat different from this ideal scheme. Leisure held the first place at the start, and came to hold a rank very much above wasteful consumption of goods, both as a direct exponent of wealth and as an element in the standard of decency, during the quasi-peaceable culture. From that point onward, consumption has gained ground, until, at present, it unquestionably holds the primacy, though it is still far from absorbing the entire margin of production above the subsistence minimum.

The early ascendency of leisure as a means of reputability is traceable to the archaic distinction between noble and ignoble employments. Leisure is honourable and becomes imperative partly because it shows exemption from ignoble labour. The archaic differentiation into noble and ignoble classes is based on an invidious distinction between employments as honorific or debasing; and this traditional distinction grows into an imperative canon of decency during the early quasi-peaceable stage. Its ascendency is furthered by the fact that leisure is still fully as effective an evidence of wealth as consumption. Indeed, so effective is it in the relatively small and stable human environment to which the individual is exposed at that cultural stage, that, with the aid of the archaic tradition which deprecates all productive labour, it gives rise to a large impecunious leisure class, and it even tends to limit the production of the community's industry to the subsistence minimum. This extreme inhibition of industry is avoided because slave labour, working under a compulsion more rigorous than that of reputability, is forced to turn out a product in excess of the subsistence minimum of the working class. The subsequent relative decline in the use of conspicuous leisure as a basis of repute is due partly to an increasing relative effectiveness of consumption as an evidence of wealth; but in part it is traceable to another force, alien, and in some degree antagonistic, to the usage of conspicuous waste.

This alien factor is the instinct of workmanship. Other circumstances permitting, that instinct disposes men to look with favour upon productive efficiency and on whatever is of human use. It disposes them to deprecate waste of substance or effort. The instinct of workmanship is present in all men, and asserts itself even under very adverse circumstances. So that however wasteful a given expenditure may be in reality, it must at least have some colourable excuse in the way of an ostensible purpose. The manner in which, under special circumstances, the instinct eventuates in a taste for exploit and an invidious discrimination between noble and ignoble classes has been indicated in an earlier chapter. In so far as it comes into conflict with the law of conspicuous waste, the instinct of workmanship expresses itself not so much in insistence on substantial usefulness as in an abiding sense of the odiousness and aesthetic impossibility of what is obviously futile. Being of the nature of an instinctive affection, its guidance touches chiefly and immediately the obvious and apparent violations of its requirements. It is only less promptly and with less constraining force that it reaches such substantial violations of its requirements as are appreciated only upon reflection.

So long as all labour continues to be performed exclusively or usually by slaves, the baseness of all productive effort is too constantly and deterrently present in the mind of men to allow the instinct of workmanship seriously to take effect in the direction of industrial usefulness; but when the quasi-peaceable stage (with slavery and status) passes into the peaceable stage of industry (with wage labour and cash payment) the instinct comes more effectively into play. It then begins aggressively to shape men's view of what is meritorious, and asserts itself at least as an auxiliary canon of self-complacency. All extraneous considerations apart, those persons (adults) are but a vanishing minority to-day who harbour no inclination to the accomplishment of some end, or who are not impelled of their own motion to shape some object or fact or relation for human use. The propensity may in large measure be overborne by the more immediately constraining incentive to a reputable leisure and an avoidance of indecorous usefulness, and it may therefore work itself out in make-believe only; as for instance in "social duties," and in quasi-artistic or quasi-scholarly accomplishments, in the care and decoration of the house, in sewing-circle activity or dress reform, in proficiency at dress, cards, yachting, golf, and various sports. But the fact that it may under stress of circumstances eventuate in inanities no more disproves the presence of the instinct than the reality of the brooding instinct is disproved by inducing a hen to sit on a nestful of china eggs.

This latter-day uneasy reaching-out for some form of purposeful activity that shall at the same time not be indecorously productive of either individual or collective gain marks a difference of attitude between the modern leisure class and that of the quasi-peaceable stage. At the earlier stage, as was said above, the all-dominating institution of slavery and status acted resistlessly to discountenance exertion directed to other than naïvely predatory ends. It was still possible to find some habitual employment for the inclination to action in the way of forcible aggression or repression directed against hostile groups or against the subject classes within the group; and this served to relieve the pressure and draw off the energy of the leisure class without a resort to actually useful, or even ostensibly useful employments. The practice of hunting also served the same purpose in some degree. When the community developed into a peaceful industrial organisation, and when fuller occupation of the land had reduced the opportunities for the hunt to an inconsiderable residue, the pressure of energy seeking purposeful employment was left to find an outlet in some other direction. The ignominy which attaches to useful effort also entered upon a less acute phase with the disappearance of compulsory labour; and the instinct of workmanship then came to assert itself with more persistence and consistency.

The line of least resistance has changed in some measure, and the energy which formerly found a vent in predatory activity, now in part takes the direction of some ostensibly useful end. Ostensibly purposeless leisure has come to be deprecated, especially among that large portion of the leisure class whose plebeian origin acts to set them at variance with the tradition of the *otium cum dignitate*. But that canon of reputability which discountenances all employment that is of the nature of productive effort is still at hand, and will permit nothing beyond the most transient vogue to any employment that is substantially useful or productive. The consequence is that a change has been wrought in the conspicuous leisure practised by the leisure class; not so much in substance as in form. A reconciliation between the two conflicting requirements is effected by a resort to make-believe. Many and intricate polite observances and social duties of a ceremonial nature are developed; many organisations are founded, with some specious object of amelioration embodied in their official style and title; there is much coming and going, and a deal of talk, to the end that the talkers may not have occasion to reflect on what is the effectual economic value of their traffic. And along with the make-believe of purposeful employment, and woven inextricably into its texture, there is commonly, if not invariably, a more or less appreciable element of purposeful effort directed to some serious end.

In the narrower sphere of vicarious leisure a similar change has gone forward. Instead of simply passing her time in visible idleness, as in the best days of the patriarchal régime, the housewife of the advanced peaceable stage applies herself assiduously to household cares. The salient features of this development of domestic service have already been indicated.

Throughout the entire evolution of conspicuous expenditure, whether of goods or of services or human life, runs the obvious implication that in order to effectually mend the consumer's good fame it must be an expenditure of superfluities. In order to be reputable it must be wasteful. No merit would accrue from the consumption of the bare necessaries of life, except by comparison with the abjectly poor who fall short even of the subsistence minimum; and no standard of expenditure could result from such a comparison, except the most prosaic and unattractive level of decency. A standard of life would still be possible which should admit of invidious comparison in other respects than that of opulence; as, for instance, a comparison in various directions in the manifestation of moral, physical, intellectual, or aesthetic force. Comparison in all these directions is in vogue today; and the comparison made in these respects is commonly so inextricably bound up with the pecuniary comparison as to be scarcely distinguishable from the latter. This is especially true as regards the current rating of expressions of intellectual and aesthetic force or proficiency; so that we frequently interpret as aesthetic or intellectual a difference which in substance is pecuniary only.

The use of the term "waste" is in one respect an unfortunate one. As used in the speech of everyday life the word carries an undertone of deprecation. It is here used for want of a better term that will adequately describe the same range of motives and of phenomena, and it is not to be taken in an odious sense, as implying an illegitimate expenditure of human products or of human life. In the view of economic theory the expenditure in question is no more and no less legitimate than any other expenditure. It is here called "waste" because this expenditure does not serve human life or human well-being on the whole, not because it is waste or misdirection of effort or expenditure as viewed from the standpoint of the individual consumer who chooses it. If he chooses it, that disposes of the question of its relative utility to him, as compared with other forms of consumption that would not be deprecated on account of their wastefulness. Whatever form of expenditure the consumer chooses, or whatever end he seeks in making his choice, has utility to him by virtue of his preference. As seen from the point of view of the individual consumer, the question of wastefulness does not arise within the scope of economic theory proper. The use of the word "waste" as a technical term, therefore, implies no deprecation of the motives or of the ends sought by the consumer under this canon of conspicuous waste.

But it is, on other grounds, worth noting that the term "waste" in the language of everyday life implies deprecation of what is characterised as wasteful. This common-sense implication is itself an outcropping of the instinct of workmanship. The popular reprobation of waste goes to say that in order to be at peace with himself the common man must be able to see in any and all human effort and human enjoyment an enhancement of life and well-being on the whole. In order to meet with unqualified approval, any economic fact must approve itself under the test of impersonal usefulness—usefulness as seen from the point of view of the generically human. Relative or competitive advantage of one individual in comparison

with another does not satisfy the economic conscience, and therefore competitive expenditure has not the approval of this conscience.

In strict accuracy nothing should be included under the head of conspicuous waste but such expenditure as is incurred on the ground of an invidious pecuniary comparison. But in order to bring any given item or element in under this head it is not necessary that it should be recognised as waste in this sense by the person incurring the expenditure. It frequently happens that an element of the standard of living which set out with being primarily wasteful, ends with becoming, in the apprehension of the consumer, a necessary of life; and it may in this way become as indispensable as any other item of the consumer's habitual expenditure. As items which sometimes fall under this head, and are therefore available as illustrations of the manner in which this principle applies, may be cited carpets and tapestries, silver table service, waiter's services, silk hats, starched linen, many articles of jewellery and of dress. The indispensability of these things after the habit and the convention have been formed, however, has little to say in the classification of expenditures as waste or not waste in the technical meaning of the word. The test to which all expenditure must be brought in an attempt to decide that point is the question whether it serves directly to enhance human life on the whole—whether it furthers the life process taken impersonally. For this is the basis of award of the instinct of workmanship, and that instinct is the court of final appeal in any question of economic truth or adequacy. It is a question as to the award rendered by a dispassionate common sense. The question is, therefore, not whether, under the existing circumstances of individual habit and social custom, a given expenditure conduces to the particular consumer's gratification or peace of mind; but whether, aside from acquired tastes and from the canons of usage and conventional decency, its result is a net gain in comfort or in the fulness of life. Customary expenditure must be classed under the head of waste in so far as the custom on which it rests is traceable to the habit of making an invidious pecuniary comparison—in so far as it is conceived that it could not have become customary and prescriptive without the backing of this principle of pecuniary reputability or relative economic success.

It is obviously not necessary that a given object of expenditure should be exclusively wasteful in order to come in under the category of conspicuous waste. An article may be useful and wasteful both, and its utility to the consumer may be made up of use and waste in the most varying proportions. Consumable goods, and even productive goods, generally show the two elements in combination, as constituents of their utility; although, in a general way, the element of waste tends to predominate in articles of consumption, while the contrary is true of articles designed for productive use. Even in articles which appear at first glance to serve for pure ostentation only, it is always possible to detect the presence of some, at least ostensible, useful purpose; and on the other hand, even in special machinery and tools contrived for some particular industrial process, as well as in the rudest appliances of human industry, the traces of conspicuous waste, or at least of the habit of ostentation, usually become evident on a close scrutiny. It would be hazardous to assert that a useful purpose is ever absent from the utility of any article or of any service, however obviously its prime purpose and chief element is conspicuous waste; and it would be only less hazardous to assert of any primarily useful product that the element of waste is in no way concerned in its value, immediately or remotely.

16. Business Depression*

WESLEY CLAIR MITCHELL

I. HOW CRISIS BREEDS DEPRESSION

1. ABORTIVE REVIVALS OF ACTIVITY

In both 1893 and 1907 the passing of the panic in America was promptly followed by an increase in business activity. Newspapers and technical journals reported the reopening of mills and factories that had been closed during the panic, the return to the road of commercial travelers who had been recalled, the freer buying of goods, and so forth. Optimists, encouraged by such reports, began to predict a speedy revival of prosperity. The crisis, they argued, had arisen from impaired confidence. If confidence could be restored, no real reason would remain why business should not be resumed on the scale prevailing before the panic. The supply of labor, the stock of raw materials, the equipment for transporting and manufacturing goods had not been reduced in quantity or quality by runs upon the banks or by insolvencies. Everyone was eager to be at work. Let businessmen "look on the bright side," combat skep-

*Source: Reprinted from Wesley Clair Mitchell Business Cycles, chapter 4 (Berkeley: University of California Press, 1913). Footnotes and parenthetical cross-references deleted.

tics by talking prosperity instead of hard times, prove their faith by their works, and all would be well once more.

After both panics a few weeks sufficed to prove the falsity of such predictions and the futility of such a policy. The little burst of activity that followed the panic subsided and hope gave place to renewed discouragement. The acute strain that had marked the panics did not recur, but a slow liquidation dragged on through many months.

The failure of these "sunshine movements" lends point to the question, Why are crises followed by depressions? Why do so many mills that reopen their gates after the season of severe stress is over presently close again? Is the reason solely that the majority of businessmen will not or cannot shake off their gloomy forebodings? Or are there elements in the business situation as left by the crises that make a period of depression inevitable—elements beyond the control of sentiment?

While a decline in current new orders and contracts for future performance begins some months before the crisis ..., yet the close of the crisis finds many factories, mines, contracting firms, and the like with a considerable amount of work still to be performed. A temporary stoppage of operations during a panic may be caused by inability to obtain money for pay rolls, or by doubts concerning the ability of consignees to pay for goods when delivered. But when the banks have ceased to limit payments, and when indiscriminate distrust of the solvency of business enterprises has disappeared, then work is promptly resumed upon these leftover orders and contracts. Other concerns find themselves caught with stocks of raw materials, already on hand or contracted for, far larger than are required by current consumption when orders are light. Their best way of raising money to meet maturing obligations is often to work up and sell these materials, even though very low prices have to be quoted to force a market. Such

conditions account for the reopening of many business enterprises in the weeks immediately following a panic.

But, unless large new orders and contracts are obtained speedily, these business enterprises soon reach the end of their order books or surplus stocks. Then they reduce their working forces, put their plants on part time, or close altogether. As a matter of fact, in neither 1894 nor 1908 did the new business prove sufficient to support the mills that had reopened. Hence the reports of the second, third, and fourth months after the panics told a disappointing tale of new suspensions of industrial operations.

It is the paucity of new orders, then, that blights the hope of a quick restoration of prosperity after a severe crisis. Businessmen may be ready to talk prosperity in the hope that others may be induced to buy; but in their own purchases they practice extreme conservatism. Confidence may be restored in the sense that no one longer doubts the solvency of the banks, or the ability of anyone fairly entitled to credit to borrow. But confidence in the sense of sanguine expectations of profitable prices and a large volume of business is not restored, and cannot be restored by cheerful conversation. Experience enforces the contrary belief that prices will fall and business shrink for some time to come. The processes that work out these results must now be described.

2. THE CUMULATION OF DEPRESSION

A. *The volume of business.* The wholesale discharges of workingmen, which occur during a crisis and again when the leftover contracts and accumulated stocks of materials have been worked off, cause a decline in consumers' demand. Many business and professional men likewise are compelled to retrench their family expenditures. Few people may starve; but tens and hundreds of thousands are forced to put up with a less varied or a less abundant diet. Other lines of expenditure are reduced more sharply than the purchases of food. Clothing and furniture are used longer before being discarded and are replaced at urgent need by cheap articles. Fuel and light are economized to an uncomfortable degree; amusements, travel, and all the dispensable adjuncts to comfort are pared down. Accumulated savings, personal credit at retail shops, and personal property that can be pawned are gradually eaten up by those hardest pressed. As these resources are exhausted, the straits of many families become worse and their purchases of commodities are progressively reduced. Hence the calls upon private and public charity usually increase and consumers' demand usually decreases as the period of hard times drags on.

In general, the current business demand for the raw materials and partly finished products from which consumers' goods are made shrinks with the shrinkage of family expenditure. Indeed, for a time this business demand shrinks even faster than consumers' demand; for either merchants or manufacturers may fill their orders for a while after the crisis from their leftover stocks, which are likely to be larger than they care to carry in a dull market. On the other hand, in order to keep at least a skeleton organization together, manufacturers sometimes make goods for which they have no present sale. But operations of this last kind must necessarily be small.

Information concerning the current demand for such producers' goods as are used in repairs and renewals of existing plants is scanty. Every period of intense activity brings out all the weak points of the active establishments, and leaves many of them in a somewhat run-down condition. The first lull in activity affords a favorable opportunity for overhauling plants and bringing their equipment up to the highest standard of efficiency. But what has been proved to be technically desirable may not be financially expedient. Many alterations

are planned as soon as the reduction in orders gives the managing staffs leisure; but their execution is often deferred until a resumption of active demand for products is in sight. On the whole, a leisurely course is probably taken by the majority of enterprises, so that the demand for repairs and renewals is light during at least the first quarter or two of depression.

Concerning the demand for all the variety of goods that enter into new construction work it is possible to speak with more confidence. While many of the existing factories are standing idle, while many buildings lack tenants, while the railways have light traffic, etc., there is little inducement to enter upon the provision of new equipment. While investors have the recent decline in the price of securities fresh in mind, there is little use in issuing any but the best accredited grade of bonds. Finally, while a further fall of prices is in prospect, it is vain to expect the larger capitalists to take up new projects which can probably be executed more cheaply after the lapse of a year or two. Engineers, architects, and the like may be kept busy preparing plans for future use; but in the early stages of depression few contracts for new construction are actually started. Hence the demand for this kind of work continues the decline that began in the latter days of prosperity.

The processes that cause this shrinking in trade, like the processes that cause an increase in times of revival, are cumulative in their effects. The more workmen discharged, the smaller becomes consumers' demand. Every reduction in consumers' demand causes a further decline in the business demand for the materials from which consumers' goods are made. On the one hand, the latter decline causes more workmen to be discharged, and on the other hand it discourages managers from making the repairs and renewals they have in mind, and discourages capitalists from putting their new projects under contract. The longer these plans for improving and extending the industrial equipment are deferred, the less grows employment in the enterprises that provide materials. And the longer men remain wholly or partly idle, the more are their families forced to scrimp expenditures, so that consumers' demand shrinks still further, and this shrinkage further intensifies the influences that are constricting business.

Nevertheless, the lowest ebb in the physical volume of industrial production usually comes in either the first or second year after a severe crisis. The statistics presented . . . [earlier], and the index numbers of trade compiled by Kemmerer and Irving Fisher, all point to this conclusion. Agricultural production, of course, is more erratic, increasing during depression quite as often as it decreases. What forces counteract the cumulative shrinkage in the physical volume of trade within two or three years after a crisis is a question that must be deferred to the concluding section of this chapter. . . .

B. The fall in prices. As a crisis subsides, the confusion that reigns in the markets for commodities . . . gradually disappears. But, while the extremely low prices made in a few forced sales may not be matched again, the trend of fluctuations continues downward for a considerable period. Thus the fall in wholesale prices after the crisis of 1890 lasted at least four years in Germany and at least six years in England and France; that after the crisis of 1893 lasted four years in America; that after the crisis of 1900 lasted three years in England and four years in Germany and France; that after the crisis of 1907 lasted from one to two years in different places. So far as the evidence of recorded quotations goes, then, the lowest level of commodity prices is reached, not during the crisis, but toward the close of the subsequent depression, or even early in the final revival of business activity. . . .

The chief cause of this fall is the shrinkage in the demand for consumers' goods, raw materials, producers' supplies, and construction work analyzed in the preceding section. On the other side of the market stands a reserve army of capital and labor capable of producing the much larger supplies of commodities for which there was call during the recent expansion. The eagerness of these enterprises now standing idle or working below their capacity to get more business intensifies competition in those branches of trade where it already exists, and often extends competition into branches of trade whence it had been banished by agreements to sustain prices. Pools, working agreements, and combinations of other kinds become far more difficult to sustain in the face of a buyers' market, and many of them go to pieces because their members begin to suspect one another of secret undercutting of rates. Moreover, enterprises verging on bankruptcy and enterprises in the hands of receivers are peculiarly dangerous competitors for solvent firms. They often disregard supplementary charges altogether and seek to defray their operating costs by taking work at prices that rivals who are keeping up interest on their bonds find it hard to match. Finally, the fall in prices is cumulative. It spreads from one part of the system of prices to other parts . . . , and then spreads back again from the parts that are slow to be affected to the parts in which the decline began.

As on the rise, so on the fall, there are marked differences in the promptness with which different classes of commodity prices begin to change and in the degree to which the change extends. Retail prices lag behind producers' goods; manufactured commodities lag behind the raw materials from which they are made; farm and forest products are less regular in their fluctuations than mineral products. These differences arise partly from the differences in the shrinkage of demand pointed out above, partly from technical circumstances affecting the possibility of adjusting current production to current consumption, and partly from the effort to adjust selling prices to the total costs incurred by business enterprises rather than to the buying prices of particular wares.

For reasons sufficiently explained, the prices of labor fall less rapidly than the prices of commodities at wholesale. Interest rates on long-time loans behave like wage rates in that they decline at a slow pace, but unlike wage rates in that they fall for a longer time. Short-time interest rates, on the contrary, fall faster and further than commodity prices. There is less hesitation to lend funds freely at low rates for three months than for ten years, and large sums which the owners will later invest in more permanent ways are transferred during depressions from the bond to the money market, checking the fall of rates in the first and accelerating the fall in the second.

As for the prices of securities, high-grade bonds rise because of the decline in long-time interest rates, while, at the other end of the scale, common stocks fall under the combined influence of diminished earnings and dull prospects. Securities that stand between these extremes, like speculative bonds, stocks with a good dividend-paying record, and preferred stocks, rise or fall according as they partake more of the character of gilt-edged bonds or of common stocks. Usually, their relation to common stocks is closer and prices decline, though less than the prices of ordinary shares.

C. *Savings and investments.* What is known concerning changes in money incomes during depressions suggests that the amount saved declines heavily—a conclusion that receives at least a measure of statistical support from data on deposits in savings banks. That the funds required for current investments in the extension of old or the construction of new concerns also shrink seriously is attested by abundant evidence. Finally, the often noted change in the preference of investors— their neglect of speculative shares which were the favorites of flush days and their taste for ultraconservative bonds—is also demonstrated.

All this corresponds to expectations. But the investment market presents one peculiar feature. The first year of depression often brings an exceedingly heavy issue of securities by large corporations. The apparent anomaly, however, has a simple explanation. During the high tide of prosperity preceding a crisis, many great enterprises provide for their most pressing financial needs by selling short-time notes or by borrowing directly from banks. . . . After the crisis when interest rates have begun to relax, they seek the first opportunity to fund these floating debts into long-time bonds. Of course, large issues of securities made for such purposes represent neither extensions of new equipment nor investments of fresh capital, but at most a shifting from one form of obligation to another, and from one set of lenders to another.

D. *The currency and the banks.* Upon the production of gold, the proportion of the output applied to monetary uses, and the international movements of the existing monetary stock, depression exercises a complicated set of influences which need not be described in detail because they are the precise opposites of the influence exercised by prosperity. . . . The net outcome of all the factors involved differs from one depression to the next. In the United States, the one country for which we have adequate data, the stock of gold currency declined in the dull months January to July 1891, February to November 1894, July to September 1895, April to July 1896, March to May 1908, and July 1909 to April 1910; but it rose during the dull months January to May 1897, May to November 1908, April 1910 to May 1911, and during the dull years 1903–04. Thus the belief that the quantity of gold currency contracts regularly with the pecuniary volume of business is not supported by the available evidence.

As for other kinds of money, bank notes alone possess pretensions to elasticity that merit serious consideration. But a survey of the records for England, France, and Germany, as well as for the United States, shows that the amount outstanding has seldom shrunk in years of business depression.

Much more decided than its influence upon the volume of the currency is the influence of depression upon the distribution of the money in circulation between the banks and the public. As soon as the strain of a severe crisis relaxes, current deposits of cash in the banks begin to exceed current withdrawals, so that presently the banks hold a decidedly larger proportion of the monetary stock than in seasons of active trade.

Of course, this process increases the deposits of the banks so far as deposits represent actual cash. In addition, the large reserves increase the ability of the banks to lend their own credit, and therefore to extend the deposits that result from discounts. Nevertheless, deposit currency usually shrinks when prosperity merges into depression. The elasticity of this element in the circulating medium, indeed, is decidedly greater than that of money. As a result, the ratio between deposits subject to check and money in circulation falls in dull years.

. . . the velocity of the circulation of money, and in higher degree the velocity of the circulation of checks, declines with the activity of trade.

By these changes in the quantity of money and of deposit currency and in the velocities at which both money and checks circulate, the volume of payments is reduced in harmony with the fall of prices and the shrinkage in the physical volume of trade. In this complicated series of readjustments the causative influences, however, are not all on the side of the business situation. The failure of the quantity of money to contract promptly when a crisis turns into depression results in monetary re-dundancy, of which the visible sign is the accumulation of idle cash in the banks. This accumulation, we have seen, does not produce the expansion in loans and deposits that would occur if the prospects of profits were bright. But it does increase the competition among banks for such business as is to be had, and aids in producing that fall in the discount rates which we have seen to be more rapid than the fall of prices at wholesale. . . . In so far, the quantity of money is a factor in accelerating the readjustment of costs to selling prices that ultimately restores the prospects of profits and ushers in a period of expanding trade and rising prices. . . . Hence such an increase in the world's production of gold as has been going on in recent years tends to cut short and to mitigate depressions as well as to prolong and to intensify prosperity. By thus altering somewhat both the intensity and the relative duration of these two phases of business cycles, it tends to give an upward direction to those long-period movements of the price curve in which the years of depression and of prosperity are averaged.

II. HOW DEPRESSION BREEDS PROSPERITY

1. READJUSTMENT OF PRIME COSTS

The shrinkage in orders that depression brings and the accompanying decline in selling prices put severe pressure upon the managers of business enterprises to reduce their expenses within the narrowest feasible limits. Certain of the price phenomena . . . indicate that the resulting efforts are successful at least in part.

That wholesale prices fall faster than retail prices, that the prices of producers' goods fall faster than those of consumers' goods, and that the prices of raw materials fall faster than the prices of manufactured products means, of course, that in these cases buying prices are reduced more than the corresponding selling prices. Further, since short-time interest rates fall much faster than wholesale prices, the cost of loans declines in proportion to the prices of products. Wages also are reduced in seasons of severe depression, but in this case the reduction is less than that in commodity prices. It does not necessarily follow, however, that the cost of labor increases in proportion to the selling prices of what labor produces. For there is strong evidence that the efficiency of labor becomes much greater in dull years than it is in brisk years. Overtime ceases, and with it ceases not only the payment of extra rates but also the weariness of long hours. When working forces are reduced in size they are raised in quality by weeding out the less desirable hands. Most important of all, the fear of being discharged at a time when thousands of men are already looking in vain for work disposes every man who is kept to do his best— to keep any pace that may be set, even at grave danger of overtaxing his strength. . . . The heightening of the physical productivity of labor that results from these changes does more than the fall of wages to diminish the ratio between money cost of labor and money value of products.

When selling prices have been materially reduced, enterprises that are poorly equipped, disadvantageously located, or inefficiently managed are often compelled to close altogether, because they cannot get back even their prime costs on an output sold at current rates. Within the stronger enterprises the poorer portions of the equipment are allowed to stand idle for the same reason. Consequently producers who remain in the race during depressions can "figure" on the basis of prime costs considerably lower than the average that prevails during prosperity.

Finally, depression checks the numerous small wastes that grow up within most business enterprises during years of intense activity. There is not only a strong incentive but also sufficient leisure to economize materials, to

make the most of by-products, to supervise the work of every employee, to adjust each successive step of each process accurately to the other steps, and to change the organization in any ways that promise a saving of cost without entailing a heavy investment of fresh capital.

2. READJUSTMENT OF SUPPLEMENTARY COSTS

Reductions in prime costs begin promptly upon the passing of prosperity. But, for a while at least, they are accompanied by an increase of supplementary costs per unit of product, arising from the distribution of the existing fixed charges over a declining volume of sales. To determine the average net effect of these opposing changes upon total cost per unit is impossible for lack of information, detailed in character and extensive in scope, regarding the quantitative importance of the numerous factors involved. But, whatever these net effects, it is certain that the policy of making selling prices cover total costs is perforce abandoned by many enterprises when business enters upon the phase of depression. Competition for what business is to be had often results in a temporary disregard of supplementary costs and the basing of quotations upon estimates that include little beyond the prices of materials, freight, and labor.

Obviously such a disregard of supplementary costs in fixing selling prices cannot continue long without threatening insolvency. Unless the coupons of bondholders and the rents of lessors are met, the creditors will insist on the appointment of a receiver to manage the property in their interest. But, under the modern form of business organization, insolvency does not necessarily involve suspension of operations. When a considerable sum has been invested in real estate, plant, machinery, or good will, so specialized in form that it cannot be diverted to other uses without serious loss, then an insolvent concern is usually kept running as long as it can pay even a slight margin above the indispensable current expenses. The financial obligations of the enterprise, however, are so reorganized as to turn the temporary disregard of supplementary costs into a permanent reduction of fixed charges. The bondholders may be forced to concede a reduction in the rate of interest or in the nominal value of their principal, lessors may be compelled to scale down their rents, preferred shares may be turned into common, outsiders may buy the whole company under foreclosure at a price that leaves little for the common stockholders, or some other plan of reorganization may be arranged among the various parties at interest that enables the enterprise to continue its business with some prospect of meeting all its obligations.

Such forced reductions of supplementary costs are a common feature not only of the months succeeding a crisis but also of the years of depression that follow. For many enterprises that weather the violent storm are so weakened that they cannot withstand the prolonged strain of low prices and meager business. And both the weak enterprises still struggling desperately to avoid receiverships and the enterprises that have been reorganized are especially dangerous competitors for solvent concerns, and make it difficult for the latter to avoid a similar compromise with their creditors. But just as fast as the process of reorganization is carried through, the prospects of profits are improved by the scaling down of costs.

A somewhat similar, but less drastic, reduction of supplementary costs is gradually effected in many enterprises that never pass through the hands of receivers. Reluctantly managers write down the book value of plants and equipment that are not paying their way. New men buy into old enterprises and estimate the selling prices they must charge on the basis of the moderate sums they have invested. As old leases

run out they may well be renewed at lower rents, and as old bonds mature they may well be replaced at lower rates of interest. More in general, businessmen are constrained to admit to themselves and to their bankers that the capitalized values of their enterprises have suffered somewhat the same decline that the stock exchange records for listed securities. While these reduced capitalizations arise primarily from the reduction of profits, they also become the basis for reduced expectations of return, and justify a smaller capital charge in fixing selling prices.

Finally, such new enterprises as may be set on foot during depression have the advantage not only of low prime costs, conferred by improved processes and machinery, but also of low supplementary costs, conferred by the low prices for construction work and the low interest on bonds.

3. INCREASE IN THE PHYSICAL VOLUME OF BUSINESS

In section I, 2, A, evidence is cited that the physical volume of business reaches its lowest ebb within the first or second year after a crisis. In other words, the second or third year of depression usually ushers in an expansion in the quantity of goods turned out by factories, transported by railways, and handled by merchants. What are the processes that bring about this result in the face of the many discouraging circumstances of dull times?

First, the accumulated stocks of goods carried over from the preceding period of prosperity are gradually disposed of. Even when current consumption is small, manufacturers and merchants can reduce their stocks of raw materials and finished wares by filling orders chiefly from what is on hand and confining purchases to the small quantities needed to keep full assortments. But when these stocks have once been reduced to the smallest dimensions allowed by the regular filling of orders, then current purchases and current production are perforce increased, even though current consumption does not grow larger.

In somewhat similar fashion, families can get on for a time with the clothing and furnishings purchased in the later days of prosperity, and business enterprises with their old equipment—not, however, indefinitely. As these articles are gradually worn out and discarded, it becomes necessary to buy new ones, if money can be found for the purpose. Then the demand for both consumers' and producers' goods begins to pick up.

Third, aggregate consumers' demand depends in large part upon the population, and the number has been shown to increase at almost the same rate in depression as in good times. This factor counts for nothing in France, but for much in Germany, and for something in England. Its importance in the United States is uncertain, because we have no adequate statistics comparing the excess of births over deaths with the excess of emigrants over immigrants.

Once more, the development of new tastes among consumers, the appearance of new materials, and the introduction of new processes do not come to a standstill even during depressions. While changes in demand may restrict the market for commodities that are being superseded, the losses of their producers are gradually written off and the stimulating effect of activity among producers of the novelties remains.

Finally, and most important of all, demand for new construction increases markedly during the later stages of depression. While the amount saved each year by the people of any country probably declines in hard times, certainly saving never ceases. For a time, however, the fresh accumulations of capital are not accompanied by a corresponding volume of fresh investments in business ventures. Refunding operations constitute a large proportion of the business done in the investment market, for governments and business enterprises alike are keen to take advantage

of the low interest rates that then prevail. Of the money seeking fresh investments, whether it is the product of current savings or of refunding, much goes into the purchase of property that embarrassed holders are forced to sell. That is, certainly a considerable and probably an extremely large share of the liquid capital provided by certain individuals during depressions is used merely to cancel part of the losses incurred by other individuals. Such investments represent a redistribution of ownership, but no new creations of industrial equipment. Finally, a part of the funds that in the prosperous phase of the business cycle seek the investment market are left during the earlier stages of depression on deposit in the banks, and used, so far as a use can be found, in making short-time loans. . . .

Changes in the business situation that in the later stages of depression direct investment funds once more to the construction of new equipment are numerous.

1) When most of the weaker owners of business enterprises have once been squeezed out and forced to sell their holdings, and when the necessary corporate reorganizations have been largely completed, the opportunities to buy into old enterprises on favorable terms become less numerous. Thereafter more of the men seeking business openings build for themselves.

2) The timidity inspired among investors by the crisis gradually wears off, and capitalists large and small become more ready to risk their funds in business ventures.

3) The low rate of interest at which money can be borrowed on long time, provided good security is offered, means that the more enterprising spirits can borrow whatever funds they require in addition to their own means on terms that will keep the fixed charges moderate for years to come.

4) Even more important in most cases in its bearing on fixed charges is the low initial cost at which contracts for construction can be let when labor is efficient and materials are cheap.

5) Under the influence of systematic research in recent times the progress of industrial technique has become fairly steady and continuous. Hence, the longer the period during which new construction is checked by business depression the greater becomes the accumulation of technical improvements of which new plants can take advantage, and therefore the greater becomes the inducement to invest in new equipment.

6) The gradual growth of the current demand for consumers' and producers' goods, brought about in the manner already explained, stimulates the investment demand with which we are now dealing. When current orders begin to increase, the managers of existing enterprises are encouraged to begin the improvements in their facilities that perhaps have been planned for several years, and the organizers of new ventures are encouraged to let their contracts. Both sets of investors are eager to make their bargains for construction before the cost of building advances and to have their new plants ready for operation by the time a revival of activity becomes pronounced.

Under the combined pressure of these various business forces, then, a marked increase in demand for all the innumerable kinds of commodities and labor required for construction occurs in the later stages of depression. Of course this increase in the volume of demand from investors causes fuller employment of labor and assures more orders to the existing producers of producers' goods. A new expansion in consumers' and producers' demand follows, which reacts in the way suggested to enhance investment demand. Thus the increase in business is cumulative. Unless the processes we have traced are checked by some untoward event such as a serious failure of crops, within a year or two they carry the physical volume of business to higher levels than those reached at the close of the preceding period of prosperity.

4. THE END OF LIQUIDATION

The various processes just described combine reductions in both prime costs and fixed charges with an expansion in the physical volume of business. In this fashion depression ultimately brings about revival. For of course these changes increase prospective profits, and in the money economy prospective profits are the great incentive to activity.

But for many months the processes by which depression works its own ending are kept down to a slow pace by the continued fall of prices. For the data . . . [shown earlier], indicate that the price level and even the pecuniary volume of business usually continue to fall for some time after the physical volume of business has begun to rise. The rate at which prices fall, however, is slower in the later than in the earlier stages of depression. And the effect of the fall in reducing profits is mitigated, if not wholly offset, by increasing sales. For to the various factors already mentioned as reducing supplementary costs per unit another factor is added when fixed charges begin to be distributed over an increasing output.

The business situation into which depression evolves, then, differs radically from the situation in which it began. Most of the heavy stocks of goods that hung menacingly over the market at the close of the crisis have been disposed of, so that every increase of consumption leads to an equivalent increase of production. The "floating" debts and the heavy fixed charges that threatened widespread insolvency have been paid off, written down, or otherwise readjusted, so that the enterprises can once more live within their incomes. Even the great mass of business enterprises that did not change hands and that did not compromise with their creditors are now assigned a lower capitalized value corresponding to their moderate expectations of profit. Outstanding credits are well within the limits mercantile houses and banks can support. Investors have ceased to be foolishly timid, and they have not yet become recklessly bold. Prices are still declining, but at a slackening pace. Costs of doing business have been so reduced as to leave a narrow margin of profit despite the low scale of selling prices. The demand for goods of many kinds—though not such as to tax the existing equipment to its utmost—is already large and growing steadily larger.

In fine, this . . . [is] the situation out of which a revival of activity presently develops. Having thus come round again to its point of departure, after tracing the processes of cumulative change by which prosperity breeds crisis, crisis evolves into depression, and depression paves the way for a return of prosperity, the present theory of business cycles has reached its appointed end.

17. Transactions and Concerns*

JOHN R. COMMONS

1. FROM CORPORATIONS TO GOING CONCERNS

In the year 1893 the people of the State of Indiana made a demand upon the legislature for an equalization of taxes upon the property of the great public utility corporations—such as railways running across the state—with the property of farmers, manufacturers, and business men. Property at that time meant corporeal property and incorporeal property, the physical goods of lands, buildings, railway tracks, stocks of inventories on hand; and the debts and shares of stock owned by individuals or corporations. The incorporeal property escaped the assessors, partly because concealed, partly because the *situs* for taxation purposes followed the domicile of the owner, which, in the case of corporations, was deemed to be the state under whose laws the charter was granted and in which the corporation was required to have its legal office. In response to the demand the legislature of Indiana changed the assessment of these corporations from the valuation of their physical property in Indiana to the total market value of their stocks and bonds, as bought and sold on the New York Stock Exchange, and then prorated that value to the State of Indiana in the proportion that the mileage in Indiana bore to the total mileage in all the states.

What happened was that a corporation which hitherto had only a legal existence in the state of its incorporation, because it was an invisible legal entity existing only in contemplation of law, now became an economic going concern existing in its transactions wherever it carried on business and gained thereby the net income which gave value to its stocks and bonds on the stock exchange.

The State of Ohio copied this legislation and it went from Ohio to the United States Supreme Court where it was sustained in 1897. The Court found that the sum total of all the corporeal property of the Adams Express Company in Ohio was only $23,400; but Ohio's share, according to mileage, of the total market value of all the stocks and bonds was $450,000, an intangible property about twelve times as valuable as the corporeal property. The Adams Express Company, instead of a corpora-

*Source: Reprinted from John R. Commons, *Institutional Economics*, section 2, chapter 2 (New York: The Macmillan Company, 1934). Reprinted by permission of the publisher. Footnotes deleted.

tion located in New York, becomes a going concern existing wherever it does business.

A similar transition from the legal to the economic meaning was made by the Supreme Court in the dissolution suit against the United States Steel Company in 1920. The company was incorporated as a holding company in the State of New Jersey. The Department of Justice brought suit to have the holding company dissolved, as a violation of the anti-trust laws, but the Court investigated the practices of its subsidiaries in different parts of the country and found them to be reasonable restraints of trade. One of these practices, not brought before the Court in 1920, the so-called "Pittsburgh Plus" practice of discrimination, came before the Federal Trade Commission in 1923, on petition of a wide-spread Western Association of Rolled Steel Consumers. The practice consisted in quoting all prices of steel at Pittsburgh, plus the freight to the point of delivery, no matter where manufactured. The buyer, according to the contract, did not obtain title at Pittsburgh, but obtained title only at the point where he used the steel. This practice, it was claimed by the lawyers in prosecution, created a monopoly located at the legal *situs* of the holding company in New Jersey. If this claim was correct, the remedy was dissolution of the holding company as a subterfuge to evade the anti-trust laws. Similar dissolutions, on that ground, had been ordered in the Standard Oil and Tobacco Company cases.

But the economists in the Pittsburgh Plus case, Fetter, Ripley, and Commons, argued that it was a discrimination rather than a monopoly, the discrimination existing wherever the corporation did business, and that the proper remedy was not dissolution, but the transfer of legal title to the product at any point where the steel was manufactured, whether Pittsburgh, Chicago, Duluth, or Birmingham. The company owned plants in all of these places, and the cost

of production *plus freight* might be *less* when manufactured in Chicago and shipped to Iowa, *away* from Pittsburgh, than when manufactured in Pittsburgh and shipped to Iowa. But Iowa did not get the advantage of lower costs and shorter haul when the Chicago plant quoted its price on the Pittsburgh base plus freight from Pittsburgh. Furthermore the plant at Chicago selling *towards* Pittsburgh charged a *lower* delivered price to its customer than its delivered price to a customer who used the steel at a point nearer Chicago. This was the practice of "dumping," or selling in a distant market at lower prices than those charged in the home market. The issue was, whether there was a free competitive market when the thirty-year-old custom of the steel business designated as the *place of alienating legal control* the thousands of places of physical delivery to customers, or whether the ideal of equal opportunity and free competition required that *legal control* should pass at the point of manufacture.

The Federal Trade Commission, on this interpretation, ordered discontinuance of Pittsburgh as the basing point and the substitution of the places of actual manufacture as the basing points. The order did not fully carry out the interpretation of the economists that legal title should pass to the customer at the place of manufacture in order that all customers might have equal opportunity to *compete for legal control* at that place, but it substantially accomplished what the economists intended.

The significant point, however, is that in the Adams Express and U.S. Steel cases mentioned, the Court or the Federal Trade Commission disregarded the domicile of the corporation in the state of its creation, and passed from a legal corporation existing only in law to an economic going concern existing wherever it does business.

This transition in meaning, while it had been going on in many other cases, involved still another transition from the older economists' meaning of an "exchange," as a physical transfer of commodities, to the institutional meaning of a transaction as a legal transfer of ownership. It was ownership that fixed prices and permitted competition, and it was the transfer of ownership, instead of physical exchange, that determined whether competition was fair or discriminatory.

2. FROM EXCHANGE TO TRANSACTIONS

John Locke's meaning of Labor was his personification of Law, Economics, and Ethics. Labor, with him, meant justification of ownership as well as the existence of material things that were owned. This double meaning of Ownership and Material Wealth continued to be the meaning of the orthodox economists for two hundred years, and they therefore concealed the field of institutional economics. It was this concealed ownership side of the double meaning of Wealth that angered the heterodox economists from Marx and Proudhon in the middle of the Nineteenth Century to Sorel at the opening of the Twentieth Century. We shall distinguish the two meanings and yet discover a correlation of materials and ownership, not in Locke's personification of Labor, but in a *unit of economic activity*, a Transaction, and in that expectation of beneficial transactions which is a larger unit of economic activity, a Going Concern.

This falls in with an analogy to the recent correlation of the separate sciences of physics, chemistry, and astronomy, by the discovery of a unit of activity common to all of them. Roughly speaking, the former units in physics had been molecules, the units in chemistry had been atoms, the units in astronomy had been planets and stars. And the "energies" which made these units go were heat, electricity, chemical affinity, gravity. But nowadays the unit common

to all of them is a unit of activity, the interaction of corpuscular wave-lengths, and the concept of "energy" disappears. Four hundred million million vibrations per second are the color red in the human mind, but they are that many wave-lengths in physics, chemistry, and astronomy.

This analogy roughly describes the problem of correlating law, economics, and ethics. It is the problem of discovering a unit of activity common to them.

In the field of economics the units had been, first, Locke's and Ricardo's material *commodities owned* and the *individuals* who owned the commodities, while the "energy" was human *labor*. Next, the units continued to be the same or similar physical commodities and their ownership, but the individuals became those who *consumed* commodities and the "energy" became the stimuli of *wants*, depending upon the quantity and kind of commodity wanted. The first was the objective side, the other the subjective side of the same relation between the individual and the forces of nature, the latter, however, in the form of materials, owned by the individuals. An "exchange," so called, was a labor process of delivering and receiving commodities, or a "subjective exchange-value." In any case, by analogy to the older physical science, these opposing energies of labor and want, magnified into "elasticities" of supply and demand, could be physically correlated by the materialistic metaphor of an automatic tendency towards equilibrium of commodities in exchange against each other, analogous to the atoms of water in the ocean, but personified as "seeking their level" at Ricardo's "margin of cultivation" or Menger's "marginal utility." This equilibrium was accomplished by the "neo-classicists," led by Alfred Marshall (1890).

There was no need of a further correlation with law or ethics—in fact these latter were necessarily excluded, because the relations on which the economic units were constructed were relations between man and nature, not between man and man. One was Ricardo's relation between human labor and the resistance of nature's forces; the other was Menger's relation between the quantity wanted of nature's forces and the quantity available. Neither statute law, nor ethics, nor custom, nor judicial decision had anything to do with either of these relationships; or rather, all these might be eliminated by assuming that ownership was identical with the materials owned, in order to construct a theory of pure economics based solely on the physical exchange of materials and services.

The latter was done. This identity of ownership and materials was accepted as a matter of custom, without investigation. It was assumed that all commodities were owned, but the ownership was assumed to be identical with the physical thing owned, and therefore was overlooked as something to be taken for granted. The theories were worked out as physical materials, omitting anything of property rights, because they were "natural."

The historical and ethical schools of economists, led by Roscher, Schmoller, and others, revolted against these eliminations of ownership. These schools, even in their culminating form of the "ideal typus" as proposed by Rickert and Max Weber, never were able to incorporate into what remained merely descriptions or subjective ideals of historical process, the economic principles derived from Ricardo and Menger. This, however, can be done if we discover a unit of activity common to law, economics, and ethics.

If the subject-matter of political economy is not only individuals and nature's forces, but is human beings getting their living out of each other by mutual transfers of property rights, then it is to law and ethics that we look for the critical turning points of this human activity.

The courts of law deal with human activity in its relation, not of man to na-

ture, but to the *ownership* of nature by man. But they deal with this activity only at a certain point, the point of *conflict of interests* between plaintiff and defendant. But classical economic theory, based on relations of man to nature, had no conflict of interests in its units of investigation, since its units were *commodities* and *individuals* with ownership omitted. These ultimate units produced, in fact, along with the analogy of equilibrium, a *harmony* of interests rather than a *conflict* of interests. Hence the ultimate unit to be sought in the problem of correlating law, economics, and ethics is a unit of conflicting interests of ownership.

But this is not enough. The ultimate unit of activity must also be a unit of *mutually dependent interests*. The relation of man to man is one of interdependence as well as conflict.

Still further, this ultimate unit must be one which not only is continually *repeating* itself, with variations, but also one whose repetitions are expected by the participants to continue, in the future, substantially similar to what they are in the present and have been in the past. The unit must contain security of expectations. This kind of expectation we name *Order*.

This meaning of Order is derived from the fact that the future is wholly uncertain except as based upon reliable inferences drawn from experiences of the past; and also from the fact that it may properly be said that man lives in the future but acts in the present. For these reasons the unit of activity contains a factor that indicates anticipation, or, literally, the act of seizing beforehand the limiting or strategic factors upon whose present control it is expected the outcome of the future may also be more or less controlled, provided there is security of expectations. This is indeed the dominant characteristic of human activity, distinguishing it from all the physical sciences. We shall later separate it out abstractedly and give it the general name of *Futurity*. But the orderly expectations, assumed by all economists under the name of "security," which is a special case of the general principle of Futurity, we name, for our present purposes, simply Order.

Thus, the ultimate unit of activity, which correlates law, economics, and ethics, must contain in itself the three principles of *conflict, dependence,* and *order*. This unit is a Transaction. A transaction, with its participants, is the smallest unit of institutional economics. Transactions intervene between the production of labor, of the classical economists, and the pleasures of consumption, of the hedonic economists, simply because it is society that, by its rules of order, controls ownership of and access to the forces of nature. Transactions, as thus defined, are not the "exchange of commodities," in the physical sense of "delivery," they are the alienation and acquisition, between individuals, of the *rights* of future ownership of physical things, as determined by the collective working rules of society. The *transfer of these rights* must therefore be negotiated between the parties concerned, according to the working rules of society, before labor can produce, or consumers can consume, or commodities be physically delivered to other persons.

When we analyze transactions, which are the transfers of ownership, we find that they resolve themselves into three types, which may be distinguished as Bargaining, Managerial, and Rationing transactions. These are functionally interdependent and together constitute the whole which we name a Going Concern. A going concern is a joint expectation of beneficial bargaining, managerial, and rationing transactions, kept together by "working rules" and by control of the changeable strategic or "limiting" factors which are expected to control the others. When the expectations cease then the concern quits going and production stops.

This going concern is itself a larger unit, and is analogous to that which in biology is Filmer's "organism," or in physics is Locke's "mechanism." But its components are not living cells, nor electrons, nor atoms—they are Transactions.

We shall here anticipate our subsequent investigational trials and errors and shall set up the conclusions of our historical research by constructing a formula of a bargaining transaction, and then distinguish it from the formulae of managerial and rationing transactions.

1. BARGAINING TRANSACTIONS

By a study of the theories of economists, in the light of decisions of courts, the bargaining unit is found to consist of *four* parties, two buyers and two sellers, all of whom are treated legally as *equals* by the ruling authority that decides disputes. The resulting formula may be pictured in terms of the offers made by the participants, as follows, where the buyers offer to pay $100 and $90 respectively, for a commodity, and the sellers offer to accept $110 and $120 respectively.

Formula of Bargaining Transaction—Legal Equals

B	$100	B^1	$ 90
S	$110	S^1	$120

On the other hand, managerial and rationing transactions are, in law and economics, the relation of a superior to an inferior. In the managerial transaction the superior is an individual or a hierarchy of individuals, giving orders which the inferiors must obey, such as the relations of foreman to worker, or sheriff to citizen, or manager to managed. But in the rationing transaction the superior is a collective superior or its official spokesman. These are of various kinds, such as a board of directors of a corporation, or a legislature, or a court of law, or an arbitration tribunal, or a communist or fascist government, or a cartel, or a trade union, or a taxing authority, which prorates among inferiors the burdens and benefits of the concern. The formula of a managerial or rationing transaction is therefore the picture of a relation between *two* parties instead of four, as follows:

Formula of Managerial and
Rationing Transactions

Legal Superior

Legal Inferior

It should be kept in mind that the formula of a transaction is not a copy of nature or reality—it is merely a mental configuration of the least unit of economic theory—a unit of investigation by means of which reality may be understood.

Here it is first necessary to distinguish the double and even triple meaning of the word Exchange, already referred to as used by the early economists, which served to conceal the marketing process of bargaining from the labor process of managing, and from the authoritative process of rationing, as well as the legal from the economic process.

The concept of exchange had its historical origin in the precapitalistic period of markets and fairs. The merchant then was a peddler who carried his goods or coins to market and physically exchanged them with other merchants. Yet he really combined in himself two entirely different activities not made use of by the economists: the labor activity of physical delivery and physical acceptance of commodities, and the legal activity of alienation and acquisition of their ownership. The one was physical delivery of physical control over commodities or metallic money, the other was legal transfer of legal control. The one was an Exchange, the other a Transaction.

The difference is fundamental and was not incorporated in economic theory, because materials were not distinguished from their ownership. The *individual* does not tranfer ownership. Only the state, or, in medieval times, the "market overt," by operation of law as interpreted by the courts, transfers ownership by reading intentions into the minds of participants in a transaction. The two kinds of transfer have been separated in capitalistic industry. Legal control is transferred at the centers of capitalism, like New York, London, or Paris, but physical control is transferred at the ends of the earth by laborers acting under the commands of those who have legal control. The transfer of legal control is the outcome of a Bargaining Transaction. The transportation of commodities and the delivery of physical control is a labor process of adding "place utility" to a material thing. This labor process, from the legal standpoint, we distinguish as Managerial Transactions.

The individualistic economists necessarily added to their meaning of Exchange the mutual grant of considerations. But this was treated, not objectively as alienation of ownership, but subjectively as a pleasure-pain choice between commodities; whereas, from the legal bargaining standpoint, it is the volitional negotiations of the persuasion or coercion between persons deemed to be legally equal and free, which terminate in reciprocal transfers of *legal control* of commodities and money by operation of existing law in view of the expectations of what the courts will do in case of dispute.

It was the latter meaning of an Exchange which the common-law judges of England, in the Sixteenth Century, recognized in their decisions of disputes between conflicting merchants, by taking over the bargaining customs of merchants on the markets and deciding disputes in conformity with those customs, in so far as they approved the custom. These customs, when taken over by the courts, became, in Anglo-American law, technically known as the doctrines of *assumpsit* and *quantum meruit*.

Broadly interpreted these doctrines run as follows: Let it be inferred, in the ordinary course of trade according to the custom of merchants, that, when a person had acquired a commodity or money from another person, he did not intend robbery or theft or deceit, but intended to accept responsibility to pay for it or to deliver a commodity or service in exchange (implied assumpsit); and further, he did not intend, by economic coercion or physical duress, to overcome the will of the other person as to the terms of the transfer of ownership, but intended to pay or perform what was fair or reasonable (quantum meruit).

This inference of intention to accept responsibility and a moral duty to pay or perform was necessary because the courts were called upon, in case of a dispute, to create a legal duty by enforcing obedience of payment or performance implied in the negotiations. And this applied not only to deferred performance or payment, usually known as debt, but also to immediate performance or payment, usually known as a sale or cash transaction. It is these negotiations and intended alienation and acquisition of legal ownership, in consideration of payment or performance, that we name a Bargaining Transaction, leaving the physical "exchange" to the labor process, which we name physical delivery, enforced by the law of managerial transactions if necessary.

Parallel to these doctrines of assumpsit and quantum meruit the courts, in developing the law of freedom from duress, constructed an ethical standard of the "willing buyer and willing seller" by making inferences as to what was going on in the minds of participants. This willingness has been, since then, the standard set up for the decision of disputes arising from bargaining transactions, whether commodity bargains on the produce markets, wage bargains on the labor markets, stock and bond bargains on the stock exchange, interest bargains on the money markets, or rent and land bargains on the real estate markets. In all of these bargains the doctrines of assumpsit, quantum meruit, and duress have had an explicit or implied influence in questions of transfer of ownership.

How, then, shall the economist construct a unit of activity, the bargaining transaction, which shall fit this evolution of the common law, derived, as it is, from thousands of decisions of courts? We have found that economists had already constructed the formula as above, applicable to markets. The bargaining consists of four parties, two buyers and two sellers, each, however, governed by the past and expected decisions of the courts in case of dispute, if a conflict of interests reaches that crisis. Out of a universal formula which may thus be constructed so as to include these four participants offering to transfer ownership, and acting in line with customs approved in legal decisions, may be derived four economic and legal relations between man and man, so intimately bound together that a change in one of them will change the magnitudes of one or more of the other three. They are the issues derived from a fourfold conflict of interests latent in every bargaining transaction, and the decisions of the American courts on economic disputes are readily classified in these four directions. Each decision has for its object the establishment of working rules as precedents which shall bring expectation of mutuality and order out of the conflict of interests. All of these relate to ownership of materials and not to the materials.

1) The first issue is, Equal or Unequal Opportunity, which is the legal doctrine of Reasonable and Unreasonable Discrimination. Each buyer is choosing between the best two sellers, and each seller is choosing between the best two buyers. If a seller, for example a railroad company, or telegraph company, or steel corporation, charges a higher price to one buyer and therefore a lower price to that buyer's competitor, for exactly similar service, then the first buyer, under modern conditions of narrow margins of profit, is unreasonably discriminated against, and eventually may be bankrupted. But if there is

good ground for the discrimination, such as a difference in quantity, cost, or quality, then the discrimination is reasonable and therefore lawful. The same doctrine appears in many cases of labor arbitration and commercial arbitration.

2) Another issue, inseparable from the first, is that of Fair or Unfair Competition. The two buyers are competitors and the two sellers are competitors, and may use unfair methods in their competition. The decisions on unfair competition have built up, during three hundred years, the modern asset of good-will, the biggest asset of modern business.

3) The third issue, inseparable from the other two, is that of Reasonable or Unreasonable Price or Value. One of the two buyers will buy from one of the two sellers. The price will depend on the three economic conditions, Opportunity for Choice, Competition of buyer with buyer and seller with seller, and Equality or Inequality of Bargaining Power between the actual buyer and the actual seller, who are nevertheless equals in law. This reasonable price is gradually constructed, in the minds of successive courts, on the three prerequisites of Equal Opportunity, Fair Competition, and Equality of Bargaining Power.

4) Finally, in the American decisions appears the dominant issue of Due Process of Law. It is this issue which we name a "working rule," which regulates individual transactions. The Supreme Court of the United States has acquired authority to overrule state legislatures, the Federal Congress, and all executives, in all cases where these are deemed by the Court to deprive individuals or corporations of property or liberty "without due process of law." Due process of law is the working rule of the Supreme Court for the time being. It changes with changes in custom and class dominance, or with changes in judges, or with changes in the opinions of judges, or with changes in the customary meanings of property and liberty. If a state legislature or the Federal Congress, or a lower court, or an executive, deprives any of the four participants in a transaction of his equal choice of opportunities, or his liberty of competition, or his bargaining power in fixing a price, that act of deprivation is a "taking" of both his property and his liberty. If the deprivation cannot be justified to the satisfaction of the Court, then it is a deprivation of property and liberty *without* due process of law, and is therefore unconstitutional and void, and will be enjoined.

Thus, if the formula of a bargaining transaction is properly constructed in the minds of both the economists and the lawyers, with its four participants ruled by the Supreme Court, with its essential attributes of conflict, dependence, and order (due process of law)— just as the formula of the atom or star is being reconstructed in physics, chemistry, and astronomy, with its constituents of protons, electrons, radio-activity, etc.—so also a unit of activity is constructed, common to law, economics, politics, and social ethics.

2. MANAGERIAL TRANSACTIONS

But there are two other, yet inseparable units of activity: the Managerial and Rationing Transactions, each exhibiting a legal, economic, and ethical correlation.

A managerial transaction grows out of a relation between two persons instead of four. While the habitual assumption back of the decisions in bargaining transactions is that of equality of willing buyers and willing sellers, the assumption back of managerial transactions is that of superior and inferior. One person is a legal superior who has legal right to issue commands. The other is a legal inferior who, while the relation lasts, is bound by the legal duty of obedience. It is the relation of foreman and worker, sheriff and citizen, manager and managed, master and servant, owner and slave. The superior gives orders, the inferior must obey.

From the economic standpoint the managerial transaction is the one whose purpose is the production of wealth, including what we have already named as the physical meaning of Exchange considered as the adding of "place utilities" by transportation and delivery of commodities; whereas the bargaining transaction has for its purpose the distribution of wealth and the inducements to produce and deliver wealth. The universal principle of bargaining transactions is scarcity, while that of managerial transactions is efficiency.

Psychologically and ethically, also, the managerial transaction differs from the bargaining transaction. The ethical psychology, or what we name negotiational psychology of bargaining transactions is that of *persuasion or coercion*, depending on opportunity, competition, and bargaining power; because the parties, although deemed to be legally equal, may be economically unequal (coercion) or economically equal (persuasion). The negotiational psychology of managerial transactions is *command and obedience*, because one of the parties is both legally and economically inferior.

This managerial transaction, in the case of labor, is inseparable from, but distinguishable from, the bargaining transaction. As a bargainer, the modern wage-earner is deemed to be the legal *equal* of his employer, induced to enter the transaction by persuasion or coercion; but once he is permitted to enter the *place of employment* he becomes legally *inferior*, induced by commands which he is required to obey. The distinction is clear if the two sets of terms are distinguished as the bargaining terms of employer and employee, or rather of owner and wage-earner, and the managerial terms of foreman or superintendent, and workman.

Here again is a double meaning of the historic word "exchange," based on failure to make use of the distinction between bargaining and managing. The proprietor, in modern industry, has two representatives, the agent and the foreman, often combined in one person. The agent is one whose acts are deemed legally to bind his principal, the employer, on the doctrine of Agency, which began long before the doctrines of *assumpsit* and *quantum meruit* but had the same underlying principle of implying an intention to transfer the ownership of property. The foreman is

an agent for certain important purposes, such as liability of the employer for accidents or accepting an employee's output, where his behavior binds the employer to an assumed debt. He is, as such, an agent, but he is also only another employee placed in charge of the technological process. The distinction has been made clear by the modern differentiation of the "employment department" from the "production department." The employment department is governed by the law of principal and agent; the production department by the law of manager and managed.

Historically the failure of economists to distinguish, in their theories, between agent and employee traces back to the double meaning—legal and technological—of the terms employer and employee, master and servant, owner and slave. But this modern differentiation of two departments gives us the clue for going back and making the historical difference of meaning.

Apparently, therefore, no place was left, in the traditional economic meaning of the word "exchange," for this institutional distinction. Hence the word "exchange" is now found to have had a third meaning—the "exchange" of the laborer's product with a foreman, which is both a physical delivery under order and a transfer of ownership by the laborer of his product to the employer, acting through the employer's agent, in consideration of the transfer of ownership of money by the proprietor, or his agent, to the laborer. The latter transfer of ownership is a detail of the bargaining transaction, with its doctrine of persuasion or coercion, and the laborer is a wage-earner. The former is the managerial transaction of command and obedience, and the laborer is just a bundle of the mechanical labor-power of Ricardo and Marx.

Recent economic theory, since the incoming of "scientific management," has furnished two pairs of terms and two units of measurement which permit the above-mentioned double meaning of "exchange" to be clearly distinguished. The units of measurement are the man-hour and the dollar. The pairs of terms are input-output and outgo-income. Scientific management has restored the labor-theory of Ricardo and Marx, but under the name of Efficiency. The ratio of output per hour (physical use-values) to input per hour (average labor) is the measure of efficiency. This is not an "exchange" at all—between the worker and the foreman—it is the physical process of overcoming the resistance of nature under the supervision of management. The unit of measurement of efficiency is the man-hour.

But the unit of measurement in the bargaining transaction is the dollar. It measures the ratio of outgo to income. The outgo is the alienation of ownership. The income is the acquisition of ownership. The dollar, then, is the measure of relative scarcities in bargaining transactions, while the man-hour is the measure of relative efficiencies in managerial transactions.

There are many cases at common law setting down the rights and duties of these managerial transactions, distinguished from bargaining transactions. They may be brought under the more general rule of the right of an owner to control the behavior of those who enter upon his premises, either as customers, visitors, trespassers, or employees. Hence, in the case of employees, the managerial transaction consists of the superior and the inferior, each governed by the law of command and obedience that has been created by the common-law method of making new law by deciding disputes which arise out of managerial transactions.

The managerial transaction has come to the front in recent years out of the investigations of scientific management. It involves, like the bargaining transaction, a certain amount of negotiation,

Job Analysis of Managing

Understanding	**Observing** (Watching the operation, supervising, includes selecting what to observe and method of recording, mental or physical.) **Evaluating** (Interpreting the observed facts; relating them to other facts and to policies; determining relative significance.)
Devising	**Conceiving** (Imaging possibilities—goals.) **Analyzing** (Analyzing goal and possibilities and relating observed and evaluated facts thereto.) **Contriving** (Determining methods, means, incentives, operatives.)
Persuading	**Directing** (Giving orders—in absolute strictness not managing, but operating.) **Teaching** (Establishing the necessary understanding of goals, means, methods, and incentives.) **Inducing** (Inspiring—"instructing the desires"; the emotional partner to teaching.)

even though, in law it is based solely upon the will of the superior. This inclusion of negotiation arises mainly from the modern freedom of labor, with its liberty of the laborer to quit without giving a reason. Under such an institutional set-up, it is inevitable that something that may look like bargaining comes to the front in managerial transactions. But it is not bargaining—it is managing, though it is an important phase in the negotiations of the bargaining transaction which accompany it. As it is stated figuratively by an eminent manager of a great corporation, "We never give an order; we sell the idea to those who must carry it out." And Mr. Henry S. Dennison, from his own managing experience, has given the most careful analysis of the up-to-date managerial transaction, under the title, "job analysis of managing." His own summary gives an adequate idea of the most recent advance of scientific management in the meaning of managerial transactions.

3. RATIONING TRANSACTIONS

Finally, Rationing Transactions differ from Bargaining and Managing Transactions in that they are the negotiations of reaching an agreement among several participants who have authority to apportion the benefits and burdens to members of a joint enterprise. A borderline case is a partnership transaction as to sharing the future burdens and benefits of a joint undertaking. A little more explicit is the activity of a board of directors of a corporation in making up its budget for the ensuing year. Quite similar, and more distinctive, is the activity of members of a legislative body in apportioning taxes or agreeing on a protective tariff—known as "log-rolling" in America. The so-called "collective bargaining," or "trade agreement," is a rationing transaction between an association of employers and an association of employees, or between any association of buyers and an association of sellers.

Dictatorship and all associations for control of output, like cartels, are a series of rationing transactions. A judicial decision of an economic dispute is a rationing of a certain quantity of the national wealth, or equivalent purchasing power, to one person by taking it forcibly from another person. In these cases there is no bargaining, for that would be bribery, and no managing which is left to subordinate executives. Here is simply that which is sometimes named "policy-shaping," sometimes named "justice," but which, when reduced to economic quantities, is the rationing of wealth or purchasing power, not by parties deemed equal, but by an authority superior to them in law.

We can distinguish two kinds of rationing, output-rationing and price-rationing. Fixing the quantities apportioned to participants without fixing the prices is output-rationing, but fixing the prices and leaving the quantities to the will of the buyer or seller is price-rationing. Soviet Russia and many cartels ration the output, but Soviet Russia also, in many of its "state trusts," like the post-office, fixes prices and leaves to individuals the decision as to quantities. The great field of taxation is a price-rationing, by charging to taxpayers the cost of public services, such as education or highways, without any bargaining by the taxpayer or any regard to the individual benefits he receives from the public services rendered.

These three units of activity exhaust all the activities of the science of economics. Bargaining transactions *transfer ownership* of wealth by voluntary agreement between legal equals. Managerial transactions *create wealth* by commands of legal superiors. Rationing transactions apportion the burdens and benefits of wealth creation by the *dictation* of legal superiors. Since they are units of social activity among equals, or between superiors and inferiors, they are ethical in character as well as legal and economic.

4. INSTITUTIONS

These three types of transactions are brought together in a larger unit of economic investigation, which, in British and American practice, is named a Going Concern. It is these going concerns, with the working rules that keep them agoing, all the way from the family, the corporation, the trade union, the trade association, up to the state itself, that we name Institutions. The passive concept is a "group"; the active is a "going concern."

The difficulty in defining a field for the so-called Institutional Economics is the uncertainty of meaning of the word institution. Sometimes an institution seems to be analogous to a building, a sort of framework of laws and regulations, within which individuals act like inmates. Sometimes it seems to mean the "behavior" of the inmates themselves. Sometimes anything additional to or critical of the classical or hedonic economics is deemed to be institutional. Sometimes anything that is "dynamic" instead of "static," or a "process" instead of commodities, or activity instead of feelings, or management instead of equilibrium, or control instead of laissez-faire, seems to be institutional economics.

All of these notions are doubtless involved in institutional economics, but they may be said to be metaphors or descriptions, whereas a *science* of economic behavior requires analysis into principles—which are similarities of cause, effect, or purpose—and a synthesis in a unified system of principles. And institutional economics, furthermore, cannot separate itself from the marvellous discoveries and insight of the pioneer classical and psychological economists. It should incorporate, however, in addition, the equally important discoveries of the communistic, anarchistic, syndicalistic, fascistic, cooperative, and unionistic economists. Doubtless it is the effort to cover by enumeration all of these uncoordinated activities that gives to the name institutional economics that reputation of a miscellaneous, nondescript, yet merely descriptive character, similar to that which has long since relegated from economics the early crude Historical School.

If we endeavor to find a universal principle, common to all behavior known as institutional, we may define an institution as Collective Action in Control of Individual Action.

Collective action ranges all the way from unorganized Custom to the many organized Going Concerns, such as the family, the corporation, the holding company, the trade association, the trade union, the Federal Reserve System, the "group of affiliated interests," the State. The principle common to all of them is more or less control of individual action by collective action.

This control of the acts of one individual always results in, and is intended to result in, a benefit to other individuals. If it be the enforcement of a contract, then the debt is exactly equal to the credit created for the benefit of the other person. A debt is a duty capable of being enforced collectively, while a credit is an equivalent right created by creating the duty. The resulting social relation is an Economic Status, consisting of the expectations towards which each party is directing his economic behavior. On the debt and duty side it is the status of Conformity to collective action. On the credit and right side it is a status of Security created by the expectation of said Conformity. This is known as "incorporeal" property.

Or, the collective control takes the form of a *tabu* or prohibition of certain acts, such as interference, infringement, trespass, and this prohibition creates an economic status of Liberty for the person thus made immune. But the liberty of one person may be accompanied by prospective benefit or damage to a correlative person, and the economic status thus created is Exposure to the Liberty of the other. An employer is exposed to the liberty of the employee to work or quit, and the employee is exposed to the liberty of the employer to hire or fire. This exposure-liberty relation is coming to be distinguished as "intangible" property, such as the good-will of a business, franchises to do business, patents, trademarks, and so on in great variety.

The working rules which determine for individuals the limits of these correlative and reciprocal economic relationships may be laid down and enforced by a corporation, or a cartel, or a holding company, or a cooperative association, or a trade union, or an employers' association, or a trade association, or a joint trade agreement of two associations, or a stock exchange or board of trade, or a political party, or the state itself through the United States Supreme Court in the American system. Indeed, these economic collective acts of private concerns are at times more powerful than the collective action of the political concern, the State.

Stated in the language of ethics and law, to be developed below, all collective acts established social relations of right, duty, no right, and no duty. Stated in the language of individual behavior, what they require is performance, avoidance, forbearance by individuals. Stated in the language of the resulting economic status of individuals, what they provide is Security, Conformity, Liberty, and Exposure. Stated in language of cause, effect, or purpose, the common principles running through all economic behavior as a limiting and complementary interdependent relationship are Scarcity, Efficiency, Futurity, the Working Rules of collective action, and Sovereignty. Stated in language of the operation of working rules on individual action they are expressed by the auxiliary verbs of what the individual can, cannot, must, must not, may, or may not *do*. He "can" or "cannot," because collective action will or will not come to his aid. He "must" or "must not," because collective action

will compel him. He "may," because collective action will permit him and protect him. He "may not," because collective action will prevent him.

It is because of these behavioristic auxiliary verbs that the familiar term "working rules" is appropriate to indicate the universal principle of cause, effect, or purpose, common to all collective action. Working rules are continually changing in the history of an institution, including the state and all private associations, and they differ for different institutions. They are sometimes known as *maxims* of conduct. Adam Smith names them *canons* of taxation, and the Supreme Court names them the *Rule of Reason*, or *Due Process of Law*. But, whatever their differences and different names, they have this similarity, that they indicate what individuals can, must, or may, do or not do, enforced by Collective Sanctions.

Analysis of these collective sanctions furnishes that correlation of economics, jurisprudence, and ethics, which is prerequisite to a theory of institutional economics. David Hume found the unity of these social sciences in the principle of scarcity and the resulting conflict of interests. Adam Smith isolated economics on the assumptions of divine providence, earthly abundance, and the resulting harmony of interests. Institutional economics goes back to Hume. Taking our cue from Hume and the modern rise of such a term as "business ethics," ethics deals with the rules of conduct arising from conflict of interests and enforced by the *moral* sanctions of collective opinion. Economics deals with the same rules of conduct enforced by the collective sanctions of economic *gain* or *loss*. Jurisprudence deals with the same rules enforced by the organized sanctions of *physical force*. Institutional economics is continually dealing with the relative merits of these three types of sanctions.

From this universal principle of collective action in control of individual action by different kinds of sanctions arise the ethical and legal relations of rights, duties, no-rights, and the economic relations not only of Security, Conformity, Liberty, and Exposure, but also of Assets and Liabilities. In fact, it is from the field of corporation finance, with its changeable assets and liabilities, rather than from the field of individual wants and labor, or pains and pleasures, or wealth and happiness, or utility and disutility, that institutional economics derives a large part of its data and methodology. Institutional economics is concerned with the Assets and Liabilities of Concerns contrasted with Adam Smith's Wealth of Nations. Between nations it is the Credits and Debits in the balance of international payments.

Collective action is even more universal in the unorganized form of Custom than it is in the organized form of Concerns. Yet even a going concern is also a Custom. Custom has not given way to free contract and competition, as was asserted by Sir Henry Maine. Customs have merely changed with changes in economic conditions, and they may today be so mandatory that even a dictator cannot overrule them. The business man who refuses or is unable to make use of the modern customs of the credit system, by refusing to accept or issue checks on solvent banks, although the checks are merely private arrangements and not legal tender, simply cannot continue in business by carrying on transactions. These instruments are customary tender, instead of legal tender, backed by the powerful sanctions of profit, loss, and competition, which compel conformity. Other mandatory customs might be mentioned, such as coming to work at seven o'clock and quitting at six, or the customary standards of living.

But these customary standards are always changing; they lack precision, and therefore give rise to disputes over conflicts of interest. If such disputes arise, then the officers of an organized concern, such as a credit association, the manager of a corporation, a stock exchange, a board of trade, a commercial or labor arbitrator, or finally, the courts of law up to the Supreme Court of the United States, reduce the custom to precision and add an organized legal or economic sanction.

This is done through the Common-Law Method of Making Law by the Decision of Disputes. The decisions, by becoming precedents, become the working rules, for the time being, of the particular organized concern. The historic "common law" of Anglo-American jurisprudence is only a special case of the universal principle common to all concerns that survive, of making new law by deciding conflicts of interest, thus giving greater precision and organized compulsion to the unorganized working rules of custom or ethics. The common-law *method* is universal in all collective action, but the technical "common law" of the English and American lawyers is a body of decisions going back to feudal times. In short, the common-law *method*, or way of acting, is itself a custom, with variabilities, like other customs. It is the way in which collective action of all going concerns acts on individual action in time of conflict. It differs from statutory law in that it is judge-made law at the time of decision of disputes.

Collective Action is more than *control* of individual action—it is, by the very act of control, as indicated by the auxiliary verbs, a *liberation* of individual action from coercion, duress, discrimination, or unfair competition, by means of restraints placed on other individuals.

And Collective Action is more than restraint and liberation of individual action—it is *expansion* of the will of the individual far beyond what he can do by his own puny acts. The head of a great corporation gives orders which execute his will at the ends of the earth.

Since liberation and expansion for some persons consist in restraint, for their benefit, of other persons, and while the short definition of an institution is collective action in control of individual action, the derived definition is: collective action in restraint, liberation, and expansion of individual action.

These individual actions are really *trans*-actions—that is, actions between individuals—as well as individual behavior. It is this shift from commodities, individuals, and exchanges to transactions and working rules of collective action that marks the transition from the classical and hedonic schools to the institutional schools of economic thinking. The shift is a change in the ultimate unit of economic investigation, from commodities and individuals to transactions between individuals.

If it be considered that, after all, it is the individual who is important, then the individual with whom we are dealing is the Institutionalized Mind. Individuals begin as babies. They learn the custom of language, of cooperation with other individuals, of working towards common ends, of negotiations to eliminate conflicts of interest, of subordination to the working rules of the many concerns of which they are members. They meet each other, not as physiological bodies moved by glands, nor as "globules of desire" moved by pain and pleasure, similar to the forces of physical and animal nature, but as prepared more or less by habit, induced by the pressure of custom, to engage in those highly artificial transactions created by the collective human will. They are not found in physics, or biology, or subjective psychology, or in the German Gestalt psychology, but are found where conflict, interdependence, and order among human beings are preliminary to getting a living. Instead of individuals the participants are citizens of a going concern. Instead of forces of nature they are forces of human nature. Instead of the mechanical uniformities of desire of the hedonistic economists, they are highly variable personalities. Instead of isolated individuals in a state of nature they are always participants in transactions, members of a concern in which they come and go, citizens of an institution that lived before them and will live after them.

VI

Neoclassicism

Introduction. Although it is useful to separate the marginalists and the neoclassicists in the categorical device used here, this division is highly arbitrary, since all neoclassical economists were in some sense marginalists too. However, given that this arbitrary grouping is being employed, it would certainly be a mistake to exclude Alfred Marshall from the neoclassical group, since he was not only its founding father but also its most outstanding member. Alfred Marshall (1842-1924) was born and reared in London. His father, who was employed by the Bank of England as a cashier, tried to steer him into the ministry. When nineteen, Marshall enrolled at St. John's College in Oxford, where he was captivated by mathematics. With financial assistance from his uncle, he pursued this interest at St. John's College in Cambridge. It was Marshall's intention that mathematics prepare him for a career as a molecular physicist, but his growing fascination with economics changed his choice of careers. After graduation he was given a lectureship and fellowship at St. John's, Cambridge. He lost this position nine years later when—at the age of thirty-five—he married Mary Paley, because the school had a restrictive marriage rule concerning fellows. Marshall taught for a few years at Balliol College until 1885, at which time Cambridge dropped the restrictive rule and rehired him. Marshall's first book, *Economics of Industry* (1879), was written with the help of his wife, who had earlier been his pupil. His greatest achievement was *Principles of Economics* (1890), a book which went through eight editions in Marshall's lifetime and which had a greater influence on economic thought than any other book since Smith's *Wealth of Nations*. Despite the smashing success of *Principles*, Marshall did not become idle; he went on to write *Industry and Trade* (1919) and *Money, Credit, and Commerce* (1923), both of which were well-received by the profession.

Although he was an overly modest writer, Marshall made many significant contributions in his *Principles*. Some of the better known are the coefficient of elasticity, quasi-rent, the principle of marginal substitution, internal and external economies, and the distinction between the short run and long run. Of course, the concept with which Marshall's name is most strongly associated is the demand curve. The first appearance of this curve in *Principles* occurs in book 3, chapter 3, which is reproduced in this section under its title, "Gradations of Consumers' Demand." Here the student will be able to see firsthand why economists began violating the mathematician's convention of placing the dependent variable on the vertical axis. Although Cournot had correctly placed price on the horizontal axis, Marshall places it on the vertical axis. This made it easier for Marshall to graphically show market demand as a sum of individual demands, since he preferred a horizontal summation to a vertical summation of curves. More important, however, Marshall regarded price as the dependent variable and quantity the independent variable, the opposite of what Walras had believed. This is especially evident in book 5, chapter 3, titled "Equilibrium of Normal Demand and Supply." In the chapter's last two sections, which are included here, the reader may observe that market equilibrium is stated in terms of an equality of demand price with supply price—not an equality of quantities demanded and supplied. In addition, our excerpt contains Marshall's famous scissors analogy of supply and demand curves. This analogy put to rest the old argument that cost was the sole determinant of price. The final chapter of book 5 is also reproduced below, since it is an excellent summary of Marshall's entire discussion of demand and supply equilibrium.

A writer who was a master of synthesizing the most important contributions of his predecessors was Knut Wicksell (1851-1926), a Swedish economist with a mathematical bent of mind. At the age of thirty-four he was graduated from the University of Uppsala with a degree in philosophy and mathematics. Wicksell then spent several years studying in France, Austria, Germany and England. Upon returning to Sweden, he re-enrolled at Uppsala to work on his Ph.D. degree in political economy, which he completed at the age of forty-four. Before he joined the faculty at the University of Lund five years later (in 1900), Wicksell had already published *Value, Capital, and Rent* (1893), *Studies in Finance Theory* (1896), and *Interest and Prices* (1898)—all three of which were written in German.

The analytical system that Wicksell had developed in the first of these three books reappeared in a more mature form in the first volume of his *Lectures on Political Economy*. This two-volume work, written in Swedish, is considered his finest achievement. The first volume is so technical and mathematical that it is one of the most difficult books to read in the category of "economic classics." That volume is a brilliant presentation of the neoclassical theory of production and distribution. The second volume explores the relationship between the general price level and the nominal rate of interest. Several of his most important ideas in this volume are summarized in his 1907 *Economic Journal* article, "The Influence of the Rate of Interest on Prices," which is reprinted in this section.

Walras picked Vilfredo Pareto (1848-1923) to succeed him in his chair at the University of Lausanne. Pareto was born in Paris, where he was reared for ten years until his wealthy Italian parents were able to return to Italy. Their return to the homeland was made possible by the receipt of political amnesty. Pareto was educated at the University of Turin, where he undertook extensive studies of mathematics and engineering. After graduating, he worked as an engineer for the railroad and as a manager for an iron manufacturer. After winning the economics chair in 1892 at Lausanne, Switzerland, Pareto published his *Lectures on Political Economy* (1896 and 1897), *Socialist Systems* (volume 1 in 1900 and volume 2 in 1902), and *Manual of Political Economy* (1906, Italian; 1909, French). The best of these is unquestionably the *Manual*, which makes heavy use of mathematics to extend general equilibrium analysis—designed by Walras for a competitive model—to a monopolistic framework. To accomplish this, Pareto also extended the indifference curve model that Edgeworth had developed and used this new tool in his general equilibrium framework. It is important to note that Pareto bases his indifference map on ordinal—not cardinal—utility. Our selections from the *Manual* are taken from chapters 3 and 6, which reveal Pareto's use of indifference curves and contain his famous statement that

> the members of a collectivity enjoy *maximum ophelimity* in a certain position when it is impossible to find a way of moving from that position very slightly in such a manner that the ophelimity enjoyed by each of the individuals of that collectivity increases or decreases.

In this description of what we now call a "Pareto optimum," Pareto used the term "ophelimity" to mean "use value" or "utility." He shunned these latter two terms to avoid confusing readers who find it difficult to believe, for example, that a drug addict could obtain "utility" from a drug that is killing him.

Philip H. Wicksteed (1844-1927) was born at Leeds in Yorkshire. Greatly influenced by his father, who was a minister in the Unitarian church, Philip entered the ministry after receiving his undergraduate degree from University College, London. He became minister of Little Portland Street Chapel in 1874 and retained that position for over twenty years. During this time, Wicksteed developed a deep interest in the philosophy of Dante and the discipline of economics. Due to his gift for speaking, he was one of the most popular lecturers at the University Extension. Partly because his religious views were becoming increasingly unorthodox and partly because he was able to support his family entirely by lecturing and writing, Wicksteed resigned the ministry in 1897. His best work includes *Alphabet of Economic Science* (1888), a book that is of historical interest because of its introduction of the term "marginal utility," a translation of the Austrian term "Grenz-nutzen" and a welcome replacement for Jevons' term "final utility." Wicksteed intended that the book be used by non-mathematical students who were trying to grasp mathematical concepts like diminishing marginal utility. Although unsuccessful with the general public, the book was highly successful among economists.

Wicksteed later published his famous *Essay on the Co-ordination of the Laws of Distribution* (1894) and *The Common Sense of Political Economy* (1910), his magnum opus. The latter book is sadly misnamed: it is far too technical to be comprehended by readers having anything less than un-common sense; and it does not really deal with *political* economy. Instead, it is the most extensive, non-mathematical treatment of "marginalist" eco-nomic theory ever written. This treatise consists of three books published in two volumes. The most famous chapter in the treatise is the sixth chapter of book 2. That chapter is "The Diagrammatic Exposition of the Law of Rent and Its Implications," two-thirds of which is excerpted here. In this chapter Wicksteed showed that land rent can be graphically represented as either the rectilinear area under the marginal product curve of land or the mix-tilinear area under the marginal product curve of labor. As is apparent from his numerical examples (which have been deleted from the reprinted selec-tion), Wicksteed made the necessary assumption of constant returns to scale. Consequently, although he failed to specify that the production func-tion is linearly homogeneous, this assumption may be inferred from his examples. By geometrically portraying rent as a rectangle (as the other fac-tor payments are normally shown), he drove home the point that rent—like any other factor payment—is determined by marginal efficiency of the in-put. That is, rent is not simply the product left after other inputs are paid (as might be suggested by its normal representation as a mixtilinear area). This and other important arguments from *Common Sense* are summarized in Wicksteed's 1913 presidential address to Section F of the British Associa-tion. Titled "The Scope and Method of Political Economy in the Light of the 'Marginal' Theory of Value and Distribution," it is reprinted here. This address was described by Lionel Robbins (in his introduction to *Common Sense*) as the most outstanding ". . . explanation of the methodological sig-nificance of the subjective theory of value. . . ."

As one of Marshall's most outstanding students and successor to his chair in economics at Cambridge, Cecil Arthur Pigou (1877-1959) became one of the founders of welfare economics. Pigou was regarded the most out-standing member of the Cambridge School of Economics after Keynes left it in 1936 and—except for Keynes—was the most celebrated economist that Britain had to offer. Pigou's best work is *The Economics of Welfare* (1920), which greatly extends the welfare theory that Marshall had established. Our selections from this treatise are taken from part 2, chapters 2 and 3, which show that national production is maximized when factors are dis-tributed so as to equate the "values of the marginal social net products." Also reprinted here is Pigou's 1951 article in *The American Economic Re-*

view on "Some Aspects of Welfare Economics." Written at the invitation of the journal's editor, this article updates *The Economics of Welfare*. Among the issues discussed therein are Pigou's position on interpersonal comparisons of utility, the proposition that an addition to a person's real income increases his satisfaction, and the proposition that society is better off when money income is taken from the rich and given to the poor.

The microeconomics of the classical writers and Marshall had considered only two extremes: pure competition and monopoly, with great emphasis placed on the former. Marshall's failure to make a clear distinction between perfect and imperfect competition greatly retarded the economists' understanding of these concepts. In this regard Samuelson has written that "much of the work from 1920 to 1933 was merely the negative task of getting Marshall out of the way." As a result, the economics profession was rediscovering in 1930 the monopoly theory that Cournot had formulated in 1838—almost a century earlier! Moreover, except for the duopoly models developed by Cournot and Edgeworth, practically none of the theory was relevant to firms falling between the two extremes. In the wake of Piero Sraffa's 1926 article, which argued that nonprice competition is more the rule than the exception, Chamberlin and Robinson pointed the way to bridging the gap by publishing work (that each had developed independently of the other) in 1933. They showed that imperfectly competitive firms do not simply differ from the two extremes by a matter of degree. For example, the pricing behavior of an oligopolist cannot be approximated by averaging together the pricing behavior of a monopolist with that of a purely competitive firm. This would make no more sense than approximating the temperature at the earth's equator by averaging together the temperatures found at the north and south poles. The conclusion that imperfect competition must be described by a whole series of models is clearly stated by Chamberlin: "Oligopoly is not one problem, but several. The solution varies, depending upon the conditions assumed."

Edward Hastings Chamberlin (1899-1967) was born and raised in Washington state. He received his B.S., M.A., and Ph.D. degrees from the University of Iowa (1920), the University of Michigan (1922), and Harvard University (1927), respectively. (He also earned a second master's degree in 1924 at Harvard.) His entire teaching career was spent at Harvard, where he began at the instructor's level in 1922.

Chamberlin's best work is unquestionably *The Theory of Monopolistic Competition* (1933), which is essentially a refinement of the doctoral dissertation he completed at Harvard in 1927. Our selections from this book include the introduction, in which the term "pure competition" makes its first appearance in economic literature. Chamberlin drew a careful distinction between this "pure competition" and "perfect competition," a term that had long been used. Also included here is part of his famous chapter

3, which explains "Duopoly and Oligopoly." Here Chamberlin contended that oligopolists can hardly ignore their interdependent relationship when they are few in number and their products are standardized. Because each fears that a price cut will invite retaliation, "no one will cut, and although the sellers are entirely independent, the equilibrium result is the same as though there were a monopolistic agreement between them." He showed that explicit collusion is not needed for oligopolists to arrive at monopoly pricing, a conclusion that has since had enormous impact on antitrust policy.

Excerpts have also been taken from the fifth chapter, which discusses "Product Differentiation and the Theory of Value." This includes his familiar graph of monopolistic competition, which is still reproduced in almost every principles- and intermediate-level textbook. Despite the frequency with which it is taught, the case of monopolistic competition is of little practical importance, considering that its occurrence in the real world is almost as rare as that of pure competition. The real importance of Chamberlin's *Monopolistic Competition* is that it explains why firms will behave in ways inconsistent with the popular model of pure competition. His book is able to predict, for example, that firms will advertise and attempt to differentiate their products. In this way Chamberlin's book showed economists that—instead of just examining monopoly and pure competition—they would have to study many different types of market structure. Hence, Chamberlin was as revolutionary in microeconomic theory as Keynes was in macroeconomic theory, and he literally opened up the field of industrial organization.

Joan Robinson (b. 1903) received her formal training in London and Cambridge and has since become one of the most prolific writers that England has produced. In 1926 she married E. A. G. Robinson, an outstanding economist who became joint editor in 1944 of the prestigious *Economic Journal*. In 1931 Mrs. Robinson joined the faculty of Cambridge University, with which she has been associated ever since. At Cambridge she was promoted to the position of university lecturer in 1937, reader in 1949, and professor in 1965. Her list of publications is staggering, but an abbreviated list of her best known books would likely include *The Economics of Imperfect Competition* (1933), *Introduction to the Theory of Employment* (1937), *Essays in the Theory of Employment* (1937), *Essay on Marxian Economics* (1942), *The Rate of Interest and Other Essays* (1952), *Collected Economic Papers* (three volumes released in 1951, 1960, and 1965), *The Accumulation of Capital* (1956), *Economic Philosophy* (1962), *Essays in the Theory of Economic Growth* (1962), and *Economics: An Awkward Corner* (1966).

Like Chamberlin, Robinson studied the intermediate ground lying between monopoly and pure competition and used the same marginal terms to specify equilibrium conditions for all market types. However, while

Chamberlin focused on monopolistic competition and product differentiation, Robinson devoted most of her attention to the problems of monopoly, monopsony, and price discrimination. This is especially true of her most famous book, *The Economics of Imperfect Competition*. It was published in 1933 only a few months after Chamberlin's *The Theory of Monopolistic Competition*. Although these two books cover similar terrain and were released almost simultaneously, it is known that they were developed independently of each other. In comparison to Chamberlin's book, Robinson's *Imperfect Competition* is more rigorous, more concisely written, and—all in all—more difficult to read. This is not true, however, of the book's introduction, most of which is excerpted below. Here she stated that the book is intended to present the economic profession with graphical techniques, a "box of tools" for economic analysis. She also explained the manner in which monopoly, as an all-inclusive categorical device, "engulfs competitive analysis." The book's rigor is apparent, however, in our excerpt from the far-famed chapter 15, devoted to "Price Discrimination." Our selection contains the now-familiar equilibrium solution for third-degree price discrimination. In standard textbooks, this solution is explained with several pages of text that accompany two or three diagrams. As the reader will see, Robinson's concise presentation employs very little text and a single diagram containing all five of the revenue curves plus the marginal cost curve.

Robinson is even more prolific with journal articles than with books. Our third selection is one of the most delightful of these articles. Titled "What Is Perfect Competition?" it appeared in a 1934 issue of *The Quarterly Journal of Economics*. Robinson's answer to the title's question is that perfect competition exists whenever the firm's demand curve is perfectly elastic. This surprisingly simple condition contrasts sharply with the long list of conditions that were given by other writers of that day—and which even now appear in almost every principles text. These conditions include freedom of entry and exit, perfect knowledge, homogeneous products, and so on. Robinson dispatched each of these common assumptions one at a time with surprising insights. For example, the usual assumption of a large number of buyers is dismissed with the observation that "the larger the number of buyers who are potential customers of any one firm the more likely is the market to be imperfect, since the more likely are differences of preference to occur." Students should compare Robinson's definition of *perfect* competition with Chamberlin's definition of *pure* competition, which is included here in the excerpt from the introduction to his book. Robinson chose to define *perfect* competition in much the same way that Chamberlin defined *pure* competition. As she noted in her article, Chamberlin did not actually specify a horizontal demand curve for pure competition, but this condition is implied by his assumption of an "absence of monopoly."

18. Principles of Economics*

ALFRED MARSHALL

GRADATIONS OF CONSUMERS' DEMAND

When a trader or a manufacturer buys anything to be used in production, or be sold again, his demand is based on his anticipations of the profits which he can derive from it. These profits depend at any time on speculative risks and on other causes, which will need to be considered later on. But in the long run the price which a trader or manufacturer can afford to pay for a thing depends on the prices which consumers will pay for it, or for the things made by aid of it. The ultimate regulator of all demands is therefore consumers' demand. And it is with that almost exclusively that we shall be concerned in the present Book.

Utility is taken to be correlative to Desire or Want. It has been already argued that desires cannot be measured directly, but only indirectly by the outward phenomena to which they give rise: and that in those cases with which economics is chiefly concerned the measure is found in the price which a person is willing to pay for the fulfilment or satisfaction of his desire. He may have desires and aspirations which are not consciously set for any satisfaction: but for the present we are concerned chiefly with those which do so aim; and we assume that the resulting satisfaction corresponds in general fairly well to that which was anticipated when the purchase was made.[1]

There is an endless variety of wants, but there is a limit to each separate want. This familiar and fundamental tendency of human nature may be stated in the *law of satiable wants* or of *diminishing utility* thus:—The *total utility* of a thing to anyone (that is, the total pleasure or other benefit it yields him) increases with every increase in his stock of it, but not as fast as his stock increases. If his stock of it increases at a uniform rate the benefit derived from it increases at a diminishing rate. In other words, the additional benefit which a person derives from a given increase of his stock of a thing, diminishes with every increase in the stock that he already has.

That part of the thing which he is only just induced to purchase may be called his *marginal purchase*, because he is on the margin of doubt whether it is worth his while to incur the outlay required to obtain it. And the utility of his marginal purchase may be called the *marginal utility* of the thing to him. Or, if instead of buying it, he makes the thing himself, then its marginal utility is the utility of that part which he thinks is only just worth his while to make. And thus the law just given may be worded:—

The marginal utility of a thing to anyone diminishes with every increase in the amount of it he already has.

There is however an implicit condition in this law which should be made clear. It is that we do not suppose time to be allowed for any alteration in the

---

Source: Excerpted from the 8th edition (New York: The Macmillan Company, 1920). The selection reprinted here originally appeared as parts of book 3, chapter 3 and book 5, chapters 3 and 15. All margin notes and some footnotes deleted, others renumbered.

character or tastes of the man himself. It is therefore no exception to the law that the more good music a man hears, the stronger is his taste for it likely to become; that avarice and ambition are often insatiable; or that the virtue of cleanliness and the vice of drunkenness alike grow on what they feed upon. For in such cases our observations range over some period of time; and the man is not the same at the beginning as at the end of it. If we take a man as he is, without allowing time for any change in his character, the marginal utility of a thing to him diminishes steadily with every increase in his supply of it.[2]

Now let us translate this law of diminishing utility into terms of price. Let us take an illustration from the case of a commodity such as tea, which is in constant demand and which can be purchased in small quantities. Suppose, for instance, that tea of a certain quality is to be had at 2s. per lb. A person might be willing to give 10s. for a single pound once a year rather than go without it altogether; while if he could have any amount of it for nothing he would perhaps not care to use more than 30 lbs. in the year. But as it is, he buys perhaps 10 lbs. in the year; that is to say, the difference between the satisfaction which he gets from buying 9 lbs. and 10 lbs. is enough for him to be willing to pay 2s. for it: while the fact that he does not buy an eleventh pound, shows that he does not think that it would be worth an extra 2s. to him. That is, 2s. a pound measures the utility to him of the tea which lies at the margin or terminus or end of his purchases; it measures the marginal utility to him. If the price which he is just willing to pay for any pound be called his *demand price*, then 2s. is his *marginal demand price*. And our law may be worded:—

The larger the amount of a thing that a person has the less, other things being equal (*i.e.* the purchasing power of money, and the amount of money at his command being equal), will be the price which he will pay for a little more of it: or in other words his marginal demand price for it diminishes.

His demand becomes *efficient*, only when the price which he is willing to offer reaches that at which others are willing to sell.

This last sentence reminds us that we have as yet taken no account of changes in the marginal utility of money, or general purchasing power. At one and the same time, a person's material resources being unchanged, the marginal utility of money to him is a fixed quantity, so that the prices he is just willing to pay for two commodities are to one another in the same ratio as the utility of those two commodities.

A greater utility will be required to induce him to buy a thing if he is poor than if he is rich. We have seen how the clerk with £100 a year will walk to business in a heavier rain than the clerk with £300 a year. But although the utility, or the benefit, that is measured in the poorer man's mind by twopence is greater than that measured by it in the richer man's mind; yet if the richer man rides a hundred times in the year and the poorer man twenty times, then the utility of the hundredth ride which the richer man is only just induced to take is measured to him by twopence; and the utility of the twentieth ride which the poorer man is only just induced to take is measured to him by twopence. For each of them the marginal utility is measured by twopence; but this marginal utility is greater in the case of the poorer man than in that of the richer.

In other words, the richer a man becomes the less is the marginal utility of money to him; every increase in his resources increases the price which he is willing to pay for any given benefit. And in the same way every diminution of his resources increases the marginal utility of money to him, and diminishes the price that he is willing to pay for any benefit.

To obtain complete knowledge of demand for anything, we should have to ascertain how much of it he would be willing to purchase at each of the prices at which it is likely to be offered; and the circumstance of his demand for, say, tea can be best expressed by a list of the prices which he is willing to pay; that is, by his several demand prices for different amounts of it. (This list may be called his *demand schedule*.)

Thus for instance we may find that he would buy

6 lbs.	at	50d.	per lb.
7 "	40	"	
8 "	33	"	
9 "	28	"	
10 "	24	"	
11 "	21	"	
12 "	19	"	
13 "	17	"	

If corresponding prices were filled in for all intermediate amounts we should have an exact statement of his demand.[3] We cannot express a person's demand for a thing by the "amount he is willing to buy," or by the "intensity of his eagerness to buy a certain amount," without reference to the prices at which he would buy that amount and other amounts. We can represent it exactly only by lists of the prices at which he is willing to buy different amounts.[4]

When we say that a person's demand for anything increases, we mean that he will buy more of it than he would before at the same price, and that he will buy as much of it as before at a higher price. A general increase in his demand is an increase throughout the whole list of prices at which he is willing to purchase different amounts of it, and not merely that he is willing to buy more of it at the current prices.[5]

So far we have looked at the demand of a single individual. And in the particular case of such a thing as tea, the demand of a single person is fairly representative of the general demand of a whole market: for the demand for tea is a constant one; and, since it can be purchased in small quantities, every variation in its price is likely to affect the

amount which he will buy. But even among those things which are in constant use, there are many for which the demand on the part of any single individual cannot vary continuously with every small change in price, but can move only by great leaps. For instance, a small fall in the price of hats or watches will not affect the action of every one; but it will induce a few persons, who were in doubt whether or not to get a new hat or a new watch, to decide in favour of doing so.

There are many classes of things the need for which on the part of any individual is inconstant, fitful, and irregular. There can be no list of individual demand prices for wedding-cakes, or the services of an expert surgeon. But the economist has little concern with particular incidents in the lives of individuals. He studies rather "the course of action that may be expected under certain conditions from the members of an industrial group," in so far as the motives of that action are measurable by a money price; and in these broad results the variety and the fickleness of individual action are merged in the comparatively regular aggregate of the action of many.

In large markets, then—where rich and poor, old and young, men and women, persons of all varieties of tastes, temperaments and occupations are mingled together,—the peculiarities in the wants of individuals will compensate one another in a comparatively regular gradation of total demand. Every fall, however slight in the price of a commodity in general use, will, other things being equal, increase the total sales of it; just as an unhealthy autumn increases the mortality of a large town, though many persons are uninjured by it. And therefore if we had the requisite knowledge, we could make a list of prices at which each amount of it could find purchasers in a given place during, say, a year.

The total demand in the place for, say, tea, is the sum of the demands of all the individuals there. Some will be richer and some poorer than the individual consumer whose demand we have just written down; some will have a greater and others a smaller liking for tea than he has. Let us suppose that there are in the place a million purchasers of tea, and that their average consumption is equal to his at each several price. Then the demand of that place is represented by the same list of prices as before, if we write a million pounds of tea instead of one pound.[6]

There is then one general *law of demand*:—

> The greater the amount to be sold, the smaller must be the price at which it is offered in order that it may find purchasers; or, in other words, the amount demanded increases with a fall in price, and diminishes with a rise in price.

There will not be any uniform relation between the fall in price and the increase of demand. A fall of one-tenth in the price may increase the sales by a twentieth or by a quarter, or it may double them. But as the numbers in the left-hand column of the demand schedule increase, those in the right-hand column will always diminish.[7]

The price will measure the marginal utility of the commodity to each purchaser individually: we cannot speak of price as measuring marginal utility in general, because the wants and circumstances of different people are different.

The demand prices in our list are those at which various quantities of a thing can be sold in a market *during a given time and under given conditions*. If the conditions vary in any respect the prices will probably require to be changed; and this has constantly to be done when the desire for anything is materially altered by a variation of custom, or by a cheapening of the supply of a rival commodity, or by the invention of a new one. For instance, the list of demand prices for tea is drawn out on the assumption that the price of coffee is known; but a failure of the coffee harvest would raise the prices for tea. The demand for gas is liable to be reduced by an improvement in electric lighting; and in the same way a fall in the price of a particular kind of tea may cause it to be substituted for an inferior but cheaper variety.[8]

Our next step will be to consider the general character of demand in the cases of some important commodities ready for immediate consumption. We shall thus be continuing the inquiry made in the preceding chapter as to the variety and satiability of wants; but we shall be treating it from a rather different point of view, viz. that of price-statistics. . . .

EQUILIBRIUM OF NORMAL DEMAND AND SUPPLY

When therefore the amount produced (in a unit of time) is such that the demand price is greater than the supply price, then sellers receive more than is sufficient to make it worth their while to bring goods to market to that amount; and there is at work an active force tending to increase the amount brought forward for sale. On the other hand, when the amount produced is such that the demand price is less than the supply price, sellers receive less than is sufficient to make it worth their while to bring goods to market on that scale; so that those who were just on the margin of doubt as to whether to go on producing are decided not to do so, and there is an active force at work tending to diminish the amount brought forward for sale. When the demand price is equal to the supply price, the amount produced has no tendency either to be increased or to be diminished; it is in equilibrium.

When demand and supply are in equilibrium, the amount of the commodity which is being produced in a unit of time may be called the *equilibirum-amount*, and the price at which it is being sold may be called the *equilibrium-price*.

Such an equilibrium is *stable*; that is,.

the price, if displaced a little from it, will tend to return, as a pendulum oscillates about its lowest point; and it will be found to be a characteristic of stable equilibria that in them the demand price is greater than the supply price for amounts just less than the equilibrium amount, and *vice versa*. For when the demand price is greater than the supply price, the amount produced tends to increase. Therefore, if the demand price is greater than the supply price for amounts just less than an equilibrium amount; then, if the scale of production is temporarily diminished somewhat below that equilibrium amount, it will tend to return; thus the equilibrium is stable for displacements in that direction. If the demand price is greater than the supply price for amounts just less than the equilibrium amount, it is sure to be less than the supply price for amounts just greater: and therefore, if the scale of production is somewhat increased beyond the equilibrium position, it will tend to return and the equilibrium will be stable for displacements in that direction also.

When demand and supply are in stable equilibrium, if any accident should move the scale of production from its equilibrium position, there will be instantly brought into play forces tending to push it back to that position; just as, if a stone hanging by a string is displaced from its equilibrium position, the force of gravity will at once tend to bring it back to its equilibrium position. The movements of the scale of production about its position of equilibrium will be of a somewhat similar kind.[9]

But in real life such oscillations are seldom as rhythmical as those of a stone hanging freely from a string; the comparison would be more exact if the string were supposed to hang in the troubled waters of a mill-race, whose stream was at one time allowed to flow freely, and at another partially cut off. Nor are these complexities sufficient to illustrate all the disturbances with which the economist and the merchant alike are forced to concern themselves. If the person holding the string swings his hand with movements partly rhythmical and partly arbitrary, the illustration will not outrun the difficulties of some very real and practical problems of value. For indeed the demand and supply schedules do not in practice remain unchanged for a long time together, but are constantly being changed; and every change in them alters the equilibrium amount and the equilibrium price, and thus gives new positions to the centres about which the amount and the price tend to oscillate.

These considerations point to the great importance of the element of time in relation to demand and supply, to the study of which we now proceed. We shall gradually discover a great many different limitations of the doctrine that the price at which a thing can be produced represents its real cost of production, that is, the efforts and sacrifices which have been directly and indirectly devoted to its production. For, in an age of rapid change such as this, the equilibrium of normal demand and supply does not thus correspond to any distinct relation of a certain aggregate of pleasures got from the consumption of the commodity and an aggregate of efforts and sacrifices involved in producing it: the correspondence would not be exact, even if normal earnings and interest were exact measures of the efforts and sacrifices for which they are the money payments. This is the real drift of that much quoted, and much-misunderstood doctrine of Adam Smith and other economists that the normal, or "natural," value of a commodity is that which economic forces tend to bring about *in the long run*. It is the average value which economic forces would bring about if the general conditions of life were stationary for a run of time long enough to enable them all to work out their full effect.

But we cannot foresee the future perfectly. The unexpected may happen; and the existing tendencies may be modified before they have had time to accomplish what appears now to be their full and complete work. The fact that the general conditions of life are not stationary is the source of many of the difficulties that are met with in applying economic doctrines to practical problems.

Of course Normal does not mean Competitive. Market prices and Normal prices are alike brought about by a multitude of influences, of which some rest on a moral basis and some on a physical; of which some are competitive and some are not. It is to the persistence of the influences considered, and the time allowed for them to work out their effects that we refer when contrasting Market and Normal price, and again when contrasting the narrower and the broader use of the term Normal price.

The remainder of the present volume will be chiefly occupied with interpreting and limiting this doctrine that the value of a thing tends in the long run to correspond to its cost of production. . . . But it may be well to say a word or two here on this last point.

We might as reasonably dispute whether it is the upper or the under blade of a pair of scissors that cuts a piece of paper, as whether value is governed by utility or cost of production. It is true that when one blade is held still, and the cutting is effected by moving the other, we may say with careless brevity that the cutting is done by the second; but the statement is not strictly accurate, and is to be excused only so long as it claims to be merely a popular and not a strictly scientific account of what happens.

In the same way, when a thing already made has to be sold, the price which people will be willing to pay for it will be governed by their desire to have it, together with the amount they can afford to spend on it. Their desire to have it depends partly on the chance that, if they do not buy it, they will be able to get another thing like it at as low a price: this depends on the causes that

govern the supply of it, and this again upon cost of production. But it may so happen that the stock to be sold is practically fixed. This, for instance, is the case with a fish market, in which the value of fish for the day is governed almost exclusively by the stock on the slabs in relation to the demand: and if a person chooses to take the stock for granted, and say that the price is governed by demand, his brevity may perhaps be excused so long as he does not claim strict accuracy. So again it may be pardonable, but it is not strictly accurate to say that the varying prices which the same rare book fetches, when sold and resold at Christie's auction room, are governed exclusively by demand.

Taking a case at the opposite extreme, we find some commodities which conform pretty closely to the law of constant return; that is to say, their average cost of production will be very nearly the same whether they are produced in small quantities or in large. In such a case the normal level about which the market price fluctuates will be this definite and fixed (money) cost of production. If the demand happens to be great, the market price will rise for a time above the level; but as a result production will increase and the market price will fall: and conversely, if the demand falls for a time below its ordinary level.

In such a case, if a person chooses to neglect market fluctuations, and to take it for granted that there will anyhow be enough demand for the commodity to insure that some of it, more or less, will find purchasers at a price equal to this cost of production, then he may be excused for ignoring the influence of demand, and speaking of (normal) price as governed by cost of production— provided only he does not claim scientific accuracy for the wording of his doctrine, and explains the influence of demand in its right place.

Thus we may conclude that, *as a general rule*, the shorter the period which we are considering, the greater must be the share of our attention which is given to the influence of demand on value; and the longer the period, the more important will be the influence of cost of production on value. For the influence of changes in cost of production takes as a rule a longer time to work itself out than does the influence of changes in demand. The actual value at any time, the market value as it is often called, is often more influenced by passing events and by causes whose action is fitful and short lived, than by those which work persistently. But in long periods these fitful and irregular causes in large measure efface one another's influence; so that in the long run persistent causes dominate value completely. Even the most persistent causes are however liable to change. For the whole structure of production is modified, and the relative costs of production of different things are permanently altered, from one generation to another.

When considering costs from the point of view of the capitalist employer, we of course measure them in money; because his direct concern with the efforts needed for the work of his employees lies in the money payments he must make. His concern with the real costs of their effort and of the training required for it is only indirect, though a monetary assessment of his own labour is necessary for some problems, as will be seen later on. But when considering costs from the social point of view, when inquiring whether the cost of attaining a given result is increasing or diminishing with changing economic conditions, then we are concerned with the real costs of efforts of various qualities, and with the real cost of waiting. If the purchasing power of money, in terms of effort has remained about constant, and if the rate of remuneration for waiting has remained about constant, then the money measure of costs corresponds to the real costs: but such a correspondence is never to be assumed lightly. These considerations will generally suffice for the interpretation of the term Cost in what follows, even where no distinct indication is given in the context. . . .

SUMMARY OF THE GENERAL THEORY OF EQUILIBRIUM OF DEMAND AND SUPPLY

[Paragraph deleted.]

. . . we have studied the theory of the mutual relations of demand and supply in their most general form; taking as little account as possible of the special incidents of particular applications of the theory, and leaving over for the following Book the study of the bearings of the general theory on the special features of the several agents of production, Labour, Capital, and Land.

The difficulties of the problem depend chiefly on variations in the area of space, and the period of time over which the market in question extends; the influence of time being more fundamental than that of space.

Even in a market of very short period, such as that of a provincial corn-exchange on market-day, the "higgling and bargaining" might probably oscillate about a mean position, which would have some sort of a right to be called the equilibrium price: but the action of dealers in offering one price or refusing another would depend little, if at all, on calculations with regard to cost of production. They would look chiefly at present demand on the one hand, and on the other at the stocks of the commodity already available. It is true that they would pay some attention to such movements of production in the near future as might throw their shadow before; but in the case of perishable goods they would look only a very little way beyond the immediate present. Cost of production has for instance no perceptible influence on the day's bargaining in a fish-market.

In a rigidly stationary state in which supply could be perfectly adjusted to demand in every particular, the normal expenses of production, the marginal expenses, and the average expenses (rent being counted in) would be one and the same thing, for long periods and for short. But, as it is, the language both of professed writers on economics and of men of business shows much elasticity in the use of the term Normal when applied to the causes that determine value. And one fairly well marked division needs study.

On the one side of this division are long periods, in which the normal action of economic forces has time to work itself out more fully; in which therefore a temporary scarcity of skilled labour, or of any other of the agents of production, can be remedied; and in which those economies that normally result from an increase in the scale of production—normally, that is without the aid of any substantive new invention—have time to develop themselves. The expenses of a representative firm, managed with normal ability and having normal access to the internal and external economies of production on a large scale, may be taken as a standard for estimating normal expenses of production: and when the period under survey is long enough to enable the investment of capital in building up a new business to complete itself and to bear full fruits; then the marginal supply price is that, the expectation of which in the long run just suffices to induce capitalists to invest their material capital, and workers of all grades to invest their personal capital in the trade.

On the other side of the line of division are periods of time long enough to enable producers to adapt their production to changes in demand, in so far as that can be done with the existing provision of specialized skill, specialized capital, and industrial organization; but not long enough to enable them to make any important changes in the supplies of these factors of production. For such periods the stock of material and personal appliances of production has to be taken in a great measure for granted; and the marginal increment of supply is determined by estimates of producers as to the amount of production it is worth their while to get out of those appliances. If trade is brisk all energies are strained to their utmost, overtime is worked, and then the limit to production is given by want of power rather than by want of will to go further or faster. But if trade is slack every producer has to make up his mind how near to prime cost it is worth his while to take fresh orders. And here there is no definite law, the chief operative force is the fear of spoiling the market; and that acts in different ways and with different strengths on different individuals and different industrial groups. For the chief motive of all open combinations and of all informal silent and "customary" understandings whether among employers or employed is the need for preventing individuals from spoiling the common market by action that may bring them immediate gains, but at the cost of a greater aggregate loss to the trade.

We next turned aside to consider the relations of demand and supply with reference to things that need to be combined together for the purposes of satisfying a joint demand; of which the most important instance is that of the specialized material capital, and the specialized personal skill that must work together in any trade. For there is no direct demand on the part of consumers for either alone, but only for the two conjointly; the demand for either separately is a derived demand, which rises, other things being equal, with every increase in the demand for the common products, and with every diminution in the supply price of the joint factors of production. In like manner commodities of which there is a joint supply, such as gas and coke, or beef and hides, can each of them have only a derived supply price, governed by the expenses of the whole process of production on the one hand, and on the other by the demand for the remaining joint products.

The composite demand for a thing, resulting from its being used for several different purposes, and the composite supply of a thing, that has several sources of production, present no great difficulty; for the several amounts demanded for the different purposes, or supplied from different sources, can be added together . . . for combining the demands of the rich, the middle classes and the poor for the same commodity.

Next we made some study of the division of the supplementary costs of a business—and especially those connected with building up a trade connection, with marketing, and with insurance—among the various products of that business.

Returning to those central difficulties of the equilibrium of normal demand and supply which are connected with the element of time, we investigated more fully the relation between the value of an appliance for production and that of the things produced by it.

When different producers have different advantages for producing a thing, its price must be sufficient to cover the expenses of production of those producers who have no special and exceptional facilities; for if not they will withhold or diminish their production, and the scarcity of the amount supplied, relatively to the demand, will raise the price. When the market is in equilibrium, and the thing is being sold at a price which covers these expenses, there remains a surplus beyond their expenses for those who have the assistance of any exceptional advantages. If these advantages arise from the command over free gifts of nature, the surplus is called a producer's surplus or producer's rent: there is a surplus in any case, and if the owner of a free gift of nature lends it out to another, he can generally get for its use a money income equivalent to this surplus.

The price of the produce is equal to the cost of production of that part of it, which is raised on the margin, that is under such unfavourable conditions as to yield no rent. The cost of this part can be reckoned up without reasoning in a circle; and the cost of other parts cannot.

If land which had been used for growing hops, is found capable of yielding a higher rent as market-garden land, the area under hops will undoubtedly be diminished; and this will raise their marginal cost of production and therefore their price. The rent which land will yield for one kind of produce, calls attention to the fact that a demand for the land for that kind of produce increases the difficulties of supply of other kinds; though it does not directly enter into those expenses. And similar arguments apply to the relation between the site values of urban land and the costs of things made on it.

Thus when we are taking a broad view of normal value, when we are investigating the causes which determine normal value "in the long run," when we are tracing the "ultimate" effects of economic causes; then the income that is derived from capital in these forms enters into the payments by which the expenses of production of the commodity in question have to be covered; and estimates as to the probable amount of that income directly control the action of the producers, who are on the margin of doubt as to whether to increase the means of production or not. But, on the other hand, when we are considering the causes which determine normal prices for a period which is short relatively to that required for largely increasing the supply of those appliances for production; then their influence on value is chiefly indirect and more or less similar to that exerted by the free gifts of nature. The shorter the period which we are considering, and the slower the process of production of those appliances, the less part will variations in the income derived from them play in checking or increasing the supply of the commodity produced by them, and in raising or lowering its supply price.

This leads to the consideration of

some difficulties of a technical character connected with the marginal expenses of production of a commodity that obeys the law of increasing return. The difficulties arise from the temptation to represent supply price as dependent on the amount produced, without allowing for the length of time that is necessarily occupied by each individual business in extending its internal, and still more its external organization; and in consequence they have been most conspicuous in mathematical and semi-mathematical discussions of the theory of value. For when changes of supply price and amount produced are regarded as dependent exclusively on one another without any reference to gradual growth, it appears reasonable to argue that the marginal supply price for each individual producer is the addition to his aggregate expenses of production made by producing his last element; that this marginal price is likely in many cases to be diminished by an increase in his output much more than the demand price in the general market would be by the same cause.

The statical theory of equilibrium is therefore not wholly applicable to commodities which obey the law of increasing return. It should however be noted that in many industries each producer has a special market in which he is well known, and which he cannot extend quickly; and that therefore, though it might be physically possible for him to increase his output rapidly, he would run the risk of forcing down very much the demand price in his special market, or else of being driven to sell his surplus production outside on less favourable terms. And though there are industries in which each producer has access to the whole of a large market, yet in these there remain but few internal economies to be got by an increase of output, when the existing plant is already well occupied. No doubt there are industries as to which neither of these statements is true: they are in a transitional state, and it must be conceded that the statical

theory of equilibrium of normal demand and supply cannot be profitably applied to them. But such cases are not numerous; and with regard to the great bulk of manufacturing industries, the connection between supply price and amount shows a fundamentally different character for short periods and for long.

For short periods, the difficulties of adjusting the internal and external organization of a business to rapid changes in output are so great that the supply price must generally be taken to rise with an increase, and to fall with a diminution in the amount produced.

But in long periods both the internal and the external economies of production on a large scale have time to develop themselves. The marginal supply price is not the expenses of production of any particular bale of goods: but it is the whole expenses (including insurance, and gross earnings of management) of a marginal increment in the aggregate process of production and marketing.

Some study of the effects of a tax, regarded as a special case of a change in the general conditions of demand and supply suggests that, when proper allowance is made for the interests of consumers, there is on abstract grounds rather less *prima facie* cause than the earlier economists supposed, for the general doctrine of so-called "Maximum Satisfaction"; *i.e.* for the doctrine that the free pursuit by each individual of his own immediate interest, will lead producers to turn their capital and labour, and consumers to turn their expenditure into such courses as are most conducive to the general interests. We have nothing to do at this stage of our inquiry, limited as it is to analysis of the most general character, with the important question how far, human nature being constituted as it is at present, collective action is likely to be inferior to individualistic action in energy and elasticity, in inventiveness and directness of purpose; and whether it is not therefore likely to waste through practical inefficiency more than it could save by taking account of all the interests affected by any course of action. But even without taking account of the evils arising from the unequal distribution of wealth, there is *prima facie* reason for believing that the aggregate satisfaction, so far from being already a maximum, could be much increased by collective action in promoting the production and consumption of things in regard to which the law of increasing return acts with especial force.

This position is confirmed by the study of the theory of monopolies. It is the immediate interest of the monopolist so to adjust the production and sale of his wares as to obtain for himself the maximum net revenue, and the course which he thus adopts is unlikely to be that which affords the aggregate maximum satisfaction. The divergence between individual and collective interests is *prima facie* less important with regard to those things which obey the law of diminishing return, than with regard to those which obey the law of increasing return: but, in the case of the latter, there is strong *prima facie* reason for believing that it might often be to the interest of the community directly or indirectly to intervene, because a largely increased production would add much more to consumers' surplus than to the aggregate expenses of production of the goods. More exact notions on the relations of demand and supply, particularly when expressed in the form of diagrams, may help us to see what statistics should be collected, and how they should be applied in the attempt to estimate the relative magnitudes of various conflicting economic interests, public and private.

Ricardo's theory of cost of production in relation to value occupies so important a place in the history of economics that any misunderstanding as to its real character must necessarily be very mischievous; and unfortunately it is so expressed as almost to invite misunderstanding. In consequence there is a widely spread belief that it has needed to be reconstructed by the present generation of economists. Cause is shown . . . for not accepting this opinion; and for holding on the contrary that the foundations of the theory as they were left by Ricardo remain intact; that much has been added to them, and that very much has been built upon them, but that little has been taken from them. It is there argued that he knew that demand played an essential part in governing value, but that he regarded its action as less obscure than that of cost of production, and therefore passed it lightly over in the notes which he made for the use of his friends, and himself; for he never essayed to write a formal treatise: also that he regarded cost of production as dependent—not as Marx asserted him to have done on the mere quantity of labour used up in production, but—on the quality as well as quantity of that labour; together with the amount of stored up capital needed to aid labour, and the length of time during which such aid was invoked.

NOTES

1. It cannot be too much insisted that to measure directly, or *per se*, either desires or the satisfaction which results from their fulfilment is impossible, if not inconceivable. . . .

2. It may be noticed here, though the fact is of but little practical importance, that a small quantity of a commodity may be insufficient to meet a certain special want; and then there will be a more than proportionate increase of pleasure when the consumer gets enough of it to enable him to attain the desired end. Thus, for instance, anyone would derive less pleasure in proportion from ten pieces of wall paper than from twelve, if the latter would, and the former would not, cover the whole of the walls of his room. Or again a very short concert or a holiday may fail of its purpose of soothing and recreating: and one of double length might be of more than double total utility. This case corre-

sponds to the fact, which we shall have to study in connection with the tendency to diminishing return, that the capital and labour already applied to any piece of land may be so inadequate for the development of its full powers, that some further expenditure on it even with the existing arts of agriculture would give a more than proportionate return; and in the fact that an improvement in the arts of agriculture may resist that tendency, we shall find an analogy to the condition just mentioned in the text as implied in the law of diminishing utility.

3. Such a demand schedule may be translated, on a plan now coming into familiar use, into a curve that may be called his *demand curve*. Let Ox and Oy be drawn the one horizontally, the other vertically. Let an inch measured along Ox represent 10 lbs. of tea, and an inch measured along Oy represent 40*d*.

	tenths of an inch.			fortieths of an inch.
take	$Om_1 = 6$,	and	draw	$m_1p_1 = 50$
	$Om_2 = 7$	''	''	$m_2p_2 = 40$
	$Om_3 = 8$	''	''	$m_3p_3 = 33$
	$Om_4 = 9$	''	''	$m_4p_4 = 28$
	$Om_5 = 10$	''	''	$m_5p_5 = 24$
	$Om_6 = 11$	''	''	$m_6p_6 = 21$
	$Om_7 = 12$	''	''	$m_7p_7 = 19$
	$Om_8 = 13$	''	''	$m_8p_8 = 17$

m_1 being on Ox and m_1p_1 being drawn vertically from m_1; and so for the others. Then p_1 $p_2 \ldots p_8$ are points on his demand curve for tea; or as we may say *demand points*. If we could find demand points in the same manner for every possible quantity of tea, we should get the whole continuous curve DD' as shown in the figure. This account of the

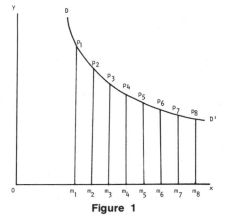

Figure 1

demand schedule and curve is provisional; several difficulties connected with it are deferred to chapter v.

4. Thus Mill says that we must

mean by the word demand, the quantity demanded, and remember that this is not a fixed quantity, but in general varies according to the value. *(Principles,* III, II, §4.)

This account is scientific in substance; but it is not clearly expressed and it has been much misunderstood. Cairnes prefers to represent

demand as the desire for commodities and services, seeking its end by an offer of general purchasing power, and supply as the desire for general purchasing power, seeking its end by an offer of specific commodities or services.

He does this in order that he may be able to speak of a ratio, or equality, of demand and supply. But the quantities of two desires on the part of two different persons cannot be compared directly; their measures may be compared, but not they themselves. And in fact Cairnes is himself driven to speak of supply as "limited by the quantity of specific commodities offered for sale, and demand by the quantity of purchasing power offered for their purchase." But sellers have not a fixed quantity of commodities which they offer for sale unconditionally at whatever price they can get: buyers have not a fixed quantity of purchasing power which they are ready to spend on the specific commodities, however much they pay for them. Account must then be taken in either case of the relation between quantity and price, in order to complete Cairnes' account, and when this is done it is brought back to the lines followed by Mill. He says, indeed, that

Demand, as defined by Mill, is to be understood as measured, not, as my definition would require, by the quantity of purchasing power offered in support of the desire for commodities, but by the quantity of commodities for which such purchasing power is offered.

It is true that there is a great difference between the statements, "I will buy twelve eggs," and "I will buy a shilling's worth of eggs." But there is no substantive difference between the statement, "I will buy twelve eggs at a penny each, but only six at three halfpence each," and the statement, "I will spend a shilling on eggs at a penny each, but if they cost three halfpence each I will spend ninepence on them." But while Cairnes' account when completed becomes substantially the same as Mill's, its present form is even more misleading.

5. We may sometimes find it convenient to speak of this as a *raising of his demand schedule*. Geometrically it is represented by raising his demand curve, or, what comes to the same thing, moving it to the right, with perhaps some modification of its shape.

6. The demand is represented by the same curve as before, only an inch measured along Ox now represents ten million pounds instead of ten pounds. And a formal definition of the demand curve for a market may be given thus:—The demand curve for any commodity in a market during any given unit of time is the locus of demand points for it. That is to way, it is a curve such that if from any point P on it, a straight line PM be drawn perpendicular to Ox, PM represents the price at which purchasers will be forthcoming for an amount of the commodity represented by OM.

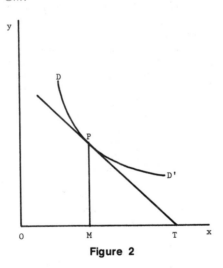

Figure 2

7. That is, if a point moves along the curve away from Oy it will constantly approach Ox. Therefore if a straight line PT be drawn touching the curve at P and meeting Ox in T, the angle PTx is an obtuse angle. It will be found convenient to have a short way of expressing this fact; which may be done by saying that PT is *inclined negatively*. Thus the one universal rule to which the demand curve conforms is that it is *inclined negatively* throughout the whole of its length.

8. It is even conceivable, though not probable, that a simultaneous and propor-

tionate fall in the price of all teas may diminish the demand for some particular kind of it; if it happens that those whom the increased cheapness of tea leads to substitute a superior kind for it are more numerous than those who are led to take it in the place of an inferior kind. The question where the lines of division between different commodities should be drawn must be settled by convenience of the particular discussion. For some purposes it may be best to regard Chinese and Indian teas, or even Souchong and Pekoe teas, as different commodities; and to have a separate demand schedule for each of them. While for other purposes it may be best to group together commodities as distinct as beef and mutton, or even as tea and coffee, and to have a single list to represent the demand for the two combined; but in such a case of course some convention must be made as to the number of ounces of tea which are taken as equivalent to a pound of coffee.

9. . . . to represent the equilibrium of demand and supply geometrically we may draw the demand and supply curves together as in Fig. 3. If then OR represents the rate at which production is being actually carried on, and Rd the demand price is greater than Rs the supply price, the production is exceptionally profitable, and will be increased. R, the *amount-index*, as we may call it, will move to the right. On the other hand, if Rd is less than Rs, R will move to the left. If Rd is equal to Rs, that is, if R is vertically under a point of intersection of the curves, demand and supply are in equilibrium.

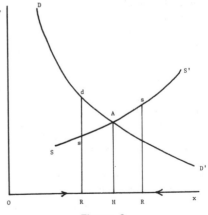

Figure 3

This may be taken as the typical diagram for stable equilibrium for a commodity that obeys the law of diminishing return. But if we had made SS' a horizontal straight line, we should have represented the case of "constant return," in which the supply price is the same for all amounts of the commodity. And if we had made SS' inclined negatively, but less steeply than DD' (the neces-sity for this condition will appear more fully later on), we should have got a case of stable equilibrium for a commodity which obeys the law of increasing return. In either case the above reasoning remains unchanged without the alteration of a word or a letter; but the last case introduces difficulties which we have arranged to postpone.

19. The Influence of the Rate of Interest on Prices*

KNUT WICKSELL

The thesis which I humbly submit to criticism is this. If, other things remaining the 'same, the leading banks of the world were to lower their rate of inter-est, say 1 per cent below its ordinary level, and keep it so for some years, then the prices of all commodities would rise and rise and rise without any limit whatever; on the contrary, if the leading banks were to *raise* their rate of interest, say 1 per cent above its normal level, and keep it so for some years, then all prices would *fall* and fall and fall without any limit except Zero.

Now this proposition cannot be proved directly by experience, because the fact required in its hypothesis never happens.

The supposition was that the banks were to lower or raise their interest, *other things remaining the same*, but that, of course, the banks never do; why, indeed, should they? Other things remaining the same, the bank-rate is sure to remain the same too, or if, by any chance, e.g., by mistake, it were al-tered, it would very soon come round to its proper level. My thesis is, therefore, only an abstract statement, and some-body, perhaps, will ask: what is the use of it then? But I venture to assert that it may be of very great use all the same. Everybody knows the statement of New-ton that, if the attraction of the sun were suddenly to cease, then the planets would leave their orbits in the tangential direction; this, too, of course, is only an abstract proposition, because the solar attraction never ceases, but it is most useful nevertheless; indeed, it is the very corner-stone of celestial mechan-ics; and in the same way I believe that the thesis here propounded, if proved to be true, will turn out to be the corner-stone of the mechanics of prices, or rather one of its corner-stones, the influ-ence of the supply of precious metals and of the demand for commodities from the gold-producing countries being the other.

Before going further, however, we must answer one more question. Our supposition might be not only unreal as to facts, but even logically impossible; and then, of course, its use would be *nil*. According to the general opinion among economists, the interest on money is regulated in the long run by the profit on capital, which in its turn is determined by the productivity and rela-tive abundance of real capital, or, in the terms of modern political economy, by

*Source: From Economic Journal (June 1907), pp. 213-20.

its *marginal productivity*. This remaining the same, as, indeed, by our supposition it is meant to do, would it be at all possible for the banks to keep the rate of interest either higher or lower than its normal level, prescribed by the simultaneous state of the average profit on capital?

This question deserves very careful consideration, and, in fact, its proper analysis will take us a long way towards solving the whole problem.

Interest on money and profit on capital are not the same thing, nor are they *immediately* connected with each other; if they were, they could not differ at all, or could only differ a certain amount at every time. There is no doubt *some* connecting link between them, but the proper nature and extent of this connection is not so very easy to define.

If we look only at credit transactions between individuals, without any interference of banks, the connection between interest and profit indeed seems obvious. If by investing your capital in some industrial enterprise you can get, after due allowance for risk, a profit of, say, 10 per cent, then, of course, you will not lend it at a much cheaper rate; and if the borrower has no recourse but to individuals in the same situation as you, he will not be able to get the money much cheaper than that.

But it is a very different thing with the modern forms of credit, which almost always imply the mediation of some bank or professional money-lender. The banks in their lending business are not only not limited by their own capital; they are not, at least not immediately, limited by any capital whatever; by concentrating in their hands almost all payments, they themselves create the money required, or, what is the same thing, they accelerate *ad libitum* the rapidity of the circulation of money. The sum borrowed to-day in order to buy commodities is placed by the seller of the goods on his account at the same bank or some other bank, and can be lent the very next day to some other person with the same effect. As the German author, Emil Struck, justly says in his well-known sketch of the English money market: in our days demand and supply of money have become about the same thing, the demand to a large extent creating its own supply.

In a *pure* system of credit, where all payments were made by transference in the bank-books, the banks would be able to grant at any moment any amount of loans at any, however diminutive, rate of interest.

But then, what becomes of the connecting link between interest and profit? In my opinion there is no such link, except precisely *the effect on prices*, which would be caused by their difference.

When interest is low in proportion to the existing rate of profit, and if, as I take it, *the prices thereby rise*, then, of course, trade will require more sovereigns and bank-notes, and therefore the sums lent will *not* all come back to the bank, but part of them will remain in the boxes and purses of the public; in consequence, the bank reserves will melt away while the amount of their liabilities very likely has increased, which will force them to raise their rate of interest.

The reverse of all this, of course, will take place when the rate of interest has accidentally become too high in proportion to the average profit on capital. So far, you will easily remark, my proposition is quite in accordance with well-known facts of the money market. If it be not true, if, on the contrary, as Thomas Tooke asserted, and even Ricardo in his earlier writings seems to have believed, a low rate of interest, by cheapening, as they put it, one of the elements of production, would lower prices, and a high rate of interest raise them—a most specious argument, resting, however, on the unwarrantable assumption that the remuneration of the other factors of production could, under such circumstances, remain the same— then the policy of banks must be the very reverse of what it really is; they would lower their rates when prices were getting high and reserves becoming low, they would raise them in the opposite case.

A more direct proof of my thesis is required, however, and might be given in some such way as this. If as a merchant I have sold my goods to the amount of £100 against a bill or promissory note of three months, and I get it discounted at once by a bank or a bill broker, the rate of discount being 4 per cent per annum, then in fact I have received a cash price for my goods amounting to £99. If, however, the bill is taken by the bank at 3 per cent, then the cash price of my goods have *ipso facto* risen, if only a quarter of 1 per cent; very likely not even that, because competition probably will force me to cede part of my extra profit to the buyer of the goods. In other cases, however, when long-term credit comes into play, the immediate rise of prices might be very much greater than that. If the rate of discount remains low, the interest on long loans is sure to go down too; building companies and railway companies will be able to raise money, say at 4 per cent instead of 5 per cent, and therefore, other things being the same, they can offer, and by competition will be more or less compelled to offer for wages and materials, anything up to 25 per cent *more* than before, 4 per cent on £125 being the same as 5 per cent on £100.

But, further—and this is the essential point to which I would call your special attention—the upward movement of prices, whether great or small in the first instance, *can never cease* so long as the rate of interest is kept lower than its normal rate, *i.e.*, the rate consistent with the then existing marginal productivity of real capital. When all commodities have risen in price, a *new level of prices* has formed itself which in its turn will serve as basis for all calculations for the future, and all contracts. Therefore, if the bank-rate now goes up to its normal

height, the level of prices will not go down; it will simply remain where it is, there being no forces in action which could press it down; and, consequently, if the bank-rate *remains lower* than its normal height, a new impetus towards forcing up the prices will follow, and so on. The opposite of all this will take place when the rate of interest has become too high in proportion to average profit, and so in both cases a difference between the two rates remaining, the movement of prices can never cease, just as the electric current never ceases as long as the difference of tension between the poles remains.

The proposition that a low rate of interest will raise prices, a high rate of interest lower prices, is in some respects anything but new; it has been stated more than once, but a formidable objection was always triumphantly brought against it in the shape of statistical facts; indeed, if you consider the figures given, *e.g.*, by Sauerbeck in his well-known tables in the *Journal of the Statistical Society*, you will generally find that high prices do not correspond with a low rate of interest, and *vice versa*; it rather comes the opposite way, interest and prices very often rising and falling together. But this objection quite loses its importance; nay, more, it turns into a positive support of our theory, as soon as we fix our eyes on the relativity of the conception of interest on money, its necessary connection with profit on capital. The rate of interest is never high or low in itself, but only in relation to the profit which people can make with the money in their hands, and this, of course, varies. In good times, when trade is brisk, the rate of profit is high, and, what is of great consequence, is generally expected to remain high; in periods of depression it is low, and expected to remain low. The rate of interest on money follows, no doubt, the same course, but not at once, not of itself; it is, as it were, dragged after the rate of profit by the movement of prices and the consequent changes in the state of bank reserve, caused by the difference between the two rates. In the meantime this difference acts on prices in just the same way as would be the case if, according to our original supposition, profit on capital were to remain constant, and interest on money were to rise or fall spontaneously. In one word, the interest on money is, in reality, very often low when it seems to be high, and high when it seems to be low. This I believe to be the proper answer to the objection stated above, as far as the influence of credit on prices is regarded; occasionally, of course, as in times of wild specualtion or panics, the problem is complicated very much by the action of other factors, which need not here be taken into consideration.

Granted, then, our theory to be true in the main or in the abstract, what will be its practical consequences? to what extent would the leading money institutions be able to regulate prices?

A single bank, of course, has no such power whatever; indeed, it cannot put its rates, whether much higher or much lower than prescribed by the state of the market; if it did, it would in the former case lose all profitable business; in the latter case its speedy insolvency would be the inevitable consequence.

Not even all the banks of a single country united could do it in the long run; a too high or too low rate would influence its balance of trade, and thereby cause an influx or reflux of gold in the well-known way, so as to force the banks to apply their rates to the state of the universal money market.

But supposing, as, indeed, we have done, that all the leading banks of the commercial world were to follow the same course, then gold could have no reason to go to one place more than to another, and so the action exercised on prices would have its sway without any hindrance from the international movement of money. Still, even then it would, under the present circumstances, have its obvious limits. As I remarked at the outset, the influence of credit or the rate of interest is only one of the factors acting on prices; the other is the volume of metallic money itself, especially, in our times, the supply of gold, and so long as the gold itself remains the standard of value, this factor evidently will take the lead in the long run. Were the production of gold materially to diminish while the demand for money be unaltered, the banks no doubt, by lowering their rate of interest, might for a while profitably react against the otherwise inevitable pressure on prices, but only for a while, because, even if the rather unnecessary stiffness of present bank legislations could be slackened, the ever-growing demand for gold for industrial purposes would gradually reduce the bank stores, and could only be checked by raising the price of gold—that is, by lowering the average money prices.

The other extreme, which at present seems much more likely to occur: a plethora of gold supply, and the rise of prices thereby caused, could not be effectually met in any way, so long as free coinage of gold exists.[1]

On the other hand, if this most essential step on the way to a rational monetary system should be taken, if the free coining of gold, like that of silver, should cease, and eventually the bank-note itself, or rather the unity in which the accounts of banks are kept, should become the standard of value, then, and not till then, the problem of keeping the value of money steady, the average level of money prices at a constant height, which evidently is to be regarded as the fundamental problem of monetary science, would be solvable theoretically and practically to any extent. And the means of solving it need not be sought in some more or less fantastic scheme like that of a central issuing bank for all the world, as it is sometimes proposed, but simply in a proper manipulation of general bank-rates, lowering them when prices are getting low, and raising them when prices are getting high.

Nor would this system be at all artificial, because the point about which the rate of interest would then oscillate, and to which it would constantly gravitate, would be precisely what I have called above its normal level, that one prescribed by the simultaneous state of the marginal productivity of real capital, the alterations of which we, of course, cannot control, but only have to comply with.

P.S.—When this paper was read at the British Association meeting it was objected by Mr. Palgrave that the banks could not possibly be charged with the regulation of prices, their liberty of action—if I understood him right—being, in his view, restricted by the necessity of protecting their own reserves as well from getting too low in consequence of an unfavourable balance of trade, as from running to an unprofitable height by an influx of gold. This, no doubt, is true, but it must not be forgotten that the international rate policy of banks has, as it were, *two degrees of freedom*, in so far as the international movement of gold can be checked or modified, not only by raising the rate of discount in the country *from* which the metal flows, but also by lowering it in the country, or countries, *to* which gold is flowing. In other words, the action of the banks against each other, which has for its object the proper distribution of money, or the levelling of the *niveau* of prices between different countries, might logically be concomitant with a *common* action for the purpose of keeping the universal value of money and level of prices at a constant height, which, however, under present circumstances only can be done within the limits prescribed by the general supply of gold.

On the other hand, it was remarked by Professor Edgeworth that if the free coinage of gold be suppressed, the Governments themselves have in their hand the regulating of general prices. This, too, is true, at any rate so long as the present large production of gold persists; and even if it should cease, and gold become scarce, the Governments, no doubt, might supplant the lack in currency by a judicious emission of paper-money. But a single Government has in this respect only the choice between two alternatives: it may try to keep the value of its money steady *towards the commodities*, but then it necessarily sacrifices the parity of its exchanges; or else it may manage to keep its exchanges strictly at par, but then it has of itself no power over the level of prices. Some international agreement, either regarding the amount of gold to be coined by each country or else involving a common rate-policy of the banks as described above, must needs come into play, shall both those purposes—the steadiness of the average value of money and the parity of exchanges—be fulfilled together; and it seems to me, although I may be mistaken, that for several reasons such agreements could be far more easily and effectually made by the banks, with the support, that is, of the Governments, than by the Governments themselves exclusive of the banks.

NOTE

1. It is not easy to describe or imagine the exact manner in which an excess or deficiency in the ordinary gold supply affects prices, although its ultimate effect on them cannot well be doubted. As in our days the new gold generally finds its way as soon as possible to the banks, the common impression seems to be that it by so much increases the loanable funds of the banks, and therefore in the first instance causes the rate of interest to go down. This, no doubt, would be true if the new gold in its totality were deposited by its owners as *capital* for lending purposes, and in so far as this may be the case it indeed affords an illustration, and the only practical one, of the lowering of bank rates effecting a rise of prices. But mostly, I suppose, the gold comes to us not as lending capital, but as payment for the imports of the gold-producing countries, and if so its acting on the prices will be much more immediate and its effect on the rate of interest very slight. It is even possible that the rise of prices, caused by the increased demand for commodities from the gold countries, will *forerun* the arriving of the gold, the necessary medium of exchange being in the meantime supplied by an extension of the credit, so that the rate of interest perhaps will rise from the beginning. In any case the *ultimate* effect of

an increased gold supply will be a *rise*, not a fall, in the rate of interest (and *vice versa* with a lacking supply of gold), because the large mining enterprises and the buying up of gold by the non-producing countries have actually destroyed large amounts of real capital and thereby given the rate of profit a tendency to rise. This all may be the explanation of some rather perplexing features in economic history, a rise of prices even when apparently caused by a surplus of gold supply very seldom being accompanied by a low rate of interest, but generally by a high one.

20. Manual of Political Economy*

VILFREDO PARETO

GENERAL NOTION OF ECONOMIC EQUILIBRIUM

[Paragraphs deleted.]

There are two large classes of theories. The object of the first is to compare the sensations of one man in different situations, and to determine which of these he would choose. Political economy deals with this class of theories primarily; and, since it is customary to assume that man will be guided in his choice exclusively by consideration of his own advantage, of his self-interest, we say that this class is made up of theories of egotism. But it would be made up of theories of *altruism* (if the meaning of that term could be defined rigorously), or, in general, of theories which rest on any rule which man follows in comparing his sensations. It is not an essential characteristic of this class of theories that a man choosing between two sensations choose the most agreeable; he could choose a different one, following a rule which could be fixed arbitrarily. What does constitute the essential characteristic of this class of theories is that we compare the different sensations of one man, and not those of different men.

The second class of theories compares the sensations of one man with those of another man, and determines the conditions in which the men must be placed relative to each other if we want to attain certain ends. This study is one of the most unsatisfactory in social science. . . .

The principal subject of our study is economic equilibrium. We will see shortly that this equilibrium results from the opposition between men's tastes and the obstacles to satisfying them. Our study includes, then, three very distinct parts: (1) the study of tastes; (2) the study of obstacles; (3) the study of the way in which these two elements combine to reach equilibrium.

The best order to follow would consist of beginning with the study of tastes and exhausting that subject; to go then to the study of obstacles and exhaust it too; and finally to study equilibrium, without returning to the study of tastes or of obstacles.

But it would be difficult for the author, as well as for the reader, to proceed in that way. It is impossible to exhaust one of these subjects without frequently bringing in notions which pertain to the other two. If these notions are not thoroughly explained, the reader cannot follow the exposition; if they are explained, we are mixing together the subjects which it was proposed to sepa-

*Source: Excerpted from the American edition, trans. Ann S. Schwier (New York: Augustus M. Kelley, Publishers, 1971), pp. 105-33 and 259-63. Reprinted by permission. Some footnotes and parenthetical references deleted; remaining footnotes and figures renumbered.

rate. Moreover, the reader easily tires of a long study the purpose of which he does not see. The writer realizes this and will treat tastes and obstacles, not haphazardly, but only insofar as may be necessary to determine equilibrium. The reader also has the justifiable desire to know where the long road which we want him to travel is leading. . . .

Let us assume that certain things capable of satisfying men's tastes exist. We will call these things economic goods. If we pose this problem—how to divide one of these goods among these individuals?—we are faced with a question which involves the second class of theories. . . . In fact, each man experiences only one sensation, the one which corresponds to the quantity of the economic good which is assigned to him. We are not dealing with different sensations of the same individual which we could compare with each other, hence we may only compare the sensation experienced by one individual with that which another individual experiences.

If there are two or more things, each individual experiences two or more different sensations, depending on the quantity of the things at his disposal. In that case we can compare these sensations and determine which of the different possible combinations will be chosen by that individual. This is a question which belongs to the first class of theories. . . .

If all the quantities of goods which an individual has at his disposal increase (or decrease), we will see immediately that, with the exception of one case which we will discuss later . . . , the new position will be more advantageous (or less advantageous) for that individual than the old one. Hence in this case there is no problem to solve. But if, on the other hand, certain quantities increase while others decrease, there is occasion for investigating whether the new combination is, or is not, advantageous to the individual. It is to this category that economic problems be-

long. In real life we see them arise in connection with the exchange contract, in which one thing is given up in order to receive another, and in connection with production, in which certain things are transformed into certain others. We will deal with these problems first.

The elements which we must combine are, on the one hand, man's tastes, and on the other, the obstacles to satisfying them. If, instead of having to deal with men, we had to study ethereal beings with neither tastes nor needs, not even experiencing the material needs of eating and drinking, there would be no economic problem to solve at all. Going to the opposite extreme, it would be the same if we were to assume that no obstacles prevented men from satisfying all their tastes and all their desires. There is no economic problem for one who has everything without limit.

The problem arises because tastes encounter certain obstacles, and it is so much the more difficult to solve if there are several ways of satisfying these tastes and overcoming these obstacles. Thus there is occasion for investigating how and why such and such a means may be preferred by the individuals.

Let us examine the problem more closely.

If one only had to choose between two or a few things, the problem to solve would be qualitative and its solution would be easy. Which do you prefer, a cask of wine or a watch? The answer is easy. But in actual fact there is a very great number of things from which choice may be made; and even for two things, the combinations of quantities among which one may choose are innumerable. In one year a man can drink 100, 101, 102, . . . litres of wine; if his watch does not run perfectly, he can get another one immediately, or wait one month, two months, . . . one year, two years, . . . before making that purchase, and keep his watch while waiting. In other words, the variations in the quantity of things among which one must choose are infinite, and these variations can be very slight, almost imperceptible. We must construct a theory which enables us to solve this type of problem.

Consider a series of these combinations of different quantities of goods. A man can pass from one to another of these combinations finally settling upon one of them. It is very important to know which is this final one, and we achieve that by the theory of economic equilibrium.

ECONOMIC EQUILIBRIUM

It can be defined in different ways which come to the same thing in the end. We may say that economic equilibrium is the state which would maintain itself indefinitely if there were no changes in the conditions under which it is observed. If, for the moment, we consider only stable equilibrium, we may say that it is determined in such a way that, if it is but slightly modified, it immediately tends to reestablish itself, to return to its original position. The two definitions are equivalent.

For example, certain circumstances or conditions being given, an individual buys 1 kilogram of bread every day. If one day he is obliged to buy 900 grams, and if the next day he again becomes free to do so, he will again buy 1 kilogram of bread. If nothing is changed in the existing conditions, he will continue to buy 1 kilogram of bread indefinitely. This is what is called the state of equilibrium.

It will be necessary to express mathematically that, this state of equilibrium being attained, these variations, or, if you will, these movements, do not occur, which comes down to saying that the system maintains itself indefinitely in the state we have considered.

The movements necessary actually to reach equilibrium can be called *real*. Those which we assume could occur to move us away from the state of equilibrium, but which do not appear in reality because the equilibrium continues, can be called *virtual*.

Political economy studies real movements in order to know how things take place; and it studies virtual movements to understand the properties of certain economic states.

Given an economic state, if we were able to move away from it by any kind of movement whatsoever, we could continue indefinitely movements which increase the quantities of all the goods which man may desire; in this way we would reach a state in which man would have everything to satiety. Obviously this would be a position of equilibrium; but it is also obvious that things do not happen that way in real life, and that we will have to determine other positions of equilibrium at which one must stop, because only certain movements are possible. In other words, there are obstacles which limit movements, which do not allow man to follow certain paths, which prevent certain variations from taking place. Equilibrium results precisely from this opposition of tastes and obstacles. The two extreme cases which we have just considered, and which are not encountered in reality, are the one in which there are no tastes and the one in which there are no obstacles.

If the obstacles or the constraints were such that they determined each movement in a precise way, we would not have to be concerned with tastes; and consideration of the obstacles would be enough to determine equilibrium. In reality things are not like that, at least in general. The obstacles do not determine all movements in an absolute fashion. They simply establish certain limits; they impose certain restrictions; but they do allow the individual to move according to his own tastes within a more or less restricted domain. And among all the admissable movements we must look for those which will occur in real life.

Tastes and obstacles refer to each of the individuals considered. For one individual the tastes of other men with whom he has relationships appear among the obstacles.

In order to have all the data for the problem of equilibrium, it is necessary to add to the tastes and obstacles the factual conditions which determine the state of the individuals and of the transformations of goods. For example, the quantities of goods possessed by the individuals, the means for transforming goods, etc. We will understand this better as our study advances.

To determine equilibrium we will set up the condition that at the moment when it occurs, movements permitted by the obstacles are prevented by the tastes; or conversely, what comes to the same thing, that at this moment, movements permitted by the tastes are prevented by the obstacles. Indeed, it is obvious that in these two ways we express the condition that no movement occurs, and this is, by definition, the equilibrium characteristic.

Thus we must investigate, at the equilibrium point, what movements are prevented and what movements are permitted by tastes; and similarly what movements are prevented and what ones are permitted by the obstacles.

MEN'S TASTES

Means must be found for subjecting them to calculation. Some writers have had the idea of deducing them from the pleasure which certain things cause men to experience. If a thing satisfies the needs or desires of a man, they would say that it had *value in use, utility.*

This notion was imperfect and ambiguous on several points. (1) It was not sufficiently demonstrated that this *value in use,* this *utility,* was exclusively a relation between a man and a thing. Moreover, they spoke of it, perhaps unconsciously, as an objective property of the things. Others, who came closer but yet not close enough to the truth, spoke of it as a relation between men in general and a thing. (2) It was not seen that this *value in use* depended on (was a function of, as the mathematicians say) the quantities consumed. For example,

to speak of the *value in use* of water does not make sense unless something more is said; and it does not suffice to add, as we have just seen, that this *value in use* is relative to a certain man. It is very different depending on whether that man is dying of thirst or has already drunk as much as he desires. To be precise, it is necessary to speak of the value in use of a certain quantity of water added to a known quantity already consumed.

It was principally through the correction of this error in earlier economics that pure economics arose. It appeared with Jevons as a rectification of the then current theories on *value;* with Walras it became, and this was very great progress, the theory of a special case of economic equilibrium, that is, that of free competition; another case, the case of monopoly, had already been studied, but in a completely different manner, by Cournot. Marshall, Edgeworth and Irving Fisher studied the economic phenomenon in a still more extensive and more general way. In our *Cours* [*Abbreviated French title of Pareto's* Lectures on Political Economy, *published in 1896–97.—Needy.*] it became the general theory of economic equilibrium, and we are going still farther along this path in the present work. (3) In political economy the word *utility* has come to mean something quite different from what it can mean in everyday language. Thus morphine is not useful, in the ordinary sense of the word, since it is harmful to the morphine addict; on the other hand it is economically *useful* to him, even though it is unhealthful, because it satisfies one of his wants. Although the older economists had mentioned this ambiguity, it is still forgotten occasionally; also, it is essential not to use the same word to mean such different things. In our *Cours* we proposed to designate economic *utility* by the word *ophelimity,* which some other authors have since adopted. . . .

For an individual, the ophelimity of a

certain quantity of a thing, added to another known quantity (it can be equal to zero) which he already possesses, is the pleasure which this quantity affords him.

If this quantity is very small (infinitely small) and if the pleasure which it gives is divided by the quantity itself, we have **elementary ophelimity.**

Finally, if we divide the elementary ophelimity by the price, we have **weighted elementary ophelimity.**

The theory of ophelimity has been improved. There is a weak point, pointed out principally by Professor Irving Fisher, in all the reasoning used to establish it. We have taken this thing called *pleasure, value in use, economic utility, ophelimity,* to be a quantity; but a demonstration of this has not been given. Assuming this demonstration accomplished, how would this quantity be measured? It is an error to believe that we could in general deduce the value of ophelimity from the law of supply and demand. We can do so only in one particular case, the unit of measure of ophelimity alone remaining arbitrary; this is when it is a case of goods of a kind such that the ophelimity of each of them depends only on the quantity of that good, and remains independent of the quantities of other goods consumed. . . . But in general, that is, when the ophelimity of a good A, consumed at the same time as goods B, C, . . . , depends not only on the consumption of A, but also on the consumption of B, C, . . . , the ophelimity remains indeterminate, even after the unit which serves to measure it has been fixed. . . .

Hereafter, when we speak of ophelimity it must always be understood that we simply mean one of the systems of indices of ophelimity. . . .

The notions of *value in use, utility,* ophelimity, indices of ophelimity, etc., greatly facilitate the exposition of the theory of economic equilibrium, but they are not necessary to construct this theory. . . .

INDIFFERENCE LINES OF TASTES

Take a man who allows himself to be governed only by his tastes and who possesses 1 kilogram of bread and 1 kilogram of wine. His tastes being given, he is willing to obtain a little less bread and a little more wine, or *vice versa.* For example, he consents to having only 0.9 kilogram of bread provided he had 1.2 of wine. In other terms, this signifies that these two combinations, 1 kilogram of bread and 1 kilogram of wine or 0.9 kilogram of bread and 1.2 kilograms of wine, are equal for him; he does not prefer the second to the first, nor the first to the second; he would not know which to choose; possessing the one or the other of these combinations is *indifferent* to him.

Starting from that combination, 1 kilogram of bread and 1 kilogram of wine, we find a great number of others among which the choice is indifferent, and we have for example

Bread 1.6 1.4 1.2 1.0 0.8 0.6
Wine 0.7 0.8 0.9 1.0 1.4 1.8

We call this series, which could be extended indefinitely, an *indifference series.*

The use of graphs greatly facilitates understanding this point.

Draw two perpendicular axes, OA and OB [Figure 1]; let OA express quantities of bread and OB quantities of

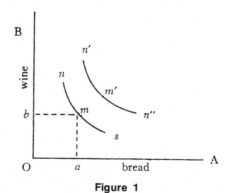

Figure 1

wine. For example, Oa represents one of bread, Ob one of wine; the point m, where these two ordinates intersect, denotes the combination 1 kilogram of bread and 1 kilogram of wine.

We can represent all of the preceding series in this way, and joining all the points of that series by a continuous line, we will have the line nms which is called an **indifference line** or **indifference curve.**[1]

Let us give each of these combinations an index which must satisfy the following two conditions, and which is arbitrary in other respects: (1) Two combinations between which the choice is indifferent must have the same index; (2) of two combinations, the one which is preferred to the other must have a larger index.

Thus we have the **indices of ophelimity**, or of the pleasure which an individual feels when he enjoys a combination which corresponds to a given index.

It follows from the above that all the combinations in one indifference series have the same index; that is, all the points on an indifference line have the same index.

Let 1 be the index of line nms of Figure 1; let m' (for example 1.1 of bread and 1.1 of wine) be another combination which the individual prefers to combination m, and give it the index 1.1. Starting from this combination m' we find another indifference series; that is, we describe another curve n'm'n''. We can continue in this fashion, of course considering not only combinations which are, for the individual, better than combination m, but also those which are worse. We will thus have several indifference series, each one having its index; in other words, we will cover the part of the plane OAB which we want to consider with an infinite number of indifference curves each of which has its index.

This gives us a complete representation of the tastes of the individual with

regard to bread and wine, and that is enough to determine economic equilibrium. The individual can disappear, provided he leaves us this photograph of his tastes.

Clearly what we have said about bread and wine can be repeated for all goods.

The reader who has used topographical maps knows that it is customary to draw certain curves which represent the points which have, for the given curve, the same height above sea level, or above any other level.

The curves in Figure 1 are contour lines if we consider the indices of ophelimity to represent the height of the points of a hill above the plane OAB which is assumed horizontal. It can be called the hill of the indices of pleasure. There are other similar ones, infinite in number, depending on the arbitrary system of indices chosen.

If pleasure can be measured, if ophelimity exists, one of these index systems will be precisely that of the values of ophelimity . . . , and the corresponding hill will be the hill of pleasure or of ophelimity.

An individual who possesses a certain combination of bread and wine can be represented by a point on that hill. The pleasure which this individual will experience will be represented by the height of this point above the plane OAB. The individual will experience a greater pleasure insofar as he is at a greater height; of two combinations he will always prefer the one which is represented by a higher point on the hill.

THE PATHS

Assume an individual who possesses the quantity of bread represented by oa and the quantity of wine represented by ab [Figure 2]. We say that the individual finds himself at the point on the hill which is projected into b on the horizontal plane xy, or in an elliptical fashion, that he is at b. Assume that at another time the individual has oa' of

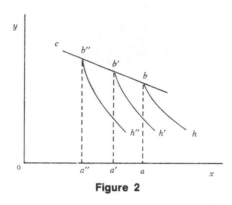

Figure 2

bread and a'b' of wine; leaving b he will be at b'. Next if he has oa'' of bread and a''b'' of wine, he will have gone from b' to b'', and so on up to c. Assume that the points b, b', b'', are very close together, and join them by a line; we will say that the individual who has successively the quantity oa of bread and ab of wine, oa' of bread and a'b' of wine, etc., has traveled, on the hill, along a *path;* or route, or road, which is projected into the line bb'b'' . . . c on the horizontal plane oxy, or, in an elliptical fashion, that he *has traveled along* the path bc.

Note that if an individual traveled along an infinite number of paths hb, h'b', h''b'', . . . , and if he stopped at the points b, b', b'', . . . , we would have to consider him as in fact traveling along the path b, b', b'', . . . , c. . . .

EQUILIBRIUM

As we have seen before, equilibrium occurs when the movements which tastes would induce are prevented by the obstacles, and *vice versa.* Consequently the general problem of equilibrium is divided into three others consisting of: (1) determining equilibrium with respect to tastes; (2) determining equilibrium with respect to obstacles, or with respect to producers; (3) finding a point common to both these equilibria which will constitute a point of general equilibrium.

As for the paths, we must: (1) con-

sider equilibrium on one fixed path; (2) consider it on a class of paths and see how the one which will be followed is chosen.

So far as the types of phenomena are concerned we must first of all study Type I for those who exchange and for those who produce. We will next study Type II which can generally occur only for those individuals who deal with others who act according to Type I. [*A Type I transaction is made when a person, accepting price as given, tries to maximize his own welfare (i.e., a shopper buying apples at the going price). Type II occurs when the person tries to alter price to maximize his own welfare (i.e., a monopolist or large investor in stocks).—Needy.*]

EQUILIBRIUM WITH RESPECT TO TASTES

Let us begin by considering an individual who follows a fixed path and who endeavors to reach the point on this path where his tastes will be best satisfied.

If obstacles of the first kind place upon this path a point beyond which he cannot go, and if the positions which precede that point are less advantageous for the individual, he obviously will go up to that point and stop there.

At that point there is equilibrium with respect to tastes. That point may be a point of tangency of the path and an indifference curve, or a terminal point . . . , in any event, it is the highest point on the segment of the path along which the individual can travel.

The point of tangency could also be the lowest point on the path, and at that point the equilibrium would be unstable. We are not concerned with this case for the time being.

Henceforth we will consider only rectilinear paths because they occur most often in reality; but our reasoning is general and, by means of slight modifications or restrictions, can be applied to other types of paths.

Consider an individual for whom t, t', t'', . . . represent indifference curves of tastes, the indices of ophelimity increasing from t to t''' [Figure 3]. Each week this individual has om of A. Assume that to transform A into B he follows the rectilinear path mn. At the point a, where the path meets indifference curve t, there is no equilibrium because it is better for the individual to go from a to b, on curve t', where he will have a larger index of ophelimity. We can say the same for all the points where the path intersects the indifference curves, but not for the point c'' where the path is tangent to an indifference curve. Indeed, the individual may move from c'' only toward b or toward b', and in both of these cases the index of ophelimity decreases. Hence, if the individual has reached c'' via the path mn, any further movement is opposed by tastes. Con-

sequently c'' is an equilibrium point. Similarly for the analogous points c, c', c'', c''' located on other paths which we assume can be taken by the individual. If we join these points by a line, we will obtain the line of equilibrium with respect to tastes; it is also called the **line of exchanges.**[2]

Terminal points which, in starting from m, precede the points of the line of exchanges may also be points of equilibrium.

It could happen that a path leads to having zero of A without being tangent to any indifference line. In this case we would have a terminal point where the path cuts the oB axis, and that would signify that on this path the individual is disposed to give not only the whole quantity of A which he possesses in

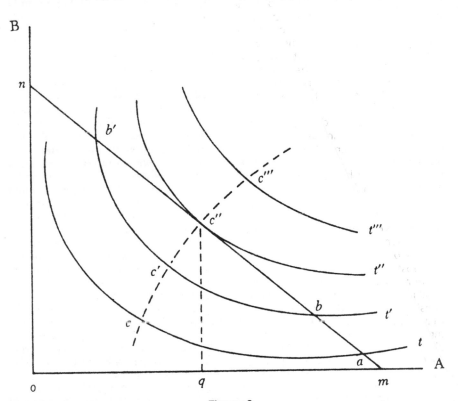

Figure 3

order to have some B, but that even if he had a larger quantity of A, he would give it to have more B.

By adding the quantities of goods transformed by each individual the line of exchanges for the collectivity made up of these individuals is obtained. And if desired, the indifference curves for that collectivity can be depicted in the same way; they will follow from the indifference curves of the individuals. . . .

ECONOMIC EQUILIBRIUM

[Paragraphs deleted.]

THE EQUILIBRIUM OF TASTES AND PRODUCTION

Let us consider a closed economy . . . and assume that the individual's expenditures are all made on goods which he purchases, and that his receipts all come from the sales of his labor, services of capital, or other goods.

In these circumstances economic equilibrium is determined by the conditions which we have already set forth . . . with regard to tastes and obstacles. We have seen that tastes, and the consideration of the existing quantities of certain goods, determine the relationships between prices and the quantities sold or purchased. Furthermore, the theory of production tells us that, given these relationships, the quantities and the prices are determined. The problem of equilibrium is thus completely solved.

EQUILIBRIUM IN GENERAL

The theoretical case above differs greatly from reality in one respect. Actually, the receipts of the individual are far from having their origin only in goods which that individual sells for production. The public debt of civilized peoples is enormous; only a very small part of that debt has been used in production, and often very poorly. The individuals who enjoy the interest on that debt certainly cannot then be considered as persons who have surrendered economic goods to production. Similar

observations could be made with regard to the salaries of the ever increasing bureaucracy of modern states, with regard to expenditures on war, naval forces, and many of the expenditures on public works. We are not investigating here whether, and in what measure, these expenditures are more or less useful to society, and in which cases they are indispensable to it; we simply claim that their utility, when it exists, is a different species from that which results from economic production.

Furthermore, the expenditures of individuals are far from being restricted to the economic goods which they purchase. Taxes make up an appreciable part of them.

By a very rough calculation, but one which is perhaps not so very far from the truth, it is estimated that in certain countries of Europe about 25 percent of the income of individuals is taken by taxes. Hence the theory which we have expounded would only be of value for at most three-fourths of the total income of a nation.

It is easy to modify that theory so as to make allowance for the phenomena we have just pointed out. To do so it is sufficient to distinguish the part of individuals' incomes which comes from economic phenomena and the part which does not, and to do the same for their expenditures.

The part of the income which is left to the individuals is spent by them in accordance with their tastes; and its allocation among the various expenditures comes within the theory of equilibrium regarding tastes which we have already given. The part taken by the public authority is spent according to other rules which economic science does not have to study. Economic science should assume that these rules are part of the given data of the problem to be solved. The laws of demand and supply will follow from the consideration of both of these categories of expenditures. If only one of them alone were to be considered, the divergence from the concrete phenomenon could be considerable. For example, for iron and steel the demands of government involve a considerable part of the output.

So far as the equilibrium of obstacles is concerned, allowance must be made for the fact that the expenditure by the enterprises is not equal to the total income of the individuals as before, but that the former constitutes only a part of the latter since the rest has another origin (public debt, government salaries, etc.). The allocation of the part destined to purchase goods transformed by production is determined by the theory of equilibrium with reference to obstacles. The allocation of the other part of incomes is determined by considerations which, as in the analogous case above, lie outside the investigations of economic science, and which consequently must be borrowed from other sciences; hence this allocation should appear among the given data of the problem.

PROPERTIES OF EQUILIBRIUM

Depending on the conditions in which it occurs, equilibrium possesses certain properties which it is important to be familiar with.

We will begin by defining a term which is desirable to use in order to avoid prolixity. We will say that the members of a collectivity enjoy *maximum ophelimity* in a certain position when it is impossible to find a way of moving from that position very slightly in such a manner that the ophelimity enjoyed by each of the individuals of that collectivity increases or decreases. That is to say, any small displacement in departing from that position necessarily has the effect of increasing the ophelimity which certain individuals enjoy, and decreasing that which others enjoy, of being agreeable to some and disagreeable to others.

EQUILIBRIUM IN EXCHANGE

We have the following theorem:

For phenomena of Type I, when equilibrium takes place at a point where the indifference curves of the contracting parties are tangent, the members of the collectivity under consideration enjoy maximum ophelimity.

Let us note that this position of equilibrium can be reached either by a rectilinear path, that is, with constant prices, or by any path whatsoever.

A rigorous demonstration of this theorem can only be given with the help of mathematics; here we shall merely give a sketch of it.

Let us begin by considering exchange between two individuals [Figure 4]. The axes are ox and oy for the first, and ωa and $\omega \beta$ for the second. Now let us arrange them so that the paths traveled by the two individuals merge into a single line. . . . The indifference lines are t, t', t'', . . . for the first individual, and s, s', s'', . . . for the second. For the first one the hill of pleasure rises from o toward ω, and for the second, on the other hand, it rises from ω toward o.

For phenomena of Type I, we know that the equilibrium point must be at a point of tangency of the indifference curves of the two individuals. Let c be one of these points. If we move away from it following the route cc', we as-

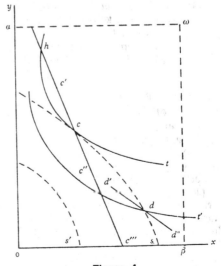

Figure 4

cend the first individual's hill of pleasure and descend that of the second; and conversely, if we follow the route cc''. Hence it is not possible to move away from c helping, or harming, both individuals at one and the same time; but necessarily, if it is agreeable to the one, it is disagreeable to the other.

It is not the same for points, such as d, where two indifference curves intersect. If we follow the route dd' we increase the satisfaction of both individuals; if we follow the line dd'' we decrease it for both.

For phenomena of Type I equilibrium occurs at a point such as c; for phenomena of Type II, equilibrium occurs at a point such as d; therein lies the difference between these two types of phenomena so far as maximum ophelimity is concerned.

NOTES

1. This expression is due to Professor F. Y. Edgeworth. He assumed the existence of *utility* (ophelimity) and deduced the indifference curves from it. On the other hand, I consider the indifference curves as given, and deduce from them all that is necessary for the theory of equilibrium, without resorting to ophelimity.

2. We could cover the plane with a large number of lines of exchanges. In this way we would have a representation of the hill of indices of ophelimity, which would be analogous to that which is obtained by covering the plane with indifference lines. . . .

21. The Diagrammatic Exposition of the Law of Rent and Its Implications*

PHILIP H. WICKSTEED

The roots of the error concerning the exceptional treatment of land . . . go down far deeper than the point to which we have as yet traced them, and the process of extirpation cannot be completed without an elaborate examination of the current exposition of the theory of rent. We will therefore go on to the examination of the ordinary diagram given to illustrate both the supposed "law of decreasing returns" and the "law of rent" derived from it. In Figure 1 increments of "labour" applied to a constant of land are reckoned along the axis of X, and rates of increment to the crop per unit increment of labour along the axis of Y. The total yield for Ox_1 "labour" is Orw_1x_1, and labour being rewarded at the rate of x_1w_1 per unit receives the area Ow_1 altogether, the balance y_1rw_1 being rent. If Ox_2 only had been applied to the same amount of land the total yield would have been the smaller area of Orw_2x_2, but the reward of "labour" *per unit* would have been higher, namely, x_2w_2. Rent would only be y_2rw_2, a smaller proportion of a smaller total. Thus decreasing returns to land per unit and increasing returns to "labour" per unit are read as we recede from the margin, and decreasing returns to "labour" per unit and increasing returns to land per unit as we advance from the origin. More labour bestowed on the same land means less land under the same labour. So we have these re-

Source: From Philip H. Wicksteed, *The Common Sense of Political Economy*, book 2, chapter 6 (London: Routledge & Kegan Paul, Limited, 1910). Marginal notes deleted; figure renumbered.

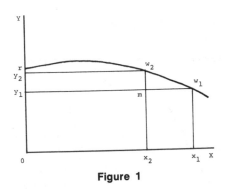

Figure 1

sults: More labour on the same land or *less land under the same labour* means a larger rent per unit of land and a less "wage" per unit of "labour"; whereas less labour on the same land or *more land under the same labour* means a lower rent per unit of land and a higher "wage" per unit of "labour." Those of the results just formulated which are directly illustrated in the figure are very familiar to all students of Political Economy, and familiarity has made them appear axiomatically true. But those of them which are just as explicitly contained in the data, but are only indirectly illustrated by the figure, and which have been italicised in the statement just made, are unfamiliar to most students of Political Economy, and may appear startling and perplexing, though they are absolutely identical with those expressed in the more familiar form and at once accepted as axiomatic.

Thus every one sees that if (after a certain point) more labour is applied to the same land the return to the land will be higher. But every one does not see that this is exactly the same as saying that after that point if more land is brought under the same "labour" the return to labour will be higher.

In our figure rent appears as a mixtilinear area and "wages" as a rectilinear one; and this has usually been asssumed to be due to some special characteristic of land, but if we work out our data under the other form of statement we shall find that these

graphic forms are simply due to the fact that land was taken as the constant. Had we thought in terms of less or more land under the same cultivation instead of more or less cultivation bestowed upon the same land, we should have found "wages" represented by a mixtilinear area and rent by a rectilinear one. This I shall go on to shew in detail. But before proceeding to the demonstration it will be well to note certain special points.

I have explained why certain phrases have been italicised above. I must now explain why I have put "wages" and "labour" between inverted commas. It is because labour is taken to include capital. In short, "labour" means all the factors of production except land. And "wages" means the remuneration of all these factors. To measure them all in one unit implies that they have all been reduced to a common denominator. . . . It would be useless to attempt to express such a unit accurately every time we have occasion to speak of it. Even to call it a "unit of labour-and-capital-reduced-to-a-common-denominator" would be too cumbrous. To call it a unit of labour is in the highest degree dangerous; but the danger is reduced, though not altogether avoided, by systematically writing "labour" for this complex of factors, and "wages" for its remuneration. We must add that the distinction between "labour" in this sense and "land" is artificial and arbitrary; for all the land we ever deal with embodies capital, and so does "labour" as now defined.

We have next to note that the figure, and the argument that usually accompanies it, do not really give us any theory of rent at all. They assume our own law of remuneration in proportion to efficiency for all the other factors (tacitly reduced to a common denomination), and then simply tell us that whatever is not anything else is rent.

Further, we must note with extreme care that the number of units of "labour," Ox_1 or Ox_2, applied to the constant of land, will be fixed by the alternatives open to land and "labour" respectively. "Labour" is devoted to, say, wheat-growing till the marginal return is only x_1w_1, because it cannot find any more eligible alternative, and it is not devoted to it beyond that point, at a lower marginal significance, because it can find alternatives as eligible. And in like manner so much land and no more offers itself at a declining marginal significance to a given amount of wheat-growing "labour," because it cannot find anything else better, but can find other things as good, to do with itself. So land will not come to a man unless he offers it as good terms as it can get anyway else, and men will not come to land unless it offers them as good terms as they can get anyway else. The quantities Ox_1, x_1w_1, y_1rw_1, are determined by the general conditions of industry and the markets; and if under conditions which would justify these proportions an individual should choose to take land and work on it at the rate represented by Ox_2, instead of earning Ow_2 and paying y_2rw_2 in rent, he would find that out of his total crop of Ow_2 he would have to pay a rent of y_1rw_1, and would only have Om minus the mixtilinear triangle w_2mw_1 for himself. If rent were at the rate of y_2rw_2, and "wages" at x_2w_2, it would be because more eligible alternatives had been opened to "labour," or a more abundant supply of land had become available to it as against the conditions that determined y_1rw_1, and Ow_1. It should be noted incidentally that any such change would be sure to affect the internal constitution of the complex unit of what we have called "labour"; it would not act upon interest on capital and wages for every different grade and character of work, for instance, in exactly the same proportion.

Lastly, we may note that the figure deals with yield per unit of land of a given quality, as it is plied with more and more "labour." It takes no account of different grades of land, each of which would present a curve of dif-

ferent form. Neither does the figure take account of the different conditions that might prevail on larger and smaller holdings. . . .

The essential and all-important point of the demonstration, up to this point, is that in the ordinary diagrams rent is set forth as a mixtilinear and "wages" as a rectangular area, not because there is any inherent appropriateness in these geometrical forms as representatives severally of the respective industrial factors, but simply because return to the constant, whatever it happens to be, will always come out as a mixtilinear area, and that to the variable as a rectangular one. And whether a distributive share is represented as a mixtilinear or a rectangular area, it is the same quantity and it is marginally determined. . . .

We have now thoroughly established the important conclusion that there is no special propriety in regarding rent as a residual share in the product, nor is there any special or necessary appropriateness in representing rent diagrammatically as a mixtilinear area, in contrast to the representation of wages, for example, as a rectilinear area. But the mistaken conceptions now dissipated have led to what I cannot but regard as disastrous confusions both in thought and nomenclature which may long impede the progress of Economics. It has been assumed, in the first place, that every economic quantity that presents itself graphically, under any treatment, in the form of a mixtilinear area has some specific analogy to rent. And here we may note that what is known as the "Ricardian" law of rent may be presented in this same form. Thus a diagram of the form in Figure 1 . . . might be regarded not as shewing the relation between marginal-return-per-unit-of-labour-and-capital and ratio-of-labour-and-capital-to-land, but as an arrangement of the several units of labour and capital employed in the wheat industry, referred to the varying fertility of the land to which they are applied. We should then have the mixtilinear area representing the excess of the yield of the more fertile over the yield of the least fertile land under cultivation. The Ricardian theory of rent usually (though quite unnecessarily) assumes that the least fertile land will bear no rent at all, and in that case the mixtilinear area would represent the whole rent; otherwise it would represent the excess of rent over a minimum. Now, if you take a number of persons who possess different talents and arrange them in the order of the marginal value to the community of the exercise of their talents, you will have near the origin an individual the product of whose efforts per annum is relatively high, and as you go forward you will come to individuals the exercise of whose talents produces a smaller and smaller pecuniary return. If we draw a line on the level of the return to the efforts of the least efficient of the men in question, the area above it will represent the excess over that minimum return that accrues to the more able individuals; and simply because this is a curvilinear figure the revenue it represents has actually been called "rent of ability."

It is clear that at this rate any excess in the value of one article above another that is nominally the same would be entitled to the name of "rent." Thus, if a pound of one kind of manure produces the same result as two pounds of another, and so forth, you might register pounds of the different manures, in order of their efficiency, along the axis of X, and treat the excess of efficiency of a pound of the one over a pound of the other as "rent of superior efficiency." Indeed, if any two things could perform the same function, but one of them could perform more of it than the other, you might regard the excess of the price of one over the price of the other as a case of "rent." And in very truth that is all that the Ricardian law of rent amounts to. If two pieces of land can each of them yield wheat to labour and capital, but one yields more wheat than the other, the value of that land will be proportionately higher, just as the value

of an apple-tree that bore an average of two hundred apples of given quality per annum would be higher than that of one that only bore an average of one hundred and fifty of the same quality. In fact the Ricardian law of rent is nothing whatever but a statement that the better article commands an advanced price in proportion to its betterness. The introduction of the hypothesis that the lowest quality of the article is to be had for nothing would make the whole price of the better article due to its "betterness." If there is no such gratuitous supply, then only the excess of the price of the more expensive article in the market would be due to its "betterness," and the rest to its "goodness" up to the point of lowest goodness in the market.

Again, reverting to our former interpretation of the figure (waiving all scruples as to the course of the curve in the neighbourhood of the origin), and bearing in mind that the form of the mixtilinear area is determined simply by the fact that land is constant, we shall see that by representing any other factor as constant we shall obtain a representation of it as a mixtilinear area. Thus, in all the individual and communal curves which represent the declining marginal significance of successive supplies of any commodity, we may regard the *psyche* or sensitive organism as the constant, and the areas as psychic. If the sensitive organism, or body of sensitive organisms, remains constant, successive increments of the provocative or stimulus will, after a certain point, produce decreasing revenues or volumes of the experience in question, and we shall therefore have the mixtilinear area representing an excess in the experience provoked by the earlier over those provoked by the marginal increments. When students perceived this they promptly dubbed that excess "consumer's rent."

But misleading as these uses of "rent" appear to me to be, they constitute but a small part of the evil that we have to deal with.

We have seen that the figure constructed on the hypothesis of land being constant, and labour and capital variable, may equally well be regarded as an illustration of the Ricardian theory of rent when associated, as it usually is, with the hypothesis of "no-rent" land being under cultivation. The general attitude of mind with regard to rent that results from all this may be thus described:—Rent is a residuum which is determined by the subtraction of the shares of the other factors of production, and what those shares are is determined by the remuneration they can secure on "no-rent" land—that is to say at the margin of cultivation.

We may notice in passing that this treatment of rent as a residuum incidentally stultifies the claim of the current economic science to have established a "law of rent" at all. For if rent is simply what is left when the other factors have been satisfied, we have not established a law of rent, but have assumed that we know how to determine the shares of everything except land, and then simply stated that what is not anything else is rent. If we start from $x=a+b+c+$etc., we cannot determine a simply by the equation $a=x-b-c-$etc., unless we have independently determined the values of b, c, etc. Thus, what is usually given as a derivation of the law of rent from the law of decreasing efficiency of successive doses of labour and capital on the same land is really an assumption that every other factor of production obeys the law of marginal efficiency which we have taken as our guide to the whole theory of distribution. Instead of elaborating a theory of rent the current exposition tacitly assumes a (correct) theory with reference to everything except land, and then claims that no theory at all is necessary for land. But our elaborate examination has shewn that the diagrammatic exposition strictly involves the conclusion that that same law really applies to land just as much as to the other factors. In truth, then, the mixtilinear area repre-

sents rent, not because it is all that is left when the other claimants have been satisfied, but because it represents the marginal efficiency of land, and would be represented by an ordinate if we had taken labour as the constant, just as labour is represented by an ordinate when we take land as the constant.

But we are concerned at present not with the inconsistencies already involved in regarding rent as a residuum but with the further conclusions that have flowed from it. If rent, it is argued, is a surplus or residuum which can be arrived at by deducting the remuneration of the other agents, as measured by the return to them on marginal or "no-rent" land, why should not profits be regarded as the residuum or surplus to be arrived at by deducting the remuneration of other agents, as measured by their returns in a marginal or "no-profit" business? And when, by these or similar processes, we have arrived at satisfactory "laws" which determine rent, profits, and so forth, surely we can determine wages (as General Walker did) by making them, too, a residuum when the other factors have been paid off. It is clear that all such attempts are based on the system of equations $a=x-b-c-$etc., $b=x-a-c-$etc., $c=x-a-b-$etc., and so on, none of which adds anything to the original datum $x=a+b+c+$etc., but each of which assumes that data have been independently obtained, with respect to all agents except that one to which it specially refers.

Nor is this the last or the worst of it. The reader will have noticed that the use of "margin" or "marginal" which we are now examining is quite different from that in which we have . . . used it throughout this work. "Marginal land," for instance, or "marginal ability," in this connection, is not land or ability considered with reference to the volume of the supply, at the margin of which it is added or subtracted, but land or ability of the lowest intrinsic quality which is devoted to the industry in question.

And the marginal conditions are not the conditions determined throughout the industry by the "margin" in our sense, that is to say, by the marginal significance of adding or subtracting a small increment, but are certain specified conditions applying to the production of specified units of the product. On this conception of margins many writers have conceived of one distributive category after another as consisting of an actually existing "surplus," mounting backwards towards the origin from the "margin," and constituting a great reservoir untapped by marginal distribution; and bewildered and bewildering attempts have been made to get at the marginal (least efficient) man working with the marginal (least efficient or least abundant) capital on the marginal (least efficient) land, and to calculate everything backwards from this point. But it must now be clear to the reader that all such attempts are based either on the mere arrangement of units on the abscissa in the order of their efficiency, which neither illustrates nor proves anything except that the better article commands the better price, or else are based on a misunderstanding of the geometrical form necessarily assumed by the area that represents the constant, whatever it may happen to be, in a diagram constructed on the principles of Figure 1. . . . The ambiguous use of the term "margin" has obviously added to the confusion. We now see once for all that the marginal distribution in our sense (that is to say, the distribution of the product amongst the claimants in proportion to the significance of the addition or withdrawal of a small increment, at the margin determined by the present supply), exhausts the whole product. The curvilinear area represents a margin just as much as the linear ordinate does, and may just as well be represented in the same geometrical form.

In our phraseology a unit "at the margin of x" is not contrasted with the other units in the group, which are in some way superior to it. All the units in the group are at the margin. The distinction is not between the x units of the group severally, but between the significance of each of a number of qualitatively indistinguishable units when forming one of a group of x and when forming one of a group of x + 1. The one use of the term implies qualitative differences, the other presupposes qualitative identity, within the group. In our sense of the term, therefore, all the units of every group are always marginal units, whatever the margin may be; and therefore, naturally, the marginal distribution accounts for the whole product.

It is open to any one to examine or to dispute the ethical or social claim of any factor of production to a share, in accordance with its marginal significance, or to argue that there is no industrial necessity to allow such a claim; but it is not open to any one who understands the facts to argue that when, by a marginal distribution, every factor, reduced to the common term . . . , has been satisfied, there remains any residuum or surplus whatever to be divided or appropriated. The vague and fervid visions of this unappropriated reserve, ruling upward as we recede from the marginal distribution, must be banished for ever to the limbo of ghostly fancies.

Before we bid farewell to the current or recently current expositions of the law of rent, we have still to notice one curious and instructive point. There is no connection whatever between the definition of rent given by the economists and the demonstrations by which they seek to determine its amount; for the economists first carefully define land as the primitive and inalienable properties of the soil, and explain that any ordinary piece of agricultural land is, to an indefinite extent, not land at all, but capital; and then proceed to examine the law of rent (almost invariably drawing their illustrations from agricultural land) on principles that take no account whatever of this distinction; for, as far as concerns the "Ricardian" law, it is clear that if one man commands a rich alluvial soil, and another man commands soil which by drainage, permanent manuring, and other devices, has been made equally desirable, both the one and the other, and both in equal degree, will pay a higher rent than they would pay for unmanipulated moorland which it is just worth while for some one to cultivate. And again (to take the law of rent as expounded in connection with the principle of "decreasing returns"), whether the land which we rent has been made what it is by mixing marl with the original soil, by drainage, or by other deliberate process, or is what it is by virtue of its original properties, or has become valuable because of the opening of a railway line or the building of a number of houses in the neighbourhood, in any case it will be cultivated more or less intensively on exactly the same principles. The law of rent, then, as expounded by the economists, has no connection with land as defined by them, but connects itself readily enough with land in the popular sense, which is an amalgam of economic land and economic capital.

There is nothing surprising in this, for we have seen over and over again that it is impossible to draw the line either between land as a primitive gift of nature and land as embodying capital or the results of human effort, or between a change in the value of a piece of land caused by something that has been done to it and that caused by changes that have taken place elsewhere. And, finally, since we know that land and capital are remunerated on one identical principle, in conformity with their marginal efficiency, we can see that the attempt to distinguish accurately between them is as unnecessary as it is hopeless.

Indeed it may be roughly said that everything that we read in Economic books as to the pure theory of distribution, whether it refers to wages, interest, rent, or profit, is either false when asserted of the category under discussion, or else true of all the others as well.

22. The Scope and Method of Political Economy in the Light of the "Marginal" Theory of Value and Distribution*

PHILIP H. WICKSTEED

I.

I address myself primarily to those who already accept the marginal theory of Value and Distribution, inviting their attention to the modifications it is already introducing into current conceptions of Political Economy and of its relation to other studies, and urging the necessity of accepting the change more frankly and pressing it further. But at the same time I think we shall find that the best approach to our proper subject is through a summary exposition, if not a defence, of the theory itself.

Let us begin by attempting to determine the characteristic of the economic

*Source: Reprinted from The Economic Journal, vol. 24 (March 1914), pp. 1-23.

field of investigation. Naturally there is no sharp line that marks off the economic life, and we must not expect to arrive at any rigid definition of it; but I take it that if I am doing a thing because I want it done for its own sake (not necessarily *my* own sake, in any restricted sense, for it may primarily concern some one else in whom I am interested out of pure goodwill), or am making a thing that I require for the supply of my own desires or the accomplishment of my own purposes; if, in fact, I am engaged in the direct pursuit of my own purposes, or expression of my own impulses, my action is not economic. But if I am making or doing anything not because I have any direct interest in it, but because some one else wants it, and that other person will either do what I want done or put me in command of it, then I am furthering his purposes as a means of furthering my own. I am indirectly forwarding my purposes by directly forwarding his. This is the nature of the economic relation, and the mechanism or articulation of the whole complex of such economic relations is the proper subject of economic investigation. Thus, if a peasant adorns his ox-yoke with carving because he likes doing it and likes it when done, or if he carves a stool for his friend because he loves him and likes doing it for him and believes he will like it when done, the action is not economic; but if he gets a reputation for carving and other peasants want his work, he may become a professional carver and may carve a yoke or a stool because other people want them and he finds that supplying their wants is the easiest way for him to get food and clothes and leisure for his own art, and all things else that he desires. His artistic work now puts him into an economic relation with his fellows; but this example serves to remind us that there may be an indefinite area of coincidence between the economic and non-economic aspects of a man's occupations and relations. That man is happy indeed who

finds that in expressing some part of his nature he is providing for all his natural wants; or that in rendering services to friends in which he delights he is putting himself in command of all the services he himself needs for the accomplishment of his own purposes. A perfect coincidence of this nature is the dream of modern Utopias; but my present subject is only the economic side of the shield.

The economic organism, then, of an industrial society represents the instrumentality whereby every man, by doing what he can for some of his fellows, gets what he wants from others. It is true, of course, that those for whom he makes or does something *may* be the same as those from whom he gets the particular things he wants. But this is not usual. In such a society as ours the persons whom a man serves are usually incapable of serving him in the way he desires, but they can put him in command of the services he requires, though they cannot render them. This is accomplished by the instrumentality of money, which is a generalised command of the services and commodities in the circle of exchange; "money" being at once a standard in which all market prices are expressed, and a universal commodity which every one who wishes to exchange what he has for what he wants will accept as a medium, or middle term, by which to effect the transformation. Thus in most commercial transactions one party furthers a specific purpose of the other, and receives in exchange a command, defined in amount but not in kind, of services and commodities in general; the scale of equivalence being a publicly recognised thing announced in current market prices. Every member of the community who stands in economic relations with others alternately generalises his special resources and then specialises his general resources, first directly furthering some one else's purposes and then picking out the persons who can directly further his. Thus each of us puts in what he has at one point of the circle of exchange and takes out what he wants at another. Being out of work is being unable to find any one who values our special service enough to relinquish in our favour such a command of services in general as we are prepared to accept in return.

Our economic relations, therefore, are built up on a recognised scale of equivalences amongst the various commodities and services in the circle of exchange; or, in other words, upon market values. And our first step must be to formulate the "marginal" theory of exchange, or market, values. It is capable of very easy and precise formulation in mathematical language; for it simply regards value in exchange as the first derived or "differential" function of value in use; which is as much as to say, in ordinary language, that what a man will give for anything sooner than go without it is determined by a comparison of the difference which he conceives its possession will make to him, compared with the difference that anything he gives for it or could have had instead of it will or would make; and, further, that we are generally considering in our private budgets, and almost always in our general speculations, not the significance of a total supply of any commodity—coals, bread, or clothes, for instance—but the significance of the difference between, say, a good and a very good wheat harvest to the public, or the difference between ten and eleven loaves of bread per week to our own family, or perhaps between ten days and a fortnight spent at the seaside. In short, when we are considering whether we will contract or enlarge our expenditure upon this or that object, we are normally engaged in considering the difference to our satisfaction which differences of adjustment in our several supplies will make. We are normally engaged, then, not in the consideration of totals, either of supplies or of satisfactions, but of differences of satisfaction dependent upon differences of supplies.

According to this theory, then, what I am willing to give for an increase in my supply of anything is determined by the difference it will make to my satisfaction, but what I shall have to give for it is determined by the difference it would make to the satisfaction of certain other people; for if there is anyone to whom it will make more difference than it will to me, he will be ready to give more for it, and he will get it, while I go without. But again, since the more he has the less difference will a still further increase make to him, and the less I have the more difference will a still further decrease make to me, we shall ultimately arrive at an equilibrium; what I am willing to give and what I am compelled to give will coincide, and the difference that a little more or a little less of any commodity which I habitually consume makes to my estimated satisfaction will be identical with a similar estimated difference to any other habitual consumer.

Or we may attack the problem from the point of view of the individual. We have pointed out that to any individual the differential significance of a unit of supply of any commodity or service declines as the supply increases. In our own expenditure, we find that current prices (our individual reaction on the market being insensible) fix the terms on which the various alternatives offered by the whole range of commodities and services in the circle of exchange are open to us. Obviously, so long as the differential satisfaction anticipated from one purchase exceeds that which the same money would procure from another, we shall take the preferable alternative (thereby reducing its differential superiority) until we have so regulated our expanding or contracting supplies that the differential satisfactions gained or lost from a given small increase or decrease of expenditure upon any one of our different objects of interest is identical. Into the practical difficulties that prevent our ever actually reaching this ideal equilibrium of expenditure I will not here enter; but I must call attention to the identity in principle of this analysis of the internal economy of our own choice between alternatives, tending to a subjective equilibrium between the differential significances of different supplies to the same person, and the corresponding analysis, just given, of the process by which an objective equilibrium is approached between the differential significances of the same supplies to different persons.

And this observation introduces another of extreme importance. In our private administration of resources we are concerned both with things that are and with things that are not in the circle of exchange, and the principle of distribution of resources is identical in both cases. The independent student who is apportioning his time and energy between pursuing his own line of research and keeping abreast of the literature of his subject is forming estimates of differential significances and is equating them to each other just as directly as the housewife who is hesitating between two stalls in the market. And when we are considering whether we will live in the country or the town, we may find, on examination, that we are carefully equating increments and decrements of such apparently heterogeneous indulgences as those associated with fresh eggs and friendship. Or, more generally, the inner core of our life problems and the gratification of all our ultimate desires (which are indeed inextricably interlaced with our command of exchangeable things, but are the ends to which the others are but means) obey the same all-permeating law. Virtue, wisdom, sagacity, prudence, success, imply different schemes of values, but they all submit to the law formulated by Aristotle with reference to virtue, and analysed by modern writers with reference to business, for they all consist in combining factors . . . , in the right proportion, as fixed by that distribution of resources which establishes the

e-uilibrium of their differential significances in securing the object contemplated, whether that object be tranquillity of mind, the indulgence of an overmastering passion or affection, the command of things and services in the circle of exchange, or a combination of all these, or of any other conceivable factors of life.

Now this dominating and universal principle of the distribution of resources, as we have seen, tends, by the instrumentality of the market, to secure an identity in the relative positions of increments of all exchangeable things upon the scales of all the members of the community amongst whom they are distributed. For if, amongst the things he possesses, A finds one, a given decrement in which would make less difference to him, as measured in increments of other exchangeable things, than the corresponding increment would make to B (who is assumed to have a certain command of exchangeable things in general), obviously there is a mutual gain in B giving for the increment in question what is less than worth it to him but more than worth it to A. There is equilibrium therefore only when a decrement in any man's stock of any exchangeable thing would make more difference to him, as measured in other exchangeable things, than the corresponding increment (measured in the same terms) would make to any one else. Hence all those who possess anything must, in equilibrium, value it more, differentially or incrementally, than any one who does not possess it, provided that this latter does possess something, and provided that "value" is measured in exchangeable things.

But this last qualification is all-important. The market tends to establish an identity of the place of the differential value of any commodity amongst all exchangeable things on everybody's scale of preferences, and further to secure that it is higher on the scale of every one that has it than on the scale of any one who has it not; so that to that extent, and in that sense, things must always tend to go and to stay where they are most significant. But then exchangeable things are never really the ultimately significant things at all. They are means. The ends, which are always subjective experiences of some kind, whether of the senses or the will or the emotions, are not in any direct way exchangeable; and there is no machinery to secure that increments and decrements of exchangeable things shall in industrial equilibrium take the same place and have the same differential significance on the scales of any two men when measured not in terms of other means, but in terms of ends. . . .

The ground is now clear for a step forward along the main line of our advance. The differential theory of exchange values carries with it a corresponding theory of distribution, whether we use this term in its technical sense of the division of a product amongst the factors that combine for its production, or whether we employ it as equivalent to "administration," and are thinking of the administration of our personal resources; that is to say, their distribution amongst the various objects that appeal to us; or again, the distribution, under economic pressures, of the sum of the industrial resources of a society amongst the objects that appeal to its members.

Land, manifold apparatus, various specialised faculties of hand, eye, and brain, are essential, let us say, to the production of some commodity valued by some one (it does not matter whom), for some purpose (it does not matter what). None of these heterogeneous factors can be dispensed with, and therefore the product in its totality is dependent upon the co-operation of each one severally. But there is room for wide variety in the proportions in which they are combined, and whatever the existing proportion may be each factor has a differential significance, and all these differential significances can be expressed in a common unit; that is to say, all

can be expressed in terms of each other, by noting the increment or decrement of any one that would be the equivalent of a given decrement or increment of any other; equivalance being measured by the neutralising of the effect upon the product, or rather, not upon the material product itself, but the command of generalised resources in the circle of exchange for the sake of which it is produced. The manager of a business is constantly engaged in considering, for instance, how much labour such-and-such a machine would save; how much raw material a man of such-and-such character would save; what equivalent an expansion or reconstruction of his premises would yield in ease and smoothness in the conduct of business; how much economy in the shop would be effected by a given addition to the staff in the office, and so on. This is considering differential significances and their equivalences as they affect his business. And all the time he is also considering the prices at which he can obtain these several factors, dependent upon their differential significances to other people in other businesses. His skill consists, like that of the housewife in the market, in expanding and contracting his expenditure on the several factors of production so as to bring their differential significances to himself into coincidence with their market prices. And note that the same principle can be applied without any difficulty to such immaterial factors of efficiency as "goodwill" or notoriety; but it would delay us too long to work this out or to anticipate possible objections. A hint must suffice.

Here, then, we have a firm theoretical basis for the study of distribution, independent of the particular form of organisation of a business. Whether those in command of the several factors of production meet and discuss the principles upon which the actual proceeds of the business shall be divided, when they are realised; or whether some one person takes the risks (on his own behalf or on behalf of a group of others), and discounts the estimated significance of the several factors, buying up their several interests in the product, by paying wages and salaries, interest, and rent, and by purchasing machinery and raw material, and so forth; or whatever other mechanism may be adopted, the underlying principle is the same. The differential equivalence of the factors of production reduces them to a common measure, and when they are all expressed in the same unit the problem of the division of the product amongst them is solved in principle.

Now I conceive that the application of this differential method to economics must tend to enlarge and to harmonise our conception of the scope of the study, and to keep it in constant touch with the wider ethical, social, and sociological problems and aspirations from which it must always draw its inspiration and derive its interest; for if we really understand and accept the principle of differential significances we shall realise, as already pointed out, that Aristotle's system of ethics and our reconstructed system of economics are twin applications of one identical principle or law, and that our conduct in business is but a phase or part of our conduct in life, both being determined by our sense, such as it is, of differential significances and their changing weights as the integrals of which they are the differences expand or contract. . . .

A full realisation of this will produce two effects. In the first place, it will put an end to all attempts to find "laws" proper to our conduct in economic relations. There are none. Hitherto economists for the most part have been vaguely conscious that the ultimate laws of economic conduct must be psychological, and, feeling the necessity of determining some defining boundaries of their study, have sought to make a selection of the motives and aims that are to be recognised by it. Hence the

simplified psychology of the "economic man," now generally abandoned—but abandoned grudgingly, by piecemeal, under pressure, and with constant attempts to patch up what ought to be cast away. There is no occasion to define the economic motive, or the psychology of the economic man, for economics study a type of relation, not a type of motive, and the psychological law that dominates economics dominates life. We may either ignore all motives or admit all to our consideration, as occasion demands, but there is no rhyme or reason in selecting certain motives that shall and certain others that shall not be recognised by the economist.

In the second place, when taken off the wrong track we shall be able to find the right one, and shall understand that the proper field of economic study is, in the first instance, the type of relationship into which men spontaneously enter, when they find that they can best further their own purposes by approaching them indirectly. . . .

Again, the realisation of the exact nature of the economic organisation as a machinery for combining in mutual helpfulness persons whose ends are diverse, will drive it home to our consciousness that one man's want is another man's opportunity, and that it may serve a man's turn to create a want or a passion in another in order that he may find his opportunity in it. All along the line, from a certain type of ingenious advertiser to the financier (if he really exists) who engineers a war in order that he may arrange a war loan, we may study the creation of wants and passions, destructive of general welfare, for the sake of securing wealth to individuals. And we may realise the deeply significant truth that to any individual the full discharge of his industrial function—that is to say, the complete satisfaction or disappearance, by whatever means, of the want which he is there to satisfy—must be, if he contemplates it, a nightmare; for it would mean that he would be "out of work," that because no one wants what he can give no one wants him, and neither will any one give him what he wants.

Yet again, in our industrial relations the thing we are doing is indeed an end, but it is some one else's end, not ours; and as far as the relation is really economic, the significance *to us* of what we are doing is measured not by its importance to the man for whom it is done, but by the degree to which it furthers our own ends. There can, therefore, be no presumption of any coincidence between the social significance of our work and the return we receive for it. We cannot say, "What men most care for they will pay most for, therefore what is most highly paid is most cared for," for (sometimes to our positive knowledge, and generally "for all we know") it is different men who express their eagerness for the different things we are comparing, by offering such-and-such prices, and those who offer little money for a thing may do so not because what they demand signifies so little, but because what they would have to give, or to forgo, for it signifies so much. They may offer little for a thing not because its possession matters so little but because their possession of anything, including this particular thing, matters so much.

These and other such considerations will not directly affect our exposition of the mechanism of the market, the central phenomenon of the industrial world, but they will profoundly affect the spirit in which we approach, and in which we conduct, our investigation of it. For we shall not only know but shall always feel that the economic machine is constructed and moved by individuals for individual ends, and that its social effect is incidental. It is a means and its whole value consists in the nature of the ends it subserves and its efficacy in subserving them. The collective wealth of a community ceases to be a matter of much direct significance to us, for if one

man has a million pounds, and a hundred others have ten pounds each, the collective wealth is the same as if the hundred and one men had a thousand each. What are we to expect from a survey made from a point of view from which these two things are indistinguishable? The market does not tell us in any fruitful sense what are the "national," "social," or "collective" wants, or means of satisfaction, of a community, for it can only give us *sums,* and the significance of a sum varies indefinitely according to its distribution.

If we reflect on these things—and the study of differential significances forces us to reflect upon them—we shall never for a moment, in our economic investigations, be able to escape from the pressure of the consciousness that they derive their whole significance from their social and vital bearings, and that the categories under which we usually discuss them conceal rather than reveal their meaning. We shall understand that this ultimate significance is determined by ethical considerations; that the sanity of men's desires matters more than the abundance of their means of accomplishing them; that the chief dangers of poverty and wealth alike are to be found in degeneracy of desire, and that the final goal of education and of legislation alike must be to thwart corrupt and degrading ends, to stimulate worthy desires, to infect the mind with a wholesome scheme of values, and to direct means into the channels where they are likeliest to conduce to worthy ends.

To sum up this branch of our examination, the differential theory of economics will never allow us to forget that organised "production," which is the proper economic field, is a means only, and derives its whole significance from its relation to "consumption" or "fruition," which is the vital field, and covers all the ends to which production is a means; and, moreover, the economics laws must not be sought and cannot be found on the properly economic field. It is on the vital field, then, that the laws of economics must be discovered and studied, and the data of economics interpreted. To recognise this will be to humanise economics.

The merit of our present organisation of industry is to be found in the extent to which it is spontaneous, and lays every man, whatever his ends, under the necessity of seeking some other man whom he can serve, in order to accomplish them. So far it is social, for it compels the individual to relate himself to others. But the more we analyse the life of society the less can we rest upon the "economic harmonies"; and the better we understand the true function of the "market," in its widest sense, the more fully shall we realise that it never has been left to itself, and the more deeply shall we feel that it never must be. Economics must be the handmaid of sociology.

II.

Let me now proceed to the consideration of a few points in which I think the traditional methods of technical exposition need reconsideration in the light of the differential theory.

At the root of all lies a profound modification of our conception of the nature and function of the "market" itself. The differential theory when applied to exchangeable things tells us that there is equilibrium only when an exchangeable commodity is so distributed that every one who possesses it assigns the same place to its differential value, amongst those of other commodities of which he has a supply; and that this place is a higher one than it occupies on the relative scale of any one who does not possess it. What this place is—that is to say, the differential equivalence of the commodity in terms of other commodities, when equilibrium is established—is fixed absolutely by two determinants. These are:

1) The tastes, desires, and resources of the individuals constituting the society. When objectively measured and expres-

sed, these individual desires for any one commodity can be represented by curves capable of being summed; and the resultant curve, objectively homogeneous but covering undefined differences of vital or subjective significance, is usually called, so far as it is understood and realised, the "curve of demand." This is one of the determinants we are examining, and it represents a series of hypothetically co-existing relations between given hypothetical supplies and corresponding differential significances. It is a curve representing a function.

2) The amount of the actual supply existing in the community. This is not a curve at all, but an actual quantity. It is not a series of co-existing relations, but one single fact, and it determines which of the series of hypothetical or potential relations represented by the curve shall be actually realised.

But what about the "supply curve" that usually figures as a determinant of price, co-ordinate with the demand curve? I say it boldly and baldly: There is no such thing. When we are speaking of a marketable commodity, what is usually called the supply curve is in reality the demand curve of those who possess the commodity; for it shows the exact place which every successive unit of the commodity holds in their relative scale of estimates. The so-called supply curve, therefore, is simply a part of the total demand curve which we have already described as factor (1). The separating out of this portion of the demand curve and reversing it in the diagram is a process which has its meaning and its legitimate function . . . but is wholly irrelevant to the determination of the price.

The intercourse of the market enables all the parties concerned to find their places with respect to each other on the general demand curve. Each individual, whether or not he possesses a stock of the commodity, brings his own individual curve of demand into the market, and there relates it to all the other individual curves of demand, thus constituting the collective curve, which (together with the amount of the commodity available) determines the price, *i.e.* the (objective) height of the lowest demand for a unit of the commodity which the available amount will suffice to reach.

The ordinary method of presenting the demand curve in two sections tells us the extent to which the present distribution of the commodity departs from that of equilibrium, and therefore the extent of the transactions that will be required to reach equilibrium. But it is the single combined curve alone that tells us what the equilibrium price will be. The customary representation of cross curves confounds the process by which the price is discovered with the ultimate facts that determine it.

Diagrams of intersecting curves (and corresponding tables) of demand prices and supply prices are therefore profoundly misleading. They co-ordinate as two determinants what are really only two separated portions of one; and they conceal altogether the existence and operation of what is really the second determinant. For it will be found on a careful analysis that the construction of a diagram of intersecting demand and "supply" curves always invlve, but never reveals, a definite assumption as to the amount of the total supply possessed by the supposed buyers and the supposed sellers taken together as a single homogeneous body, and that if this total is changed the emerging price changes too. . . .

. . . But what is cost of production? In the market of commodities I am ready to give as much as the article is worth to me, and I cannot get it unless I give as much as it is worth to others. In the same way, if I employ land or labour or tools to produce something, I shall be ready to give as much as they are worth to me, and I shall have to give as much as they are worth to others—always, of course, differentially. Their worth to me is determined by their differential effect upon *my* product, their worth to others by the like effect upon *their* products (or direct fruitions, if they do not apply them industrially). Again we have an *alias* merely. Cost of production is merely the form in which the desiredness a thing possesses for some one else presents itself to me.[1] When we take the collective curve of demand for any factor of production we see again that it is entirely composed of demands, and my adjustment of my own demands to the conditions imposed by the demands of others is of exactly the same nature whether I am buying cabbages or factors for the production of steel plates. I have to adjust my desire for a thing to the desires of others for the same thing, not to find some principle other than that of desiredness, co-ordinate with it as a second determinant of market price. The second determinant, here as everywhere, is the supply. It is not until we have perfectly grasped the truth that costs of production of one thing are nothing whatever but an *alias* of efficiencies in production of other things that we shall be finally emancipated from the ancient fallacy we have so often thrust out at the door, while always leaving the window open for its return.

I now turn to some of the most obvious consequences of the differential theory of distribution. They are all included in the one statement that when fully grasped this theory must destroy the very conception of separate laws of distribution such as the law of rent, the law of iterest, or the law of wages. It is by determining the differential equivalence of all the factors of production, however heterogeneous, that we reduce them to a common measure and establish the theory of distribution; just as it is by determining the differential equivalence of all our pursuits and possessions that we attempt to place a shilling or an hour or an effort of the mind where it will tell best, and so distribute our money or time or mental energy well. There can no more be a law of rent than there can be a law of the price of shoes distinct from the general law of the market. The way in which the several factors render their service to production differs, but the differential service they render is in every case identical, and it is on this identity or equivalence of service that the possibility of co-ordinated distribution rests. So the economist, though he may begin by giving precision to the student's idea of *how* "waiting," for example, or tools, or mere command of "extension" in space, or manual skill, or experience, or honesty, may affect the value of the product, must end by showing him that their distributive share of the product depends not upon *the way in which* they affect the product (wherein they are all heterogeneous), but on the differential *amount* of their effect (wherein they are all alike). The law of distribution, then, is one, and is governed not by the differences of nature in the factors, but by the identity of their differential effect. With this searchlight we must scrutinise the body of current economic teaching, and must cast out the mischievous survivals that deform it.

On the present occasion severe selection and limitation is, of course, necessary, and I think we cannot do better than take up a few of the current phrases, or conceptions and diagrammatic illustrations connected with the phenomenon of rent. Antecedently we must expect that as there is no theoretical difference between the part played by land and that played by other factors of production (or more direct ministrants to enjoyment), so there can be no general assertion about rent and land which is at once true and distinctive; for, if true, it must be based on that aspect of land which expresses its function in a unit common, say, to capital, and which brings its differential significance, upon which all depends, under the same law; and therefore it cannot be distinctive of land.

Let us test the truth of these anticipations. Ricardo's celebrated law of rent really asserts nothing except that the superior article fetches the superior price, in proportion to its superiority; and it is obvious that all "superiorities"

in land, whether arising from "inalienable" properties or from expenditure of capital, tell in exactly the same way upon the rent.

Again, a diagram may easily be constructed in which different qualities of land are represented along the axis of X and their supposed relative fertilities to a fixed application of labour and capital along the axis of Y. The "marginal" land will occupy the extreme place to the right. This is not a functional curve; for the height of y does not depend upon the length of x, the units being expressly so placed on OX as to produce a declining y. It is applicable to land or to anything else of which typical units can be arranged in ascending or descending order of efficiency.

But the same figure has been used as a functional curve in connection with the theory of rent. Take a given fixed area of land of a certain quality and consider what would be its yield if it were "dosed" with a certain quantity of labour and capital represented by a unit on the axis of X. Increase the doses till a further increment of labour and capital would not produce as large an increment in the yield of this land as it would if applied to some other piece of land of the same or different quality, or if turned to some non-agricultural business. The last increment actually applied is the "marginal" increment, and it measures the distributive share of a unit "dose" in the product. The figure and the details of the argument are too familiar to need elaboration; nor can I stay to show that such a curve ought really to pass through the origin, for important as the point is, it does not affect our present investigation; but it is essential to point out that the descriptive and the functional curves just described both present the same appearance, both represent "rent" by a curvilinear surface, both use the term "margin," though in entirely different senses, as determining rent, and are both just as applicable to anything else as to land, and (specifically) ignore the difference between "economic" and "commercial" rent, being just as applicable to one as to the other.

The ambiguous use of "marginal" has naturally caused some confusion (a point to which I shall soon revert), but at present the descriptive curve and "margin" have only been introduced to be dismissed. In the discussion of the functional curve, which we must now continue, I have used the term "marginal" in the sense of "differential" as applied throughout our whole investigation. It is not any peculiarity of the "marginal" increment that makes it yield less than the others. It does not. They all have exactly the same differential effect on the yield, as to which none is after or afore the other. The height of this differential or marginal yield is dependent not upon the nature of each several dose, but upon their aggregate number. What we have here, then, is not a law or theory of rent at all, but the tacit assumption that the differential theory of distribution is true of every factor of production except land, and that rent is what is left after everything that is not rent is taken away. For, observe, land-and-labour is treated as a homogeneous quantity, so that the reduction of heterogeneous factors to a common unit is assumed, and how is this to be done except by comparing their several efficiencies on the product, and so combining them as to keep those efficiencies in differential equivalence to their market prices, *i.e.* their efficiencies on other land or in other industries? And thus the principle of marginal or differential efficiency as determining distributive shares in the product has long been quite definitely, though naively and unconsciously, asserted in saying that the "marginal" efficiency of this compound factor of production will find the same level in the specified industry and out of it, and will determine its remuneration.

This so-called statement of the law of rent, then, assumes our differential laws of exchange value and distribution, with all their implications, as ruling everywhere *except* in land and rent. Rent is merely what is left when everything except rent is taken away. This can hardly be called a "law," but, such as it is, it is again common to all factors of production. Wages are all that is left when everything that is not wages is taken out. And this is actually the statement of Walker's "law of wages." And so with the rest.

But this is not all. In the treatment of rent that we are examining the differential theory of distribution is avowed with respect to every factor except land; but it is implied with respect to land also. This can be rigidly proved mathematically, as is now beginning to be acknowledged; and even the non-mathematical student can easily perceive that the forms of the figures representing the shares of "land" and "labour-and-capital" respectively are determined not by any peculiarity of land, but by the fact that land is supposed to remain constant, while labour-and-capital vary. But three pounds sterling applied to one acre is the same thing as a third of an acre coming under one pound's worth of culture, and five pounds per acre is a fifth of an acre per pound. Instead of taking an acre, therefore, and considering the difference of yield, as two, three, four, five pounds are expended upon it, let us take one pound and consider the differences of yield, as one-fifth, one-fourth, one-third, one-half of an acre come under it, or in other words, as it spreads itself over these different areas. You will then find that you have a figure in which the same identical data are presented and the same identical results obtained, but the return to land is represented as a rectangle cut off by a line parallel to *OX*, and the return to labour-and-capital by a curvilinear "surplus" or residuum. So that the supposed law of rent again turns out, in so far as it is true of land, to be true of all the other factors of production. But the unhappy confusion between the geometric properties of an arbitrarily selected constant factor in a diagram and the economic properties of land has brought dire confusion into economic thought and economic terminology. The Augean stables must be cleansed. We must understand that when the differential distribution is effected there is no surplus or residuum at all; and that any diagram of distribution that represents the shares of the different factors under different geometrical forms is sure to be misleading, and is likely to be particularly mischievous in its misdirection of social imagination and aspiration.

And note, finally, that even in practical problems the supposed peculiar conditions introduced by the rigidly determined quantity of land in existence are non-existent. Any individual can have as much land as he likes if he will pay the price, and he is conscious of no difference in principle whether he is bidding for a certain quality and site of land, or a certain grade of labour or kind of ability, unless it be that in the latter case he is *more* conscious of the limits of supply that no offer of remuneration can stretch.

In conclusion, I will revert to the point, incidentally raised in connection with rent, of the difficulties and confusions connected with terminology.

I have throughout spoken of *differential*, rather than *marginal* significances; for there is a fatal ambiguity in the use of the word "marginal." And yet, after all, I have felt like the man who "did flee from a lion and a bear met him; or went into the house and leaned his hand on the wall, and a serpent bit him," for by a singular perversity of fate or fashion a closely similar ambiguity besets the word "differential" itself, and yet another and equally appropriate term "incremental." All these words have been preoccupied; and curiously enough it is speculations on the nature of rent or projects concerning land that have done the mischief in every case. "Increment," instead of suggesting a small homogeneous addition to any magnitude whatever, at once suggests to the reader of economic literature the "unearned increment of land," so that the "incremental value," "efficacy," or "significance" of anything cannot conveniently carry its proper meaning of the value attached to a small increment or decrement of anything, varying with the expansion or contraction of the supply. This is the conception I have indicated by the term "differential." But here again we are forestalled. "Differential payment," for instance, would generally be understood by readers of economic literature to mean payment made for some articles in excess of that made for others, in consideration of their superiority. Thus, if I were to say that "rent is a differential charge," I should be supposed to mean that what you pay for a certain piece of land as rent represents the superiority of that piece of land to another that you can get for nothing. In this use of the word everything depends upon the different *quality* of the things compared. But what we want is a word which shall always carry the underlying assumption that we are considering the expansion and contraction of a *homogeneous* supply, the "differential" value of that supply being a function of its breadth or magnitude.

Again, the same theory of rent which regards it as a differential charge, in the sense of a charge due to an inherent difference of quality in the things charged for, assumes that there is some land which bears no rent at all. This is the land on the "margin" of cultivation. Hence "marginal" has come to be used in economic literature to signify the lowest grade or quality of any commodity, or service, or the least favourable set of conditions, that just hold their footing in any industry. Thus the marginal land would mean the worst land under cultivation, the marginal workman the least efficient man in actual employment, the marginal conditions of an industry the least advantageous conditions under which it is actually conducted, and, I suppose, the marginal grade of potatoes or wheat the worst quality actually in the market; or to the hungry individual the marginal mouthful of beef would be the one just not rejected and left on the plate because too largely composed of "veins" to be eaten, even if no more of any kind were to be had.

Now attempts have been made to erect a theory of distribution upon the consideration of "margins" in this sense. The "marginal" man, working on the "marginal" land, under the "marginal" conditions, and with the "marginal" appliances, is taken as the ultimate basis of the pile, and wages, rent and interest are explained as "differential" in their nature; that is to say, as due to the superiority in quality, position, or point of application, of such-and-such work, land, or apparatus, over the "marginal" specimens.

I do not stay to examine this theory on its merits; but it is necessary to insist on the almost incredible fact that there is constant confusion between it and what I have tried to expound as the "differential" theory of distribution, simply because they can both be described as "marginal," and the term "differential," though in quite divergent senses, may be introduced in the exposition of either.

Once again, then, if I speak of the differential or marginal significance of my supply of bread and milk, and say that it depends, *ceteris paribus,* upon how many loaves of bread and how many pints of milk I take, I am supposing all the bread and milk to be of the same quality. And if I speak of the differential or marginal significance of labour in a particular industry, I am either speaking of a uniform grade of labour or of different grades reduced to some common measure and expressed in one and the same unit, and I mean the significance which such a unit has when it is one out of so many others like itself. Thus, in my use of the word, there is no ear-marked

marginal unit, which is such in virtue of its special quality. Any one of 100 units has exactly the same marginal value; but as soon as one unit is withdrawn, all the remaining 99 have a higher marginal value; and when one is added, all the 101 a lower.

The only word I can think of free from misleading associations would be "quotal"; for *quotus* means (amongst other things) "one out of how many," and so *quotal* significance might mean the significance which a unit has when associated with such-and-such a number of others *homogeneous with itself.*

Here I must close these almost random indications of some of the directions in which I think that convinced apostles of the differential economics should revise the methods of economic exposition. For myself I cannot but believe that if this were accomplished, all serious opposition to the doctrine would cease, that there would once again be a body of accepted economic doctrine, and that Jevons's dream would be accomplished and economic science re-established "on a sensible basis."

It is impossible to exaggerate the importance of such a consummation. Social reformers and legislators will never be economists, and they will always work on economic theory of one kind or another. They will quote and apply such dicta as they can assimilate, and such acknowledged principles as seem to serve their turn. Let us suppose there were a recognised body of economic doctrine the truth and relevancy of which perpetually revealed itself to all who looked below the surface, which taught men what to expect and how to analyse their experience; which insisted at every turn on the illuminating relation between our conduct in life and our conduct in business; which drove the analysis of our daily administration of our individual resources deeper, and thereby dissipated the mist that hangs about our economic relations, and concentrated attention upon the uniting and all-penetrating principles of our study.

Economics might even then be no more than a feeble barrier against passion, and might afford but a feeble light to guide honest enthusiasm, but it would exert a steady and a cumulative pressure, making for the truth. While the experts worked on severer methods than ever, popularisers would be found to drive homely illustrations and analogies into the general consciousness; and the roughly understood dicta bandied about in the name of Political Economy would at any rate stand in some relation to truth and to experience, instead of being, as they too often are at present, a mere armoury of consecrated paradoxes that cannot be understood because they are not true, that every one uses as weapons while no one grasps them as principles.

NOTE

1. I do not deny that, as we recede from the market and deal with long periods and the ultimate conditions on which nature yields her stores, cases may arise in which something like a "supply curve" seems legitimate. The terms on which nature yields increasing supplies of some raw material, for instance, cannot legitimately be regarded as the reserve prices in which she expresses her own demand! But even here in the last analysis, and when we consider the enormous range of the principle of "substitution" and the pressures that determine the directions taken by inventive genius, I believe we shall be thrown back in all important cases upon modifications in the demands upon human energy and expressions of human vitality and their distribution amongst all the utilities and fruitions that appeal to them.

23. The Economics of Welfare*

ARTHUR CECIL PIGOU

THE DEFINITION OF MARGINAL SOCIAL AND PRIVATE NET PRODUCTS

Concerned as we are with the national dividend as a continuing flow, we naturally understand by the resources directed to making it, not a stock of resources, but a similarly continuing flow; and we conceive the distribution of these resources among different uses or places on the analogy, not of a stagnant pond divided into a number of sections, but rather a river divided into a number of streams. This conception involves, no doubt, many difficulties in connection both with the varying durability of the equipment employed in different industries and with the dynamic, or changing, tendencies of industry as a whole. In spite of these difficulties, however, the general idea is exact enough for the present purpose. That purpose is to provide a suitable definition for the concepts which are fundamental throughout this Part, namely, *the value of marginal private* and *the value of the marginal social net product*. The essential point is that these too must be conceived as flows—as the result *per year* of the employment *per year* of the marginal increment of some given quantity of resources. On this basis we may proceed to work out our definition.

For complete accuracy it is necessary to distinguish between two senses in which the term marginal increment of resources may be employed. It may be

*Source: Reprinted from *The Economics of Welfare* by Arthur Cecil Pigou, 4th ed., chapters 2 and 3 (London: Macmillan & Co., Limited, 1932). Reprinted by permission of Macmillan, London and Basingstoke. Several footnotes deleted; others renumbered.

conceived either as being added, so to speak, from outside, thus constituting a net addition to the sum total of resources in existence, or as being transferred to the particular use or place we are studying from some other use or place. If the effect on production in a particular use or place of adding an increment of resources is independent of the quantity of resources employed elsewhere, the net products of these two sorts of marginal increment will be the same. It often happens, however, that this condition of independence is not satisfied. Thus, as will be shown more fully in a later chapter, the nth unit of resources employed in a particular firm will yield different quantities of produce according as the quantity of resources employed in other firms in the same industry is larger or smaller. The net products derived from marginal increments of resources, interpreted in the above two ways, might perhaps be distinguished as additive marginal net products and substitutive marginal net products. In general, however, the net products derived from the two sorts of marginal increment of resources in any use or place are not likely to differ sensibly from one another, and for most purposes they may be treated as equivalent.

Waiving, then, this point, we have next to define more precisely what is meant when we speak of the marginal net product of the resources employed in any use or place as *the result of* the marginal increment of resources employed there. This is tantamount to saying that the marginal net product of a given quantity of resources is equal to the difference that would be made to the total product of these resources by adding to or subtracting from them a small increment. This, however, is not by itself sufficient. For the addition or subtraction of a small increment can be accomplished in several different ways with correspondingly different results. We are here concerned with a particular way. For us the marginal net product of any flow of resources employed in any use or place is equal to the difference between the aggregate flow of product for which that flow of resources, *when appropriately organised*, is responsible and the aggregate flow of product for which a flow of resources differing from that flow by a small (marginal) increment, *when appropriately organised*, would be responsible. In this statement the phrase *when appropriately organised* is essential. If we were thinking of marginal net product in the sense of the difference between the products of two adjacent *quantities* of resources, we should normally imagine the resources to be organised suitably to one of these quantities and, therefore, not to the other. Since, however, our interest is in the difference between the products of two adjacent *flows* of resources, it is natural to conceive each of the two flows as organised in the manner most appropriate to itself. This is the conception we need. It is excellently illustrated by Professor J. B. Clark. The marginal increment of capital invested in a railway corporation is in reality, he writes,

> a difference between two kinds of plant for carrying goods and passengers. One of these is the railroad as it stands, with all its equipment brought up to the highest pitch of perfection that is possible with the present resources. The other is the road built and equipped as it would have been if the resources had been by one degree less. A difference in all-round quality between an actual and a possible railroad is in reality the final increment of capital now used by the actual corporation. The product of that last unit of capital is the difference between what the road actually produces and what it would have produced if it had been made one degree poorer.[1]

One further point must be made clear. The marginal net product of a factor of production is the difference that would be made to the aggregate product by withdrawing *any* (small) unit of the factor. The marginal unit is thus not any particular unit. Still less is it the worst unit in existence—the most incompetent workman who is employed at all—as some writers have supposed! It is *any* (small) unit out of the aggregate of units, *all exactly alike*, into which we imagine this aggregate to be divided. Though, however, the marginal unit is thus *any* unit, it is not any unit *however placed*. On the contrary, it is any unit *conceived as placed at the margin*. The significance of this is best understood with the help of an illustration. To withdraw a man attending a new machine or working in an easy place in any industry and to do nothing else would, of course, affect aggregate output more seriously than to withdraw a man attending an obsolete machine or working in a difficult place would do. The marginal net product of work in that industry is then the difference that would be made to aggregate output by withdrawing for a day any (similar) man and redistributing, if necessary, the men that are left in such wise that the machine consequently left unattended or place of work left unfilled is the least productive machine or place of work of which use has hitherto been made.

So much being understood, we have next to distinguish precisely between the two varieties of marginal net product which I have named respectively *social* and *private*. The marginal social net product is the total net product of physical things or objective services due to the marginal increment of resources in any given use or place, no matter to whom any part of this product may accrue. It might happen, for example, as will be explained more fully in a later chapter, that costs are thrown upon people not directly concerned, through, say, uncompensated damage done to surrounding woods by sparks from railway engines. All such effects must be included—some of them will be positive, others negative elements—in reckoning up the social net product of the marginal increment of any volume of resources turned into any use or place. Again an increase in the quantity of resources employed by one firm in an industry may give rise to external economies in the industry as a whole and so lessen the real costs involved in the production by other firms of a given output. Everything of this kind must be counted in. For some purposes it is desirable to count in also indirect effects induced in people's tastes and in their capacity to derive satisfaction from their purchases and possessions. Our principal objective, however, is the national dividend and changes in it. . . . Therefore psychical consequences are excluded, and the marginal social net product of any given volume of resources is taken, except when special notice to the contrary is given, to consist of physical elements and objective services only. The marginal private net product is that part of the total net product of physical things or objective services due to the marginal increment of resources in any given use or place which accrues in the first instance—*i.e.* prior to sale—to the person responsible for investing resources there. In some conditions this is equal to, in some it is greater than, in others it is less than the marginal social net product.

The *value* of the marginal social net product of any quantity of resources employed in any use or place is simply the sum of money which the marginal social net product is worth in the market. In like manner the value of the marginal private net product is the sum of money which the marginal private net product is worth in the market. Thus, when the marginal social net product and the marginal private net product are identical and the person responsible for the investment sells what accrues to him, the value of both sorts of marginal net product in respect of a given volume of resources is equal to the increment of product multiplied by the price per unit at which the product is sold when that volume of resources is being employed in producing it.[2] For example, the two sorts of marginal net product per year of a million units of resources invested in weaving being assumed to be identical, the value of both is equal to the number of bales of cloth by which the output of a million *plus* a small increment, say a million and one, exceeds the output of a million units, multiplied by the money value of a bale of cloth when this output is being produced.[3] This, it should be observed in passing, is different from, and must by no means be confused with, the excess—if there is an excess—of the money value of the whole product when a million and one units of resources are being employed over the money value of the whole product when a million units are being employed.

THE VALUES OF MARGINAL SOCIAL NET PRODUCTS AND THE SIZE OF THE NATIONAL DIVIDEND

Let us suppose that a given quantity of productive resources is being employed, that there are no costs of movement between different occupations and places, and that conditions are such that only one arrangement of resources will make the values of marginal social net products everywhere equal. On these suppositions it is easy to show that this arrangement of resources will make the national dividend larger than it would be under any other arrangement. . . . The value of the marginal social net product of resources in any use is the money measure of the satisfaction which the marginal increment of resources in that use is yielding. Whenever, therefore, the value of the marginal social net product of resources is less in any one use than it is in any other, the money measure of satisfaction in the aggregate can be increased by transferring resources from the use where the value of the marginal social net product is smaller to the use where it is larger. It follows that, since, *ex hypothesi*, there is only one arrangement of resources that will make the values of the marginal social net products equal in all uses, this arrangement

is necessarily the one that makes the national dividend, as here defined, a maximum.[4]

This conclusion may be extended to show that, when complete equality among the values of marginal social net products is wanting, a diminution in the degree of inequality that exists among them is likely to benefit the national dividend. This result cannot, however, be set down without explanation. If the uses in which resources are employed were only two in number, its meaning would be perfectly clear and its validity undoubted. In fact, however, these uses are very numerous. This circumstance gives rise to a difficulty, which has already been referred to in another connection. The meaning of the concept of greater or less equality among a large number of values is ambiguous. Are we to measure the degree of equality by the mean deviation from the average value, or by the standard deviation, or by the "probable error," or by some other statistical measure? If we use the standard deviation as our criterion . . . a decrease in the degree of inequality subsisting among the values of marginal social net products in different uses will *probably* lead to an increase in the national dividend. But it is not certain to do this unless the decrease of inequality is brought about by a group of (one or more) changes of individual values, *each one of which taken by itself* tends to decrease inequality. Thus, if the distribution of resources is so altered that a number of values of marginal social net products which are below the average are all increased, or if a number which are above the average are all diminished, it is certain that the dividend will be increased. But, if a cause comes into play, which, while decreasing the degree of inequality among the values of marginal social net products on the whole, yet increases *some* values that are above the average and diminishes *some* that are below it, this is not certain. This type of difficulty is not, however, of great practical importance, because the obstacles to equality with which we have to deal are, for the most part, general obstacles, and operate in the same sense at nearly all points where they operate at all.

Let us next take account of the fact that in real life costs are often involved in moving resources from one place or occupation to another, and let us inquire in what, if any, respects this fact makes it necessary to modify the conclusions set out above. The kernel of the matter can be displayed as follows. Suppose that between two points A and B the movement of a unit of resources can be effected at a capital cost equivalent to an annual charge of n shillings for every year during which a unit that is moved continues in productive work in its new home. In these circumstances the national dividend will be increased by the movement of resources from A to B, so long as the annual value of the marginal social net product as B exceeds that at A by more than n shillings; and it will be injured by any movement of resources which occurs after the excess of the value of the marginal social net product at B has been reduced below n shillings. If the initial distribution of resources between A and B is such that the value of the marginal social net product at B exceeds (or falls short of) the value of the marginal social net product at A by any number of shillings less than n, say by (n − h) shillings, the existing arrangement—that under which the values of the marginal social net products at the two points differ by (n − h) shillings—is the best arrangement, not indeed absolutely, since, if there were no costs, a better arrangement would be possible, but relatively to the fact of the initial distribution and the existing costs of movement. It is not, be it noted, the best arrangement relatively to the existing costs of movement alone. We cannot say that, when the costs of movement are equivalent to n shillings, the national dividend is best served by a distribution under which the values of the marginal social net prod-

ucts at A and B differ by such and such a defined number of shillings. The only accurate statement is: when the costs of movement between A and B are equivalent to n shillings, the national dividend is best served by the maintenance of the existing distribution, whatever that may be, provided that this distribution does not involve a divergence in the values of marginal social net products greater than n shillings; and, if the existing distribution does involve a divergence greater than n shillings, by a new distribution brought about by the transference of sufficient resources to bring the divergence down to n shillings.

The results set out in the two preceding sections rest upon the assumption that there is only one arrangement of resources which makes the values of marginal social net products everywhere equal—or as nearly equal as, in view of costs of movement, it is to the interest of the national dividend that they should be made. This assumption would be justified if the value of the marginal social net product of resources employed in each several use was always smaller, the greater the volume of resources employed there. There are, however, two sets of conditions in which this is not so. First, the employment of additional resources in the production of a commodity may, after a time, enable improved methods of organisation to be developed. This means that decreasing supply price prevails, in such wise that the marginal (physical) net product of a greater quantity of resources exceeds the marginal (physical) net product of a smaller quantity: and, whenever this happens, it is possible, though, of course, it is not necessary, that the value of the marginal social net product of several different quantities of resources that might be engaged in producing the commodity will be the same. Secondly, the employment of additional resources in the production of a commodity may, after a time, lead to an increase in the price per unit offered by consumers of any given quantity of it. For their taste for it may be lastingly enhanced—obvious examples are afforded by the taste for music and tobacco—through experience of it. When this happens the value per unit of a larger product will (after an appropriate interval of time) be greater than the value per unit of a smaller product. It follows that, even for commodities whose production is not subject to conditions of decreasing supply price in the sense defined above, there *may* be, though, of course, there need not be, several different quantities of invested resources, the values of whose marginal social net products are the same.[5] Hence, the conclusions set out above require to be restated in a modified form. Allowance being made for costs of movement, it is true that the dividend cannot reach the maximum attainable amount *unless* the values of the marginal social net products of resources in all uses are equal. For, if they are not equal, the dividend can always be increased by a transference of resources from the margin of some uses to the margin of others. But, when the values of the marginal social net products in all uses are equal, the dividend *need not* attain an unequivocal maximum. For, if several arrangements are possible, all of which make the values of the marginal social net products equal, each of these arrangements does, indeed, imply what may be called a *relative maximum* for the dividend; but only one of these maxima is the unequivocal, or absolute, maximum. All of the relative maxima are, as it were, the tops of hills higher than the surrounding country, but only one of them is the highest hill-top of all. Furthermore, it is not necessary that all positions of relative maximum should represent larger dividends than all positions which are not maxima. On the contrary, a scheme of distribution approximating to that which yields the absolute maximum, but not itself fulfilling the condition of equal marginal yields, would probably imply a larger dividend than most of the schemes which do fulfil this condition

and so constitute relative maxima of a minor character. A point *near* the summit of the highest hill may be higher than any summit except the highest itself.

These considerations show that, even though the values of marginal social net products were everywhere equal or differed only in ways "justified" by the costs of movement, there might still be scope for State action designed to increase the magnitude of the national dividend and augment economic welfare. Benefit might be secured by a *temporary* bounty (or temporary protection) so arranged as to jerk the industrial system out of its present poise at a position of relative maximum, and induce it to settle down again at the position of absolute maximum—the highest hill-top of all. This is the analytical basis of the argument for the *temporary* protection, or other encouragement, of infant industries; and, if the right infants are selected, the right amount of protection accorded, and this protection removed again at the right time, the argument is perfectly valid. Benefit might also be secured by a *permanent* bounty at a different rate from that contemplated above, so arranged as to force the industrial system from the summit of the hill-top on which it is found to any position, that overtops its present site, on the slope of a higher hill. The conditions in which bounties are likely to have this effect, rather than that of shifting the economic system to a different position on the hill that it is on already, are somewhat special. But it can be proved that, in certain states of demand and supply, *some* rates of bounty *must* have this effect.[6]

NOTES

1. *The Distribution of Wealth*, p. 250. I have substituted "produced" for "earned" in the sentence quoted above.
2. This definition tacitly assumes that the

realised price is equal to the (marginal) demand price. If government limitation of price causes it to be temporarily less than this, the value of the marginal net product will need to be interpreted as the marginal (physical) net product multiplied by the marginal demand price, and the marginal demand price in these conditions will not be equal to the actual selling price.

3. Cf. Alfred Marshall, *Principles of Economics*, p. 847. It will be noticed by the careful reader that, even when the *additive* marginal net product and the *substitute* marginal net product are equal, the *value* of the marginal net product will be different according as marginal net product is interpreted as additive and as substitute marginal net product. The difference will, however, in general, be of the second order of smalls.

4. A minor point should be noticed in passing. In occupations in which *no* resources are employed, the value of the marginal net product of resources will, in general, be smaller than it is in occupations where *some* resources are employed. This circumstance clearly does not imply the existence of inequality among the values of marginal net products in any sense incompatible with the maximisation of the national dividend. But, if it should anywhere happen that the value of the marginal net product of resources in an occupation where no resources are employed is larger than it is in occupations where some resources are

employed,—e.g. a profitable venture which for some reason people have failed to exploit,—*that* inequality would be an effective inequality and would be incompatible with the maximisation of the dividend.

5. If equality of the values of marginal net products is attained when 1000 units of resources are devoted to the production of a particular thing, and also, *because of decreasing supply price,* when 5000 units are so devoted, the national dividend is necessarily larger under the latter arrangement. If equality is attained with 1000 units and also, *because of reactions upon tastes,* with 5000 units, both economic welfare and the national dividend, from the point of view of the period in which the 5000 units are operating, are necessarily larger under the latter arrangement. But the national dividend, from the point of view of the other period, may be smaller under the 5000 units arrangement. In these circumstances . . . from an absolute point of view, the dividends under the two arrangements are incommensurable.

6. The shapes of the demand and supply curves and the size of the bounty must be such that, when the demand curve is raised by the bounty, it does not cut the supply curve at any point corresponding to its former point of intersection, but does cut it at a point corresponding to a point of stable equilibrium further to the right than this. This condition can readily be depicted in a diagram.

24. Some Aspects of Welfare Economics*

ARTHUR CECIL PIGOU

I have been invited by the editor of the *American Economic Review* to write an article on "Some Aspects of Welfare Economics"; and I have accepted. Whether I ought to have accepted is more than doubtful. For a great deal has been written on this subject in recent years and most of it I have not read. Nevertheless, having agreed to write the

article, I must do what I can. My book *The Economics of Welfare,* not revised since 1932, stood aside from some significant logical problems which arise out of the fact that real income is made up of a number of different things, the quantities of which vary in different proportions. It is with these problems, together with some semiphilosophical

*Source: From *American Economic Review*, vol. 41 (June 1951), pp. 287-302. Reprinted by permission of the American Economic Association.

questions about utility, that "the new Welfare Economics," as it likes to be named, principally deals. The technique of indifference curves, preference maps and so on, which it employs, is, of course, machinery. Here I shall confine myself to fundamental issues.

I. THE PURPOSE OF WELFARE ECONOMICS

Welfare Economics is concerned to investigate the dominant influences through which the economic welfare of the world, or of a particular country, is likely to be increased. The hope of those who pursue it is to suggest lines of action—or non-action—on the part of the State or of private persons that might foster such influences. Nobody supposes that economic welfare is coincident with the whole of welfare or that the State ought to pursue it relentlessly without regard for other goods—liberty, for instance, the amenities of the family, spiritual needs and so on. But here we are not concerned with these things; only with economic welfare, that is to say, the part of welfare that is associated with the economic aspects of life. First and foremost we have to satisfy ourselves as to what that is and, more particularly, to decide whether or not it is the sort of thing to which the notions of greater or less and increase or decrease can properly be applied. For, if they cannot, Welfare Economics, every part and aspect of it, vanishes and leaves not a wrack behind.

II. THE MEANING OF ECONOMIC WELFARE

Let us consider first a single individual. What do we mean by the economic welfare of such an individual? It will be generally agreed that this must be somehow resident in his state of mind or consciousness. When we speak loosely of "material welfare," in the sense of a man's income or possessions, that is not welfare as we are thinking of

it here. Material welfare may be a *means* to welfare, but it certainly is not identical with or a part of it. As it seems to me, welfare must be taken to refer either to the goodness of a man's state of mind or to the satisfactions embodied in it. If we were prepared to say that the goodness of satisfactions depended simply on their intensity it might not be necessary to make this distinction. But it is generally felt, in a vague way, that some sorts of satisfaction are in their nature better than others, and that quite irrespective of whether or not they entail dissatisfactions later on. If this is right, a situation containing more satisfaction is not necessarily "better" than one containing less. For the present purpose, I propose to make welfare refer to satisfactions, not goodness, thus leaving it possible that in certain circumstances, a government "ought"—granted that it "ought" to promote goodness—to foster a situation embodying less welfare (but more goodness) in preference to one embodying more welfare.

A man's welfare then consists in his satisfactions. But what does satisfaction mean? Not simply happiness or pleasure; for a man's desires may be directed to other things than these and may be satisfied. It might seem that, when his desire attitude is given, his satisfaction depends straightforwardly on the extent to which his desires are fulfilled. But the satisfaction yielded when a desire is satisfied does not always bear the same proportion to the intensity of the desire. Not only may people make mistakes, desiring certain objects in the hope of satisfactions which they do not in fact yield, but also, as Sidgwick observed, "I do not judge pleasures to be greater or less exactly in proportion as they exercise more or less influence in stimulating the will to actions likely to sustain or produce them."[1] Some economists, neglecting this point, have employed the term "utility" indifferently for satisfactions and for desiredness. I shall employ it here to mean satisfactions, so that we may say that a man's economic welfare is made up of his utilities. For a full treatment we should need to bring into account also such dissatisfactions or disutilities as men may suffer from work, or, what is not quite the same thing, such further satisfactions or utilities as leisure yields to them. It would not be difficult to do this but doing it would complicate and lengthen the discussion. I shall not, therefore, trespass into that field.

III. MEASURABILITY AND COMPARABILITY IN PRINCIPLE OF SATISFACTIONS ENJOYED BY THE SAME INDIVIDUAL

I said in Section I that, if economic welfare were not something to which the notion of greater or less were applicable, Welfare Economics would vanish away. It is sometimes thought that this notion *cannot* be applicable unless satisfactions are measurable.

Now for magnitudes of any kind to be measurable means that a unique and reciprocal correspondence, a one-one relation, can be established between the magnitudes in question and cardinal numbers. Extensive magnitudes, such as length, are in general measurable in this sense. Pleasures, satisfactions, utilities, are intensive magnitudes and are not measurable. They are not the sort of thing that we can correlate with a series of cardinal numbers.

It is true, no doubt, that an intensive magnitude may sometimes be correlated with an extensive magnitude and so may be capable of being measured indirectly. This would be true of satisfactions if, by a miracle, they were correlated rigidly with levels of temperature or speed of pulse. Moreover, there is in fact available in our field an "extensive" magnitude of the kind required, namely the amount of money that a man would be willing to pay in order to avoid losing a given satisfaction, or pleasure. Marshall, it will be remembered, laid stress on the advantage which economics has over other social

sciences in possessing this measuring rod. Apart, however, from complications about the relation between the intensity of desires and the intensity of the satisfactions that result when a desired object is secured, to which I have already referred, neither Marshall nor anybody else claims that money enables us to measure anything more than small parts of a man's satisfaction. If I have an income of £1,000, it is reasonable to say that the satisfaction I get (or, more strictly expect) when I spend £2 on a small increment of one commodity is likely to be twice as great as what I get when I spend £1 on a small increment of another. But nobody supposes that the satisfaction I get from the whole of my £1,000 income will be only 1,000 times as large as what I get from the expenditure of a single marginal pound. Money does not, therefore, enable us to correlate satisfactions with a series of cardinal numbers, that is, to measure it in the sense understood here. We must concede that they are not measurable in that sense.

This, however, is far from entailing that satisfactions are not in principle *comparable*. The following passage from Bertrand Russell makes this clear.

Those mathematicians who are accustomed to an exclusive emphasis on numbers will think that not much can be said with definiteness concerning magnitudes incapable of measurement. This, however, is by no means the case. The immediate judgments of equality, upon which (as we saw) all measurements depend, are still possible where measurement fails, as are also the immediate judgments of greater and less. Doubt only arises where the difference is small; and all that measurement does in this respect is to make the margin of doubt smaller—an achievement which is purely psychological and of no philosophical importance. Quantities not susceptible of numerical measurement can thus be arranged in a scale of greater and smaller magnitudes, and this is the only strictly quantitative achievement of even numerical measurement. We can know that one magnitude is greater than another and that a third is intermediate between them; also, since the differences of magnitudes are always magnitudes, there is always (theoretically at least) an answer to the question whether the difference of one pair of magnitudes is greater than, less than or the same as, the difference of another pair of the same kind. . . . Without numerical measurement, therefore, the quantitative relations of magnitudes have all the definiteness of which they are capable—nothing is added, from the theoretical standpoint, by the assignment of correlated numbers.[2]

A corollary follows—or seems to follow. Given that we are able in principle to say that the difference between one pair of magnitudes is greater or less than the difference between another pair, we must presumably also be able to say that about differences between differences. This entails that, in spite of the fact that utilities are not measurable, it is still legitimate in principle to imagine a marginal utilities curve and to say, not merely that it slopes down or up, but also that it slopes more or less steeply as we move along it from right to left.

It is indeed impossible even in principle to draw a base line for the curve. Non-measurability entails that. It is thus meaningless to say that the utility derived by one individual in a given period from x units of a commodity is twice, or any other multiple, of the utility derived from y units, or to say, for example, that the curve is a rectangular hyperbola or bears some specifiable relation to a rectangular hyperbola. This entails that we cannot compare the damage done to welfare by a given proportionate change in a man's income when he is enjoying incomes of different sizes. Such questions as whether a tax proportioned to income will inflict equal sacrifice upon him whatever the size of his income or whether a tax progressive in some given form and degree is required to do this, are unanswerable, not merely from lack of data, but in principle. Thus the non-measurability of utility rules out one type of question, which, were utility measurable, it would be legitimate to ask—and which, assum-

ing that it *is* measurable, I did ask in Chapter 7, Part II of my *Study in Public Finance*. This does not, however, reduce the domain of Welfare Economics very seriously, nor does it seriously matter that such questions as whether aggregate welfare would be increased if the population were larger but individual satisfactions smaller are in principle, not merely in practice, unanswerable.

IV. COMPARABILITY IN FACT

So far I have been discussing comparability in principle; are satisfactions or utilities the sort of things which can be held in the relation of greater or less or is it nonsense to maintain this of them in the way that it is nonsense to maintain that one is more red or more liquid than another? I have answered that question. But, granted that these things are comparable in principle, it is a quite different question whether they can be actually compared. If we found that they could not be actually compared, it would not follow that they are incomparable in principle. If all thermometers and kindred gadgets were destroyed, this would not upset at all the comparability in principle of temperatures. *Per contra*, to find, as we have done, that utilities, differences among utilities and differences among these differences are comparable in principle does not imply that all or any of them can be compared in fact. Subject, however, to a qualification to be mentioned presently, it is generally agreed that, when an individual chooses satisfaction A in preference to satisfaction B, this *indicates* that satisfaction A is or, more strictly, is expected to be greater than satisfaction B. Choice thus provides an objective test of the comparative magnitudes of different utilities or satisfactions to a given individual. It does the same for marginal utilities or satisfactions, that is the utilities derived from marginal increments of different sorts of goods. But nobody chooses or can choose between the *excess* of marginal utility A over marginal utility B and the *excess* of marginal utility C over marginal utility D. Hence these second differences, though, as I have maintained, comparable in principle, are not comparable in fact—at all events by means of this kind of test. The point, however, is not important for our main argument.

V. INTER-PERSONAL COMPARISONS

So far we have been considering only the comparability of satisfactions as affecting the same person. Once we reject solipsism and admit the existence of other people, what has already been said should suffice to show that the utilities enjoyed by different people are not in their nature incomparable—it is not nonsense to say that A is happier than B. But the question whether they are comparable in fact is a more difficult one. The test of choice is not available here as it is for intra-personal comparisons. No doubt, a parent can choose satisfaction A for one of his sons as against satisfaction B for another; and, if he is impartial between them, this should mean that he judges satisfaction A to be the greater. But I do not think we can appeal to this because the parent's choice is not a direct one and, in framing his decision, he is really faced with the very problem that confronts us here. We cannot, therefore, shift our burden upon him. The issue for Welfare Economics is important. For, if the satisfactions of different individuals cannot be compared, a large part of that subject is undermined. We are not, indeed, precluded from saying that, if one person has more of something and nobody else has less of anything, the welfare of the whole group, so long as their desires are unchanged, is increased. But we are precluded from saying anything about the implication of transfers between richer and poorer persons. To ask whether inter-personal comparisons of

satisfactions or utilities are in fact possible is thus not an idle question.

Now, if we take random groups of people of the same race and brought up in the same country, we find that in many features that *are* comparable by objective tests they are on the average pretty much alike; and, indeed, for fundamental characters we need not limit ourselves to people of the same race and country. On this basis we are entitled, I submit, to infer by analogy that they are probably pretty much alike in other respects also. In all practical affairs we act on that supposition. We cannot prove that it is true. But we do not need to do so. Nobody can prove that anybody besides himself exists, but, nevertheless, everybody is quite sure of it. We do not, in short, and there is no reason why we should, start from a *tabula rasa*, binding ourselves to hold every opinion which the natural man entertains to be guilty until it is proved innocent. The burden is the other way. To deny this is to wreck, not merely Welfare Economics, but the whole apparatus of practical thought. On the basis of analogy, observation and intercourse, inter-personal comparisons *can*, as I think, properly be made; and, moreover, unless we have a special reason to believe the contrary, a given amount of stuff may be presumed to yield a similar amount of satisfaction, not indeed as between *any* one man and any other, but as between representative members of groups of individuals, such as the citizens of Birmingham and the citizens of Leeds. This is all that we need to allow this branch of Welfare Economics to function. Of course, in working it out, positive conclusions can only be reached subject to very important qualifications—of which something will have to be said presently.

VI. PROGRAMME

With this background I shall now review the implications and limitations of two propositions in Welfare Economics, on the assumption that satisfactions or utilities, though not measurable, are comparable in principle and can in fact be compared both intra-personally and inter-personally. The two propositions, put at their crudest, are: first, any additions to the real income of an individual makes satisfaction larger; secondly, transfers of money income from better-to-do people to worse-to-do people make satisfaction larger.

VII. THE FIRST PROPOSITION IN A ONE-COMMODITY WORLD

In the conditions supposed the amount of satisfaction that our individual gets depends partly on the state of his desires and partly on how much of the commodity is available to him. If the state of his desires is fixed, it will be generally agreed that in all ordinary circumstances his utility will be greater the more of the commodity that he has. If the state of his desires changes spontaneously, this changing is an additional factor affecting welfare, and nothing can be said about its consequences until the exact nature of the change is known. We rule out, therefore, spontaneous changes in desire attitudes. Our proposition is obviously subject to the condition that such spontaneous changes are excluded. On this basis, if the state of an individual's desires were independent of the amount that he has, nothing further would need to be said. But the amount that he has may react upon and partly determine the state of his desires. What are the implications of this possibility, and in what conditions is it to be expected that these reactions will make our proposition invalid?

It is commonly supposed that, besides more stuff with a given desire attitude entailing more utility, so also does a keener desire attitude with a given quantity of stuff. If this were always so, when an increase of stuff, in the familiar manner of appetite growing with eating, made desire more intense, the increase

of stuff would enhance satisfaction in a double way, partly through itself and partly through its effects. In fact, however, enhanced desire with a given quantity of stuff does not necessarily entail more utility or satisfaction. For unsatisfied desire may be painful. If a man with a given income of food per day becomes hungrier, the utility associated with the food he has increases, but the disutility of the food he has not increases too; and the last state of that man may be worse than the first. The ordinary form of diagrammatic analysis fails to bring out this point, though it could easily be modified so as to make it do so. The point, however, is not, I think, of large practical importance, and, for a broad view, may be left out of account. In general, then, an enhancement of desire increases the utility derived from a given provision of our commodity and a contraction of desire has the opposite effect.

It follows that an increase in the quantity of stuff available, not only when it leaves a man's desire attitude unaltered, but also, a fortiori, when it expands it, must entail an increase of utility. But having more of a thing may cause a man's desire attitude towards it to become less keen, not more. Or, to put the same thing the other way round, when he has become accustomed to having less he may find himself more happy with any given quantity than he used to be. It may even happen that the total satisfaction he gets from the smaller is as large as what he used to get from the larger quantity.

Thus—for this illustration we may waive the assumptions of one individual and a one-commodity world—consider two undergraduates precisely alike in temperament and constitution. One is poor and goes on a cheap Continental holiday, stopping the night at youth hostels; the other does an exactly similar tour at much greater expense and stopping at luxury hotels. Each of them is conditioned by habit and experience to his circumstances. Is there any reason to suppose that the rich undergraduate has a better time—achieves more utility—than the poor one? Yet again in prewar days well-to-do people had elaborate meals and had a number of servants to work for them. Now they have much simpler meals and do their own work. After they have become accustomed to the new conditions, are they less happy than before? It is very doubtful whether a moderately well-to-do man is appreciably happier now than he would be if transplanted back to the pre-railway age and attuned to the conditions of that age. This is in no way incompatible with a man preferring *at any given moment* to have more rather than less. Nor is it incompatible with the fact that the process of *becoming* better-off often yields satisfaction. In the process there is a prize, and, so far, progress, even among the fairly well-to-do, is not merely illusion. But there is a great deal of illusion about it. From a long-run standpoint, *after incomes in excess of a certain moderate level have been attained*, further increases in it may well not be significant for economic welfare.

The italicised words in that sentence are, of course, vital. What the "certain moderate level of income," to which they refer, is can only be guessed at. My own guess is that, even in this country and most certainly, for example, in Asia, a large number of people have incomes well below it. It follows that over a very wide area, in spite of reactions of having on desiring, having more does in fact entail more satisfaction.

VIII. THE FIRST PROPOSITION IN A MANY-COMMODITY WORLD

Let us now abandon the assumption that real income consists of a single sort of commodity—or of bundles of different commodities in each of which the proportions of these commodities are the same. When we do this it is still possible to say, in a straightforward physical sense, that one real income is larger than another, provided that it contains more of some item and not less of any item. There is, therefore, still meaning in the assertion that, other things being equal, a man's economic welfare is increased if his real income becomes larger; and the discussion of the preceding section remains appropriate without fundamental change.

It may perhaps be suggested that for most practical issues this is good enough, for, while technical knowledge and skill are always going forward in some fields, it is unlikely that they are actually going backwards in any. This may be thought to imply that the representative man's real income is unlikely to expand in some of its parts and at the same time to contract in others. That, however, is wrong. This is immediately obvious as regards agricultural products; some crops will often have a better harvest this year than last, others a worse one. But, over and above that, it is easy to see that, when technique improves as regards some commodity, the quantity of another commodity where it has not improved may not remain stationary, but may fall off. Even when technique has improved in respect of both of two commodities, the output of one of them may fall off. What happens, as a moment's reflection shows, depends on the general conditions of demand. The case, therefore, of some commodities available to our representative man increasing while others decrease is far from being a freak case of no practical importance. On the contrary, it is very important indeed. The relation between alterations of this kind in real income and in economic welfare cannot be ignored.

When this kind of alteration has taken place it is plainly impossible to say in any physical sense that actual real income has become larger or has become smaller. As physical entities the first and second actual real incomes are incommensurable.[3] Fortunately, however, we need not stop here. As was said just now, if a man with given desire attitudes comes to have more of something and not less of anything else, his satisfaction will be increased. Moreover, we may presume, in a general way and subject to qualifications, that, alike before and after a change in his real income, he will dispose of his purchasing power among different commodities in a way that gives him more satisfaction than he would get from any other disposition. If then the conditions are such that in the new situation he *could* get more income of the old proportionate pattern, or more of some items and not less of any, we may infer that his economic welfare is greater in the new situation than in the old. That is to say, if in the second situation his *potential* real income of the first situation's pattern is greater than his actual real income in the first, we can infer that his utility or satisfaction will be greater in the second situation. *Per contra*, if in the first situation his potential real income (of the second situation's pattern) is greater than the actual real income in the second, his satisfaction will be greater in the first situation.

There is indeed a difficulty. For may it not happen that, not only is the potential real income of the pattern proper to the first situation larger in the second situation than the actual real income of the first situation, but *also* the potential real income of the pattern proper to the second situation is larger in the first situation than the actual real income of the second situation? If this happens, we are forced to the absurd conclusion that our man's aggregate satisfaction is at once greater in the second situation than in the first, and also greater in the first situation than in the second. The emergence of this contradiction proves that the state of things we are supposing cannot exist. If the potential real income of the pattern of the first situation is larger in the second situation than the actual real income of the first situation, it *must* happen that the potential real income of the pattern proper to the second situation is smaller, not larger, in

the first situation than the actual real income of the second situation.

This conclusion seems inevitable in logic, but, none the less, unless we can see *how* it comes about that this must happen, we shall be left with the feeling of intellectual discomfort. Why then must it happen? The explanation is that a man's tastes help to determine what his actual real incomes in the two situations are. The discord we have been contemplating is impossible because, though it would occur *if* his actual real incomes were such and such, in fact his tastes, being, on our assumptions, the same in the two situations, *prevent* his actual real incomes from being such and such.[4]

This analysis, it will be observed, does not in all circumstances enable us in principle to decide whether the economic welfare of an individual with a given desire attitude is greater in one situation than in another. For it may happen that in each situation his potential real income of the other situation's pattern is *less* than the actual real income of that situation. When this is so, it is easy to see that no inference about his comparative economic welfare in the two situations can be drawn. If this is not obvious immediately, it can easily be made so with the help of algebraic symbols.

IX. THE FIRST PROPOSITION AS REGARDS GROUPS OF PEOPLE

Our first proposition when applied to a group of people is obviously subject to all the limitations which we have found to be necessary as regards a single individual. Are there any further limitations?

Suppose first that our group consists of a number of exactly similar persons enjoying identical real incomes and that in consequence of technical advance all these real incomes are increased by equal amounts of some items unaccompanied by a decrease in any others. If people *only* wanted things so as not to be inferior to other people, this development would clearly leave economic welfare unaltered. And no doubt to some extent people do want things for this sort of distinction motive. If it were not for this, it would be difficult for an academic person like myself to conceive how anybody could possibly have ever wanted such things as top hats or frock coats or crinolines or bustles. But it would be absurd to suggest that people *only* want things as a means to distinction. Though, therefore, the economic welfare of groups is not in fact increased by an expansion in real income as much as we should expect it to be if we ignored this characteristic, there is no ground for suggesting that it is not increased at all. So far what is true of individuals is also true for groups.

But in real life changes in technique do not affect all members of a group—a national group for instance—similarly. This opens up new possibilities. Even in a one-commodity world it might happen that a development which increased potential real income as a whole injured particular sections of the group—landlords, for example, or capitalists or wage-earners. If all the persons affected were similiar and were initially in receipt of identical incomes, a contraction in the incomes of some might outweigh from the standpoint of welfare a more than equivalent expansion in the incomes of others. With people of different tastes and different initial incomes the same thing is true, and the likelihood of a decrease in aggregate welfare is greater. The change in productivity, since we are supposing it to entail an increase in aggregate income, *could*, of course, be accompanied by a set of transfers—compensations—so arranged that in the final result some persons had more real income and none had less. In that event aggregate economic welfare *would be* increased. But to say that in that event it *is* increased is, to my mind, to use

words in a misleading way. The correct statement is, I think, that the improvement in productivity necessarily entails a *potential* increase in aggregate economic welfare, but does not necessarily entail an actual increase.

In a many-commodity world we saw in Section VII that it is often impossible in principle to say whether or not actual real income has increased between two years, but usually possible to say whether potential real income has. With a single person, we have found that an increase in potential real income over the actual income of an earlier time necessarily entails an increase in economic welfare, provided that the person's desire attitudes are the same before and after the change. With a group within which distribution is different after the change from what it was before, we can only say that an increase in potential real income necessarily entails a potential increase, not an *actual* increase, in economic welfare. If productivity changes make things predominantly consumed by poor persons (or by persons specially keen on those things) more abundant and things predominantly consumed by rich persons (or by persons indifferent to those things) less abundant, aggregate economic welfare may be increased even though aggregate potential real income is diminished; just as in opposite conditions it may be diminished even though aggregate potential real income is increased.

All this is true and from an academic point of view significant. But the paradox that technical advance may for this sort of reason be adverse to welfare is not I think—apart from advance in the machinery of war—significant practically. For our paradox can only become a fact if technical advances that increase potential real income as a whole at the same time damage the relatively poor. But experience hitherto does not suggest that technical advance in fact acts in that way. On the contrary, mechanical improvements are more readily made in respect of mass-produced goods, which poor people predominantly buy, and in transport, which directly or indirectly cheapen poor men's goods in a larger proportion than rich men's goods. As Leroy-Beaulieu observed long ago:

> The man of fashion who is fitted for his clothes by a tailor gains nothing from the great reduction of prices which shops selling clothes ready-made offer to the less comfortable section of the population.[5]

Moreover, as the history of the motor car, culminating in the petrol dirven lorry and motor omnibus, illustrates even those improvements which were originally designed exclusively for the luxuries of the rich are apt soon to spread themselves to the comforts of other classes.[6] Nobody, of course, can be certain that the experience of the past will not refute itself in the future. But subject to that general caution we may, I think, feel confident that what was said in the last section about the relation of changes in potential real income to the economic welfare of a single individual is true also without serious limitations of national or other groups.[7]

X. THE SECOND PROPOSITION

Let us now pass, once more beginning with the assumption of a one-commodity world, to the second of the two propositions set out in Section VI, namely, that transfers of money income from relatively rich to relatively poor persons increase aggregate satisfaction. In a one-commodity world transfers of money income imply unambiguously transfers of real income. It will not, I think, be disputed that, provided people's desire attitudes are not affected by differences in the size of their incomes, the law of diminishing utility in respect of real income will prevail. It follows immediately that, as between any two people with similar desire attitudes, a transfer of real and so of money income from the better-to-do to the worse-to-do—apart from reactions on real income, of which something will be said presently—increases aggregate satisfaction. Nor does it matter that the rich from whom transfers are made are likely to be much less numerous than the poor by whom they are received. Thus suppose that there is one rich man and ten poor ones. A pound is taken from the rich man and given to the first poor one. Aggregate satisfaction is increased. But the rich man is still richer than the second poor man. So the transfer of a pound to him again increases aggregate satisfaction. And so on until the originally rich man is no richer than anybody else. What is true of a transfer from one rich man to one poor one is also true of a set of transfers from few rich men to many poor ones.

No doubt at the moment if a rich man accustomed to a high standard of living has £5,000 cut off his income and given to a poor man, the rich man will suffer a good deal, while the poor man may have no idea of what to do with his new-found gains. But it is proper here to take a long-run view and to think of transfers, not as single, casual acts, but as lasting modifications of income distribution. From this standpoint, as we have already argued, cutting down large incomes probably leaves the people whose incomes are cut with substantially as much satisfaction as before, while the poor, whose incomes are increased, gain both directly and also indirectly by having their desire attitudes pushed up. This reasoning will not appeal to anyone who believes that people now rich are different in kind from people now poor, having, in their fundamental nature, greater *capacities* for enjoyment—real high-grade Herrenvolk. For myself, however, I see no reason for believing anything of the sort. If we agree that representative members of the two groups are probably by and large pretty much alike, the argument from the law of diminishing utility holds.

There are also incidental considerations available to support it. Thus it may well be that on the whole, in spite of the pleasure that some people take in contemplating the glories of Royalty and of "high-ups" generally, inequality itself damages happiness. For the odds are that the dwellers in hell are more annoyed at seeing the rich in heaven than the rich are pleased at seeing the poor in hell. To be "all in the same boat" is, for many, a consolation, even though the boat be a leaky one. On the whole then, for a one-commodity world we may feel reasonably confident, apart from possible reactions on potential real income, in this second crude welfare proposition.

In a many-commodity world, as we have seen, it is physically meaningless to say that one real income is larger than another, except in the special case where the one contains more of some commodities and not less of any. In like manner, it is meaningless to say that A is richer than B in respect of real income unless A's income contains more of some kind of commodities and not less of any. In like manner again, we cannot say that real income is transferred from A to B unless some commodities of some kinds are so transferred and none of any kind are transferred the other way. Thus plainly we cannot now appeal to the law of diminishing utility in respect of real income in the straightforward way that we were able to do in a one-commodity world.

There is, however, a way round. Money income being homogeneous, the law diminishing utility *can*, of course apply to it. If it *does* apply to it, we can infer that transfers of money income from richer people to poorer people of similar desire attitudes increase economic welfare in exactly the same way as we can infer this about transfers in a one-commodity world.

But are we entitled to say that the law of diminishing utility in fact holds of money income? A man does not buy different commodities in the same proportions when he has £100 as when he has £99. We must suppose that he will adjust his expenditure in the optimum manner for each several amount of income and associated set of prices. Hence, to say that the marginal utility of money income to him decreases as its amount increases must mean that the difference of satisfaction yielded by the marginal pound of a hundred pounds expended in the optimum manner is less than that yielded by the marginal pound of ninety-nine pounds so expended. This proposition cannot be derived from the Law of Diminishing Utility in respect of individual commodities. It is a separate proposition. If it is to be accepted, this must be upon broad grounds of experience, reflection and conversation. On these grounds I myself feel reasonably confident that it is true. Granted this, again apart from possible reactions on potential real income, it follows that in a many-commodity world, no less than in a one-commodity world, transfers of money income from the relatively rich to the relatively poor (of similar desire attitudes) will increase economic welfare. This is so in spite of the fact that a large change in the distribution of money income in favour of the poor would probably reduce the volume of saving, thus leading indirectly to a rise in the rate of interest and, through that, to a rise in aggregate money income. So long as potential real income is not also affected, this does not matter. The transfers and their direct consequences are still there, irrespective of the fact that *also* the aggregate number of counters that go to make up money income has been increased.

Our conclusion in this matter is, however, as has already been indicated in cautionary parentheses, subject to a very important limitation. As everybody knows, transfers of money income from the better-to-do to the worse-to-do sections of the community must in practice be accomplished, if they are at all large, with the help of steeply graduated taxes. These are likely in some measure to check effort, enterprise and the development of capital equipment; and so indirectly to reduce potential real income. On the other hand, the fact that the relatively poor are made better off will certainly increase their ability to acquire skill and to work hard, and may also increase their willingness. What will actually happen it is, of course, not possible to guess without a detailed study of the particular circumstances; and very likely not even then. No doubt, our fathers and grandfathers over-emphasized the dark and under-emphasized the bright side of the picture. None the less, it remains true that transfers may indirectly damage potential income so much that in the end they make against rather than in favour of economic welfare. Badly constructed schemes for giving poor people a "fairer share" of the national cake may even make the cake so much smaller that the absolute amount which they receive is actually reduced. These considerations do not, of course, warrant our standing still and doing nothing at all. But they do suggest that in going forward we should move with reasonable care and probe for hidden minefields.

NOTES

1. *Methods of Ethics* (Macmillan & Co., England, 1893), p. 126.
2. Bertrand Russell, *Principles of Mathematics* (Cambridge University Press, England, 1903), pp. 182-83.
3. In the *Economics of Welfare*, I *defined* an increase in actual real income as an alteration in its content such that, with tastes and distribution constant, more satisfaction would be yielded by it after the alteration than before (p. 54). On that basis our problem was to find an *index* of real income changes that would, or probably would, move up or down as real income so defined moved up or down. The problem here is es-

sentially the same but approached from a different angle.
4. Professor Paul A. Samuelson's "Evaluation of Real National Income" in *Oxford Economic Papers*, Vol. 2, No. 1 (Jan., 1950), p. 24, when he corrects a mistake in the *Economics of Welfare*.
5. *La Repartition des Richesses*, p. 87.
6. Compare the *Economics of Welfare*, p. 678 and Alfred Marshall's *Principles of Economics*, p. 541.
7. It seems proper to say a word here about quantity index numbers. These purport to represent variations in "production"—an important part of real income—over a series of years, despite the fact that some items have increased and others diminished; a task that in a physical sense is impossible. Great labour has been expended on the construction of these index numbers, and in political discussions appeal is frequently made to them. A quantity index is usually constructed by weighting the several elements in accordance with the amount of expenditure on them in some base year. If then we suppose that this expenditure is proportionate to the productive power—ambiguities about the definition of productive power being ignored—then employed in producing the several items, if we suppose that tastes (and distributions) have not changed, and if we also suppose that constant returns operate everywhere in both the base year and the year with which a comparison is being made, a quantity index number will show how the quantity of productive resources at work in the aggregate would have had to change, if there had been no change in technique, in order to allow the output actually found in the latter year to be produced. It, therefore, measures, granted constant tastes (and distribution) and constant returns, the proportion in which *potential* output of *the pattern ruling in the base year* is greater or less in the year we are studying than in the base year. This information, resting, as it does, on assumptions that must often depart seriously from the facts, is very different from the precise and definite information which quantity index numbers are popularly supposed to give. The moral is, however, not to leave these investigations unattempted, but to be cautious about the uses to which we put their results.

25. The Theory of Monopolistic Competition*

EDWARD HASTINGS CHAMBERLIN

INTRODUCTION

Economic literature affords a curious mixture, confusion and separation, of the ideas of competition and monopoly. On the one hand, analysis has revealed the differences between them and has led to the perfection and refinement of a separate body of theory for each. Although the two forces are complexly interwoven, with a variety of design, throughout the price system, the fabric has been undone and refashioned into two, each more simple than the original and bearing to it only a partial resemblance. Furthermore, it has, in the main, been assumed that the price system is like this—that all the phenomena to be explained are *either* competitive *or* monopolistic, and therefore that the expedient of two purified and extreme types of theory is adequate.

On the other hand, the facts of intermixture in real life have subtly worked against that complete theoretical distinction between competition and monopoly which is essential to a clear understanding of either. Because *actual* competition (rarely free of monopoly elements) is supposedly explained by the theory of *pure* competition, familiar results really attributable to monopolistic forces are readily associated with a theory which denies them. This association of the theory of competition with facts which it does not fit has not only

led to false conclusions about the facts; it has obscured the theory as well. This is the more serious because the mixture of the two forces is a chemical process and not merely a matter of addition. Slight elements of monopoly have a way of playing unexpected logical tricks, with results quite out of proportion to their seeming importance.

For example, Cournot and Edgeworth, in the problem of "duopoly," or price determination where there are only two competing sellers, arrive at wholly different solutions, although each is attacking, with the precision of mathematical methods, the same problem. Cournot's solution is that price is determinate and will lie between the monopoly price and the "perfectly" competitive price (where the number of sellers is infinite). Edgeworth's is that it is indeterminate, oscillating continually between the two extremes. The differences are explained in part by the fact that competition, supposedly pure except for the fewness of sellers, really contains, in the case as put by Edgeworth, certain other monopoly elements which affect the result.

As another instance, we have the paradoxical reasoning of Professor J. M. Clark, in his analysis of the market:

> If all the competitors followed suit instantly the moment any cut was made, each would gain his quota of the resulting increase in output, and no one would gain

any larger proportion of his previous business than a monopoly would gain by a similar cut in prices. Thus the competitive cutting of prices would naturally stop exactly where it would if there were no competition.[1]

Perfect competition, it would seem, gives the same price as perfect monopoly![2] His conclusion, that it is the "qualified monopoly" enjoyed by each producer which makes the market really competitive after all, and which accordingly permits price reductions, seems only still further to confuse the matter. From a somewhat different point of view, Professor Knight comments that "there does seem to be a certain Hegelian self-contradiction in the idea of theoretically perfect competition after all."[3] These contradictions and paradoxes arise, however, because supposedly perfect competition is really imperfect. The first step in the formulation of a theory of prices must be a clear definition of the two fundamental forces of competition and monopoly, and an examination of each in isolation.

The second step must be a synthesis of the two. This brings us back to the assertion that price theories have followed, in the main, the two extreme channels, without (conscious) recognition of a middle course. Quantitatively, competitive theory has dominated—indeed, the theory of competition has been so generally accepted as the underlying explanation of the price system that the presumption is in its favor; its inadequacy remains to be proved. Hints at the ubiquity of monopoly elements and at the possibility of an intermediate theory are not entirely lacking, however. Thus Professor Knight remarks that

in view of the fact that practically every business is a partial monopoly, it is remarkable that the theoretical treatment of economics has related so exclusively to complete monopoly and perfect competition,

and Veblen,

. . . it is very doubtful if there are any successful business ventures within the range

of modern industries from which the monopoly element is wholly absent.[4]

Such fragmentary recognition of the problem is not hard to find. Yet, with the exception of the theory of duopoly, the middle ground between competition and monopoly remains virtually unexplored and the possibilities of applying such a theory relatively little appreciated.

"Pure competition" is taken as a point of departure, the adjective "pure" being chosen deliberately to describe competition unalloyed with monopoly elements. It is a much simpler and less inclusive concept than "perfect" competition, for the latter may be interpreted to involve perfection in many other respects than in the absence of monopoly. It may imply, for instance, an absence of friction in the sense of an ideal fluidity or mobility of factors such that adjustments to changing conditions which actually involve time are accomplished instantaneously in theory. It may imply perfect knowledge of the future and the consequent absence of uncertainty. It may involve such further "perfection" as the particular theorist finds convenient and useful to his problem. Two illustrations will serve to bring out the contrast between pure and perfect competition. The actual price of wheat approximates very inaccurately its normal price, yet the individual wheat farmer possesses not a jot of monopoly power. The market, though a very imperfect one, is purely competitive.[5] On the other hand, monopoly may exist under conditions which are "perfect," or "ideal," in other respects. The static state and perfect competition are wrongly treated as synonymous by J. B. Clark. There is no reason whatever why monopoly of all sorts and degrees should not be present in a state where the conditions as to population, the supply of capital, technology, organization, and wants remained unchanged. "Pure" and "perfect" competition must not be identified; and to consider the theory of monopolistic competition vaguely as a theory of "imperfect" competition is to confuse the issues.

Monopoly ordinarily means control over the supply, and therefore over the price. A sole prerequisite to pure competition is indicated—that no one have any degree of such control.[6] This, however, may be analyzed into two phases. In the first place, there must be a large number of buyers and sellers so that the influence of any one or of several in combination is negligible. There is no need that their numbers be infinite (although to treat them for certain purposes as though they were is perfectly legitimate and necessary), but they must be large enough so that, even though any single individual has, in fact, a slight influence upon the price, he does not exercise it because it is not worth his while. If the individual seller produces on the assumption that his entire output can be disposed of at the prevailing or market price, and withholds none of it, there is pure competition so far as numbers are concerned, no matter at what price he actually disposes of it, and how much influence he actually exerts.

Secondly, control over price is completely eliminated only when all producers are producing the identical good and selling it in the identical market. Goods must be perfectly homogeneous, or standardized, for if the product of any one seller is slightly different from those of others, he has a degree of control over the price of his own variety, whereas under pure competition he can have no control over the price of anything. If his product is slightly different from others, it would be a mistake for the producer to proceed on the assumption that he can sell any amount of it at the going price, since buyers might prefer other varieties and take larger amounts of his own only at a price sacrifice or through the persuasion of advertising. (This is the circumstance in which the ordinary business man finds himself, and this is why most markets are not purely competitive.)

Not only goods, but sellers, must be "standardized" under pure competition. Anything which makes buyers prefer one seller to another, be it personality, reputation, convenient location, or the tone of his shop, differentiates the thing purchased to that degree, for what is bought is really a bundle of utilities, of which these things are a part. The utilities offered by all sellers to all buyers must be identical, otherwise individual sellers have a degree of control over their individual prices. Under such conditions it is evident that buyers and sellers will be paired in "random" fashion in a large number of transactions. It will be entirely a matter of chance from which seller a particular buyer makes his purchase, and purchases over a period of time will be distributed among all according to the law of probability. After all, this is only another way of saying that the product is homogeneous.

The two requirements for pure competition suggest at once the two ways in which monopolistic and competitive elements may be blended. In the first place, there may be one, few, or many selling the identical product in the identical market. Here the common market is shared by all, and such control over price as any one has is a control over the single price at which all must sell. A condition of monopoly shades gradually into one of pure competition as the sellers increase in number. The theory of value for the intermediate ground in this case has been treated, mainly by the mathematical economists, with particular reference to the problem of two sellers, or "duopoly," and we may extend this terminology, adding "oligopoly" for a few sellers.[7] . . .

In the second place, sellers may be offering identical, slightly different, or very different products. If they are identical, competition is pure (provided also that the number of sellers is very large). With differentiation appears monopoly, and as it proceeds further the element of monopoly becomes greater. Where there is any degree of differentiation whatever, each seller has an absolute monopoly of his own product, but is subject to the competition of more or less imperfect substitutes. Since each is a monopolist and yet has competitors, we may speak of them as "competing monopolists," and, with peculiar appropriateness, of the forces at work as those of "monopolistic competition."[8]. . .

It is this latter problem which is of especial interest and importance. In all of the fields where individual products have even the slightest element of uniqueness, competition bears but faint resemblance to the pure competition of a highly organized market for a homogeneous product. Consider, for instance, the competitive analysis as applied to the automobile industry. How is one to conceive of demand and supply curves for "automobiles in general" when, owing to variations in quality, design, and type, the prices of individual units range from several hundred to many thousands of dollars? How define the number of units which would be taken from or put upon the market at any particular price? How fit into the analysis a wide variety of costs based mostly upon a correspondingly wide variety of product? These difficulties are great; perhaps they are not insurmountable. The real one is neither of definition nor of interpretation, and cannot be surmounted. Competitive theory does not fit because competition throughout the group is only partial and is highly uneven. The competition between sport roadsters and ten-ton trucks must be virtually zero; and there is probably more justification for drawing up a joint demand schedule for Fords and house room than for Fords and Locomobiles. These are, perhaps, extreme cases, but the fact that each producer throughout the group has a market at least partially distinct from those of the others introduces forces, absent under pure competition, which materially alter the result. Prices throughout are adjusted in some measure according to the monopoly principle. Furthermore, advertising and selling outlays are invited by the fact that the market of each seller is limited, whereas the very nature of a purely competitive market precludes a selling problem. The theory of pure competition, in explaining the adjustment of economic forces in such an industry, is a complete misfit.

Because most prices involve monopoly elements, it is monopolistic competition that most people think of in connection with the simple word "competition." In fact, it may almost be said that under pure competition the buyers and sellers do not really compete in the sense in which the word is currently used. One never hears of "competition" in connection with the great markets, and the phrases "price cutting," "underselling," "unfair competition," "meeting competition," "securing a market," etc., are unknown. No wonder the principles of such a market seem so unreal when applied to the "business" world where these terms have meaning. They are based on the supposition that each seller accepts the market price and can dispose of his entire supply without materially affecting it. Thus there is no problem of choosing a price policy, no problem of adapting the product more exactly to the buyers' (real or fancied) wants, no problem of advertising in order to change their wants. The theory of pure competition could hardly be expected to fit facts so far different from its assumptions. But there is no reason why a theory of value cannot be formulated which will fit them—a theory concerning itself specifically with goods which are not homogeneous. This is the purpose of the later chapters of this book. We turn first to the theory of pure competition. . . .

DUOPOLY AND OLIGOPOLY

[Paragraphs deleted.]

MUTUAL DEPENDENCE RECOGNIZED

I pass now to a new phase of the problem. None of the solutions yet given conforms perfectly to the hypothesis that each seller acts so as to render his profit a maximum. In order to do this, he will take account of his *total* influence upon the price, indirect as well as direct. When a move by one seller evidently forces the other to make a counter move, he is very stupidly refusing to look further than his nose if he proceeds on the assumption that it will not. As already argued, the assumption of independence cannot be construed as requiring the sellers to compete as though their fortunes were independent, for this is to belie the very problem of oligopoly itself. It can refer only to independence of action—the absence of agreement or of "tacit" agreement. For one competitor to take into account the alterations of policy which he forces upon the other is simply for him to consider the indirect consequences of his own acts. Let each seller, then, in seeking to maximize his profit, reflect well, and look to the total consequences of his move. He must consider not merely what his competitor is doing now, but also what he will be forced to do in the light of the change which he himself is contemplating. . . .

The result is the same when the sellers adjust their prices. . . . Since the result of a cut by any one is inevitably to decrease his own profits, no one will cut, and, although the sellers are entirely independent, the equilibrium result is the same as though there were a monopolistic agreement between them.

As in the case where amounts are adjusted, the break towards purely competitive levels comes when the number of sellers is so large that each is led to neglect his influence upon the price. Neglect of either indirect or direct influence gives, by the theory of contract, or competitive bidding, the same result as if there were pure competition, so long as there are at least two sellers, or, by recognition of the full power of each, oscillation at a somewhat higher level, as shown above. It must again be emphasized, however, that *this result does not flow from the assumption that each seeks independently to maximize his profit.* On the contrary, this latter leads to the conclusion of a monopoly price for any fairly small number of sellers. No one will cut from the monopoly figure because he would force others to follow him, and thereby work his own undoing. As their numbers increase, it is impossible to say at just what point this consideration ceases to be a factor. If there were 100 sellers, a cut by any one which doubled his sales would, if his gains were taken equally from each of his competitors, reduce the sales of each of them by only 1/99, and this might be so small as not to force them, *because* of the cut, to do anything which they would not do without it. At whatever point this becomes true, the barrier to the downward movement of price from the point which will maximize the joint profits of all is removed. No one seller will look upon himself as *causing* the dislodgment, since he secures his gains with comparatively little disturbance to any of his rivals. Under these circumstances there is no reason for him to withhold a shading of his price which is to his advantage, and which has no repercussions. Nor is there any reason for the others not to do likewise, and the price becomes the purely competitive one.

All of the above has been reasoned on the assumption that the response of each seller to a move by his rival is instantaneous. If one cuts, the others are supposed to cut at once, leaving him no interval in which to enjoy the larger profits he anticipated. Indeed, there being no interval, the very conception of one reducing his price below the rest may well be dropped. The prices of all move together, and from this it follows at once that the equilibrium price will be the monopoly one. The same conclusion is reached if the idea of "recontract" is introduced, for this insures that, although the provisional contracts may diverge, final ones do not. There is no incentive to make a new provisional contract (with a larger number of buyers at a slightly lower price), which is advantageous, if the very act of making it puts into motion forces which must destroy it and substitute one less advantageous than the original one. Such is the case unless the number of sellers is very large. In fact, "re-contract" is another way of expressing the absence of friction. The results are the same whether the friction is never permitted or whether it is permitted and then removed.

The results are different, however, if friction is permitted and is not removed. If an interval, no matter how long, elapses between price adjustments (and if every sale is final), the one who cuts his price will enjoy an advantage during that interval which will be a factor in his decision as to price policy. This phase of the matter may be summed up by the general statement that the *ultimate* consequences of his price cut (through his indirect influence upon price) are a factor of more or of less significance to the seller, depending on whether the time lag is short or long *relative* to the period he expects to continue selling. If he is in business permanently, the temporary gains of a price cut are of negligible importance. He will give full weight to the indirect, or ultimate, consequences of his acts, and make no move which will force future sales at a lower figure. On the other hand, if he is in the market only temporarily, bent on disposing of a certain amount of product, the ultimate consequences do not enter into his calculations at all. If he can effect a sale of his goods at a slight sacrifice from the prevailing price, he has not more to sell, and cares nothing for the figure at which subsequent sales are made. Midway between these two extremes lie cases where immediate gains must be balanced against ultimate losses, direct and indirect influence upon price being given such weight as is appropriate.

THE EFFECT OF UNCERTAINTY

There remains to take account of the factor of uncertainty on the part of one seller as to what the other is going to do. This factor has been deferred until last in order not to throw a haze prematurely over the working of the various forces *about which* there may be uncertainty. We have seen that the solutions varied all the way from the equilibrium price defined by monopolistic agreement to the one defined by conditions of pure competition, depending upon the various assumptions which one seller might make as to the conduct of his rival. If, now, he does not know what assumption to make, the conclusions must be that the price may be anything between these limits, depending upon the one which chance, shrewdness, or desperation leads him to choose, and depending also upon whether his rival chooses the same one. Such uncertainty cannot be asserted, however, without establishing a reason for it. What basis is there, then, for doubt on the part of one seller as to what his competitor will do?

The first element of uncertainty lies within the limits of the problem as stated with reference only to the direct influence of each seller upon price. If each assumes his rival's present policy to continue, unaffected by his own, he still has no way of knowing whether this fixity of policy will express itself with regard to his rival's supply or his price. The general answer here must therefore be a price ranging anywhere from Cournot's solution to the purely competitive figure. If, on the contrary, he is certain that his rival's policy *is* affected by his own, there is no indeterminateness on this score, for it makes no difference then whether it is his price or his supply which is affected—the result when *total* influence upon price is taken into account is always the monopoly figure.

A second possible element of uncertainty has regard to the degree of intelligence and far-sightedness of the competitors. It is true that, for relatively small numbers, if *each one could see* the ultimate consequences of his price cut there would be no downward movement of price from the monopoly figure. But even though some can thus pursue their interests coolly, there may be others so eager for economic gain that they see nothing but the immediate profits from cutting under their rivals. Any one seller may be perfectly aware of his own indirect influence upon the price, but uncertain as to how many of his competitors are aware of theirs. He will then be in doubt as to the effectiveness of his own foresight in maintaining the price, and therefore in doubt as to whether he should lower or maintain it.

A third element of uncertainty arises when numbers are such as to leave doubt in the the mind of any one as to the extent of the incursions which his move will make upon the sales of the others. (Let the previous element of uncertainty be laid aside and kept distinct by the assumption here that each and every seller is aware of his own indirect influence and aware that the others are aware of theirs.) Uncertainty and hence indeterminateness are now present, not when numbers are small, but when they are fairly large yet not large enough to make the conditions those of pure competition. If numbers are fairly small, any one seller can be *certain* that his incursions upon the others by a price cut will be large enough to cause them to follow suit; and therefore no one will cut. If they are very large, he can be certain thathis incursions will be such a negligible factor to each other seller that no one will "follow suit" (*i.e.,* cut *because* he did); and therefore everyone will cut. But in between there is a range of doubt. At what point exactly do the effects of a price cut upon others become "negligible"? It is undeniable that they are not so when numbers are small and that they become so when numbers are very large. Between these limits the result is unpredictable.

A fourth element of uncertainty appears in the case where there is "friction" in the working of the market. It arises with regard to the length of the time lag. (The question of the relative certainty of the final result has already been considered.) The "immediate" effects of a price cut (*i.e.,* those enjoyed before the rival also cuts) are not realized immediately in point of time, but with a delay the length of which is uncertain, depending upon the rapidity with which knowledge of the cut spreads and buyers are brought to alter established relationships. This creates uncertainty as to the result of a price cut by one seller, even though his rival were sure to maintain his price; but especially important is the added uncertainty as to (a) *how soon* pressure will actually be brought to bear upon the other, by the reduction in his sales, to follow suit, and (b) the degree to which he will anticipate it. This leaves each competitor in doubt, not as to what his rival will do, but as to when he will do it, which suffices, however, to make him uncertain as to what to do in the first place. Under these circumstances, no assumption as to the intelligence which the sellers apply to the pursuit of their maximum gain, short of omniscience, would render the outcome determinate.

SUMMARY

The most important conclusions of this chapter may now be summarized:

1. Oligopoly is not one problem, but several. The solution varies, depending upon the conditions assumed. Putting to one side the factor of uncertainty, it is (with minor exceptions) determinate for each set of assumptions made. . . .

2. If sellers have regard to their *total* influence upon price, the price will be the monopoly one. Independence of the producers and the pursuit of their self-interest are not sufficient to lower it. Only if the number is large enough to render negligible the effect of an adjustment by any one upon each of the others is the equilibrium price the purely competitive one. If the market is imperfect, however, true self-interest requires the neglect of indirect influence to a degree depending upon the degree of imperfection.

3. If sellers neglect their indirect influence upon price, each determining upon his policy as though his competitors were uninfluenced by what he did, the results vary, depending upon further circumstances. If each assumes his competitors' supplies to be unchanged, the equilibrium price is continually lower than the monopoly one as the sellers are more numerous, descending to the purely competitive level only when their numbers are infinite. If each assumes his competitors' prices unchanged, and if competitive bidding, or "re-contract," continues until no further price change can be made without disadvantage to someone, the equilibrium price is the purely competitive one for only two sellers, and, of course, for any greater number. If the full power of the seller to alter his price, even to the disadvantage of the buyer, is recognized, however, price will oscillate over an area which becomes narrower and approaches more closely the purely competitive figure as the number of sellers becomes larger.

4. If sellers neglect both their indirect and their direct influence upon price, the outcome will be the purely competitive price, *regardless of numbers*.

5. Uncertainty, where present, as to (a) whether other competitors will hold their amounts or their prices constant, (b) whether they are far-sighted, (c) the extent of the possible incursions upon their markets, and (d) in the case of a time lag, its length, renders the outcome indeterminate for the particular reasons indicated in each case. . . .

PRODUCT DIFFERENTIATION AND THE THEORY OF VALUE

[*Paragraphs deleted.*]

GROUP EQUILIBRIUM

Let us turn now to what we may call the group problem, or the adjustment of prices and "products" of a number of producers whose goods are fairly close substitutes. The group contemplated initially is one which has *ordinarily* been regarded as composing one imperfectly competitive market: a number of automobile manufacturers, of producers of pots and pans, of magazine publishers, or of retail shoe dealers. From our point of view, each producer within the group is a monopolist, yet his market is interwoven with those of his competitors, and he is no longer to be isolated from them. The question now to be asked is: what characterizes the system of relationships into which the group tends to fall as a result of their influence one upon another? The conclusions reached will be especially illuminating when considered alongside of those yielded by the theory of pure competition, ordinarily applied to the same phenomena.

One difficulty encountered in describing the group equilibrium is that the widest variations may exist in all respects between the different component firms. Each "product" has distinctive features and is adapted to the tastes and needs of those who buy it. Qualitative differences lead to wide divergences in the curves of cost of production, and buyers' preferences account for a corresponding variety of demand curves, both as to shape (elasticity) and as to position (distance from the x and y axes). The result is heterogeneity of prices, and variation over a wide range in outputs (scales of production) and in profits. Many such variations are, of course, temporary, and are constantly in process of being eliminated. Our main concern, however, is with those which persist over a long period of time. To a very considerable extent the scheme of prices is the result of conditions unique to each product and to its market—it defies comprehensive description as a "group" problem, even when monopolistic forces are given their full value in the explanation.

The matter may be put in another way by saying that the "imperfection" of competition is not uniform. It is not as though a few elements of friction, such as imperfect knowledge, or partial indifference to economic gain, spread an even haze over the whole; nor as though immobility of resources gave a general tendency for "normal" results to be retarded in working themselves out.

These factors would apply with equal force in all portions of the field, at least over periods long enough for chance short time irregularities to be ironed out. But the differentiation of the product is not, so to speak, "uniformly spaced"; it is not distributed homogeneously among all of the products which are grouped together. Each has its own individuality, and the size of its market depends on the strength of the preference for it over other varieties. Again, if high average profits lead new competitors to invade the general field, the markets of different established producers cannot be wrested from them with equal facility. Some will be forced to yield ground, but not enough to reduce their profits below the minimum necessary to keep them in business. Others may be cut to the minimum, and still others may be forced to drop out because only a small demand exists or can be created for their particular variety of product. Others, protected by a strong prejudice in favor of theirs, may be virtually unaffected by an invasion of the general field—their monopoly profits are beyond the reach of competition.

These variations will give no real difficulty in the end. Exposition of the group theory is facilitated, however, by ignoring them for the present. We therefore proceed under the heroic assumption that both demand and cost curves for all the "products" are uniform throughout the group. We shall return later to a recognition of their diversity, and to the manner in which allowance for it is to be made. Meanwhile, it may be remarked that diversity of "product" is not entirely eliminated under our assumption. It is required only that consumers' preferences be evenly distributed among the different varieties, and that differences between them be not such as to give rise to differences in cost. This might be approximately true where very similar products were differentiated by trade-marks. It is also approximately realized in the fairly even geographical distribution of small retail

establishments in the outlying districts of a city.

Another complication in the group problem arises in connection with the number of competitors included within the group and the manner in which their markets "overlap." . . . This complication may be adequately recognized by considering first the case where numbers are very large, then the case where they are small. Specifically, we assume *for the present* that any adjustment of price or of "product" by a single producer spreads its influence over so many of his competitors that the impact felt by any one is negligible and does not lead him to any readjustment of his own situation. A price cut, for instance, which increases the sales of him who made it, draws inappreciable amounts from the markets of each of his many competitors, achieving a considerable result for the one who cut, but without making incursions upon the market of any single competitor sufficient to cause him to do anything he would not have done anyway.

As in the case of individual equilibrium, we shall first focus attention upon the price adjustment by assuming "products" stable; then reverse the process; and finally combine the two results.

Let the demand and cost curves for the "product" of *each* of the competing monopolists in the group be *DD'* and *PP'* respectively (Figure 1). Each seller will at once set his price at *AR*, since his profits, *GHRE*, at that point are a maximum. In spite of the extra profit which all are enjoying, there is no reason for any one to reduce his price below this figure, since the business gained would not make up for the price sacrifice. The extra profit will, however, attract new competitors into the field, with a resulting shift in the demand curves and possibly in the cost curves. The demand curve for the "product" of each seller will be moved to the left, since the total purchases must now be distributed among a larger number of

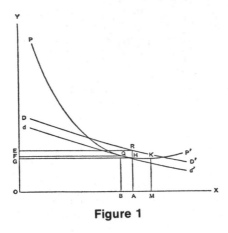

Figure 1

sellers. The cost curve we shall assume for the moment to be unaffected. With each shift in the demand curve will come a price readjustment so as to leave the area corresponding to *GHRE* a maximum, the process continuing until the demand curve for each "product" is tangent to its cost curve, and the area of surplus profit is wiped out. The price is now *BQ*, and the ultimate demand curve, *dd'*. The same final adjustment would have been reached if the original demand curve had lain to the left of and below *dd'*, through an exodus of firms caused by the general realization of losses, and the movement of the demand curve to the right and upwards as the total sales were shared by a smaller number of competitors, until it settled in the position of *dd'*. Here is a position of equilibrium. Price equals cost of production and any seller will lose by either raising or lowering it; it is therefore stable. There will be no further flow of resources into or out of the field, since profits are just adequate to maintain the amount then invested.

Let us now return to the question of the cost curves in the adjustment. As new resources flow into the field, these curves may be raised (by an increase in the price of the productive factors employed); they may be lowered (by improvements in the organization of the group as a whole—"external econo-

mies"); or they may remain the same (owing to the absence of both of these tendencies or to their cancellation one against the other). These three possibilities correspond respectively to the familiar increasing, decreasing, and constant cost of competitive theory. In the simple illustration just given no allowance was made for a shift in the curves; in other words, the assumption was implicitly made that conditions of constant cost obtained for the group as a whole. This assumption will be continued throughout, and for two reasons: (1) the theory in this form is widely applicable to the facts, and (2) where it is not applicable, its extension to cover cases of increasing and decreasing cost for the group is easily made.

First, as to its applicability. . . . "variations" in output by a single producer will, if he is one of many producers, have a negligible effect upon the total output for all and hence upon cost tendencies for the product as a whole. Similarly, whenever the quantity of resources employed in one field of production is small relative to their quantity employed generally, an increase or decrease in output within this one field will have a negligible effect upon the prices of the productive factors employed and hence upon costs. An increase in the manufacture of scissors will not appreciably affect the price of steel. Nor will an increased output of rubber boots raise the price of rubber. What conditions obtain in any particular case is, of course, a question of fact. It is only meant to point out that tendencies towards increasing (or decreasing) cost with respect to particular kinds of resources or factors of production are transmitted to finished products almost always with diminished force and often with a force which is negligible. To this must be added the fact that the resources themselves may be obtainable at fairly constant cost. If increased supplies of cement, sand, and gravel are readily available, expansion of the building industry will be possible at constant costs so far as these materials are a factor. In sum, it is likely that many fields of production are subject to conditions of approximately constant cost so far as the prices of the resources involved are concerned.

Do improvements in the organization of resources with larger output—"external economies"—result generally in a tendency to diminishing cost? The answer is yes, where they are appreciable. But it must be realized that such economies include only those made possible by the expansion of this particular field, exclusive of (a) those arising from the expansion of smaller fields (the individual establishments) within it—"internal economies"—and (b) those arising from the expansion of larger fields of which it is a part—the largest of which would be industry generally. The former are excluded because they may be realized to the full, independently of the output of the group . . . ; the latter, for a similar reason, because, since the group in question is small relative to larger fields of which it is a part, its expansion or contraction has a negligible effect upon economies in this larger field. To illustrate, an expansion of the retail grocery trade does not enable the individual grocer to approximate any more closely the most effective conditions of production within his own shop; neither does it contribute appreciably to such economies as are made possible by a large volume of retailing generally. In the group problem, then, the only economies which may be admitted as lowering the cost curves with increase of output are those which are due to the expansion of the group itself. Whether such economies exist in any particular case is, again, a matter of fact. Wherever they do not or where they are of only negligible importance, the result is a tendency to constant cost for the group.

The theory as developed for the case of constant cost may also be applicable if there are opposing tendencies of increasing and decreasing cost which approximately offset each other. Thus, expansion of the automobile industry may lead to (1) higher costs because of increased demand for materials, and (2) lower costs because of improved organization within the industry, the two roughly balancing each other and giving a net result of constant cost.

Secondly, the theory is not developed to include the cases of increasing and decreasing cost for the group because to do so in detail is not necessary. Where increasing costs obtain, the curves of all producers will rise as the resources employed in the field are increased, and fall as they are diminished, equilibrium being reached at a higher or at a lower point as the case may be. (Rents will be affected as in purely competitive theory, and are here to be included within the cost curves of the individual producers.) Similarly, in the case of decreasing cost the curves of all producers will fall as resources are increased and rise as they are diminished, the equilibrium being correspondingly lower or higher. These observations need not be repeated at every stage of the argument. Regardless of the cost tendency for the group, the equilibrium is always defined in the same manner with respect to the individual curves, and the divergences from the norms of purely competitive theory are always of the same sort. Our interest lies primarily in these matters, and they are most clearly revealed in the simple case of constant cost, to which attention will be confined from this point on.

Before introducing further complications, we may note some general conclusions as to monopolistic competition which follow from the first very simple putting of the case. In the first place, we see the necessity for distinguishing carefully between competitive prices and competitive profits. If there were no monopoly elements, prices would correspond to the cost of production under the most efficient conditions, MK in the figure. The demand curve for the product of any single producer would be a horizontal line, and would be lowered by competition until it was tangent to *PP'* at *K*. The monopoly elements inevitably carry it higher, although the profits made by the individual producer are no greater, costs being exactly covered in both cases. Competition, in so far as it consists of a movement of resources into the industry, reduces profits to the competitive level, but leaves prices higher to a degree dependent upon the strength of the monopoly elements. Competitive profits, then, never mean competitive prices under monopolistic competition, for the demand curve is never tangent to the cost curve at its lowest point.

In the second place, the price is inevitably higher and the scale of production inevitably smaller under monopolistic competition than under pure competition. It might be argued that a price reduction on the part of one seller, although it would increase his sales only within limits, would conceivably increase them to *OM*, and that successive moves on the part of all would establish the price *MK*. But this is impossible. It is true that for the position of *DD'* shown in Figure 2 a reduction, if made, would in fact give the price of *MK* and the most efficient scale of production, *OM*. But such a reduction would not be made, for any seller could increase his profits by raising his price to *AR*, where *FHRE* is a maximum; and equilibrium

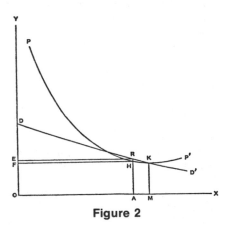

Figure 2

will be reached, as described earlier, when *DD'* has moved to the left until it is tangent to *PP'*, the price at this point being higher than *MK* and the scale of production smaller than *OM*.

A third conclusion is that general uniformity of price proves nothing as to the freedom of competition from monopoly elements. The general explanation of such tendency towards a uniform price as exists in actuality is that the demand curve for the product of each seller is of about the same elasticity, so that each finds his maximum profit at the same point. In the field of retailing, for instance, if the market of each seller is a random sample of the whole population, prices in an entire area will be fairly uniform, and grouped about a modal, or most prevalent, price according to the law of probability. Of course, such freedom of movement as exists among buyers contributes to this result, for the more elastic the demand schedules, the more closely will price deviations be grouped about the mode. But apart from such freedom of movement (the elasticity of demand), they will also be grouped more closely about the mode as each sample is more nearly the same in composition as the whole. If each dealer's market were made up of exactly the same proportion of rich and poor, and of those of different tastes and preferences, prices would everywhere be the same, even though a wall separated the province of each seller, isolating his market completely from those of his competitors. General uniformity of prices, therefore, proves nothing as to the purity of competition, or, we might say, as to the relative proportions of monopoly and competition in the admixture.

Let us return to the main thread of the argument. The nature of the equilibrium adjustment pictured in Figure 1 will be better understood if another route by which it may be reached is described. The maladjustment which was corrected in the movement towards this equilibrium was one of an unduly small number of firms, which gave to each one a larger market and the possibility of profits above the minimum level. It was corrected by an influx of new firms until markets were diminished and the extra profits eliminated. Let us now suppose the number of firms to be that corresponding to the equilibrium adjustment and to remain unchanged while a ruling price higher than the equilibrium one is corrected. Graphic representation of this situation requires the introduction of a new type of demand curve.

The curve *DD'*, as heretofore drawn, describes the market for the "product" of any one seller, *all* "products" and *all other* prices being given. It shows the increase in sales which he could realize by cutting his price, *provided* others did not also cut theirs; and conversely, it shows the falling off in sales which would attend an increase in price, *provided* other prices did not also increase. Another curve may now be drawn which shows the demand for the product of any one seller at various prices on the assumption that his competitors' prices are always identical with his. Evidently this latter curve will be much less elastic than the former, since the concurrent movement of all prices eliminates incursions by one seller, through a price cut, upon the markets of others. Such a curve will, in fact, be a fractional part of the demand curve for the general class of product, and will be of the same elasticity. If there were 100 sellers, it will show a demand at each price which will be exactly 1/100 of the total demand at that price (since we have assumed all markets to be of equal size). Let *DD'* in Figure 3 be such a curve, and let the price asked by all producers be, for the moment, *BQ*. The sales of each are *OB*, and the profits of each (in excess of the minimum contained within the cost curve) are *FHQE*. Now let *dd'* be drawn through *Q*, showing the increased sales which any one producer may enjoy by lowering his price, provided the others hold theirs fast at

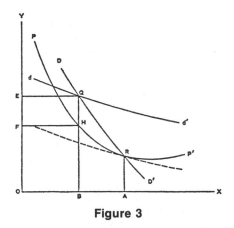

Figure 3

BQ.[9] Evidently, profits may be increased for any individual seller by moving to the right along *dd'*; and he may do this without fear of ultimately reducing his gains through forcing others to follow him because his competitors are so numerous that the market of each of them is inappreciably affected by his move. (Each loses only 1/99 of the total gained by the one who cuts his price.) The same incentive of larger profits which prompts one seller to reduce his price leads the others to do likewise. The curve *dd'*, then, explains why each seller is led to reduce his price; the curve *DD'* shows his actual sales as the *general* downward movement takes place. The former curve "slides" downwards along the latter as prices are lowered, and the movement comes to a stop at the price of *AR*.[10] Evidently it will pay no one to cut beyond that point, for his costs of producing the larger output would exceed the price at which it could be sold.

The position of *DD'* depends upon the number of sellers in the field. It lies further to the left as there are more of them, since the share of each in the total is then smaller; and further to the right as there are fewer of them, since the share of each in the total is then larger. It was drawn through *R*, the point of tangency of *dd'* with *PP'*, in the example just given, since the number of sellers was assumed to be that consistent with the final equilibrium adjustment. Let us now suppose that, at prices in the neighborhood of *BQ*, temporarily prevailing, additional sellers are attracted by the high profits, and intrench themselves in the field before the price-cutting corrective takes place. Such an inflow of resources may conceivably continue until *DD'* is pushed leftwards to a position of tangency with *PP'*, as in Figure 4, the price being *BQ* and the output per firm *OB*. Here cost exactly equals price, because the uneconomical scale at which each is producing has raised costs to meet it. The situation is unstable, however, because of the possibility of increased profits, represented for any producer by the demand curve *dd'*, drawn through *Q*. That each, and hence all, will cut prices is evident from *dd'*; and that each, and hence all, are involved in ever increasing losses as the process continues is evident from *DD'*, which shows the sales of each as the prices of all are lowered. When the price has fallen to *CQ'*, for instance, the sales of each are *OC*, and his losses *FQ'HE*. An escape is offered to anyone by further cuts, however, as is indicated by the dotted line passing through *Q'*. Any seller, by cutting to *AR*, will avoid losses and exactly cover his costs. It might seem that

equilibrium has been reached at this point, since *dd'* is now tangent to *PP'*, as required. However, the number of sellers is so great that when all cut to *AR*, as they must, the sales of each are not *OA*, but *OM*, as indicated by *DD'*, and losses are larger than ever. Equilibrium can be achieved only by the elimination of firms.

Before this takes place, however, price cutting may continue still further. Although, for positions of *dd'* lower than the dotted line, it is no longer possible to escape losses of some magnitude, it is still possible to reduce them. Evidently, if *dd'* is only slightly lower than the dotted line passing through *R*, this will be true. Soon, however, a lower limit will be reached, represented by the dot-dash line, where departure by any one from the adjustment for all on *DD'* will no longer diminish his losses, and here the movement will stop.

The curve *dd'* having reached any position below that of tangency, there is no escape from general losses until the number of firms is reduced. As this takes place, *DD'* will move to the right, and the movement must continue until it passes through *R*—in other words, until the output of each producer when all are charging the same price is *OA*. Equilibrium, then, is defined by two conditions: *(a) dd'* must be tangent to *PP'*, and *(b) DD'* must intersect both *dd'* and *PP'* at the point of tangency.

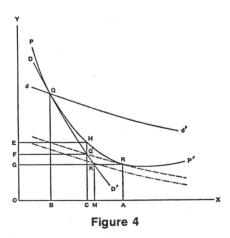

Figure 4

NOTES

1. J. M. Clark, *The Economics of Overhead Costs* (1923) p. 417.

2. And if we now regard perfect competition as a norm which prices under imperfect competition more or less closely approximate, we reach the startling conclusion that they approximate monopoly prices.

3. *Risk, Uncertainty and Profit,* p. 193.

4. *The Theory of Business Enterprise,* p. 54.

5. It is the long run market which is meant. The market, of course, is not free from manipulation which is a form of partial monopoly control over short periods.

6. I do not mean to assert, as did Cournot, that all of my conclusions are derived from a single hypothesis!

7. It came to my attention (in 1936) that the term "oligopoly" was used as early as 1914 by Karl Schlesinger, *Theorie der Geld- und Kreditwirtschaft*, pp. 17, 18, 57.

8. The term "monopolistic competition" seems a better fit for this second type of problem than for the first, since, where product is differentiated, each seller is truly both a monopolist and a competitor. . . . It may also be used, however, in a more general sense (as in this book) merely to describe the blending of monopolistic and competitive elements, thus embracing both types of hybrid problems.

9. It may seem that anyone reducing his price from BQ would enjoy all the additional demand at the lower price for the entire market, i.e., 100 times that shown by DD' in Figure 3; and that this fact alone would, by the reasoning developed in connection with pure competition, make the curve dd' virtually horizontal. This is not the case, however. The increased demand when all lower their prices, indicated by the so-called demand curve for the general market, contains its due proportion of those who prefer each variety of the product, and the lower price offer by one producer will attract only a portion of them. In fact, the very concept of a demand curve for the general market of a differentiated product is open to the objection that people do not demand the product "in general," but particular varieties of it, so that the amount which any buyer will take depends not only upon the price which is offered him but upon the variety which is offered him.

10. At any particular stage of this movement the *position* of dd' depends on the uniform price which momentarily obtains for all sellers. Its *elasticity* is represented as roughly unchanged throughout the movement because there seems to be no way of telling a *priori* how it would be affected by higher or lower *general* prices, and some reason to think that it would be affected very little.

26. The Economics of Imperfect Competition*

JOAN ROBINSON

INTRODUCTION

Such conduct, though it springs from an admirable humility, is a scandalous breach of faith with the practical man. It would be far better that the economist should take a sardonic pleasure in shocking the practical man by the brutal frankness with which he sets out his assumptions—consoling himself for the disgust that this conduct will inspire by his own conviction, which he cannot expect the practical man to share, that he is approaching the problem that has been set to him by the only route along which there is even a chance of finding the answer.

My book attempts to live up to this standard, and if anywhere a necessary assumption is missing from the list, it must be taken to show that I have fallen into the third trap which besets the path of the economist: the danger that he does not himself quite know what his own assumptions are.

In the older text-books it was customary to set out upon the analysis of value from the point of view of perfect compe-

*Source: Reprinted from *The Economics of Imperfect Competition* by Joan Robinson, introduction and chapter 15 (London: Macmillan & Co., Limited), Copyright Q 1933. Reprinted by permission of Macmillan, London and Basingstoke. Two footnotes deleted; others renumbered. Figures renumbered.

tition. The whole scheme appeared almost homogeneous and it had some aesthetic charm. But somewhere, in an isolated chapter, the analysis of monopoly had to be introduced. This presented a hard, indigestible lump which the competitive analysis could never swallow. To quote Mr. Sraffa's comment:

> Of course, when we are supplied with theories in respect to the two extreme cases of monopoly and competition as part of the equipment required in order to undertake the study of the actual conditions in the different industries, we are warned that these generally do not fit exactly one or other of the categories, but will be found scattered along the intermediate zone, and that the nature of an industry will approximate more closely to the monopolist or the competitive system according to its particular circumstances.[1]

But the books never contained any very clear guidance as to how these intermediate cases should be treated; as a picture of the real world the theory was unconvincing, and as a pure analytical construction it had a somewhat uncomfortable air.

Moreover, the relations between the real world and the competitive analysis of value were marred by frequent misunderstandings. The economists, misled by the logical priority of perfect competition in their scheme, were somehow trapped into thinking that it must be of equal importance in the real world. When they found in the real world some phenomenon, such as "economics internal to the firm," which is inconsistent with the assumptions of perfect competition, they were inclined to look for some complicated explanation of it, before the simple explanation occurred to them that the real world did not fulfil the assumptions of perfect competition. Or they were tempted to introduce into the theoretical scheme elements which, at a superficial glance, appeared to account for the phenomena of the real world, but which completely destroyed the logical self-consistency of the theoretical scheme.

It was at such a moment of confusion that Mr. Sraffa declared: "It is necessary, therefore, to abandon the path of free competition and turn in the opposite direction, namely, towards monopoly."[2]

Now no sooner had Mr. Sraffa released the analysis of monopoly from its uncomfortable pen in a chapter in the middle of the book than it immediately swallowed up the competitive analysis without the smallest effort. The whole scheme of analysis, composed of just the same elements as before, could now be arranged in a perfectly uniform manner, with no awkward cleavage in the middle of the book. Two simple examples will show this process at work.

First consider the problem of defining a monopoly. It was tempting, under the old scheme, to arrange actual cases in a series of which pure monopoly would be the limit at one end and pure competition at the other, but a definition of pure monopoly which would correspond to the definition of pure competition was extremely hard to find. At first sight it seems easy enough to say that competition exists when the demand for a commodity in a certain market is met by a number of producers, and that monopoly exists when it is met by only one. But what is a commodity? Must we group together as a single commodity all articles which compete against each other to satisfy a single demand? In that case, since every article must have some rivals, and since in the last resort every article represents a use of money which is rival to every other, we should be compelled to say that no such thing as complete monopoly exists at all. Or must we define as a single commodity only a group of articles which is perfectly homogeneous? Then the slightest degree of difference, from the point of view of their customers, between rival producers even of one sufficiently homogeneous commodity, must be taken as a sign that we are dealing not with one commodity but with several. For if the individual buyer has any reason to prefer one producer to another, the articles which they sell are not perfectly interchangeable from the point of view of the buyer, and we are reduced to regarding the output of each producer as a separate commodity. Thus any attempt at a logical definition of a monopolist drives either monopoly or competition quite out of the field. It is easy enough to find the limiting case at the competitive end of the scale. The limiting case occurs when the demand for the product of an individual producer is perfectly elastic. But what is the limiting case at the other end? The case in which the demand for the product of the individual is the same as the total demand for the commodity? Then we are back at the original problem of how to define a commodity. We know what we mean by "selling in a perfect market," but what is a perfectly imperfect market?

Now as soon as we abandon the attempt to confine monopoly in a pen by itself the whole of this difficulty disappears. Every individual producer has the monopoly of his own output—that is sufficiently obvious—and if a large number of them are selling in a perfect market the state of affairs exists which we are accustomed to describe as perfect competition. We have only to take the word monopoly in its literal sense, a single seller, and the analysis of monopoly immediately swallows up the analysis of competition.

The reader may object that there is clearly some sense in which Messrs. Coats have got a monopoly of sewing cotton, and in which a Bedfordshire market gardener has not got a monopoly of brussels-sprouts. But this objection is easily answered. All that "monopoly" means, in this old-fashioned sense, is that the output of the individual producer happens to be bounded on all sides by a marked gap in the chain of substitutes. Such a gap in nature provides us with a rough-and-ready definition of a single commodity—sewing cotton or brussels-

sprouts—which is congenial to common sense and causes no trouble. When a single producer controls the whole output of such a commodity the plain man's notion of a monopolist and the logical definition of a monopolist as a single seller coincide, and the difficulty disappears.

A second example of the manner in which monopoly analysis engulfs competitive analysis can be illustrated from the technique of analysis itself. When Mr. Sraffa declared that the time had come to re-write the theory of value, starting from the conception of the firm as a monopolist, he suggested that the familiar tool, "maximum monopoly net revenue," was ready to hand and that the job could begin at once. But that tool is at best a clumsy one and is inappropriate to many of the operations which are required of it. In its place the "marginal" technique must be borrowed from the competitive chapters of the old textbooks, and adapted to new purposes.

Whilst many pieces of technical apparatus have no intrinsic merit, and are used merely for convenience, the use of marginal curves for the analysis of monopoly output contains within itself the heart of the whole matter. The single assumption which it is necessary to make in order to set that piece of apparatus at work is the assumption that the individual firm will always arrange its affairs in such a way as to make the largest profits that can be made in the particular situation in which it finds itself. Now it is this assumption that makes the analysis of value possible. If individuals act in an erratic way only statistical methods will serve to discover the laws of economics, and if individuals act in a predictable way, but from a large number of complicated motives, the economist must resign his task to the psychologist. It is the assumption that any individual, in his economic life, will never undertake an action that adds more to his losses than to his gains, and will always undertake an action which adds more to his gains than to his losses, which makes the analysis of value possible. And it is this assumption that underlies the device of drawing marginal curves. With bricks of this one simple pattern the whole structure of analysis is built up.

The main theme of this book is the analysis of value. It is not easy to explain what the analysis of value is, without making it appear extremely mysterious and extremely foolish. The point may be put like this: You see two men, one of whom is giving a banana to the other, and is taking a penny from him. You ask, How is it that a banana costs a penny rather than any other sum? The most obvious line of attack on this question is to break it up into two fresh questions: How does it happen that the one man will take a penny for a banana? and: How does it happen that the other man will give a penny for a banana? In short, the natural thing is to divide up the problem under two heads: Supply and Demand.

Under the first head the question is: How does it come about that an individual seller sells his commodity for the price at which he does sell it, rather than any other price? Now the price at which he sells is determined on the one side by what he can get for it, and on the other side by what it costs him to make it. Here we come once more upon the dichotomy between demand and supply. But in this context the conditions of demand are regarded objectively, from the point of view of the seller, and form part of the general circumstances which determine what he will decide to do. Next it is obvious that when a number of sellers each acting upon sensible and predictable motives, but each acting independently, are trying to sell the same commodity, their decisions may set up some complicated interactions which must be carefully examined. And whis this has been done the analysis of value has not very much more to say about Supply.

Then, turning to the second heading under the main question, the analyst examines price from the point of view of the individual buyer. In this context the conditions of supply are looked at objectively, as part of the general circumstances which will determine what the buyer decides to do. And, after that, there is not much more to be said about Demand. Perhaps this account of the process of the analysis of value removes the mystery only too thoroughly, but not it appears more foolish than ever. "I thought that at least you were going to tell me," the reader protests,

> why, in some fundamental sense, a banana costs a penny. All you have done is to provide a complicated filing system for a few perfectly obvious ideas with which I have always been quite familiar.

But this filing system is an essential part of the equipment of the analytical economist, whose ultimate aim is to find answers to the practical questions presented to him by the real world, and it is in the hope of assisting him in this task that I have fitted out my toolbox. . . .

PRICE DISCRIMINATION

1

It often happens that a monopolist finds it possible and profitable to sell a single commodity at different prices to different buyers. This can occur when he is selling in several markets which are divided from one another in such a way that goods which are sold in the cheaper market cannot be bought from the monopolist and resold in the dearer market; and when customers in the dearer market cannot transfer themselves into the cheaper market to get the benefit of the lower price. The act of selling the same article, produced under a single control, at different prices to different buyers is known as *price discrimination*.

Under conditions of perfect competition price discrimination could not exist even if the market could be easily divided into separate parts. In each section of the market the demand would be perfectly elastic, and every seller would prefer to sell his whole output in that section of the market in which he could obtain the highest price. The attempt to do so, of course, would drive the price down to the competitive level, and there would be only one price throughout the whole market. So long as the market is perfect it is only if all sellers are combined or are acting in agreement that they can take advantage of the barriers between one part of a market and another to charge different prices for the same thing.

But if there is some degree of market imperfection there can be some degree of discrimination. The market is imperfect because customers will not move readily from one seller to another, and if it is possible for an individual seller to divide his market into separate parts, price discrimination becomes practicable. But since under ordinary competitive conditions the demand curves for the individual sellers are likely to be very elastic, price discrimination will not usually lead to any very great differences in the prices charged to different buyers by any one seller.

When a single seller is not subject to close competition, or when there is an agreement between rival sellers, price discrimination is more likely to occur. The most usual case is in the sale of direct personal services, where there is no possibility of a transfer from one market to another. For instance surgeons commonly grade the fee for an operation according to the wealth of the patient. This practice is maintained by a tradition among doctors, and would break down if they chose to compete among themselves by underbidding one another in the fees charged to rich patients. Or discrimination may occur when the markets in which a monopolist is selling are divided from each other geographically or by tariff barriers, so that there would be a considerable expense in transferring goods from a cheaper market to be resold in a dearer market;

when this type of discrimination leads to a concern selling at a lower price in an export market and a higher price at home it is commonly described as "dumping." Or discrimination may occur when several groups of buyers require the same service in connection with clearly differentiated commodities. Thus a railway can charge different rates for the transport of cotton goods and of coal without any fear that bales of cotton will be turned into loads of coal in order to enjoy a cheaper rate.

There is probably also a good deal of rather haphazard discrimination wherever goods are sold on special orders, so that the individual buyer has no means of knowing what price is being charged to other buyers for a similar commodity.

Even when there is no natural barrier between the groups of customers there are various devices by which the market may be broken up so as to make price discrimination possible. Various brands of a certain article which in fact are almost exactly alike may be sold as different qualities under names and labels which induce rich and snobbish buyers to divide themselves from poorer buyers; and in this way the market is split up, and the monopolist can sell what is substantially the same thing at several prices. The device of making the same thing appear in different guises will also serve to save the monopolist from the reproaches of injustice between customers which sometimes put difficulties in the way of price discrimination.

2

In some cases the demand in one market will depend upon the price that is being charged in another market. The case of first- and third-class railway fares, analysed by Edgeworth, is of this nature.[3] In the following argument we shall only consider cases in which the demand curve in each separate market is independent of the prices charged in the other markets.

An analysis of price discrimination can then be built up from the analysis already given for simple monopoly when only one price can be charged for a single commodity. If it is possible for a monopolist to sell the same commodity in separate markets it will clearly be to his advantage to charge different prices in the different markets, provided that the elasticities of demand in the separate markets are not equal. For if he charges the same price in each market he will find that, at that price, the marginal revenue obtained by selling an increment of output in each market separately is greater in some markets that in others. He can therefore increase his profit by selling less in those markets where the elasticity of demand is less and the marginal revenue smaller, and selling more in those markets where the elasticity of demand is higher and the marginal revenue greater. He will therefore adjust his sales in such a way that the marginal revenue obtained from selling an additional unit of output in any one market is the same for all the markets. And his profits will be at a maximum when the marginal revenue in each market is equal to the marginal cost of the whole output.[4] The method by which prices will be determined can be shown by the following method.

Suppose that there are two markets, I and II, in which the conditions of demand are different. With the same system of axes, draw the demand curves (D_1 and D_2) of the two markets with the corresponding marginal revenue curves, and sum them laterally, so as to obtain an aggregate demand curve showing the total amount that would be sold at each price if the price were the same in both markets, and an aggregate marginal revenue curve showing the amount of sales that would correspond to each value of the marginal revenue if the marginal revenue were the same in both markets. This curve will show the marginal revenue obtained by the discriminating monopolist.

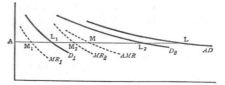

Figure 1

This construction can be exhibited thus:

Draw any line AL parallel to the x axis, to cut D_1 in L_1, D_2 in L_2, and the aggregate demand curve (AD) in L.
Let it cut MR_1 in M_1, MR_2 in M_2, and the aggregate marginal revenue curve (AMR) in M.
Then $AL = AL_1 + AL_2$, and $AM = AM_1 + AM_2$.

The monopoly output under price discrimination is determined by the intersection of the monopolist's marginal cost curve with the aggregate marginal revenue curve. This total output is made up of the amounts sold in the two markets, in each of which marginal revenue is equal to the marginal cost of the whole output. The price in each market will be the demand price for the amount of output sold there.[5]

OM is the total output, and is equal to $OM_1 + OM_2$.
MC is the marginal cost of the output OM.

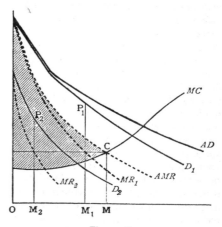

Figure 2

OM_1 is sold at the price M_1P_1 in market I. OM_2 is sold at the price M_2P_2 in market II. The shaded area shows the monopoly revenue, which is equal to the area lying under the aggregate marginal revenue curve (total revenue) *minus* the area lying under the marginal cost curve (total costs).

In Figure 2 marginal costs are rising, but whether marginal costs are constant, rising, or falling, output will be determined by the point at which the aggregate marginal revenue curve cuts the marginal cost curve, and the amount sold in each market will be the amount for which marginal revenue is equal to the marginal cost of the whole output.[6] [*Page of original text omitted.*]

4

The existence of price discrimination, as we have seen, depends on a difference between the elasticities of the demands in the markets in which it is possible to sell. If the demand curves of the separate markets were iso-elastic, so that at any price the elasticity of demand was the same in each market, then the same price would be charged in all of them; for when the marginal revenues were equal in each market, the prices would then also be equal, and the result would be the same as though the market was not divisible. This would occur, for example, if the demand curves of individual buyers were all identical. One market might contain more buyers than another, so that one demand curve was simply an enlargement of the other. The same result would be produced if the demand curves of individuals were of various shapes, but each market was made up of the same proportions of individual demands of various types. If the only practicable subdivisions of a market were such that the demand curves in each were iso-elastic, there would be no advantage from price discrimination. It might be possible for a village barber to charge a differential price for shaving red-haired clients, but if the red-haired members of the village had the same wealth and the same desire to be shaved as the rest of the inhabitants, the barber would find it profitable to charge them the same price as the rest.

The profitability of the monopoly will depend upon the manner in which the market is broken up. In many cases the division into sub-markets will be arbitrarily dictated by circumstance; for instance geographical or tariff barriers may divide the markets. But it may often happen that even when the monopolist can fix only a small number of different prices he can influence to some extent the manner in which buyers are distributed between the markets in which the different prices rule. In the rate-schedules of railway companies the types of goods which are to be charged at various rates are grouped together at the will of the company. Moreover, when the monopolist divides up his market by the introduction of various "brands" of the same article, he will attempt to divide the customers from each other, so as to be able to charge a higher price for the higher class "brands" of the article. In this way the markets will be divided up in a manner which is partly under the control of the monopolist.

It is therefore necessary to inquire in what way a monopolist would divide his market if he were perfectly free to do so in the manner most profitable to himself. Let us suppose that the monopolist is in possession of some device which enables him to separate buyers from each other at will, and let us suppose that he is at first charging a single monopoly price throughout the market, and then proceeds to divide it up by successive stages. The total demand of the market is made up of the demands of individual buyers, and if at the single monopoly price the elasticities of the demands of individuals are all the same there is nothing to be gained by discrimination, and the market will not be divided. But if the elasticities of demand are different he will first divide all individual buyers into two classes such that the highest elasticity of demand in the one class is less than the least elasticity of demand in the other class. To the first class he will raise the price, and to the second class he will lower it. Now if at the new prices the elasticities of demand of all individual buyers within each class are the same there can be no gain from further subdivision. But if they are not alike each sub-market will be split into two on the same principle as before, the parts will again be subdivided, and so forth, until the point is reached at which each sub-market consists of a single buyer, or a group of buyers whose elasticities of demand are the same. As long as any two individual buyers with different elasticities of demand are being charged the same price the monopolist can increase his gains by selling to each of them at a different price, if it is possible to do so.[7]

In most cases, of course, it will not be possible for the monopolist to divide the market at will, and there will be an arbitrary element in the possible barriers between individual buyers which will prevent him from achieving the most profitable division of the market.[8] But however the market is divided, once the division has been achieved the sub-markets will be arranged in ascending order of their elasticities, the highest price being charged in the least elastic market, and the lowest price in the most elastic market.[9]

NOTES

1. "The Laws of Returns under Competitive Conditions," *Economic Journal*, December 1926, p. 542.

2. *Loc. cit.*

3. *Papers Relating to Political Economy*, vol. i. p. 174.

4. Professor Pigou does not make use of this method, but he is evidently aware of the underlying fact, though he expresses it in a somewhat obscure mathematical form (*Economics of Welfare*, p. 302, note 1).

5. Professor Yntema makes use of this construction (see "The Influence of Dumping on Monopoly Price," *Journal of Political Economy*, December 1928), but he confines himself to establishing with its aid a proposition which can be proved without resort to any such complicated apparatus. . . .

6. The points at which the separate marginal revenue curves cut the marginal cost curve have no significance, since these points (except when costs happen to be constant) do not show the marginal cost of the whole output which is actually being produced.

7. This treatment of the matter is somewhat different from that given by Professor Pigou (*Economics of Welfare*, pp. 279-82). He envisages the monopolist as dividing, not the individual buyers, but the separate units of the commodity, between the different markets, but he does not make it clear how this can be done.

8. Even if the monopolist is able to charge a separate price to each buyer he will not necessarily have achieved what Professor Pigou describes as "discrimination of the first degree." For discrimination of the first degree (which may be called *perfect discrimination*) is only achieved when it is possible to sell each separate unit of output at a different price (*loc. cit.* p. 279), and this condition will not be fulfilled if each separate buyer varies the amount of his purchases with the price that he is charged. Perfect discrimination could only occur if each consumer bought only one unit of the product and was forced to pay a price which represented his maximum offer for it (prisoners of war might have been held to ransom on this principle in mediaeval times, and so may the victims of kidnappers in modern America). Or if the monopolist knew the average price which each buyer would give for that quantity of output whose marginal cost to the monopolist is equal to its marginal utility to the buyer, and made to each buyer an all-or-none offer at that amount at that price; as long as the total sum which he was forced to pay did not exceed his estimate of the total utility of that amount of the commodity, the buyer would prefer to purchase rather than go without, so that the price per unit charged to each buyer would represent the average utility of the amount which he purchased. . . .

Professor Pigou's discrimination of the second degree would obtain if a monopolist were able to make *n* separate prices, in such wise that all units with a demand price greater than x were sold at a price x, all with a demand price less than x and greater than y at a price y, and so on (loc. cit. p. 279).

This could only be achieved if each individual buyer had a perfectly inelastic demand for the commodity below a certain maximum price, above which he would buy none at all.

9. Professor Pigou states that

it is not, indeed, true, as is sometimes supposed, that the relative rates [prices] charged to different markets will depend . . . simply upon the comparative elasticities (in respect of some unspecified amount of output) of the demands of these markets (loc. cit. p. 302).

But it is true that the prices will depend on, and be in the same order as, the elasticities of demand in the separate markets at the prices charged in these markets. This follows

$$\frac{\text{Marginal Revenue}}{1 - 1/\epsilon}$$

from the formula, Price = Marginal Revenue, where ϵ is the elasticity of demand; for the marginal revenue is the same in each market. Professor Pigou, in a footnote to the above passage, finds the price in each market for straight-line demand curves by considering "the demand price of the unit that is most keenly demanded," overlooking the fact that this highest demand price can be deduced (for a straight line) from the value of the elasticity of demand at any given price.

27. What Is Perfect Competition?*

JOAN ROBINSON

What do we mean by "perfect competition"? The phrase is made to cover so many separable ideas, and is used in so many distinct senses, that it has become almost valueless as a means of communication. It seems best therefore to begin with a definition. By perfect competition I propose to mean a state of affairs in which the demand for the output of an individual seller is perfectly elastic.

This is a far more restricted definition than that which is to be found in many modern writings. To Professor Knight, for instance, perfect competition entails rational conduct on the part of buyers and sellers, full knowledge, absence of frictions, perfect mobility and perfect divisibility of factors of production, and completely static conditions [1] This definition is unusually wide. More commonly these various strands of thought

are separated from each other and the term "perfect competition" applied only to some of them. There are, however, two notions which seem to be very closely linked in many minds and lumped together as "perfect competition." These are, first, a situation in which a single seller cannot influence price (that is perfect competition in my terminology) and second, a situation in which a single seller cannot make more than normal profits. Leaving all the rest on one side I wish to confine myself to discussing only these two meanings of the phrase "perfect competition."

Mr. Sraffa, whose article of 1926 took such an important part in the work of emancipating economic analysis from the tyranny of the assumption of perfect competition, was not himself completely aware of the freedom that he was winning for us.[2] He was content to

*Source: Reprinted by permission of the publishers from Joan Robinson, The Quarterly Journal of Economics (November 1934). Cambridge, Mass.: Harvard University Press. Copyright, 1934, by the President and Fellows of Harvard College, pp. 104-120.

say that when competition is imperfect there is no need to consider the problem of normal profits and the entry of new firms into an industry, since the entry of new firms into an imperfect market must necessarily be difficult.[3] But it is a simple step to carry Mr. Sraffa's own argument to its logical conclusion. He had shown that in the real world almost every market is imperfect, and it would be impossible to contend that in the real world new firms hardly ever enter any industry. In 1930 Mr. Shove was still adopting a somewhat ambiguous attitude to the question and failed to snap completely the connection between the notion of perfect competition and the notion of free entry into an industry.[4]

Professor Chamberlin in 1933 performed a useful service in categorically separating the two ideas. He distinguishes between "pure competition" and "perfect competition."[5] Pure competition is a state of affairs in which the demand for the output of each firm is perfectly elastic.[6] while perfect competition may be conceived to require the further conditions of "an ideal fluidity or mobility of factors," "absence of uncertainty,"[7] or "such further 'perfection' as the particular theorist finds convenient and useful to his problem." Here the issue is clearly stated. But Professor Chamberlin's terminology is somewhat misleading, and pays a verbal tribute to the old confusion. It seems better boldly to define perfect competition in the terms which he confines to pure competition and so to force the particular theorist to state specifically what further conditions he finds it useful to assume for the purposes of each problem.

In his article on "Doctrines of Imperfect Competition" Mr. Harrod appears at first sight to follow this procedure, and his definition of "perfect competition" is the same as my own.[8] But in the course of his argument it becomes clear that even for him "perfect competition" implies free entry.[9] It therefore seems desirable, before discussing the conception of a perfectly elastic demand, for the output of an individual seller to say something about the other strand of thought which has been entangled with it—the notion of normal profits.

The idea of normal profits in its most naïve form is the idea of a single general level of profits. Profits in any one industry, on this view, are normal when they are the same as profits in the generality of other industries. But there is obviously no more reason to expect a uniform level of profit for enterprise than there is to expect a uniform level of rent for land. In the world depicted in the well-known beginners' question, in which all land is alike in respect of fertility and site value, there is a uniform rate of rent per acre in the long period. In a world in which all entrepreneurs are alike there would be a uniform rate of profit in all industries in the long period. In the real world entrepreneurship is no more homogeneous than land in the real world. This view of uniform normal profits may therefore be dismissed as a beginner's simplification. The idea that there is one level of profits which obtains in competitive industries, and that when competition is not perfect profits must exceed this level, is clearly untenable.

Indeed, this is one of those problems in which the main difficulty is to see what the difficulty is. Normal profits are simply the supply price of entrepreneurship to a particular industry. The essence of the notion of normal profits is that when profits are more than normal, new firms will enter the trade, and normal profits are simply the profits which prevail when there is no tendency for the number of firms to alter. It is possible, of course, that the number of firms may be arbitrarily restricted. The firms may require a license from some controlling authority, or the existing firms may be so strong that they are able to fend off fresh competition by the threat of a price war. They may even resort to violence to prevent fresh rivals from appearing on the scene. In such cases no level of profits, however high, will be great enough to tempt new firms into the trade, and the supply of enterprise to that trade is perfectly inelastic at the existing amount. For such an industry any level of profits is normal, and the term ceases to have a useful application.

In all less extreme cases there will be some elasticity of supply of new enterprise, which may be small or great according to the circumstances of the trade. The normal level of profits will be different in different industries and different at different scales of the same industry, and the level of normal profits will depend upon the conditions of supply of enterprise. Trades which require unusual personal ability or special qualifications, such as the power to command a large amount of capital for the initial investment, will tend to have a high level of normal profits; trades which are easy to enter will have a lower level.

Now there is nothing in all this which is connected with the notion of perfect competition, in the sense in which I use that phrase. It is true that a high level of normal profits will often be found where competition is imperfect. The fact that an old established firm enjoys "good will" has the effect both of giving it a hold upon the market which enables it to influence the price of the commodity which it sells and of increasing the cost of entry to new rivals. And the powerful firm which uses the methods of "unfair competition" to strangle rivals is highly unlikely to be selling in a perfect market. But this association of high normal profits (not abnormally high profits) with imperfect competition is a purely empirical one. The two conceptions are analytically quite distinct, and we shall have made a considerable advance towards clear analysis when we have learned habitually to distinguish them.

But quite apart from this gratuitous confusion the whole notion of normal profits is beset with difficulties. Mr. Shove has pointed out that there is not one level of normal profits, but two.[10] The level of profits which will attract new enterprise into an industry is usually higher than the level which is just sufficient to retain existing enterprise. Entry into a trade is likely to involve considerable initial expense, and often involves, as Marshall was fond of pointing out, a lean period of low profits before the name of the firm becomes known. To move out of this trade into another would involve fresh sacrifice. "When you are in you are in" and if demand falls after you are established you will prefer to stay where you are at a level of reward that would not have tempted you to enter the trade if you had the choice still to make.

This notion of a gap between the two levels of normal profits is associated by Mr. Harrod with imperfect competition.[11] And it must be conceded that a gap is likely to occur wherever good will is important, so that in fact the phenomenon is likely to be found in many industries where the market is imperfect. But it is important to realize that there is no necessary connection between the two ideas. The existence of the gap depends upon costs of movement from one industry to another, and these may very well occur when competition is perfect. Moreover, competition may be imperfect, for instance from differential transport charges, when there are no costs of movement. A gap between the upper level of reward, necessary to tempt new resources into an industry, and the lower level, necessary to drive old resources out, will exist wherever there is cost of movement between one trade and another, and the double level of normal profits is merely one example of a phenomenon which may affect every factor of production equally.

A general discussion of the phenomenon of the gap would lead us far afield, and in the present paper I propose only to inquire whether the existence of the gap destroys the usefulness of the notion of normal profits. Before tackling this question it is necessary to make a digression upon the manner in which equilibrium is attained. When we are considering discontinuous changes in the number of firms in an industry the existence of the gap between the two levels of profits is a very serious matter. When profits are more than normal in a certain industry a number of fresh entrepreneurs (each in ignorance of the others' action) come into the trade. With this new competition actual profits are depressed much below the level that tempted in the new entrepreneurs, but they are not perhaps low enough to drive out any existing firms. The industry will continue at this swollen size, and it will be in equilibrium in the sense that no new enterprise tends to enter it or old enterprise to leave it. Yet the actual size of the industry, the price of the commodity, and the level of profits ruling, are determined by the number of firms, which is determined by the excessive optimism of the latest entrants. In such a case the supply price of any amount of output depends to a large extent upon the immediate past history of the industry. If fewer firms had happened to enter in the period of high profits the present price of a given output would have been higher; if more had entered it would have been lower. The whole notion of a unique long-period supply curve breaks down, and with the notion of a supply curve the notion of normal profits goes by the board.

In order therefore to justify the notion of a supply curve at all we must make the artificial assumption that equilibrium is attained by a gradual and continuous movement. When profits are more than normal a few firms enter. Profits decline; if they are still more than normal a new firm comes in, and another, and another, until profits are just reduced to the upper normal level and there is no incentive for one fresh firm to enter. Equilibrium is thus reached without oscillation. Similarly, when profits fall below the lower nor-

mal level first one then another decides to abandon the struggle, and profits for those that remain are gradually raised till each of the remaining firms is contented with its lot, and no more find it worth while to leave.

This account of the matter is obviously extremely unrealistic if we have to do with large erratic movements of demand. But if demand is expanding or contracting continuously it is plausible to suppose that firms enter or leave the industry one by one. I think, therefore, that in order to retain the idea of a long-period supply curve we may permit ourselves to take this view of the process of reaching equilibrium. And then the existence of two levels of profits introduces only a minor complication into the analysis.

There are two supply curves, one above the other. The upper one applies only to expansions of the industry, and the lower one applies only to contractions. Each point on the upper curve is joined to that point on the lower curve at which the number of firms is the same by what I call a "quasi-long-period supply curve"[12]—the supply curve of a fixed number of firms. This is determined under perfect competition by the marginal cost curves of the given

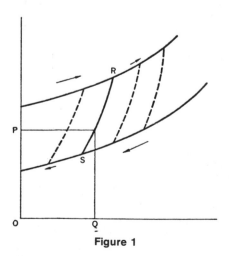

Figure 1

number of firms. Suppose we are considering an expansion of demand, and we start from a position in which price is *OP* and output *OQ*. Then as demand is raised supply price climbs up the quasi-long-period supply curve to *R*, and then proceeds (for further increases of demand) along the upper long-period supply curve to the right. Now suppose that we start from the same point and consider a contraction of demand. Then supply price slides down the quasi-long-period curve to *S* and for further contractions of demand supply price follows the lower long-period curve to the left.

The quasi-long-period position does of course depend upon past history. There is a continuous series of quasi-long-period curves, and which curve we are on at any moment depends upon the number of firms in existence at that moment, just as the familiar short-period curve depends upon the amount of fixed plant that there happens to be in the industry. But the pair of long-period curves is as much uniquely determined as the old-style single long-period curve ever was.[13] By making an admittedly unrealistic assumption about the way in which equilibrium is attained we can rescue the long-period supply curve from the perils of the gap between the upper and lower levels of normal profits.

So much for normal profits. Leaving all this on one side let us return to the main question. What is perfect competition? Let us take our stand boldly on the formal definition and see what it requires of us.

Competition is perfect when the demand for the output of any one firm individually is perfectly elastic. In what conditions can this be true? We are accustomed to say that there are two conditions:

1. That the market must be perfect.
2. That the number of firms must be large.

Let us examine these two conditions in turn.

The first condition, that the market must be perfect, was dealt with by Mr. Sraffa. Marshall writes,

> The more nearly perfect a market is, the stronger is the tendency for the same price to be paid for the same thing at the same time in all parts of the market; but of course if the market is large, allowance must be made for the expense of delivering the goods to different purchasers.[14]

Mr. Sraffa pointed out that absence of frictions is not sufficient to make a market perfect, since buyers may have good and permanent reasons for preferring the output of one firm to that of another, while the presence of differential transport costs may be sufficient by itself to make the market imperfect.[15] Moreover, he showed that the condition that the same price shall rule throughout the market is not adequate to define perfection, for if all the firms in an industry are alike in respect both to the costs and the conditions of demand, the same price will rule throughout the market no matter how imperfect it may be.

Professor Chamberlin's attitude to the perfection of the market is not quite clear. He seems to associate imperfection simply with differentiation of the product.[16] But the relationship between differentiation of the commodity and imperfection of the market is somewhat complicated. Physical differentiation is not a *necessary* condition for market imperfection. Two commodities may be alike in every respect except the names of the firms producing them, and yet the market in which they are sold will be imperfect if different buyers have different scales of preference as between the two firms. Nor is differentiation a *sufficient* condition for market imperfection. Two firms may be producing two distinct commodities and yet these two commodities may be sold against each other in a perfect market. Suppose that every individual buyer will pay 6d. more for *A* than for *B*, and that everyone buys either *A* or *B*, never some of each. Then when *B* is selling at 1/- the smallest rise in the price of *A* above 1/6 will cause every buyer to transfer his custom to B, and the sales of A will cease; and the smallest fall in the price of A below 1/6 will increase its sales by an amount equal to the whole output of B. The demand for either A or B, given the price of the other, is perfectly elastic, although they are two distinct commodities.

On the other hand the market will not necessarily be perfect if all buyers have the same scale of preferences as between A and B. Suppose that when the price of A rises each buyer purchases somewhat less of A, and somewhat more of B, but does not forsake A entirely. Then the market as between A and B would not be perfect, even though all buyers were alike. Similarity of buyers is a necessary, but not a sufficient condition for the market to be perfect. For the market to be perfect it is necessary first that all buyers should be alike in respect to preferences, and second that each buyer should deal with only one firm at any one time. When these conditions are fulfilled a rise in the price charged by any one firm would, if other prices remained the same, lead to a complete cessation of its sales. And this is the criterion of a perfect market.

The definition of a commodity is completely arbitrary, and the definition of a market depends upon the definition of a commodity. Suppose that we start with a single quality of a certain perfectly homogeneous product, offered for sale by a firm at a single place and time, and group with it all other products which satisfy the condition of market perfection. In most cases we shall reach the boundary of the perfect market even before we have reached the boundary of the output of a single firm. Now let us agree upon a certain degree of imperfection in the market and group together all products in respect to which the imperfection has less than the agreed value. This group of products may be described as a single commodity. Often we can fix a convenient boundary by

obvious natural landmarks, so that within it we have products which are all obviously in an everyday sense a single commodity (steam-coal, or chewing-gum) and all products outside the boundary are other commodities. But at best there must be some arbitrary element in drawing the boundary, and all products must be regarded as a continuous series in more or less close rivalry with each other. Thus the first prerequisite of perfect competition is a "commodity" clearly demarcated from others by a boundary of natural gaps in the chain of substitutes, within which the market is perfect.

The second condition required for perfect competition is that the number of firms selling within the market is such that when any one firm alters its price there is no consequent alteration in the prices charged by the others. It is this condition that we must now examine.

First it is necessary to stop up a blind alley that might lead us astray. It is sometimes supposed that for competition to be perfect it is necessary that the number of buyers should be large.[17] But this is the reverse of the truth. If there is only one buyer the market for each firm must be perfect, since a relative lowering of the price by any firm would cause the single buyer to prefer its output to that of the others. And if there is more than one buyer it is necessary for perfection of the market that the buyers should all be exactly alike in respect of their preferences. The larger the number of buyers who are potential customers of any one firm the more likely is the market to be imperfect, since the more likely are differences of preference to occur.[18]

To return to the main argument—the number of sellers necessary to secure perfect competition in a perfect market. On this point there seems to be a considerable amount of confusion. Cournot stated that competition will be perfect if each seller provides so small a part of the total output of a commodity that his removal from production would make no appreciable difference to price.[19] On this view the number of firms required for even approximately perfect competition must be extremely great. Now there is nothing unrealistic in the notion of a firm so small that its total disappearance would leave price unaffected. A certain farmer may very well root up his three acres of strawberries without producing any effect upon the price of strawberries in Covent Garden market. But is this not because, in the real world, demand curves always contain small but perceptible discontinuities? Until amount is reduced enough to put say a half-penny on to price no one will notice that anything has happened. But if we assume (as we must do at this level of abstraction) a perfectly continuous demand curve, the conception of a number of firms so great that each produces a negligibly small proportion of the output of an industry, is a somewhat uncomfortable one. But it is clear that Cournot's condition is much too severe.

More commonly it is said to be sufficient for perfect competition that an increase in the output of any one firm should produce a negligible effect upon price. But this way of stating the matter is extremely unsatisfactory. How exactly does the number of firms come into the picture? Is the individual firm conceived to increase its output by a certain definite amount (one ton of coal)? In that case the effect upon price (given the elasticity of the total demand curve) depends upon the ratio of this amount (one ton) to the total output of the industry and the number of firms has nothing to do with the case. Or is the firm conceived to increase its output by a certain proportion, say 5 per cent? Then certainly the smaller is the share of this firm in the total output, the less will be the effect upon price; but why should we be concerned with a *proportionate* change in the output of a firm? The apparent simple statement dissolves into a haze of ambiguities as soon as it is closely examined.

From this fog we emerge when the condition is stated in a third way. A small increase in output made by a single firm, the output of other firms remaining the same, will produce a perceptible effect upon the price of the commodity. But if the total output of the firm is sufficiently small, the price cut upon its whole output, when a unit is added to the output of the industry, will be negligible. Marginal revenue is equal to price *minus* the fall in value of the old output when output is increased by one unit. If the output of the firm is very small the difference between marginal revenue and price will be very small. Marginal revenue will be almost equal to price and the demand curve for the firm will have an elasticity sufficiently near to infinity for us to say that competition is almost perfect. The point is, not that the change in price due to a change in output is negligible when the number of firms is large, but the effect of the change of price upon any one firm is negligible. Competition will be more perfect the smaller is the ratio of the output of one firm to the output of the industry, and more perfect the greater is the elasticity of the total demand curve. At first sight it may appear strange that the degree of competition *within* an industry should be affected by the elasticity of the total demand curve. But after all it is natural that this should be so. For the form of the demand curve represents the degree of competition between the product of this industry and other commodities. The stronger the competition from substitutes for this commodity the smaller the degree of competition within the industry necessary to secure any given elasticity of demand for each separate producer.

This third statement appears to give a far more reasonable account of the matter than the account given in the first two statements. It was at this stage I had arrived when I wrote my book on the *Economics of Imperfect Competition*. I was then too much under the influence of tradition to imagine that there was anything more to be said about the matter, but I now feel that the argument must be pushed a stage further.

The difficulty lies in the assumption that when one firm in a competitive industry adds a unit to output, the output of the other firms remains unchanged. Clearly if we take the continuity of the demand curve and of the marginal cost curves seriously this assumption is unwarranted. A small increase in the output of the industry will produce a small but perceptible fall in price. The fall in price will lead all other firms to reduce output by some fraction of a unit, since each equates marginal cost to price. We thus reach the conclusion that an increase in the output of one firm by one unit will *not* increase the output of the industry by a whole unit, but by something less. If competition is absolutely perfectly perfect an increase in the output of one firm by one unit would leave the output of the industry unchanged and there would be no change in price at all. Competition will be near enough to perfection for practical purposes if an increase in the output of one firm by one unit increases the output of the industry by so much less than one unit that the effect upon price is negligible.

This argument is different from the argument of the third stage. At the third stage we said that an increase in the output of a firm by one unit *would* produce a perceptible effect upon price, but the share of the firm in the loss due to the price cut would be so small as not to affect its conduct. At the stage where I now stand we say that a unit increase in the output of one firm will not produce a perceptible effect upon price at all.

If we adopt this position it remains to inquire what effect will be produced upon the output of the other firms when one firm increases its output. This will clearly depend upon the slopes of the marginal cost curves of the other firms. The proposition to which my lengthy preamble leads up is this—it is impossible to discuss the number of firms required to ensure perfect competition without discussing the marginal cost curves of the firms composing the industry.[20]

First consider the case in which the firms have falling marginal costs for all outputs. Then so long as the market is perfect it is impossible for two firms to survive in the industry. If there are two firms each will be anxious to increase its output at the expense of the other and any cut in price made by one of them will be answered by an equal cut by the other. Price will be driven down to the point at which one or other of the firms is forced out of the industry, and when only one firm is left in possession of the field it is impossible that competition should be perfect. Of course both firms may survive if each is afraid to begin the war. The price may then be at any level, but the situation cannot be regarded as an equilibrium position, since any accidental increase in output by either firm would precipitate price cutting.

Next consider the case in which marginal costs are constant. Then if there are two firms competition will be perfect. Either by lowering its price to a level infinitesimally less than the marginal cost of the other can drive it from the field, and either by raising its price infinitesimally above the marginal cost of the other will lose its whole market. Here then we have perfect competition. But this situation cannot persist in the long period. For a firm with constant marginal costs long-period average costs must be falling, since there must always be some fixed element in the cost of a firm, if only the minimum income of the entrepreneur. Thus when price is equal to marginal cost it is less than average cost and one or other of the firms must ultimately disappear.

We are brought back therefore to the familiar conclusion that marginal costs must be rising if more than one firm is to survive in a perfect market. Consider, then, an industry consisting of several firms for each of which marginal costs are rising. For each firm marginal cost will be equal to price. Suppose that one of these firms makes a unit increase in ouput. In the first instance the price of the commodity will fall to an extent depending upon the slope of the total demand curve. This fall in price will lead the remaining firms to contract output to an extent determined by the slope of their marginal cost curves. In the new position the output of one firm is greater by a unit, the output of each other firm is less by a fraction of a unit, and the price is lower than before. It follows that the cut in price associated with a unit increase in the output of one firm will be smaller, given the number of firms, the less is the slope of the marginal cost curves of the other firms. And it will be smaller, given the slopes of the marginal cost curves, the greater is the number of firms. Competition can only be absolutely perfect, given rising marginal costs, if the number of firms is infinite. Absolute perfection of competition is therefore an impossibility. Let us agree to call competition perfect if the price cut associated with a unit increase of output by one firm is less than a certain small finite value. Then for any given slope of the marginal cost curves there is a certain number of firms which will make competition perfect. This number will be smaller the smaller the slope of the marginal cost curves, and greater the greater the slope of the marginal cost curves.

In the limiting case, where the marginal cost curves are rising vertically, we revert to our third account of the matter in which it was assumed that the output of the other firms was fixed. We are thus led to the conclusion that when supply for each firm is completely inelastic the number of firms required to give even a reasonable approximation to perfect competition must be indefinitely great.

At first sight this conclusion appears rather strange. If we are really required to believe that in the well-known case of the fish market on Saturday night there is not quite perfect competition,

must we conclude that the competitive output is not sold? That some of the fish is always allowed to rot? This would certainly be hard to accept. But here another proposition comes to our rescue. When supply is perfectly inelastic it makes no difference whether competition is perfect or not. Marginal revenue is equal to marginal cost at the same output as price is equal to marginal cost, provided that the elasticity of the individual demand curve is greater than unity. Therefore price and output are the same whatever the individual elasticity of demand. Thus, although there is not, strictly speaking, perfect competition among the fishmongers on Saturday night, yet the competitive output will be sold at the competitive price unless the demand curve for fish is highly inelastic.[21]

We have thus reached the conclusion that there is not one universal value for the "large number of firms" which ensures perfect competition.[22] In each particular case, with given slopes of the marginal cost curves, there is a certain definite number of firms which will produce competition of an agreed degree of perfection, and this number, in some cases, may be quite small.

NOTES

1. *Risk, Uncertainty, and Profit*, pp. 76-80.

2. "The Laws of Returns under Competitive Conditions," *Economic Journal*, December 1926.

3. *Ibid.*, p. 549.

4. "Symposium on Increasing Returns and the Representative Firm," *Economic Journal*, March 1930.

5. *The Theory of Monopolistic Competition*, p. 6.

6. Professor Chamberlin does not give quite this account of "pure competition." He says, "Purity requires only the absence of monopoly, which is realized when there are many buyers and sellers of the *same* (perfectly standardized) product" (*op. cit.*, p. 25). These conditions, as we shall find, are un-

necessarily severe, but by "absence of monopoly" he appears to mean a state of affairs in which no one firm can raise its price without sacrificing the whole of its sales, and this is the essential point.

7. Professor Chamberlin is here referring to Professor Knight, *loc. cit.*

8. In this Journal, May 1934, p. 443.

9. *Loc. cit.*, p. 460.

10. *Economic Journal,* March 1933, pp. 119-121.

11. See Harrod, *Economic Journal,* June 1933, p. 337 and this Journal, May 1934, p. 457. In the latter article Mr. Harrod, if I understand him aright, uses the phrase "excess profit" to describe any surplus above the lower normal level.

12. *Economics of Imperfect Competition,* p. 47.

13. The width of the gap depends upon the length of the period in respect to which the curves are drawn. For some industries, in a sufficiently long period, there will be no gap at all; for others a considerable gap would be found even if an indefinitely long period were taken into account. The familiar short-period supply curve bridges the gap at its widest point.

14. *Principles of Economics,* p. 325.

15. *Loc. cit.*, p. 542.

16. *Op. cit.*, Chapter IV. Mr. Harrod adopts the same view, in this Journal, May 1934, p. 445.

17. E.g., Chamberlin, see above, p. 105, note 6.

18. Similarly, the larger the number of sellers supplying any one buyer the more likely is the market to be imperfect from the point of view of buyers. The fact that the market must be perfect, from the point of view of sellers, if there is only one buyer, and is likely to be imperfect from the point of view of a buyer if there are many sellers, throws some light upon the question of "bargaining strength" between employers and workers. In the ordinary case a single buyer, that is, one employer, will be buying from a fairly large number of sellers—the workers. Thus the workers are necessarily in the weak position of selling in a perfect market, whereas the employer is very likely to be in the strong position of buying in an imperfect market. For the employer there will be some element of what I call "monopsony" in the situation, whereas for unorganized workers there is no element of monopoly. Cf. Harrod, *loc. cit.*, p. 460.

19. *Mathematical Principles of the Theory of Wealth* (Bacon's translation), p. 90.

20. Cf. Harrod, *Economic Journal,* December 1933, p. 664.

21. The elasticity of the demand for one seller will be less than unity if the elasticity of the total demand falls short of unity to a sufficient extent.

22. Professor Chamberlin (*op. cit.*, p. 49) rather weakly suggests that 100 would be a "large number," though in the particular case that he is considering two would have been enough.

VII

Modern Period

Introduction. John Maynard Keynes (1883-1946), now considered one of the greatest economists of all time, was born and reared in Cambridge, where his father was an economist, logician, and administrator at Cambridge University. In some measure due to the personal training that his father had given him, Keynes won a highly valued scholarship in 1897 to attend Eton, where he excelled in academic studies. This outstanding performance at Eton opened doors for him at King's College in Cambridge. He enrolled there in 1902 and was graduated with the Mathematics Tripos in 1905. After graduation Keynes developed an interest in economics, and he attended a series of lectures given by Marshall, who tried to persuade Keynes to make economics his profession. Nonetheless, in 1906 Keynes passed a civil service exam and accepted a post in the India Office, where he worked for the next two years. Bored with the work, Keynes studied probability theory during this period, leading him to write *A Treatise on Probability* (1921) many years later. In 1908 he became an economics lecturer at Cambridge, where only three years later he was made coeditor (with Edgeworth) of the *Economic Journal*. In 1913 Keynes published his first important work, *Indian Currency and Finance*, and in 1915 went to work for the British Treasury until the end of World War I. After the war he served as a representative of the Treasury at the Paris Peace Conference. However, he became so disgusted with the harsh conditions specified by the Allies for German reparation payments that he withdrew from the conference and quickly wrote *The Economic Consequences of the Peace* (1919).

Following the war, Keynes taught at King's College and began speculating in the foreign exchange market. He did so well in the latter endeavor that his fortune was to eventually exceed a million dollars (in 1937), and he later built an active business as a consultant for companies seeking his advice on money management. In 1922 Keynes published another book on the problem of reparations payments, *A Revision of the Treaty*, which was quickly followed by *A Tract on Monetary Reform* (1923), in which he argued that Britain's return to the gold standard would be detrimental to the country. The year 1925 was bad and good for Keynes: he witnessed Britain's return to the gold standard; he married a Russian ballerina named Lydia Lopokova. During the next several years Keynes was forming ideas in his course at Cambridge that were to crystalize in his *Treatise on Money*, a two-volume work published in 1930. A classic in its own right, this book has been overshadowed by the fame of his epic *General Theory of Employment, Interest and Money* (1936).

In the introduction to the *General Theory*, Keynes calls attention to "General" in the title. He argues that "the postulates of the classical theory are applicable to a special case only and not to the general case, the situation which it assumes being a limiting point of the possible positions of equilibrium." Keynes's rejection of "classical" theory is especially evident in his contentions that the rate of interest does not necessarily equate investment demand with savings supply, that a fall in money wages may not decrease unemployment, and that unemployment is not simply caused by frictional factors in the economy. In truth, however, these propositions were accepted in whole or in part by many classical and neoclassical economists who were at that time—as economists are today—a diverse group of men. So, while Keynes's conclusions were not entirely new, his *General Theory* buttressed these conclusions with the first consistent, well-integrated model of the national economy. Because the neoclassicists had been largely preoccupied with microeconomics, it is no exaggeration to say that the *General Theory* created a macroeconomic revolution. Moreover, because this book carefully specified the key economic variables and constructed a testable macroeconomic model, it propelled econometrics forward to the elevated status which it now enjoys.

Our selections below are taken from the *General Theory* and three famous articles by Keynes. Students who have not yet seen the *General Theory* will be surprised to learn that it contains only one graph, which is buried in the middle of the book. The elegant textbook geometry that introduces us all to Keynesian theory was developed and refined over the years by Hansen, Hicks, and others. By way of contrast, the original theory is scattered in bits and pieces throughout the *General Theory*. Like most creative books that are on the forefront of knowledge, this one is unpolished and, therefore, difficult to follow. Nevertheless, two of the most important chapters are reprinted in this section that, together with the three articles, should provide the reader with an understanding of Keynes's approach to macroeconomics and the manner in which he made his contributions.

John R. Hicks (b. 1904), one of the most famous Oxford economists, has taught at the London School of Economics, Cambridge, Manchester, and Oxford. Before his recent retirement from Oxford, he held the Drummond Chair in Political Economy at that university. Along with Arrow, he won the Nobel Prize in economics in 1972. Hicks first became prominent in the profession when he published *Theory of Wages* in 1932. Five years later he published his famous article, "Mr. Keynes and the 'Classics'; A Suggested Interpretation," in the *Econometrica*. This article, which we have included here, contains his invention of the IS-LM diagram, an apparatus that he created to clarify the relation between Keynesian and Classical theory. Because this device was also independently developed by Hansen, it is now referred to as the Hicks-Hansen diagram. In 1939 Hicks published his best known work, *Value and Capital*. It does much to refine utility theory and general equilibrium analysis. Although this work was based on an extensive use of mathematical reasoning, Hicks swept the mathematics away into appendices at the end of the book to avoid intimidating most of his readers. Our selections include the first two chapters, which contain the textbook-famous exposition of income- and price-consumption curves, which Hicks developed in a 1934 article written jointly with Allen. Actually, the same results had been independently discovered in 1913 and 1915 by Johnson and Slutsky, respectively. Even so, this graphical technique did not become popular until it was later invented by Hicks and Allen. Finally, we have also reprinted a note from *Value and Capital* that discusses the relation between saving and investment. In order to clear up an ambiguity in Keynes's *General Theory*, Hicks explained why *planned* savings and investment are never likely to be equal even though *realized* savings and investment are always equal. This is accomplished by providing both an *ex ante* and *ex post* definition of savings and investment. This distinction—like several other Hicksian contributions—is now common fare in modern principles texts.

Joseph A. Schumpeter (1883-1950) was born in a region called Moravia, which is now an area of Czechoslovakia, and was raised primarily in Vienna. He studied law and economics at the University of Vienna, where he received his law degree at the age of twenty-three. At this university, which probably had Europe's finest economics department in that day, Schumpeter studied economics under Bohm-Bawerk and Menger. When only twenty-five years old, he attracted favorable attention with his first book, *Nature and Contents of Economic Theory* (1908). In 1912 he published *Theory of Economic Development* and was at that time teaching at the University of Graz. Following World War I Schumpeter briefly held the position of minister of finance in Austria. He resumed his teaching career in 1925 at the University of Bonn in Germany. He took leaves of absence from this institution in 1927 and 1931 to be a visiting professor at Harvard University, where he taught for seventeen years after joining it permanently in 1932. While at Harvard he published *Business Cycles* (1939) and the controversial *Capitalism, Socialism, and Democracy* (1942). From the latter we have excerpted chapters 6-8, in which he argued that the most frequently criticized elements of capitalism are largely responsible for the rapid advances in productivity and technology that capitalism has enjoyed. These three chapters reveal his meticulous attention to detail.

Schumpeter was a founding member—and, for a few years, president—of the Econometric Society. He also served as president of the American Economic Association in 1948. He was still working on his greatest book, *History of Economic Analysis,* when he died in 1950. Thanks to the editing work of his wife, the book was published in 1954, proving Schumpeter to be a man of encyclopedic learning.

Friedrich A. Hayek (b. 1899) was born and reared in Vienna, where he was graduated with a doctorate from the University of Vienna in 1923. (Twenty years later he was given a D.Sc. degree in economics by the University of London.) He served as director of the Austrian Institute of Economic Research, lecturered at his alma mater, and taught at the London School of Economics. He taught economics at the University of Chicago from 1950 to 1962, at which time he joined the faculty at the University of Freilburg, Germany. In 1974 he was awarded the Nobel Prize in economics. Hayek's impressive list of publications includes the following books: *Prices and Production* (1931); *Monetary Theory and the Trade Cycle* (1933); *Collectivist Economic Planning* (1935); *Profit, Interest, and Investment* (1939); *The Pure Theory of Capital* (1941); *Individualism and the Economic Order* (1948); *Capitalism and the Historians* (1954); and *Studies in Philosophy, Politics, and Economics* (1967). Among the other books not listed above is *The Road to Serfdom* (1944), Hayek's most famous and best selling work. Written during World War II, it mirrored Hayek's fear of totalitarianism and concern with England's drift toward socialism and the controlled economy. (Hayek became a naturalized British citizen in 1938.) He argued that liberal socialism ultimately leads to a totalitarian regime and requires far more central planning than is generally recognized. As Hayek readily admitted in the book's preface, "This is a political book." The reader will find chapters 4 and 5 reproduced here. As our excerpts will make clear, this book produces an eloquent defense of capitalism and individual liberty.

Paul A. Samuelson (b. 1915) is as highly regarded by the profession as any other living economist. Reared in Indiana, he completed his undergraduate degree at the University of Chicago in 1935, at which time he enrolled at Harvard to pursue graduate studies. There he eagerly joined the Keynesian Revolution and was greatly influenced by Hansen. By the time he received his Ph.D. from Harvard in 1941, he had already published eleven articles and been invited to join the Society of Junior Fellows in Cambridge. In addition, he received the annual David A. Wells Award for writing the best economics thesis at Harvard. Although this dissertation had been conceived and mostly written in 1937, it was not completed until

1941. The war effort delayed its publication until 1947, at which time it was released under the title, *Foundations of Economic Analysis*. The first purpose of the book is to translate many prominent economic theories into a mathematical language. Samuelson was convinced that mathematics would reveal a general theory that was the basis of particular theories. The book's second purpose is to produce testable economic theorems which are capable of being supported or refuted by empirical data.

After graduating in 1941, Samuelson was not offered a teaching position at Harvard as he had hoped. Although he had the pick of all other institutions, his determination to stay in Cambridge led him to accept a job offer from Massachusetts Institute of Technology (MIT), where he has remained ever since. His presence at MIT was such an attraction to other members of the profession that, within the next ten years, MIT had assembled one of the nation's best economics departments. In 1947—when he was only thirty-two—Samuelson saw his *Foundations* published, was promoted to full professor at MIT, and was honored with the first John Bates Clark Award (given in recognition of the most outstanding work by economists under the age of 40). Moreover, in that same year he published the first edition of his textbook, which was one of the earliest principles books to simplify Hansen's synthesis of the Keynesian doctrine. Samuelson's *Principles* has been translated into more than a dozen languages and has already gone through ten editions. Approximately two million copies of it have been sold! The year 1947, then, was a very good year for Samuelson. In 1951 he became president of the Econometric Society, in 1961 president of the American Economic Association, and in 1970 the first American to be awarded the Nobel Prize in economics. In spite of his association with the Econometric Society, it should be noted that Samuelson has published relatively little in the area of econometrics. Nevertheless, his development of mathematical economic models has been of great assistance to econometricians.

Our first selection by Samuelson is "Economic Theory and Mathematics—An Appraisal" (1952). In this article he discussed the importance of mathematical economics, a methodology for which he is famous. His skepticism about accuracy of econometric models is very apparent in our second selection, "Economic Forecasting and Science" (1965). The third selection, "Wage-Price Guideposts and the Need for Informal Controls in aMixed Economy," is an excerpt from the Rational Debate Seminar held at George Washington University in 1967. The topic of the debate, in which Samuelson was pitted against Arthur Burns, was "Full Employment, Guideposts and Economic Stability." Although Samuelson argued in favor of the guideposts, his mixed feelings about their implementation will be apparent to the reader. Finally, in the fourth selection—which Samuelson presented to the American Economic Association in late 1973—he explained what lessons can be learned from the economic expansion of the early 1970s.

Another contemporary economist and Nobel Laureate is Kenneth J. Arrow (b. 1921). He received his B.S. degree from The City College of New York in 1940, his M.A. from Columbia University in 1941, and his Ph.D. from Columbia University in 1951. While undertaking his doctorate, Arrow worked as a research associate on the Cowles Commission for Research in Economics from 1947 to 1949. He left this position when invited to join the faculty at Stanford University, where he was professor of economics, statistics, and operations research until 1968. In that year he began teaching at Harvard, where he still remains. Arrow won the Nobel Prize (along with Hicks) in 1972 and was elected president of the American Economic Association for the following year. His earlier research interests included theory of choice, welfare economics, and economic growth. This early research produced his best known book, *Social Choice and Individual Values* (1951), and his classic article, "A Difficulty in the Concept of Social Welfare" (1950). From the latter we have taken a brief excerpt that contains his exposition of the "paradox of voting." It is now known that this contradiction in the system of majority rule was earlier discovered by Condorcet (1785). In his article, Arrow acknowledged that the paradox is "well-known" and makes no pretense of having discovered it. Nonetheless, modern textbook presentations of the paradox use the procedure employed by Arrow, since he was the first to explain the paradox with symbolic logic (instead of differential calculus).

In the past decade Arrow's research efforts have focused on uncertainty information and organization, an interest that is recently reflected in *The Limits of Organization* (1974)—one of the few things he has written for the nonmathematical reader. From this book we have taken chapters 2 and 3, in which Arrow examined the successes and failures of the price system. He said that organizations are formed so the members may reap the benefit "of collective action in situations in which the price system fails." Although there are many failures of the price system, the one that Arrow stressed is the existence of uncertainty, which he held to be the primary cause of the need for organizations. Consequently, he took up a discussion of the significance of information channels within an organization.

Of all economists testifying before congressional committees on economic matters, none commands greater respect than Milton Friedman (b. 1912), who may well rival Keynes as the most influential economist of our century. Friedman was born in Brooklyn, New York, and reared in Rahway, New Jersey. He received his B.A. degree from Rutgers University in 1932. He earned his master's degree in 1933 at the University of Chicago, where he studied under Knight, Simons, Shultz, and Viner. In 1946 he received his doctorate from Columbia University, where he was influenced by Hotelling. As was true for Samuelson, anti-Semitism in the academic community was initially a hindrance for Friedman, leading him to work for the U.S. Treasury until after the Second World War. In the period 1948-1963 he was professor of economics at the University of Chicago, where in 1963 he was promoted to Paul Snowden Russell Distinguished Service Professor of Economics, a position that he still retains. Since 1977 he has also held the position of senior research fellow at Stanford University's Hoover Institute.

Among his many awards, Friedman was the third recipient of the John Bates Clark Medal (1951), president of the American Economic Association (1967), and winner of the Nobel Prize (1976). His most outstanding books include *Essays in Positive Economics* (1953), *A Theory of the Consumption Function* (1957), *A Program for Monetary Stability* (1960), and—what he considers his best work—*A Monetary History of the United States, 1867-1960* (written with Anna Schwartz; published in 1963). He is well known for his careful empirical testing of the quantity theory·of money, his conservative views on the role of the state, his conviction that the Great Depression was primarily due to the "Great Contraction" of the money supply, and his belief that monetary policy—though powerful—should not be used in an attempt to fine tune the economy. Moreover, he is known to be a gifted orator and the best debater in the profession. As with Samuelson, he has been reaching a wide audience of laymen for over a decade with his articles in *Newsweek* magazine.

Friedman's clarity of expression is evident in his classic essay, "The Methodology of Positive Economics," included here. In this essay he emphasized the importance of keeping value judgments about "what should be" separate from rational judgments of "what is." Believing that there is general agreement on the goals while most of the controversy concerns predictions of actual events, he argued that the controversy can be resolved if the hypotheses are worked in such a way that they are empirically testable. The best hypothesis, then, is the one yielding the most accurate predictions. This essay shows the care that Friedman has taken to keep his philosophical work separate from his scientific work. Also included in this section is "A Monetary and Fiscal Framework for Economic Stability," a famous 1948 article in which Friedman outlined the four main elements of his proposed program for economic stability. These four elements call for reforms in the monetary system, government expenditure policy, government transfer payments, and tax structure. In essence, this proposal recommends that the nation eliminate discretionary monetary and fiscal policy and rely, instead, upon the competitive forces of the market mechanism to achieve economic stability.

28. General Theory of Employment, Interest and Money*

JOHN MAYNARD KEYNES

THE THEORY OF PRICES

I

So long as economists are concerned with what is called the Theory of Value, they have been accustomed to teach that prices are governed by the conditions of supply and demand; and, in particular, changes in marginal cost and the elasticity of short-period supply have played a prominent part. But when they pass in volume II, or more often in a separate treatise, to the Theory of Money and Prices, we hear no more of these homely but intelligible concepts and move into a world where prices are governed by the quantity of money, by its income-velocity, by the velocity of circulation relatively to the volume of transactions, by hoarding, by forced saving, by inflation and deflation *et hoc genus omne;* and little or no attempt is made to relate these vaguer phrases to our former notions of the elasticities of supply and demand. If we reflect on what we are being taught and try to rationalise it, in the simpler discussions it seems that the elasticity of supply must have become zero and demand proportional to the quantity of money; whilst in the more sophisticated we are lost in a haze where nothing is clear and everything is possible. We have all of us become used to finding ourselves sometimes on the one side of the moon and sometimes on the other, without knowing what route or journey connects them, related, apparently, after the fashion of our waking and our dreaming lives.

. . . The division of Economics between the Theory of Value and Distribution on the one hand and the Theory of Money on the other hand is, I think, a false division. The right dichotomy is, I suggest, between the Theory of the Individual Industry or Firm and of the rewards and the distribution between different uses of a *given* quantity of resources on the one hand, and the Theory of Output and Employment *as a whole* on the other hand. So long as we limit ourselves to the study of the individual industry or firm on the assumption that the aggregate quantity of employed resources is constant, and, provisionally, that the conditions of other industries or firms are unchanged, it is true that we are not concerned with the significant characteristics of money. But as soon as we pass to the problem of what determines output and employment as a whole, we require the complete theory of a Monetary Economy.

Or, perhaps, we might make our line of division between the theory of stationary equilibrium and the theory of shifting equilibrium—meaning by the latter the theory of a system in which changing views about the future are capable of influencing the present situation. *For the importance of money essentially flows from its being a link be-*

*Source: From *The Collected Writings of John Maynard Keynes,* volume 7, pp 292-309 and 372-384, copyright © 1973 The Royal Economic Society. Reprinted by permission of Cambridge University Press. Footnotes deleted.

tween the present and the future. We can consider what distribution of resources between different uses will be consistent with equilibrium under the influence of normal economic motives in a world in which our views concerning the future are fixed and reliable in all respects;—with a further division, perhaps, between an economy which is unchanging and one subject to change, but where all things are foreseen from the beginning. Or we can pass from this simplified propaedeutic to the problems of the real world in which our previous expectations are liable to disappointment and expectations concerning the future affect what we do to-day. It is when we have made this transition that the peculiar properties of money as a link between the present and the future must enter into our calculations. But, although the theory of shifting equilibrium must necessarily be pursued in terms of a monetary economy, it remains a theory of value and distribution and not a separate "theory of money." Money in its significant attributes is, above all, a subtle device for linking the present to the future; and we cannot even begin to discuss the effect of changing expectations on current activities except in monetary terms. We cannot get rid of money even by abolishing gold and silver and legal tender instruments. So long as there exists any durable asset, it is capable of possessing monetary attributes and, therefore, of giving rise to the characteristic problems of a monetary economy.

II

In a single industry its particular price-level depends partly on the rate of remuneration of the factors of production which enter into its marginal cost, and partly on the scale of output. There is no reason to modify this conclusion when we pass to industry as a whole. The general price-level depends partly on the rate of remuneration of the factors of production which enter into marginal cost and partly on the scale of output as a whole, *i.e.* (taking equipment and technique as given) on the volume of employment. It is true that, when we pass to output as a whole, the costs of production in any industry partly depend on the output of other industries. But the more significant change, of which we have to take account, is the effect of changes in *demand* both on costs and on volume. It is on the side of demand that we have to introduce quite new ideas when we are dealing with demand as a whole and no longer with the demand for a single product taken in isolation, with demand as a whole assumed to be unchanged.

III

If we allow ourselves the simplification of assuming that the rates of remuneration of the different factors of production which enter into marginal cost all change in the same proportion, *i.e.* in the same proportion as the wage-unit, it follows that the general price-level (taking equipment and technique as given) depends partly on the wage-unit and partly on the volume of employment. Hence the effect of changes in the quantity of money on the price-level can be considered as being compounded of the effect on the wage-unit and the effect on employment.

To elucidate the ideas involved, let us simplify our assumptions still further, and assume (1) that all unemployed resources are homogeneous and interchangeable in their efficiency to produce what is wanted, and (2) that the factors of production entering into marginal cost are content with the same money-wage so long as there is a surplus of them unemployed. In this case we have constant returns and a rigid wage-unit, so long as there is any unemployment. It follows that an increase in the quantity of money will have no effect whatever on prices, so long as there is any unemployment, and that employment will increase in exact proportion to any increase in effective demand brought about by the increase in the quantity of money; whilst as soon as full employment is reached, it will thence-forward be the wage-unit and prices which will increase in exact proportion to the increase in effective demand. Thus if there is perfectly elastic supply so long as there is unemployment, and perfectly inelastic supply so soon as full employment is reached, and if effective demand changes in the same proportion as the quantity of money, the Quantity Theory of Money can be enunciated as follows:

> So long as there is unemployment, *employment* will change in the same proportion as the quantity of money; and when there is full employment, *prices* will change in the same proportion as the quantity of money.

Having, however, satisfied tradition by introducing a sufficient number of simplifying assumptions to enable us to enunciate a Quantity Theory of Money, let us now consider the possible complications which will in fact influence events:

(1) Effective demand will not change in exact proportion to the quantity of money.

(2) Since resources are not homogeneous, there will be diminishing, and not constant, returns as employment gradually increases.

(3) Since resources are not interchangeable, some commodities will reach a condition of inelastic supply whilst there are still unemployed resources available for the production of other commodities.

(4) The wage-unit will tend to rise, before full employment has been reached.

(5) The remunerations of the factors entering into marginal cost will not all change in the same proportion.

Thus we must first consider the effect of changes in the quantity of money on the quantity of effective demand; and the increase in effective demand will, generally speaking, spend itself partly in increasing the quantity of employment and partly in raising the level of prices. Thus instead of constant prices in conditions of unemployment, and of prices rising in proportion to the quantity of money in conditions of full employ-

ment, we have in fact a condition of prices rising gradually as employment increases. The Theory of Prices, that is to say, the analysis of the relation between changes in the quantity of money and changes in the price-level with a view to determining the elasticity of prices in response to changes in the quantity of money, must, therefore, direct itself to the five complicating factors set forth above.

We will consider each of them in turn. But this procedure must not be allowed to lead us into supposing that they are, strictly speaking, independent. For example, the proportion, in which an increase in effective demand is divided in its effect between increasing output and raising prices, may affect the way in which the quantity of money is related to the quantity of effective demand. Or, again, the differences in the proportions, in which the remunerations of different factors change, may influence the relation between the quantity of money and the quantity of effective demand. The object of our analysis is, not to provide a machine, or method of blind manipulation, which will furnish an infallible answer, but to provide ourselves with an organised and orderly method of thinking out particular problems; and, after we have reached a provisional conclusion by isolating the complicating factors one by one, we then have to go back on ourselves and allow, as well as we can, for the probable interactions of the factors amongst themselves. This is the nature of economic thinking. Any other way of applying our formal principles of thought (without which, however, we shall be lost in the wood) will lead us into error. It is a great fault of symbolic pseudo-mathematical methods of formalising a system of economic analysis, such as we shall set down in section VI of this chapter, that they expressly assume strict independence between the factors involved and lose all their cogency and authority if this hypothesis is disallowed; whereas, in ordinary discourse where we are not blindly manipulating but know all the time what we are doing and what the words mean, we can keep "at the back of our heads" the necessary reserves and qualifications and the adjustments which we shall have to make later on, in a way in which we cannot keep complicated partial differentials "at the back" of several pages of algebra which assume that they all vanish. Too large a proportion of recent "mathematical" economics are mere concoctions, as imprecise as the initial assumptions they rest on, which allow the author to lose sight of the complexities and interdependencies of the real world in a maze of pretentious and unhelpful symbols.

IV

(1) The primary effect of a change in the quantity of money on the quantity of effective demand is through its influence on the rate of interest. If this were the only reaction, the quantitative effect could be derived from the three elements—

(a) the schedule of liquidity-preference which tells us by how much the rate of interest will have to fall in order that the new money may be absorbed by willing holders,

(b) the schedule of marginal efficiencies which tells us by how much a given fall in the rate of interest will increase investment, and

(c) the investment multiplier which tells us by how much a given increase in investment will increase effective demand as a whole.

But this analysis, though it is valuable in introducing order and method into our enquiry, presents a deceptive simplicity, if we forget that the three elements (a), (b) and (c) are themselves partly dependent on the complicating factors (2), (3), (4) and (5) which we have not yet considered. For the schedule of liquidity-preference itself depends on how much of the new money is absorbed into the income and industrial circulations, which depends in turn on how much effective demand increases and how the increase is divided between the rise of prices, the rise of wages, and the volume of output and employment. Furthermore, the schedule of marginal efficiencies will partly depend on the effect which the circumstances attendant on the increase in the quantity of money have on expectations of the future monetary prospects. And finally the multiplier will be influenced by the way in which the new income resulting from the increased effective demand is distributed between different classes of consumers. Nor, of course, is this list of possible interactions complete. Nevertheless, if we have all the facts before us, we shall have enough simultaneous equations to give us a determinate result. There will be a determinate amount of increase in the quantity of effective demand which, after taking everything into account, will correspond to, and be in equilibrium with, the increase in the quantity of money. Moreover, it is only in highly exceptional circumstances that an increase in the quantity of money will be associated with a *degree* in the quantity of effective demand.

The ratio between the quantity of effective demand and the quantity of money closely corresponds to what is often called the "income-velocity of money";—except that effective demand corresponds to the income the expectation of which has set production moving, not to the actually realised income, and to gross, not net, income. But the "income-velocity of money" is, in itself, merely a name which explains nothing. There is no reason to expect that it will be constant. For it depends, as the foregoing discussion has shown, on many complex and variable factors. The use of this term obscures, I think, the real character of the causation, and has led to nothing but confusion.

(2) . . . the distinction between diminishing and constant returns partly depends on whether workers are remunerated in strict proportion to their efficiency. If so, we shall have constant

labour-costs (in terms of the wage-unit) when employment increases. But if the wage of a given grade of labourers is uniform irrespective of the efficiency of the individuals, we shall have rising labour-costs, irrespective of the efficiency of the equipment. Moreover, if equipment is non-homogeneous and some part of it involves a greater prime cost per unit of output, we shall have increasing marginal prime costs over and above any increase due to increasing labour-costs.

Hence, in general, supply price will increase as output from a given equipment is increased. Thus increasing output will be associated with rising prices, apart from any change in the wage-unit.

(3) Under (2) we have been contemplating the possibility of supply being imperfectly elastic. If there is perfect balance in the respective quantities of specialised unemployed resources, the point of full employment will be reached for all of them simultaneously. But, in general, the demand for some services and commodities will reach a level beyond which their supply is, for the time being, perfectly inelastic, whilst in other directions there is still a substantial surplus of resources without employment. Thus as output increases, a series of "bottle-necks" will be successively reached, where the supply of particular commodities ceases to be elastic and their prices have to rise to whatever level is necessary to divert demand into other directions.

It is probable that the general level of prices will not rise very much as output increases, so long as there are available efficient unemployed resources of every type. But as soon as output has increased sufficiently to begin to reach the "bottle-necks", there is likely to be a sharp rise in the prices of certain commodities.

Under this heading, however, as also under heading (2), the elasticity of supply partly depends on the elapse of time. If we assume a sufficient interval for the quantity of equipment itself to change, the elasticities of supply will be decidedly greater eventually. Thus a moderate change in effective demand, coming on a situation where there is widespread unemployment, may spend itself very little in raising prices and mainly in increasing employment; whilst a larger change, which, being unforeseen, causes some temporary "bottle-necks" to be reached, will spend itself in raising prices, as distinct from employment, to a greater extent at first than subsequently.

(4) That the wage-unit may tend to rise before full employment has been reached, requires little comment or explanation. Since each group of workers will gain, cet. par., by a rise in its own wages, there is naturally for all groups a pressure in this direction, which entrepreneurs will be more ready to meet when they are doing better business. For this reason a proportion of any increase in effective demand is likely to be absorbed in satisfying the upward tendency of the wage-unit.

Thus, in addition to the final critical point of full employment at which money-wages have to rise, in response to an increasing effective demand in terms of money, fully in proportion to the rise in the prices of wage-goods, we have a succession of earlier semi-critical points at which an increasing effective demand tends to raise money-wages though not fully in proportion to the rise in the price of wage-goods; and similarly in the case of a decreasing effective demand. In actual experience the wage-unit does not change continuously in terms of money in response to every small change in effective demand; but discontinuously. These points of discontinuity are determined by the psychology of the workers and by the policies of employers and trade unions. In an open system, where they mean a change relatively to wage-costs elsewhere, and in a trade cycle, where even in a closed system they may mean a change relatively to expected wage-costs in the future, they can be of considerable practical significance. These points, where a further increase in effective demand in terms of money is liable to cause a discontinuous rise in the wage-unit, might be deemed, from a certain point of view, to be positions of semi-inflation, having some analogy (though a very imperfect one) to the absolute inflation . . . which ensues on an increase in effective demand in circumstances of full employment. They have, moreover, a good deal of historical importance. But they do not readily lend themselves to theoretical generalisations.

(5) Our first simplification consisted in assuming that the remunerations of the various factors entering into marginal cost all change in the same proportion. But in fact the rates of remuneration of different factors in terms of money will show varying degrees of rigidity and they may also have different elasticities of supply in response to changes in the money-rewards offered. If it were not for this, we could say that the price-level is compounded of two factors, the wage-unit and the quantity of employment.

Perhaps the most important element in marginal cost which is likely to change in a different proportion from the wage-unit, and also to fluctuate within much wider limits, is marginal user cost. For marginal user cost may increase sharply when employment begins to improve, if (as will probably be the case) the increasing effective demand brings a rapid change in the prevailing expectation as to the date when the replacement of equipment will be necessary.

Whilst it is for many purposes a very useful first approximation to assume that the rewards of all the factors entering into marginal prime-cost change in the same proportion as the wage-unit, it might be better, perhaps, to take a weighted average of the rewards of the factors entering into marginal prime-cost, and call this the *cost-unit*. The cost-unit, or, subject to the above ap-proximation, the wage-unit, can thus be regarded as the essential standard of value; and the price-level, given the state of technique and equipment, will depend partly on the cost-unit and partly on the scale of output, increasing, where output increases, *more* than in proportion to any increase in the cost-unit, in accordance with the principle of diminishing returns in the short period. We have full employment when output has risen to a level at which the marginal return from a representative unit of the factors of production has fallen to the minimum figure at which a quantity of the factors sufficient to produce this output is available.

V

When a further increase in the quantity of effective demand produces no further increase in output and entirely spends itself on an increase in the cost-unit fully proportionate to the increase in effective demand, we have reached a condition which might be appropriately designated as one of true inflation. Up to this point the effect of monetary expansion is entirely a question of degree, and there is no previous point at which we can draw a definite line and declare that conditions of inflation have set in. Every previous increase in the quantity of money is likely, in so far as it increases effective demand, to spend itself partly in increasing the cost-unit and partly in increasing output.

It appears, therefore, that we have a sort of asymmetry on the two sides of the critical level above which true inflation sets in. For a contraction of effective demand below the critical level will reduce its amount measured in cost-units; whereas an expansion of effective demand beyond this level will not, in general, have the effect of increasing its amount in terms of cost-units. This result follows from the assumption that the factors of production, and in particular the workers, are disposed to resist a reduction in their money-rewards, and that there is no corresponding motive to resist an increase. This assumption is, however, obviously well founded in the facts, due to the circumstance that a change, which is not an all-round change, is beneficial to the special factors affected when it is upward and harmful when it is downward.

If, on the contrary, money-wages were to fall without limit whenever there was a tendency for less than full employment, the asymmetry would, indeed, disappear. But in that case there would be no resting-place below full employment until either the rate of interest was incapable of falling further or wages were zero. In fact we must have *some* factor, the value of which in terms of money is, if not fixed, at least sticky, to give us any stability of values in a monetary system.

The view that *any* increase in the quantity of money is inflationary (unless we mean by *inflationary* merely that prices are rising) is bound up with the underlying assumption of the classical theory that we are *always* in a condition where a reduction in the real rewards of the factors of production will lead to a curtailment in their supply.

VI

. . .we can, if we wish, express the substance of the above in symbolic form.

Let us write $MV = D$ where M is the quantity of money, V its income-velocity (this definition differing in the minor respects indicated above from the usual definition) and D the effective demand. If, then, V is constant, prices will change in the same proportion as the quantity of money provided that e_p $\left(= \dfrac{Ddp}{pdD} \right)$ is unity. This condition is satisfied . . . if $e_o = 0$ or if $e_w = 1$. The condition $e_w = 1$ means that the wage-unit in terms of money rises in the same proportion as the effective demand, since $e_w = \dfrac{DdW}{WdD}$; and the condition $e_o = 0$ means that output no longer shows any response to a further increase in ef-

fective demand, since $e_o = \dfrac{DdO}{OdD}$. Output in either case will be unaltered.

Next, we can deal with the case where income-velocity is not constant, but introducing yet a further elasticity, namely the elasticity, of effective demand in response to changes in the quantity of money,

$$e_d = \frac{MdD}{DdM}.$$

This gives us

$$\frac{Mdp}{pdM} = e_p.e_d \text{ where } e_p = 1 - e_e.e_o\,(1 - e_w);$$

so that
$$e = e_d - (1 - e_w)e_d.e_e.e_o$$
$$= e_d\,(1 - e_e.e_o + e_e.e_o.e_w)$$

where e without suffix $= \dfrac{Mdp}{pdM}$

stands for the apex of this pyramid and measures the response of money-prices to changes in the quantity of money.

Since this last expression gives us the proportionate change in prices in response to a change in the quantity of money, it can be regarded as a generalised statement of the Quantity Theory of Money. I do not myself attach much value to manipulations of this kind; and I would repeat the warning, which I have given above, that they involve just as much tacit assumption as to what variables are taken as independent (partial differentials being ignored throughout) as does ordinary discourse, whilst I doubt if they carry us any further than ordinary discourse can. Perhaps the best purpose served by writing them down is to exhibit the extreme complexity of the relationship between prices and the quantity of money, when we attempt to express it in a formal manner. It is, however, worth pointing out that, of the four terms e_d, e_w, e_e and e_o upon which the effect on prices of changes in the quantity of money depends, e_d stands for the liquidity factors which determine the demand for money in each situation, e_w for the labour factors (or, more strictly, the factors entering into prime-cost) which determine the extent to which money-wages are raised as employment increases, and e_e and e_o for the physical factors which determine the rate of decreasing returns as more employment is applied to the existing equipment.

If the public hold a constant proportion of their income in money, $e_d = 1$; if money-wages are fixed, $e_w = 0$; if there are constant returns throughout so that marginal return equals average return, $e_e \, e_o = 1$; and if there is full employment either of labour or of equipment, $e_e \, e_o = 0$.

Now $e = 1$, if $e_d = 1$ and $e_w = 1$; or if $e_d = 1$, $e_w = 0$ and $e_e.e_o = 1$; or if $e_d = 1$ and $e_o = 0$. And obviously there is a variety of other special cases in which $e = 1$. But in general e is not unity; and it is, perhaps, safe to make the generalisation that on plausible assumptions relating to the real world, and excluding the case of a "flight from the currency" in which e_d and e_w become large, e is, as a rule, less than unity.

VII

So far, we have been primarily concerned with the way in which changes in the quantity of money affect prices in the short period. But in the long run is there not some simpler relationship?

This is a question for historical generalisation rather than for pure theory. If there is some tendency to a measure of long-run uniformity in the state of liquidity-preference, there may well be some sort of rough relationship between the national income and the quantity of money required to satisfy liquidity-preference, taken as a mean over periods of pessimism and optimism together. There may be, for example, some fairly stable proportion of the national income more than which people will not readily keep in the shape of idle balances for long periods together, provided the rate of interest exceeds a certain psychological minimum; so that if the quantity of money beyond what is required in the active circulation is in excess of this proportion of the national income, there will be a tendency sooner or later for the rate of interest to fall to the neighbourhood of this minimum. The falling rate of interest will then, cet. par., increase effective demand, and the increasing effective demand will reach one or more of the semicritical points at which the wage-unit will tend to show a discontinuous rise, with a corresponding effect on prices. The opposite tendencies will set in if the quantity of surplus money is an abnormally low proportion of the national income. Thus the net effect of fluctuations over a period of time will be to establish a mean figure in conformity with the stable proportion between the national income and the quantity of money to which the psychology of the public tends sooner or later to revert.

These tendencies will probably work with less friction in the upward than in the downward direction. But if the quantity of money remains very deficient for a long time, the escape will be normally found in changing the monetary standard or the monetary system so as to raise the quantity of money, rather than in forcing down the wage-unit and thereby increasing the burden of debt. Thus the very long-run course of prices has almost always been upward. For when money is relatively abundant, the wage-unit rises; and when money is relatively scarce, some means is found to increase the effective quantity of money.

During the nineteenth century, the growth of population and of invention, the opening-up of new lands, the state of confidence and the frequency of war over the average of (say) each decade seem to have been sufficient, taken in conjunction with the propensity to consume, to establish a schedule of the marginal efficiency of capital which allowed a reasonably satisfactory average level of employment to be compatible with a rate of interest high enough to be psychologically acceptable to wealth-owners. There is evidence that for a period of almost one hundred and fifty years the long-run typical rate of interest in the leading financial centres was about 5 per cent., and the gilt-edged rate between 3 and 3½ per cent.; and that these rates of interest were modest enough to encourage a rate of investment consistent with an average of employment which was not intolerably low. Sometimes the wage-unit, but more often the monetary standard or the monetary system (in particular through the development of bank-money), would be adjusted so as to ensure that the quantity of money in terms of wage-units was sufficient to satisfy normal liquidity-preference at rates of interest which were seldom much below the standard rates indicated above. The tendency of the wage-unit was, as usual, steadily upwards on the whole, but the efficiency of labour was also increasing. Thus the balance of forces was such as to allow a fair measure of stability of prices;—the highest quinquennial average for Sauerbeck's index number between 1820 and 1914 was only 50 per cent. above the lowest. This was not accidental. It is rightly described as due to a balance of forces in an age when individual groups of employers were strong enough to prevent the wage-unit from rising much faster than the efficiency of production, and when monetary systems were at the same time sufficiently fluid and sufficiently conservative to provide an average supply of money in terms of wage-units which allowed to prevail the lowest average rate of interest readily acceptable by wealth-owners under the influence of their liquidity-preferences. The average level of employment was, of course, substantially below full employment, but not so intolerably below it as to provoke revolutionary changes.

To-day and presumably for the future the schedule of the marginal efficiency of capital is, for a variety of reasons, much lower than it was in the nineteenth century. The acuteness and the peculiarity of our contemporary problem arises, therefore, out of the possibility that the average rate of interest which will allow a reasonable average level of employment is one so unacceptable to wealth-owners that it cannot be readily established merely by manipulating the quantity of money. So long as a tolerable level of employment could be attained on the average of one or two or three decades merely by assuring an adequate supply of money in terms of wage-units, even the nineteenth century could find a way. If this was our only problem now—if a sufficient degree of devaluation is all we need—we, to-day, would certainly find a way.

But the most stable, and the least easily shifted, element in our contemporary economy has been hitherto, and may prove to be in future, the minimum rate of interest acceptable to the generality of wealth-owners. If a tolerable level of employment requires a rate of interest much below the average rates which ruled in the nineteenth century, it is most doubtful whether it can be achieved merely by manipulating the quantity of money. From the percentage gain, which the schedule of marginal efficiency of capital allows the borrower to expect to earn, there has to be deducted (1) the cost of bringing borrowers and lenders together, (2) income and sur-taxes and (3) the allowance which the lender requires to cover his risk and uncertainty, before we arrive at the net yield available to tempt the wealth-owner to sacrifice his liquidity. If, in conditions of tolerable average employment, this net yield turns out to be infinitesimal, time-honoured methods may prove unavailing.

To return to our immediate subject, the long-run relationship between the national income and the quantity of money will depend on liquidity-preferences. And the long-run stability or instability of prices will depend on the strength of the upward trend of the wage-unit (or, more precisely, of the cost-unit) compared with the rate of increase in the efficiency of the productive system.

CONCLUDING NOTES ON THE SOCIAL PHILOSOPHY TOWARDS WHICH THE GENERAL THEORY MIGHT LEAD

The outstanding faults of the economic society in which we live are its failure to provide for full employment and its arbitrary and inequitable distribution of wealth and incomes. The bearing of the foregoing theory on the first of these is obvious. But there are also two important respects in which it is relevant to the second.

Since the end of the nineteenth century significant progress towards the removal of very great disparities of wealth and income has been achieved through the instrument of direct taxation—income tax and surtax and death duties—especially in Great Britain. Many people would wish to see this process carried much further, but they are deterred by two considerations; partly by the fear of making skilful evasions too much worth while and also of diminishing unduly the motive towards risk-taking, but mainly, I think, by the belief that the growth of capital depends upon the strength of the motive towards individual saving and that for a large proportion of this growth we are dependent on the savings of the rich out of their superfluity. Our argument does not affect the first of these considerations. But it may considerably modify our attitude towards the second. For we have seen that, up to the point where full employment prevails, the growth of capital depends not at all on a low propensity to consume but is, on the contrary, held back by it; and only in conditions of full employment is a low propensity to consume conducive to the growth of capital. Moreover, experience suggests that in existing conditions saving by in-

stitutions and through sinking funds is more than adequate, and that measures for the redistribution of incomes in a way likely to raise the propensity to consume may prove positively favourable to the growth of capital.

The existing confusion of the public mind on the matter is well illustrated by the very common belief that the death duties are responsible for a reduction in the capital wealth of the country. Assuming that the State applies the proceeds of these duties to its ordinary outgoings so that taxes on incomes and consumption are correspondingly reduced or avoided, it is, of course, true that a fiscal policy of heavy death duties has the effect of increasing the community's propensity to consume. But inasmuch as an increase in the habitual propensity to consume will in general (i.e. except in conditions of full employment) serve to increase at the same time the inducement to invest, the inference commonly drawn is the exact opposite of the truth.

Thus our argument leads towards the conclusion that in contemporary conditions the growth of wealth, so far from being dependent on the abstinence of the rich, as is commonly supposed, is more likely to be impeded by it. One of the chief social justifications of great inequality of wealth is, therefore, removed. I am not saying that there are no other reasons, unaffected by our theory, capable of justifying some measure of inequality in some circumstances. But it does dispose of the most important of the reasons why hitherto we have thought it prudent to move carefully. This particularly affects our attitude towards death duties; for there are certain justifications for inequality of incomes which do not apply equally to inequality of inheritances.

For my own part, I believe that there is social and psychological justification for significant inequalities of incomes and wealth, but not for such large disparities as exist to-day. There are valuable human activities which require the motive of money-making and the environment of private wealth-ownership for their full fruition. Moreover, dangerous human proclivities can be canalised into comparatively harmless channels by the existence of opportunities for money-making and private wealth, which, if they cannot be satisfied in this way, may find their outlet in cruelty, the reckless pursuit of personal power and authority, and other forms of self-aggrandisement. It is better that a man should tyrannise over his bank balance than over his fellow-citizens; and whilst the former is sometimes denounced as being but a means to the latter, sometimes at least it is an alternative. But it is not necessary for the stimulation of these activities and the satisfaction of these proclivities that the game should be played for such high stakes as at present. Much lower stakes will serve the purpose equally well, as soon as the players are accustomed to them. The task of transmuting human nature must not be confused with the task of managing it. Though in the ideal commonwealth men may have been taught or inspired or bred to take no interest in the stakes, it may still be wise and prudent statesmanship to allow the game to be played, subject to rules and limitations, so long as the average man, or even a significant section of the community, is in fact strongly addicted to the money-making passion.

II

There is, however, a second, much more fundamental inference from our argument which has a bearing on the future of inequalities of wealth; namely, our theory of the rate of interest. The justification for a moderately high rate of interest has been found hitherto in the necessity of providing a sufficient inducement to save. But we have shown that the extent of effective saving is necessarily determined by the scale of investment and that the scale of investment is promoted by a *low* rate of interest, provided that we do not attempt to

stimulate it in this way beyond the point which corresponds to full employment. Thus it is to our best advantage to reduce the rate of interest to that point relatively to the schedule of the marginal efficiency of capital at which there is full employment.

There can be no doubt that this criterion will lead to a much lower rate of interest than has ruled hitherto; and, so far as one can guess at the schedules of the marginal efficiency of capital corresponding to increasing amounts of capital, the rate of interest is likely to fall steadily, if it should be practicable to maintain conditions of more or less continuous full employment—unless, indeed, there is an excessive change in the aggregate propensity to consume (including the State).

I feel sure that the demand for capital is strictly limited in the sense that it would not be difficult to increase the stock of capital up to a point where its marginal efficiency had fallen to a very low figure. This would not mean that the use of capital instruments would cost almost nothing, but only that the return from them would have to cover little more than their exhaustion by wastage and obsolescence together with some margin to cover risk and the exercise of skill and judgment. In short, the aggregate return from durable goods in the course of their life would, as in the case of short-lived goods, just cover their labour-costs of production *plus* an allowance for risk and the costs of skill and supervision.

Now, though this state of affairs would be quite compatible with some measure of individualism, yet it would mean the euthanasia of the rentier, and, consequently, the euthanasia of the cumulative oppressive power of the capitalist to exploit the scarcity-value of capital. Interest to-day rewards no genuine sacrifice, any more than does the rent of land. The owner of capital can obtain interest because capital is scarce, just as the owner of land can obtain rent because land is scarce. But whilst there may be intrinsic reasons for the scarcity of land, there are no intrinsic reasons for the scarcity of capital. An intrinsic reason for such scarcity, in the sense of a genuine sacrifice which could only be called forth by the offer of a reward in the shape of interest, would not exist, in the long run, except in the event of the individual propensity to consume proving to be of such a character that net saving in conditions of full employment comes to an end before capital has become sufficiently abundant. But even so, it will still be possible for communal saving through the agency of the State to be maintained at a level which will allow the growth of capital up to the point where it ceases to be scarce.

I see, therefore, the rentier aspect of capitalism as a transitional phase which will disappear when it has done its work. And with the disappearance of its rentier aspect much else in it besides will suffer a sea-change. It will be, moreover, a great advantage of the order of events which I am advocating, that the euthanasia of the rentier, of the functionless investor, will be nothing sudden, merely a gradual but prolonged continuance of what we have seen recently in Great Britain, and will need no revolution.

Thus we might aim in practice (there being nothing in this which is unattainable) at an increase in the volume of capital until it ceases to be scarce, so that the functionless investor will no longer receive a bonus; and at a scheme of direct taxation which allows the intelligence and determination and executive skill of the financier, the entrepreneur et hoc genus omne (who are certainly so fond of their craft that their labour could be obtained much cheaper than at present), to be harnessed to the service of the community on reasonable terms of reward.

At the same time we must recognise that only experience can show how far the common will, embodied in the policy of the State, ought to be directed to increasing and supplementing the inducement to invest; and how far it is safe to stimulate the average propensity to consume, without forgoing our aim of depriving capital of its scarcity-value within one or two generations. It may turn out that the propensity to consume will be so easily strengthened by the effects of a falling rate of interest, that full employment can be reached with a rate of accumulation little greater than at present. In this event a scheme for the higher taxation of large incomes and inheritances might be open to the objection that it would lead to full employment with a rate of accumulation which was reduced considerably below the current level. I must not be supposed to deny the possibility, or even the probability, of this outcome. For in such matters it is rash to predict how the average man will react to a changed environment. If, however, it should prove easy to secure an approximation to full employment with a rate of accumulation not much greater than at present, an outstanding problem will at least have been solved. And it would remain for separate decision on what scale and by what means it is right and reasonable to call on the living generation to restrict their consumption, so as to establish, in course of time, a state of full investment for their successors.

III

In some other respects the foregoing theory is moderately conservative in its implications. For whilst it indicates the vital importance of establishing certain central controls in matters which are now left in the main to individual initiative, there are wide fields of activity which are unaffected. The State will have to exercise a guiding influence on the propensity to consume partly through its scheme of taxation, partly by fixing the rate of interest, and partly, perhaps, in other ways. Furthermore, it seems unlikely that the influence of banking policy on the rate of interest will be sufficient by itself to determine an optimum rate of investment. I conceive, therefore, that a somewhat comprehensive socialisation of investment will prove the only means of securing an approximation to full employment; though this need not exclude all manner of compromises and of devices by which public authority will co-operate with private initiative. But beyond this no obvious case is made out for a system of State Socialism which would embrace most of the economic life of the community. It is not the ownership of the instruments of production which it is important for the State to assume. If the State is able to determine the aggregate amount of resources devoted to augmenting the instruments and the basic rate of reward to those who own them, it will have accomplished all that is necessary. Moreover, the necessary measures of socialisation can be introduced gradually and without a break in the general traditions of society.

Our criticism of the accepted classical theory of economics has consisted not so much in finding logical flaws in its analysis as in pointing out that its tacit assumptions are seldom or never satisfied, with the result that it cannot solve the economic problems of the actual world. But if our central controls succeed in establishing an aggregate volume of output corresponding to full employment as nearly as is practicable, the classical theory comes into its own again from this point onwards. If we suppose the volume of output to be given, i.e. to be determined by forces outside the classical scheme of thought, then there is no objection to be raised against the classical analysis of the manner in which private self-interest will determine what in particular is produced, in what proportions the factors of production will be combined to produce it, and how the value of the final product will be distributed between them. Again, if we have dealt otherwise with the problem of thrift, there is no objection to be raised against the modern classical theory as to the degree of

consilience between private and public advantage in conditions of perfect and imperfect competition respectively. Thus, apart from the necessity of central controls to bring about an adjustment between the propensity to consume and the inducement to invest, there is no more reason to socialise economic life than there was before.

To put the point concretely, I see no reason to suppose that the existing system seriously misemploys the factors of production which are in use. There are, of course, errors of foresight; but these would not be avoided by centralising decisions. When 9,000,000 men are employed out of 10,000,000 willing and able to work, there is no evidence that the labour of these 9,000,000 men is misdirected. The complaint against the present system is not that these 9,000,000 men ought to be employed on different tasks, but that tasks should be available for the remaining 1,000,000 men. It is in determining the volume, not the direction, of actual employment that the existing system has broken down.

Thus I agree with Gesell that the result of filling in the gaps in the classical theory is not to dispose of the "Manchester System," but to indicate the nature of the environment which the free play of economic forces requires if it is to realise the full potentialities of production. The central controls necessary to ensure full employment will, of course, involve a large extension of the traditional functions of government. Furthermore, the modern classical theory has itself called attention to various conditions in which the free play of the economic forces may need to be curbed or guided. But there will still remain a wide field for the exercise of private initiative and responsibility. Within this field the traditional advantages of individualism will still hold good.

Let us stop for a moment to remind ourselves what these advantages are. They are partly advantages of efficiency—the advantages of decentralisation and of the play of self-interest. The advantage to efficiency of the decentralisation of decisions and of individual responsibility is even greater, perhaps, than the nineteenth century supposed; and the reaction against the appeal to self-interest may have gone too far. But, above all, individualism, if it can be purged of its defects and its abuses, is the best safeguard of personal liberty in the sense that, compared with any other system, it greatly widens the field for the exercise of personal choice. It is also the best safeguard of the variety of life, which emerges precisely from this extended field of personal choice, and the loss of which is the greatest of all the losses of the homogeneous or totalitarian state. For this variety preserves the traditions which embody the most secure and successful choices of former generations; it colours the present with the diversification of its fancy; and, being the handmaid of experiment as well as of tradition and of fancy, it is the most powerful instrument to better the future.

Whilst, therefore, the enlargement of the functions of government, involved in the task of adjusting to one another the propensity to consume and the inducement to invest, would seem to a nineteenth-century publicist or to a contemporary American financier to be a terrific encroachment on individualism, I defend it, on the contrary, both as the only practicable means of avoiding the destruction of existing economic forms in their entirety and as the condition of the successful functioning of individual initiative.

For if effective demand is deficient, not only is the public scandal of wasted resources intolerable, but the individual enterpriser who seeks to bring these resources into action is operating with the odds loaded against him. The game of hazard which he plays is furnished with many zeros, so that the players *as a whole* will lose if they have the energy and hope to deal all the cards. Hitherto the increment of the world's wealth has

fallen short of the aggregate of positive individual savings; and the difference has been made up by the losses of those whose courage and initiative have not been supplemented by exceptional skill or unusual good fortune. But if effective demand is adequate, average skill and average good fortune will be enough.

The authoritarian state systems of to-day seem to solve the problem of unemployment at the expense of efficiency and of freedom. It is certain that the world will not much longer tolerate the unemployment which, apart from brief intervals of excitement, is associated—and, in my opinion, inevitably associated—with present-day capitalistic individualism. But it may be possible by a right analysis of the problem to cure the disease whilst preserving efficiency and freedom.

IV

I have mentioned in passing that the new system might be more favourable to peace than the old has been. It is worth while to repeat and emphasise that aspect.

War has several causes. Dictators and others such, to whom war offers, in expectation at least, a pleasurable excitement, find it easy to work on the natural bellicosity of their peoples. But, over and above this, facilitating their task of fanning the popular flame, are the economic causes of war, namely, the pressure of population and the competitive struggle for markets. It is the second factor, which probably played a predominant part in the nineteenth century, and might again, that is germane to this discussion.

I have pointed out in the preceding chapter that, under the system of domestic *laissez-faire* and an international gold standard such as was orthodox in the latter half of the nineteenth century, there was no means open to a government whereby to mitigate economic distress at home except through the competitive struggle for markets. For all measures helpful to a state of chronic or intermittent under-employment were ruled out, except measures to improve the balance of trade on income account.

Thus, whilst economists were accustomed to applaud the prevailing international system as furnishing the fruits of the international division of labour and harmonising at the same time the interests of different nations, there lay concealed a less benign influence; and those statesmen were moved by common sense and a correct apprehension of the true course of events, who believed that if a rich, old country were to neglect the struggle for markets its prosperity would droop and fail. But if nations can learn to provide themselves with full employment by their domestic policy (and, we must add, if they can also attain equilibrium in the trend of their population), there need be no important economic forces calculated to set the interest of one country against that of its neighbours. There would still be room for the international division of labour and for international lending in appropriate conditions. But there would no longer be a pressing motive why one country need force its wares on another or repulse the offerings of its neighbour, not because this was necessary to enable it to pay for what it wished to purchase, but with the express object of upsetting the equilibrium of payments so as to develop a balance of trade in its own favour. International trade would cease to be what it is, namely, a desperate expedient to maintain employment at home by forcing sales on foreign markets and restricting purchases, which, if successful, will merely shift the problem of unemployment to the neighbour which is worsted in the struggle, but a willing and unimpeded exchange of goods and services in conditions of mutual advantage.

V

Is the fulfilment of these ideas a vi-

sionary hope? Have they insufficient roots in the motives which govern the evolution of political society? Are the interests which they will thwart stronger and more obvious than those which they will serve?

I do not attempt an answer in this place. It would need a volume of a different character from this one to indicate even in outline the practical measures in which they might be gradually clothed. But if the ideas are correct—an hypothesis on which the author himself must necessarily base what he writes—it would be a mistake, I predict, to dispute their potency over a period of time. At the present moment people are unusually expectant of a more fundamental diagnosis; more particularly ready to receive it; eager to try it out, if it should be even plausible. But apart from this contemporary mood, the ideas of economists and political philosophers, both when they are right and when they are wrong, are more powerful than is commonly understood. Indeed the world is ruled by little else. Practical men, who believe themselves to be quite exempt from any intellectual influences, are usually the slaves of some defunct economist. Madmen in authority, who hear voices in the air, are distilling their frenzy from some academic scribbler of a few years back. I am sure that the power of vested interests is vastly exaggerated compared with the gradual encroachment of ideas. Not, indeed, immediately, but after a certain interval; for in the field of economic and political philosophy there are not many who are influenced by new theories after they are twenty-five or thirty years of age, so that the ideas which civil servants and politicians and even agitators apply to current events are not likely to be the newest. But, soon or late, it is ideas, not vested interests, which are dangerous for good or evil.

29. The Theory of the Rate of Interest*

JOHN MAYNARD KEYNES

Perhaps the following is a useful way of indicating the precise points of departure of the theory of the rate of interest expounded in my *General Theory of Employment, Interest and Money* from what I take to be the orthodox theory. Let us begin with four propositions, which, although they may be unfamiliar in form, are not inconsistent with the orthodox theory and which that theory has no reason, so far as I am aware, to reject.

(1) Interest on money *means* precisely what the books on arithmetic say that it means; that is to say, it is simply the premium obtainable on current cash over deferred cash, so that it measures the marginal preference (for the community as a whole) for holding cash in hand over cash for deferred delivery. No one would pay this premium unless the possession of cash served some purpose, *i.e.*, had some efficiency. Thus we can conveniently say that interest on money measures the marginal efficiency of money measured in terms of itself as a unit.[1]

(2) Money is not peculiar in having a marginal efficiency measured in terms of itself. Surplus stocks of commodities in excess of requirements and other capital assets representing surplus capacity may, indeed, have a negative marginal efficiency in terms of themselves, but normally capital assets of all kinds have a positive marginal efficiency measured in terms of themselves. If we know the relation between the present and expected prices of an asset in terms of money we can convert the measure of its marginal efficiency in terms of itself into a measure of its mar-

ginal efficiency in terms of money by means of a formula which I have given in my *General Theory*.

(3) The effort to obtain the best advantage from the possession of wealth will set up a tendency for capital assets to exchange, in equilibrium, at values proportionate to their marginal efficiencies in terms of a common unit. That is to say, if r is the money rate of interest (*i.e.*, r is the marginal efficiency of money in terms of itself) and y is the marginal efficiency of a capital asset A in terms of money, then A will exchange in terms of money at a price such as to make $y = r$.

(4) If the demand price of our capital asset A thus determined is not less than its replacement cost, new investment in A will take place, the scale of such investment depending on the capacity available for the production of A, *i.e.*, on its elasticity of supply, and on the rate at which y, its marginal efficiency, declines as the amount of investment in A increases. At a scale of new investment at which the marginal cost of producing A is equal to its demand price as above, we have a position of equilibrium. Thus the price system resulting from the relationships between the marginal efficiencies of different capital assets including money, measured in terms of a common unit, determines the aggregate rate of investment.

These propositions are not, I think, inconsistent with the orthodox theory, or in any way open to doubt. They establish that relative prices (and, under the influence of prices, the scale of output) move until the marginal efficiencies of all kinds of assets are equal when

*Source: From *The Collected Writings of John Maynard Keynes*, volume 14, pp. 101-108, copyright © 1973 The Royal Economic Society. Reprinted by permission of Cambridge University Press.

measured in a common unit; and consequently that the marginal efficiency of capital is equal to the rate of interest. But they tell us nothing as to the forces which determine what this common level of marginal efficiency will tend to be. It is when we proceed to this further discussion that my argument diverges from the orthodox argument.

Put shortly, the orthodox theory maintains that the forces which determine the common value of the marginal efficiency of various assets are independent of money, which has, so to speak, no autonomous influence, and that prices move until the marginal efficiency of money, *i.e.*, the rate of interest, falls into line with the common value of the marginal efficiency of other assets as determined by other forces. My theory, on the other hand, maintains that this is a special case and that over a wide range of possible cases almost the opposite is true, namely, that the marginal efficiency of money is determined by forces partly appropriate to itself, and that prices move until the marginal efficiency of other assets fall into line with the rate of interest.

Let me proceed to give the further propositions, which, I suggest, the orthodox theory requires.

(5) The marginal efficiency of money in terms of itself has the peculiarity that it is independent of its quantity. In this respect it differs from other capital assets. This is a consequence of the Quantity Theory of Money strictly stated (a matter to which we shall return later). Thus, unless we import considerations from outside, the money rate of interest is indeterminate, for the demand schedule for money is a function solely of its supply. Nevertheless, a determinate value for r can be derived from the condition that the value of an asset A, of which the marginal efficiency in terms of money is y, must be such that $y = r$. For provided that we know the scale of investment, we know y and the value of A, and hence we can deduce r. In other words, the rate of interest depends on the marginal efficiency of capital assets other than money. This must, however, be

supplemented by another proposition; for it requires that we should already know the scale of investment. This further proposition is as follows.

(6) The scale of investment will not reach its equilibrium level until the point is reached at which the elasticity of supply of output as a whole has fallen to zero.

Hence follows the final synthesis of this theory. The equilibrium rate of aggregate investment, corresponding to the level of output for a further increase in which the elasticity of supply is zero, depends on the readiness of the public to save. But this in turn depends on the rate of interest. Thus for each level of the rate of interest we have a given quantity of saving. This quantity of saving determines the scale of investment. The scale of investment settles the marginal efficiency of capital, to which the rate of interest must be equal. Our system is therefore determinate. To each possible value of the rate of interest there corresponds a given volume of saving; and to each possible value of the marginal efficiency of capital there corresponds a given volume of investment. Now the rate of interest and the marginal efficiency of capital must be equal. Thus the position of equilibrium is given by that common value of the rate of interest and of the marginal efficiency of capital at which the saving determined by the former is equal to the investment determined by the latter.

Now my departure from the orthodox theory takes place, as I have said, at propositions (5) and (6), for which I substitute:

(5)* The marginal efficiency of money in terms of itself is, in general, a function of its quantity (though not of its quantity alone), just as in the case of other capital assets.

(6)* Aggregate investment may reach its equilibrium rate under proposition (4) above, before the elasticity of supply of output as a whole has fallen to zero.

Before we examine the grounds for substituting (5)* and (6)* for (5) and (6), let us stop for a moment to consider more fully the meaning and the practical implications of the special postulates of the orthodox theory.

Let us begin with proposition (5). So far as the active circulation is concerned, it is sufficiently correct as a first approximation to regard the demand for money as proportionate to the effective demand, i.e., to the level of money income; which amounts to saying that the income velocity of the active circulation is independent of the quantity of money. This is, I say, only a first approximation because the demand for money in the active circulation is also to some extent a function of the rate of interest, since a higher rate of interest may lead to a more economical use of active balances, though this only means that the active balances are partially under the same influence as the inactive balances. But we also require the postulate that the amount of the inactive balances is independent of the rate of interest. I do not see, however, how this can be the case, except in conditions of long-period equilibrium, by which I mean a state of expectation which is both definite and constant and has lasted long enough for there to be no hangover from a previous state of expectation.

In ordinary conditions, on the other hand, this postulate would have awkward consequences quite incompatible with experience. It would mean, for example, that "open-market operations" by a central bank would have no effect, other than momentary, on the rate of interest, the price of bonds remaining the same whatever quantity of them the central bank may buy or sell; the effect of the central bank's action on prices being such as to modify the demand for money to just the same extent as that by which the central bank was altering the supply of money.

Let us now turn to proposition (6). A zero elasticity of supply for output as a whole means that an increase of demand in terms of money will lead to no change in output; that is to say, prices will rise in the same proportion as the money demand rises. Inflation will have no effect on output or employment, but only on prices. This is what I mean by saying that the orthodox theory of the rate of interest involves a strict interpretation of the Quantity Theory of Money, namely that P changes in the same proportion as M. This does not, of course, mean that T and V in the equation $PT = MV$ are irrevocably fixed; but the above, in conjunction with proposition (5), does mean that T and V are neither of them a function of M and that they do not change merely as a result of inflation in the quantity of money. Otherwise interpreted, a zero elasticity of supply for output as a whole involves a zero elasticity of supply for employment, i.e., there is, in my terminology, full employment. Indeed the condition in which the elasticity of supply for output as a whole is zero, is, I now think, the most convenient criterion for defining full employment.

It seems, therefore, that the orthodox theory requires (1) that there should be a state of definite and constant expectation and (2) that there should be a state of full employment. These limitations mean that it is a particular theory applicable only to certain conditions; and this is my justification for calling my own theory a general theory, of which the orthodox theory is a limiting case. Perhaps I am wrong in making the orthodox theory employ these postulates. For I am under the disadvantage that no one has ever thought it worth while to write down the postulates which the orthodox theory is supposed to require. But I do not at present see any alternative.

If I am right, the orthodox theory is wholly inapplicable to such problems as those of unemployment and the trade cycle, or, indeed, to any of the day-to-day problems of ordinary life. Nevertheless it is often in fact applied to such problems. The postulates which it requires, not having been stated, have escaped notice, with the result that deep-seated inconsistencies have been introduced into economic thought. The orthodox theory of the rate of interest properly belongs to a different stage of economic assumptions and abstractions from that in which any of us are thinking today. For the rate of interest and the marginal efficiency of capital are particularly concerned with the *indefinite* character of actual expectations; they sum up the effect on men's market decisions of all sorts of vague doubts and fluctuating states of confidence and courage. They belong, that is to say, to a stage of our theory where we are no longer assuming a definite and calculable future. The orthodox theory, on the other hand, is concerned with a simplified world where there is always full employment, and where doubt and fluctuations of confidence are ruled out, so that there is no occasion to hold inactive balances, and prices must be constantly at a level which, merely to satisfy the transactions motive and without leaving any surplus to be absorbed by the precautionary and speculative motives, causes the whole stock of money to be worth a rate of interest equal to the marginal efficiency of capital which corresponds to full employment. The orthodox theory is, for example, particularly applicable to the stationary state? For in such conditions, not only is proposition (5) valid for the same reasons that apply in the case of the long period; but the stock of capital being fixed and new investment being zero, the marginal efficiency of capital must depend on the amount of this given stock and prices must be at a level which equates the amount of money, demanded for active balances at a rate of interest equal to this fixed marginal efficiency of capital, to the fixed supply of money in existence.

There is one other comment worth making. It leads to considerable difficulties to regard the marginal efficiency of money as wholly different in character from the marginal efficiency of other assets. Equilibrium requires, as we have seen above (proposition 3), that the prices of different kinds of assets measured in the same unit must move until their marginal efficiencies measured in that unit are equal. But if the marginal efficiency of money in terms of itself is always equal to the marginal efficiency of other assets, irrespective of the price of the latter, the whole price system in terms of money becomes indeterminate. It is the elements of elasticity (a) in the desire to hold inactive balances and (b) in the supply of output as a whole, which permits a reasonable measure of stability in prices. If these elasticities are zero there is a necessity for the whole body of prices and wages to respond immediately to every change in the quantity of money. This assumes a state of affairs very different from that in which we live. For the two elasticities named above are highly characteristic of the real world; and the assumption that both of them are zero assumes away three-quarters of the problems in which we are interested.

NOTES

1. This implies a slightly different definition of marginal efficiency from that which I have given in my *General Theory*, namely the substitution of "market value" for "replacement cost." The meaning of "marginal efficiency of capital" of which I make use—and which is, in my opinion, the only definition of the term which makes good sense—was first introduced into economic theory by Irving Fisher in his *Theory of Interest* (1930), under the designation "the rate of return over cost." This conception of his is, I think, the most important and fruitful of his recent original suggestions.

2. Unless we suppose that a constant money wage is compatible with a constant level of employment which is less than full employment.

30. The General Theory of Employment*

JOHN MAYNARD KEYNES

It is generally recognized that the Ricardian analysis was concerned with what we now call long-period equilibrium. Marshall's contribution mainly consisted in grafting on to this the marginal principle and the principle of substitution, together with some discussion of the passage from one position of long-period equilibrium to another. But he assumed, as Ricardo did, that the amounts of the factors of production in use were given and that the problem was to determine the way in which they would be used and their relative rewards. Edgeworth and Professor Pigou and other later and contemporary writers have embroidered and improved this theory by considering how different peculiarities in the shapes of the supply functions of the factors of production would affect matters, what will happen in conditions of monopoly and imperfect competition, how far social and individual advantage coincide, what are the special problems of exchange in an open system and the like. But these more recent writers like their predecessors were still dealing with a system in which the amount of the factors employed was given and the other relevant facts were known more or less for certain. This does not mean that they were dealing with a system in which change was ruled out, or even one in which the disappointment of expectation was ruled out. But at any given time facts and expectations were assumed to be given in a definite and calculable form; and risks, of which, tho admitted, not much notice was taken, were supposed to be capable of an exact actuarial computation. The calculus of probability, tho mention of it was kept in the background, was supposed to be capable of reducing uncertainty to the same calculable status as that of certainty itself; just as in the Benthamite calculus of pains and pleasures or of advantage and disadvantage, by which the Benthamite philosophy assumed men to be influenced in their general ethical behavior.

Actually, however, we have, as a rule, only the vaguest idea of any but the most direct consequences of our acts. Sometimes we are not much concerned with their remoter consequences, even tho time and chance may make much of them. But sometimes we are intensely concerned with them, more so, occasionally, than with the immediate consequences. Now of all human activities which are affected by this remoter preoccupation, it happens that one of the most important is economic in character, namely, Wealth. The whole object of the accumulation of Wealth is to produce results, or potential results, at a comparatively distant, and sometimes at an *indefinitely* distant, date. Thus the fact that our knowledge of the future is fluctuating, vague and uncertain, renders Wealth a peculiarly unsuitable subject for the methods of the classical economic theory. This theory might work very

*Source: From The Collected Writings of John Maynard Keynes, volume 14, pp. 112-23, copyright © 1973 The Royal Economic Society. Reprinted by permission of Cambridge University Press.

well in a world in which economic goods were necessarily consumed within a short interval of their being produced. But it requires, I suggest, considerable amendment if it is to be applied to a world in which the accumulation of wealth for an indefinitely postponed future is an important factor; and the greater the proportionate part played by such wealth-accumulation the more essential does such amendment become.

By "uncertain" knowledge, let me explain, I do not mean merely to distinguish what is known for certain from what is only probable. The game of roulette is not subject, in this sense, to uncertainty; nor is the prospect of a Victory bond being drawn. Or, again, the expectation of life is only slightly uncertain. Even the weather is only moderately uncertain. The sense in which I am using the term is that in which the prospect of a European war is uncertain, or the price of copper and the rate of interest twenty years hence, or the obsolescence of a new invention, or the position of private wealth-owners in the social system in 1970. About these matters there is no scientific basis on which to form any calculable probability whatever. We simply do not know. Nevertheless, the necessity for action and for decision compels us as practical men to do our best to overlook this awkward fact and to behave exactly as we should if we had behind us a good Benthamite calculation of a series of prospective advantages and disadvantages, each multiplied by its appropriate probability, waiting to be summed.

How do we manage in such circumstances to behave in a manner which saves our faces as rational, economic men? We have devised for the purpose a variety of techniques, of which much the most important are the three following:

(1) We assume that the present is a much more serviceable guide to the future than a candid examination of past experience would show it to have been hitherto.

In other words we largely ignore the prospect of future changes about the actual character of which we know nothing.

(2) We assume that the *existing* state of opinion as expressed in prices and the character of existing output is based on a *correct* summing up of future prospects, so that we can accept it as such unless and until something new and relevant comes into the picture.

(3) Knowing that our own individual judgment is worthless, we endeavor to fall back on the judgment of the rest of the world which is perhaps better informed. That is, we endeavor to conform with the behavior of the majority or the average. The psychology of a society of individuals each of whom is endeavoring to copy the others leads to what we may strictly term a *conventional* judgment.

Now a practical theory of the future based on these three principles has certain marked characteristics. In particular, being based on so flimsy a foundation, it is subject to sudden and violent changes. The practice of calmness and immobility, of certainty and security, suddenly breaks down. New fears and hopes will, without warning, take charge of human conduct. The forces of disillusion may suddenly impose a new conventional basis of valuation. All these pretty, polite techniques, made for a well-panelled Board Room and a nicely regulated market, are liable to collapse. At all times the vague panic fears and equally vague and unreasoned hopes are not really lulled, and lie but a little way below the surface.

Perhaps the reader feels that this general, philosophical disquisition on the behavior of mankind is somewhat remote from the economic theory under discussion. But I think not. Tho this is how we behave in the market place, the theory we devise in the study of how we behave in the market place should not itself submit to market-place idols. I accuse the classical economic theory of being itself one of these pretty, polite techniques which tries to deal with the present by abstracting from the fact that we know very little about the future.

I daresay that a classical economist would readily admit this. But, even so, I think he has overlooked the precise nature of the difference which his abstraction makes between theory and practice, and the character of the fallacies into which he is likely to be led. This is particularly the case in his treatment of Money and Interest. And our first step must be to elucidate more clearly the functions of Money.

Money, it is well known, serves two principal purposes. By acting as a money of account it facilitates exchanges without its being necessary that it should ever itself come into the picture as a substantive object. In this respect it is a convenience which is devoid of significance or real influence. In the second place, it is a store of wealth. So we are told, without a smile on the face. But in the world of the classical economy, what an insane use to which to put it! For it is a recognized characteristic of money as a store of wealth that it is barren; whereas practically every other form of storing wealth yields some interest or profit. Why should anyone outside a lunatic asylum wish to use money as a store of wealth?

Because, partly on reasonable and partly on instinctive grounds, our desire to hold Money as a store of wealth is a barometer of the degree of our distrust of our own calculations and conventions concerning the future. Even tho this feeling about Money is itself conventional or instinctive, it operates, so to speak, at a deeper level of our motivation. It takes charge at the moments when the higher, more precarious conventions have weakened. The possession of actual money lulls our disquietude; and the premium which we require to make us part with money is the measure of the degree of our disquietude.

The significance of this characteristic of money has usually been overlooked; and in so far as it has been noticed, the essential nature of the phenomenon has been misdescribed. For what has attracted attention has been the *quantity* of money which has been hoarded; and importance has been attached to this because it has been supposed to have a direct proportionate effect on the price-level through affecting the velocity of circulation. But the *quantity* of hoards can only be altered either if the total quantity of money is changed or if the quantity of current money-income (I speak broadly) is changed; whereas fluctuations in the degree of confidence are capable of having quite a different effect, namely, in modifying not the amount that is actually hoarded, but the amount of the premium which has to be offered to induce people not to hoard. And changes in the propensity to hoard, or in the state of liquidity-preference as I have called it, primarily affect, not prices, but the rate of interest; any effect on prices being produced by repercussion as an ultimate consequence of a change in the rate of interest.

This, expressed in a very general way, is my theory of the rate of interest. The rate of interest obviously measures—just as the books on arithmetic say it does—the premium which has to be offered to induce people to hold their wealth in some form other than hoarded money. The quantity of money and the amount of it required in the active circulation for the transaction of current business (mainly depending on the level of money-income) determine how much is available for inactive balances, *i.e.* for hoards. The rate of interest is the factor which adjusts at the margin the demand for hoards to the supply of hoards.

Now let us proceed to the next stage of the argument. The owner of wealth, who has been induced not to hold his wealth in the shape of hoarded money, still has two alternatives between which to choose. He can lend his money at the current rate of money-interest or he can purchase some kind of capital-asset. Clearly in equilibrium these two alternatives must offer an equal advantage to the marginal investor in each of them. This is brought about by shifts in the money-prices of capital-assets relative to the prices of money-loans. The prices of capital-assets move until, having regard to their prospective yields and account being taken of all those elements of doubt and uncertainty, interested and disinterested advice, fashion, convention and what else you will which affect the mind of the investor, they offer an equal apparent advantage to the marginal investor who is wavering between one kind of investment and another.

This, then, is the first repercussion of the rate of interest, as fixed by the quantity of money and the propensity to hoard, namely, on the prices of capital-assets. This does not mean, of course, that the rate of interest is the only fluctuating influence on these prices. Opinions as to their prospective yield are themselves subject to sharp fluctuations, precisely for the reason already given, namely, the flimsiness of the basis of knowledge on which they depend. It is these opinions taken in conjunction with the rate of interest which fix their price.

Now for stage three. Capital-assets are capable, in general, of being newly produced. The scale on which they are produced depends, of course, on the relation between their costs of production and the prices which they are expected to realize in the market. Thus if the level of the rate of interest taken in conjunction with opinions about their prospective yield raise the prices of capital-assets, the volume of current investment (meaning by this the value of the output of newly produced capital-assets) will be increased; while if, on the other hand, these influences reduce the prices of capital-assets, the volume of current investment will be diminished.

It is not surprising that the volume of investment, thus determined, should fluctuate widely from time to time. For it depends on two sets of judgments about the future, neither of which rests on an adequate or secure foundation—on the propensity to hoard and on opinions of the future yield of capital-assets. Nor is

there any reason to suppose that the fluctuations in one of these factors will tend to offset the fluctuations in the other. When a more pessimistic view is taken about future yields, that is no reason why there should be a diminished propensity to hoard. Indeed, the conditions which aggravate the one factor tend, as a rule, to aggravate the other. For the same circumstances which lead to pessimistic views about future yields are apt to increase the propensity to hoard. The only element of self-righting in the system arises at a much later stage and in an uncertain degree. If a decline in investment leads to a decline in output as a whole, this may result (for more reasons than one) in a reduction of the amount of money required for the active circulation, which will release a larger quantity of money for the inactive circulation, which will satisfy the propensity to hoard at a lower level of the rate of interest, which will raise the prices of capital-assets, which will increase the scale of investment, which will restore in some measure the level of output as a whole.

This completes the first chapter of the argument, namely, the liability of the scale of investment to fluctuate for reasons quite distinct (a) from those which determine the propensity of the individual to save out of a given income and (b) from those physical conditions of technical capacity to aid production which have usually been supposed hitherto to be the chief influence governing the marginal efficiency of capital.

If, on the other hand, our knowledge of the future was calculable and not subject to sudden changes, it might be justifiable to assume that the liquidity-preference curve was both stable and very inelastic. In this case a small decline in money-income would lead to a large fall in the rate of interest, probably sufficient to raise output and employment to the full. In these conditions we might reasonably suppose that the whole of the available resources would normally be employed; and the conditions required by the orthodox theory would be satisfied.

My next difference from the traditional theory concerns its apparent conviction that there is no necessity to work out a theory of the demand and supply of output *as a whole*. Will a fluctuation in investment, arising for the reasons just described, have any effect on the demand for output as a whole, and consequently on the scale of output and employment? What answer can the traditional theory make to this question? I believe that it makes no answer at all, never having given the matter a single thought; the theory of effective demand, that is the demand for output as a whole, having been entirely neglected for more than a hundred years.

My own answer to this question involves fresh considerations. I say that effective demand is made up of two items—investment-expenditure determined in the manner just explained and consumption-expenditure. Now what governs the amount of consumption-expenditure? It depends mainly on the level of income. People's propensity to spend (as I call it) is influenced by many factors such as the distribution of income, their normal attitude to the future and—tho probably in a minor degree—by the rate of interest. But in the main the prevailing psychological law seems to be that when aggregate income increases, consumption-expenditure will also increase but to a somewhat lesser extent. This is a very obvious conclusion. It simply amounts to saying that an increase in income will be divided in some proportion or another between spending and saving, and that when our income is increased it is extremely unlikely that this will have the effect of making us either spend less or save less than before. This psychological law was of the utmost importance in the development of my own thought, and it is, I think, absolutely fundamental to the theory of effective demand as set forth in my book. But few critics or commentators so far

have paid particular attention to it.

There follows from this extremely obvious principle an important, yet unfamiliar, conclusion. Incomes are created partly by entrepreneurs producing for investment and partly by their producing for consumption. The amount that is consumed depends on the amount of income thus made up. Hence the amount of consumption-goods which it will pay entrepreneurs to produce depends on the amount of investment-goods which they are producing. If, for example, the public are in the habit of spending nine-tenths of their income on consumption-goods, it follows that if the entrepreneurs were to produce consumption-goods at a cost more than nine times the cost of the investment-goods they are producing, some part of their output could not be sold at a price which would cover its cost of production. For the consumption-goods on the market would have cost more than nine-tenths of the aggregate income of the public and would therefore be in excess of the demand for consumption-goods, which by hypothesis is only the nine-tenths. Thus entrepreneurs will make a loss until they contract their output of consumption-goods down to an amount at which it no longer exceeds nine times their current output of investment goods.

The formula is not, of course, quite so simple as in this illustration. The proportion of their income which the public will choose to consume will not be a constant one, and in the most general case other factors are also relevant. But there is always a formula, more or less of this kind, relating the output of consumption-goods which it pays to produce to the output of investment-goods; and I have given attention to it in my book under the name of the *Multiplier*. The fact that an increase in consumption is apt in itself to stimulate this further investment merely fortifies the argument.

That the level of output of consumption-goods, which is profitable to the entrepreneur, should be related by a formula of this kind to the output of investment-goods depends on assumptions of a simple and obvious character. The conclusion appears to me to be quite beyond dispute. Yet the consequences which follow from it are at the same time unfamiliar and of the greatest possible importance.

The theory can be summed up by saying that, given the psychology of the public, the level of output and employment as a whole depends on the amount of investment. I put it in this way, not because this is the only factor on which aggregate output depends, but because it is usual in a complex system to regard as the *causa causans* that factor which is most prone to sudden and wide fluctuation. More comprehensively, aggregate output depends on the propensity to hoard, on the policy of the monetary authority as it affects the quantity of money, on the state of confidence concerning the prospective yield of capital-assets, on the propensity to spend and on the social factors which influence the level of the money-wage. But of these several factors it is those which determine the rate of investment which are most unreliable, since it is they which are influenced by our views of the future about which we know so little.

This that I offer is, therefore, a theory of why output and employment are so liable to fluctuation. It does not offer a ready-made remedy as to how to avoid these fluctuations and to maintain output at a steady optimum level. But it is, properly speaking, a Theory of Employment because it explains *why*, in any given circumstances, employment is what it is. Naturally I am interested not only in the diagnosis, but also in the cure; and many pages of my book are devoted to the latter. But I consider that my suggestions for a cure, which, avowedly, are not worked out completely, are on a different plane from the diagnosis. They are not meant to be definitive; they are subject to all sorts of special assumptions and are necessarily related to the particular conditions of the time. But my main reasons for departing from the traditional theory go much deeper than this. They are of a highly general character and are meant to be definitive.

I sum up, therefore, the main grounds of my departure as follows:

(1) The orthodox theory assumes that we have a knowledge of the future of a kind quite different from that which we actually possess. This false rationalization follows the lines of the Benthamite calculus. The hypothesis of a calculable future leads to a wrong interpretation of the principles of behavior which the need for action compels us to adopt, and to an underestimation of the concealed factors of utter doubt, precariousness, hope and fear. The result has been a mistaken theory of the rate of interest. It is true that the necessity of equalizing the advantages of the choice between owning loans and assets requires that the rate of interest should be *equal* to the marginal efficiency of capital. But this does not tell us at what *level* the equality will be effective. The orthodox theory regards the marginal efficiency of capital as setting the pace. But the marginal efficiency of capital depends on the price of capital-assets; and since this price determines the rate of new investment, it is consistent in equilibrium with only one given level of money-income. Thus the marginal efficiency of capital is not determined, unless the level of money-income is given. In a system in which the level of money-income is capable of fluctuating, the orthodox theory is one equation short of what is required to give a solution. Undoubtedly the reason why the orthodox system has failed to discover this discrepancy is because it has always tacitly assumed that income is given, namely, at the level corresponding to the employment of all the available resources. In other words it is tacitly assuming that the monetary policy is such as to maintain the rate of

interest at that level which is compatible with full employment. It is, therefore, incapable of dealing with the general case where employment is liable to fluctuate. Thus, instead of the marginal efficiency of capital determining the rate of interest, it is truer (tho not a full statement of the case) to say that it is the rate of interest which determines the marginal efficiency of capital.

(2) The orthodox theory would by now have discovered the above defect, if it had not ignored the need for a theory of the supply and demand of output as a whole. I doubt if many modern economists really accept Say's Law that supply creates its own demand. But they have not been aware that they were tacitly assuming it. Thus the psychological law underlying the Multiplier has escaped notice. It has not been observed that the amount of consumption-goods which it pays entrepreneurs to produce is a function of the amount of investment-goods which it pays them to produce. The explanation is to be found, I suppose, in the tacit assumption that every individual spends the whole of his income either on consumption or on buying, directly or indirectly, newly produced capital goods. But, here again, whilst the older economists expressly believed this, I doubt if many contemporary economists really do believe it. They have discarded these older ideas without becoming aware of the consequences.

31. The Future*

JOHN MAYNARD KEYNES

Let us, for the sake of argument, suppose that a hundred years hence we are all of us, on the average, eight times better off in the economic sense than we are to-day. Assuredly there need be nothing here to surpise us.

Now it is true that the needs of human beings may seem to be insatiable. But they fall into two classes—those needs which are absolute in the sense that we feel them whatever the situation of our fellow human beings may be, and those which are relative in the sense that we feel them only if their satisfaction lifts us above, makes us feel superior to, our fellows. Needs of the second class, those which satisfy the desire for superiority, may indeed be insatiable; for the higher the general level, the higher still are they. But this is not so true of the absolute needs—a point may soon be reached, much sooner perhaps than we are all of us aware of, when these needs are satisfied in the sense that we prefer to devote our further energies to non-economic purposes.

Now for my conclusion, which you will find, I think, to become more and more startling to the imagination the longer you think about it.

I draw the conclusion that, assuming no important wars and no important increase in population, the *economic*

*Source: From The Collected Writings of John Maynard Keynes, volume 9, pp. 326-32, copyright © 1972 The Royal Economic Society. Reprinted by permission of Cambridge University Press.

problem may be solved, or be at least within sight of solution, within a hundred years. This means that the economic problem is not—if we look into the future—*the permanent problem of the human race.*

Why, you may ask, is this so startling? It is startling because—if, instead of looking into the future, we look into the past—we find that the economic problem, the struggle for subsistence, always has been hitherto the primary, most pressing problem of the human race—not only of the human race, but of the whole of the biological kingdom from the beginnings of life in its most primitive forms.

Thus we have been expressly evolved by nature—with all our impulses and deepest instincts—for the purpose of solving the economic problem. If the economic problem is solved, mankind will be deprived of its traditional purpose.

Will this be a benefit? If one believes at all in the real values of life, the prospect at least opens up the possibility of benefit. Yet I think with dread of the readjustment of the habits and instincts of the ordinary man, bred into him for countless generations, which he may be asked to discard within a few decades.

To use the language of to-day—must we not expect a general "nervous breakdown"? We already have a little experience of what I mean—a nervous breakdown of the sort which is already common enough in England and the United States amongst the wives of the well-to-do classes, unfortunate women, many of them, who have been deprived by their wealth of their traditional tasks and occupations—who cannot find it sufficiently amusing, when deprived of the spur of economic necessity, to cook and clean and mend, yet are quite unable to find anything more amusing.

To those who sweat for their daily bread leisure is a longed-for sweet—until they get it.

There is the traditional epitaph written for herself by the old charwoman:

Don't mourn for me, friends, don't weep for me never,
For I'm going to do nothing for ever and ever.

This was her heaven. Like others who look forward to leisure, she conceived how nice it would be to spend her time listening-in—for there was another couplet which occurred in her poem:

With psalms and sweet music the heavens'll be ringing,
But I shall have nothing to do with the singing.

Yet it will only be for those who have to do with the singing that life will be tolerable—and how few of us can sing!

Thus for the first time since his creation man will be faced with his real, his permanent problem—how to use his freedom from pressing economic cares, how to occupy the leisure, which science and compound interest will have won for him to live wisely and agreeably and well.

The strenuous purposeful moneymakers may carry all of us along with them into the lap of economic abundance. But it will be those peoples, who can keep alive, and cultivate into a fuller perfection, the art of life itself and do not sell themselves for the means of life, who will be able to enjoy the abundance when it comes.

Yet there is no country and no people, I think, who can look forward to the age of leisure and of abundance without a dread. For we have been trained too long to strive and not to enjoy. It is a fearful problem for the ordinary person, with no special talents, to occupy himself, especially if he no longer has roots in the soil or in custom or in the beloved conventions of a traditional society. To judge from the behaviour and the achievements of the wealthy classes to-day in any quarter of the world, the outlook is very depressing! For these are, so to speak, our advance guard—those who are spying out the promised land for the rest of us and pitching their camp there. For they have most of them failed disastrously, so it seems to me—those who have an independent income but no associations or duties or ties—to solve the problem which has been set them.

I feel sure that with a little more experience we shall use the new-found bounty of nature quite differently from the way in which the rich use it to-day, and will map out for ourselves a plan of life quite otherwise than theirs.

For many ages to come the old Adam will be so strong in us that everybody will need to do *some* work if he is to be contented. We shall do more things for ourselves than is usual with the rich to-day, only too glad to have small duties and tasks and routines. But beyond this, we shall endeavour to spread the bread thin on the butter—to make what work there is still to be done to be as widely shared as possible. Three-hour shifts or a fifteen-hour week may put off the problem for a great while. For three hours a day is quite enough to satisfy the old Adam in most of us!

There are changes in other spheres too which we must expect to come. When the accumulation of wealth is no longer of high social importance, there will be great changes in the code of morals. We shall be able to rid ourselves of many of the pseudo-moral principles which have hag-ridden us for two hundred years, by which we have exalted some of the most distasteful of human qualities into the position of the highest virtues. We shall be able to afford to dare to assess the money-motive at its true value. The love of money as a possession—as distinguished from the love of money as a means to the enjoyments and realities of life—will be recognised for what it is, a somewhat disgusting morbidity, one of those semi-criminal, semi-pathological propensities which one hands over with a shudder to the specialists in mental disease. All kinds of social customs and economic practices, affecting the distribution of wealth and of economic rewards and penalties, which we now maintain at all costs, however distasteful and unjust they may be in themselves, because they are tremendously useful in promoting the accumulation of capital, we shall then be free, at last, to discard.

Of course there will still be many people with intense, unsatisfied purposiveness who will blindly pursue wealth—unless they can find some plausible substitute. But the rest of us will no longer be under any obligation to applaud and encourage them. For we shall inquire more curiously than is safe to-day into the true character of this "purposiveness" with which in varying degrees Nature has endowed almost all of us. For purposiveness means that we are more concerned with the remote future results of our actions than with their own quality or their immediate effects on our own environment. The "purposive" man is always trying to secure a spurious and delusive immortality for his acts by pushing his interest in them forward into time. He does not love his cat, but his cat's kittens; nor, in truth, the kittens, but only the kittens' kittens, and so on forward for ever to the end of cat-dom. For him jam is not jam unless it is a case of jam to-morrow and never jam to-day. Thus by pushing his jam always forward into the future, he strives to secure for his act of boiling it an immortality.

Let me remind you of the Professor in *Sylvie and Bruno:*

"Only the tailor, sir, with your little bill," said a meek voice outside the door.

"Ah, well, I can soon settle *his* business," the Professor said to the children, "if you'll just wait a minute. How much is it, this year, my man?" The tailor had come in while he was speaking.

"Well, it's been a-doubling so many years, you see," the tailor replied, a little gruffly, "and I think I'd like the money now. It's two thousand pound, it is!"

"Oh, that's nothing!" the Professor carelessly remarked, feeling in his pocket, as if he always carried at least *that* amount about with him. "But wouldn't you like to wait just another year and make it *four* thousand? Just think how rich you'd be! Why, you might be a *king*, if you liked!"

"I don't know as I'd care about being a

king," the man said thoughtfully. "But it *dew* sound a powerful sight o' money! Well, I think I'll wait——"

"Of course you will!" said the Professor. "There's good sense in *you*, I see. Good-day to you, my man!"

"Will you ever have to pay him that four thousand pounds?" Sylvie asked as the door closed on the departing creditor.

"*Never*, my child!" the Professor replied emphatically. "He'll go on doubling it till he dies. You see, it's *always* worth while waiting another year to get twice as much money!"

Perhaps it is not an accident that the race which did most to bring the promise of immortality into the heart and essence of our religions has also done most for the principle of compound interest and particularly loves this most purposive of human institutions.

I see us free, therefore, to return to some of the most sure and certain principles of religion and traditional virtue—that avarice is a vice, that the exaction of usury is a misdemeanour, and the love of money is detestable, that those walk most truly in the paths of virtue and sane wisdom who take least thought for the morrow. We shall once more value ends above means and prefer the good to the useful. We shall honour those who can teach us how to pluck the hour and the day virtuously and well, the delightful people who are capable of taking direct enjoyment in things, the lilies of the field who toil not, neither do they spin.

But beware! The time for all this is not yet. For at least another hundred years we must pretend to ourselves and to every one that fair is foul and foul is fair; for foul is useful and fair is not. Avarice and usury and precaution must be our gods for a little longer still. For only they can lead us out of the tunnel of economic necessity into daylight.

I look forward, therefore, in days not so very remote, to the greatest change which has ever occurred in the material environment of life for human beings in the aggregate. But, of course, it will all happen gradually, not as a catastrophe. Indeed, it has already begun. The course of affairs will simply be that there will be ever larger and larger classes and groups of people from whom problems of economic necessity have been practically removed. The critical difference will be realised when this condition has become so general that the nature of one's duty to one's neighbour is changed. For it will remain reasonable to be economically purposive for others after it has ceased to be reasonable for oneself.

The *pace* at which we can reach our destination of economic bliss will be governed by four things—our power to control population, our determination to avoid wars and civil dissensions, our willingness to entrust to science the direction of those matters which are properly the concern of science, and the rate of accumulation as fixed by the margin between our production and our consumption; of which the last will easily look after itself, given the first three.

Meanwhile there will be no harm in making mild preparations for our destiny, in encouraging, and experimenting in, the arts of life as well as the activities of purpose.

But, chiefly, do not let us overestimate the importance of the economic problem, or sacrifice to its supposed necessities other matters of greater and more permanent significance. It should be a matter for specialists—like dentistry. If economists could manage to get themselves thought of as humble, competent people, on a level with dentists, that would be splendid!

32. Mr. Keynes and the "Classics"; A Suggested Interpretation*

JOHN R. HICKS

I

It will be admitted by the least charitable reader that the entertainment value of Mr. Keynes' *General Theory of Employment* is considerably enhanced by its satiric aspect. But it is also clear that many readers have been left very bewildered by this Dunciad. Even if they are convinced by Mr. Keynes' arguments and humbly acknowledge themselves to have been "classical economists" in the past, they find it hard to remember that they believed in their unregenerate days the things Mr. Keynes says they believed. And there are no doubt others who find their historic doubts a stumbling block, which prevents them from getting as much illumination from the positive theory as they might otherwise have got.

One of the main reasons for this situation is undoubtedly to be found in the fact that Mr. Keynes takes as typical of "Classical economics" the later writings of Professor Pigou, particularly *The Theory of Unemployment*. Now *The Theory of Unemployment* is a fairly new book, and an exceedingly difficult book; so that it is safe to say that it has not yet made much impression on the ordinary teaching of economics. To most people its doctrines seem quite as strange and novel as the doctrines of Mr. Keynes himself; so that to be told that he has believed these things himself leaves the ordinary economist quite bewildered.

For example, Professor Pigou's theory runs, to a quite amazing extent, in real terms. Not only is his theory a theory of real wages and unemployment; but numbers of problems which anyone else would have preferred to investigate in money terms are investigated by Professor Pigou in terms of "wage-goods." The ordinary classical economist has no part in this *tour de force*.

But if, on behalf of the ordinary classical economist, we declare that he would have preferred to investigate many of those problems in money terms, Mr. Keynes will reply that there is no classical theory of money wages and employment. It is quite true that such a theory cannot easily be found in the textbooks. But this is only because most of the textbooks were written at a time when general changes in money wages in a closed system did not present an important problem. There can be little doubt that most economists have thought that they had a pretty fair idea of what the relation between money wages and employment actually was.

In these circumstances, it seems worth while to try to construct a typical "classical" theory, built on an earlier and cruder model than Professor Pigou's. If we can construct such a theory, and show that it does give results which have in fact been commonly taken for granted, but which do not agree with Mr. Keynes' conclusions, then we shall at last have a satisfactory basis of comparison. We may hope to

Source: From *Econometrica*, vol. 5 (1937), pp. 147-59. Reprinted by permission of The Econometric Society.

be able to isolate Mr. Keynes' innovations, and so to discover what are the real issues in dispute.

Since our purpose is comparison, I shall try to set out my typical classical theory in a form similar to that in which Mr. Keynes sets out his own theory; and I shall leave out of account all secondary complications which do not bear closely upon this special question in hand. Thus I assume that I am dealing with a short period in which the quantity of physical equipment of all kinds available can be taken as fixed. I assume homogeneous labour. I assume further that depreciation can be neglected, so that the output of investment goods corresponds to new investment. This is a dangerous simplification, but the important issues raised by Mr. Keynes in his chapter on user cost are irrelevant for our purposes.

Let us begin by assuming that w, the rate of money wages per head, can be taken as given.

Let x, y, be the outputs of investment goods and consumption goods respectively, and N_x, N_y, be the numbers of men employed in producing them. Since the amount of physical equipment specialised to each industry is given, $x = f_x(N_x)$ and $y = f_y(N_y)$, where f_x, f_y, are *given* functions.

Let M be the *given* quantity of money.

It is desired to determine N_x and N_y.

First, the price-level of investment goods = their marginal cost = $w(dN_x/dx)$. And the price-level of consumption goods = their marginal cost = $w(dN_y/dy)$.

Income earned in investment trades (value of investment, or simply Investment) = $wx(dN_x/dx)$. Call this I_x.

Income earned in consumption trades = $wy(dN_y/dy)$.

Total Income = $wx(dN_x/dx) + wy(dN_y/dy)$. Call this I.

I_x is therefore a given function of N_x, I of N_x and N_y. Once I and I_x are determined, N_x and N_y can be determined.

Now let us assume the "Cambridge Quantity equation"—that there is some definite relation between Income and the demand for money. Then, approximately, and apart from the fact that the demand for money may depend not only upon total Income, but also upon its distribution between people with relatively large and relatively small demands for balances, we can write

$$M = kI.$$

As soon as k is given, total Income is therefore determined.

In order to determine I_x, we need two equations. One tells us that the amount of investment (looked at as demand for capital) depends upon the rate of interest:

$$I_x = C(i).$$

This is what becomes the marginal-efficiency-of-capital schedule in Mr. Keynes' work.

Further, Investment = Saving. And saving depends upon the rate of interest and, if you like, Income. $\therefore$ $I_x = S(i, I)$. (Since, however, Income is already determined, we do not need to bother about inserting Income here unless we choose.)

Taking them as a system, however, we have three fundamental equations,

$$M = kI, \ I_x = C(i), \ I_x = S(i, I),$$

to determine three unknowns, I, I_x, i. As we have found earlier, N_x and N_y can be determined from I and I_x. Total employment, $N_x + N_y$, is therefore determined.

Let us consider some properties of this system. It follows directly from the first equation that as soon as k and M are given, I is completely determined; that is to say, total income depends directly upon the quantity of money. Total employment, however, is not necessarily determined at once from income, since it will usually depend to some extent upon the proportion of income saved, and thus upon the way production is divided between investment and consumption-goods trades. (If it so happened that the elasticities of supply were the same in each of these trades, then a shifting of demand between them would produce compensating movements in N_x and N_y, and consequently no change in total employment.)

An increase in the inducement to invest (i.e., a rightward movement of the schedule of the marginal efficiency of capital, which we have written as $C(i)$) will tend to raise the rate of interest, and so to affect saving. If the amount of saving rises, the amount of investment will rise too; labour will be employed more in the investment trades, less in the consumption trades; this will increase total employment if the elasticity of supply in the investment trades is greater than that in the consumption-goods trades—diminish it if vice versa.

An increase in the supply of money will necessarily raise total income, for people will increase their spending and lending until incomes have risen sufficiently to restore k to its former level. The rise in income will tend to increase employment, both in making consumption goods and in making investment goods. The total effect on employment depends upon the ratio between the expansions of these industries; and that depends upon the proportion of their increased incomes people desire to save, which also governs the rate of interest.

So far we have assumed the rate of money wages to be given; but so long as we assume that k is independent of the level of wages, there is no difficulty about this problem either. A rise in the rate of money wages will necessarily diminish employment and raise real wages. For an unchanged money income cannot continue to buy an unchanged quantity of goods at a higher price-level; and, unless the price-level rises, the prices of goods will not cover their marginal costs. There must therefore be a fall in employment; as employment falls, marginal costs in terms of labour will diminish and therefore real wages rise. (Since a change in money wages is always accompanied by a change in real wages in the same direction, if not in the same proportion, no harm will be done, and some advantage will perhaps be secured, if one prefers to work in terms of real wages. Naturally most "classical economists" have taken this line.)

I think it will be agreed that we have here a quite reasonably consistent theory, and a theory which is also consistent with the pronouncements of a recognizable group of economists. Admittedly it follows from this theory that you may be able to increase employment by direct inflation; but whether or not you decide to favour that policy still depends upon your judgment about the probable reaction on wages, and also—in a national area—upon your views about the international standard.

Historically, this theory descends from Ricardo, though it is not actually Ricardian; it is probably more or less the theory that was held by Marshall. But with Marshall it was already beginning to be qualified in important ways; his successors have qualified it still further. What Mr. Keynes has done is to lay enormous emphasis on the qualifications, so that they almost blot out the original theory. Let us follow out this process of development.

II

When a theory like the "classical" theory we have just described is applied to the analysis of industrial fluctuations, it gets into difficulties in several ways. It is evident that total money income experiences great variations in the course of a trade cycle, and the classical theory can only explain these by variations in M or in k, or, as a third and last alternative, by changes in distribution.

(1) Variation in M is simplest and most obvious, and has been relied on to a large extent. But the variations in M that are traceable during a trade cycle are variations that take place through the banks—they are variations in bank loans; if we are to rely on them it is urgently necessary for us to explain the connection between the supply of bank money and the rate of interest. This can be done roughly by thinking of banks as persons who are strongly inclined to

pass on money by lending rather than spending it. Their action therefore tends at first to lower interest rates, and only afterwards, when the money passes into the hands of spenders, to raise prices and incomes.

> The new currency, or the increase of currency, goes, not to private persons, but to the banking centers; and therefore, it increases the willingness of lenders to lend in the first instance, and lowers the rate of discount. But it afterwards raises prices; and therefore it tends to increase discount.[1]

This is superficially satisfactory; but if we endeavoured to give a more precise account of this process we should soon get into difficulties. What determines the amount of money needed to produce a given fall in the rate of interest? What determines the length of time for which the low rate will last? These are not easy questions to answer.

(2) In so far as we rely upon changes in k, we can also do well enough up to a point. Changes in k can be related to changes in confidence, and it is realistic to hold that the rising prices of a boom occur because optimism encourages a reduction in balances; the falling prices of a slump because pessimism and uncertainty dictate an increase. But as soon as we take this step it becomes natural to ask whether k has not abdicated its status as an independent variable, and has not become liable to be influenced by others among the variables in our fundamental equations.

(3) This last consideration is powerfully supported by another, of more purely theoretical character. On grounds of pure value theory, it is evident that the direct sacrifice made by a person who holds a stock of money is a sacrifice of interest; and it is hard to believe that the marginal principle does not operate at all in this field. As Lavington put it:

> The quantity of resources which (an individual) holds in the form of money will be such that the unit of money which is just and only just worth while holding in this form yields him a return of convenience and security equal to the yield of satisfaction derived from the marginal unit spent on consumables, and equal also to the net rate of interest.[2]

The demand for money depends upon the rate of interest! The stage is set for Mr. Keynes.

As against the three equations of the classical theory,

$$M = kI, \quad I_x = C(i), \quad I_x = S(i,I),$$

Mr. Keynes begins with three equations,

$$M = L(i), \quad I_x = C(i), \quad I_x = S(I).$$

These differ from the classical equations in two ways. On the one hand, the demand for money is conceived as depending upon the rate of interest (Liquidity Preference). On the other hand, any possible influence of the rate of interest on the amount saved out of a given income is neglected. Although it means that the third equation becomes the multiplier equation, which performs such queer tricks, nevertheless this second amendment is a mere simplification, and ultimately insignificant.[3] It is the liquidity preference doctrine which is vital.

For it is now the rate of interest, not income, which is determined by the quantity of money. The rate of interest set against the schedule of the marginal efficiency of capital determines the value of investment; that determines income by the multiplier. Then the volume of employment (at given wage-rates) is determined by the value of investment and of income which is not saved but spent upon consumption goods.

It is this system of equations which yields the startling conclusion, that an increase in the inducement to invest, or in the propensity to consume, will not tend to raise the rate of interest, but only to increase employment. In spite of this, however, and in spite of the fact that quite a large part of the argument runs in terms of this system, and this system alone, *it is not the General Theory*. We may call it, if we like, Mr. Keynes' *special theory*. The General Theory is something appreciably more orthodox.

Like Lavington and Professor Pigou, Mr. Keynes does not in the end believe that the demand for money can be determined by one variable alone—not even the rate of interest. He lays more stress on it than they did, but neither for him nor for them can it be the only variable to be considered. The dependence of the demand for money on interest does not, in the end, do more than qualify the old dependence on income. However much stress we lay upon the "speculative motive," the "transactions" motive must always come in as well.

Consequently we have for the General Theory

$$M = L(I,i), \ I_x = C(i), \ I_x = S(I).$$

With this revision, Mr. Keynes takes a big step back to Marshallian orthodoxy, and his theory becomes hard to distinguish from the revised and qualified Marshallian theories, which, as we have seen, are not new. Is there really any difference between them, or is the whole thing a sham fight? Let us have recourse to a diagram (Figure 1).

Against a given quantity of money, the first equation, $M = L(I, i)$, gives us a relation between Income (I) and the rate of interest (i). This can be drawn out as a curve (LL) which will slope upwards, since an increase in income tends to raise the demand for money, and an increase in the rate of interest tends to lower it. Further, the second two equations taken together give us another relation between Income and interest. (The marginal-efficiency-of-capital schedule determines the value of investment at any given rate of interest, and the multiplier tells us what level of income will be necessary to make savings equal to that value of investment.) The curve IS can therefore be drawn showing the relation between Income and interest which must be maintained in order to make saving equal to investment.

Income and the rate of interest are now determined together at P, the point of intersection of the curves LL and IS. They are determined together; just as price and output are determined together in the modern theory of demand and supply. Indeed, Mr. Keynes' innovation is closely parallel, in this respect, to the innovation of the marginalists. The quantity theory tries to determine income without interest, just as the labour theory of value tried to determine price without output; each has to give place to a theory recognising a higher degree of interdependence.

III

But if this is the real "General Theory," how does Mr. Keynes come to make his remarks about an increase in the inducement to invest not raising the rate of interest? It would appear from our diagram that a rise in the marginal-efficiency-of-capital schedule must raise the curve IS; and, therefore, although it will raise Income and employment, it will also raise the rate of interest.

This brings us to what, from many points of view, is the most important thing in Mr. Keynes' book. It is not only possible to show that a given supply of

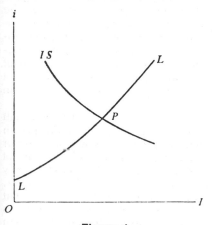

Figure 1

money determines a certain relation between Income and interest (which we have expressed by the curve *LL*); it is also possible to say something about the shape of the curve. It will probably tend to be nearly horizontal on the left, and nearly vertical on the right. This is because there is (1) some minimum below which the rate of interest is unlikely to go, and (though Mr. Keynes does not stress this) there is (2) a maximum to the level of income which can possibly be financed with a given amount of money. If we like we can think of the curve as approaching these limits asymptotically (Figure 2).

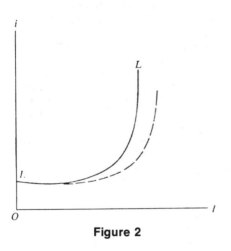

Figure 2

Therefore, if the curve *IS* lies well to the right (either because of a strong inducement to invest or a strong propensity to consume), *P* will lie upon that part of the curve which is decidedly upward sloping, and the classical theory will be a good approximation, needing no more than the qualification which it has in fact received at the hands of the later Marshallians. An increase in the inducement to invest will raise the rate of interest, as in the classical theory, but it will also have some subsidiary effect in raising income, and therefore employment as well. (Mr. Keynes in 1936 is not the first Cambridge economist to

have a temperate faith in Public Works.) But if the point *P* lies to the left of the *LL* curve, then the *special* form of Mr. Keynes' theory becomes valid. A rise in the schedule of the marginal efficiency of capital only increases employment, and does not raise the rate of interest at all. We are completely out of touch with the classical world.

The demonstration of this minimum is thus of central importance. It is so important that I shall venture to paraphrase the proof, setting it out in a rather different way from that adopted by Mr. Keynes.[4]

If the costs of holding money can be neglected, it will always be profitable to hold money rather than lend it out, if the rate of interest is not greater than zero. Consequently the rate of interest must always be positive. In an extreme case, the shortest short-term rate may perhaps be nearly zero. But if so, the long-term rate must lie above it, for the long rate has to allow for the risk that the short rate may rise during the currency of the loan, and it should be observed that the short rate can only rise, it cannot fall.[5] This does not only mean that the long rate must be a sort of average of the probable short rates over its duration, and that this average must lie above the current short rate. There is also the more important risk to be considered, that the lender on long term may desire to have cash before the agreed date of repayment, and then, if the short rate has risen meanwhile, he may be involved in a substantial capital loss. It is this last risk which provides Mr. Keynes' "speculative motive" and which ensures that the rate for loans of indefinite duration (which he always has in mind as *the* rate of interest) cannot fall very near zero.[6]

It should be observed that this minimum to the rate of interest applies not only to one curve *LL* (drawn to correspond to a particular quantity of money) but to any such curve. If the supply of money is increased, the curve *LL* moves to the right (as the dotted curve in Figure 2), but the horizontal parts of the curve are almost the same. Therefore, again, it is this doldrum to the left of the diagram which upsets the classical theory. If *IS* lies to the right, then we can indeed increase employment by increasing the quantity of money; but if *IS* lies to the left, we cannot do so; merely monetary means will not force down the rate of interest any further.

So the General Theory of Employment is the Economics of Depression.

IV

In order to elucidate the relation between Mr. Keynes and the "Classics," we have invented a little apparatus. It does not appear that we have exhausted the uses of that apparatus, so let us conclude by giving it a little run on its own.

With that apparatus at our disposal, we are no longer obliged to make certain simplifications which Mr. Keynes makes in his exposition. We can reinsert the missing *i* in the third equation, and allow for any possible effect of the rate of interest upon saving; and, what is much more important, we can call in question the sole dependence of investment upon the rate of interest, which looks rather suspicious in the second equation. Mathematical elegance would suggest that we ought to have *I* and *i* in all three equations, if the theory is to be really General. Why not have them there like this:

$$M = L(I,i), \; I_x = C(I,i), \; I_x = S(I,i)?$$

Once we raise the question of Income in the second equation, it is clear that it has a very good claim to be inserted. Mr. Keynes is in fact only enabled to leave it out at all plausibly by his device of measuring everything in "wage-units," which means that he allows for changes in the marginal-efficiency-of-capital schedule when there is a change in the level of money wages, but that other changes in Income are deemed not to affect the curve, or at least not in the same immediate manner. But why

draw this distinction? Surely there is every reason to suppose that an increase in the demand for consumers' goods, arising from an increase in employment, will often directly stimulate an increase in investment, at least as soon as an expectation develops that the increased demand will continue. If this is so, we ought to include *I* in the second equation, though it must be confessed that the effect of *I* on the marginal efficiency of capital will be fitful and irregular.

The Generalized General Theory can then be set out in this way. Assume first of all a given total money Income. Draw a curve *CC* showing the marginal efficiency of capital (in money terms) at that given Income; a curve *SS* showing the supply curve of saving at that *given* Income (Figure 3). Their intersection will determine the rate of interest which makes savings equal to investment at that level of income. This we may call the "investment rate."

If Income rises, the curve *SS* will move to the right; probably *CC* will move to the right too. If *SS* moves more than *CC*, the investment rate of interest will fall; if *CC* more than *SS*, it will rise. (How much it rises and falls, however, depends upon the elasticities of the *CC* and *SS* curves.)

The *IS* curve (drawn on a separate diagram) now shows the relation between Income and the corresponding investment rate of interest. It has to be confronted (as in our earlier constructions) with an *LL* curve showing the relation between Income and the "money" rate of interest; only we can now generalise our *LL* curve a little. Instead of assuming, as before, that the supply of money is given, we can assume that there is a given monetary system—that up to a point, but only up to a point, monetary authorities will prefer to create new money rather than allow interest rates to rise. Such a generalised *LL* curve will then slope upwards only gradually—the elasticity of the curve depending on the elasticity of the monetary system (in the ordinary monetary sense).

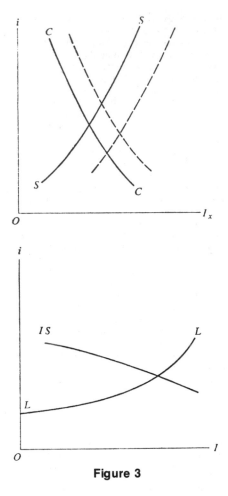

Figure 3

As before, Income and interest are determined where the IS and LL curves intersect—where the investment rate of interest equals the money rate. Any change in the inducement to invest or the propensity to consume will shift the IS curve; any change in liquidity preference or monetary policy will shift the LL curve. If, as the result of such a change, the investment rate is raised above the money rate, Income will tend to rise; in the opposite case, Income will tend to fall; the extent to which Income rises or falls depends on the elasticities of the curves.[7]

When generalised in this way, Mr. Keynes' theory begins to look very like Wicksell's; this is of course hardly surprising.[8] There is indeed one special case where it fits Wicksell's construction absolutely. If there is "full employment" in the sense that any rise in Income immediately calls forth a rise in money wage rates; then it is *possible* that the CC and SS curves may be moved to the right to exactly the same extent, so that IS is horizontal. (I say possible, because it is not unlikely, in fact, that the rise in the wage level may create a presumption that wages will rise again later on; if so, CC will probably be shifted more than SS, so that IS will be upward sloping.) However that may be, if IS is horizontal, we do have a perfectly Wicksellian construction;[9] the investment rate becomes Wicksell's *natural rate*, for in this case it may be thought of as determined by real causes; if there is a perfectly elastic monetary system, and the money rate is fixed below the natural rate, there is cumulative inflation; cumulative deflation if it is fixed above.

This, however, is now seen to be only one special case; we can use our construction to harbour much wider possibilities. If there is a great deal of unemployment, it is very likely that $\partial C/\partial I$ will be quite small; in that case IS can be relied upon to slope downwards. This is the sort of Slump Economics with which Mr. Keynes is largely concerned. But one cannot escape the impression that there may be other conditions when expectations are tinder, when a slight inflationary tendency lights them up very easily. Then $\partial C/\partial I$ may be large and an increase in Income tend to *raise* the investment rate of interest. In these circumstances, the situation is unstable at *any* given money rate; it is only an imperfectly elastic monetary system—a rising LL curve—that can prevent the situation getting out of hand altogether.

These, then, are a few of the things we can get out of our skeleton apparatus. But even if it may claim to be a slight extension of Mr. Keynes' similar skeleton, it remains a terribly rough and ready sort of affair. In particular, the concept of "Income" is worked monstrously hard; most of our curves are not really determinate unless something is said about the distribution of Income as well as its magnitude. Indeed, what they express is something like a relation between the price-system and the system of interest rates; and you cannot get that into a curve. Further, all sorts of questions about depreciation have been neglected; and all sorts of questions about the timing of the processes under consideration.

The General Theory of Employment is a useful book; but it is neither the beginning nor the end of Dynamic Economics.

NOTES

1. Marshall, Money, Credit, and Commerce, p. 257.

2. Lavington, English Capital Market, 1921, p. 30. See also Pigou, "The Exchange-value of Legal-tender Money," in Essays in Applied Economics, 1922, pp. 179-181.

3. This can be readily seen if we consider the equations

$$M = kI, \ I_x = C(i), \ I_x = S(I),$$

which embody Mr. Keynes' second amendment without his first. The third equation is already the multiplier equation, but the multiplier is shorn of his wings. For since I still depends only on M, I_x depends only on M, and it is impossible to increase investment without increasing the willingness to save or the quantity of money. The system thus generated is therefore identical with that which, a few years ago, used to be called the "Treasury View." But Liquidity Preference

transports us from the "Treasury View" to the "General Theory of Employment."

4. Keynes, General Theory, pp. 201-202.

5. It is just conceivable that people might become so used to the idea of very low short rates that they would not be much impressed by this risk; but it is very unlikely. For the short rate may rise, either because trade improves, and income expands; or because trade gets worse, and the desire for liquidity increases. I doubt whether a monetary system so elastic as to rule out both of these possibilities is really thinkable.

6. Nevertheless something more than the "speculative motive" is needed to account for the system of interest rates. The shortest of all short rates must equal the relative valuation, at the margin, of money and such a bill; and the bill stands at a discount mainly because of the "convenience and security" of holding money—the inconvenience which may possibly be caused by not having cash immediately available. It is the chance that you may want to discount the bill which matters, not the chance that you will then have to discount it on unfavourable terms. The "precautionary motive," not the "speculative motive," is here dominant. But the prospective terms of rediscounting are vital, when it comes to the difference between short and long rates.

7. Since $C(I,i)$

$$\frac{dI}{di} = - \frac{\partial S/\partial i - \partial C/\partial i}{\partial S/\partial I - \partial C/\partial I}$$

The savings investment market will not be stable unless $\partial S/\partial i + (-\partial C/\partial i)$ is positive. I think we may assume that this condition is fulfilled.

If $\partial S/\partial i$ is positive, $\partial C/\partial i$ negative, $\partial S/\partial I$ and $\partial C/\partial I$ positive (the most probable state of affairs), we can say that the IS curve will be more elastic, the greater the elasticities of the CC and SS curves, and the larger is $\partial C/\partial I$ relatively to $\partial S/\partial I$. When $\partial C/\partial I > \partial S/\partial I$, the IS curve is upward sloping.

8. Cf. Keynes, General Theory, p. 242.

9. Cf. Myrdal, "Gleichgewichtsbegriff," in Beitrage zur Geldtheorie, ed. Hayek.

33. Value and Capital*

JOHN R. HICKS

UTILITY AND PREFERENCE

1. The pure theory of consumer's demand, which occupied a good deal of the attention of Marshall and his contemporaries, has received far less notice in the present century. The third book of Marshall's *Principles* still remains the last word on the subject so far as books written in English are concerned. Now Marshall's theory of demand is no doubt admirable, but it is remarkable that it has remained so long upon such an unquestioned eminence. This would be explicable if there were really no more to say on the subject, and if every step in Marshall's analysis were beyond dispute. But this is clearly not the case; several writers have felt very uncomfortable about Marshall's treatment, and it is actually the first step, on which everything else depends, which is the most dubious.

Let us first remind ourselves of the bare outline of Marshall's main argument. A consumer with a given money income is confronted with a market for consumption goods, on which the prices of those goods are already determined; the question is, How will he divide his expenditure among the different goods? It is supposed, for convenience, that the goods are available in very small units. It is assumed that the consumer derives from the goods he purchases so much "utility," the amount of utility being a function of the quantities of goods acquired; and that he will spend his income in such a way as to bring in the maximum possible amount of utility. But utility will be maximized when the marginal unit of expenditure in each direction brings in the same increment of utility. For, if this is so, a transference of expenditure from one direction to another will involve a greater loss of utility in the direction where expenditure is reduced than will be compensated by the gain in utility in the direction where expenditure is increased (from the principle of diminishing marginal utility). Total utility must therefore be diminished, whatever transfer is made. Since, with small units, the differences between the marginal utilities of two successive units of a commodity may be neglected, we can express the conclusion in another way: the marginal utilities of the various commodities bought must be proportional to their prices.

Marshall's argument therefore proceeds from the notion of maximizing total utility, by way of the law of diminishing marginal utility, to the conclusion that the marginal utilities of commodities bought must be proportional to their prices.

But now what is this "utility" which the consumer maximizes? And what is the exact basis for the law of diminishing marginal utility? Marshall leaves one uncomfortable on these subjects. However, further light on them was thrown by Pareto.

2. Pareto's *Manuel d'économie*

---

*Source: From *Value and Capital* by J. R. Hicks (2nd ed., 1946), part 1, chapters 1 and 2; part 3, chapter 14. Reprinted by permission of Oxford University Press. Most footnotes deleted; others renumbered.

politique (1909) has to be reckoned as the other classical treatment of the theory of consumer's demand, from which any modern investigation must begin. It is not that Pareto's book, as a whole, is at all comparable with Marshall's. The *Manuel* purports to be a sort of general *Principles*; but most problems are treated by it quite superficially, while its famous theory of General Equilibrium is nothing else but a more elegant restatement of the doctrines of Walras. However, on this particular matter of utility theory Pareto was a specialist, and his investigations well deserve attention. Since they are not very familiar to English readers, I shall summarize the relevant arguments rather carefully.

Pareto started off, originally, from the same utility theory as Marshall; the argument we have just summarized would have been quite acceptable to him also in the first stage of the development of his ideas. But instead of proceeding afterwards, as Marshall did, to concentrate attention upon the demand for a single commodity (and thus to investigate the relation between the curve of diminishing marginal utility and the demand curve), Pareto turned his attention to the problem of related—complementary and competitive—goods. Here he made an extension of the earlier analysis; or rather, something which started as an extension but ended as a revolution.

For the purpose of studying related goods, Pareto took over from Edgeworth a geometrical device—the Indifference Curve. When we are concerned, like Marshall, with one commodity only, we can draw a total utility curve, measuring amounts of that commodity along one axis, and total amounts of utility derived from those various amounts of commodity along the other axis. Just in the same way, when we are interested in two commodities, we can draw a utility surface. Measuring quantities of the two commodities X and Y along two horizontal axes, we get a diagram in which

any point P represents a collection of given quantities (PM and PN) of the two commodities. From every such point, we can erect an ordinate in a third dimension whose length represents the amount of utility derived from that particular collection of quantities. Joining the tops of these ordinates, we get a "utility surface" (Figure 1).

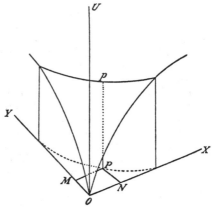

Figure 1

In principle, this is simple enough; but three-dimensional diagrams are awkward things to handle. Fortunately, having once visited the third dimension, we need not stay there. The third dimension can be eliminated, and we can return to two.

Instead of using a three-dimensional model, we can use a map (Figure 2). Keeping quantities of the two commodities X and Y along the two axes, we can mark off on the horizontal diagram the contour lines of the utility surface (the broken line in Figure 1). These are the indifference curves. They join all those points which correspond to the same height in the third dimension, that is, to the same total utility. If P and P' are on the same indifference curve, that means that the total utility derived from having PM and PN is the same as that derived from having P'M' and P'N'. If P'' is on a higher indifference curve than

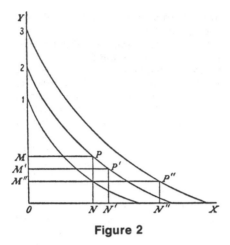

Figure 2

P (the curves will have to be numbered so as to distinguish higher from lower), then P"M" and P"N" will give a higher total utility than PM and PN.

What will be the shape of these indifference curves? So long as each commodity has a positive marginal utility, the indifference curves must slope downwards to the right. For if X has a positive marginal utility, an increase in the quantity of X, unaccompanied by any change in the quantity of Y (that is to say, a simple movement to the right on the diagram), must increase total utility, and so bring us on to a higher indifference curve. Similarly, a simple movement upwards must lead on to a higher indifference curve. It is only possible to stay on the same indifference curve if these movements are compensated—X increased and Y diminished, or X diminished and Y increased. The curves must therefore slope downwards to the right.

The slope of the curve passing through any point P has indeed a very definite and important meaning. It is the amount of Y which is needed by the individual in order to compensate him for the loss of a small unit of X. Now the gain in utility got by gaining such an amount of Y equals amount of Y gained × marginal utility of Y; the loss in utility

got from losing the corresponding amount of X equals amount of X lost × marginal utility of X (so long as the quantities are small). Therefore, since the gain equals the loss, the slope of the curve

$$= \frac{\text{amount of Y gained}}{\text{amount of X lost}} = \frac{\text{marginal utility of X}}{\text{marginal utility of Y}}.$$

The slope of the curve passing through P measures the ratio of the marginal utility of X to the marginal utility of Y, when the individual has quantities PM and PN of X and Y respectively.

Have we any further information about the shapes of the curves? There ought, it would seem, to be some way of translating into terms of this diagram the principle of diminishing marginal utility. At first sight, it looks as if such a translation were possible. As one moves along an indifference curve one gets more X and less Y. The increase in X diminishes the marginal utility of X, the diminution in Y increases the marginal utility of Y. On both grounds, therefore, the slope of the curve must diminish. Falling curves, whose slope diminishes as we move to the right, will be convex to the origin, as they have been drawn in the diagram.

But does this quite necessarily follow? As far as the direct effects just taken into account are concerned, it must; but there are other indirect effects to take into account too. The increase in X may affect not only the marginal utility of X, it may also affect the marginal utility of Y. With such related goods the above argument does not necessarily follow. Suppose that the increase in X lowers the marginal utility of Y, and the diminution in Y raises the marginal utility of X; and that these cross-effects are considerable. Then the cross-effects may actually offset the direct effects, and a movement along the indifference curve to the right may actually increase the slope of the curve. This is no doubt a very queer case, but it is consistent with diminishing marginal utility. Diminishing marginal utility and convexity of the indifference curves are not the same thing.

3. We come now to the really remarkable thing about indifference curves—the discovery which shunted Pareto's theory on to a different line from Marshall's, and opened a way to new results of wide economic significance.

Suppose that we have a consumer with a given money income, who is spending the whole of that income upon the two commodities X and Y, no others entering into the picture. Suppose that the prices of those commodities are given on the market. Then we can read off the amounts that he will buy directly from his indifference map, without any information about the amounts of utility he derives from the goods.

Mark off a length OL along the X-axis (Figure 3), representing the amount of X which he could buy if he spent all of his income upon X; and an amount OM on the Y-axis, representing the amount of Y he could buy if he spent all his income upon Y; and join LM. Then any point on the line LM represents a pair of quantities of the two commodities which he could buy out of his income. Starting from L, in order to acquire some Y, he will have to give up X in the proportion indicated by the ratio of their prices;

and the price-ratio is indicated by the slope of the line LM.

Through any point on the line LM there will pass an indifference curve; but usually the line LM will intersect the indifference curve. If this happens the point cannot be one of equilibrium. For, by moving along the line LM in one direction or the other, the consumer will always be able to get on to a higher indifference curve, which gives him greater utility. He is therefore not maximizing his utility at that particular point.

It is only when the line LM touches an indifference curve that utility will be maximized. For at a point of tangency, the consumer will get on to a lower indifference curve if he moves in either direction.

Tangency between the price-line and an indifference curve is the expression, in terms of indifference curves, of the proportionality between marginal utilities and prices.

4. Thus we can translate the marginal utility theory into terms of indifference curves; but, having done that, we have accomplished something more remarkable than a mere translation. For, in the process of translation, we have left behind some of the original data; and yet we have arrived at the desired result all the same.

In order to determine the quantities of goods which an individual will buy at given prices, Marshall's theory implies that we must know his utility surface; Pareto's theory only assumes that we must know his indifference map. And that conveys less information than the utility surface. It only tells us that the individual prefers one particular collection of goods to another particular collection; it does not tell us, as the utility surface purports to do, *by how much* the first collection is preferred to the second.

The numbers which we give to the indifference curves are indeed wholly arbitrary; it will be convenient for them to rise as we go on to higher curves, but

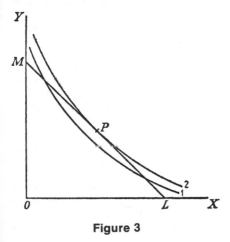

Figure 3

the numbers can be 1, 2, 3, 4 . . . , 1, 2, 4, 7 . . . , 1, 2, 7, 10 . . . , or any ascending series we like to take.

Pareto's little piece of geometry thus resulted in a conclusion of wide methodological importance. It is necessary, in any theory of value, to be able to define just what we mean by a consumer of "given wants" or "given tastes". In Marshall's theory (like that of Jevons, and Walras, and the Austrians) "given wants" is interpreted as meaning a given utility function, a given intensity of desire for any particular collection of goods. This assumption has made many people uncomfortable, and it appears from Pareto's work that it is not a necessary assumption at all. "Given wants" can be quite adequately defined as a given *scale of preferences;* we need only suppose that the consumer has a preference for one collection of goods rather than another, not that there is ever any sense in saying that he desires the one collection 5 per cent more than the other, or anything like that.

Now of course this does not mean that if any one has other ground for supposing that there exists some suitable quantitative measure of utility, or satisfaction, or desiredness, there is anything in the above argument to set against it. If one is a utilitarian in philosophy, one has a perfect right to be a utilitarian in one's economics. But if one is not (and few people are utilitarians nowadays), one also has the right to an economics free of utilitarian assumptions.

From this point of view, Pareto's discovery only opens a door, which we can enter or not as we feel inclined. But from the technical economic point of view there are strong reasons for supposing that we ought to enter it. The quantitative concept of utility is not necessary in order to explain market phenomena. Therefore, on the principle of Occam's razor, it is better to do without it. For it is not, in practice, a matter of indifference if a theory contains unnecessary entities. Such entities are irrelevant to the problem in hand, and their presence is likely to obscure the vision. How important this is can only be shown by experience; I shall hope to convince the reader that it is of some considerable importance in this case.

5. Acting on this principle, we have now to inquire whether a full theory of consumer's demand at least as thoroughgoing as Marshall's cannot be built up from the assumption of a *scale of preference.* In constructing such a theory it will be necessary every time to reject any concept which is at all dependent upon quantitative utility, so that it cannot be derived from the indifference map alone. We start off from the indifference map alone; nothing more can be allowed.

In undertaking this reconsideration we lose the help of Pareto; for even after Pareto had established his great proposition, he continued to use concepts derived from the earlier set of ideas. The reason was, perhaps, that he did not take the trouble to work his earlier conclusions in the light of a proposition which he only reached at a rather late stage of his work in economics. However that may be, he missed an opportunity.

The first person to take the opportunity was the Russian economist and statistician Slutsky, in an article published in the Italian *Giornale degli Economisti* in 1915. The theory to be set out in this chapter and the two following is essentially Slutsky's; although the exposition is modified by the fact that I never saw Slutsky's work until my own was very far advanced, and some time after the substance of these chapters had been published in *Economica* by R. G. D. Allen and myself. Slutsky's work is highly mathematical, and he does not give much discussion about the significance of his theory. These things (and the date of its publication) perhaps explain why it remained for so long without influence, and had to be rediscovered. The present volume is the first systematic exploration of the territory which Slutsky opened up.

6. We have now to undertake a purge, rejecting all concepts which are tainted by quantitative utility, and replacing them, so far as they need to be replaced, by concepts which have no such implication.

The first victim must evidently be marginal utility itself. If total utility is arbitrary, so is marginal utility. But we can still give a precise meaning to the ratio of two marginal utilities, when the quantities possessed of both commodities are given. For this quantity is represented by the slope of an indifference curve; and that is independent of the arbitrariness in question.

In order to avoid the danger of misleading associations, let us give this quantity a new name, and call it the Marginal Rate of Substitution between the two commodities. We may define the marginal rate of substitution of X for Y as the quantity of Y which would just compensate the consumer for the loss of a marginal unit of X. This definition is entirely free from any dependence upon a quantitative measure of utility.

If an individual is to be in equilibrium with respect to a system of market prices, it is directly evident that his marginal rate of substitution between any two goods must equal the ratio of their prices. Otherwise he would clearly find an advantage in substituting some quantity of one for an equal value (at the market price) of the other. This is therefore the form in which we must now write the condition of equilibrium on the market.

It may be observed that in this formulation we have, as yet, scarcely departed from Marshall. The marginal rate of substitution of X for Y is what he would have called the marginal utility of X in terms of Y. We may transcribe Marshall if we like, and say that the price of a commodity equals the marginal rate of substitution of that commodity for money.

7. The second victim (a more serious one this time) must be the principle of Diminishing Marginal Utility. If marginal utility has no exact sense, diminishing marginal utility can have no exact sense either. But by what shall we replace it?

By the rule that the indifference curves must be convex to the axes. This may be called, in our present terminology, the principle of Diminishing Marginal Rate of Substitution. It may be expressed in the following terms: Suppose we start with a given quantity of goods, and then go on increasing the amount of X and diminishing that of Y in such a way that the consumer is left neither better off nor worse off on balance; then the amount of Y which has to be subtracted in order to set off a second unit of X will be less than that which has to be subtracted in order to set off the first unit. In other words, the more X is substituted for Y, the less will be the marginal rate of substitution of X for Y.

But what is the exact reason why we must replace diminishing marginal utility by precisely this principle—the principle of diminishing marginal rate of substitution? As we have seen already, they are not exactly the same thing. The replacement is therefore not a mere translation; it is a positive change in the foundation of the theory, and requires a very definite justification.

The justification is this. We need the principle of diminishing marginal rate of substitution for the same reason as Marshall's theory needed the principle of diminishing marginal utility. Unless, at the point of equilibrium, the marginal rate of substitution is diminishing, equilibrium will not be stable. Even if the marginal rate of substitution equals the price ratio, so that the acquisition of one unit of X would not yield any appreciable advantage; nevertheless, if the marginal rate of substitution is increasing, the acquisition of a larger quantity would be advantageous. It is instructive to set this out on the indifference diagram (Figure 4).

At the point Q on the diagram, the

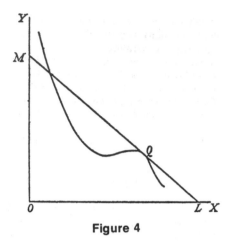

Figure 4

marginal rate of substitution equals the price-ratio, so that the price-line touches the indifference curve through Q. But the marginal rate of substitution is increasing (the indifference curve is concave to the axes), so that a movement away from Q in either direction along LM would lead the individual on to a higher indifference curve. Q is therefore a point of minimum, not maximum, utility, and cannot be a point of equilibrium.

It is clear, therefore, that for any point to be a possible rate of equilibrium at appropriate prices the marginal rate of substitution at that point must be diminishing. Since we know from experience that some points of possible equilibrium do exist on the indifference maps of nearly every one (that is to say, they do decide to buy such-and-such quantities of commodities, and do not stay hesitating indefinitely like Buridan's ass), it follows that the principle of diminishing marginal rate of substitution must sometimes be true.

However, for us to make progress in economics, it is not enough for us that the principle should be true sometimes; we require a more general validity than that. The law of diminishing marginal utility used to be assumed generally valid (with perhaps some special exceptions), and on that general validity important economic conclusions were based. We shall have to investigate those conclusions afresh; but, if they are to have any chance at all, they need as their basis a property of the indifference map which is more than *sometimes* true.

What were in fact the grounds upon which economists used to base their general principle of diminishing marginal utility? Usually an appeal to experience; though to experience of that uncomfortably vague sort which does not offer any opportunity for actual testing. Critics have not been lacking to point out that this procedure was not very scientific, and the doubts which have been thrown by our present discussion upon the intelligibility of the "law of diminishing marginal utility" itself can only strengthen the case against the traditional procedure. If, however, we throw over diminishing marginal utility as being in any case dubious, and now certainly irrelevant, can we base upon similar "experience" a general principle of diminishing marginal rate of substitution? Again, I suppose, we might get away without being challenged; but one would like a surer foundation.

8. We can, I think, get that surer foundation if we reflect on the purpose for which we require our principle. We want to deduce from it laws of market conduct—laws, that is, which deal with the reaction of the consumer to changes in market conditions. When market conditions change, the consumer moves from one point of equilibrium to another point of equilibrium; at each of these positions the condition of diminishing marginal rate of substitution must hold, or he could not take up such a position at all. So much is clear directly; but to proceed from this to the law of diminishing marginal rate of substitution, as we need it in economic theory, an assumption is necessary. We have to assume that the condition holds at all intermediate points, so that there are no kinks in the curves between the two positions of equilibrium. (If there are kinks in the curves, curious consequences follow, such that there will be some systems of prices at which the consumer will be unable to choose between two different ways of spending his income.) The general principle of diminishing marginal rate of substitution merely rules out these oddities; by that principle we select the simplest of the various possibilities before us.

As we go on, we shall find that most of the "laws" of pure economic theory can be looked at in this sort of way. Pure economics has a remarkable way of producing rabbits out of a hat— apparently a *priori* propositions which apparently refer to reality. It is fascinating to try to discover how the rabbits got in; for those of us who do not believe in magic must be convinced that they got in somehow. I have become convinced myself that they get in in two ways. One is by the assumption, at the beginning of every economic argument, that the things to be dealt with in the argument are the only things that matter in some practical problem. (This is always a dangerous assumption, and nearly always more or less wrong—which is why the application of economic theory is such a ticklish matter.) That takes us much of the way, but it does not take us the whole way. The other assumption is that which we have just isolated, the assumption that kinks can be neglected, that there is a sufficient degree of regularity in the system of wants (and also, as we shall see later, in the productive system) for any set of quantities in the neighborhood of those with which we are concerned to be a possible position of equilibrium at some system of prices. Again, this assumption may be wrong; but, being the simplest assumption possible, it is a good assumption to start with; and in fact its accordance with experience seems definitely good.

The road which lies before us now begins to be distinguishable. If this is the true foundation of the principle of diminishing marginal rate of substitution among consumption goods, other prin-

ciples can be discovered whose foundation is exactly similar. These principles can be enumerated, and their consequences worked out. . . . What begins as an analysis of the consumer's choice among consumption goods ends as a theory of economic choice in general. We are in sight of a unifying principle for the whole of economics.

9. But this is running ahead. Before we can explore these long avenues much preparation is needed. One necessary piece of preparation may conclude this chapter.

During most of the above discussion we have made the extreme simplification that the consumer had his choice restricted to expenditure on two sorts of goods. It is high time that we abandoned this simplification, for if our theory were confined to this simple case there would not be much to be said for it. It is in fact one of the main defects of the indifference-curve technique that it encourages concentration upon this simple case, concentration that can easily prove very dangerous.

When expenditure is distributed between more than two goods, the indifference diagram loses its simplicity; for three goods we need three dimensions, and for more than three goods geometry fails us altogether. However, the principles which we have established in this chapter remain substantially unaffected. The marginal rate of substitution can be defined as before, with the added proviso that the quantities consumed of all other commodities $(Z \ldots)$ must remain unchanged. The consumer is only in full equilibrium if the marginal rate of substitution between any two goods equals their price-ratio. Over the principle of diminishing marginal rate of substitution there is a slight difference.

In order that equilibrium should be stable, when expenditure is distributed among many commodities, it is necessary that no possible substitution of equal market values should lead the consumer to a preferred position. This means not only that we must have a diminishing marginal rate of substitution between each pair of commodities, but also that more complicated substitutions (of some X for some Y and some Z) must be ruled out in the same way. We may express this by saying that the marginal rate of substitution must diminish for substitutions in every direction. This is a rather complicated condition, but it will appear, as we proceed, that it leads directly to conclusions of great importance.

On the same grounds as before, we shall assume that the marginal rate of substitution diminishes in every direction at every position with which we shall be concerned in our analysis. I do not think this could be established introspectively, or from "experience," but it can be justified in the same way as we have justified the simpler condition. It becomes clear now, however, that it is a fairly drastic hypothesis, which gives us a good deal to go on, and from which we can expect to deduce some positive results.

THE LAW OF CONSUMER'S DEMAND

1. We have now, from the conditions of equilibrium and the basic assumption of regularity, set out in the preceding chapter, to deduce laws of market conduct—to find out what can be said about the way the consumer will react when prices change. Discussion of equilibrium conditions is always a means to an end; we seek information about the conditions governing quantities bought at given prices in order that we may use them to discover how the quantities bought will be changed when prices change.

This stage of our investigation corresponds to the stage in Marshall's theory where he deduces the downward slope of the demand curve from the law of diminishing marginal utility. The particular way in which Marshall carries out that deduction is worth noting. He assumes that the marginal utility of

money is constant.[1] Therefore, the ratio between the marginal utility of a commodity and its price is a constant ratio. If the price falls, the marginal utility must be reduced too. But, by the law of diminishing marginal utility, this implies an increase in the amount demanded. A fall in price therefore increases the amount demanded. This is the argument we have to reconsider.

What is meant by the marginal utility of money being constant? Making our translation, it would appear to mean that changes in the consumer's supply of money (that is, with respect to the problem in hand, his income) will not affect the marginal rate of substitution between money and any particular commodity X. (For the marginal rate of substitution equals the ratio of the marginal utilities of X and money.) Therefore, if his income increases, and the price of X remains constant, the price of X will still equal the marginal rate of substitution, without any change in the amount of X bought. The demand for X is therefore independent of income. His demand for any commodity is independent of his income.

It will appear in what follows that this is actually what the constancy of the marginal utility of money did mean for Marshall; not that he really supposed that people's demands for commodities do not depend upon their incomes, but that in his theory of demand and price he generally neglected the income side. We shall find that he had quite good reasons for doing so, that the constancy of the marginal utility of money is in fact an ingenious simplification, which is quite harmless for most of the applications Marshall gave it himself. But it is not harmless for all applications; it is not always a good thing to be vague about the effects of changes in income on demand. There are distinct advantages to be gained from having a theory of value in which the relations of demand, price, and income are all made quite clear.

2. Let us now revert to the indifference diagram, and begin by investigating the effects of changes in income. We shall go on to investigate the effects of price-changes later, but price-changes will be easier to deal with if we examine the effects of income-changes first. Let us therefore continue to suppose, as in the last chapter, that the prices of X and Y are given, but now suppose the consumer's income to vary.

We have seen before that if his income is OL (measured in terms of X) or OM (measured in terms of Y), the point of equilibrium will be at P, where LM touches an indifference curve (Figure 5). If now his income increases, LM will move to the right, but the new line L'M' will still be parallel to LM, so long as the prices of X and Y are unchanged. (For, then, OM'/OL' = OM/OL, the unchanged price-ratio.) The new point of equilibrium will be at P', where L'M' touches an indifference curve.

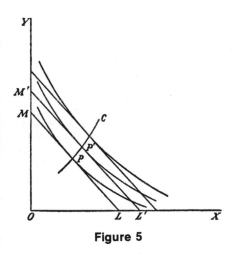

Figure 5

As income continues to increase, L'M' continues to move to the right, and the point P' traces out a curve, which we may call the *income-consumption curve*.[2] It shows the way in which consumption varies, when income increases and prices remain unchanged. Through any point P on the diagram an income-consumption curve could be

drawn; thus there will be an income-consumption curve corresponding to each possible system of prices.

What can be said about the form of the income-consumption curve? Mere experience in drawing diagrams is enough to convince one that it will ordinarily slope upwards and to the right; but that is not enough to show that it will necessarily behave in this way. In fact, there is only one necessary restriction on its shape. An income-consumption curve cannot intersect any particular indifference curve more than once. (For if it did so, that would mean that the indifference curve had two parallel tangents—which is impossible, if the indifference curves are always convex to the origin.) Consequently, while there is most "room" for the income-consumption curves to slope upwards and to the right, it is also possible for them to creep round to the left or downwards (PC₁ or PC₂ in Figure 6) without ever cutting an indifference curve more than once.

And clearly that is as it should be. Curves such as PC₁ do occur. They are found whenever the commodity X is an "inferior" good, largely consumed at low levels of income, but replaced, or partially replaced, by goods of higher quality when income rises. Margarine is

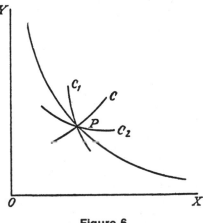

Figure 6

obviously a case in point; its inferiority is well attested by statistical investigation. But it can hardly be doubted that there are a great many others. Most of the poorer qualities of goods offered for sale are probably, in our sense, inferior goods.

Although the diagrammatic apparatus we have just been using is only valid for the case of two goods (X and Y), it is evident that a similar argument must hold however many are the goods among which income is being distributed. If income increases, and the increased income is spent, then there must be increased consumption in some directions, perhaps most directions or even all; but it is perfectly possible that there will be a limited number of goods whose consumption will be actually diminished. This is a very negative result and obviously needs no further elaboration.

3. Let us now pass on to consider the effects of a change in price. Here again we begin with the case of two goods. Income is now to be taken as fixed, and the price of Y as fixed; but the price of X is variable. The possibilities of consumption now open are presented on the diagram (Figure 7) by straight lines joining M (OM is income measured in terms of Y, and is therefore fixed) to

points on OX which vary as the price of X varies. Each price of X will determine a line LM (OL increasing as the price falls); and the point of equilibrium corresponding to each price will be given by the point at which the line LM touches an indifference curve. The curve MPQ joining these points may be called a *price-consumption curve*. It shows the way in which consumption varies, when the price of X varies and other things remain equal.

Starting off from a particular position of LM, we have thus two sets of straight lines, and corresponding points of contact. We have the lines parallel to LM, whose points of contact tract out the income-consumption curve. We have the lines passing through M, whose points of contact tract out the price-consumption curve. Any particular indifference curve must be touched by one line from each of these sets. Take an indifference curve I_2, which is higher than the indifference curve I_1, touched by LM. The curve I_2 is touched by a line parallel to LM at P', by a line through M at Q. Not it is at once obvious from the diagram (it follows from the convexity of the indifference curve) that Q must lie to the right of P'. This property must hold for all indifference curves which are higher than the original curve; and it therefore follows that as we go up on to higher indifference curves the price-consumption curve through P must always lie to the right of the income-consumption curve through P (Figure 8).

This proposition, which looks like a mere piece of geometry, turns out to have much economic significance, and to be indeed quite fundamental to a large part of the theory of value. Let us try to see its implications.

When the price of X falls, the consumer moves along the price-consumption curve from P to Q. We now see that this movement from P to Q is equivalent to a movement from P to P' along the income-consumption curve, and a movement from P' to Q along an indifference curve. We shall

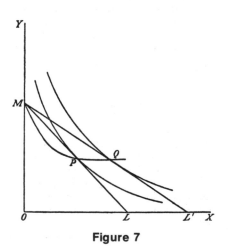

Figure 7

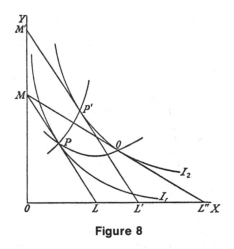

Figure 8

find it very instructive to think of the effect of price on demand as falling into these two separate parts.

A fall in the price of a commodity does actually affect the demand for that commodity in two different ways. On the one hand, it makes the consumer better off, it raises his "real income," and its effect along this channel is similar to that of an increase in income. On the other hand, it changes relative prices; and therefore, apart from the change in real income, there will be a tendency to substitute the commodity whose price has fallen for other commodities. The total effect on demand is the sum of these two tendencies.

The relative importance of these tendencies can be further shown to depend upon the proportions in which the consumer was dividing his expenditure between this commodity (X) and other goods. For the extent to which he is made better off by a fall in the price of X will depend upon the amount of X which he was initially buying; if that amount was large relatively to his income, he will be made much better off, and the first effect (the Income Effect, we may call it) will be very important; but if the amount was small, the gain is small, and the income effect is likely to be swamped by the Substitution Effect.

It is this last point which is the justification of Marshall's "constant marginal utility." It will be observed that our two effects stand on a different footing as regards the certainty of their operation. It follows from the principle of diminishing marginal rate of substitution that the substitution effect is absolutely certain—it must always work in favour of an increase in the demand for a commodity when the price of that commodity falls. But the income effect is not so reliable; ordinarily it will work the same way, but it will work in the opposite way in the case of inferior goods. It is therefore a consideration of great importance that this unreliable income effect will be of relatively little importance in all those cases where the commodity in question plays a fairly small part in the consumer's budget; for it is only in these cases (fortunately, they are most important cases) that we have a quite unequivocal law of demand. It is only in these cases that we can be quite sure that a fall in price will necessarily lead to a rise in the amount demanded.

Marshall concentrated his attention upon these cases; and therefore he neglected the income effect. He did this by means of his assumption that the marginal utility of money could be treated as constant, which meant that he neglected the effect on demand of the charges in real income which result from changes in price. For many purposes this was a quite justifiable simplification, and it certainly did simplify his theory enormously. It is indeed one of those simplifications of genius, of which there are several instances in Marshall. Economists will continue to use these simplifications, though their path is made safer when they know exactly what it is that they are neglecting. We shall find, as we proceed, that there are other problems, not much considered by Marshall, that are made definitely easier when we are clear in our minds about the income effect.

4. The geometrical argument of the

preceding section appears to apply only to the case when the consumer divides his expenditure between two commodities and no more; but it is not actually as limited as that. For suppose we regard X and Y, not as bread and potatoes, or tea and margarine (physical commodities in that sense), but as bread (some physical commodity) for one, and general purchasing power (Marshall's "money") for the other. The choice of the consumer is a choice between spending his money on bread or keeping it available for expenditure on other things. If he decides not to spend it on bread, he will subsequently convert it into some other form by buying some other commodity or commodities with it. But even if Y were potatoes, it might still be converted into other forms, some of the potatoes being roasted, some being boiled. These possibilities do not prevent us from drawing up a determinate indifference system for bread and potatoes. Similarly, so long as the terms on which money can be converted into other commodities are given, there is no reason why we should not draw up a determinate indifference system between any commodity X and money (that is to say, purchasing power in general). The distribution of purchasing power among other commodities is exactly similar to the distribution of a commodity among various uses, which may take place even if there is only one other commodity in a physical sense.

This principle is of quite general application. A collection of physical things can always be treated as if they were divisible into units of a single commodity so long as their relative prices can be assumed to be unchanged, in the particular problem in hand. So long as the prices of other consumption goods are assumed to be given, they can be lumped together into one commodity "money" or "purchasing power in general." Similarly, in other applications, if changes in relative wages are to be neglected, it is quite legitimate to assume all labour homogeneous. There will be other applications still to notice as we go on.[3]

For the present, we shall only use this principle to assure ourselves that the classification of the effects of price on demand into income effects and substitution effects, and the law that the substitution effect, at least, always tends to increase demand when price falls, are valid, however the consumer is spending his income.

5. In all our discussions so far, we have been concerned with the behaviour of a single individual. But economics is not, in the end, much interested in the behavior of single individuals. Its concern is with the behaviour of groups. A study of individual demand is only a means to the study of market demand. Fortunately, with our present methods we can make the transition very easily.

Market demand has almost exactly the same properties as individual demand. This can be seen at once if we reflect that it is the actual change in the amount demanded (brought about by a small change in price) which we can divide into two parts, due respectively to the income effect and the substitution effect. The change in the demand of a group is the sum of changes in individual demands; it is therefore also divisible into two parts, one corresponding to the sum of the individual income effects, the other to the sum of the individual substitution effects. Similar propositions to those which held about the individual effects hold about the group effects.

(1) Since all the individual substitution effects go in favour of increased consumption of the commodity whose price has fallen, the group substitution effect must do so also.

(2) Individual income effects are not quite reliable in direction; therefore group income effects cannot be quite reliable either. A good may, of course, be inferior for some members of a group, and not be inferior for the group as a whole; the negative income effects of this section being offset by positive income effects from the rest of the group.

(3) The group income effect will usually be negligible if the group as a whole spends a small proportion of its total income upon the commodity in question.

6. We are therefore in a position to sum up about the law of demand. The demand curve for a commodity must slope downwards, more being consumed when the price falls, in all cases when the commodity is not an inferior good. Even if it is an inferior good, so that the income effect is negative, the demand curve will still behave in an orthodox manner so long as the proportion of income spent upon the commodity is small, so that the income effect is small. Even if neither of these conditions is satisfied, so that the commodity is an inferior good which plays an important part in the budgets of its consumers, it still does not necessarily follow that a fall in price will diminish the amount demanded. For even a large negative income effect may be outweighed by a large substitution effect.

It is apparent what very stringent conditions need to be fulfilled before there can be any exception to the law of demand. Consumers are only likely to spend a large proportion of their incomes upon what is for them an inferior good if their standard of living is very low. The famous Giffen case, quoted by Marshall,[4] exactly fits these requirements. At a low level of income, consumers may satisfy the greater part of their need for food by one staple foodstuff (bread in the Giffen case), which will be replaced by a more varied diet if income rises. If the price of this staple falls, they have a quite considerable surplus available for expenditure, and they may spend this surplus upon more interesting foods, which then take the place of the staple, and reduce the demand for it. In such a case as this, the negative income effect may be strong enough to outweigh the substitution effect. But it is evident how rare such cases must be.

Thus, as we might expect, the simple law of demand—the downward slope of the demand curve—turns out to be almost infallible in its working. Exceptions to it are rare and unimportant. It is not in this direction that our present technique has anything new to offer.

7. But as soon as we pass beyond this standard case, we do begin to get some effective clarification.

So far we have assumed the consumer's income to be fixed in terms of money. What happens if this is not so, if he comes to the market not only as a buyer but also as a seller? Suppose he comes with a fixed stock of some commodity X, of which he is prepared to hold back some for his own consumption, if price-conditions are favourable to that course of action.

It is clear that so long as the price of X remains fixed, our previous arguments are unaffected. We may suppose, if we like, that he exchanges his whole stock into money at the fixed price, when he will find himself in exactly the same position as our consumer whose income was fixed in terms of money. He can then buy back some of his X if he wants to.

But what happens if the price of X varies? The substitution effect will be the same as before. A fall in the price of X will encourage substitution of X for other goods; this must favour increased demand for X, that is to say, diminished supply. But the income effect will not be the same as before. A fall in the price of X will make a *seller* of X worse off; this will diminish his demand (increase his supply) unless X is for him an inferior good.

The significant difference between the position of the seller and that of the buyer thus comes out at once. In the case of the buyer income effect and substitution effect work in the same direction—save in the exceptional case of inferior goods. In the case of the seller, they only work in the same direction in that exceptional case. Ordinarily they work in opposite directions.

The position is made more awkward by the fact that sellers' income effects

can much more rarely be neglected.
Sellers usually derive large parts of their
incomes from some particular thing
which they sell. We shall therefore expect to find many cases in which the income effect is just as powerful as the
substitution effect, or is dominant. We
must conclude that a fall in the price of
X may either diminish its supply or increase it.

The practical importance of such a
supply curve is no doubt most evident
in the case of the factors of production.
Thus a fall in wages may sometimes
make the wage-earner work less hard,
sometimes harder; for, on the one hand,
reduced piece-rates make the effort
needed for a marginal unit of output
seem less worth while, or would do so,
if income were unchanged; but on the
other, his income is reduced, and the
urge to work harder in order to make up
for the loss in income may counterbalance the first tendency.

Such a supply curve will appear,
however, whenever there is a possibility
of reservation demand; that is to say,
whenever the seller would prefer, other
things being equal, to give up less,
rather than more. The supply of agricultural products from not too specialized
farms is thus another good example.
Any such supply curve, drawn on a

price-quantity diagram, is likely to turn
back on itself at some point. We cannot
be at all confident that it will be
upward-sloping (Figure 9).

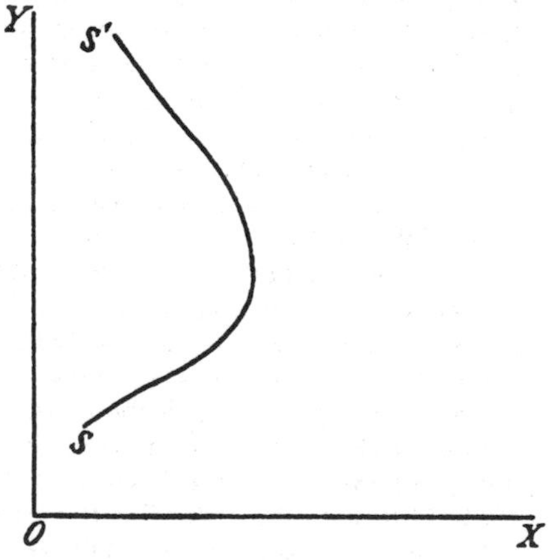

That there existed this asymmetry between supply and demand has long
been familiar; it should perhaps be
reckoned as one of the discoveries of
Walras. But so long as the reason for the
asymmetry was not made clear, it was
rather too easy to forget its existence. To
have cleared up this matter may be regarded as the first-fruits of our new
technique. It is itself a good thing to
have cleared up, and, we shall find as
we go on, it opens the way to some very
convenient analytical methods.

CONSUMER'S SURPLUS[5]

The doctrine of Consumer's Surplus
has caused more trouble and controversy than anything else in book iii of
Marshall's *Principles*; the results we
have just reached throw some light
upon it; consequently, although it lies
off the main track of our present inquiry,
it may usefully be examined here.

Consumer's surplus is the one instance in this field where Marshall was,
perhaps, just a shade too ingenious; but
he was very ingenious, and we must be
careful not to fall into the most common
error of writers on this matter, which is
to fail to give him the credit for the ingenuity he showed. We are dealing with
one of those deceptive doctrines which
appear to be a good deal simpler than
they are. It can easily be stated in a way
which is altogether fallacious; and it is
easy to overlook the fact that Marshall
did go to some considerable trouble in
order not to state it in a fallacious way.

It is thus useful to begin by contrasting Marshall's argument with that of the
original inventor of consumer's
surplus—Dupuit. Dupuit, writing in
1844, gave a version that has none of
Marshall's refinement. He held
straightforwardly that 'l' économie
politique doit prendre pour mesure de
l'utilité d'un objet le sacrifice maximum

Figure 9

que chaque consommateur serait disposé à faire pour se le procurer' (p. 40), and therefore that the "utility" secured by being able to purchase *on* units of a commodity at the price *pn* is given by the area *dpk* on the price-quantity demand diagram (p. 63). This without any qualification. Marshall uses the same diagram (Figure 10) and arrives at the same result; but he makes the significant qualification that the marginal utility of money must be supposed constant.

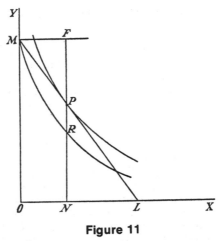

Figure 11

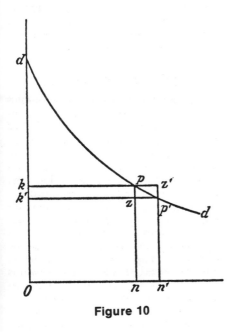

Figure 10

The force of this can be readily shown on the indifference diagram, measuring, as before, the commodity *X* along one axis and money on the other (Figure 11). If the consumer's income is *OM*, and the price of *X* is indicated by the slope of *ML*, which touches an indifference curve at *P*, *ON* will be the amount of *X* purchased, and *PF* the amount of money paid for it. Now *P* is on a higher indifference curve than *M*, and what is wanted is a money measure of this gain in "utility." Like Dupuit,

Marshall takes "the excess of the price which (the consumer) would be willing to pay rather than go without the thing, over that which he actually does pay." The price he actually does pay is measured on our diagram by *PF*, the price he would be willing to pay by *RF*, where *R* lies on the same indifference curve as *M* (so that if he bought *ON* and paid *RF* for it, he would be no better off by making the transaction). Consumer's surplus is therefore the length of the line *RP*.

RP is a perfectly general representation of consumer's surplus, independent of any assumption about the marginal utility of money. But it is not necessarily equal to the area under the demand curve in Marshall's diagram, unless the marginal utility of money is constant. This can be seen as follows. If the marginal utility of money is constant, the slope of the indifference curve at *R* must be the same as the slope of the indifference curve at *P*, that is to say, the same as the slope of the line *MP*. A slight movement to the right along the indifference curve *MR* will therefore increase *RF* by the same amount as a slight movement along *MP* will increase *PF*. But the increment in *PF* is the additional amount paid for a small increment in the amount purchased at the price given by *MP*, an amount measured by the area *pnn'z'* in Figure 10. The length *RF* is built up out of a series of such increments, and must therefore be represented on Figure 10 by the area built up out of increments such as *pnn'z'*. This is nothing else than *dpno*.

RP will therefore be represented on Figure 10 by *dpk*—Marshall's consumer's surplus.

This is valid so long as the marginal utility of money is constant—so long as income effects can be neglected. But how legitimate is it in this case to follow Marshall in neglecting income effects? This is not a case in which they can be very safely ignored. Marshall neglects the difference between the slope of the indifference curve at *P* and the slope of the indifference curve at *R*. It is true that this difference is likely to be less important, the less important in the consumer's budget is the commodity we are considering. But the difference may still be important, even if the proportion of income spent upon the commodity is small; it will still be important, if *RP* itself is large, if the consumer's surplus is large, so that the loss of the opportunity of buying the commodity is equivalent to a large loss of income.

This is the weakness which remains even in Marshall's version of the consumer's surplus theory; but there is really no reason why it should be allowed to remain. We must remember that the notion of consumer's surplus is not wanted for its own sake; it is wanted as a means of demonstrating a very important proposition, which was supposed to depend upon it. However, in fact that proposition can be demonstrated without begging any questions at all.

As we have seen, the best way of looking at consumer's surplus is to regard it as a means of expressing, in terms of money income, the gain which accrues to the consumer as a result of a fall in price. Or better, it is the *compensating variation* in income, whose loss would just offset the fall in price, and leave the consumer no better off than before. Now it can be shown that this compensating variation cannot be less than a certain amount, and will ordinarily be greater than that amount. This is all that is needed.

Suppose the price of oranges is 2*d.* each; and at this price a person buys 6 oranges. Now suppose that the price falls to 1*d.*, and at the lower price he buys 10 oranges. What is the compensating variation in income? We cannot say exactly, but we can say that it cannot be less than 6*d.* For suppose again that, at the same time as the price of oranges fell, his income had been reduced by 6*d.* Then, in the new circumstances, he can, if he chooses, buy the same amount of oranges as before, and the same amounts of all other commodities; what had previously been his most preferred position is still open to him; so he cannot be worse off. But with the change in relative prices, it is probable that he will be able to substitute some quantity of oranges for some quantities of other things, and so make himself better off. But if he can lose 6*d.* and still remain better off, 6*d.* must be less than the compensating variation; he would have to lose more than 6*d.* in order to be just as well off as before.[6]

This is all that is necessary in order to establish the important consequences in the theory of taxation which follow from the consumer's surplus principle. It shows, for example, why (apart from distributional effects) a tax on commodities lays a greater burden on consumers than an income tax. If the price of oranges falls from 2*d.* to 1*d.* as the result of a reduction in taxation, then (assuming constant costs) the reduction in tax receipts from our particular consumer is 6*d.* If this is taken from him by an income tax, he is still left better off, and the government no worse off.

Other deductions which have been drawn from the consumer's surplus principle can presumably be tested out in a similar way.

Selection continues with an excerpt of chapter 14 of part 3—Needy.

SAVING AND INVESTMENT[7]

The principle difficulty in this matter of saving and investment evidently arises from the multiplicity of ways in which the terms can be defined. Without involving ourselves in any of the more recondite definitions which have been put forward, it is directly obvious that there is a definition of saving to correspond with each of the definitions of income set out in the preceding chapter. Saving can be defined *ex ante* or *ex post*; it can be defined to match definitions of Income Nos. 1, 2, or 3. To each of these definitions of saving there corresponds a definition of investment. This provides a good many ways in which argument may get at cross-purposes!

As soon as we have these different definitions spread out before us it becomes clear that there is no reason, in general, for expecting any sort of significant correspondence between the saving that relates to one definition of income, and the investment that relates to another. The different definitions of income move on quite different planes, and take different things into account. It is only between those sorts of saving and investment which spring from the same definition of income that we can expect to find a correspondence worth studying.

This first remark clears out a good many of the possible issues, but it still leaves us with quite a wide choice. We have still to decide whether to concern ourselves with the saving and investment which correspond to Income No. 1, No. 2, or No. 3; and whether to consider them *ex ante* or *ex post*. Now I do not believe that the first decision is a very important one; we can start with any sort of approximation to the concept of income, and we shall find things working out very similarly. But the *ex ante-ex post* distinction is of course very important.

For brevity I shall confine myself here to those definitions of saving and investment which correspond to Income No. 1. If we were to start with, say, Income No. 3, the whole argument would be exactly duplicated; but I think I may leave the reader to test this for himself. If we start from Income No. 1, we define a person's saving *(ex ante)* as the difference between his actual consumption during the week and that level of consumption which would leave the money value of the prospect he can expect to have at the end of the week the same as it actually was at the beginning. If we take the week to be short enough in length for the accretion of interest during the week to be negligible, we may say that his saving is the increment in the money value of his prospect planned to accrue during the week. Further, if we neglect any changes in his prospect due to changes in his own personal earning power, his saving may also be written as the planned increment in the value of his property. All this is saving *ex ante*; saving *ex post* will be the realized increment in the value of his property.

Savings *ex post* may be aggregated for all members of the community. Their sum total will equal the total increment in the money value of all persons' property which accrues during the week. Now property has three forms: it may consist of physical goods (real capital), or securities, or money. But money, as we have seen, is either a physical good, like gold, or a security, like notes or bank deposits. Our three categories thus reduce to two. Further, securities are simply debts of various sorts from one person (or concern) to another; and therefore, when all property is aggregated, they cancel out. Total savings *ex post* therefore reduce to nothing else but the increment in the value of physical capital; which is what seems to be meant by investment—of course investment *ex post*.

Equality between saving *ex post* and investment *ex post* is thus necessarily assured, for the community taken as a whole. But this equality is a mere truism—it expresses nothing else but the mere fact that all the capital goods in the economy belong to somebody. And that is not a consideration of very profound theoretical significance.

The relation between saving *ex ante* and investment *ex ante* is more interesting. By analogy, investment *ex ante* must equal the planned increment in the value of physical capital, including both producers' goods and durable consumers' goods. Now, following out this definition, a particular person (or concern) can plan to save more than he plans to invest, only if he plans to acquire, during the week, property of the non-material kind—property in securities. Similarly, he can only plan to invest more than he plans to save if he intends to diminish his holding of securities; which, as we have seen, includes issuing securities, creating securities against himself. Thus the difference between planned saving and planned investment is the difference between the planned demand and planned supply for securities in general—including money.

Now it will be remembered that, under the special assumptions of the model with which we are working throughout, the "week" is a period of temporary equilibrium, characterized by the condition that all demands and corresponding supplies are equal during the week. This rule applies to the demand and supply for securities. The planned demands and supplies for securities are supposed to be at once made actual on the market on "Monday." They are therefore necessarily equal for the community as a whole. Therefore, during the week, not only does saving *ex post* equal investment *ex post*; saving *ex ante* also equals investment *ex ante*.[8]

This equality between the *ex ante* magnitudes is not, however, a mere truism, like the equality between the *ex post* magnitudes. It is an expression of the equation of supply and demand for securities; and that, as we have seen, forms part of the system of equations determining the price-system. I do not

think, however, that we ought to admit any particular connexion between this savings-investment equation and the rate of interest. There is, as we have seen, a sense in which the rate of interest is particularly determined by the equation of supply and demand for securities—excluding money; but the equation here is one including money, and that has no special connexion with the rate of interest. Since the equation of supply and demand for securities, including money, is the same thing as the equation of supply and demand for real goods in general (producers' goods *plus* consumers' goods *plus* factors of production); if we are to allow ourselves to connect the savings-investment equation with the determination of any particular part or aspect of the price-system, it is the general price-level which ought to be chosen. Still, when we remember how the whole system is interconnected, this relating of particular equations to particular prices becomes rather idle.

Thus, during the week, savings *ex ante* equal investment *ex ante*; but this is a property of the week, and not of any longer period. The *ex post* magnitudes will be equal whatever period we take, but the *ex ante* magnitudes will only be necessarily equal if plans are consistent. Equality between savings *ex ante* and investment *ex ante* is then one of the conditions of equilibrium over time. In conditions of disequilibrium, it is perfectly possible for planned saving to exceed planned investment, if we look forward for a longer period than a week. And it is through the working of this inequality that the disequilibrium is likely to show itself. If an attempt is made to carry through the plans without readjustment, supplies of commodities will begin to exceed demands, and (so far as we can see at present) prices will tend to fall. Similarly, if planned investment exceeds planned saving, there will be a tendency for prices to rise.

What a tricky business this all is! In his *Treatise on Money*, Mr. Keynes told the world that savings and investment are only equal in conditions of equilibrium; that an excess of investment over saving means rising prices, and vice versa. In his *General Theory*, he told us that savings and investment are always equal, and that this is a mere identity or truism, without significance for the determination of prices. As far as I can make out, there are relevant and important senses in which all these four statements are each of them right and each of them wrong.

NOTES

1. This, of course, abolishes any distinction between the diminishing marginal utility of a commodity and the diminishing marginal rate of substitution of that commodity for money. Consequently, it explains why Marshall was satisfied with diminishing marginal utility.

2. In "A Reconsideration of the Theory of Value" I called this the expenditure curve. It was clearly a bad name.

3. Beyond this, it does not seem necessary to worry about the definition of a "commodity." What collections of things we regard as composing a commodity must be allowed to vary with the problem in hand.

4. *Principles*, p. 132.

5. *Note to chapter 2 of part 1—Needy.*

6. The compensating variation can thus be proved to be greater than the area *kpzk'* on Figure 10. Can it also be proved to be less than the area *kz'p'k'*? At first sight, one might think so; but in fact it is not possible to give an equally rigorous proof on this side. This comes out clearly if we use the indifference diagram (Figure 11). The line exhibiting opportunities of purchase, when the price of oranges falls by 1*d.*, and income is reduced by 10*d.*, no longer passes through the original point of equilibrium *P*. Thus we have no reliable information about the indifference curve it touches. We are left to infer from our earlier argument that the compensating variation will be less than the larger rectangle, so long as the marginal utility of money can be taken as constant.

7. *Note to part 3, chapter 14—Needy.*

8. At the same time, there is of course no necessity for the *ex ante* magnitudes and the *ex post* magnitudes to be equal to one another.

34. Capitalism, Socialism, and Democracy*

JOSEPH A. SCHUMPETER

PLAUSIBLE CAPITALISM

[*Paragraphs deleted.*]

On the one hand, we have a considerable body of statistical data descriptive of a rate of "progress" that has been admired even by very critical minds. On the other hand, we have a body of facts about the structure of the economic system of that period and about the way it functioned; from these facts, analysis has distilled what is technically called a "model" of capitalist reality, *i.e.*, a generalized picture of its essential features. We wish to know whether that type of economy was favorable, irrelevant, or unfavorable to the performance we observe and, if favorable, whether those features may be reasonably held to yield adequate explanation of this

*Source: From pp. 73-92 in *Capitalism, Socialism, and Democracy* by Joseph A. Schumpeter. Copyright © 1942, 1947 by Joseph A. Schumpeter. Copyright © 1950 by Harper & Row, Publishers. Reprinted by permission. Most footnotes deleted; remaining one renumbered.

performance. Waiving technicalities as much as possible, we shall approach the question in a common-sense spirit.

1. Unlike the class of feudal lords, the commercial and industrial bourgeoisie rose by business success. Bourgeois society has been cast in a purely economic mold: its foundations, beams and beacons are all made of economic material. The building faces toward the economic side of life. Prizes and penalties are measured in pecuniary terms. Going up and going down means making and losing money. This, of course, nobody can deny. But I wish to add that, within its own frame, that social arrangement is, or at all events was, singularly effective. In part it appeals to, and in part it creates, a schema of motives that is unsurpassed in simplicity and force. The promises of wealth and the threats of destitution that it holds out, it redeems with ruthless promptitude. Wherever the bourgeois way of life asserts itself sufficiently to dim the beacons of other social worlds, these promises are strong enough to attract the large majority of supernormal brains and to identify success with business success. They are not proffered at random; yet there is a sufficiently enticing admixture of chance: the game is not like roulette, it is more like poker. They are addressed to ability, energy and supernormal capacity for work; but if there were a way of measuring either that ability in general or the personal achievement that goes into any particular success, the premiums actually paid out would probably not be found proportional to either. Spectacular prizes much greater than would have been necessary to call forth the particular effort are thrown to a small minority of winners, thus propelling much more efficaciously than a more equal and more "just" distribution would, the activity of that large majority of businessmen who receive in return very modest compensation or nothing or less than nothing, and yet do their utmost because they have the big prizes before their eyes and

overrate their chances of doing equally well. Similarly, the threats are addressed to incompetence. But though the incompetent men and the obsolete methods are in fact eliminated, sometimes very promptly, sometimes with a lag, failure also threatens or actually overtakes many an able man, thus whipping up *everyone,* again much more efficaciously than a more equal and more "just" system of penalties would. Finally, both business success and business failure are ideally precise. Neither can be talked away.

One aspect of this should be particularly noticed, for future reference as well as because of its importance for the argument in hand. In the way indicated and also in other ways which will be discussed later on, the capitalist arrangement, as embodied in the institution of private enterprise, effectively chains the bourgeois stratum to its tasks. But it does more than that. The same apparatus which conditions for performance the individuals and families that at any given time form the bourgeois class, *ipso facto* also selects the individuals and families that are to rise into that class or to drop out of it. This combination of the conditioning and the selective function is not a matter of course. On the contrary, most methods of social selection, unlike the "methods" of biological selection, do not guarantee performance of the selected individual; and their failure to do so constitutes one of the crucial problems of socialist organization that will come up for discussion at another stage of our inquiry. For the time being, it should merely be observed how well the capitalist system solves that problem: in most cases the man who rises first *into* the business class and then *within* it is also an able businessman and he is likely to rise exactly as far as his ability goes—simply because in that schema rising to a position and doing well in it generally is or was one and the same thing. This fact, so often obscured by the auto-therapeutic effort of the unsuccessful to deny it, is much more important for an appraisal of capitalist society and its civilization than anything that can be gleaned from the pure theory of the capitalist machine.

2. But is not all that we might be tempted to infer from "maximum performance of an optimally selected group" invalidated by the further fact that that performance is not geared to social service—production, so we might say, for consumption—but to money-making, that it aims at maximizing profits instead of welfare? Outside of the bourgeois stratum, this has of course always been the popular opinion. Economists have sometimes fought and sometimes espoused it. In doing so they have contributed something that was much more valuable than were the final judgments themselves at which they arrived individually and which in most cases reflect little more than their social location, interests and sympathies or antipathies. They slowly increased our factual knowledge and analytic powers so that the answers to many questions we are able to give today are no doubt much more correct although less simple and sweeping than were those of our predecessors.

To go no further back, the so-called classical economists[1] were practically of one mind. Most of them disliked many things about the social institutions of their epoch and about the way those institutions worked. They fought the landed interest and approved of social reforms—factory legislation in particular—that were not all on the lines of *laissez faire*. But they were quite convinced that within the institutional framework of capitalism, the manufacturer's and the trader's self-interest made for maximum performance in the interest of all. Confronted with the problem we are discussing, they would have had little hesitation in attributing the observed rate of increase in total output to relatively unfettered enterprise and the profit motive—perhaps they would have

mentioned "beneficial legislation" as a condition but by this they would have meant the removal of fetters, especially the removal or reduction of protective duties during the nineteenth century.

It is exceedingly difficult, at this hour of the day, to do justice to these views. They were of course the typical views of the English bourgeois class, and bourgeois blinkers are in evidence on almost every page the classical authors wrote. No less in evidence are blinkers of another kind: the classics reasoned in terms of a particular historical situation which they uncritically idealized and from which they uncritically generalized. Most of them, moreover, seem to have argued exclusively in terms of the English interests and problems of their time. This is the reason why, in other lands and at other times, people disliked their economics, frequently to the point of not even caring to understand it. But it will not do to dismiss their teaching on these grounds. A prejudiced man may yet be speaking the truth. Propositions developed from special cases may yet be generally valid. And the enemies and successors of the classics had and have only different but not fewer blinkers and preconceptions; they envisaged and envisage different but not less special cases.

From the standpoint of the economic analyst, the chief merit of the classics consists in their dispelling, along with many other gross errors, the naïve idea that economic activity in capitalist society, because it turns on the profit motive, must by virtue of that fact alone necessarily run counter to the interests of consumers; or, to put it differently, that moneymaking necessarily deflects producing from its social goal; or, finally, that private profits, both in themselves and through the distortion of the economic process they induce, are always a net loss to all excepting those who receive them and would therefore constitute a net gain to be reaped by socialization. If we look at the logic of these and similar propositions which no trained economist ever thought of defending, the classical refutation may well seem trivial. But as soon as we look at all the theories and slogans which, consciously or subconsciously, imply them and which are once more served up today, we shall feel more respect for that achievement. Let me add at once that the classical writers also clearly perceived, though they may have exaggerated, the role of saving and accumulation and that they linked saving to the rate of "progress" they observed in a manner that was fundamentally, if only approximately, correct. Above all, there was practical wisdom about their doctrine, a responsible long-run view and a manly tone that contrast favorably with modern hysterics.

But between realizing that hunting for a maximum of profit and striving for maximum productive performance are not necessarily incompatible, to proving that the former will necessarily—or in the immense majority of cases—imply the latter, there is a gulf much wider than the classics thought. And they never succeeded in bridging it. The modern student of their doctrines never ceases to wonder how it was possible for them to be satisfied with their arguments or to mistake these arguments for proofs; in the light of later analysis their *theory* was seen to be a house of cards whatever measure of truth there may have been in their *vision.*

3. This later analysis we will take in two strides—as much of it, that is, as we need in order to clarify our problem. Historically, the first will carry us into the first decade of this century, the second will cover some of the postwar developments of scientific economics. Frankly I do not know how much good this will do the non-professional reader; like every other branch of our knowledge, economics, as its analytic engine improves, moves fatally away from that happy stage in which all problems, methods and results could be made ac-

cessible to every educated person without special training. I will, however, do my best.

The first stride may be associated with two great names revered to this day by numberless disciples—so far at least as the latter do not think it bad form to express reverence for anything or anybody, which many of them obviously do—Alfred Marshall and Knut Wicksell. Their theoretical structure has little in common with that of the classics—though Marshall did his best to hide the fact—but it conserves the classic proposition that in the case of perfect competition the profit interest of the producer tends to maximize production. It even supplied almost satisfactory proof. Only, in the process of being more correctly stated and proved, the proposition lost much of its content—it does emerge from the operation, to be sure, but it emerges emaciated, barely alive. Still it can be shown, within the general assumptions of the Marshall-Wicksell analysis, that firms which cannot by their own individual action exert any influence upon the price of their products or of the factors of production they employ—so that there would be no point in their weeping over the fact that any increase in production tends to decrease the former and to increase the latter—will expand their output until they reach the point at which the additional cost that must be incurred in order to produce another small increment of product (marginal cost) just equals the price they can get for that increment, *i.e.*, that they will produce as much as they can without running into loss. And this can be shown to be as much as it is in general "socially desirable" to produce. In more technical language, in that case prices are, from the standpoint of the individual firm, not variables but parameters; and where this is so, there exists a state of equilibrium in which all outputs are at their maximum and all factors fully employed. This case is usually referred to as perfect competition. . . .

4. Let us take the second stride. The Marshall-Wicksell analysis of course did not overlook the many cases that fail to conform to that model. Nor, for that matter, had the classics overlooked them. They recognized cases of "monopoly," and Adam Smith himself carefully noticed the prevalence of devices to restrict competition and all the differences in flexibility of prices resulting therefrom. But they looked upon those cases as exceptions and, moreover, as exceptions that could and would be done away with in time. Something of that sort is true also of Marshall. Although he developed the Cournot theory of monopoly and although he anticipated later analysis by calling attention to the fact that most firms have special markets of their own in which they set prices instead of merely accepting them, he as well as Wicksell framed his general conclusions on the pattern of perfect competition so as to suggest, much as the classics did, that perfect competition was the rule. Neither Marshall and Wicksell nor the classics saw that perfect competition is the exception and that even if it were the rule there would be much less reason for congratulation than one might think.

If we look more closely at the conditions—not all of them explicitly stated or even clearly seen by Marshall and Wicksell—that must be fulfilled in order to produce perfect competition, we realize immediately that outside of agricultural mass production there cannot be many instances of it. A farmer supplies his cotton or wheat in fact under those conditions: from his standpoint the ruling prices of cotton or wheat are data, though very variable ones, and not being able to influence them by his individual action he simply adapts his output; since all farmers do the same, prices and quantities will in the end be adjusted as the theory of perfect competition requires. But this is not so even with many agricultural prod-ucts—with ducks, sausages, vegetables and many dairy products for instance. And as regards practically all the finished products and services of industry and trade, it is clear that every grocer, every filling station, every manufacturer of gloves or shaving cream or handsaws has a small and precarious market of his own which he tries—must try—to build up and to keep by price strategy, quality strategy—"product differentiation"—and advertising. Thus we get a completely different pattern which there seems to be no reason to expect to yield the results of perfect competition and which fits much better into the monopolistic schema. In these cases we speak of Monopolistic Competition. Their theory has been one of the major contributions to postwar economics.

There remains a wide field of substantially homogeneous products—mainly industrial raw materials and semi-finished products such as steel ingots, cement, cotton gray goods and the like—in which the conditions for the emergence of monopolistic competition do not seem to prevail. This is so. But in general, similar results follow for that field inasmuch as the greater part of it is covered by largest-scale firms which, either individually or in concert, are able to manipulate prices even without differentiating products—the case of Oligopoly. Again the monopoly schema, suitably adapted, seems to fit this type of behavior much better than does the schema of perfect competition.

As soon as the prevalence of monopolistic competition or of oligopoly or of combinations of the two is recognized, many of the propositions which the Marshall-Wicksell generation of economists used to teach with the utmost confidence become either inapplicable or much more difficult to prove. This holds true, in the first place, of the propositions turning on the fundamental concept of equilibrium, i.e., a determinate state of the economic organism, toward which any given state of it is always gravitating and which displays certain simple properties. In the general case of oligopoly there is in fact no determinate equilibrium at all and the possibility presents itself that there may be an endless sequence of moves and countermoves, an indefinite state of warfare between firms. It is true that there are many special cases in which a state of equilibrium theoretically exists. In the second place, even in these cases not only is it much harder to attain than the equilibrium in perfect competition, and still harder to preserve, but the "beneficial" competition of the classic type seems likely to be replaced by "predatory" or "cutthroat" competition or simply by struggles for control in the financial sphere. These things are so many sources of social waste, and there are many others such as the costs of advertising campaigns, the suppression of new methods of production (buying up of patents in order not to use them) and so on. And most important of all: under the conditions envisaged, equilibrium, even if eventually attained by an extremely costly method, no longer guarantees either full employment or maximum output in the sense of the theory of perfect competition. It *may* exist without full employment; it is *bound* to exist, so it seems, at a level of output below that maximum mark, because profit-conserving strategy, impossible in conditions of perfect competition, now not only becomes possible but imposes itself.

Well, does not this bear out what the man in the street (unless a businessman himself) always thought on the subject of private business? Has not modern analysis completely refuted the classical doctrine and justified the popular view? Is it not quite true after all, that there is little parallelism between producing for profit and producing for the consumer and that private enterprise is little more than a device to curtail production in order to extort profits which then are correctly described as tolls and ransoms?

THE PROCESS OF CREATIVE DESTRUCTION

[*Paragraphs deleted.*]

The conclusions alluded to at the end of the preceding chapter are in fact almost completely false. Yet they follow from observations and theorems that are almost completely true. Both economists and popular writers have once more run away with some fragments of reality they happened to grasp. These fragments themselves were mostly seen correctly. Their formal properties were mostly developed correctly. But no conclusions about capitalist reality as a whole follow from such fragmentary analyses. If we draw them nevertheless, we can be right only by accident. That has been done. And the lucky accident did not happen.

The essential point to grasp is that in dealing with capitalism we are dealing with an evolutionary process. It may seem strange that anyone can fail to see so obvious a fact which moreover was long ago emphasized by Karl Marx. Yet that fragmentary analysis which yields the bulk of our propositions about the functioning of modern capitalism persistently neglects it. Let us restate the point and see how it bears upon our problem.

Capitalism, then, is by nature a form or method of economic change and not only never is but never can be stationary. And this evolutionary character of the capitalist process is not merely due to the fact that economic life goes on in a social and natural environment which changes and by its change alters the data of economic action; this fact is important and these changes (wars, revolutions and so on) often condition industrial change, but they are not its prime movers. Nor is this evolutionary character due to a quasi-automatic increase in population and capital or to the vagaries of monetary systems of which exactly the same thing holds true. The fundamental impulse that sets and keeps the capitalist engine in motion comes from the new consumers' goods, the new methods of production or transportation, the new markets, the new forms of industrial organization that capitalist enterprise creates.

As we have seen in the preceding chapter, the contents of the laborer's budget, say from 1760 to 1940, did not simply grow on unchanging lines but they underwent a process of qualitative change. Similarly, the history of the productive apparatus of a typical farm, from the beginnings of the rationalization of crop rotation, plowing and fattening to the mechanized thing of today—linking up with elevators and railroads—is a history of revolutions. So is the history of the productive apparatus of the iron and steel industry from the charcoal furnace to our own type of furnace, or the history of the apparatus of power production from the overshot water wheel to the modern power plant, or the history of transportation from the mailcoach to the airplane. The opening up of new markets, foreign or domestic, and the organizational development from the craft shop and factory to such concerns as U.S. Steel illustrate the same process of industrial mutation—if I may use that biological term—that incessantly revolutionizes the economic structure *from within,* incessantly destroying the old one, incessantly creating a new one. This process of Creative Destruction is the essential fact about capitalism. It is what capitalism consists in and what every capitalist concern has got to live in. This fact bears upon our problem in two ways.

First, since we are dealing with a process whose every element takes considerable time in revealing its true features and ultimate effects, there is no point in appraising the performance of that process *ex visu* of a given point of time; we must judge its performance

over time, as it unfolds through decades or centuries. A system—any system, economic or other—that at *every* given point of time fully utilizes its possibilities to the best advantage may yet in the long run be inferior to a system that does so at *no* given point of time, because the latter's failure to do so may be a condition for the level or speed of long-run performance.

Second, since we are dealing with an organic process, analysis of what happens in any particular part of it—say, in an individual concern or industry—may indeed clarify details of mechanism but is inconclusive beyond that. Every piece of business strategy acquires its true significance only against the background of that process and within the situation created by it. It must be seen in its role in the perennial gale of creative destruction; it cannot be understood irrespective of it or, in fact, on the hypothesis that there is a perennial lull.

But economists who, *ex visu* of a point of time, look for example at the behavior of an oligopolist industry—an industry which consists of a few big firms—and observe the well-known moves and countermoves within it that seem to aim at nothing but high prices and restrictions of output are making precisely that hypothesis. They accept the data of the momentary situation as if there were no past or future to it and think that they have understood what there is to understand if they interpret the behavior of those firms by means of the principle of maximizing profits with reference to those data. The usual theorist's paper and the usual government commission's report practically never try to see that behavior, on the one hand, as a result of a piece of past history and, on the other hand, as an attempt to deal with a situation that is sure to change presently—as an attempt by those firms to keep on their feet, on ground that is slipping away from under them. In other words, the problem that is usually being visualized is how capitalism administers existing structures, whereas the relevant problem is how it creates and destroys them. As long as this is not recognized, the investigator does a meaningless job. As soon as it is recognized, his outlook on capitalist practice and its social results changes considerably.

The first thing to go is the traditional conception of the *modus operandi* of competition. Economists are at long last emerging from the stage in which price competition was all they saw. As soon as quality competition and sales effort are admitted into the sacred precincts of theory, the price variable is ousted from its dominant position. However, it is still competition within a rigid pattern of invariant conditions, methods of production and forms of industrial organization in particular, that practically monopolizes attention. But in capitalist reality as distinguished from its textbook picture, it is not that kind of competition which counts but the competition from the new commodity, the new technology, the new source of supply, the new type of organization (the largest-scale unit of control for instance)—competition which commands a decisive cost or quality advantage and which strikes not at the margins of the profits and the outputs of the existing firms but at their foundations and their very lives. This kind of competition is as much more effective than the other as a bombardment is in comparison with forcing a door, and so much more important that it becomes a matter of comparative indifference whether competition in the ordinary sense functions more or less promptly; the powerful lever that in the long run expands output and brings down prices is in any case made of other stuff.

It is hardly necessary to point out that competition of the kind we now have in mind acts not only when in being but also when it is merely an ever-present threat. It disciplines before it attacks. The businessman feels himself to be in a competitive situation even if he is alone in his field or if, though not alone, he holds a position such that investigating government experts fail to see any effective competition between him and any other firms in the same or a neighboring field and in consequence conclude that his talk, under examination, about his competitive sorrows is all make-believe. In many cases, though not in all, this will in the long run enforce behavior very similar to the perfectly competitive pattern.

Many theorists take the opposite view which is best conveyed by an example. Let us assume that there is a certain number of retailers in a neighborhood who try to improve their relative position by service and "atmosphere" but avoid price competition and stick as to methods to the local tradition—a picture of stagnating routine. As others drift into the trade that quasi-equilibrium is indeed upset, but in a manner that does not benefit their customers. The economic space around each of the shops having been narrowed, their owners will no longer be able to make a living and they will try to mend the case by raising prices in tacit agreement. This will further reduce their sales and so, by successive pyramiding, a situation will evolve in which increasing potential supply will be attended by increasing instead of decreasing prices and by decreasing instead of increasing sales.

Such cases do occur, and it is right and proper to work them out. But as the practical instances usually given show, they are fringe-end cases to be found mainly in the sectors furthest removed from all that is most characteristic of capitalist activity. Moreover, they are transient by nature. In the case of retail trade the competition that matters arises not from additional shops of the same type, but from the department store, the chain store, the mail-order house and the supermarket which are bound to destroy those pyramids sooner or later. Now a theoretical construction which neglects this essential element of the case neglects all that is most typically capitalist about it; even if correct in logic as well as in fact, it is like *Hamlet* without the Danish prince.

MONOPOLISTIC PRACTICES

What has been said so far is really sufficient to enable the reader to deal with the large majority of the practical cases he is likely to meet and to realize the inadequacy of most of those criticisms of the profit economy which, directly or indirectly, rely on the absence of perfect competition. Since, however, the bearing of our argument on some of those criticisms may not be obvious at a glance, it will be worth our while to elaborate a little in order to make a few points more explicit.

1. We have just seen that, both as a fact and as a threat, the impact of new things—new technologies for instance—on the existing structure of an industry considerably reduces the long-run scope and importance of practices that aim, through restricting output, at conserving established positions and at maximizing the profits accruing from them. We must now recognize the further fact that restrictive practices of this kind, as far as they are effective, acquire a new significance in the perennial gale of creative destruction, a significance which they would not have in a stationary state or in a state of slow and balanced growth. In either of these cases restrictive strategy would produce no result other than an increase in profits at the expense of buyers except that, in the case of balanced advance, it might still prove to be the easiest and most effective way of collecting the means by which to finance additional investment. But in the process of creative destruction, restrictive practices may do much to steady the ship and to alleviate temporary difficulties. This is in fact a very familiar argument which always turns up in times of depression and, as everyone knows, has become very popular with governments and their economic advisers—witness the NRA. While it has been so much misused and so faultily acted upon that most economists heartily despise it, those same advisers who are responsible for this invariably fail to see its much more general rationale.

Practically any investment entails, as a necessary complement of entrepreneurial action, certain safeguarding activities such as insuring or hedging. Long-range investing under rapidly changing conditions, especially under conditions that change or may change at any moment under the impact of new commodities and technologies, is like shooting at a target that is not only indistinct but moving—and moving jerkily at that. Hence it becomes necessary to resort to such protecting devices as patents or temporary secrecy of processes or, in some cases, long-period contracts secured in advance. But these protecting devices which most economists accept as normal elements of rational management are only special cases of a larger class comprising many others which most economists condemn although they do not differ fundamentally from the recognized ones.

If for instance a war risk is insurable, nobody objects to a firm's collecting the cost of this insurance from the buyers of its products. But that risk is no less an element in long-run costs, if there are no facilities for insuring against it, in which case a price strategy aiming at the same end will seem to involve unnecessary restriction and to be productive of excess profits. Similarly, if a patent cannot be secured or would not, if secured, effectively protect, other means may have to be used in order to justify the investment. Among them are a price policy that will make it possible to write off more quickly than would otherwise be rational, or additional investment in order to provide excess capacity to be used only for aggression or defense. Again, if long-period contracts cannot be entered into in advance, other means may have to be devised in order to tie prospective customers to the investing firm.

In analyzing such business strategy *ex visu* of a given point of time, the investigating economist or government agent sees price policies that seem to him predatory and restrictions of output that seem to him synonymous with loss of opportunities to produce. He does not see that restrictions of this type are, in the conditions of the perennial gale, incidents, often unavoidable incidents, of a long-run process of expansion which they protect rather than impede. There is no more of paradox in this than there is in saying that motorcars are traveling faster than they otherwise would *because* they are provided with brakes.

2. This stands out most clearly in the case of those sectors of the economy which at any time happen to embody the impact of new things and methods on the existing industrial structure. The best way of getting a vivid and realistic idea of industrial strategy is indeed to visualize the behavior of new concerns or industries that introduce new commodities or processes (such as the aluminum industry) or else reorganize a part or the whole of an industry (such as, for instance, the old Standard Oil Company).

As we have seen, such concerns are aggressors by nature and wield the really effective weapon of competition. Their intrusion can only in the rarest of cases fail to improve total output in quantity or quality, both through the new method itself—even if at no time used to full advantage—and through the pressure it exerts on the preexisting firms. But these aggressors are so circumstanced as to require, for purposes of attack and defense, also pieces of armor other than price and quality of their product which, moreover, must be strategically manipulated all along so that at any point of time they seem to be doing nothing but restricting their output and keeping prices high.

On the one hand, largest-scale plans could in many cases not materialize at all if it were not known from the outset that competition will be discouraged by heavy capital requirements or lack of experience, or that means are available to discourage or checkmate it so as to gain the time and space for further developments. Even the conquest of financial control over competing concerns in otherwise unassailable positions or the securing of advantages that run counter to the public's sense of fair play— railroad rebates—move, as far as long-run effects on total output alone are envisaged, into a different light they *may* be methods for removing obstacles that the institution of private property puts in the path of progress. In a socialist society that time and space would be no less necessary. They would have to be secured by order of the central authority.

On the other hand, enterprise would in most cases be impossible if it were not known from the outset that exceptionally favorable situations are likely to arise which if exploited by price, quality and quantity manipulation will produce profits adequate to ride over exceptionally unfavorable situations provided these are similarly managed. Again this requires strategy that in the short run is often restrictive. In the majority of successful cases this strategy just manages to serve its purpose. In some cases, however, it is so successful as to yield profits far above what is necessary in order to induce the corresponding investment. These cases then provide the baits that lure capital on to untried trails. Their presence explains in part how it is possible for so large a section of the capitalist world to work for nothing: in the midst of the prosperous twenties just about half of the business corporations in the United States were run at a loss, at zero profits, or at profit which, if they had been foreseen, would have been inadequate to call forth the effort and expenditure involved.

Our argument however extends beyond the cases of new concerns methods and industries. Old concerns and established industries, whether or not directly attacked, still live in the perennial gale. Situations emerge in the process of creative destruction in which many firms may have to perish that nevertheless would be able to live on vigorously and usefully if they could weather a particular storm. Short of such general crises or depressions, sectional situations arise in which the rapid change of data that is characteristic of that process so disorganizes an industry for the time being as to inflict functionless losses and to create avoidable unemployment. Finally, there is certainly no point in trying to conserve obsolescent industries indefinitely; but there is point in trying to avoid their coming down with a crash and in attempting to turn a rout, which may become a center of cumulative depressive effects, into orderly retreat. Correspondingly there is, in the case of industries that have sown their wild oats but are still gaining and not losing ground, such a thing as orderly advance.

All this is of course nothing but the tritest common sense. But it is being overlooked with a persistence so stubborn as sometimes to raise the question of sincerity. And it follows that, within the process of creative destruction, all the realities of which theorists are in the habit of relegating to books and courses on business cycles, there is another side to industrial self-organization than that which these theorists are contemplating. "Restraints of trade" of the cartel type as well as those which merely consist in tacit understandings about price competition may be effective remedies under conditions of depression. As far as they are, they may in the end produce not only steadier but also greater expansion of total output than could be secured by an entirely uncontrolled onward rush that cannot fail to be studded with catastrophes. Nor can it be argued that these catastrophes occur in any case. We know what has happened in each historical case. We have a very imperfect idea of what might have happened,

considering the tremendous pace of the process, if such pegs had been entirely absent.

Even as now extended however, our argument does not cover all cases of restrictive or regulating strategy, many of which no doubt have that injurious effect on the long-run development of output which is uncritically attributed to all of them. And even in the cases our argument does cover, the net effect is a question of the circumstances and of the way in which and the degree to which industry regulates itself in each individual case. It is certainly as conceivable that an all-pervading cartel system might sabotage all progress as it is that it might realize, with smaller social and private costs, all that perfect competition is supposed to realize. This is why our argument does not amount to a case against state regulation. It does show that there is no general case for indiscriminate "trust-busting" or for the prosecution of everything that qualifies as a restraint of trade. Rational as distinguished from vindictive regulation by public authority turns out to be an extremely delicate problem which not every government agency, particularly when in full cry against big business, can be trusted to solve. But our argument, framed to refute a prevalent *theory* and the inferences drawn therefrom about the relation between modern capitalism and the development of total output, only yields another *theory,* i.e., another outlook on facts and another principle by which to interpret them. For our purpose that is enough. For the rest, the facts themselves have the floor.

NOTE

1. The term Classical Economists will in this book be used to designate the leading English economists whose works appeared between 1776 and 1848. Adam Smith, Ricardo, Malthus, Senior and John Stuart Mill are the outstanding names. It is important to keep this in mind because a much broader use of the term has come into fashion of late.

35. The Road to Serfdom*

FRIEDRICH A. HAYEK

THE "INEVITABILITY" OF PLANNING

It is a revealing fact that few planners are content to say that central planning is desirable. Most of them affirm that we can no longer choose but are compelled by circumstances beyond our control to substitute planning for competition. The myth is deliberately cultivated that we are embarking on the new course not out of free will but because competition is spontaneously eliminated by technological changes which we neither can reverse nor should wish to prevent. This argument is rarely developed at any length—it is one of the assertions taken over by one writer from another until, by mere iteration, it has come to be accepted as an established fact. It is, nevertheless, devoid of foundation. The tendency toward monopoly and planning is not the result of any "objective facts" beyond our control but the product of opinions fostered and propagated for half a century until they have come to dominate all our policy.

Of the various arguments employed to demonstrate the inevitability of planning, the one most frequently heard is that technological changes have made competition impossible in a constantly increasing number of fields and that the only choice left to us is between control of production by private monopolies and direction by the government. This belief derives mainly from the Marxist doctrine of the "concentration of industry," although, like so many Marxist

ideas, it is now found in many circles which have received it at third or fourth hand and do not know whence it derives.

The historical fact of the progressive growth of monopoly during the last fifty years and the increasing restriction of the field in which competition rules is, of course, not disputed—although the extent of the phenomenon is often greatly exaggerated. The important question is whether this development is a necessary consequence of the advance of technology or whether it is simply the result of the policies pursued in most countries. We shall presently see that the actual history of this development strongly suggests the latter. But we must first consider in how far modern technological developments are of such a kind as to make the growth of monopolies in wide fields inevitable.

The alleged technological cause of the growth of monopoly is the superiority of the large firm over the small, owing to the greater efficiency of modern methods of mass production. Modern methods, it is asserted, have created conditions in the majority of industries where the production of the large firm can be increased at decreasing costs per unit, with the result that the large firms are everywhere underbidding and driving out the small ones; this process must go on until in each industry only one or at most a few giant firms are left. This argument singles out one effect sometimes accompanying technological progress; it disregards others which work in the opposite direction; and it receives little support from a serious study of the facts. We cannot here investigate this question in detail and must be content to accept the best evidence available. The most comprehensive study of the facts undertaken in recent times is that by the Temporary National Economic Committee on the *Concentration of Economic Power.* The final report of this committee (which certainly cannot be accused of an undue liberal bias) arrives at the conclusion that the view according to which the greater efficiency of large-scale production is the cause of the disappearance of competition "finds scant support in any evidence that is now at hand." And the detailed monograph on the question which was prepared for the committee sums up the answer in this statement:

The superior efficiency of large establishments has not been demonstrated; the advantages that are supposed to destroy competition have failed to manifest themselves in many fields. Nor do the economies of size, where they exist, invariably necessitate monopoly. . . . The size or the sizes of the optimum efficiency may be reached long before the major part of a supply is subjected to such control. The conclusions that the advantage of large-scale production must lead inevitably to the abolition of competition cannot be accepted. It should be noted, moreover, that monopoly is frequently the product of factors other than the lower costs of greater size. It is attained through collusive agreement and promoted by public policies. When these agreements are invalidated and when these policies are reversed, competitive conditions can be restored.

An investigation of conditions in England would lead to very similar results. Anyone who has observed how aspiring monopolists regularly seek and frequently obtain the assistance of the power of the state to make their control effective can have little doubt that there is nothing inevitable about this development.

This conclusion is strongly supported by the historical order in which the decline of competition and the growth of monopoly manifested themselves in different countries. If they were the result of technological developments or a necessary product of the evolution of "capitalism," we should expect them to appear first in the countries with the most advanced economic system. In fact, they appeared first during the last third of the nineteenth century in what were then comparatively young industrial countries, the United States and Germany. In the latter country especially, which came to be regarded as the model country typifying the necessary evolution of capitalism, the growth of cartels and syndicates has since 1878 been systematically fostered by deliberate policy. Not only the instrument of protection but direct inducements and ultimately compulsion were used by the governments to further the creation of monopolies for the regulation of prices and sales. It was here that, with the help of the state, the first great experiment in "scientific planning" and "conscious organization of industry" led to the creation of giant monopolies, which were represented as inevitable growths fifty years before the same was done in Great Britain. It is largely due to the influence of German socialist theoreticians, particularly Sombart, generalizing from the experience of their country, that the inevitable development of the competitive system into "monopoly capitalism" became widely accepted. That in the United States a highly protectionist policy made a somewhat similar development possible seemed to confirm this generalization. The development of Germany, however, more than that of the United States, came to be regarded as representative of a universal tendency; and it became a commonplace to speak—to quote a widely read political essay of recent date—of "Germany where all the social and political forces of modern civilization have reached their most advanced form."

How little there was of inevitability in all this, and how much is the result of deliberate policy, becomes clear when we consider the position in England until 1931 and the development since that year in which Great Britain also embarked upon a policy of general protection. It is only a dozen years since, except for a few industries which had obtained protection earlier, British industry was on the whole as competitive as, perhaps, at any time in its history. And, although during the 1920's it suffered severely from incompatible policies followed with regard to wages and to money, at least the years up to 1929 compare with regard to employment and general activity not unfavorably with the 1930's. It is only since the transition to protection and the general change in British economic policy accompanying it that the growth of monopolies has proceeded at an amazing rate and has transformed British industry to an extent the public has scarcely yet realized. To argue that this development has anything to do with the technological progress during this period, that technological necessities which in Germany operated in the 1880's and 1890's, made themselves felt here in the 1930's, is not much less absurd than the claim, implied in a statement of Mussolini, that Italy had to abolish individual freedom before other European people because its civilization had marched so far in advance of the rest!

In so far as England is concerned, the thesis that the change in opinion and policy merely follows an inexorable change in the facts can be given a certain appearance of truth, just because the nation has followed at a distance the intellectual developments elsewhere. It could thus be argued that monopolistic organization of industry grew up in spite of the fact that public opinion still favored competition but that outside events frustrated their wishes. The true relation between theory and practice becomes, however, clear as soon as we look to the prototype of this development—Germany. That *there* the suppression of competition was a matter of deliberate policy, that it was undertaken in the service of the ideal which we now call planning, there can be no doubt. In the progressive advance toward a completely planned society the Germans, and all the people who are imitating their example, are merely following the course which nineteenth-century thinkers, particularly Germans, have mapped out for them. The intellectual history of the last sixty or eighty years is indeed a perfect illustration of the truth that in social evolution nothing is inevitable but thinking makes it so.

The assertion that modern technological progress makes planning inevitable can also be interpreted in a different manner. It may mean that the complexity of our modern industrial civilization creates new problems with which we cannot hope to deal effectively except by central planning. In a sense this is true—yet not in the wide sense in which it is claimed. It is, for example, a commonplace that many of the problems created by a modern town, like many other problems caused by close contiguity in space, are not adequately solved by competition. But it is not these problems, like those of the "public utilities," etc., which are uppermost in the minds of those who invoke the complexity of modern civilization as an argument for central planning. What they generally suggest is that the increasing difficulty of obtaining a coherent picture of the complete economic process makes it indispensable that things should be co-ordinated by some central agency if social life is not to dissolve in chaos.

This argument is based on a complete misapprehension of the working of competition. Far from being appropriate only to comparatively simple conditions, it is the very complexity of the division of labor under modern conditions which makes competition the only method by which such co-ordination can be adequately brought about. There would be no difficulty about efficient control or planning were conditions so simple that a single person or board could effectively survey all the relevant facts. It is only as the factors which have to be taken into account become so numerous that it is impossible to gain a synoptic view of them that decentralization becomes imperative. But, once decentralization is necessary, the problem of co-ordination arises—a co-ordination which leaves the separate agencies free to adjust their activities to the facts which only they can know and yet brings about a mutual adjustment of their respective plans. As decentralization has become necessary because nobody can consciously balance all the considerations bearing on the decisions of so many individuals, the coordination can clearly be effected not by "conscious control" but only by arrangements which convey to each agent the information he must possess in order effectively to adjust his decisions to those of others. And because all the details of the changes constantly affecting the conditions of demand and supply of the different commodities can never be fully known, or quickly enough be collected and disseminated, by any one center, what is required is some apparatus of registration which automatically records all the relevant effects of individual actions and whose indications are at the same time the resultant of, and the guide for, all the individual decisions.

This is precisely what the price system does under competition, and which no other system even promises to accomplish. It enables entrepreneurs, by watching the movement of comparatively few prices, as an engineer watches the hands of a few dials, to adjust their activities to those of their fellows. The important point here is that the price system will fulfil this function only if competition prevails, that is, if the individual producer has to adapt himself to price changes and cannot control them. The more complicated the whole, the more dependent we become on that division of knowledge between individuals whose separate efforts are co-ordinated by the impersonal mechanism for transmitting the relevant information known by us as the price system.

It is no exaggeration to say that if we had had to rely on conscious central planning for the growth of our industrial system, it would never have reached the degree of differentiation, complexity, and flexibility it has attained. Compared with this method of solving the economic problem by means of decentralization plus automatic co-ordination, the more obvious method of central direction is incredibly clumsy, primitive, and limited in scope. That the division of labor has reached the extent which makes modern civilization possible we owe to the fact that it did not have to be consciously created but that man tumbled on a method by which the division of labor could be extended far beyond the limits within which it could have been planned. Any further growth of its complexity, therefore, far from making central direction more necessary, makes it more important than ever that we should use a technique which does not depend on conscious control.

There is yet another theory which connects the growth of monopolies with technological progress, and which uses arguments almost opposite to those we have just considered; though not often clearly stated, it has also exercised considerable influence. It contends not that modern technique destroys competition but that, on the the contrary, it will be impossible to make use of many of the new technological possibilities unless protection against competition is granted, i.e., a monopoly is conferred. This type of argument is not necessarily fraudulent, as the critical reader will perhaps suspect: the obvious answer— that if a new technique for satisfying our wants is really better, it ought to be able to stand up against all competition— does not dispose of all instances to which this argument refers. No doubt in many cases it is used merely as a form of special pleading by interested parties. Even more often it is probably based on a confusion between technical excellence from a narrow engineering point of view and desirability from the point of view of society as a whole.

There remains, however, a group of instances where the argument has some force. It is, for example, at least conceivable that the British automobile industry might be able to supply a car cheaper and better than cars used to be in the United States if everyone in England were made to use the same kind of car or that the use of electricity for all purposes could be made cheaper than coal or gas if everybody could be made to use only electricity. In instances like these it is at least possible that we might all be better off and should prefer the new situation if we had the choice—but that no individual ever gets the choice, because the alternative is either that we should all use the same cheap car (or all should use only electricity) or that we should have the choice between these things with each of them at a much higher price. I do not know whether this is true in either of the instances given. But it must be admitted that it is possible that, by compulsory standardization or the prohibition of variety beyond a certain degree, abundance might be increased in some fields more than sufficiently to compensate for the restriction of the choice of the consumer. It is even conceivable that a new invention may be made some day whose adoption would seem unquestionably beneficial but which could be used only if many or all people were made to avail themselves of it at the same time.

Whether such instances are of any great or lasting importance, they are certainly not instances where it could be ligitimately claimed that technical progress makes central direction inevitable. They would merely make it necessary to choose between gaining a particular advantage by compulsion and

not obtaining it—or, in most instances, obtaining it a little later, when further technical advance has overcome the particular difficulties. It is true that in such situations we may have to sacrifice a possible immediate gain as the price of our freedom—but we avoid, on the other hand, the necessity of making future developments dependent upon the knowledge which particular people now possess. By sacrificing such possible present advantages, we preserve an important stimulus to further progress. Though in the short run the price we have to pay for variety and freedom of choice may sometimes be high, in the long run even material progress will depend on this very variety, because we can never predict from which of the many forms in which a good or service can be provided something better may develop. It cannot, of course, be asserted that the preservation of freedom at the expense of some addition to our present material comfort will be thus rewarded in all instances. But the argument for freedom is precisely that we ought to leave room for the unforeseeable free growth. It applies, therefore, no less when, on the basis of our present knowledge, compulsion would seem to bring only advantages, and although in a particular instance it may actually do no harm.

In much of the current discussion on the effects of technological progress this progress is presented to us as if it were something outside us which could compel us to use the new knowledge in a particular way. While it is true, of course, that inventions have given us tremendous power, it is absurd to suggest that we must use this power to destroy our most precious inheritance: liberty. It does mean, however, that if we want to preserve it, we must guard it more jealously than ever and that we must be prepared to make sacrifices for it. While there is nothing in modern technological developments which forces us toward comprehensive economic planning, there is a great deal in them which makes infinitely more dangerous the power a planning authority would possess.

While there can thus be little doubt that the movement toward planning is the result of deliberate action and that there are no external necessities which force us to it, it is worth inquiring why so large a proportion of the technical experts should be found in the front rank of the planners. The explanation of this phenomenon is closely connected with an important fact which the critics of the planners should always keep in mind: that there is little question that almost every one of the technical ideals of our experts could be realized within a comparatively short time if to achieve them were made the sole aim of humanity. There is an infinite number of good things, which we all agree are highly desirable as well as possible, but of which we cannot hope to achieve more than a few within our lifetime, or which we can hope to achieve only very imperfectly. It is the frustration of his ambitions in his own field which makes the specialist revolt against the existing order. We all find it difficult to bear to see things left undone which everybody must admit are both desirable and possible. That these things cannot all be done at the same time, that any one of them can be achieved only at the sacrifice of others, can be seen only by taking into account factors which fall outside any specialism, which can be appreciated only by a painful intellectual effort—the more painful as it forces us to see against a wider background the objects to which most of our labors are directed and to balance them against others which lie outside our immediate interest and for which, for that reason, we care less.

Every one of the many things which, considered in isolation, it would be possible to achieve in a planned society creates enthusiasts for planning who feel confident that they will be able to instil into the directors of such a society their sense of the value of the particular objective; and the hopes of some of them would undoubtedly be fulfilled, since a planned society would certainly further some objectives more than is the case at present. It would be foolish to deny that the instances of planned or semiplanned societies which we know do furnish illustrations in point, good things which the people of these countries owe entirely to planning. The magnificent motor roads in Germany and Italy are an instance often quoted—even though they do not represent a kind of planning not equally possible in a liberal society. But it is equally foolish to quote such instances of technical excellence in particular fields as evidence of the general superiority of planning. It would be more correct to say that such extreme technical excellence out of line with general conditions is evidence of a misdirection of resources. Anyone who has driven along the famous German motor roads and found the amount of traffic on them less than on many a secondary road in England can have little doubt that, so far as peace purposes are concerned, there was little justification for them. Whether it was not a case where the planners decided in favor of "guns" instead of "butter" is another matter. But by our standards there is little ground for enthusiasm.

The illusion of the specialist that in a planned society he would secure more attention to the objectives for which he cares most is a more general phenomenon than the term "specialist" at first suggests. In our predilections and interests we are all in some measure specialists. And we all think that our personal order of values is not merely personal but that in a free discussion among rational people we would convince the others that ours is the right one. The lover of the countryside who wants above all that its traditional appearance should be preserved and that the blots already made by industry on its fair face should be removed, no less than the health enthusiast who wants all the picturesque but insanitary old cottages cleared away, or the motorist who wishes the country cut up by big motor roads, the efficiency fanatic who desires the maximum of specialization and mechanization no less than the idealist who for the development of personality wants to preserve as many independent craftsmen as possible, all know that their aim can be fully achieved only by planning—and they all want planning for that reason. But, of course, the adoption of the social planning for which they clamor can only bring out the concealed conflict between their aims.

The movement for planning owes its present strength largely to the fact that, while planning is in the main still an ambition, it unites almost all the single-minded idealists, all the men and women who have devoted their lives to a single task. The hopes they place in planning, however, are the result not of a comprehensive view of society but rather of a very limited view and often the result of a great exaggeration of the importance of the ends they place foremost. This is not to underrate the great pragmatic value of this type of men in a free society like ours, which makes them the subject of just admiration. But it would make the very men who are most anxious to plan society the most dangerous if they were allowed to do so—and the most intolerant of the planning of others. From the saintly and single-minded idealist to the fanatic is often but a step. Though it is the resentment of the frustrated specialist which gives the demand for planning its strongest impetus, there could hardly be a more unbearable—and more irrational—world than one in which the most eminent specialists in each field were allowed to proceed unchecked with the realization of their ideals. Nor can "co-ordination," as some planners seem to imagine, become a new specialism. The economist is the last to claim that he has the knowledge which the co-ordinator would need. His plea is for a method which effects such co-ordination without the need for an omniscient dictator. But that means precisely the retention of some such impersonal, and often unintelligible, checks on individual efforts as those against which all specialists chafe.

PLANNING AND DEMOCRACY

The common features of all collectivist systems may be described, in a phrase ever dear to socialists of all schools, as the deliberate organization of the labors of society for a definite social goal. That our present society lacks such "conscious" direction toward a single aim, that its activities are guided by the whims and fancies of irresponsible individuals, has always been one of the main complaints of its socialist critics.

In many ways this puts the basic issue very clearly. And it directs us at once to the point where the conflict arises between individual freedom and collectivism. The various kinds of collectivism, communism, fascism, etc., differ among themselves in the nature of the goal toward which they want to direct the efforts of society. But they all differ from liberalism and individualism in wanting to organize the whole of society and all its resources for this unitary end and in refusing to recognize autonomous spheres in which the ends of the individuals are supreme. In short, they are totalitarian in the true sense of this new word which we have adopted to describe the unexpected but nevertheless inseparable manifestations of what in theory we call collectivism.

The "social goal," or "common purpose," for which society is to be organized is usually vaguely described as the "common good," the "general welfare," or the "general interest." It does not need much reflection to see that these terms have no sufficiently definite meaning to determine a particular course of action. The welfare and the happiness of millions cannot be measured on a single scale of less and more. The welfare of a people, like the happiness of a man, depends on a great many things that can be provided in an infinite variety of combinations. It cannot be adequately expressed as a single end, but only as a hierarchy of ends, a comprehensive scale of values in which every need of every person is given its place. To direct all our activities according to a single plan presupposes that every one of our needs is given its rank in an order of values which must be complete enough to make it possible to decide among all the different courses which the planner has to choose. It presupposes, in short, the existence of a complete ethical code in which all the different human values are allotted their due place.

The conception of a complete ethical code is unfamiliar, and it requires some effort of imagination to see what it involves. We are not in the habit of thinking of moral codes as more or less complete. The fact that we are constantly choosing between different values without a social code prescribing how we ought to choose does not surprise us and does not suggest to us that our moral code is incomplete. In our society there is neither occasion nor reason why people should develop common views about what should be done in such situations. But where all the means to be used are the property of society and are to be used in the name of society according to a unitary plan, a "social" view about what ought to be done must guide all decisions. In such a world we should soon find that our moral code is full of gaps.

We are not concerned here with the question whether it would be desirable to have such a complete ethical code. It may merely be pointed out that up to the present the growth of civilization has been accompanied by a steady diminution of the sphere in which individual actions are bound by fixed rules. The rules of which our common moral code consists have progressively become fewer and more general in character. From the primitive man, who

was bound by an elaborate ritual in almost every one of his daily activities, who was limited by innumerable taboos, and who could scarcely conceive of doing things in a way different from his fellows, morals have more and more tended to become merely limits circumscribing the sphere within which the individual could behave as he liked. The adoption of a common ethical code comprehensive enough to determine a unitary economic plan would mean a complete reversal of this tendency.

The essential point for us is that no such complete ethical code exists. The attempt to direct all economic activity according to a single plan would raise innumerable questions to which the answer could be provided only by a moral rule, but to which existing morals have no answer and where there exists no agreed view on what ought to be done. People will have either no definite views or conflicting views on such questions, because in the free society in which we have lived there has been no occasion to think about them and still less to form common opinions about them.

Not only do we not possess such an all-inclusive scale of values: it would be impossible for any mind to comprehend the infinite variety of different needs of different people which compete for the available resources and to attach a definite weight to each. For our problem it is of minor importance whether the ends for which any person cares comprehend only his own individual needs, or whether they include the needs of his closer or even those of his more distant fellows—that is, whether he is egoistic or altruistic in the ordinary senses of these words. The point which is so important is the basic fact that it is impossible for any man to survey more than a limited field, to be aware of the urgency of more than a limited number of needs. Whether his interests center round his own physical needs, or whether he takes a warm interest in the welfare of every human being he knows, the ends about which he can be concerned will always be only an infinitesimal fraction of the needs of all men.

This is the fundamental fact on which the whole philosophy of individualism is based. It does not assume, as is often asserted, that man is egoistic or selfish or ought to be. It merely starts from the indisputable fact that the limits of our powers of imagination make it impossible to include in our scale of values more than a sector of the needs of the whole society, and that, since, strictly speaking, scales of value can exist only in individual minds, nothing but partial scales of values exist—scales which are inevitably different and often inconsistent with each other. From this the individualist concludes that the individuals should be allowed, within defined limits, to follow their own values and preferences rather than somebody else's; that within these spheres the individual's system of ends should be supreme and not subject to any dictation by others. It is this recognition of the individual as the ultimate judge of his ends, the belief that as far as possible his own views ought to govern his actions, that forms the essence of the individualist position.

This view does not, of course, exclude the recognition of social ends, or rather of a coincidence of individual ends which makes it advisable for men to combine for their pursuit. But it limits such common action to the instances where individual views coincide; what are called "social ends" are for it merely identical ends of many individuals—or ends to the achievement of which individuals are willing to contribute in return for the assistance they receive in the satisfaction of their own desires. Common action is thus limited to the fields where people agree on common ends. Very frequently these common ends will not be ultimate ends to the individuals but means which different persons can use for different purposes. In fact, people are most likely to agree on common action where the common end is not an ultimate end to them but a means capable of serving a great variety of purposes.

When individuals combine in a joint effort to realize ends they have in common, the organizations, like the state, that they form for this purpose are given their own system of ends and their own means. But any organization thus formed remains one "person" among others, in the case of the state much more powerful than any of the others, it is true, yet still with its separate and limited sphere in which alone its ends are supreme. The limits of this sphere are determined by the extent to which the individuals agree on particular ends; and the probability that they will agree on a particular course of action necessarily decreases as the scope of such action extends. There are certain functions of the state on the exercise of which there will be practical unanimity among its citizens; there will be others on which there will be agreement of a substantial majority; and so on, until we come to fields where, although each individual might wish the state to act in some way, there will be almost as many views about what the government should do as there are different people.

We can rely on voluntary agreement to guide the action of the state only so long as it is confined to spheres where agreement exists. But not only when the state undertakes direct control in fields where there is no such agreement is it bound to suppress individual freedom. We can unfortunately not indefinitely extend the sphere of common action and still leave the individual free in his own sphere. Once the communal sector, in which the state controls all the means, exceeds a certain proportion of the whole, the effects of its actions dominate the whole system. Although the state controls directly the use of only a large part of the available resources, the effects of its decisions on the remaining part of the economic system become so great that indirectly it controls almost everything. Where, as was, for example, true in Germany as early as 1928, the central and local authorities directly control the use of more than half the national income (according to an official German estimate then, 53 per cent), they control indirectly almost the whole economic life of the nation. There is, then, scarcely an individual end which is not dependent for its achievement on the action of the state, and the "social scale of values" which guides the state's action must embrace practically all individual ends.

It is not difficult to see what must be the consequences when democracy embarks upon a course of planning which in its execution requires more agreement than in fact exists. The people may have agreed on adopting a system of directed economy because they have been convinced that it will produce great prosperity. In the discussions leading to the decision, the goal of planning will have been described by some such term as "common welfare," which only conceals the absence of real agreement on the ends of planning. Agreement will in fact exist only on the mechanism to be used. But it is a mechanism which can be used only for a common end; and the question of the precise goal toward which all activity is to be directed will arise as soon as the executive power has to translate the demand for a single plan into a particular plan. Then it will appear that the agreement on the desirability of planning is not supported by agreement on the ends the plan is to serve. The effect of the people's agreeing that there must be central planning, without agreeing on the ends, will be rather as if a group of people were to commit themselves to take a journey together without agreeing where they want to go: with the result that they may all have to make a journey which most of them do not want at all. That planning creates a situation in which it is necessary for us to agree on a much larger number of topics than we have been used to, and that in a planned sys-

tem we cannot confine collective action to the tasks on which we can agree but are forced to produce agreement on everything in order that any action can be taken at all, is one of the features which contributes more than most to determining the character of a planned system.

It may be the unanimously expressed will of the people that its parliament should prepare a comprehensive economic plan, yet neither the people nor its representatives need therefore be able to agree on any particular plan. The inability of democratic assemblies to carry out what seems to be a clear mandate of the people will inevitably cause dissatisfaction with democratic institutions. Parliaments come to be regarded as ineffective "talking shops," unable or incompetent to carry out the tasks for which they have been chosen. The conviction grows that if efficient planning is to be done, the direction must be "taken out of politics" and placed in the hands of experts—permanent officials or independent autonomous bodies.

The difficulty is well known to socialists. It will soon be half a century since the Webbs began to complain of "the increased incapacity of the House of Commons to cope with its work." More recently, Professor Laski has elaborated the argument:

> It is common ground that the present parliamentary machine is quite unsuited to pass rapidly a great body of complicated legislation. The National Government, indeed, has in substance admitted this by implementing its economy and tariff measures not by detailed debate in the House of Commons but by a wholesale system of delegated legislation. A Labour Government would, I presume, build upon the amplitude of this precedent. It would confine the House of Commons to the two functions it can properly perform: the ventilation of grievances and the discussion of general principles of its measures. Its Bills would take the form of general formulae conferring wide powers on the appropriate government departments; and those powers would be exercised by Order in Coun-

cil which could, if desired, be attacked in the House by means of a vote of no confidence. The necessity and value of delegated legislation has recently been strongly reaffirmed by the Donoughmore Committee; and its extension is inevitable if the process of socialisation is not to be wrecked by the normal methods of obstruction which existing parliamentary procedure sanctions.

And to make it quite clear that a socialist government must not allow itself to be too much fettered by democratic procedure, Professor Laski at the end of the same article raised the question "whether in a period of transition to Socialism, a Labour Government can risk the overthrow of its measures as a result of the next general election"—and left it significantly unanswered.

It is important clearly to see the causes of this admitted ineffectiveness of parliaments when it comes to a detailed administration of the economic affairs of a nation. The fault is neither with the individual representatives nor with parliamentary institutions as such but with the contradictions inherent in the task with which they are charged. They are not asked to act where they can agree, but to produce agreement on everything—the whole direction of the resources of the nation. For such a task the system of majority decision is, however, not suited. Majorities will be found where it is a choice between limited alternatives; but it is a superstition to believe that there must be a majority view on everything. There is no reason why there should be a majority in favor of any one of the different possible courses of positive action if their number is legion. Every member of the legislative assembly might prefer some particular plan for the direction of economic activity to no plan, yet no one plan may appear preferable to a majority to no plan at all.

Nor can a coherent plan be achieved by breaking it up into parts and voting on particular issues. A democratic assembly voting and amending a comprehensive economic plan clause by clause, as it deliberates on an ordinary bill, makes nonsense. An economic plan, to deserve the name, must have a unitary conception. Even if a parliament could, proceeding step by step, agree on some scheme, it would certainly in the end satisfy nobody. A complex whole in which all the parts must be most carefully adjusted to each other cannot be achieved through a compromise between conflicting views. To draw up an economic plan in this fashion is even less possible than, for example, successfully to plan a military campaign by democratic procedure. As in strategy it would become inevitable to delegate the task to the experts.

Yet the difference is that, while the general who is put in charge of a campaign is given a single end to which, for the duration of the campaign, all the means under his control have to be exclusively devoted, there can be no such single goal given to the economic planner, and no similar limitation of the means imposed upon him. The general has not got to balance different independent aims against each other; there is for him only one supreme goal. But the ends of an economic plan, or of any part of it, cannot be defined apart from the particular plan. It is the essence of the economic problem that the making of an economic plan involves the choice between conflicting or competing ends—different needs of different people. But which ends do so conflict, which will have to be sacrificed if we want to achieve certain others, in short, which are the alternatives between which we must choose, can only be known to those who know all the facts; and only they, the experts, are in a position to decide which of the different ends are to be given preference. It is inevitable that they should impose their scale of preferences on the community for which they plan.

This is not always clearly recognized, and delegation is usually justified by the technical character of the task. But this does not mean that only the technical detail is delegated, or even that the inability of parliaments to understand the technical detail is the root of the difficulty. Alterations in the structure of civil law are no less technical and no more difficult to appreciate in all their implications; yet nobody has yet seriously suggested that legislation there should be delegated to a body of experts. The fact is that in these fields legislation does not go beyond general rules on which true majority agreement can be achieved, while in the direction of economic activity the interests to be reconciled are so divergent that no true agreement is likely to be reached in a democratic assembly.

It should be recognized, however, that it is not the delegation of law-making power as such which is so objectionable. To oppose delegation as such is to oppose a symptom instead of the cause and, as it may be a necessary result of other causes, to weaken the case. So long as the power that is delegated is merely the power to make general rules, there may be very good reasons why such rules should be laid down by local rather than by the central authority. The objectionable feature is that delegation is so often resorted to because the matter in hand cannot be regulated by general rules but only by the exercise of discretion in the decision of particular cases. In these instances delegation means that some authority is given power to make with the force of law what to all intents and purposes are arbitrary decisions (usually described as "judging the case on its merits").

The delegation of particular technical tasks to separate bodies, while a regular feature, is yet only the first step in the process whereby a democracy which embarks on planning progressively relinquishes its powers. The expedient of delegation cannot really remove the causes which make all the advocates of comprehensive planning so impatient with the impotence of democracy. The delegation of particular powers to separate agencies creates a new obstacle to the achievement of a single co-ordinated plan. Even if, by this expedient, a democracy should succeed in planning every sector of economic activity, it would still have to face the problem of integrating these separate plans into a unitary whole. Many separate plans do not make a planned whole—in fact, as the planners ought to be the first to admit, they may be worse than no plan. But the democratic legislature will long hesitate to relinquish the decisions on really vital issues, and so long as it does so it makes it impossible for anyone else to provide the comprehensive plan. Yet agreement that planning is necessary, together with the inability of democratic assemblies to produce a plan, will evoke stronger and stronger demands that the government or some single individual should be given powers to act on their own responsibility. The belief is becoming more and more widespread that, if things are to get done, the responsible authorities must be freed from the fetters of democratic procedure.

The cry for an economic dictator is a characteristic stage in the movement toward planning. It is now several years since one of the most acute of foreign students of England, the late Élie Halévy, suggested that,

> if you take a composite photograph of Lord Eustace Percy, Sir Oswald Mosley, and Sir Stafford Cripps, I think you would find this common feature—you would find them all agreeing to say: "We are living in economic chaos and we cannot get out of it except under some kind of dictatorial leadership."

The number of influential public men whose inclusion would not materially alter the features of the "composite photograph" has since grown considerably.

In Germany, even before Hitler came into power, the movement had already progressed much further. It is important to remember that, for some time before 1933, Germany had reached a stage in which it had, in effect, had to be governed dictatorially. Nobody could then doubt that for the time being democracy had broken down and that sincere democrats like Brüning were no more able to govern democratically than Schleicher or von Papen. Hitler did not have to destroy democracy; he merely took advantage of the decay of democracy and at the critical moment obtained the support of many to whom, though they detested Hitler, he yet seemed the only man strong enough to get things done.

The argument by which the planners usually try to reconcile us with this development is that, so long as democracy retains ultimate control, the essentials of democracy are not affected. Thus Karl Mannheim writes:

> The only [sic] way in which a planned society differs from that of the nineteenth century is that more and more spheres of social life, and ultimately each and all of them, are subjected to state control. But if a few controls can be held in check by parliamentary sovereignty, so can many. . . . In a democratic state sovereignty can be boundlessly strengthened by plenary powers without renouncing democratic control.

This belief overlooks a vital distinction. Parliament can, of course, control the execution of tasks where it can give definite directions, where it has first agreed on the aim and merely delegates the working-out of the detail. The situation is entirely different when the reason for the delegation is that there is no real agreement on the ends, when the body charged with the planning has to choose between ends of whose conflict parliament is not even aware, and when the most that can be done is to present to it a plan which has to be accepted or rejected as a whole. There may and probably will be criticism; but as no majority can agree on an alternative plan, and the parts objected to can almost always be represented as essential parts of the whole, it will remain quite ineffective. Parliamentary discussion may be retained as a useful safety valve and even more as a convenient medium

through which the official answers to complaints are disseminated. It may even prevent some flagrant abuses and successfully insist on particular shortcomings being remedied. But it cannot direct. It will at best be reduced to choosing the persons who are to have practically absolute power. The whole system will tend toward that plebiscitarian dictatorship in which the head of the government is from time to time confirmed in his position by popular vote, but where he has all the powers at his command to make certain that the vote will go in the direction he desires.

It is the price of democracy that the possibilities of conscious control are restricted to the fields where true agreement exists and that in some fields things must be left to chance. But in a society which for its functioning depends on central planning this control cannot be made dependent on a majority's being able to agree; it will often be necessary that the will of a small minority be imposed upon the people, because this minority will be the largest group able to agree among themselves on the question at issue. Democratic government has worked successfully where, and so long as, the functions of government were, by a widely accepted creed, restricted to fields where agreement among a majority could be achieved by free discussion; and it is the great merit of the liberal creed that it reduced the range of subjects on which agreement was necessary to one on which it was likely to exist in a society of free men. It is now often said that democracy will not tolerate "capitalism." If "capitalism" means here a competitive system based on free disposal over private property, it is far more important to realize that only within this system is democracy possible. When it becomes dominated by a collectivist creed, democracy will inevitably destroy itself.

We have no intention, however, of making a fetish of democracy. It may well be true that our generation talks and thinks too much of democracy and too little of the values which it serves. It cannot be said of democracy, as Lord Acton truly said of liberty, that it

> is not a means to a higher political end. It is itself the highest political end. It is not for the sake of a good public administration that it is required, but for the security in the pursuit of the highest objects of civil society, and of private life.

Democracy is essentially a means, a utilitarian device for safeguarding internal peace and individual freedom. As such it is by no means infallible or certain. Nor must we forget that there has often been much more cultural and spiritual freedom under an autocratic rule than under some democracies—and it is at least conceivable that under the government of a very homogeneous and doctrinaire majority democratic government might be as oppressive as the worst dictatorship. Our point, however, is not that dictatorship must inevitably extirpate freedom but rather that planning leads to dictatorship because dictatorship is the most effective instrument of coercion and the enforcement of ideals and, as such, essential if central planning on a large scale is to be possible. The clash between planning and democracy arises simply from the fact that the latter is an obstacle to the suppression of freedom which the direction of economic activity requires. But in so far as democracy ceases to be a guaranty of individual freedom, it may well persist in some form under a totalitarian regime. A true "dictatorship of the proletariat," even if democratic in form, if it undertook centrally to direct the economic system, would probably destroy personal freedom as completely as any autocracy has ever done.

The fashionable concentration on democracy as the main value threatened is not without danger. It is largely responsible for the misleading and unfounded belief that, so long as the ultimate source of power is the will of the majority, the power cannot be arbitrary. The false assurance which many people derive from this belief is an important cause of the general unawareness of the dangers which we face. There is no justification for the belief that, so long as power is conferred by democratic procedure, it cannot be arbitrary; the contrast suggested by this statement is altogether false: it is not the source but the limitation of power which prevents it from being arbitrary. Democratic control may prevent power from becoming arbitrary, but it does not do so by its mere existence. If democracy resolves on a task which necessarily involves the use of power which cannot be guided by fixed rules, it must become arbitrary power.

36. Economic Theory and Mathematics— An Appraisal*

PAUL A. SAMUELSON

It has been correctly said that mathematical economics is flying high these days. So I come, not to praise mathematics, but rather to slightly debunk its use in economics. I do so out of tenderness for the subject, since I firmly believe in the virtues of understatement and lack of pretension.

*Source: From American Economic Review, vol. 42 (May 1952), pp. 56-66. Copyright © 1952 American Economic Association. Reprinted by permission.

I realize that this is a session on methodology. Hence, I must face some basic questions as to the nature of mathematics and of its application. What I have to say on this subject is really very simple—perhaps too brief and simple. The time that I save by brief disposal of the weighty philosophical and epistemological issues of methodology I can put to good use in discussing the tactical and pedagogical issues—or what you might even call the Freudian problems that the mathematical and nonmathematical student of economics must face.

The Strict Equivalence of Mathematical Symbols and Literary Words. On the title page of my *Foundations of Economic Analysis*, I quoted the only speech that the great Willard Gibbs was supposed ever to have made before the Yale Faculty. As professors do at such meetings, they were hotly arguing the question of required subjects: Should certain students be required to take languages or mathematics? Each man had his opinion of the relative worth of these disparate subjects. Finally Gibbs, who was not a loquacious man, got up and made a four-word speech: "Mathematics is a language."

I have only one objection to that statement. I wish he had made it 25 per cent shorter—so as to read as follows: "Mathematics *is* language." Now I mean this entirely literally. In principle, mathematics cannot be worse than prose in economic theory; in principle, it certainly cannot be better than prose. For in deepest logic—and leaving out all tactical and pedagogical questions—the two media are strictly identical.

Irving Fisher put this very well in his great doctoral thesis, written exactly sixty years ago. As slightly improved by my late teacher, Joseph Schumpeter, Fisher's statement was: "There is no place you can go by railroad that you cannot go afoot." And I might add, "Vice versa!"

I do not think we should make too much of the fact that in recent years a number of universities have permitted their graduate students to substitute a reading knowledge of mathematics for a reading knowledge of one foreign language. For after all we run our universities on the principle that Satan will find work for idle hands to do; and the fact that we may permit a student to choose between ROTC and elementary badminton does not mean that these two subjects are methodologically identical. And besides, we all know just what a euphemism the expression "a graduate student's reading knowledge" really is.

INDUCTION AND DEDUCTION

Every science is based squarely on induction—on observation of empirical facts. This is true even of the very imperfect sciences, which have none of the good luck of astronomy and classical physics. This is true of meteorology, of medicine, of economics, of biology, and of a number of other fields that have achieved only modest success in their study of reality. It used to be thought that running parallel with induction there runs an equally important process called "Deduction"—spelled with a capital *D*. Indeed, certain misguided methodologists carried their enthusiasm for the latter to such extremes that they regarded Deduction as in some sense overshadowing mere pedestrian induction.

Now science is only one small part of man's activity—a part that is today given great honorific status, but which I should like to strip of all honorific status for purposes of this discussion. However, to the extent that we do agree to talk about what is ordinarily called science—and not about poetry or theology or something else—it is clear that deduction has the modest linguistic role of translating certain empirical hypotheses into their "logical equivalents." To a really good man, whose IQ is 300 standard deviations above the average, all syllogistic problems of deduction are so obvious and take place so quickly that he is scarcely aware of their existence. Now I believe that I am uttering a correct statement—in fact, it is the only irrefutable and empty truth that I shall waste your time in uttering—when I say that not everybody, nor even half of everybody, can have an IQ 300 standard deviations above the mean. So there is for all of us a psychological problem of making correct deductions. That is why pencils have erasers and electronic calculators have bells and gongs.

I suppose this is what Alfred Marshall must have had in mind when he followed John Stuart Mill in speaking of the dangers involved in *long* chains of logical reasoning. Marshall treated such chains as if their truth content was subject to radioactive decay and leakage—at the end of *n* propositions only half the truth was left, at the end of a chain of 2*n* propositions, only half of half the truth remained, and so forth in a geometric multiplier series converging to zero truth. Obviously, in making such a statement, Marshall was describing a property of that biological biped or computing machine called *homo sapiens*; for he certainly could not be describing a property of logical implication. Actually, if proposition A correctly implies proposition B, and B correctly implies proposition C, and so forth all the way to Z, then it is necessarily true that A implies Z in every sense that it implies B. There can be no leakage of truth at any stage of a valid deductive syllogism. All such syllogisms are mere translations of the type, "A rose is a rose is a rose."

All this is pretty well understood when it comes to logical processes of the form: Socrates is a man. All men are mortal. Therefore, Socrates is mortal. What is not always so clearly understood is that a literary statement of this type has its complete equivalent in the symbolism of mathematical logic. If we write it out in such symbolism, we may save paper and ink; we may even make it easier for a seventeen-year-old freshman to arrive at the answer to complex questions of the type: "Is Robinson, who smokes cigarettes and is a non-self shaver, a fascist or is it Jones?" But nonetheless, the mathematical symbolism can be replaced by words. I should hate to put six monkeys in the British Museum and wait until they had typed out in words the equivalent of the mathematical formulas involved in Whitehead and Russell's *Mathematical Principia*. But if we were to wait long enough, it could be done.

THE CASE OF NEOCLASSICAL DISTRIBUTION

Similarly, in economics. The cornerstone of the simplest and most fundamental theory of production and distribution—that of Walras and J. B. Clark—is Euler's theorem on homogeneous functions. Now it is doubtful that Clark—who rather boasted of his mathematical innocence—had ever heard of Euler. Certainly, he cannot have known what is meant by a homogeneous function. But nonetheless, in Clark's theory, there is the implicit assumption that scale does not count; that what does count is the proportions in which the factors combine; and that it does not matter which of the factors of production is the hiring factor and which the hired. If we correctly interpret the implication of all this, we see that Clark—just as he was talking prose and knowing it—was talking the mathematics of homogeneous functions and not knowing it.

I have often heard Clark criticized for not worrying more about the exhaustion-of-the-product problem. He seems never to have worried whether rent, computed as a triangular residual, would be numerically equal—down to the very last decimal place—to rent calculated as a rectangle of marginal product. Like King Canute, he seems simply to have instructed his draftsman to draw the areas so as to be equal.

As I say, Clark has often been criticized for not going into this problem of exhaustion of the product. I myself have joined in such criticism. But I now think differently—at least from the present standpoint of the nature of true logical deductive implication as distinct from the human psychological problem of perceiving truth and cramming it into the heads of one's students or readers. Even if Euler had never lived to perceive his theorem, even if Wicksell, Walras, and Wicksteed had not applied it to economic theory, Clark's doctrine is in the clear. His assumptions of constant-returns-to-scale and viable free-entry ensure for him that total revenue of each competitive firm will be exactly equal to total cost. And with this settled in the realm of cost and demand curves, there is no need for a textbook writer in some later chapter of his book dealing with production to suddenly become assailed by doubts about the "adding-up problem of exhaustion-of-the product."

Now let me linger on this case for a moment. Economists have carefully compared Wicksteed's and Clark's treatment of this problem in order to show that mathematics is certainly not inferior to words in handling such an important element of distribution theory.

What is not so clear is the answer to the reverse question: Is not literary economics, by its very nature, inferior to mathematics in handling such a complex quantitative issue. As one eminent mathematical economist put it to me:

> Euler's theorem is absolutely basic to the simplest neoclassical theory of imputation. Yet without mathematics, you simply cannot give a rigorous proof of Euler's theorem.

Now I must concede that the economics literature does abound with false proofs of Euler's theorem on homogeneous functions. But what I cannot admit—unless I am willing to

recant on all that I have been saying about the logical identity of words and symbols—I simply cannot admit that a rigorous literary proof of Euler's theorem is in principle impossible.

In fact, I tried a literary proof on my mathematical friend. He quite properly pointed out that it was not rigorous in the way it treated infinitesimals. I fully agree. My argument was heuristic. But I do claim that if my friend and I could spend a week or so talking together, so that I could describe in words the fundamental limit processes involved in the Newton-Leibniz calculus and derivatives, then this problem of lack of rigor could be met. In fact, much more subtle properties of Pfaffian partial differential equations are in principle capable of being stated in basic English. As Professor Leontief has pointed out, the final proof of the identity of mathematics and words is the fact that we teach people mathematics by the use of words, defining each symbol as we go along. It is no accident that the printer of mathematical equations is forced to put commas, periods, and other punctuation in them, for equations are sentences, pure and simple.

GEOMETRY IN RELATION TO WORDS AND MATHEMATICAL ANALYSIS

Today when an economic theorist deplores the use of mathematics, he usually speaks up for the virtues of geometrical diagrams as the alternatives. It was not always thus. Seventy years ago, when a man like Cairnes criticized the use of mathematics in economics, probably he meant by the term "mathematics" primarily geometrical diagrams. From the point of view of this lecture, the ancients were more nearly right than the modern critics. Geometry is a branch of mathematics, in exactly the same sense that mathematics is a branch of language. It is easy to understand why a man might have no use at all for economic theory, invoking, instead, a plague on mathematical economics, on diagrammatic textbooks, and on all fine-spun literary theories. It is also easy to understand why some men should want to swallow economic theory in all of its manifestations. But what is not at all clear—except in terms of human frailty—is why a man like Cairnes should be so enamored of literary theory and should then stop short of diagrams and symbols. Or why any modern methodologist should find some virtue in two-dimensional graphs but should draw the line at third or higher dimensions.

I suggest that the reason for such inconsistent methodological views must be found in the psychological and tactical problems which constitute the remaining part of my remarks.

But before leaving the discussion of the logical identity of mathematical symbols and words, I must examine its bearing on a famous utterance of Cairnes. He lived at a time when, as we now know, mathematics was helping bring into birth a great new neoclassical synthesis. Yet Cairnes went so far as to say:

> So far as I can see, economic truths are not discoverable through the instrumentality of mathematics. If this view be unsound, there is at hand an easy means of refutation—the production of an economic truth, not before known, which has been thus arrived at.

Now this view is the direct opposite of that of Marshall. Marshall in his own way also rather pooh-poohed the use of mathematics. But he regarded it as a way of arriving at truths, but not as a good way of communicating such truths—which is just the opposite of Cairnes's further remarks on the subject.

Well, what are we to think of the crucial experiment proposed by Cairnes? In the first place, he himself was both unable and unwilling to use the mathematical technique; so it might have been possible for us to produce a new truth which Cairnes could never have been capable of recognizing. Indeed, many

have cogently argued that Jevons had in fact done so. However, from the methodological viewpoint that I have been expounding, it will be clear that any truth arrived at by way of mathematical manipulation must be translatable into words; and hence, as a matter of logic, could quite possibly have been arrived at by words alone. Reading Cairnes literally, we are not required to produce a truth by mathematics that could not have been proved by words; we are only required to produce one that has not, as a matter of historical fact, been previously produced by words. I suggest that a careful review of the literature since the 1870's will show that a significant part of all truths since arrived at have in fact been the product of theorists who use symbolic techniques. In particular, Walrasian general equilibrium, which is the peak of neoclassical economics, was already enunciated in Walras' first edition of the *Elements* at the time Cairnes was writing.

Jevons, Walras, and Menger each independently arrived at the so-called "theory of subjective value." And I consider it a lucky bonus for my present thesis that Menger did arrive at his formulation without the use of mathematics. But, in all fairness, I should point out that a recent rereading of the excellent English translation of Menger's 1871 work convinces me that it is the least important of the three works cited; and that its relative neglect by modern writers was not simply the result of bad luck or scholarly negligence. I should also add that the important revolution of the 1870's had little really to do with either subjective value and utility or with marginalism; rather it consisted of the perfecting of the general relations of supply and demand. It culminated in Walrasian general equilibrium. And we are forced to agree with Schumpeter's appraisal of Walras as the greatest of theorists—not because he used mathematics, since the methods used are really quite elementary—but because of the key importance of the concept of general equilibrium itself. We may say of Walras what Lagrange ironically said in praise of Newton:

> Newton was assuredly the man of genius *par excellence*, but we must agree that he was also the luckiest: one finds only once the system of the world to be established!

And how lucky he was that "in his time the system of the world still remained to be discovered." Substitute "system of equilibrium" for "system of the world" and Walras for Newton and the equation remains valid.

SUMMARY OF BASIC METHODOLOGY

In leaving my discussion of Methodology with a capital M, let me sum up with a few dogmatic statements. All sciences have the common task of describing and summarizing empirical reality. Economics is no exception. There are no separate methodological problems that face the social scientist different in kind from those that face any other scientist. It is true that the social scientist is part of the reality he describes. The same is true of the physical scientist. It is true that the social scientist in observing a phenomenon may change it. The theory of quantum mechanics, with its Heisenberg uncertainty principle, shows that the same is true of the physical scientist making small-scale observations. Similarly, if we enumerate one by one the alleged differences between the social sciences and other sciences, we find no differences in kind.

Finally, it is clear that no a priori empirical truths can exist in any field. If a thing has a priori irrefutable truth, it must be empty of empirical content. It must be regarded as a meaningless proposition in the technical sense of modern philosophy. At the epistemological frontier, there are certain refined difficulties concerning these matters. But at the rough and ready level that concerns the scientist in his everyday work, the above facts are widely recognized by scientists in every discipline. The only exceptions are to be found in certain backwaters of economics, and I shall not here do more than point the finger of scorn at those who carry into the twentieth century ideas that were not very good even in their earlier heyday.

DIFFERENCES IN CONVENIENCE OF LANGUAGES

I now turn to the really interesting part of the subject. What are the conditions under which one choice of language is more convenient than another? If you are a stenographer required to take rapid dictation, there is no doubt that you will prefer shorthand to old-English lettering. No disinterested third party will ever be in doubt as to whether Roman numerals are less convenient than arabic numerals for the solution of problems in commercial arithmetic; and the same goes for a comparison between a decimal system of coinage and that used by the English.

A comparison between a language like French and one like German or English or Chinese is a little more difficult. We might concede that any proposition in one language is translatable into another. But that is not relevant to the psychological question as to whether one language is intrinsically more convenient for a certain purpose than another. We often hear it said that French is a very clear language, and that German is a very opaque one. This is illustrated by the story that Hegel did not really understand his philosophy until he had read the French translation!

I do not know whether there is anything in this or not. It seems to me that Böhm-Bawerk or Wicksell written in German is quite as straightforward as in English; whereas I find Max Weber or Talcott Parsons difficult to understand in any tongue. I suspect that certain cultures develop certain ways of tackling problems. In nineteenth century German economics it was popular and customary to ask about a problem like interest or value: What is the essence of interest or value? After this qualitative question is answered, then the quantitative level of the rate of interest or price-ratio can be settled. Now I happen to think that this is sterile methodology. But I cannot blame it on the German language.

It is interesting, however, that Menger wrote a letter to Walras on this very subject. As reported by Professor Jaffe's interesting article (*Journal of Political Economy*, 1936), Menger said that mathematics was all very well for certain descriptive purposes, but that it did not enable you to get at the essence of a phenomenon. I wish I thought it were true that the language of mathematics had some special faculty of drawing attention away from pseudo problems of qualitative essence. For, unlike Menger, I should consider that a great advantage.

BACONIAN AND NEWTONIAN METHODS

There are many empirical fields where translation into mathematical symbols would seem to have no advantage. Perhaps immunology is one, since I am told not a single cure for disease—vaccination against smallpox, inoculation for diphtheria, use of penicillin and sulpha, and so forth—has been discovered by anything but the crudest empiricism and with sheer accident playing a great role. Here the pedestrian methods of Francis Bacon show up to much greater advantage than do the exalted methods of a Newton. If true, we must simply accept this as a fact. I am sure that many areas of the social sciences and economics are at present in this stage. It is quite possible that many such areas will always continue to be in this stage.

Pareto regarded sociology as being of this type. But curiously enough, he goes on to argue that the chief virtue of mathematics is in its ability to represent complexly interacting and interdependent phenomena. I think we must accept this with a grain of salt. Analogies with complicated interdependent physical systems are valuable if they alert us to the dangers of theories of unilateral causation. But after mathematical notions have performed the function of reminding us that everything depends upon everything else, they may not add very much more—unless some special hypotheses can be made about the facts.

On the other hand, there are areas which over the years have fallen into the hands of the mathematically anointed. Earlier I mentioned the case of symbolic logic. There are still some girls' seminaries where literary logic rules the roost; but no sensible man expects that in the centuries ahead the field of logic will be deloused of mathematics.

Another field is that of physics. Its capture by mathematics is a fact—as solid and irreversible as the second law of thermodynamics itself.

It is dangerous to prophesy. But I suspect that in some small degree the same will hold of the field of economic theory. For a century mathematics knocked at the door. Even today it has no more than a foot in the doorway. But the problems of economic theory—such as the incidence of taxation, the effects of devaluation—are by their nature quantitative questions whose answer depends upon a superposition of many different pieces of quantitative and qualitative information. When we tackle them by words, we are solving the same equations as when we write out those equations.

Now I hold no brief for economic theory. I think the pendulum will always swing between interest in concrete description and attempts to construct abstract summaries of experience, with one decade and tradition giving more emphasis to the one process and another time and place giving emphasis to the other. But I do think that when the pendulum is swinging in favor of theory, there will be kind of a Gresham's law operating whereby the more convenient deductive method will displace the less convenient.

CONVENIENCE OF SYMBOLS FOR DEDUCTION

And make no mistake about it. To get to some destinations it matters a great deal whether you go afoot or ride by a train. No wise man studying the motion of a top would voluntarily confine himself to words, forswearing all symbols. Similarly, no sensible person who had at his command both the techniques of literary argumentation and mathematical manipulation would tackle by words alone a problem like the following: Given that you must confine all taxes to excises on goods or factors, what pattern of excises is optimal for a Robinson Crusoe or for a community subject to prescribed norms?

I could go on and enumerate other problems. But that is not necessary. All you have to do is pick up a copy of any economic journal and turn to the articles on literary economic theory, and you will prove the point a hundred times over.

The convenience of mathematical symbolism for handling certain deductive inferences is, I think, indisputable. It is going too far to say that mathematicians never make mistakes. Like everybody else, they can pull some awful boners. But it is surprising how rare pure mistakes in logic are. Where the really big mistakes are made is in the formulation of premises. Logic is no protection against false hypotheses; or against misinterpretation of reality; or against the formulation of irrelevant hypotheses. I think it is one of the advantages of the mathematical medium—or, strictly speaking, of the mathematician's customary canons of exposition of proof, whether in words or symbols—that we are forced to lay our cards on the table so that all can see our

premises. But I must confess that I have heard of card games—in fact I have participated in them myself—where knowingly or unknowingly, we have dealt cards from the bottom of the deck. So there are no absolute checks against human error.

THE HUMAN DILEMMA

In conclusion, ask yourself what advice you would have to give to a young man who steps into your office with the following surprisingly common story:

I am interested in economic theory. I know little mathematics. And when I look at the journals, I am greatly troubled. Must I give up hopes of being a theorist? Must I learn mathematics? If so, how much? I am already past twenty-one; am I past redemption?

Now you could answer him the way Marshall more or less advised Schumpeter: forget economic theory. Diminishing returns has set in there. The world is waiting for a thousand important applications.

This of course is no answer at all. Either the young man disregards your advice, as Schumpeter did. Or he accepts it, and psychologically you have dealt him the cruelest blow of all.

I think a better answer might go somewhat as follows: Some of the most distinguished economic theorists, past and present, have been innocent of mathematics. Some of the most distinguished theorists have known some degree of mathematics. Obviously, you can become a great theorist without knowing mathematics. Yet it is fair to say that you will have to be that much more clever and brilliant.

It happens to be empirically true that if you examine the training and background of all the past great economic theorists, a surprisingly high percentage had, or acquired, at least an intermediate mathematical training. Marshall, Wicksell, Wicksteed, Cassel, and even such literary economists as

Nicholson or Malthus provide examples. This is omitting economists like Edgeworth, Cournot, Walras, Pareto, and others who were avowedly mathematical economists.

Moreover, without mathematics you run grave psychological risks. As you grow older, you are sure to resent the method increasingly. Either you will get an inferiority complex and retire from the field of theory or you will get an inferiority complex and become aggressive about your dislike of it. Of course, those are the betting odds and not perfect certainties. The danger is almost greater that you will overrate the method's power for good or evil. You may even become the prey of charlatans who say to you what Euler said to Diderot to get him to leave Catherine the Great's court: "Sir, $(a + b^n)/n = x$, hence God exists; reply!" And, like Diderot, you may slink away in shame. Or reacting against the episode, you may disbelieve the next mathematician who

later comes along and gives you a true proof of the existence of the Deity.

In short—your advice will continue—mathematics is neither a necessary nor a sufficient condition for a fruitful career in economic theory. It can be a help. It can certainly be a hindrance, since it is only too easy to convert a good literary economist into a mediocre mathematical economist.

Despite the above advice, it is doubtful that when you check back five years later on that young man he will be very different. Indeed, as I look back over recent years, I am struck by the fact that the species of mathematical economist pure and simple seems to be dying out and becoming extinct. Instead, as one of my older friends complained to me: "These days you can hardly tell a mathematical economist from an ordinary economist." I know the sense in which he meant the remark, but let me reverse its emphasis by concluding with the question: Is that bad?

37. Economic Forecasting and Science*

PAUL A. SAMUELSON

If prediction is the ultimate aim of all science, then we forecasters ought to award ourselves the palm for accomplishment, bravery, or rashness. We are the end-product of Darwinian evolution and the payoff for all scientific study of economics. Around the country, students are grinding out doctoral theses by the use of history, statistics, and theory—merely to enable us to reduce the error in our next year's forecast of GNP from $10 billion down to $9 billion.

Actually, though, I am not sure that the ultimate end of science is prediction—at least in the sense of unconditional prediction about what is likely to happen at a specified future date. Students are always asking of professors, "If you are so smart, how come you ain't rich?" Some of our best economic scientists seem to be fairly poor forecasters of the future. One of our very best economists, in fact, couldn't even correctly foresee the results of the last election. Is it legitimate to ask of a

*Source: From The Michigan Quarterly Review (October 1965), pp. 274-80. Copyright © 1965 The University of Michigan. Reprinted by permission.

scholar: "If you are so scientific and learned, how come you are so stupid at predicting next year's GNP?"

I think not, and for several different reasons. In the first place, a man might be a brilliant mathematician in devising methods for the use of physicists and still be a very poor physicist. Or he might be a genius in devising statistical methods while still being rather poor at conducting statistical investigations. Let us grant then at the beginning, that a person might be poor himself at *any* predictions within a field, and still be a useful citizen. Only we would then call him a mathematician—rather than simply a physicist, statistician, or economist.

The late Sir Ronald Fisher, for instance, was a genius, as we all gladly acknowledge. And perhaps he did good empirical work in the field of agronomy and applied fertilizer. But I must say that his work on genetics—in which he blithely infers the decline of Roman and all civilizations from the dastardly habit infertile heiresses have of snatching off the ablest young men for mates, thereby making them infertile—seems awfully casual statistical inference to me. And I can't think Fisher covered himself with immortal glory at the end of his life when he doubted that cigarette smoking and inhaling has anything to do with reducing longevity.

A good scientist should be good at *some* kind of prediction. But it need not be flat prediction about future events. Thus, a physicist may be bad at telling you what the radioactivity count in the air will be next year, but be very good at predicting for you what will be the likely effects on air pollution of a given controlled experiment involving fissionable materials. If he is a master scientist, his hunches about experiments never yet performed may be very good ones.

Similarly, a good economist has good judgment about economic reality. To have good judgment means you are able to make good judgments—good predictions about what will happen under *certain specified conditions*. This is different from having a model that is pretty good at doing mechanical extrapolation of this year's trends of GNP to arrive at respectable guesses of next year's GNP. Time and again your naive model may win bets from me in office pools on next year's outcome. But neither of us would ever dream of using such a naive model to answer the question, "What will happen to GNP, compared to what it would otherwise have been, when the Kennedy-Johnson massive tax cut is put into effect?" The mechanical, naive model does not have in it, explicitly, the parameter tax rates. And if we insist upon differentiating the result with respect to such a parameter, we will end up with a zero partial derivative and with the dubious conclusion that massive tax cuts cannot have any effect on GNP. The model that I use, which is perhaps very non-mechanical and perhaps even non-naive, may be bad at predicting unconditionally next year's GNP, and still be very good at answering the other-things-equal question of the effect of a change in tax rates or in some other structural parameter of the system.

What I have been saying here can be put in technical language: to make good year-to-year predictions, you need not necessarily have accomplished good "identification" of the various structural relations of a model.

Is it possible to have everything good?—to be able to make good annual predictions as well as good predictions of identified structural relationships? The best economists I have known, in the best years of their lives, were pretty good at making just such predictions. And that is what I call good judgment in economics.

Obviously, they have to be men of much experience. In the last analysis, empirical predictions can be made only on the basis of empirical evidence. But it is an equal empirical truth that the facts do not tell their own story to scientists or historical observers, and that the men who develop topnotch judgment have an analytical framework within which they try to fit the facts. I should say that such men are constantly using the evidence of economic time series; the evidence of cross-sectional data; the evidence of case studies and anecdotes, but with some kind of judgment concerning the frequency and importance of the cases and instances. And they are even using conjectures of the form, "What if I were no smarter than these businessmen and unionists? What would I be likely to do?"

We all know the great statistical problems involved in the small samples economic statisticians must work with. We have few years of data relevant to the problem at hand. Maybe the data can be found by months or by quarters; but since there is much serial correlation between adjacent monthly data, we can by no means blithely assume that we have increased our degrees of freedom twelve-fold or more by using monthly data. Nature has simply not performed the controlled experiments that enable us to predict as we should wish.

This means that the master economist must piece together, from all the experience he has ever had, hunches relevant to the question at hand. In short, we begin to accumulate "degrees of freedom" from the first moment we draw breath and begin to take in observations of the world around us. Indeed, we could perhaps begin the integral of experience even before birth.

At any rate, just as there is a time for remembering, there is a time for forgetting. Economics is not a stationary time-series. Getting a year's extra data for 1864 is not worth nearly so much as getting extra data for 1964. We must learn both to regard experience and to disregard it. I've known men who paid dearly for every thousand dollars of profits they made from selling short in 1929-1932. They never recovered from being bears—even in 1946-1955!

But if economics does not deal with a stationary time-series, neither is igno-

rance bliss in our profession. There are thousands of ways for the really uninformed man to be wrong in the field of forecasting. Today will not simply repeat yesterday. But to think that the laws of the universe were born anew this morning when you opened your eyes is pitiful nonsense. The essence of science is mastering the art of filtering out the obsolete patterns of the past and filtering in the patterns of persistence.

If science becomes a private art, it loses its characteristic of reproducibility. Here is an example. Sumner Slichter, from 1930 to his death in the late 1950's, was a good forecaster. Dr. Robert Adams of Standard Oil (New Jersey), comparing different methods of forecasting, found that "being Sumner Slichter" was then about the best. But how did Slichter do it? I could never make this out. And neither, I believe, could he. One year he talked about Federal Reserve policy, another year about technical innovation. Somehow the whole came out better than the sum of its parts. Now what I should like to emphasize is that the private art of Sumner Slichter died with him. No less-gifted research assistant could have had transferred to him even a fraction of the Master's skill. And thus one of the principal aims of science was not achieved—namely, reproducibility by any patient person of modest ability of the empirical regularities discerned by luck or by the transcendental efforts of eminent scholars.

The models of Klein, Goldberger, Tinbergen, and Suits have at least this property. Take away Frankenstein and you still have a mechanical monster that will function for awhile. But unlike the solar system, which had to be wound up by Divine Providence only once, any economic model will soon run down if the breath of intelligent life is not pumped into it. When you see a 7094 perform well in a good year, never forget that it is only a Charlie McCarthy; without an Edgar Bergen in the background it is only a thing of paint and wood, of inert transistors and obsolescing matrices.

How well can economists forecast? The question is an indefinite one, and reminds us of the man who was asked what he thought about his wife, and had to reply, "Compared to what?"

When I say that as an economist I am not very good at making economic forecasts, that sounds like modesty. But actually, it represents the height of arrogance. For I know that bad as we economists are, we are better than anything else in heaven and earth at forecasting aggregate business trends—better than gypsy tea-leaf readers, Wall Street soothsayers and chartist technicians, hunch-playing heads of mail order chains, or all-powerful heads of state. This is a statement based on empirical experience. Over the years I have tried to keep track of various methods of forecasting, writing down in my little black book what people seemed to be saying before the event, and then comparing their prediction with what happened. The result has been a vindication of the hypothesis that there is no efficacious substitute for economic analysis in business forecasting. Some maverick may hit a home run on occasion; but over the long season, batting averages tend to settle down to a sorry level when the more esoteric methods of soothsaying are relied upon.

What constitutes a good batting average? That depends on the contest. In baseball these days, .300 or 300-out-of-1,000, is very good. In economic forecasting of the direction of change, we ought to be able to do at least .500 just by tossing a coin. And taking advantage of the undoubted upward trend in all modern economies, we can bat .750 or better just by parrot-like repeating, "Up, Up." The difference between the men and the boys, then, comes between an .850 performance and an .800 performance. Put in other terms, the good forecaster, who must in November make a point-estimate of GNP for the calendar year ahead, will, over a decade, have an average error of perhaps one per cent, being in a range of $12 billion dollars, with reality being $6 billion on either side of the estimate. And a rather poor forecaster may, over the same period, average an error of 1½ per cent. When we average the yearly results for a decade, it may be found that in the worst year the error was over 2 per cent, compensated by rather small errors in many of the years not expected to represent turning points.

In a sense this is a modest claim. But again I must insist on the arrogance underlying these appraisals. For I doubt that it is possible, on the basis of the evidence now knowable a year in advance, to do much better than this. An expert owns up to the limits of his accuracy, but goes on arrogantly to insist that the result cannot be bettered. His range of ignorance is, so to speak, based on experience. It is ignorance based on knowledge, not ignorance based on ignorance. It reminds one a little bit of Heisenberg's Uncertainty Principle in quantum mechanics. According to it, an observer cannot simultaneously determine both the position and the velocity of a particle: if he arranges his observational experiment so as to get an accurate fix on position, his recording instruments will make the velocity indeterminate with a range; and if he rearranges the observational instruments so as to get an accurate fix on velocity, the cost he must pay is giving up knowledge of position.

I do not mean to imply that this is fixed for all time. Once our profession got new surveys of businessmen's intentions to invest, of their decisions as to capital appropriations, and of consumers' responses to random polling, the critical level of imprecision was reduced. In all likelihood, the critical level of uncertainty is a secularly declining one. But is its asymptote (for forecasting a year ahead, remember) literally zero? I do not know how to answer this question. Although it may seem pessimistic to give a negative answer, I am tempted to do so. For remember, you cannot find what is in a person's mind by interrogation, before there is anything in his mind. That is why preliminary surveys of the McGraw-Hill type, taken in October before many corporations have made their capital-budgeting decisions, are necessarily of limited accuracy—which does not deny that they are of some value to us.

The imprecision inherent in forecasting raises some questions about the propriety of making simple point-estimates. If you twist my arm, you can make me give a single number as a guess about next year's GNP. But you will have to twist hard. My scientific conscience would feel more comfortable giving you my subjective probability distribution for all the values of GNP. Thus, I might reckon the rough probability to be one-half that GNP will be at most $655 billion in 1965; one-quarter that it will be at most $650 billion; and three-quarters that it will be at most $662 billion. Actually, it is a pain in the neck to have to work out the whole probability distribution rather than to give a single point-estimate. But satisfying one's scientific conscience is never a very easy task. And there is some payoff for the extra work involved.

For one thing, just what does a point-estimate purport to mean? That is often not clear even to the man issuing it. Do I give the number at which I should just be indifferent to make a bet *on either side*, if forced to risk a large sum of money on a bet whose side can be determined by an opponent or by a referee using chance devices? If that is what I mean in issuing a point-estimate, I am really revealing the *median* of my subjective probability distribution. Other times estimators have in the back of their mind that over the years they will be judged by their mean-square-error, and hence it is best for them to reveal the *arithmetic mean* of their subjective distribution.

I have known still others who aimed, consciously or unconsciously, at the mode of their distribution—sometimes perhaps using the modal value of forecasts among all their friends and acquaintances as the way of arriving at their own mode. Warning: the distribution of all point-estimates issued from a hundred different banks, insurance companies, corporations, government agencies, and academic experts is usually more bunched than the defensible *ex ante* subjective probability distribution any one of them should use in November. This is illustrated by a story I heard Roy Blough once tell at a Treasury Meeting. He said: "Economic forecasters are like six eskimos in one bed; the only thing you can be sure of is that they are all going to turn over together." Blough is right. In a few weeks time one often sees all the forecasts revised together upward or downward.

The difference between median, mean, and mode is not very significant if our expected distributions are reasonably symmetrical. But often they are not: often it will be easier to be off by $15 billion through being too pessimistic rather than too optimistic. Making your soothsayer provide you with a probability range may seem to be asking him to be more pretentiously accurate than he can be. But that is not my interpretation: using the language of arithmetical probability is my way of introducing and emphasizing the degree of uncertainty in the procedure, not its degree of finicky accuracy. There is a further advantage of using probability spreads rather than single point-estimates. One of the whizziest of the Whiz Kids in the Pentagon told me that they get better point estimates from Generals and Admirals if they make them always give high and low estimates. Before, you could never be sure whether some conservative bias or discount was not already being applied to data. Henri Theil of Rotterdam has studied how well forecasters perform and has found a similar tendency toward conservative bias in economic forecasters.

Suppose we think that GNP is likely to rise, say by $30 billion. If we issue the forecast of a rise of $20 billion, we shall certainly have been in the right direction. And we shall be in the ball park with respect to general magnitude. Why be hoggish and try for better? Particularly since GNP might go down, and then you would be standing all alone out there in right field, more than $30 billion off the mark. "Better be wrong in good company, than run the risk of being wrong all alone" is a slogan that every Trustee knows to represent wisdom for his actions.

But here I am talking about science, not about gamesmanship for the forecaster. Gamesmanship introduces a whole new set of considerations. Many forecasters, particularly amateurs, don't really care whether they turn out to be wrong or by how much they turn out to be wrong. They want to tell a good story. They want to back the longshot of possible success when their wild forecasts that depart from that of the fashionable mob might just possibly happen to be right. Then their prescience will be noted and remembered, whereas if they turn out to be woefully wrong, who is going to be there to remind people of that? If that is how you want to play the game, then naturally you should do what the rational entrant in an office pool on the election does. He does not place his bet at 61 per cent of the popular vote for Johnson, even if that is his best belief. Why not? Because there are people who are picking numbers all around that. Instead, he looks for the open spaces—measured of course in his probability metric—where few entrants in the pool have selected their estimates. Why is this rational? Because to amateurs it usually does not matter by how much you are wrong. The only prize is to be at the top. In science and in real economic life, it is terribly important not to be wrong by much. To be second-best year after year in a stock-portfolio competition would be marvel-ous for a mutual fund manager, and especially where the first-place winners are a shifting group of crap-shooters who stake all on one whim or another.

As an economic scientist, I take economic forecasting with deadly seriousness. I hate to be far wrong. Every residual is a wound on my body. And I'd rather make two small errors, than be right once at the cost of being wrong a second time by the sum of the two errors. The reason is not vanity—because forecasting serves a purpose: each dollar of error costs something in terms of corporate or national policy; and if the "loss function" or "social welfare function" is a smooth one in the neighborhood of its optimum, it will be the square of the error of forecast that gives a rough measure of local error.

If we use means-square-error as our criterion of fit, I think it will be found that forecasters have another persistent bias, namely a tendency to be too pessimistic. This is different from the conservatism that makes forecasters shade both their upward and downward forecasts below the true magnitude. Why is there this downward bias? First, because it is never easy to know where next year's dollar is going to come from, and many forecasters try to build up their total by adding up the elements that they can see. There is a second, perhaps more defensible, reason for erring on the downward or pessimistic side in making a forecast. The social consequences of unemployment and underproduction may be deemed more serious than those of over-full-employment and (mild) demand inflation. I once shocked the late John Maurice Clark at a meeting in Washington by saying, "Although the chance of a recession next year is only one-third, for policy purposes we should treat it as if it were two-thirds." He thought that a contradiction in terms. But in terms of his colleague Wald's loss-function concept, I could make sense of my statement by postulating that each dollar of deflationary gap had social consequences more serious than each dollar of inflationary gap.

Often a forecaster is forced to give a single point-estimate because his boss or consumers cannot handle a more complicated concept. Then he must figure out for himself which point-estimate will do them the most good, or the least harm. Years ago one of the publishing companies used to have every staff member make a prediction of the sales each textbook would enjoy. If people tried to play safe and guess low figures, the President of the company would penalize them for having too little faith in the company's sales staff and authors. (Incidentally, the sales manager used to come up with the least inaccurate predictions, odd as that may sound.)

A good speech should tell the audience something that it already knows to be true. Then having gained their good approval for soundness, it should tell them something they didn't previously know to be true. I don't know whether I have been able to complete the second part of this recipe, but I want to add a third requirement for a good speech. It should call attention to some problem whose true answer is not yet known. Let me conclude, therefore, by raising an unanswered question.

Naive models based upon persistence, momentum, or positive serial correlation do rather well in economics as judged by least-square-error of predictions. An extreme case is one which merely projects the current level or the current direction of change. Yet such models do badly in "calling turning points." Indeed, as described above, such naive models are like the Dow System of predicting stockmarket prices, which never even tries to call a turning point in advance and is content to learn, not too long after the fact, that one has actually taken place.

Forecasters regard models which merely say, "Up and up," or "more of the same," as rather dull affairs. When I

once explained to editors of a financial magazine that one disregarded this continuity only at one's risk, they said: "Professor, that may be good economic science, but it's darn dull journalism." But are we forecasters here to have a good time? Dullness may be part of the price we must pay for good performance. More than that. Are we here to cater to our own vanity? One hates to be wrong; but if one's average error could be reduced at the cost of being more often wrong in direction, is that not a fair bargain?

I don't pretend to know the answer to these questions. But they do have a bearing on the following issue. Often an economist presents a model which he admits does worse than some more naive model, but which he justifies for its better fit at the turning points. Is this emphasis legitimate? That question I leave open.

Is policy action most important at the turning points? Is policy action most potent at the turning points? Is a correct guess about turning points likely to lead to correct guesses for the next several quarters? And if so, why doesn't this importance of accuracy of the turning points already get duly registered in the minimum-squared-error criterion? The whole notion of a turning point would be changed in its timing if we shifted, as many dynamic economies in Europe have to do, to changes in direction of trend-deviations rather than changes in absolute direction as insisted on by the National Bureau. Does this lack of invariance cast doubt on the significance of turning points?

Finally, is it possible that public preoccupation with economics is greatest at the turning point and that we are essentially catering to our own vanity and desire for publicity when we stress accuracy at such times?

But for all that, to the scientific forecaster I say, "Always study your residuals." Charles Darwin, who lived before the age of Freud, made it a habit to write down immediately any arguments *against* his theory of evolution, for he found that he invariably tended to forget those arguments. When I have steeled myself to look back over my past economic forecasts in the London *Financial Times*, they have appeared to be a little less prescient than I had remembered them to be. Janus-like, we must look at the past to learn how to look into the future.

After I had made some innocent remarks like this in my 1961 Stamp Memorial Lecture at the University of London, I ran into Professor Frank Paish, himself one of England's best economic forecasters.

"Great mistake ever to look back," he quipped, "you'll lose your nerve."

This is almost precisely what the great Satchel Paige of baseball said. "Never look backward. Somebody may be gaining on you."

Like Sir Winston, I bring you blood, sweat, and tears. The way of the scientific forecaster is hard. Let Lot's wife, who did look back, be your mascot and guide. What Satch Paige didn't mention is that "they may be gaining on you anyway." Know the truth—and while it may not make you free—it will help rid you of your amateur standing.

38. Wage-Price Guideposts and the Need for Informal Controls in a Mixed Economy*

PAUL A. SAMUELSON

I realize that this is a debate whose title might crudely be put—"Resolved: Wage-Price Guideposts are Obnoxious, Harmful if Effective but Inevitably Ineffective." Professor Burns is the speaker for the affirmative, and I have the not completely enviable task of being speaker for the negative. . . .

Actually, I propose to treat this as a seminar, adhering literally to the title of this series. For one thing I am not a wholehearted enthusiast for guideposts; if uncritical enthusiasm were desired, one would have to go elsewhere. Many aspects of guideposts I do admire, but at points I shall have to be the devil's advocate in an adversary procedure designed to bring out truth and balance. . . .

We may with fine rhetoric or telling syllogism slay the presidential guideposts a dozen times; but still, in the opinion of the vast majority of economic experts, we shall be left with the vexing dilemma that free markets do not give us a stable consumers price index at the same time that the rate of unemployment stays down to a socially desirable minimum.

BACKGROUND OF GUIDEPOSTS

During the great slump of the 1930s economists learned that expansionary fiscal and monetary policies could bring a depressed economic system toward full employment. You might call these the days of happy and simple Keynesianism.

However, by the end of World War II

*Source: From Arthur F. Burns and Paul A. Samuelson, *Full Employment, Guideposts and Economic Stability: Rational Debate Seminars* (Washington, D.C.: American Enterprise Institute for Public Policy Research, 1967), pp. 43-66. Reprinted by permission of the American Enterprise Institute for Public Policy Research. Footnotes deleted.

when full employment had long been a reality, the honeymoon was over. The issue of price instability at full employment stared economists in the face. I suppose the famous Beveridge Report of the mid-1940s in England was the first to state forcefully this dilemma. (Parenthetically, our own Employment Act of 1946 tactfully avoided noticing the problem.)

Then there was a dramatic series of unsigned articles in the *Economist* predictive that ours would be an age of inflation. These articles asked the question:

Can any modern mixed economy simultaneously enjoy
1) full employment
2) stability of the general price index
3) free commodity and collective bargaining markets uncontrolled by government fiats?

The author, who I believe was Peter Wiles, then a young scholar at Oxford, answered his own question in the negative. Either you must give up full employment, or stand some creeping inflation. If you can't tolerate unemployment, and if you insist upon reasonable price stability, there is nothing to do but bring government into the act, invoking formal or informal price-wage controls.

Two decades have passed and one must admit that the prophet's pessimism was amply justified. Indeed, he may not have been pessimistic enough. Perhaps even with government intervention, we cannot long enjoy both high employment and reasonable price stability. That is the basic issue we face here tonight.

Since I have quoted one prophet and am here performing the role of the devil's advocate, let me now quote another prophet, John Kenneth Galbraith. Not content with the fame and affluence from his earlier works, Galbraith has brought forth a new classic, *The New Industrial State*. From it we can learn his views on the subject of guideposts.

At any reasonably high level of demand,

prices and wages in the industrial system are inherently unstable.... The ... remedy for the wage-price spiral is to regulate prices and wages by public authority.... In World War II and the Korean War ... the wage-price spiral was successfully contained by controls.... [and] there was nothing unique about the war-time situation. Economic institutions and behavior are not drastically altered either by declared or undeclared war....

This initiative [of guideposts] was, perhaps, the most important innovation in economic policy of the administration of President John F. Kennedy.... Thereafter for several years the wage guideposts, as they came to be called, and the counterpart price behavior were a reasonably accepted feature of government policy. Wage negotiations were closely consistent with the guidelines. Prices of manufactured goods were stable.

Let me quote another modern prophet, Milton Friedman, whose palette holds different paint:

Inflation is always and everywhere a monetary phenomenon.... It follows that the only effective way to stop inflation is to restrain the rate of growth of the quantity of money.... Compliance with the guideposts is harmful because it encourages delay in taking effective measures to stem inflation, distorts production and distribution, and encourages restrictions on personal freedom ... guidelines threaten the censensus of shared values which is the moral basis of a free society.

I suppose it will be argued by many that Professors Galbraith and Friedman are not middle-of-the-road men. Let me, therefore, demonstrate the capacity of our subject for arousing strong opinion by quoting Arthur F. Burns:

The fundamental point of the preceding analysis is that general observance of the guideposts would throttle the forces of competition no less effectively than those of monopoly.... Since free competitive markets would virtually cease to exist in an economy that observed the guidelines, this transformation of the economy merits serious reflection.

Let us begin by clearing up one inexcusable misunderstanding of the wage guideposts. After President Kennedy issued his 1962 recommendation that wage rates be increased only by the 3.2 percent increase in labor productivity, financial columnists and corporate executives repeatedly stated in an arithmetical falsity:

> If labor productivity grows by 3.2 percent and wages rise by 3.2 percent, then there is zero percent left over of the fruits of technological progress to go to profit. And yet much, probably most, of the improvement in labor productivity is in fact attributable to better capital tools, better management methods, and improved scientific know-how.

Indeed it would be unfair and unworkable if all the fruits of progress were to go to labor alone. The guidelines could be rejected out of hand were this their purpose and effect. But critics who use this argument have failed in their elementary arithmetic. The truth is that a 3 percent increase in labor productivity matched by a 3 percent increase in wages entails exactly a 3 percent increase in profits. To clinch this, suppose we begin with 700 of wages and 300 of profit, or 1,000 in all. Let productivity grow by 3 percent, so that we now have 1,030 to divide. A 3 percent increase in wages does not use up the whole of the extra 30, but rather .03 × 700 = 21, with 9 left over the profit. But what is this 9? It is exactly .03 × profit's original 30. Those financial columnists who wept crocodile tears for euthanaesia of the profit class engendered by guidelines could have been saved from error if the presidential directive had been enunciated as a 3.2 percent increase in profits *and* wages.

In economic argumentation, when you gain one friend you lose another. Precisely because the guidelines allow for an equal percentage increase in all factor-of-production shares, they have been criticized as "freezing the *status quo* distribution of productive incomes." I must confess that this was my initial reaction against them.

What is so sacred about the existing distribution of income that it should be frozen forever? For one thing, why should organized labor agree in perpetuity to desist from trying to raise the share of the social pie going to workers? And, if you believe that it is the purely competitive forces of the marketplace which determine the distribution of income shares, what a coincidence it would be for changes in technology and tastes to be such as lead exactly to perpetuation of any base-period sharing of the national income?

My qualms in this matter, and those of any critic, seem to be best answered by quoting the analysis of Professor Robert Solow, one of the formulators of the Kennedy guideposts.

> It seems to me that this argument has no practical weight at all. It is rendered trivial by two facts. The first is that the division of the national income between labor and property incomes is among the slower-changing characteristics of our economy, or of any Western economy. The second is that neither the guideposts nor any other such quantitative prescription can be satisfied exactly. Suppose that wage rates do follow the guideposts exactly. Then if the price level, instead of remaining constant, goes up by, say, 1 percent in a year, the share of wages in national income will fall by 1 percent—that is, by about † of 1 percentage point. If, on the other hand, the price level should fall by 1 percent, the share of wages in national income would rise by † of 1 percentage point. That may not seem like much, but actually it is quite a lot, more than enough to provide all the flexibility that our economic system is likely to need.
>
> In the twenty years since the end of the war, the proportion of "compensation of employees" to national income has moved about within a narrow range, say from 65 percent to 71 percent. There is no reason to suppose that market forces will always want to keep the figure within those bounds, but there is every reason to believe that market forces will never, or hardly ever, want to move the proportional distribution of income very rapidly. As the numerical example shows, if wages adhered to the guidelines, the distribution of income could get from one end of its postwar range to the other in about eigh

years, with an annual rate of inflation or deflation never exceeding 1 percent.

Since this is a seminar, I trust I shall be forgiven for writing down a few simple equations or arithmetical identities. The value of total product is equal to dollar-price times quantity sold; and this can be broken up into wage-cost alone plus the remainder. which is the share of profit.

$$P \times Q = W \times L + Profit$$

Now let us write the ratio depicting the relative share of profits to wages as r. Then arithmetic multiplication and division and a little rearrangement of terms will convert our equation into the guidepost form.

$$W = P (1 + r) \frac{Q}{L}$$

This says that, if the price level is to be stable and relative factor shares are not to be disturbed, wage rates can rise only in the same proportion as physical-labor productivity rises. I warn that this is a mere tautology of arithmetic. In *any* inflation, even that of purest demand pull, wage rates and money profits rise at a faster pace than physical productivity.

The above formulation permits me to concede at once certain valid objections to any one frozen guidepost target number such as 3.2 percent. If business is to be subject to higher tax rates—as for example in the 1965 step-up in social security payroll tax rates—then permitting labor a wage-rate increase fully equal to the productivity increase would be in effect to say: "Labor is to bear none of the burden of the extra social security benefits voted by Congress." I agree that that would be unfair, but add the reminder that this is a two-way street. When Congress reduces business taxes—as in the investment tax credit—labor gets none of the benefits under frozen guidepost numbers.

The same problem arises from changes in prices of nonindustrial materials. When 1965 copper and oil prices rise, any firm experiencing only a 3.2 increase in the productivity of its *own* laborers can afford to raise its workers' wages by 3.2 percent only by suffering a deterioration of relative profit share.

Because the guideposts were promulgated in a period that proved to be an exceptionally long economic expansion, with productivity and volume continuing to grow for an exceptionally long time, one could not prior to 1967 weep for the plight of the profit receiver. Profits in the 1960s have done very well. But I must point out that in the course of the business cycle there is a characteristic fluctuation of the wage-profit share: the profit share drops during recessions and pauses; it rises sharply in recoveries. Thus, we must question whether the remarks quoted from Solow fully succeed in banishing concern that guidepost formulas tend to resist natural economic forces by trying to freeze relative factor shares. This is one way of looking at the problem which vexed President Johnson's advisers. To give, at the end of a cycle, wage increases equal to average productivity growth over the cycle, is to produce inflation at the end of the cycle. On the other hand, to hold down wage increases at the end of the cycle to the low productivity advances of that period is to fly in the face of tight labor markets and invite noncompliance with the guideposts.

Let me turn from the arithmetic of the problem to what it is that wage-price guideposts are an attempt to do.

A BETTER PHILLIPS CURVE

I cannot stress too strongly that wage-price guideposts are not substitutes for proper macroeconomic fiscal and monetary policies. Economists have always known that excessively easy monetary policy and/or enlarged expenditures coupled with small tax receipts can produce demand-pull inflation. The only cure for that situation is tighter money and/or more restrictive fiscal policy.

If prices and wages were perfectly

flexible, like those in ideal auction markets, there would be no need for guideposts. The authorities would engineer fiscal and monetary expansion just up to the point of full employment. Prior to that point, the general price level would not rise and average wages would grow automatically with productivity. Relative prices and wages would have to show fluctuations in order to clear particular markets. In this ideal world, which differs dramatically from every mixed economy that now exists, the problem would be merely one of macroeconomic dosage, and there would be no dilemmas of policy.

Our mixed economy—like that of Germany, Japan, England, France, Sweden, and Belgium—reveals a tendency for prices to creep upward even when there is substantial unemployment. To keep wholesale prices stable and the implicit-GNP-deflator index growing at a moderate 1.5 percent might well require that U.S. unemployment be, in the short run, 5 percent or more.

Experience suggests that in the short run there is a trade-off between the intensity of unemployment of men and capital and the intensity of price increase. This can be plotted as a statistical scatter diagram and graphed in the form of what is called a Phillips curve—named after Professor A. W. Phillips of the London School of Economics, who measured this relationship for the United Kingdom over the past century. One must not exaggerate the exactitude of the Phillips curve but nevertheless it is one of the most important concepts of our times. Any criticism of the guideposts which does not explicitly take into account the Phillips curve concept I have to treat as having missed the fundamental point of all economic policy discussions.

Let me illustrate with a case in point. I have quoted Friedman's view that the quantity theory of money is all-important in explaining fluctuations of aggregate spending. Suppose we grant a premise that I regard as untenable,

namely that the velocity of circulation of money can be treated as a constant. Then the GNP can be rewritten as MV and by hypothesis it will move in strict proportion to the supply of M. One can still imagine two mixed economies that would differ drastically in their behavior with respect to creeping inflation. To put the matter succinctly, Economy A might have a very bad Phillips curve and Economy B might have a very good one. In Economy B the monopoly power of price-administrating corporations and of union bargainers is hardly to be observed at all. Employment can be very full indeed before the price level creeps. The problem of macroeconomic policy is the transparent one of dosage.

But how can we make mixed Economy A like that of B?

Now, maybe guideposts won't do it, which is a question that has to be examined on its merits. But don't make the mistake of thinking that macroeconomic policy can do it.

Macroeconomic policy can determine *where* you are on the Phillips curve. But if you have a bad short- or long-run curve, macroeconomic policy cannot give you a good Phillips curve.

Now, how can you get a good Phillips curve? And by a good Phillips curve I mean how can you get an economy which takes every expansion of purchasing power short of full employment and converts it into real, physical product of things that people want, an economy which lowers structural unemployment before prices creep. That's the problem for guideposts.

And that is why I think it is of the utmost superficiality for some people to say guideposts worked well from 1962 to 1964 but that they worked very badly in 1965, 1966, and 1967.

For prices to behave well in 1962-64 is a very easy victory, and it is not a victory that necessarily belongs to guideposts. And for guideposts to be judged to work badly in 1965 and 1966, you can't ask whether prices

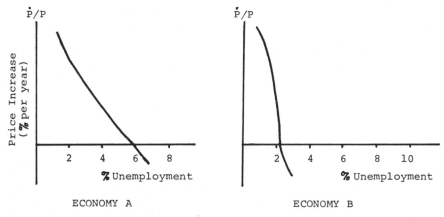

Fig. 1. On the left is shown a typical Phillips curve for a mixed economy like that of the United States. By contrast, on the right is shown Economy B with a more ideal Phillips curve. The problem posed for guidelines and for "income policies" generally is not where one should be on the Phillips curve; that is the problem of proper macroeconomic fiscal and monetary policy. Rather the guideposts attempt to achieve a better Phillips curve—to shift the curve leftward so that it will be more like that of Economy B. This is also the problem for antitrust enforcement, for labor legislation, for avoidance of too-high minimum wage laws, for manpower retraining, and mobility programs.

crept upward. You have to ask how prices and wages would have behaved in the absence of incomes policy or guideposts.

One may fairly ask what it is that critics of guideposts themselves advocate to meet this genuine problem of cost inflation.

We can all agree that the government should be careful in the way it spends its money so as not to drive up prices. And, of course, it would be nice to have better antitrust laws. I think we're all in favor of that. And if you know some way of making union behavior more like that of Economy B, then that will be very welcome. But the proposals that have been put forth, in terms of their actual feasibility, have not yet amounted to much.

The guideposts and related "incomes policies" are attempts all over the world to give us the same degree of fullness of employment with less price creep than would otherwise have been the case.

STATISTICAL ANALYSIS OF GUIDEPOSTS

Now, how would you judge whether guideposts have been influential? If this were a physical science, you might hope to make a controlled experiment, run the thing twice, with guideposts and without guideposts, and then see what the difference is. Of course, we can't do that.

One attempt by statistical multiple correlation, much quoted, was done on the subject at the Massachusetts Institute of Technology by George Perry of the University of Minnesota.

Perry first did what many people have done, such as Phillips in England. He tried to find a formula to estimate wage increases in the United States statistically. Then he related wage increases statistically to the degree of unemployment and to the amount of profits—because if the profits are very high, then concessions are given to wages—and to rates of change of these variables. This is a very familiar exercise.

I can't remember the exact date of his investigation, but I think he first used data that went up to about 1962 or 1963.

Then, on the basis of these previously established patterns, he tackled the post-1962 period in which the guideposts were operating. A number of other people have done the same thing and with much the same results.

All of these studies show that prices and wages did not rise as much in 1964, 1965, and 1966 as had been predicted for them on the basis of previous experience. For the same levels of unemployment, profitability, rates of change, and so forth, in post-1962 we did seem to have a better Phillips curve.

What was different? Well, some people say what was different were the Kennedy-Johnson guideposts. Now, that is not a conclusive argument. We can certainly think of some other things that were different. One is that in the late 1950s we ran a very sluggish economy. This has been called an investment in sadism by the old William McChesney Martin—not the new William McChesney Martin.

Although I call it an investment in sadism, it wasn't done just for kicks, and it may have had a return. Some can argue that one of its returns was the fact that we had a better Phillips curve in the 1960s under Kennedy and Johnson because of the unemployment that was tolerated in the 1950s by Eisenhower, i.e., differences in *past* history, which are not in Perry's regressions, might possibly explain it.

I think if that were the case, I would expect as the passage of time goes on that this would be a fading type of effect; and it isn't clear to me that with the passage of time this has been the case.

I don't know how you feel about the present mid-1967 wage settlements and how they are going; but 12 months ago, if you had described today's tight labor market to me and asked me to predict how the wage settlements would be going, I would have thought, frankly, they would be higher than they have been.

I do want to mention one other factor, though, which is also different and which doesn't show in Perry's regression. That is the balance-of-payments constraint and the possible constraint on

our prices and wages that come from the import picture.

As an example, I don't believe that the difference in behavior of the steel industry in the 1960s and the 1950s can be understood without reference to the import picture. I think socially the steel industry has been behaving immeasurably better in the 1960s than in the 1950s. And for the purpose of this argument I am not saying that this is because of a confrontation between President Kennedy and Roger Blough. Moreover I'm talking about better performance on the part of the union and the industry generally. I suspect that part of the reason is that the workers are beginning to realize that when they raise money wages and when that increases steel prices, they lose volume of business and employment.

And so a better Phillips curve in the 1960s—if indeed we have it—may be due to the openness of the economy and to the international competition.

Yet when all is said and done, I think that there is some influence discernible from the guidepost philosophy. Last year at a Chamber of Commerce debate, I described the guideposts as really an attempt to affect the philosophy of men in the marketplace.

Now, if you think that the marketplace is subject only to Walrasian equations of perfect competition, then the will of men, except as it affects our tastes between cheese and apples and clothing, will cancel out of everything and nobody's influence can make a difference. Then there is certainly no room for the guideposts.

By contrast, I think that there are many sectors in our modern mixed economy where the short-run behavior of people can be substantially affected through moral suasion and public attitudes.

But, if it were just that, these effects would probably be very short run. Remember, in these industrial sectors, as elsewhere, the whole is the sum of its parts. And if in the short run all of the oligopolies can be persuaded to take things easy on the upside with respect to price, that makes it much easier for every one of them to go along with this philosophy.

Sometimes what I am talking about is called the apologetics of the modern corporation. An old friend of mine from Japan once told me in the postwar period that if Japanese capitalism were like the new American capitalism, then he would not be a Socialist. He said "You are a rich country, which can afford a more gentle kind of capitalism."

The hard-boiled believers in markets say that this is rot, capitalism is just as bad as it ever was—by which they mean just as good as it ever was; they say,

> The worst thing in the world would be for capitalists to stop acting like capitalists. to stop maximizing profits and start doing what it isn't their business to do. Don't believe them when they say they are doing it: in the first place they are lying; in the second place, they don't know what they are saying; and in the third place, if they really act that way, they won't be here tomorrow, because competition will take care of them.

Again by contrast, I think that there is a lot of cushion in the 500 largest corporations, which permits them to follow independent policy that takes some account of the public welfare.

I don't think you can expect the president of American Tobacco to get religion on lung cancer. I think that if he gets a violent view about cigarettes and lung cancer, he must go; he cannot stay as president of American Tobacco. He can't take the company with him, he has to go. But I don't think that is the situation in which the typical large corporation is. Here I am not talking about a single corporation trying to buck the system, because if one corporation behaved this way and no other corporation did, I agree that ruthless competition might soon eliminate it. But if all the 500 corporations in some degree have a social philosophy and purpose, I

think that they enable each one to perform in this way.

One of my former students who works for one of the largest corporations in the world tried to get his board of directors there to admit that they maximize their profits. He said,

> Profits aren't a dirty word. All I want you to do is admit that you maximize your long-run profits. And that it's good public relations in the long run to maximize your profits.

Yet, he tells me, he cannot get them to admit that, adding,

> And why not? These people have been in this large corporation all their executive lives; they have a lot of headaches, but by no means is their biggest headache the annual meeting. And when they say that they regard themselves as *pluralistically* responding to government, to their consumers, to their workers, and to their stockholders, after years of trying to get them to say the opposite I felt forced to believe them.

Now, the background of my argument that guideposts have some effect is that all the large corporations together and the labor unions do have some discretionary power in marking up their prices. While their sectors could charge what the market will bear, every time the demand seems to be inelastic, raising the prices, I don't recognize that as realistic for the large-corporation sector. I think you can get a price spiral in which all the large corporations simultaneously goad each other into raising prices. I extend this same argument, by the way, to the wage part of the picture.

Now, mind you, guideposts have been shown not to be a substitute for macroeconomic policy. You cannot print trillions of marks or dollars per day and think that public spirit is going to hold prices stable. But what you can do is have a system which at 5 percent unemployment generates creeping inflation of 3 percent per year, or one which at 5 percent unemployment generates a lower rate of price increase, being able to go to 4 percent of unemployment and still generate reasonable stability in the price index.

I regard the Galbraith quotation as absurd—that during the big war we held prices down and it worked well; that during the Korean War we held prices down and it worked well; that there is no real difference between war and peace, so let's just hold prices and wages down. The more you are trying to push the Phillips curve down, while also operating in the inflationary part of it, the less the siutation can be maintained, particularly in the longer run. But within limits I think that the experience of the 1960s suggests to us that there has been an important role to be played by these informal controls.

WHAT LONG-RUN PHILLIPS CURVE?

Now, the time for my formal discussion is almost up, but I do raise a more complicated problem: How does the Phillips curve change over time?

I mentioned the hypothesis that unemployment in the late 1950s has made possible the good price behavior of the early 1960s. This can be expressed in different ways, and has been expressed in different ways. Professor Friedman in the cited volume expresses the matter this way: There is no tradeoff between unemployment and the rate of change of prices. (By that he means there is no such tradeoff, except in the short run.) Instead, he says, there is a tradeoff between today's unemployment and tomorrow's unemployment. And if you generate some unemployment today, you may be able to reduce unemployment tomorrow with the same price stability.

Now, I think that's true in part. I think that this effect is plausible from economic reasoning. I think there is some experience in the statistics which suggests that this is in fact the case.

But I do not think the sharper form of the doctrine is true, namely that there is a one-to-one tradeoff between today's and tomorrow's unemployment. This would suggest enunciation of a new doctrine. We have the law of conservation of energy; we have the law of conservation of matter. We are now to have a new law of conservation, the alleged law of conservation of unemployment, which says: Any mixed economy has the same amount of unemployment to be enjoyed—if that is the right verb—over the long run regardless of price behavior, that it is the same whether in the long run you are averaging a 3 percent increase in the price level or stability in the price level, or a decrease in the price level.

If this notion of a vertical long-run Phillips curve were true, and if we like price stability and can afford the long-run view, than I suppose we might as well have stable prices and get this fundamental amount of unemployment at a stable price level.

You see what all this implies in terms of a Phillips curve diagram on this blackboard. We now have a vertical line at the structural amount of unemployment which is characteristic of the mixed economy in question. And independently of the price level you are always going to return to that same vertical line which represents the same fundamental amount of unemployment.

Of course, that line could conceivably be shifted. For example, trustbusting, getting rid of a minimum wage, promoting flexibility, making various structural changes, and educating the labor force might move the line to the left, but it is a vertical line regardless of price behavior.

I have been studying the time series trying to piece together from cases of experiences of different countries what I can. I also have been thinking of what is plausible. In the end I can't really see that it is plausible that unemployment should be a fundamental long-run constant, that there should be a one-to-one tradeoff.

I think it is true that you may gain in high employment in one short period and have to pay in some amount for it later. But I don't think that you need always pay an equal amount, and that the Phillips curve will reconstitute itself always at a perverse level, and at the same perverse level.

I hope that we'll get more scientific studies trying to elucidate this. The trouble is, of course, that experience is very slow to come by when we are trying to measure long-run relationships of this sort. And we rather hope that economies won't go through the fluctuations which will give us the experience that will add to our scientific knowledge, because the guinea pigs that the experiments will involve would be ourselves and our neighbors.

39. Lessons from the Current Economic Expansion*

PAUL A. SAMUELSON

I shall take literally my assignment on this panel and discuss what lessons we have learned from recent macroeconomic experience. This means noting some surprising departures from previous patterns of experience. But it also means pinching ourselves and asking, What went right?

Here, then, in ten minutes are ten lessons learned or to be learned, which is at the rate of one lesson a minute.

Lesson 1. *Economists cannot forecast the future with precision.*

Lesson 2. *Neither can anyone else,* and the forecasts made by professional economists are systematically better than any made by brokers, bankers or businessmen. (Together, these lessons might constitute the "random dart" theory of getting a forecast: throw a coin at any one of the couple of dozen leading practitioners of the forecasting art, and you'll do about as well as if you try to pick out the very best one. In fact, it won't matter much where your coin lands, you'll get almost the same forecast anyway—which leads to the next lesson.)

Lesson 3. *Economists can succeed in forecasting like each other.* Roy Blough's dogma still holds. Economists are like eight Esquimaux in one bed—the only thing you can be sure about is that they are all going to turn over together. I may add as a corollary to Blough's Law: most economists are going to be all correct together, or all wrong together. The dispersion between forecasts by a score of university, bank, government, and corporation analysts is much less than the dispersion of their best guesses around where the future reality will lie.

Lesson 4. *Some economists manage to forecast worse than others.* But a Darwinian process of selection—often self-selection when one deals with rational men with alternative uses for their leisure time—does serve to eliminate those whose comparative advantage lies in cosmology or in futurism. After a man has said a dozen times, "If this forecast

*Source: From The American Economic Review: Papers and Proceedings of the Eighty-sixth Annual Meeting of the American Economic Association (May 1974), pp. 75-77. Copyright © 1974 American Economic Association. Reprinted by permission. Footnote added.

doesn't turn out correct, I'll hang up my gloves," he finally does. However, there are exceptions to this rule: some masochists make a nice living out of being wrong in an interesting way, predicting every other year that the Dow-Jones average will go down to 200, where it will meet the dollar price of gold. Businessmen, who like to have their adrenalin run listening to a ghost story, will pay as much to listen to these ever-losers as to informed analysts. But my Darwinian proposition becomes irrefutable when I base it on the tautology that the born losers who stay in the forecasting game cease to be regarded as economists by members of our guild.

Lesson 5. *An automatic computer can forecast better than an official government agency.* But an analyst with judgment can do better than an automatic computer. This is borne out, not only by the rather sad performance of the reduced-form monetarist model of the Federal Reserve Bank of St. Louis, but also by Ray Fair's audit of his own Princeton model, which does without any inputs of "judgment" and which thereby runs up a larger mean square error than the leading judgmental-computer models of the Wharton, Michigan, *DRI*, Chase, or other type.

Lesson 6. *Judgmental analysts cannot do without the computer.* So much of the information that comes to any man of judgment these days has been massaged by a computer that the era is past when one could have a fair contest between a nonanalytical observer such as Sumner Slichter and a giant post-Keynesian macro computer model. Were Slichter alive today, he would make his forward strides of shrewdness while riding on the escalator of the computer.

Lesson 7. *Economists can forecast (well, almost forecast) everything but prices.* In this sense they are the reverse of Oscar Wilde's cynics, who know the price of everything and the value of nothing. When it comes to next March's price of wheat, why should any Ph.D.

be able to forecast that better than people who know a lot about the crops and milling industry and who have a lot of money riding on the outcome of their best guesses? All the things that are easy to forecast—that is, easy enough for a mere professor to foresee—can be expected to have already been taken into account by the speculative market. Indeed, if there were in Las Vegas or New York a continuous casino on the money GNP of 1974's fourth quarter, it would be absurd to think that the best economic forecasters could improve upon the guess posted there. Whatever knowledge and analytical skill they possess would already have been fed into the bidding. It is a manifest contradiction to think that most economists can be expected to do better than their own best performance. But I am saying something more devastating than that. I am saying that the best forecasters have been poor in predicting the general price level's movements and level even a year ahead. By Valentine's Day 1973 the best forecasters were beginning to talk of the growth recession that we now know did set in at the end of the first quarter. Aside from their end-of-1972 forecasts, the fashionable crowd has little to blame itself for when it comes to their 1973 real GNP projections. But, of course, they did not foresee the upward surge of food and decontrolled industrial prices. This has been a recurring pattern: surprise during the event at the virulence of the inflation, wisdom after the event in demonstrating that it did, after all, fit in with past patterns of experience. I know of no exception to this generalization. Monetarists have generally done no better in this regard, although some have thought that there is somehow a closer link between M and P than between M and money $GNP = PXQ$. To be sure, some have been less unlucky in their guesses than others, but we all know what the corollary of that is. What seems to have thrown economists off is the fact that the Phillips Curve seems to have worsened, both in the eyes of those who believe in the Phillips Curve and in the eyes of those who don't (and use a different language to describe the same disappointing effect upon wages and costs generally of each degree of stagnation). Improvement in the rate of inflation is a mirage that economists see eighteen months ahead; but just as the railroad tracks never seem to meet as they appeared to do ten miles back, so that return to "normalcy" never seems to occur—not even after we have euphemistically redefined normalcy to permit of 2.5 percent annual inflation or more. Paradoxically, as soon as the analysts stopped underestimating wage increases, they began to underestimate general price increases. One suspects that two things are involved: wishful thinking and perhaps a change in the structural difficulty of the economy in having steady or slowly growing price levels. When their predictions go wrong, people usually find alibis in contrafactual predictions incapable of being falsified or corroborated. Thus, some say,

> It is price controls that cause the error in my forecasts (in either direction!); but, of course, we shall never know what the world would have been like without those price controls.

Or they say,

> If the Fed would do something (which the odds are against its doing), then the reality would agree with my forecast.

Much of the disagreement for policy, but not all, comes from differences between advisers on how much sacrifice of short-term welfare they are willing to invest in now and in the near future for some hypothetical better behavior of the economy in the more distant future. Those with a low rate of time discount, who will cheerfully recommend a flyer in sadomasochistic austerity, are likely by the Darwinian process of politics to find themselves not in power for the period of time they say their therapy requires.

Lesson 8. *In recent years the U.S. economy has been remarkably unprone to swings of inventory accumulation such as characterized our past history.*[1] Those who prior to the energy crisis predicted a genuine recession for 1974 were counting on such an inventory slingshot effect to give them their downturn. But they may have to look elsewhere for their recession.

Lesson 9. *A microeconomic event such as an Arab oil boycott can loom large as a macroeconomic depressant.* Most experts now think that if the boycott is more than a charade and a passing thing, real output will decline in the first half of 1974. But we now realize that our Fisher-Keynes macro models do not tell us how to handle such a microeconomic restriction on supply and productivity. It is not even clear that we should call such a downturn a recession, since it may not involve much wastage between our actual GNP and our producible GNP. However, to the extent that gasoline scares hurt the auto business and the suburban building market, some of the same secondary effects of conventional recession will become operative, calling for some of the conventional lean-against-the-wind policy measures.

Lesson 10. *The conventional wisdom that currency depreciation will improve the balance of payments seems in 1973, at long last, to receive some support from the factual evidence.* There have been more important things to worry about in recent years than which way the dollar would move in a regime of somewhat-flexible exchange rates.

I've still not drawn all the lessons taught by our recent times. Perhaps I may be permitted to give one final lesson, to grow wise on, so to speak.

Lesson 11. *Events of the last half dozen years have shown us how much economics remains an art rather than a science.* Economics is exciting because what we study is hard, not easy. Once again, I think, experience has taught us the hard way that eclecticism in economics is, to paraphrase Justice Holmes, not so much a desirability as a necessity.

_____

NOTE

1. [Added by author ib 1979.] I could not know at that time that the Department of Commerce was about to revise its estimates of inventory accumulation and invalidate this inference based upon their earlier estimates. There is a moral here: although our statistical data are more complete now than they used to be, they are still subject to revision and subjective judgment in reporting.

40. A Difficulty in the Concept of Social Welfare*

KENNETH J. ARROW

In a capitalist democracy there are essentially two methods by which social choices can be made: voting, typically used to make "political" decisions, and the market mechanism, typically used to make "economic" decisions. In the emerging democracies with mixed economic systems, Great Britain, France, and Scandinavia, the same two modes of making social choices prevail, though more scope is given to the method of voting and to decisions based directly or indirectly on it and less to the rule of the price mechanism. Elsewhere in the world, and even in smaller social units within the democracies, the social decisions are sometimes made by single individuals or small groups and sometimes (more and more rarely in this modern world) by a widely encompassing set of traditional rules for making the social choice in any given situation, e.g., a religious code.

The last two methods of social choice, dictatorship and convention, have in their formal structure a certain definiteness absent from voting or the market mechanism. In an ideal dictatorship, there is but one will involved in choice; in an ideal society ruled by convention, there is but the divine will or perhaps, by assumption, a common will of all individuals concerning social decisions, so that in either case no conflict of individual wills is involved. The methods of voting and of the market, on the other hand, are methods of amalgamating the tastes of many individuals in the making of social choices. The methods of dictatorship and convention are, or can be, rational in the sense that any individual can be rational in his choice. Can such consistency be attributed to collective modes of choice, where the wills of many people are involved?

It should be emphasized here that the present study is concerned only with the formal aspects of the foregoing question. That is, we ask if it is formally possible to construct a procedure for passing from a set of known individual tastes to a pattern of social decision-making, the procedure in question being required to satisfy certain natural conditions. An illustration of the problem is

*Source: Excerpted from "A Difficulty in the Concept of Social Welfare," by Kenneth J. Arrow. Journal of Political Economy (1950), pp. 328-30. Copyright © 1950 The University of Chicago Press. Reprinted by permission. Most footnotes deleted; remaining renumbered.

the following well-known "paradox of voting." Suppose there is a community consisting of three voters and this community must choose among three alternative modes of social action (e.g., disarmament, cold war, or hot war). It is expected that choices of this type have to be made repeatedly, but sometimes not all of the three alternatives will be available. In analogy with the usual utility analysis of the individual consumer under conditions of constant wants and variable price-income situations, rational behavior on the part of the community would mean that the community orders the three alternatives according to its collective preferences once for all and then chooses in any given case that alternative among those actually available which stands highest on this list. A natural way of arriving at the collective preference scale would be to say that one alternative is preferred to another if a majority of the community prefer the first alternative to the second, i.e., would choose the first over the second if those were the only two alternatives. Let A, B, and C be the three alternatives, and 1, 2, and 3 the three individuals. Suppose individual 1 prefers A to B and B to C (and therefore A to C), individual 2 prefers B to C and C to A (and therefore B to A), and individual 3 prefers C to A and A to B (and therefore C to B). Then a majority prefers A to B, and a majority prefers B to C. We may therefore say that the community prefers A to B and B to C. If the community is to be regarded as behaving rationally, we are forced to say that A is preferred to C. But, in fact, a majority of the community prefers C to A.[1] So the method just outlined for passing from individual to collective tastes fails to satisfy the condition of rationality as we ordinarily understand it. Can we find other methods of aggregating individual tastes which imply rational behavior on the part of the community and which will be satisfactory in other ways?

If we adopt the traditional identification of rationality with maximization of

some sort, then the problem of achieving a social maximum derived from individual desires is precisely the problem which has been central to the field of welfare economics. However, the search for a clear definition of optimum social welfare has been plagued by the difficulties of interpersonal comparisons. The emphasis, as is well known, has shifted to a weaker definition of optimum, namely, the determination of all social states such that no individual can be made better off without making someone worse off. As Professors Bergson, Lange, and Samuelson have argued, though, the weaker definition cannot be used as a guide to social policy; the second type of welfare economics is only important as a preliminary to the determination of a genuine social maximum in the full sense. E.g., under the usual assumptions, if there is an excise tax imposed on one commodity in the initial situation, it can be argued that the removal of the tax accompanied by a suitable redistribution of income and direct tax burdens will improve the position of all individuals in the society. But there are, in general, many redistributions which will accomplish this end, and society must have some criterion for choosing among them before it can make any change at all. Further, there is no reason for confining the range of possible social actions to those which will injure no one as compared with the initial situation, unless the status quo is to be sanctified on ethical grounds. All we can really say is that society ought to abolish the excise tax and make some redistribution of income and tax burdens; but this is no prescription for action unless there is some principle by which society can make its choice among attainable income distributions, i.e., a social indifference map.

Voting can be regarded as a method of arriving at social choices derived from the preferences of individuals. Another such method of more specifically economic content is the compensation principle, as proposed by Mr.

Kaldor: in a choice between two alternative economic states x and y, if there is a method of paying compensations under state x such that everybody can be made better off in the state resulting from making the compensations under x than they are in state y, then x should be chosen in preference to y, *even if the compensation is not actually paid.* Apart from the ethical difficulties in the acceptance of this principle, there is a formal difficulty which was pointed out by Professor Scitovszky: it is possible that simultaneously x should be preferred to y and y be preferred to x. Just as in the case of majority voting, this method of aggregating individual preferences may lead to a pattern of social choice which is not a linear ordering of the social alternatives. Note that in both cases the paradox need not occur; all that is said is that there are preference patterns which, if held by the individual members of the society, will give rise to an inconsistent pattern of social choice. Unless the trouble-breeding individual preference patterns can be ruled out by a priori assumption, both majority voting and the compensation principle must be regarded as unsatisfactory techniques for the determination of social preferences.

The aim of the present paper is to show that these difficulties are general. For *any* method of deriving social choices by aggregating individual preference patterns which satisfies certain natural conditions, it is possible to find individual preference patterns which give rise to a social choice pattern which is not a linear ordering. In particular, this is very likely to be the case if, as is frequently assumed, each individual's preferences among social states are derived purely from his personal consumption-leisure-saving situation in each.

NOTE

1. It may be added that the method of decision sketched above is essentially that used in deliberative bodies, where a whole range of alternatives usually comes up for decision in the form of successive pairwise comparisons. The phenomenon described in the text can be seen in a pure form in the disposition of the proposals before recent Congresses for federal aid to state education, the three alternatives being no federal aid, federal aid to public schools only, and federal aid to both public and parochial schools.

41. The Limits of Organization*

KENNETH J. ARROW

ORGANIZATION AND INFORMATION

[*Paragraphs deleted.*]

The purpose of organizations is to exploit the fact that many (virtually all) decisions require the participation of many individuals for their effectiveness. In particular . . . organizations are a means of achieving the benefits of collective action in situations in which the price system fails.

There is one particular failure of the price system to which I want to stress, one that is absolutely central to the understanding of organizations. I refer to the presence of uncertainty. Now there is a purely theoretical device for introducing the price system to handle uncertainty in certain aspects. Since this approach may not be familiar to all, it may be as well to sketch it here.

Uncertainty means that we do not have a complete description of the world which we fully believe to be true. Instead, we consider the world to be in one or another of a range of states. Each state of the world is a description which is complete for all relevant purposes. Our uncertainty consists in not knowing which state is the true one. The uncertainty may be about conditions of production or tastes or anything else which, if known, would affect individuals' desires to trade. Then instead of contracts to buy and sell fixed amounts of goods, it would be better to have conditional contracts, or contracts in *contingent commodities,* to use the technical term, that is, each unit contract is for the delivery of a one unit of some good *if* a specified state has occurred. Since the state of the world completely specifies demand and supply conditions, it is possible to prescribe that contingent contracts can always be carried out, since we need offer to deliver exactly as much would be available in the state which the contract is contingent. Prices can be attached to these contracts; then the standard theory of the competitive economy without uncertainty can be reinterpreted to give a theory of competitive equilibrium under uncertainty. A commodity in the ordinary sense is replaced by a contingent commodity.

From this account, it can be seen that this theoretical scheme has some parallels in the real world. Insurance policies exist; so does the necessary evil of the cost-plus contract. Much more important, the common stock market serves for the diffusion of risks. But clearly also the range of contingencies for which conditional contracts are available is much more limited than would be ide-

ally desirable in theory. The taking of desirable economic risks is inhibited by the inability to insure against business failure, for example. At a more detailed level, the coordination of complicated production processes within a firm is in part a question of uncertainty—for example, random delays in one part or another of the process. One could imagine a price system in principle for internal coordination of the firms: the department which supplies a part to another would sell it at a price which varies according to the average length of the delay. The selling department would have a clear incentive to reduce the delay. However, the risks to the buyer can be optimally allocated only if there is a system of insurance against the contingencies which can create delays; otherwise, the buying department would have to alter the scope of its operations so as to minimize uncertainty, an alteration which would result in reduced output overall. It is not hard to see that such a combination of prices and insurance would be exceedingly difficult to implement in practice.

There is more than one reason for the failure of the theoretically desirable contingent prices to exist. One doubtless is the sheer complexity of the price schedule. An insurance policy would have to specify an enormous number of contingencies with, in general, different payments for each possibility. Drawing up such contracts would be expensive, and understanding them equally so. The courts of law, on the basis of long experience, have shown little faith in the ability of the average individual to understand complicated contracts. An illustration is the treatment of the so-called exculpatory clauses. For example, when shipping goods, the transportation company frequently includes in its contract a clause exempting it from liability for damage to or loss of the goods shipped. Formally, one could regard this simply as determining the locus of risk-bearing. Once this is determined, a perfect market could permit the reshifting of risks, for example, through insurance. But courts have consistently refused to enforce such clauses and have held the transport companies liable anyway. Their argument is that it is too much to expect the average shipper, who is small compared with the transport company, to appreciate the risks in question.

Another major reason for limitation of the price system for allocating risk-bearing is the difficulty of distinguishing between genuine risks and failures to optimize, a difficulty referred to by students of insurance as *moral hazard*. For example, the outbreak of a fire may be due to a combination of exogenous circumstances and individual choice, such as carelessness or, in the extreme case, arson. Hence, a fire insurance policy creates an incentive for an individual to change his behavior and ceases to be a pure insurance against an uncontrollable event.

Roy Radner has put the matter in more general perspective by observing the key role of information in the possibility of arriving at contingent contracts. Briefly, my sketch of the pure theory of allocation of risk-bearing has implicitly assumed that all individuals know what state of nature prevails when the contracts are finally fulfilled, when the insurance payments are made. It suffices, to be precise, that they will have the same information, whatever it may be. But in most cases, this will not be so. To illustrate, consider the problem known in insurance literature as *adverse selection*. The insured may know his risks better than the insurer, for example, in life insurance. The insurer may start by choosing his rates on some actuarial basis. But then the high-risk groups will buy more of the insurance than the average, while the low-risk groups will buy less. Hence, the experience of the insurer, as weighted by dollars, will be less favorable than the actuarial. The rates will have to be raised, but this will drive still more of the low-risk groups out. Clearly a situation will be created

in which there are many whose risks are inadequately covered, because it is not known how low those risks really are. The essential cause is an inequality of information between the two parties to the contract.

Another illustration of the inequality of information among economic agents is the relation between patient and physician. It is of the essence of this or other relations between principal and agent that they differ in their information about the world. But this means that there can really be no contract which insures against the agent's failure to do his business properly. I have argued in a study of medical economics that one might regard professional ethics as an example of an institution which fills in some measure the gap created by the corresponding failure of the price system.

It follows that the information structure of individual economic agents powerfully conditions the possibilities of allocating risk-bearing through the market. By information structure here I mean not merely the state of knowledge existing at any moment of time but the possibility of acquiring relevant information in the future. We speak of the latter in communication terminology as the possession of an *information channel,* and the information to be received as *signals* from the rest of the world.

Thus the possibility of using the price system to allocate uncertainty, to insure against risks, is limited by the structure of the information channels in existence. Put the other way, the value of nonmarket decision-making, the desirability of creating organizations of a scope more limited than the market as a whole, is partially determined by the characteristics of the network of information flows.

But the presence or absence of information channels is not prescribed exogenously to the economic system. Channels can be created or abandoned, and their capacities and the types of signals to be transmitted over them are subject to choice, a choice based on a comparison of benefits and costs. I therefore turn to an examination of the characteristics of information and in particular some generalities on the benefits and costs of information channels. In the next chapter, I will discuss more specifically the organization as a processor of information.

Each individual economic agent is assumed to start with the ability to receive some signals from the natural and social environments. This capacity is not, however, unlimited, and the scarcity of information-handling ability is an essential feature for the understanding of both individual and organizational behavior. The individual also starts off with a set of expectations as to the range of signals that he or anybody else might possibly receive now or in the future and probabilities of receiving the different signals. In technical terms, the individual begins with a prior probability distribution over the space of possible signals. The concept of signal is to be interpreted broadly; some signals might inform the individual of the outcome of his decisions, some might be used as the basis of decisions, if only of implicit decisions not to act. A signal is then any event capable of altering the individual's probability distribution; in more technical language, the posterior distribution of signals conditional on the observation of one may, in general, differ from the prior. This transformation of probabilities is precisely what constitutes the acquisition of information.

This definition of information is qualitative, and so it will remain for the purposes of this volume. The quantitative definition which appears in information theory is probably of only limited value for economic analysis, for reasons pointed out by Marschak; different bits of information, equal from the viewpoint of information theory, will usually have very different benefits or costs. Thus, let A and B be any two statements about the world, for neither of which is its truth or falsity known *a priori*. Then a signal that A is true conveys exactly as much information, in the sense of Shannon, as a statement that B is true. But the value of knowing whether or not A is true may be vastly greater than the value of knowing B's truth-value; or it may be that the resources needed to ascertain the truth-value of A are much greater than those for B. In either case, the information-theoretic equivalence of the two possible signals conceals their vast economic difference.

The channels initially open to the individual may be augmented by the creation of new channels. The choice of new channels will be determined by their benefits and costs. There is little that one can say systematically about the benefits for information in general. The main remark that can be ventured on now is the familiar one that there are increasing returns to the *uses* of information. The same body of technological information, for example, can be used in production on any scale and therefore towards productive enterprises with some degree of monopoly power, in accordance with familiar principles.

Let us now turn to the costs of information, that is, to the inputs needed for the installation and operation of information channels. First and most important, the individual himself is an input, indeed the chief input if quantification is at all meaningful here, into any of his information channels. Immediately or ultimately, the information must enter his brain through his sensory organs, and both brain and senses are limited in capacity. Information may be accumulated in files, but it must be retrieved to be of use in decision-making. The psychological literature has many studies of the limits on the sensory perception abilities of human beings and some on their limits as information-processors. I do not want to argue for fixed coefficients in information-handling any more than in more conventional production activities; substitution of other factors, especially computers, for the individual's mind is possible. But the individual's very limited capacity for acquiring and using information is a fixed factor in information processing, and one may expect a sort of diminishing returns to increases in other information resources. Organization theorists have long recognized limits of this kind under the heading of "span of control."

A second key characteristic of information costs is that they are in part capital costs; more specifically, they typically represent an irreversible investment. I am not placing much weight on the physical aspects of communication, telephone lines and the like, though they are in fact non-negligible in cost and they do provide a concrete, understandable paradigm. Rather I am thinking of the need for having made an adequate investment of time and effort to be able to distinguish one signal from another. Learning a foreign language is an obvious example of what I have in mind. The subsequent ability to receive signals in French requires this initial investment. There are in practice many other examples of codes that have to be learned in order to receive messages; the technical vocabulary of any science is a case in point. The issue here is that others have found it economical to use one of a large number of possible coding methods, and for any individual it is necessary to make an initial investment to acquire it.

However, even when the codes are not deliberately contrived, there is a need for an initial attempt at understanding. The empirical scientist in any area has to make preliminary observations (or learn them from others, which also involves an investment) in order to read nature's signals. Similarly, as E. H. Gombrich has emphasized, our understanding of a particular school of art, and indeed the understanding by artists themselves, depends on a degree of familiarity with it. Thus, there tends to be a cycle in which an innovation in artistic vision first occurs and is diffused; then, as it becomes more familiar, the value of repetition of similar signals decreases, and the ability to understand new signals, *i.e.*, departures from the new tradition, increases.

One might attempt to formalize the capital aspect of information in this way. A signal hitherto unheard is useless by itself; it does not modify any probability distribution. However, a preliminary sampling experiment in which the relation between the new signal and more familiar ones can be determined or at least estimated will serve to make valuable further signals of the new type. This experiment, which may be vicarious (education, scientific literature), is an act of investment.

Such investment, being locked up in an individual's mind, is necessarily irreversible. It can of course be transmitted to others, but it remains in the possession of the individual and cannot be alienated by him, though, like most irreversible investments, it is subject to depreciation.

In the last twenty years, there has developed some theoretical literature on irreversible investment. Obviously irreversibility is of no consequence when the future is one of steadily growing demand for the capital good; but it becomes of importance when there are fluctuations, particularly stochastic fluctuations. Now by its very nature the value of an information channel is uncertain, and so we have an economic problem which resembles the demand for inventories under conditions of uncertainty. We may venture on some possible generalizations. One is that the demand for investment in information is less than it would be if the value of the information were more certain. The second, most important I would guess, is that the random accidents of history will play a bigger role in the final equilibrium. Once the investment has been made and an information channel acquired, it will be cheaper to keep on using it than to invest in new channels, especially since the scarcity of the individual as an input, already alluded to, implies that the use of new channels will diminish the product of old ones. Thus, it will be difficult to reverse an initial commitment in the direction in which information is gathered. Even if the expected value of the difference between two possible channels was relatively small and even if subsequent information suggested that the initial choice was wrong, it would not pay to reverse the decision later on.

A third basic characteristic of information costs is that they are by no means uniform in different directions. At any given moment an individual is a bundle of abilities and accumulated information. He may easily find it cheaper to open certain information channels rather than others in ways connected with these abilities and this knowledge. Thus, an explorer in hitherto unknown territory will find it easier to explore new areas near to those he has already covered. Geographical propinquity is but a special case. It is cheaper to proceed to the chemical analysis of compounds similar to those already studied. Learning generalizes naturally and cheaply in some directions, with much greater difficulty in others. A rat shocked at one point will generalize by staying some distance away; the avoidance effect falls off with distance.

It is also easier to communicate with other individuals with whom one has a common approach or a common language, literally or metaphorically. The capital accumulation of learning a code, referred to earlier, may have to be engaged in at both ends of the channel. In the usual economic analysis, known as the theory of the core, collusive agreements in an industry are not stable because there always exist alternative allocative deals involving some producers and some consumers which are preferable from the viewpoint of the participants. But if, as Adam Smith once suggested, members of the same trade find it easy to communicate with each other, presumably because of their common experiences, it may well be that the exchange of information leading to a collusive agreement among producers of one commodity is much cheaper than that needed to achieve a blocking coalition. Hence, the collusive agreement may in fact be stable. (The concept of class interest and identification may be related to ease of communication among individuals with similar life experiences.)

The relative costs of communication channels may also be influenced by activities of the individual other than the collection of information. There is a complementary between a productive activity and some kinds of information. An individual cannot help making observations while working at some task. These observations are signals which in some circumstances change his knowledge about this productive activity, so-called learning by doing. In other circumstances, they may yield information relevant in other, seemingly remote, areas of decision-making, a phenomenon known as serendipity. We are all familiar with the accomplishments of explorers who were seeking the Northwest Passage.

To sum up, the costs of information, in the general sense of utilization of scarce resources, (a) are in some sense increasing for the individual because he is himself a scarce input, (b) involve a large irreversible capital element, and (c) vary in different directions.

. . . Next . . . I will discuss more specifically the role of information channels within an organization, to illustrate and amplify the cost propositions developed today in this context, and to examine in a general way the implications for the process and outcome of organizational decision-making.

THE AGENDA OF ORGANIZATIONS

In classical maximizing theory it is implicit that the values of all relevant variables are at all moments under construction. All variables are therefore *agenda* of the organization, that is, their values have always to be chosen. On the other hand, it is a commonplace of everyday observation and of studies of organization that the difficulty of arranging that a potential decision variable be recognized as such may be much greater than that of choosing a value for it. What the Federal Government regards as appropriate agenda has changed rapidly; nor can it be maintained that the new agenda necessarily correspond to changes in demand or supply, *i.e.*, the emergence of new problems in the world or of new techniques for their solution. Unemployment insurance is an old idea, and the need for it did not emerge only in the Great Depression; but it suddenly changed from a nonagendum to an agendum. Similar examples can be cited for all sorts of organizations; innovation by firms is in many cases simply a question of putting an item on its agenda before other firms do. We can also see some items now in the process of arriving on the agenda. In the case of the Federal Government, the possibility of flexible exchange rates is at least on the horizon.

On the other hand, there is clearly a real value to putting an item on the agenda. The Employment Act of 1946 amounted to nothing more than a statement that full employment was at last on the Federal agenda, and many felt that this was a hollow victory indeed. But those who opposed it so violently were not deceived; in the long run, this recognition was decisive, though the process of implementing the responsibility was slow indeed. Once an item has arrived on the agenda, it is difficult not to treat it in a somewhat rational manner, if this is at all possible, and almost any considered solution may be better than neglect. I hasten to add that this generalization has its exceptions; there are problems for which there are no satisfactory solutions; placing such an item on the agenda may create a demand for a solution, which will of necessity be unsatisfactory. Thus there is some justification for the principle of "salutory neglect," but on the

whole this exception is not likely to be real. An unsatisfactory solution may be what is needed to provoke the needed information-gathering to produce a better one, while neglect is never productive.

I want to sketch here some thoughts on the factors determining agenda. This problem already exists for the individual, and some time will be first devoted to him. But it will be suggested that the nature and purpose of organizations create additional implications for the determination of agenda and, in particular, for sluggishness in the introduction of new items.

What will be presented is not, strictly speaking, a theory or model but the kinds of considerations that will or should enter into a formulation of such a model. There does not seem to be great difficulty in formalizing the concepts to be presented, though handling them analytically to produce strong implications may be very difficult indeed. But at this stage it seemed more appropriate to raise these questions in a broad way, to avoid concentration on analytic problems. The point of view is that of an optimizing model but in a rich framework of uncertainty and information channels. Decisions, wherever taken, are a function of information received; then when information remains unchanged, no decision is made, or, to put the matter in a slightly more precise way, the implicit decision is made not to change the values of certain variables. In turn, the acquisition of information must be analyzed, since it is itself the result of decisions.

Of course, it is essential to this argument that information is scarce or costly; it can be assumed that any free information is acquired. As will be argued, the fact that for any given individual or organization different sorts of information have different costs has many implications for organizational behavior.

The theme to be presented is that the combination of uncertainty, indivisibility, and capital intensity associated with information channels and their use imply (a) that the actual structure and behavior of an organization may depend heavily upon random events, in other words on history, and (b) the very pursuit of efficiency may lead to rigidity and unresponsiveness to further change.

Decisions are necessarily a function of information. Hence, if it is decided to collect no information relevant to a certain class of decisions, those decisions are nonagenda.

The last sentence, by its uses of the words, "decided," and, "decision," highlights the need for a distinction between two kinds of decisions, decisions to act in some concrete sense, and decisions to collect information. The distinction is very familiar in statistical decision theory; the two are referred to as "terminal acts" and "experiments," respectively, by Raiffa and Schlaifer in their standard work. A prototypical illustration occurs in what is known as acceptance sampling. A firm or government is buying large quantities of some good. The quality of the good may vary from item to item. A typical procedure, when a lot of goods arrives, is to take a sample, test each item in it, and accept or reject the entire lot on the basis of the results in the sample. The sampling and testing constitute an experiment in this sense, the decision to accept or reject is the terminal act. If the cost of testing is at all considerable, it will be much cheaper, on the average, to test a sample than to test every item in the lot. Both the experiment and the terminal act are relevant to resource utilization. The experiment has implications for resource utilization because it is costly, the terminal act because it is a decision which may be beneficial or not. The experiment yields no benefits directly, but it has the instrumental value of improving the terminal act by supplying more information.

If the resource effects of the two steps are additive, the distinction between experiments and terminal acts can be held to rigorously. Even though this additivity is not always valid, it is suggestive.

Suppose we imagine that there are a number of different decision areas for the organization within each of which we have a range of possible experiments and a range of possible terminal acts. Suppose further these decision areas are sufficiently independent so that the values of terminal acts in the different areas are more or less additive. A decision area may be *active, monitored,* or *passive.* An active area is one in which experiments are performed, signals received from them, and terminal acts chosen as functions of the signals. A monitored area is one in which some experiments are being performed; the signals received convey too little information to take terminal acts, but if appropriate signals are received it is optimal to make further experiments, which in turn will yield enough information to bring the terminal acts onto the agenda. Finally, a passive area is one in which no experiments are being conducted, and therefore neither experiments nor terminal acts are on the agenda.

The partition of decision areas among these types will depend of course on the relative benefits and costs. There is a little that can be said in a general way about anticipated benefits, but the classification of information costs in the last chapter may have some explanatory power. As an illustration, consider an individual investor choosing a portfolio of securities. There will be one class of securities in which the individual is actively investing; he has positive investments in them or else they are being watched closely, with the decision to invest or not invest being thought about steadily. The investor will be watching the market prices, receiving reports on the activities of the firms, and so forth. There will be a second class of securities which he is watching, so to speak, out of the corner of his eye. He occasionally checks prices and looks at relatively cursory information. If interesting movements or other information appears, he may increase the intensity of his surveillance and move the security into the active group. Finally, he will pay no attention whatever to the largest number of securities.

Analysis of information costs suggests some systematic reasons for classifying securities into one group or another. Familiarity with a particular firm or industry, because of previous experiences or current productive relations, will mean that information about some securities will be cheaper than about others; the investor has a background which enables him to understand the signals better. The fact that information has a strong capital component means that once an investor has chosen a selected list of securities, he will stay within that group, because additional information about the same securities is cheaper than acquiring the initial information about other securities needed to begin meaningful analysis.

He is likely to monitor securities for which some information is cheap because its acquisition is complementary to other activities. Thus, as a background for analysis of the securities he is primarily interested in, he may pick up some information about others; from the point of view of the latter group, this process amounts to inexpensive monitoring. Professional information services, brokers and the like, may supply him with broadly spread, if shallow information, at the same time they supply detailed information. General news sources about business conditions may be read simply because of their intrinsic interest and hence at virtually no cost; but these may constitute a certain amount of monitoring. Finally, simply social associations with business connections may constitute a source of information, the stronger because much evidence shows that personal influences are regarded as more reliable, which means that they convey more informa-

tion, subjectively measured, at a given cost.

How then do we expect the agenda of an individual to change, that is, how do decision areas get changed from one class to another? The monitoring process is a built-in explanation of part of the process. There are a lot of potential decision areas which are in fact being looked at a little bit. A classical illustration of monitoring is the process of quality control in industry. The quality of the product is tested on a sampling basis. So long as the results are satisfactory, nothing is done; but when deterioration occurs, there is a more thorough investigation of its causes, with the possible eventuality that a machine is repaired or replaced. But clearly there is more to the matter than agenda changes as the result of foreseen possibilities. One possibility is a sharp change in payoffs to terminal acts. In particular, the opportunity benefit, that is the change in benefits due to a change in action, may rise because of a decrease in the return to the present, unexamined, action. In plain language, we have a "crisis." In William James's term, a "coercive fact" may be more persuasive than any speculation about potential benefits from change. The sinking of the *Titanic* led to iceberg patrols.

No doubt the changes in payoffs may be changes in perceptions rather than in actuality. The current ecological concerns have grown much more rapidly than the actual problems (which is not to say that they are not important; they are). What sometimes happens is that the cost of signals goes down, for one of many reasons. There may simply be a threshold effect; beyond a certain point, the effects of, say, pollution or the low performance of our portfolio, become obvious with virtually no investment in observation or experiment. In some cases, it may be that some other individuals, for their own reasons, are supplying signals cheaply. These are the reformers and agitators of all sorts; no doubt, their work only flourishes when the value and cost structures are appropriate, but the torch, though ready, still has to be lit by someone.

Another cause of agenda changes is that information channels do not, despite the model that has been tentatively used, stand in a simple relation to the partition of decision areas which has been assumed above. Signals with quite different policy implications may be closely interrelated in origin and be received over the same channel; or it may be that an experiment for one purpose can yield additional information relevant to very different terminal acts with only slightly additional cost. An interesting paradigm is that of opportunistic replacement; when a complex mechanism, such as a missile, is being examined to check for possible malfunctioning of one subunit, it becomes much cheaper to examine or replace others.

Let us turn to the factors determining the agenda of organizations. As noted earlier, the functional role of organizations is to take advantage of the superior productivity of joint actions. In the discussion of the internal economies of the firm, this point is of course customary with regard to what has been here called terminal acts. But it is equally and even more valid with regard to experiments, that is, information channels.

An organization can require more information than any one individual, for it can have each member performing different experiments. Thus, the limitations on an individual's capacity are overcome. But as always there is a price to be paid. In fact, the relevant considerations have been adduced in some of the old discussions of the U-shaped cost curve. The information has to be coordinated if it is to be of any use to the organization. More formally stated, communication channels have to be created within the organization.

Now if all information received by any member of the organization were transmitted to all others or even to one headquarters, there would be no gain in information processing costs. Indeed, there would be a loss, since there are additional information channels within the firm. The economies of information in the organization occur because in fact much of the information received is irrelevant. The terminal acts within the competence of the organization do not require for assessment the entire probability distribution of states of the world but only some marginal distributions derived from it. Hence, in general, the information received by a member of the organization can be transformed into a much smaller volume of retransmission without losing value for choice of terminal acts. The theory of sufficient statistics is an example of this reduction of information without loss of value. In this case, the reason is that the value of any terminal act depends only on the parameters of the underlying distribution and not on the values observed in the sample; hence it suffices to transmit the values of a function of the sample which exhausts its information about the parameters.

It is this reduction in retransmission which explains the utility of an organization for information-handling. Since information is costly, it is clearly optimal, in general, to reduce the internal transmission still further. That is, it pays to have some loss in value for the choice of terminal act in order to economize on internal communication channels. The optimal choice of internal communication structures is a vastly difficult question. It underlies, not always explicitly, the great controversies on the economics of socialism and has received deep exploration in certain directions in the Marschak-Radner theory of teams.

Since it is, in general, optimal not to transmit all the relevant information, an individual member will have accumulated information which is not under present circumstances judged worthwhile to transmit. It is possible that at a later time this information will turn out to be of value, due to receipt of some other signal which is complementary to it. Whether this information will then be used depends on a number of factors; among them are the cheapness of transmission over time, by means of memory or files and subsequent retrieval. This creates the possibility that different members of the organization who have had different experiences which have not been transmitted will interpret new signals in different ways. There seem to be interesting implications for a reduction of informational efficiency in organizations whose external environment has changed considerably.

Since internal communication channels can be designed, their structure can be chosen with a view to cost minimization. In particular, the efficiency of a channel can be increased by suitable choice of a code. This term is used both literally and metaphorically. It refers to all the known ways, whether or not inscribed informal rules, for conveying information. As is well known from information theory, the optimal code will depend upon the a priori distribution of possible signals, as well as upon the costs of communicating differently coded signals.

The role of coding has two economic implications: (a) it weakens but does not eliminate the tendency to increasing costs with scale of operation; (b) it creates an intrinsic irreversible capital commitment of the organization. With regard to the first point, we have seen that the organization's gains from increasing scale are derived by having its members make different experiments, that is, by specialization. As we have seen in the last chapter's discussion of the economics of information for the individual, this means the members will be accumulating differing types of skills in information-processing, learning (acquiring capital) in the areas in which they are specializing and unlearning elsewhere. As a result, communication

among them becomes more difficult (as academic specialists are learning), and the codes used in their intercommunications have to become more complex. Hence, while coding permits a greater number of individual information sources to be pooled usefully, there are still increasing costs eventually as the scale of operations grows.

With regard to the second point, we have already argued that the learning of a code by an individual is an act of irreversible investment for him. It is therefore also an irreversible capital accumulation for the organization. It follows that organizations, once created, have distinct identities, because the costs of changing the code are those of unanticipated obsolescence.

Becker and others have stressed that a significant part of accumulation of human capital consists of training specific to the needs of a firm, an input of information to the worker which increases his value to the firm but not to other firms. If the function of labor is to cooperate in production with capital goods which are held widely by different firms, it would appear that virtually all training is general. But learning the information channels within a firm and the codes for transmitting information through them is indeed a skill of value only internally.

One might ask, as one does frequently in the theory of the firm, why all firms do not have the same codes, so that training in the code is transferable? In the first place, in this combinatorial situation, there may easily be many optimal codes, all equally good, but to be useful in a firm it is important to know the right code. The situation here is very much that of the games of coordination which have been stressed so much by Schelling. If it is valuable for two people to meet without being able to communicate with each other during their trips, the meeting-place must be agreed on beforehand. It may not matter much where the meeting is to be. But a person who learned one meeting-place is not much use to an organization which has selected another.

In the second place, history matters. The code is determined in accordance with the best expectations at the time of the firm's creation. Since the code is part of the firm's or more generally the organization's capital, as already argued, the code of a given organization will be modified only slowly over time. Hence, the codes of organizations starting at different times will in general be different even if they are competitive firms. Indeed, individuals starting firms at the same time may well have different a priori distributions and therefore different codes.

The need for codes mutually understandable within the organization imposes a uniformity requirement on the behavior of the participants. They are specialized in the information capable of being transmitted by the codes, so that, in a process already described, they learn more in the direction of their activity and become less efficient in acquiring and transmitting information not easily fitted into the code. Hence, the organization itself serves to mold the behavior of its members.

This process may well have interesting implications for the behavior of the organization. The code of the organization may be supposed governed most strongly by its primary functions. But an organization has in general many functions, auxiliary indeed to its primary ones but important to its welfare. Alternatively, it may be thought desirable to add some secondary functions to the organization because their accomplishment appears to be complementary to the primary ones. But if the code appropriate to the primary functions is inappropriate to the auxiliary or secondary functions, the organization may function badly. Burdon Klein has provided one illustration in an unpublished manuscript: the primary function of the military is the coordination of large masses

of men and material in circumstances where coordination is according to a previously planned timetable. Research and development on military weapons is, in the present era, an important auxiliary service. But, Klein has argued, it tends to be run by men who think in military terms and therefore expect coordination of achievements at predictable time points in the future. In fact, of course, research and development are prime examples of information-gathering with a considerable degree of uncertainty, and achievements are certainly not predictable. As a result the precisely laid-out timetables are dramatically unfulfilled, as Summers has shown. The costs in the end are much higher than they would have been if the uncertainty had been taken into account initially. Klein's recommended solution, indeed, is to remove military research and development from military control and put it in the hands of a separate civilian agency.

An example of the difficulty of adding functions to an existing organization is provided by the tendency to add management control functions to existing accounting and budgetary departments. Since the quantitative basis of scientific decision-making overlaps so heavily with classical accounts, it is appealing to economize by joining the two functions. But in fact the purposes differ considerably and therefore the code, the way of looking at the world, differs also. The accountant, whose aim is in part to insure against dishonesty, is interested in a degree of precision in certain data unnecessary for management science but not interested in other and rougher kinds of data. Budgetary control is also different in many ways from scientific management, and some students of public administration are highly critical of the recent addition of management control to the functions of the former Bureau of the Budget.

Because of these difficulties of communication, there has been in both the public and private sectors a tendency to hive off incompatible functions into new organizations. Stigler has pointed suggestively to the steady vertical disintegration which has accompanied the growth of large firms; the forces of the market make it profitable for the specialization in auxiliary services. Similarly, in the government, Franklin D. Roosevelt seems to have been the innovator who first saw the need of assigning new tasks to new bureaus, even though according to some logic it belonged in the sphere of an existing department.

Let us return to the original purpose of this chapter, the determination of the agenda of organizations. Basically, the possible causes of changes in the agenda of organizations are the same as those of individuals: a signal may be received in a monitored area on the basis of which it is judged worthwhile to make the area active; the payoffs to terminal acts may change or may be perceived to change abruptly; or an information channel used primarily for one purpose may turn up a signal with implications for taking action in a hitherto passive area. The discussion of organizations just concluded has been directed towards expanding the cost factors specific to organizations which change the bases on which organizations change their agenda. In many ways, indeed, the costs of change may be greater for an organization. More exactly, it has a greater ability to monitor but a lesser ability to change from a passive attitude to a monitoring or active role.

There is one effect on organization which has no parallel in individuals. An organization is typically composed of changing individuals. Now any individual typically has access to many communication channels, of which this particular organization is only one. In particular, education is such a channel. Thus, the organization is getting the benefit of a considerable amount of information which is free to it. Even though the code of the organization may make the internal transmission of such information costly, if there is enough of it, the behavior of the organization will change. In particular, new items will appear on the organization's agenda. If we think of education as the primary source of new information, then it is introduced into an organization by its youngest and newest members. Thus we have the possibility of changes in organizational agenda induced by generational changes. More generally, the prime need in organizational design is increasing capacity to handle a large agenda. To the extent that information and its handling are accumulations of personal capital, what is needed is what Pareto called the "circulation of elites," the turnover of decision-makers. More generally, what is needed is a "circulation of information and decision rules." Shortrun efficiency and even flexibility within a narrow frameworks of alternatives may be less important in the long run than a wide compass of potential activities. These are some of the considerations in the design of public and private organizations and the choice between them in carrying out the tasks of society.

42. The Methodology of Positive Economics*

MILTON FRIEDMAN[1]

In his admirable book on *The Scope and Method of Political Economy*, John Neville Keynes distinguishes among "a *positive science* . . . [,] a body of systematized knowledge concerning what is; a *normative* or *regulative science* . . . [,] a body of systematized knowledge discussing criteria of what ought to be . . . ; an *art* . . . [,] a system of rules for the attainment of a given end"; comments that "confusion between them is common and has been the source of many mischievous errors"; and urges the importance of "recognizing a distinct positive science of political economy."[2]

This paper is concerned primarily with certain methodological problems that arise in constructing the "distinct positive science" Keynes called for—in particular, the problem how to decide whether a suggested hypothesis or theory should be tentatively accepted as part of the "body of systematized knowledge concerning what is." But the confusion Keynes laments is still so rife and so much of a hindrance to the recognition that economics can be, and in part is, a positive science that it seems well to preface the main body of the paper with a few remarks about the relation between positive and normative economics.

I. THE RELATION BETWEEN POSITIVE AND NORMATIVE ECONOMICS

Confusion between positive and normative economics is to some extent inevitable. The subject matter of economics is regarded by almost everyone as vitally important to himself and within the range of his own experience and competence; it is the source of continuous and extensive controversy and the occasion for frequent legislation. Self-proclaimed "experts" speak with many voices and can hardly all be regarded as disinterested; in any event, on questions that matter so much, "expert" opinion could hardly be accepted solely on faith even if the "experts" were nearly unanimous and clearly disinterested.[3] The conclusions of positive economics seem to be, and are, immediately relevant to important normative problems, to questions of what ought to be done and how any given goal can be attained. Laymen and experts alike are inevitably tempted to shape positive conclusions to fit strongly held normative preconceptions and to reject positive conclusions if their normative implications—or what are said to be their normative implications—are unpalatable.

Positive economics is in principle independent of any particular ethical position or normative judgments. As Keynes says, it deals with "what is," not with "what ought to be." Its task is to provide a system of generalizations that can be used to make correct predictions about the consequences of any change in circumstances. Its performance is to be judged by the precision, scope, and conformity with experience of the predictions it yields. In short, positive economics is, or can be, an "objective" science, in precisely the same sense as any of the physical sciences. Of course, the fact that economics deals with the interrelations of human beings, and that the investigator is himself part of the subject matter being investigated in a more intimate sense than in the physical sciences, raises special difficulties in achieving objectivity at the same time that it provides the social scientist with a class of data not available to the physical scientist. But neither the one nor the other is, in my view, a fundamental distinction between the two groups of sciences.[4]

Normative economics and the art of economics, on the other hand, cannot be independent of positive economics. Any policy conclusion necessarily rests on a prediction about the consequences of doing one thing rather than another, a prediction that must be based— implicitly or explicitly—on positive economics. There is not, of course, a one-to-one relation between policy conclusions and the conclusions of positive economics; if there were, there would be no separate normative science. Two individuals may agree on the consequences of a particular piece of legislation. One may regard them as desirable on balance and so favor the legislation; the other, as undesirable and so oppose the legislation.

I venture the judgment, however, that currently in the Western world, and especially in the United States, differences about economic policy among disinterested citizens derive predominantly from different predictions about the economic consequences of taking action—differences that in principle can be eliminated by the progress of positive economics—rather than from fundamental differences in basic values, differences about which men can ultimately only fight. An obvious and not unimportant example is minimum-wage legislation. Underneath the welter of arguments offered for and against such legislation there is an underlying consensus on the objective of achieving a "living wage" for all, to use the ambiguous phrase so common in such discussions. The difference of opinion is largely grounded on an implicit or explicit difference in predictions about the efficacy of this particular means in furthering the agreed-on end. Proponents believe (predict) that legal minimum wages diminish poverty by raising the wages of those receiving less than the minimum wage as well as of some receiving more than the minimum wage without any counterbalancing increase in the number of people entirely unemployed or employed less advantageously than they otherwise would be. Opponents believe (predict) that legal minimum wages increase poverty by increasing the number of people who are unemployed or employed less advantageously and that this more than offsets any favorable effect on the wages of those who remain employed. Agreement about the economic consequences of the legislation might not produce complete agreement about its desirability, for differences might still remain about its political or social consequences; but, given agreement on objectives, it would certainly go a long way toward producing consensus.

Closely related differences in positive analysis underlie divergent views about the appropriate role and place of trade-unions and the desirability of direct price and wage controls and of tariffs. Different predictions about the importance of so-called "economies of scale" account very largely for divergent views about the desirability or necessity of detailed government regulation of industry and even of socialism rather than private enterprise. And this list could be extended indefinitely.[5] Of course, my judgment that the major differences about economic policy in the Western world are of this kind is itself a "positive" statement to be accepted or rejected on the basis of empirical evidence.

If this judgment is valid, it means that a consensus on "correct" economic policy depends much less on the progress of normative economics proper than on the progress of a positive economics yielding conclusions that are, and deserve to be, widely accepted. It means also that a major reason for distinguishing positive economics sharply from normative economics is precisely the contribution that can thereby be made to agreement about policy.

II. POSITIVE ECONOMICS

The ultimate goal of a positive science is the development of a "theory" or "hypothesis" that yields valid and meaningful (i.e., not truistic) predictions about phenomena not yet observed. Such a theory is, in general, a complex intermixture of two elements. In part, it is a "language" designed to promote "systematic and organized methods of reasoning."[6] In part, it is a body of substantive hypotheses designed to abstract essential features of complex reality.

Viewed as a language, theory has no substantive content; it is a set of tautologies. Its function is to serve as a filing system for organizing empirical material and facilitating our understanding of it; and the criteria by which it is to be judged are those appropriate to a filing system. Are the categories clearly and precisely defined? Are they exhaustive? Do we know where to file each individual item, or is there considerable ambiguity? Is the system of headings and subheadings so designed that we can quickly find an item we want, or must we hunt from place to place? Are the items we shall want to consider jointly filed together? Does the filing system avoid elaborate cross-references?

The answers to these questions depend partly on logical, partly on factual, considerations. The canons of formal logic alone can show whether a particular language is complete and consistent, that is, whether propositions in the language are "right" or "wrong." Factual evidence alone can show whether the categories of the "analytical filing system" have a meaningful empirical counterpart, that is, whether they are useful in analyzing a particular class of concrete problems.[7] The simple example of "supply" and "demand" illustrates both this point and the preceding list of analogical questions. Viewed as elements of the language of economic theory, these are the two major categories into which factors affecting the relative prices of products or factors of production are classified. The usefulness of the dichotomy depends on the

> empirical generalization that an enumeration of the forces affecting demand in any problem and of the forces affecting supply will yield two lists that contain few items in common.[8]

Now this generalization is valid for markets like the final market for a consumer good. In such a market there is a clear and sharp distinction between the economic units that can be regarded as demanding the product and those that can be regarded as supplying it. There is seldom much doubt whether a particular factor should be classified as affecting supply, on the one hand, or demand, on the other; and there is seldom much necessity for considering cross-effects (cross-references) between the two categories. In these cases the simple and even obvious step of filing the relevant factors under the headings of "supply" and "demand" effects a great simplification of the problem and is an effective safeguard against fallacies that otherwise tend to occur. But the generalization is not always valid. For example, it is not valid for the day-to-day fluctuations of prices in a primarily speculative market. Is a rumor of an increased excess-profits tax, for example, to be regarded as a factor operating primarily on today's supply of corporate equities in the stock market or on today's demand for them? In similar fashion, almost every factor can with about as much justification be classified under the heading "supply" as under the heading "demand." These concepts can still be used and may not be entirely pointless; they are still "right" but clearly less useful than in the first example because they have no meaningful empirical counterpart.

Viewed as a body of substantive hypotheses, theory is to be judged by its predictive power for the class of phenomena which it is intended to "explain." Only factual evidence can show whether it is "right" or "wrong" or, better, tentatively "accepted" as valid or "rejected." As I shall argue at greater length below, the only relevant test of the *validity* of a hypothesis is comparison of its predictions with experience. The hypothesis is rejected if its predictions are contradicted ("frequently" or more often than predictions from an alternative hypothesis); it is accepted if its predictions are not contradicted; great confidence is attached to it if it has survived many opportunities for contradiction. Factual evidence can never "prove" a hypothesis; it can only fail to disprove it, which is what we generally mean when we say, somewhat inexactly, that the hypothesis has been "confirmed" by experience.

To avoid confusion, it should perhaps be noted explicitly that the "predictions" by which the validity of a hypothesis is tested need not be about phenomena that have not yet occurred, that is, need not be forecasts of future events; they may be about phenomena that have occurred but observations on which have not yet been made or are not known to the person making the prediction. For example, a hypothesis may imply that such and such must have happened in 1906, given some other known circumstances. If a search of the records reveals that such and such did happen, the prediction is confirmed; if it reveals that such and such did not happen, the prediction is contradicted.

The validity of a hypothesis in this sense is not by itself a sufficient criterion for choosing among alternative hypotheses. Observed facts are necessarily finite in number; possible hypotheses, in-finite. If there is one hypothesis that is consistent with the available evidence, there are always an infinite number that are.[9] For example, suppose a specific excise tax on a particular commodity produces a rise in price equal to the amount of the tax. This is consistent with competitive conditions, a stable demand curve, and a horizontal and stable supply curve. But it is also consistent with competitive conditions and a positively or negatively sloping supply curve with the required compensating shift in the demand curve or the supply curve; with monopolistic conditions, constant marginal costs, and stable demand curve, of the particular shape required to produce this result; and so on indefinitely. Additional evidence with which the hypothesis is to be consistent may rule out some of these possibilities; it can never reduce them to a single possibility alone capable of being consistent with the finite evidence. The choice among alternative hypotheses equally consistent with the available evidence must to some extent be arbitrary, though there is general agreement that relevant considerations are suggested by the criteria "simplicity" and "fruitfulness," themselves notions that defy completely objective specification. A theory is "simpler" the less the initial knowledge needed to make a prediction within a given field of phenomena; it is more "fruitful" the more precise the resulting prediction, the wider the area within which the theory yields predictions, and the more additional lines for further research it suggests. Logical completeness and consistency are relevant but play a subsidiary role; their function is to assure that the hypothesis says what it is intended to say and does so alike for all users—they play the same role here as checks for arithmetical accuracy do in statistical computations.

Unfortunately, we can seldom test particular predictions in the social sciences by experiments explicitly designed to eliminate what are judged to be the most important disturbing influences. Generally, we must rely on evidence cast up by the "experiments" that happen to occur. The inability to conduct so-called "controlled experiments" does not, in my view, reflect a basic difference between the social and physical sciences both because it is not peculiar to the social sciences—witness astronomy—and because the distinction between a controlled experiment and uncontrolled experience is at best one of degree. No experiment can be completely controlled, and every experience is partly controlled, in the sense that some disturbing influences are relatively constant in the course of it.

Evidence cast up by experience is abundant and frequently as conclusive as that from contrived experiments; thus the inability to conduct experiments is not a fundamental obstacle to testing hypotheses by the success of their predictions. But such evidence is far more difficult to interpret. It is frequently complex and always indirect and incomplete. Its collection is often arduous, and its interpretation generally requires subtle analysis and involved chains of reasoning, which seldom carry real conviction. The denial to economics of the dramatic and direct evidence of the "crucial" experiment does hinder the adequate testing of hypotheses; but this is much less significant than the difficulty it places in the way of achieving a reasonably prompt and wide consensus on the conclusions justified by the available evidence. It renders the weeding-out of unsuccessful hypotheses slow and difficult. They are seldom downed for good and are always cropping up again.

There is, of course, considerable variation in these respects. Occasionally, experience casts up evidence that is about as direct, dramatic, and convincing as any that could be provided by controlled experiments. Perhaps the most obviously important example is the evidence from inflations on the hypothesis that a substantial increase in the quantity of money within a relatively short period is accompanied by a substantial increase in prices. Here the evidence is dramatic, and the chain of reasoning required to interpret it is relatively short. Yet, despite numerous instances of substantial rises in prices, their essentially one-to-one correspondence with substantial rises in the stock of money, and the wide variation in other circumstances that might appear to be relevant, each new experience of inflation brings forth vigorous contentions, and not only by the lay public, that the rise in the stock of money is either an incidental effect of a rise in prices produced by other factors or a purely fortuitous and unnecessary concomitant of the price rise.

One effect of the difficulty of testing substantive economic hypotheses has been to foster a retreat into purely formal or tautological analysis.[10] As already noted, tautologies have an extremely important place in economics and other sciences as a specialized language or "analytical filing system." Beyond this, formal logic and mathematics, which are both tautologies, are essential aids in checking the correctness of reasoning, discovering the implications of hypotheses, and determining whether supposedly different hypotheses may not really be equivalent or wherein the differences lie.

But economic theory must be more than a structure of tautologies if it is to be able to predict and not merely describe the consequences of action; if it is to be something different from disguised mathematics.[11] And the usefulness of the tautologies themselves ultimately depends, as noted above, on the acceptability of the substantive hypotheses that suggest the particular categories into which they organize the refractory empirical phenomena.

A more serious effect of the difficulty of testing economic hypotheses by their predictions is to foster misunderstanding of the role of empirical evidence in theoretical work. Empirical evidence is vital at two different, though closely related, stages: in constructing hypotheses and in testing their validity. Full and comprehensive evidence on the phenomena to be generalized or "explained" by a hypothesis, besides its obvious value in suggesting new hypotheses, is needed to assure that a hypothesis explains what it sets out to explain—that its implications for such phenomena are not contradicted in advance by experience that has already been observed.[12] Given that the hypothesis is consistent with the evidence at hand, its further testing involves deducing from it new facts capable of being observed but not previously known and checking these deduced facts against additional empirical evidence. For this test to be relevant, the deduced facts must be about the class of phenomena the hypothesis is designed to explain; and they must be well enough defined so that observation can show them to be wrong.

The two stages of constructing hypotheses and testing their validity are related in two different respects. In the first place, the particular facts that enter at each stage are partly an accident of the collection of data and the knowledge of the particular investigator. The facts that serve as a test of the implications of a hypothesis might equally well have been among the raw material used to construct it, and conversely. In the second place, the process never begins from scratch; the so-called "initial stage" itself always involves comparison of the implications of an earlier set of hypotheses with observation; the contradiction of these implications is the stimulus to the construction of new hypotheses or revision of old ones. So the two methodologically distinct stages are always proceeding jointly.

Misunderstanding about this apparently straightforward process centers on the phrase "the class of phenomena the hypothesis is designed to explain." The difficulty in the social sciences of get-

ting new evidence for this class of phenomena and of judging its conformity with the implications of the hypothesis makes it tempting to suppose that other, more readily available, evidence is equally relevant to the validity of the hypothesis—to suppose that hypotheses have not only "implications" but also "assumptions" and that the conformity of these "assumptions" to "reality" is a test of the validity of the hypothesis different from or additional to the test by implications. This widely held view is fundamentally wrong and productive of much mischief. Far from providing an easier means for sifting valid from invalid hypotheses, it only confuses the issue, promotes misunderstanding about the significance of empirical evidence for economic theory, produces a misdirection of much intellectual effort devoted to the development of positive economics, and impedes the attainment of consensus on tentative hypotheses in positive economics.

In so far as a theory can be said to have "assumptions" at all, and in so far as their "realism" can be judged independently of the validity of predictions, the relation between the significance of a theory and the "realism" of its "assumptions" is almost the opposite of that suggested by the view under criticism. Truly important and significant hypotheses will be found to have "assumptions" that are wildly inaccurate descriptive representations of reality, and, in general, the more significant the theory, the more unrealistic the assumptions (in this sense).[13] The reason is simple. A hypothesis is important if it "explains" much by little, that is, if it abstracts the common and crucial elements from the mass of complex and detailed circumstances surrounding the phenomena to be explained and permits valid predictions on the basis of them alone. To be important, therefore, a hypothesis must be descriptively false in its assumptions; it takes account of, and accounts for, none of the many other attendant circumstances, since its very success shows them to be irrelevant for the phenomena to be explained.

To put this point less paradoxically, the relevant question to ask about the "assumptions" of a theory is not whether they are descriptively "realistic," for they never are, but whether they are sufficiently good approximations for the purpose in hand. And this question can be answered only by seeing whether the theory works, which means whether it yields sufficiently accurate predictions. The two supposedly independent tests thus reduce to one test.

The theory of monopolistic and imperfect competition is one example of the neglect in economic theory of these propositions. The development of this analysis was explicitly motivated, and its wide acceptance and approval largely explained, by the belief that the assumptions of "perfect competition" or "perfect monopoly" said to underlie neoclassical economic theory are a false image of reality. And this belief was itself based almost entirely on the directly perceived descriptive inaccuracy of the assumptions rather than on any recognized contradiction of predictions derived from neoclassical economic theory. The lengthy discussion on marginal analysis in the *American Economic Review* some years ago is an even clearer, though much less important, example. The articles on both sides of the controversy largely neglect what seems to me clearly the main issue—the conformity to experience of the implications of the marginal analysis—and concentrate on the largely irrelevant question whether businessmen do or do not in fact reach their decisions by consulting schedules, or curves, or multivariable functions showing marginal cost and marginal revenue.[14] Perhaps these two examples, and the many others they readily suggest, will serve to justify a more extensive discussion of the methodological principles involved than might otherwise seem appropriate.

III. CAN A HYPOTHESIS BE TESTED BY THE REALISM OF ITS ASSUMPTIONS?

We may start with a simple physical example, the law of falling bodies. It is an accepted hypothesis that the acceleration of a body dropped in a vacuum is a constant—g, or approximately 32 feet per second on the earth—and is independent of the shape of the body, the manner of dropping it, etc. This implies that the distance traveled by a falling body in any specified time is given by the formula $s = \frac{1}{2} gt^2$, where s is the distance traveled in feet and t is time in seconds. The application of this formula to a compact ball dropped from the roof of a building is equivalent to saying that a ball so dropped behaves *as if* it were falling in a vacuum. Testing this hypothesis by its assumptions presumably means measuring the actual air pressure and deciding whether it is close enough to zero. At sea level the air pressure is about 15 pounds per square inch. Is 15 sufficiently close to zero for the difference to be judged insignificant? Apparently it is, since the actual time taken by a compact ball to fall from the roof of a building to the ground is very close to the time given by the formula. Suppose, however, that a feather is dropped instead of a compact ball. The formula then gives wildly inaccurate results. Apparently, 15 pounds per square inch is significantly different from zero for a feather but not for a ball. Or, again, suppose the formula is applied to a ball dropped from an airplane at an altitude of 30,000 feet. The air pressure at this altitude is decidedly less than 15 pounds per square inch. Yet, the actual time of fall from 30,000 feet to 20,000 feet, at which point the air pressure is still much less than at sea level, will differ noticeably from the time predicted by the formula—much more noticeably than the time taken by a compact ball to fall from the roof of a building to the ground. According to the formula, the velocity of the ball should be gt and should therefore increase steadily. In fact, a ball dropped at 30,000 feet will reach its top velocity well before it hits the ground. And similarly with other implications of the formula.

The initial question whether 15 is sufficiently close to zero for the difference to be judged insignificant is clearly a foolish question by itself. Fifteen pounds per square inch is 2,160 pounds per square foot, or 0.0075 ton per square inch. There is no possible basis for calling these numbers "small" or "large" without some external standard of comparison. And the only relevant standard of comparison is the air pressure for which the formula does or does not work under a given set of circumstances. But this raises the same problem at a second level. What is the meaning of "does or does not work"? Even if we could eliminate errors of measurement, the measured time of fall would seldom if ever be precisely equal to the computed time of fall. How large must the difference between the two be to justify saying that the theory "does not work"? Here there are two important external standards of comparison. One is the accuracy achievable by an alternative theory with which this theory is being compared and which is equally acceptable on all other grounds. The other arises when there exists a theory that is known to yield better predictions but only at a greater cost. The gains from greater accuracy, which depend on the purpose in mind, must then be balanced against the costs of achieving it.

This example illustrates both the impossibility of testing a theory by its assumptions and also the ambiguity of the concept "the assumptions of a theory." The formula $s = \frac{1}{2} gt^2$ is valid for bodies falling in a vacuum and can be derived by analyzing the behavior of such bodies. It can therefore be stated: under a wide range of circumstances, bodies that fall in the actual atmosphere behave as if they were falling in a vacuum. In the language so common in economics this would be rapidly translated into: the formula assumes a vacuum. Yet it clearly does no such thing. What it does say is that in many cases the existence of air pressure, the shape of the body, the name of the person dropping the body, the kind of mechanism used to drop the body, and a host of other attendant circumstances have no appreciable effect on the distance the body falls in a specified time. The hypothesis can readily be rephrased to omit all mention of a vacuum: under a wide range of circumstances, the distance a body falls in a specified time is given by the formula $s = \frac{1}{2} gt^2$. The history of this formula and its associated physical theory aside, is it meaningful to say that it assumes a vacuum? For all I know there may be other sets of assumptions that would yield the same formula. The formula is accepted because it works, not because we live in an approximate vacuum—whatever that means.

The important problem in connection with the hypothesis is to specify the circumstances under which the formula works or, more precisely, the general magnitude of the error in its predictions under various circumstances. Indeed, as is implicit in the above rephrasing of the hypothesis, such a specification is not one thing and the hypothesis another. The specification is itself an essential part of the hypothesis, and it is a part that is peculiarly likely to be revised and extended as experience accumulates.

In the particular case of falling bodies a more general, though still incomplete, theory is available, largely as a result of attempts to explain the errors of the simple theory, from which the influence of some of the possible disturbing factors can be calculated and of which the simple theory is a special case. However, it does not always pay to use the more general theory because the extra accuracy it yields may not justify the extra cost of using it, so the question under what circumstances the simpler theory works "well enough" remains important. Air pressure is one, but only one, of the variables that define these circumstances; the shape of the body, the velocity attained, and still other variables are relevant as well. One way of interpreting the variables other than air pressure is to regard them as determining whether a particular departure from the "assumption" of a vacuum is or is not significant. For example, the difference in shape of the body can be said to make 15 pounds per square inch significantly different from zero for a feather but not for a compact ball dropped a moderate distance. Such a statement must, however, be sharply distinguished from the very different statement that the theory does not work for a feather because its assumptions are false. The relevant relation runs the other way: the assumptions are false for a feather because the theory does not work. This point needs emphasis, because the entirely valid use of "assumptions" in *specifying* the circumstances for which a theory holds is frequently, and erroneously, interpreted to mean that the assumptions can be used to *determine* the circumstances for which a theory holds, and has, in this way, been an important source of the belief that a theory can be tested by its assumptions.

Let us turn now to another example, this time a constructed one designed to be an analogue of many hypotheses in the social sciences. Consider the density of leaves around a tree. I suggest the hypothesis that the leaves are positioned as if each leaf deliberately sought to maximize the amount of sunlight it receives, given the position of its neighbors, as if it knew the physical laws determining the amount of sunlight that would be received in various positions and could move rapidly or instantaneously from any one position to any other desired and unoccupied posi-

tion.[15] Now some of the more obvious implications of this hypothesis are clearly consistent with experience: for example, leaves are in general denser on the south than on the north side of trees but, as the hypothesis implies, less so or not at all on the northern slope of a hill or when the south side of the trees is shaded in some other way. Is the hypothesis rendered unacceptable or invalid because, so far as we know, leaves do not "deliberate" or consciously "seek," have not been to school and learned the relevant laws of science or the mathematics required to calculate the "optimum" position, and cannot move from position to position? Clearly, none of these contradictions of the hypothesis is vitally relevant; the phenomena involved are not within the "class of phenomena the hypothesis is designed to explain"; the hypothesis does not assert that leaves do these things but only that their density is the same *as if* they did. Despite the apparent falsity of the "assumptions" of the hypothesis, it has great plausibility because of the conformity of its implications with observation. We are inclined to "explain" its validity on the ground that sunlight contributes to the growth of leaves and that hence leaves will grow denser or more putative leaves survive where there is more sun, so the result achieved by purely passive adaptation to external circumstances is the same as the result that would be achieved by deliberate accommodation to them. This alternative hypothesis is more attractive than the constructed hypothesis not because its "assumptions" are more "realistic" but rather because it is part of a more general theory that applies to a wider variety of phenomena, of which the position of leaves around a tree is a special case, has more implications capable of being contradicted, and has failed to be contradicted under a wider variety of circumstances. The direct evidence for the growth of leaves is in this way strengthened by the indirect evidence from the other phenomena to which the more general theory applies.

The constructed hypothesis is presumably valid, that is, yields "sufficiently" accurate predictions about the density of leaves, only for a particular class of circumstances. I do not know what these circumstances are or how to define them. It seems obvious, however, that in this example the "assumptions" of the theory will play no part in specifying them: the kind of tree, the character of the soil, etc., are the types of variables that are likely to define its range of validity, not the ability of the leaves to do complicated mathematics or to move from place to place.

A largely parallel example involving human behavior has been used elsewhere by Savage and me.[16] Consider the problem of predicting the shots made by an expert billiard player. It seems not at all unreasonable that excellent predictions would be yielded by the hypothesis that the billiard player made his shots *as if* he knew the complicated mathematical formulas that would give the optimum directions of travel, could estimate accurately by eye the angles, etc., describing the location of the balls, could make lightning calculations from the formulas, and could then make the balls travel in the direction indicated by the formulas. Our confidence in this hypothesis is not based on the belief that billiard players, even expert ones, can or do go through the process described; it derives rather from the belief that, unless in some way or other they were capable of reaching essentially the same result, they would not in fact be *expert* billiard players.

It is only a short step from these examples to the economic hypothesis that under a wide range of circumstances individual firms behave *as if* they were seeking rationally to maximize their expected returns (generally if misleadingly called "profits")[17] and had full knowledge of the data needed to succeed in this attempt; *as if*, that is, they knew the relevant cost and de-

mand functions, calculated marginal cost and marginal revenue from all actions open to them, and pushed each line of action to the point at which the relevant marginal cost and marginal revenue were equal. Now, of course, businessmen do not actually and literally solve the system of simultaneous equations in terms of which the mathematical economist finds it convenient to express this hypothesis, any more than leaves or billiard players explicitly go through complicated mathematical calculations or falling bodies decide to create a vacuum. The billiard player, if asked how he decides where to hit the ball, may say that he "just figures it out" but then also rubs a rabbit's foot just to make sure; and the businessman may well say that he prices at average cost, with of course some minor deviations when the market makes it necessary. The one statement is about as helpful as the other, and neither is a relevant test of the associated hypothesis.

Confidence in the maximization-of-returns hypothesis is justified by evidence of a very different character. This evidence is in part similar to that adduced on behalf of the billiard-player hypothesis—unless the behavior of businessmen in some way or other approximated behavior consistent with the maximization of returns, it seems unlikely that they would remain in business for long. Let the apparent immediate determinant of business behavior be anything at all—habitual reaction, random chance, or whatnot. Whenever this determinant happens to lead to behavior consistent with rational and informed maximization of returns, the business will prosper and acquire resources with which to expand; whenever it does not, the business will tend to lose resources and can be kept in existence only by the addition of resources from outside. The process of "natural selection" thus helps to validate the hypothesis—or, rather, given natural selection, acceptance of the hypothesis can be based largely on the judgment that it summarizes appropriately the conditions for survival.

An even more important body of evidence for the maximization-of-returns hypothesis is experience from countless applications of the hypothesis to specific problems and the repeated failure of its implications to be contradicted. This evidence is extremely hard to document; it is scattered in numerous memorandums, articles, and monographs concerned primarily with specific concrete problems rather than with submitting the hypothesis to test. Yet the continued use and acceptance of the hypothesis over a long period, and the failure of any coherent, self-consistent alternative to be developed and be widely accepted, is strong indirect testimony to its worth. The evidence *for* a hypothesis always consists of its repeated failure to be contradicted, continues to accumulate so long as the hypothesis is used, and by its very nature is difficult to document at all comprehensively. It tends to become part of the tradition and folklore of a science revealed in the tenacity with which hypotheses are held rather than in any textbook list of instances in which the hypothesis has failed to be contradicted.

IV. THE SIGNIFICANCE AND ROLE OF THE "ASSUMPTIONS" OF A THEORY

Up to this point our conclusions about the significance of the "assumptions" of a theory have been almost entirely negative: we have seen that a theory cannot be tested by the "realism" of its "assumptions" and that the very concept of the "assumptions" of a theory is surrounded with ambiguity. But, if this were all there is to it, it would be hard to explain the extensive use of the concept and the strong tendency that we all have to speak of the assumptions of a theory and to compare the assumptions of alternative

theories. There is too much smoke for there to be no fire.

In methodology, as in positive science, negative statements can generally be made with greater confidence than positive statements, so I have less confidence in the following remarks on the significance and role of "assumptions" than in the preceding remarks. So far as I can see, the "assumptions of a theory" play three different, though related, positive roles: (a) they are often an economical mode of describing or presenting a theory; (b) they sometimes facilitate an indirect test of the hypothesis by its implications; and (c), as already noted, they are sometimes a convenient means of specifying the conditions under which the theory is expected to be valid. The first two require more extensive discussion.

A. THE USE OF "ASSUMPTIONS" IN STATING A THEORY

The example of the leaves illustrates the first role of assumptions. Instead of saying that leaves seek to maximize the sunlight they receive, we could state the equivalent hypothesis, without any apparent assumptions, in the form of a list of rules for predicting the density of leaves: if a tree stands in a level field with no other trees or other bodies obstructing the rays of the sun, then the density of leaves will tend to be such and such; if a tree is on the northern slope of a hill in the midst of a forest of similar trees, then . . . ; etc. This is clearly a far less economical presentation of the hypothesis than the statement that leaves seek to maximize the sunlight each receives. The latter statement is, in effect, a simple summary of the rules in the above list, even if the list were indefinitely extended, since it indicates both how to determine the features of the environment that are important for the particular problem and how to evaluate their effects. It is more compact and at the same time no less comprehensive.

More generally, a hypothesis or

theory consists of an assertion that certain forces are, and by implication others are not, important for a particular class of phenomena and a specification of the manner of action of the forces it asserts to be important. We can regard the hypothesis as consisting of two parts: first, a conceptual world or abstract model simpler than the "real world" and containing only the forces that the hypothesis asserts to be important; second, a set of rules defining the class of phenomena for which the "model" can be taken to be an adequate representation of the "real world" and specifying the correspondence between the variables or entities in the model and observable phenomena.

These two parts are very different in character. The model is abstract and complete; it is an "algebra" or "logic." Mathematics and formal logic come into their own in checking its consistency and completeness and exploring its implications. There is no place in the model for, and no function to be served by, vagueness, maybe's, or approximations. The air pressure is zero, not "small," for a vacuum; the demand curve for the product of a competitive producer is horizontal (has a slope of zero), not "almost horizontal."

The rules for using the model, on the other hand, cannot possibly be abstract and complete. They must be concrete and in consequence incomplete— completeness is possible only in a conceptual world, not in the "real world," however that may be interpreted. The model is the logical embodiment of the half-truth, "There is nothing new under the sun"; the rules for applying it cannot neglect the equally significant half-truth, "History never repeats itself." To a considerable extent the rules can be formulated explicitly—most easily, though even then not completely, when the theory is part of an explicit more general theory as in the example of the vacuum theory for falling bodies. In seeking to make a science as "objective" as possible, our aim should be to

formulate the rules explicitly in so far as possible and continually to widen the range of phenomena for which it is possible to do so. But, no matter how successful we may be in this attempt, there inevitably will remain room for judgment in applying the rules. Each occurrence has some features peculiarly its own, not covered by the explicit rules. The capacity to judge that these are or are not to be disregarded, that they should or should not affect what observable phenomena are to be identified with what entities in the model, is something that cannot be taught; it can be learned but only by experience and exposure in the "right" scientific atmosphere, not by rote. It is at this point that the "amateur" is separated from the "professional" in all sciences and that the thin line is drawn which distinguishes the "crackpot" from the scientist.

A simple example may perhaps clarify this point. Euclidean geometry is an abstract model, logically complete and consistent. Its entities are precisely defined—a line is not a geometrical figure "much" longer than it is wide or deep; it is a figure whose width and depth are zero. It is also obviously "unrealistic." There are no such things in "reality" as Euclidean points or lines or surfaces. Let us apply this abstract model to a mark made on a blackboard by a piece of chalk. Is the mark to be identified with a Euclidean line, a Euclidean surface, or a Euclidean solid? Clearly, it can appropriately be identified with a line if it is being used to represent, say, a demand curve. But it cannot be so identified if it is being used to color, say, countries on a map, for that would imply that the map would never be colored; for this purpose, the same mark must be identified with a surface. But it cannot be so identified by a manufacturer of chalk, for that would imply that no chalk would ever be used up; for his purposes, the same mark must be identified with a volume. In this simple example these judgments will command general agreement. Yet it seems obvious that, while general considerations can be formulated to guide such judgments, they can never be comprehensive and cover every possible instance; they cannot have the self-contained coherent character of Euclidean geometry itself.

In speaking of the "crucial assumptions" of a theory, we are, I believe, trying to state the key elements of the abstract model. There are generally many different ways of describing the model completely—many different sets of "postulates" which both imply and are implied by the model as a whole. These are all logically equivalent: what are regarded as axioms or postulates of a model from one point of view can be regarded as theorems from another, and conversely. The particular "assumptions" termed "crucial" are selected on grounds of their convenience in some such respects as simplicity or economy in describing the model, intuitive plausibility, or capacity to suggest, if only by implication, some of the considerations that are relevant in judging or applying the model.

B. The Use of "Assumptions" As an Indirect Test of a Theory

In presenting any hypothesis, it generally seems obvious which of the series of statements used to expound it refer to assumptions and which to implications; yet this distinction is not easy to define rigorously. It is not, I believe, a characteristic of the hypothesis as such but rather of the use to which the hypothesis is to be put. If this is so, the ease of classifying statements must reflect unambiguousness in the purpose the hypothesis is designed to serve. The possibility of interchanging theorems and axioms in an abstract model implies the possibility of interchanging "implications" and "assumptions" in the substantive hypothesis corresponding to the abstract model, which is not to say that any implication can be interchanged with any assumption but only that there

may be more than one set of statements that imply the rest.

For example, consider a particular proposition in the theory of oligopolistic behavior. If we assume (a) that entrepreneurs seek to maximize their returns by any means including acquiring or extending monopoly power, this will imply (b) that, when demand for a "product" is geographically unstable, transportation costs are significant, explicit price agreements illegal, and the number of producers of the product relatively small, they will tend to establish basing-point pricing systems.[18] The assertion (a) is regarded as an assumption and (b) as an implication because we accept the prediction of market behavior as the purpose of the analysis. We shall regard the assumption as acceptable if we find that the conditions specified in (b) are generally associated with basing-point pricing, and conversely. Let us now change our purpose to deciding what cases to prosecute under the Sherman Antitrust Law's prohibition of a "conspiracy in restraint of trade." If we now assume (c) that basing-point pricing is a deliberate construction to facilitate collusion under the conditions specified in (b), this will imply (d) that entrepreneurs who participate in basing-point pricing are engaged in a "conspiracy in restraint of trade." What was formerly an assumption now becomes an implication, and conversely. We shall now regard the assumption (c) as valid if we find that, when entrepreneurs participate in basing-point pricing, there generally tends to be other evidence, in the form of letters, memorandums, or the like, of what courts regard as a "conspiracy in restraint of trade."

Suppose the hypothesis works for the first purpose, namely, the prediction of market behavior. It clearly does not follow that it will work for the second purpose, namely, predicting whether there is enough evidence of a "conspiracy in restraint of trade" to justify court action. And, conversely, if it works for the second purpose, it does not follow that it will work for the first. Yet, in the absence of other evidence, the success of the hypothesis for one purpose—in explaining one class of phenomena—will give us greater confidence than we would otherwise have that it may succeed for another purpose—in explaining another class of phenomena. It is much harder to say how much greater confidence it justifies. For this depends on how closely related we judge the two classes of phenomena to be, which itself depends in a complex way on similar kinds of indirect evidence, that is, on our experience in other connections in explaining by single theories phenomena that are in some sense similarly diverse.

To state the point more generally, what are called the assumptions of a hypothesis can be used to get some indirect evidence on the acceptability of the hypothesis in so far as the assumptions can themselves be regarded as implications of the hypothesis, and hence their conformity with reality as a failure of some implications to be contradicted, or in so far as the assumptions may call to mind other implications of the hypothesis susceptible to casual empirical observation.[19] The reason this evidence is indirect is that the assumptions or associated implications generally refer to a class of phenomena different from the class which the hypothesis is designed to explain; indeed, as is implied above, this seems to be the chief criterion we use in deciding which statements to term "assumptions" and which to term "implications." The weight attached to this indirect evidence depends on how closely related we judge the two classes of phenomena to be.

Another way in which the "assumptions" of a hypothesis can facilitate its indirect testing is by bringing out its kinship with other hypotheses and thereby making the evidence on their validity relevant to the validity of the hypothesis in question. For example, a hypothesis is formulated for a particular class of behavior. This hypothesis can, as usual, be stated without specifying any "assumptions." But suppose it can be shown that it is equivalent to a set of assumptions including the assumption that man seeks his own interest. The hypothesis then gains indirect plausibility from the success for other classes of phenomena of hypotheses that can also be said to make this assumption; at least, what is being done here is not completely unprecedented or unsuccessful in all other uses. In effect, the statement of assumptions so as to bring out a relationship between superficially different hypotheses is a step in the direction of a more general hypothesis.

This kind of indirect evidence from related hypotheses explains in large measure the difference in the confidence attached to a particular hypothesis by people with different backgrounds. Consider, for example, the hypothesis that the extent of racial or religious discrimination in employment in a particular area or industry is closely related to the degree of monopoly in the industry or area in question; that, if the industry is competitive, discrimination will be significant only if the race or religion of employees affects either the willingness of other employees to work with them or the acceptability of the product to customers and will be uncorrelated with the prejudices of employers.[20] This hypothesis is far more likely to appeal to an economist than to a sociologist. It can be said to "assume" single-minded pursuit of pecuniary self-interest by employers in competitive industries; and this "assumption" works well in a wide variety of hypotheses in economics bearing on many of the mass phenomena with which economics deals. It is therefore likely to seem reasonable to the economist that it may work in this case as well. On the other hand, the hypotheses to which the sociologist is accustomed have a very different kind of model or ideal world, in which single-minded pursuit of pecuniary self-interest plays a much less important role. The indirect evidence available to the sociologist on this hypothesis is much less favorable to it than the indirect evidence available to the economist; he is therefore likely to view it with greater suspicion.

Of course, neither the evidence of the economist nor that of the sociologist is conclusive. The decisive test is whether the hypothesis works for the phenomena it purports to explain. But a judgment may be required before any satisfactory test of this kind has been made, and, perhaps, when it cannot be made in the near future, in which case, the judgment will have to be based on the inadequate evidence available. In addition, even when such a test can be made the background of the scientists is not irrelevant to the judgments they reach. There is never certainty in science, and the weight of evidence for or against a hypothesis can never be assessed completely "objectively." The economist will be more tolerant than the sociologist in judging conformity of the implications of the hypothesis with experience, and he will be persuaded to accept the hypothesis tentatively by fewer instances of "conformity."

V. SOME IMPLICATIONS FOR ECONOMIC ISSUES

The abstract methodological issues we have been discussing have a direct bearing on the perennial criticism of "orthodox" economic theory as "unrealistic" as well as on the attempts that have been made to reformulate theory to meet this charge. Economics is a "dismal" science because it assumes man to be selfish and money-grubbing, "a lightning calculator of pleasures and pains, who oscillates like a homogeneous globule of desire of happiness under the impulse of stimuli that shift him about the area, but leave him intact;[21] it rests on outmoded psychology and must be reconstructed in line with each new development in psychology; it assumes

men, or at least businessmen, to be "in a continuous state of 'alert,' ready to change prices and/or pricing rules whenever their sensitive intuitions . . . detect a change in demand and supply conditions",[22] it assumes markets to be perfect, competition to be pure, and commodities, labor, and capital to be homogeneous.

As we have seen, criticism of this type is largely beside the point unless supplemented by evidence that a hypothesis differing in one or another of these respects from the theory being criticized yields better predictions for as wide a range of phenemoena. Yet most such criticism is not so supplemented; it is based almost entirely on supposedly directly perceived discrepancies between the "assumptions" and the "real world." A particularly clear example is furnished by the recent criticisms of the maximization-of-returns hypothesis on the grounds that businessmen do not and indeed cannot behave as the theory "assumes" they do. The evidence cited to support this assertion is generally taken either from the answers given by businessmen to questions about the factors affecting their decisions—a procedure for testing economic theories that is about on a par with testing theories of longevity by asking octogenarians how they account for their long life—or from descriptive studies of the decision-making activities of individual firms.[23] Little if any evidence is ever cited on the conformity of businessmen's actual market behavior—what they do rather than what they say they do—with the implications of the hypothesis being criticized, on the one hand, and of an alternative hypothesis, on the other.

A theory or its "assumptions" cannot possibly be thoroughly "realistic" in the immediate descriptive sense so often assigned to this term. A completely "realistic" theory of the wheat market would have to include not only the conditions directly underlying the supply and demand for wheat but also the kind of coins or credit instruments used to make exchanges; the personal characteristics of wheat-traders such as the color of each trader's hair and eyes, his antecedents and education, the number of members of his famioy, their characteristics, antecedents, and education, etc.; the kind of soil on which the wheat was grown, its physical and chemical characteristics, the weather prevailing during the growing season; the personal characteristics of the farmers growing the wheat and of the consumers who will ultimately use it; and so on indefinitely. Any attempt to move very far in achieving this kind of "realism" is certain to render a theory utterly useless.

Of course, the notion of a completely realistic theory is in part a straw man. No critic of a theory would accept this logical extreme as his objective; he would say that the "assumptions" of the theory being criticized were "too" unrealistic and that his objective was a set of assumptions that were "more" realistic though still not completely and slavishly so. But so long as the test of "realism" is the directly perceived descriptive accuracy of the "assumptions"—for example, the observation that "businessmen do not appear to be either as avaricious or as dynamic or as logical as marginal theory portrays them"[24] or that "it would be utterly impractical under present conditions for the manager of a multi-process plant to attempt . . . to work out and equate marginal costs and marginal revenues for each productive factor"[25]—there is no basis for making such a distinction, that is, for stopping short of the straw man depicted in the preceding paragraph. What is the criterion by which to judge whether a particular departure from realism is or is not acceptable? Why is it more "unrealistic" in analyzing business behavior to neglect the magnitude of businessmen's costs than the color of their eyes? The obvious answer is because the first makes more difference to business behavior than the second; but there is no way of knowing

that this is so simply by observing that businessmen do have costs of different magnitudes and eyes of different color. Clearly it can only be known by comparing the effect on the discrepancy between actual and predicted behavior of taking the one factor or the other into account. Even the most extreme proponents of realistic assumptions are thus necessarily driven to reject their own criterion and to accept the test by prediction when they classify alternative assumptions as more or less realistic.[26]

The basic confusion between descriptive accuracy and analytical relevance that underlies most criticisms of economic theory on the grounds that its assumptions are unrealistic as well as the plausibility of the views that lead to this confusion are both strikingly illustrated by a seemingly innocuous remark in an article on business-cycle theory that

> economic phenomena are varied and complex, so any comprehensive theory of the business cycle that can apply closely to reality must be very complicated.[27]

A fundamental hypothesis of science is that appearances are deceptive and that there is a way of looking at or interpreting or organizing the evidence that will reveal superficially disconnected and diverse phenomena to be manifestations of a more fundamental and relatively simple structure. And the test of this hypothesis, as of any other, is its fruits—a test that science has so far met with dramatic success. If a class of "economic phenomena" appears varied and complex, it is, we must suppose, because we have no adequate theory to explain them. Known facts cannot be set on one side; a theory to apply "closely to reality," on the other. A theory is the way we perceive "facts," and we cannot perceive "facts" without a theory. Any assertion that economic phenomena are varied and complex denies the tentative state of knowledge that alone makes scientific activity meaningful; it is in a class with John Stuart Mill's justly ridiculed statement that happily, there is nothing in the laws of value which remains [1848] for the present or any future writer to clear up; the theory of the subject is complete.[28]

The confusion between descriptive accuracy and analytical relevance has led not only to criticisms of economic theory on largely irrelevant grounds but also to misunderstanding of economic theory and misdirection of efforts to repair supposed defects. "Ideal types" in the abstract model developed by economic theorists have been regarded as strictly descriptive categories intended to correspond directly and fully to entities in the real world independently of the purpose for which the model is being used. The obvious discrepancies have led to necessarily unsuccessful attempts to construct theories on the basis of categories intended to be fully descriptive.

This tendency is perhaps most clearly illustrated by the interpretation given to the concepts of "perfect competition" and "monopoly" and the development of the theory of "monopolistic" or "imperfect competition." Marshall, it is said, assumed "perfect competition"; perhaps there once was such a thing. But clearly there is no longer, and we must therefore discard his theories. The reader will search long and hard—and I predict unsuccessfully—to find in Marshall any explicit assumption about perfect competition or any assertion that in a descriptive sense the world is composed of atomistic firms engaged in perfect competition. Rather, he will find Marshall saying:

> At one extreme are world markets in which competition acts directly from all parts of the globe; and at the other those secluded markets in which all direct competition from afar is shut out, though indirect and transmitted competition may make itself felt even in these; and about midway between these extremes lie the great majority of the markets which the economist and the business man have to study.[29]

Marshall took the world as it is; he sought to construct an "engine" to analyze it, not a photographic reproduction of it.

In analyzing the world as it is, Marshall constructed the hypothesis that, for many problems, firms could be grouped into "industries" such that the similarities among the firms in each group were more important than the differences among them. These are problems in which the important element is that a group of firms is affected alike by some stimulus—a common change in the demand for their products, say, or in the supply of factors. But this will not do for all problems: the important element for these may be the differential effect on particular firms.

The abstract model corresponding to this hypothesis contains two "ideal" types of firms: atomistically competitive firms, grouped into industries, and monopolistic firms. A firm is competitive if the demand curve for its output is infinitely elastic with respect to its own price for some price and all outputs, given the prices charged by all other firms; it belongs to an "industry" defined as a group of firms producing a single "product." A "product" is defined as a collection of units that are perfect substitutes to purchasers so the elasticity of demand for the output of one firm with respect to the price of another firm in the same industry is infinite for some price and some outputs. A firm is monopolistic if the demand curve for its output is not infinitely elastic at some price for all outputs.[30] If it is a monopolist, the firm is the industry.[31]

As always, the hypothesis as a whole consists not only of this abstract model and its ideal types but also of a set of rules, mostly implicit and suggested by example, for identifying actual firms with one or the other ideal type and for classifying firms into industries. The ideal types are not intended to be descriptive; they are designed to isolate the features that are crucial for a particular problem. Even if we could estimate directly and accurately the demand curve for a firm's product, we could not proceed immediately to classify the firm as perfectly competitive or monopolistic according as the elasticity of the demand curve is or is not infinite. No observed demand curve will ever be precisely horizontal, so the estimated elasticity will always be finite. The relevant question always is whether the elasticity is "sufficiently" large to be regarded as infinite, but this is a question that cannot be answered, once for all, simply in terms of the numerical value of the elasticity itself, any more than we can say, once for all, whether an air pressure of 15 pounds per square inch is "sufficiently" close to zero to use the formula $s = \frac{1}{2}gt^2$. Similarly, we cannot compute cross-elasticities of demand and then classify firms into industries according as there is a "substantial gap in the cross-elasticities of demand." As Marshall says,

> The question where the lines of division between different commodities [i.e., industries] should be drawn must be settled by convenience of the particular discussion.[32]

Everything depends on the problem; there is no inconsistency in regarding the same firm as if it were a perfect competitor for one problem, and a monopolist for another, just as there is none in regarding the same chalk mark as a Euclidean line for one problem, a Euclidean surface for a second, and a Euclidean solid for a third. The size of the elasticity and cross-elasticity of demand, the number of firms producing physically similar products, etc., are all relevant because they are or may be among the variables used to define the correspondence between the ideal and real entities in a particular problem and to specify the circumstances under which the theory holds sufficiently well; but they do not provide, once for all, a classification of firms as competitive or monopolistic.

An example may help to clarify this point. Suppose the problem is to determine the effect on retail prices of cigarettes of an increase, expected to be permanent, in the federal cigarette tax. I venture to predict that broadly correct results will be obtained by treating cigarette firms as if they were producing an identical product and were in perfect competition. Of course, in such a case, "some convention must be made as to the" number of Chesterfield cigarettes "which are taken as equivalent" to a Marlboro.[33]

On the other hand, the hypothesis that cigarette firms would behave as if they were perfectly competitive would have been a false guide to their reactions to price control in World War II, and this would doubtless have been recognized before the event. Costs of the cigarette firms must have risen during the war. Under such circumstances perfect competitors would have reduced the quantity offered for sale at the previously existing price. But, at that price, the wartime rise in the income of the public presumably increased the quantity demanded. Under conditions of perfect competition strict adherence to the legal price would therefore imply not only a "shortage" in the sense that quantity demanded exceeded quantity supplied but also an absolute decline in the number of cigarettes produced. The facts contradict this particular implication: there was reasonably good adherence to maximum cigarette prices, yet the quantities produced increased substantially. The common force of increased costs presumably operated less strongly than the disruptive force of the desire by each firm to keep its share of the market, to maintain the value and prestige of its brand name, especially when the excess-profits tax shifted a large share of the costs of this kind of advertising to the government. For this problem the cigarette firms cannot be treated as if they were perfect competitors.

Wheat farming is frequently taken to exemplify perfect competition. Yet, while for some problems it is appropriate to treat cigarette producers as if they comprised a perfectly competitive industry, for some it is not appropriate to treat wheat producers as if they did. For example, it may not be if the problem is the differential in prices paid by local elevator operators for wheat.

Marshall's apparatus turned out to be most useful for problems in which a group of firms is affected by common stimuli, and in which the firms can be treated *as if* they were perfect competitors. This is the source of the misconception that Marshall "assumed" perfect competition in some descriptive sense. It would be highly desirable to have a more general theory than Marshall's, one that would cover at the same time both those cases in which differentiation of product or fewness of numbers makes an essential difference and those in which it does not. Such a theory would enable us to handle problems we now cannot and, in addition, facilitate determination of the range of circumstances under which the simpler theory can be regarded as a good enough approximation. To perform this function, the more general theory must have content and substance; it must have implications susceptible to empirical contradiction and of substantive interest and importance.

The theory of imperfect or monopolistic competition developed by Chamberlin and Robinson is an attempt to construct such a more general theory.[34] Unfortunately, it possesses none of the attributes that would make it a truly useful general theory. Its contribution has been limited largely to improving the exposition of the economics of the individual firm and thereby the derivation of implications of the Marshallian model, refining Marshall's monopoly analysis, and enriching the vocabulary available for describing industrial experience.

The deficiencies of the theory are revealed most clearly in its treatment of, or inability to treat, problems involving groups of firms—Marshallian "industries." So long as it is insisted that differentiation of product is essential—and it is the distinguishing feature of the

theory that it does insist on this point—the definition of an industry in terms of firms producing an identical product cannot be used. By that definition each firm is a separate industry. Definition in terms of "close" substitutes or a "substantial" gap in cross-elasticities evades the issue, introduces fuzziness and undefinable terms into the abstract model where they have no place, and serves only to make the theory analytically meaningless—"close" and "substantial" are in the same category as a "small" air pressure.[35] In one connection Chamberlin implicitly defines an industry as a group of firms having identical cost and demand curves.[36] But this, too, is logically meaningless so long as differentiation of product is, as claimed, essential and not to be put aside. What does it mean to say that the cost and demand curves of a firm producing bulldozers are identical with those of a firm producing hairpins?[37] And if it is meaningless for bulldozers and hairpins, it is meaningless also for two brands of toothpaste—so long as it is insisted that the difference between the two brands is fundamentally important.

The theory of monopolistic competition offers no tools for the analysis of an industry and so no stopping place between the firm at one extreme and general equilibrium at the other.[38] It is therefore incompetent to contribute to the analysis of a host of important problems: the one extreme is too narrow to be of great interest; the other, too broad to permit meaningful generalizations.[39]

VI. CONCLUSION

Economics as a positive science is a body of tentatively accepted generalizations about economic phenomena that can be used to predict the consequences of changes in circumstances. Progress in expanding this body of generalizations, strengthening our confidence in their validity, and improving the accuracy of the predictions they yield is hindered not only by the limitations of human ability that impede all search for knowledge but also by obstacles that are especially important for the social sciences in general and economics in particular, though by no means peculiar to them. Familiarity with the subject matter of economics breeds contempt for special knowledge about it. The importance of its subject matter to everday life and to major issues of public policy impedes objectivity and promotes confusion between scientific analysis and normative judgment. The necessity of relying on uncontrolled experience rather than on controlled experiment makes it difficult to produce dramatic and clear-cut evidence to justify the acceptance of tentative hypotheses. Reliance on uncontrolled experience does not affect the fundamental methodological principle that a hypothesis can be tested only by the conformity of its implications or predictions with observable phenomena; but it does render the task of testing hypotheses more difficult and gives greater scope for confusion about the methodological principles involved. More than other scientists, social scientists need to be self-conscious about their methodology.

One confusion that has been particularly rife and has done much damage is confusion about the role of "assumptions" in economic analysis. A meaningful scientific hypothesis or theory typically asserts that certain forces are, and other forces are not, important in understanding a particular class of phenomena. It is frequently convenient to present such a hypothesis by stating that the phenomena it is desired to predict behave in the world of observation *as if* they occurred in a hypothetical and highly simplified world containing only the forces that the hypothesis asserts to be important. In general, there is more than one way to formulate such a description—more than one set of "assumptions" in terms of which the theory can be presented. The choice among such alternative assumptions is made on the grounds of the resulting economy, clarity, and precision in presenting the hypothesis; their capacity to bring indirect evidence to bear on the validity of the hypothesis by suggesting some of its implications that can be readily checked with observation or by bringing out its connection with other hypotheses dealing with related phenomena; and similar considerations.

Such a theory cannot be tested by comparing its "assumptions" directly with "reality." Indeed, there is no meaningful way in which this can be done. Complete "realism" is clearly unattainable, and the question whether a theory is realistic "enough" can be settled only by seeing whether it yields predictions that are good enough for the purpose in hand or that are better than predictions from alternative theories. Yet the belief that a theory can be tested by the realism of its assumptions independently of the accuracy of its predictions is widespread and the source of much of the perennial criticism of economic theory as unrealistic. Such criticism is largely irrelevant, and, in consequence, most attempts to reform economic theory that it has stimulated have been unsuccessful.

The irrelevance of so much criticism of economic theory does not of course imply that existing economic theory deserves any high degree of confidence. These criticisms may miss the target, yet there may be a target for criticism. In a trivial sense, of course, there obviously is. Any theory is necessarily provisional and subject to change with the advance of knowledge. To go beyond this platitude, it is necessary to be more specific about the content of "existing economic theory" and to distinguish among its different branches; some parts of economic theory clearly deserve more confidence than others. A comprehensive evaluation of the present state of positive economics, summary of the evidence bearing on its validity, and assessment of the relative confidence that each part deserves is clearly a task for a treatise or a set of treatises, if it be possible at all, not for a brief paper on methodology.

About all that is possible here is the cursory expression of a personal view. Existing relative price theory, which is designed to explain the allocation of resources among alternative ends and the division of the product among the co-operating resources and which reached almost its present form in Marshall's *Principles of Economics*, seems to me both extremely fruitful and deserving of much confidence for the kind of economic system that characterizes Western nations. Despite the appearance of considerable controversy, this is true equally of existing static monetary theory, which is designed to explain the structural or secular level of absolute prices, aggregate output, and other variables for the economy as a whole and which has had a form of the quantity theory of money as its basic core in all of its major variants from David Hume to the Cambridge School to Irving Fisher to John Maynard Keynes. The weakest and least satisfactory part of current economic theory seems to me to be in the field of monetary dynamics, which is concerned with the process of adaptation of the economy as a whole to changes in conditions and so with short-period fluctuations in aggregate activity. In this field we do not even have a theory that can appropriately be called "the" existing theory of monetary dynamics.

Of course, even in relative price and static monetary theory there is enormous room for extending the scope and improving the accuracy of existing theory. In particular, undue emphasis on the descriptive realism of "assumptions" has contributed to neglect of the critical problem of determining the limits of validity of the various hypotheses that together constitute the existing economic theory in these areas. The abstract models corresponding to these hypotheses have been elaborated in considerable detail and greatly improved in rigor and precision. Descriptive material on the characteristics of our economic system and its operations have been amassed on an unprecedented scale. This is all to the good. But, if we are to use effectively these abstract models and this descriptive material, we must have a comparable exploration of the criteria for determining what abstract model it is best to use for particular kinds of problems, what entities in the abstract model are to be identified with what observable entities, and what features of the problem or of the circumstances have the greatest effect on the accuracy of the predictions yielded by a particular model or theory.

Progress in positive economics will require not only the testing and elaboration of existing hypotheses but also the construction of new hypotheses. On this problem there is little to say on a formal level. The construction of hypotheses is a creative act of inspiration, intuition, invention; its essence is the vision of something new in familiar material. The process must be discussed in psychological, not logical, categories; studied in autobiographies and biographies, not treatises on scientific method; and promoted by maxim and example, not syllogism or theorem.

NOTES

1. I have incorporated bodily in this article without special reference most of my brief "Comment" in *A Survey of Contemporary Economics*, Vol. II, B. F. Haley, ed. (Chicago: Richard D. Irwin, Inc., 1952), pp. 455-57....

2. (London: Macmillan & Co., 1891), pp. 34-35 and 46.

3. Social science or economics is by no means peculiar in this respect—witness the importance of personal beliefs and of "home" remedies in medicine wherever ob-

viously convincing evidence for "expert" opinion is lacking. The current prestige and acceptance of the views of physical scientists in their fields of specialization—and, all too often, in other fields as well—derives, not from faith alone, but from the evidence of their works, the success of their predictions, and the dramatic achievements from applying their results. When economics seemed to provide such evidence of its worth, in Great Britain in the first half of the nineteenth century, the prestige and acceptance of "scientific economics" rivaled the current prestige of the physical sciences.

4. The interaction between the observer and the process observed that is so prominent a feature of the social sciences, besides its more obvious parallel in the physical sciences, has a more subtle counterpart in the indeterminacy principle arising out of the interaction between the process of measurement and the phenomena being measured. And both have a counterpart in pure logic in Gödel's theorem, asserting the impossibility of a comprehensive self-contained logic. It is an open question whether all three can be regarded as different formulations of an even more general principle.

5. One rather more complex example is stabilization policy. Superficially, divergent views on this question seem to reflect differences in objectives; but I believe that this impression is misleading and that at bottom the different views reflect primarily different judgments about the source of fluctuations in economic activity and the effect of alternative countercyclical action. For one major positive consideration that accounts for much of the divergence see "The Effects of a Full-Employment Policy on Economic Stability: A Formal Analysis," infra, pp. 117-32. For a summary of the present state of professional views on this question see "The Problem of Economic Instability," a report of a subcommittee of the Committee on Public Issues of the American Economic Association, American Economic Review, XL (September, 1950), 501-38.

6. Final quoted phrase from Alfred Marshall, "The Present Position of Economics" (1885), reprinted in Memorials of Alfred Marshall, ed. A. C. Pigou (London: Macmillan & Co., 1925), p. 164. See also "The Marshallian Demand Curve," infra, pp. 56-57, 90-91.

7. See "Lange on Price Flexibility and Employment: A Methodological Criticism," infra, pp. 181-89.

8. The Marshallian Demand Curve," infra, p. 57.

9. The qualification is necessary because the "evidence" may be internally contradictory, so there may be no hypothesis consistent with it. See also "Lange on Price Flexibility and Employment," infra, pp. 181-83.

10. See "Lange on Price Flexibility and Employment," infra, passim.

11. See also Milton Friedman and L. J. Savage, "The Expected-Utility Hypothesis and the Measurability of Utility," Journal of Political Economy, LX (December, 1952), 463-74, esp. pp. 465-67.

12. In recent years some economists, particularly a group connected with the Cowles Commission for Research in Economics at the University of Chicago, have placed great emphasis on a division of this step of selecting a hypothesis consistent with known evidence into two substeps: first, the selection of a class of admissible hypotheses from all possible hypotheses (the choice of a "model" in their terminology); second, the selection of one hypothesis from this class (the choice of a "structure"). This subdivision may be heuristically valuable in some kinds of work, particularly in promoting a systematic use of available statistical evidence and theory. From a methodological point of view, however, it is an entirely arbitrary subdivision of the process of deciding on a particular hypothesis that is on a par with many other subdivisions that may be convenient for one purpose or another or that may suit the psychological needs of particular investigators.

One consequence of this particular subdivision has been to give rise to the so-called "identification" problem. As noted above, if one hypothesis is consistent with available evidence, an infinite number are. But, while this is true for the class of hypotheses as a whole, it may not be true of the subclass obtained in the first of the above two steps—the "model." It may be that the evidence to be used to select the final hypothesis from the subclass can be consistent with at most one hypothesis in it, in which case the "model" is said to be "identified"; otherwise it is said to be "unidentified." As is clear from this way of describing the concept of "identification," it is essentially a special case of the more general problem of selecting among the alternative hypotheses equally consistent with the evidence—a problem that must be decided by some such arbitrary principle as Occam's razor. The introduction of two substeps in selecting a hypothesis makes this problem arise at the two corresponding stages and gives it a special cast. While the class of all hypotheses is always unidentified, the subclass in a "model" need not be, so the problem arises of conditions that a "model" must satisfy to be identified. However useful the two substeps may be in some contexts, their introduction raises the danger that different criteria will unwittingly be used in making the same kind of choice among alternative hypotheses at two different stages. . . .

13. The converse of the proposition does not of course hold: assumptions that are unrealistic (in this sense) do not guarantee a significant theory.

14. . . . It should be noted that, along with much material purportedly bearing on the validity of the "assumptions" of marginal theory, Lester does refer to evidence on the conformity of experience with the implications of the theory, citing the reactions of employment in Germany to the Papen plan and in the United States to changes in minimum-wage legislation as examples of lack of conformity. However, Stigler's brief comment is the only one of the other papers that refers to this evidence. It should also be noted that Machlup's thorough and careful exposition of the logical structure and meaning of marginal analysis is called for by the misunderstandings on this score that mar Lester's paper and almost conceal the evidence he presents that is relevant to the key issue he raises. But, in Machlup's emphasis on the logical structure, he comes perilously close to presenting the theory as a pure tautology, though it is evident at a number of points that he is aware of this danger and anxious to avoid it. The papers by Oliver and Gordon are the most extreme in the exclusive concentration on the conformity of the behavior of businessmen with the "assumptions" of the theory.

15. This example, and some of the subsequent discussion, though independent in origin, is similar to and in much the same spirit as an example and the approach in an important paper by Armen A. Alchian, "Uncertainty, Evolution, and Economic Theory," *Journal of Political Economy*, LVIII (June, 1950), 211-21.

16. Milton Friedman and L. J. Savage, "The Utility Analysis of Choices Involving Risk," *Journal of Political Economy*, LVI (August, 1948), 298. Reprinted in American Economic Association, *Readings in Price*

Theory (Chicago: Richard D. Irwin, Inc., 1952), pp. 57-96.

17. It seems better to use the term "profits" to refer to the difference between actual and "expected" results, between *ex post* and *ex ante* receipts. "Profits" are then a result of uncertainty and, as Alchian (*op. cit.*, p. 212), following Tintner, points out, cannot be deliberately maximized in advance. Given uncertainty, individuals or firms choose among alternative anticipated probability distributions of receipts or incomes. The specific content of a theory of choice among such distributions depends on the criteria by which they are supposed to be ranked. One hypothesis supposes them to be ranked by the mathematical expectation of utility corresponding to them (see Friedman and Savage, "The Expected-Utility Hypothesis and the Measurability of Utility," *op cit.*). A special case of this hypothesis or an alternative to it ranks probability distributions by the mathematical expectation of the money receipts corresponding to them. The latter is perhaps more applicable, and more frequently applied, to firms than to individuals. The term "expected returns" is intended to be sufficiently broad to apply to any of these alternatives.

The issues alluded to in this note are not basic to the methodological issues being discussed, and so are largely by-passed in the discussion that follows.

18. See George J. Stigler, "A Theory of Delivered Price Systems," *American Economic Review*, XXXIX (December, 1949), 1143-57.

19. See Friedman and Savage, "The Expected-Utility Hypothesis and the Measurability of Utility," *op. cit.*, pp. 466-67, for another specific example of this kind of indirect test.

20. A rigorous statement of this hypothesis would of course have to specify how "extent of racial or religious discrimination" and "degree of monopoly" are to be judged. The loose statement in the text is sufficient, however, for present purposes.

21. Thorstein Veblen, "Why Is Economics Not an Evolutionary Science?" (1898), reprinted in *The Place of Science in Modern Civilization* (New York, 1919), p. 73.

22. Oliver, *op. cit.*, p. 381.

23. . . . I do not mean to imply that questionnaire studies of businessmen's or others' motives or beliefs about the forces affecting their behavior are useless for all purposes in economics. They may be extremely valuable

in suggesting leads to follow in accounting for divergencies between predicted and observed results; that is, in constructing new hypotheses or revising old ones. Whatever their suggestive value in this respect, they seem to me almost entirely useless as a means of *testing* the validity of economic hypotheses. . . .

24. Oliver, *op. cit.*, p. 382.

25. Lester, "Shortcomings of Marginal Analysis for Wage-Employment Problems," *op. cit.*, p. 75.

26. *E.g.*, Gordon's direct examination of the "assumptions" leads him to formulate the alternative hypothesis generally favored by the critics of the maximization-of-returns hypothesis as follows:

> There is an irresistible tendency to price on the basis of average total costs for some 'normal' level of output. This is the yardstick, the short-cut, that businessmen and accountants use, and their aim is more to earn satisfactory profits and play *safe* than to maximize profits (*op. cit.*, p. 175).

Yet he essentially abandons this hypothesis, or converts it into a tautology, and in the process implicitly accepts the test by prediction when he later remarks:

> Full cost and satisfactory profits may continue to be the objectives even when total costs are shaded to meet competition or exceed to take advantage of a sellers' market (*ibid.*, p. 284).

Where here is the "irresistible tendency"? What kind of evidence could contradict this assertion?

27. Sidney S. Alexander, "Issues of Business Cycle Theory Raised by Mr. Hicks," *American Economic Review*, XLI (December, 1951), 872.

28. *Principles of Political Economy* (Ashley ed.; Longmans, Green & Co., 1919), p. 436.

29. *Principles*, p. 329; see also pp. 35, 100, 341, 347, 375, 546.

30. This ideal type can be divided into two types: the oligopolistic firm, if the de-

mand curve for its output is infinitely elastic at some price for some but not all outputs; the monopolistic firm proper, if the demand curve is nowhere infinitely elastic (except possibly at an output of zero).

31. For the oligopolist of the preceding note an industry can be defined as a group of firms producing the same product.

32. *Principles*, p. 100.

33. Quoted parts from *ibid*.

34. E. H. Chamberlin, *The Theory of Monopolistic Competition* (6th ed.; Cambridge: Harvard University Press, 1950); Joan Robinson, *The Economics of Imperfect Competition* (London: Macmillan & Co., 1933).

35. See R. L. Bishop, "Elasticities, Cross-elasticities, and Market Relationships," *American Economic Review*, XLII (December, 1952), 779-803, for the recent attempt to construct a rigorous classification of market relationships along these lines. Despite its ingenuity and sophistication, the result seems to me thoroughly unsatisfactory. It rests basically on certain numbers being classified as "large" or "small," yet there is no discussion at all of how to decide whether a particular number is "large" or "small," as of course there cannot be on a purely abstract level.

36. *Op. cit.*, p. 82.

37. There always exists a transformation of quantities that will make either the cost curves or the demand curves identical; this transformation need not, however, be linear, in which case it will involve different-sized units of one product at different levels of output. There does not necessarily exist a transformation that will make both pairs of curves identical.

38. See Robert Triffin, *Monopolistic Competition and General Equilibrium Theory* (Cambridge: Harvard University Press, 1940), esp. pp. 188-89.

39. For a detailed critique see George J. Stigler, "Monopolistic Competition in Retrospect," in *Five Lectures on Economic Problems* (London: Macmillan & Co., 1949), pp. 12-24.

43. A Monetary and Fiscal Framework for Economic Stability*

MILTON FRIEDMAN

During the late 19th and early 20th centuries, the problems of the day were of a kind that led economists to concentrate on the allocation of resources and, to a lesser extent, economic growth, and to pay little attention to short-run fluctuations of a cyclical character. Since the Great Depression of the 1930's, this emphasis has been reversed. Economists now tend to concentrate on cyclical movements, to act and talk as if any improvement, however slight, in control of the cycle justified any sacrifice, however large, in the long-run efficiency, or prospects for growth, of the economic system. Proposals for the control of the cycle thus tend to be developed almost as if there were no other objectives and as if it made no difference within what general framework cyclical fluctuations take place. A consequence of this attitude is that inadequate attention is given to the possibility of satisfying both sets of objectives simultaneously.

In constructing the monetary and fiscal framework proposed in this paper, I deliberately gave primary consideration to long-run objectives. That is, I tried to design a framework that would be appropriate for a world in which cyclical movements, other than those introduced by "bad" monetary and fiscal arrangements, were of no consequence. I then examined the resulting proposal to see how it would behave in respect of cyclical fluctuations. It behaves surprisingly well; not only might it be expected not to contribute to cyclical fluctuations, it tends to offset them and therefore seems to offer considerable promise of providing a tolerable degree of short-run economic stability.

This paper is devoted to presenting the part of the analysis dealing with the implications of the proposal for cyclical stability. Nonetheless, in view of the motivation of the proposal it seems well to begin by indicating the long-run objectives adopted as a guide, even though a reasonably full discussion of these long-run objectives would not be appropriate here.

The basic long-run objectives, shared I am sure by most economists, are political freedom, economic efficiency, and substantial equality of economic power. These objectives are not, of course, entirely consistent and some compromise among them may be required. Moreover, objectives states on this level of generality can hardly guide proximate policy choices. We must take the next step and specify the general institutional arrangements we regard best suited for the attainment of these objectives. I believe—and at this stage agreement will be far less widespread—that all three objectives can best be realized by relying, as far as possible, on a market mechanism within a "competitive order" to organize the

*Source: From American Economic Review, vol. 38 (1948), pp. 245-64. Copyright © 1948 American Economic Association. Reprinted by permission. Some footnotes deleted; others renumbered.

utilization of economic resources. Among the specific propositions that follow from this general position, three are particularly relevant: (1) Government must provide a monetary framework for a competitive order since the competitive order cannot provide one for itself. (2) This monetary framework should operate under the "rule of law" rather than the discretionary authority of administrators. (3) While a truly free market in a "competitive order" would yield far less inequality than currently exists, I should hope that the community would desire to reduce inequality even further. Moreover, measures to supplement the market would need to be taken in the interim. For both purposes, general fiscal measures (as contrasted with specific intervention) are the most desirable non-free-market means of decreasing inequality.

The extremely simply proposal which these long-run objectives lead me to advance contains no new elements. Indeed, in view of the number of proposals that have been made for altering one or another part of the present monetary or fiscal framework, it is hard to believe that anything completely new remains to be added. The combination of elements that emerges is somewhat less hackneyed; yet no claim of originality can be made even for this. As is perhaps not surprising from what has already been said, the proposal is something like the greatest common denominator of many different proposals. This is perhaps the chief justification for presenting it and urging that it receive full professional discussion. Perhaps it, or some variant, can approach a minimum program for which economists of the less extreme shades of opinion can make common cause.

This paper deals only with the broad outlines of the monetary and fiscal framework and neglects, or deals superficially with, many difficult, important, and closely related problems. In particular, it neglects almost entirely the transition from the present framework to that outlined here; the implications of the adoption of the recommended framework for international monetary arrangements; and the special requirements of war finance. These associated problems are numerous and serious and are likely to justify compromise at some points. It seems well, however, to set forth the ultimate ideal as clearly as possible before beginning to compromise.

I. THE PROPOSAL

The particular proposal outlined below involves four main elements: the first relates to the monetary system; the second, to government expenditures on goods and services; the third, to government transfer payments; and the fourth, to the tax structure. Throughout, it pertains entirely to the federal government and all references to "government" should be so interpreted.[1]

1. A reform of the monetary and banking system to eliminate both the private creation or desctruction of money and discretionary control of the quantity of money by central bank authority. The private creation of money can perhaps best be eliminated by adopting the 100 per cent reserve proposal, thereby separating the depositary from the lending function of the banking system? The adoption of 100 percent reserves would also reduce the discretionary powers of the reserve system by eliminating rediscounting and existing powers over reserve requirements. To complete the elimination of the major weapons of discretionary authority, the existing powers to engage in open market operations and the existing direct controls over stock market and consumer credit should be abolished.

These modifications would leave as the chief monetary functions of the banking system the provision of depositary facilities, the facilitation of check clearance, and the like; and as the chief function of the monetary authorities, the creation of money to meet government deficits or the retirement of money when the government has a surplus?

2. A policy of determining the volume of government expenditures on goods and services—defined to exclude transfer ex-

penditures of all kinds—entirely on the basis of the community's desire, need, and willingness to pay for public services. Changes in the level of expenditure should be made solely in response to alterations in the relative value attached by the community to public services and private consumption. No attempt should be made to vary expenditures, either directly or inversely, in response to cyclical fluctuations in business activity. Since the community's basic objectives would presumably change only slowly—except in time of war or immediate threat of war—this policy would, with the same exception, lead to a relatively stable volume of expenditures on goods and services.[4]

3. A predetermined program of transfer expenditures, consisting of a statement of the conditions and terms under which relief and assistance and other transfer payments will be granted.[5] Such a program is exemplified by the present system of social security under which rules exist for the payment of old-age and unemployment insurance. The program should be changed only in response to alterations in the kind and level of transfer payments the community feels it should and can afford to make. The program should not be changed in response to cyclical fluctuations in business activity. Absolute outlays, however, will vary automatically over the cycle. They will tend to be high when unemployment is high and low when unemployment is low.[6]

4. A progressive tax system which places primary reliance on the personal income tax. Every effort should be made to collect as much of the tax bill as possible at source and to minimize the delay between the accrual of the tax liability and the actual collection of the tax. Rates, exemptions, etc., should be set in light of the expected yield at a level of income corresponding to reasonably full employment at a predetermined price level. The budget principle might be either that the hypothetical yield should balance government expenditure, including transfer payments (at the same hypothetical level of income) or that it should lead to a deficit sufficient to provide some specified secular increase in the quantity of money.[7] The tax structure should not be varied in response to cyclical fluctuations in business activity, though actual receipts will, of course, vary automatically.[8] Changes in

the tax structure should reflect changes in the level of public services or transfer payments the community chooses to have. A decision to undertake additional public expenditures should be accompanied by a revenue measure increasing taxes. Calculations of both the cost of additional public services or transfer payments and the yield of additional taxes should be made at the hypothetical level of income suggested above rather than at the actual level of income. The government would thus keep two budgets: the stable budget, in which all figures refer to the hypothetical income, and the actual budget. The principle of balancing outlays and receipts at a hypothetical income level would be substituted for the principle of balancing actual outlays and receipts.

II. OPERATION OF THE PROPOSAL

The essence of this fourfold proposal is that it uses automatic adaptations in the government contribution to the current income stream to offset, at least in part, changes in other segments of aggregate demand and to change appropriately the supply of money. It eliminates discretionary action in response to cyclical movements as well as some extraneous or perverse reactions of our present monetary and fiscal structure.[9] Discretionary action is limited to the determination of the hypothetical level of income underlying the stable budget; that is, essentially to the determination of a reasonably attainable objective. Some decision of this kind is unavoidable in drawing up the government's budget; the proposal involves a particular decision and makes it explicit. The determination of the income goal admittedly cannot be made entirely objective or mechanical. At the same time, this determination would need to be made only at rather long intervals—perhaps every five or ten years—and involves a minimum of forecasting. Further, as will be indicated later, errors in the income goal tend to be automatically neutralized and do not require a redetermination of the goal.

Under the proposal, government expenditures would be financed entirely by either tax revenues or the creation of money, that is, the issue of non-interest-bearing securities. Government would not issue interest-bearing securities to the public; the Federal Reserve System would not operate in the open market. This restriction of the sources of government funds seems reasonable for peacetime. The chief valid ground for paying interest to the public on government debt is to offset the inflationary pressure of abnormally high government expenditures when, for one reason or another, it is not feasible or desirable to levy sufficient taxes to do so. This was the justification for wartime issuance of interest-bearing securities, though, perversely, the rate of interest on these securities was pegged at a low level. It seems inapplicable in peacetime, especially if, as suggested, the volume of government expenditures on goods and services is kept relatively stable. Another reason sometimes given for issuing interest-bearing securities is that in a period of unemployment it is less deflationary to issue securities than to levy taxes. This is true. But it is still less deflationary to issue money.[10]

Deficits or surpluses in the government budget would be reflected dollar for dollar in changes in the quantity of money; and, conversely, the quantity of money would change only as a consequence of deficits or surpluses. A deficit means an increase in the quantity of money; a surplus, a decrease.[11]

Deficits or surpluses themselves become automatic consequences of changes in the level of business activity. When national money income is high, tax receipts will be large and transfer payments small; so a surplus will tend to be created, and the higher the level of income, the larger the surplus. This extraction of funds from the current income stream makes aggregate demand lower than it otherwise would be and reduces the volume of money, thereby tending to offset the factors making for a further increase in income. When national money income is low, tax receipts will be small and transfer payments large, so a deficit will tend to be created, and the lower the level of income, the larger the deficit. This addition of funds to the current income stream makes aggregate demand higher than it otherwise would be and increases the quantity of money, thereby tending to offset the factors making for a further decline in income.

The size of the effects automatically produced by changes in national income obviously depends on the range of activities government undertakes, since this will in turn determine the general order of magnitude of the government budget. Nonetheless, an essential element of the proposal is that the activities to be undertaken by government be determined entirely on other grounds. In part, this element is an immediate consequence of the motivation of the proposal. The motivation aside, however, it seems a desirable element of any proposal to promote stability. First, there is and can be no simple, reasonably objective, rule to determine the optimum share of activity that should be assigned to government—short of complete socialization—even if stability were the only objective. Changes in circumstances are likely to produce rapid and erratic variations in the share that seems desirable. But changes in the share assigned government are themselves likely to be destabilizing, both directly and through their adverse effects on anticipations. The attempt to adapt the magnitude of government operations to the requirements of stability may therefore easily introduce more instability than it corrects. Second, the share of activity assigned government is likely to have far more important consequences for other objectives—particularly political freedom and economic efficiency—than for stability.[12] Third, means other than changes in the share of activity assigned government are readily available for changing the size of the reaction to changes in income, if experience under the proposal should prove this desirable. And some of these means need not have anything like the same consequences for other objects.

Under the proposal, the aggregate quantity of money is automatically determined by the requirements of domestic stability. It follows that changes in the quantity of money cannot also be used—as they are in a fully operative gold standard—to achieve equilibrium in international trade. The two criteria will by no means always require the same changes in the quantity of money; when they conflict, one or the other must dominate. The decision, implicit in the framework recommended, to select domestic stability means that some other technique must be used to bring about adjustments to changes in the conditions of international trade. The international arrangement that seems the logical counterpart of the proposed framework is flexible exchange rates, freely determined in foreign exchange markets, preferably entirely by private dealings.[13]

III. EFFECT OF PROPOSAL UNDER PRESENT INSTITUTIONAL CONDITIONS

The fluctuations in the government contribution to the income stream under the proposed monetary and fiscal framework are clearly in the "right" direction. Nonetheless, it is not at all clear that they would, without additional institutional modifications, necessarily lead either to reasonably full employment or to a reasonable degree of stability. Rigidities in prices are likely to make this proposal, and indeed most if not all other proposals for attaining cyclical stability, inconsistent with reasonably full employment; and, when combined with lags in other types of response, to render extremely uncertain their effectiveness in stabilizing economic activity.

A. PRICE RIGIDITIES

Under existing circumstances, when many prices are moderately rigid, at least against declines, the monetary and fiscal framework described above cannot be expected to lead to reasonably full employment of resources, even though lags in other kinds of response are minor. The most that can be expected under such circumstances is a reasonably stable or moderately rising level of money income. As an extreme example, suppose that the economy is in a relatively stable position at reasonably full employment and with a roughly balanced actual government budget and that the great bulk of wage rates are rigid against downward pressure. Now, let there be a substantial rise in the wage rates of a particular group of workers as a consequence either of trade union action or of a sharp but temporary increase in the demand for that type of labor or decrease in its supply, and let this higher wage rate be rigid against downward pressure. Employment of resources as full as previously would imply a higher aggregate money income since, under the assumed conditions of rigidity, other resources would receive the same amount as previously whereas the workers whose wage rates rose would receive a larger aggregate amount if fully employed. But if this higher money income, which also of course would imply a higher price structure, were attained, the government would tend to have a surplus since receipts would rise by more than expenditures. There is nothing that has occurred that would, in the absence of other independent changes, offset the deflationary effect of the surplus. The assumed full employment position would not therefore be an equilibrium position. If attained by accident, the resultant budgetary surplus would reduce effective demand and, since prices are assumed rigid, the outcome could only be unemployment. The equilibrium level of income will be somewhat higher than before, primarily because transfer payments to the unemployed will be larger, so that some of the unemployment will be offset. But there is no mechanism for offsetting the rest. The only escape from this situation is to permit inflation.

As is widely recognized, the difficulty just described is present also in most other monetary and fiscal proposals; they, too, can produce full employment under such circumstances only by inflation. This dilemma often tends, however, to be concealed in their formulation, and, in practice, it seems fairly likely that inflation would result. The brute fact is that a rational economic program for a free enterprise system (and perhaps even for a collectivist system) must have flexibility of prices (including wages) as one of its cornerstones. This need is made clear by a proposal like the present. Moreover, the adoption of such a proposal would provide some assurance against cumulative deflation and thereby tend to make flexibility of prices a good deal easier to achieve since government support for monopolistic practices of special occupational and industrial groups derives in large measure from the obvious waste of general deflation and the need for protection against it.

B. LAGS IN RESPONSE

Our economy is characterized not only by price rigidities but also by significant lags in other types of response. These lags make impossible any definitive statement about the actual degree of stability likely to result from the operation of the monetary and fiscal framework described above. One could reasonably expect smaller fluctuations than currently exist; though our ignorance about lags and about the fundamental causes of business fluctuations prevents complete confidence even in this outcome. The lag between the creation of a government deficit and its effects on the behavior of consumers and producers could conceivably be so long and variable that the stimulating effects

of the deficit were often operative only after other factors had already brought about a recovery rather than when the initial decline was in progress. Despite intuitive feelings to the contrary, I do not believe we know enough to rule out completely this possibility. If it were realized, the proposed framework could intensify rather than mitigate cyclical fluctuations; that is, long and variable lags could convert the fluctuations in the government contribution to the income stream into the equivalent of an additional random disturbance.

About all one can say about this possibility is that the completely automatic proposal outlined above seems likely to do less harm under the circumstances envisaged than alternative proposals which provide for discretionary action in addition to automatic reactions. There is a strong presumption that these discretionary actions will in general be subject to longer lags than the automatic reactions and hence will be destabilizing even more frequently.

The basis for this presumption can best be seen by subdividing into three parts the total lag involved in any action to offset a disturbance: (1) the lag between the need for action and the recognition of this need; (2) the lag between recognition of the need for action and the taking of action; and (3) the lag between the action and its effects.

The first lag, which is nonexistent for automatic reactions of the kind here proposed, could be negative for discretionary proposals if it were possible to forecast accurately the economic changes that would occur in the absence of government action. In view of the record of forecasters, it hardly needs to be argued that it would be better to shun forecasting and rely instead on as prompt an evaluation of the current situation as possible. The lag between the need for action and the recognition of that need then becomes positive. Its exact magnitude depends on the particular discretionary proposal, though the past record of contemporary interpreters of business conditions indicates that it is not likely to be negligible.

The second lag is present even for automatic reactions because all taxes will not or cannot be collected at source simultaneously with the associated payments, and transfer payments will not or cannot be made immediately without some kind of a waiting period or processing period. It is clear, however, that this lag can be reduced to a negligible time by appropriate construction and administration of the system of taxes and transfer payments. For discretionary action, the length of the lag between the recognition of the need for action and the taking of action depends very much on the kind of action taken. Action can be taken very promptly to change the form or amount of the community's holdings of assets by open market purchases or sales of securities or by changes in rediscount rates or reserve requirements. A considerably longer time is required to change the net contribution of the government to the income stream by changing the tax structure. Even though advance prescription for alternative possibilities eliminates any delay in deciding what changes to make in tax rates, exemptions, kinds of taxes levied, or the like, administrative considerations will enforce a substantial delay before the change becomes effective. Taxpayers, businesses or individuals acting as intermediaries in collecting the taxes, and tax administrators must all be informed of the change and be given an opportunity to make the appropriate adjustments in their procedures; new forms must be printed or at least circulated; and so on.

The longest delay of all is likely to be involved in changing the net contribution of government to the income stream by changing government expenditure policy, particularly for goods and services. No matter how much advance planning may have been done, the rate of expenditure cannot be stepped up or curtailed overnight unless the number of names on the payroll is to be the only basis in terms of which the expenditure is to be controlled or judged. Time is involved in getting projects under way with any degree of efficiency; and considerable waste in ceasing work on projects abruptly.

The third lag, that between the action and its effects, is present and significant both for automatic reactions and discretionary actions, and little if anything can be done about it by either legal or administrative reform of the fiscal and monetary structure.[14] We have no trustworthy empirical evidence on the length of this lag for various kinds of action, and much further study of this problem is clearly called for. Some clues about the direction such study should take are furnished by a priori considerations which suggest, as a first approximation, that the order of the various policies with respect to the length of this lag is the reverse of their order with respect to the length of the lag between the recognition of the need for action and the taking of action. Changes in government expenditures on goods and services lead to almost immediate changes in the employment of the resources used to produce those goods and services. They have secondary effects through the changes thereby induced in the expenditures of the individuals owning the resources so employed.

The lag in these induced changes might be expected to be less than the lag in the adjustment of expenditures to changed taxes or to a changed amount or form of asset holdings. Changes in taxes make the disposable incomes of individuals larger or smaller than they would otherwise be. Individuals might be expected to react to a change in disposable income as a result of a tax change only slightly less rapidly than to a change in disposable income as a result of a change in aggregate income.

These indications are, however, none too trustworthy. These are likely to be important indirect effects that depend on such things as the kinds of goods and services directly affected by changed government expenditures, the incidence of the changes in disposable income that result from changed expenditures or taxes, and the means employed to finance government deficits. For example, if deficits are financed through increases in the quantity of money and surpluses are used to reduce the quantity of money part of the effect of changes in government expenditures or taxes will be produced by changes in interest rates and the kind and volume of assets held by the community. The entire effect of open-market operations, changes in rediscount rates and reserve requirements, and the like will be produced in this way, and it seems likely that these effects would take the longest to make themselves felt.

The automatic reactions embodied in the proposal here advanced operate in part like tax changes—in so far as tax receipts vary—and in part like expenditure changes—in so far as transfer payments vary; and like both of these, some part of their effect is through changes in the quantity of money. One might expect, therefore, that the lag between action and its effects would be roughly the same for automatic reactions than for discretionary monetary changes, and somewhat longer for automatic reactions than for discretionary changes in government expenditures on goods and services.

This analysis, much of which is admittedly highly conjectural, suggests that the total lag is definitely longer for discretionary monetary or tax changes than for automatic reactions, since each of the three parts into which the total lag has been subdivided is longer. There is doubt about the relative length of the total lag only for discretionary expenditure changes. Even for these, however, it seems doubtful that the shorter lag between action and its effects can more than offset the longer lag between the need for action and the taking of action.

Given less extreme conditions than those required to convert the present proposal into a destabilizing influence, the reduction achieved in the severity of fluctuations would depend on the extent and rapidity of price adjustments, the nature of the responses of individuals to these price changes and to the changes in their incomes and asset holdings resulting from the induced surpluses or deficits, and the lags in such responses. If these were such as to make the system operate reasonably well, the improvement would tend to be cumulative, since the experience of damped fluctuations would lead to patterns of expectations on the part of both businessmen and consumers that would make it rational for them to take action that would damp fluctuations still more. This favorable result would occur, however, only if the proposed system operated reasonably well without such aid; hence, in my view, this proposal, and all others as well, should be judged primarily on their direct effects, not on their indirect effects in stimulating a psychological climate favorable to stability. It must be granted, however, that the present proposal is less likely to stimulate such a favorable psychological climate than a proposal which has a simpler and more easily understood goal, for example, a proposal which sets a stable price level as its announced goal. *If the business world were sufficiently confident of the ability of the government to achieve the goal*, it would have a strong incentive to behave in such a way as greatly to simplify the government's task.

IV. IMPLICATIONS OF THE PROPOSAL IF PRICES ARE FLEXIBLE AND LAGS IN RESPONSE MINOR

The ideal possibilities of the monetary and fiscal framework proposed in this paper, and the stabilizing economic forces on which these possibilities depend, can be seen best if we put aside the difficulties that have been detaining us and examine the implications of the proposal in an economy in which prices of both products and factors of production are flexible[15] and lags in other types of response are minor. In such an economy, the monetary and fiscal system described above would tend toward an equilibrium characterized by reasonably full employment.

To describe the forces at work, let us suppose that the economy is initially in a position of reasonably full employment with a balanced actual budget and is subjected to a disturbance producing a decline in aggregate money demand that would be permanent if no other changes occurred.[16] The initial effect of the decline in aggregate demand will be a decline in sales and the piling up of inventories in at least some parts of the economy; followed shortly by unemployment and price declines caused by the attempt to reduce inventories to the desired level. The lengthening of the list of unemployed will increase government transfer payments; the loss of income by the unemployed will reduce government tax receipts. The deficit created in this way is a net contribution by the government to the income stream which directly offsets some of the decline in aggregate demand, thereby preventing unemployment from becoming as large as it otherwise would and serving as a shock absorber while more fundamental correctives come into play.

These more fundamental correctives, aside from changes in relative prices and interest rates, are (1) a decline in the general level of prices which affects (a) the real value of the community's assets and (b) the government contribution to the income stream, and (2) an increase in the stock of money.

The decline in the general level of prices that follows the initial decline in aggregate demand will clearly raise the real value of the community's stock of money and government bonds since the nominal value of these assets will not decrease. The real value of the remainder of the community's assets may be expected to remain roughly the same,

so the real value of the total stock of assets will rise.[17] The rise in the real value of assets will lessen the need for additional saving and hence increase the fraction of any given level of real income that the community will wish to consume. This force, in principle, would alone be sufficient to assure full employment even if the government maintained a rigidly balanced actual budget and kept the quantity of money constant, since there would presumably always be some price level at which the community could be made to feel rich enough to spend on consumption whatever fraction or multiple of its current income is required to yield an aggregate demand sufficient to permit full employment.

This effect of a lower price level in increasing the fraction of current private (disposable) income devoted to consumption is reinforced by its effect on the government's contribution to the income stream. So long as the price level, and with it money income, is below its initial level, the government will continue to run a deficit. This will be true even if employment is restored to its initial level, so that transfer payments and loss in tax receipts on account of unemployment are eliminated. The tax structure is progressive, and exemptions, rates, etc., are expressed in absolute dollar amounts. Receipts will therefore fall more than in proportion to the fall in the price level; expenditures, at most, proportionately.[18] Because of the emergence of such a deficit, the price decline required to restore employment will be smaller than if the government were to maintain a rigidly balanced actual budget, and this will be true even aside from the influence of the deficit on the stock of money. The reason is that the price level will have to fall only to the point at which the amount the community desires to add to its hoards equals the government deficit, rather than to the point at which the community desires to add nothing to its hoards.[19]

The decline in the price level may restore the initial level of employment through the combined effects of the increased average propensity to consume and the government deficit. But so long as a deficit exists, the position attained is not an equilibrium position. The deficit is financed by the issue of money. The resultant increase in the aggregate stock of money must further raise the real value of the community's stock of assets and hence the average propensity to consume. This is the same effect as that discussed above except that it is brought about by an increase in the absolute stock of money rather than by a decline in prices. Like the corresponding effect produced by a decline in prices, the magnitude of this effect is, in principle, unlimited. The rise in the stock of money and hence in the average propensity to consume will tend to raise prices and reduce the deficit. If we suppose no change to occur other than the one introduced to start the analysis going, the final adjustment would be attained when prices had risen sufficiently to yield a roughly balanced actual budget.

A disturbance increasing aggregate money demand would bring into play the same forces operating in the reverse direction: the increase in employment would reduce transfer payments and raise tax receipts, thus creating a surplus to offset part of the increase in aggregate demand; the rise in prices would decrease the real value of the community's stock of money and hence the fraction of current income spent on consumption; the rise in prices would also mean that even after "overemployment" was eliminated, the government would run a surplus that would tend to offset further the initial increase in aggregate demand;[20] and, finally, the surplus would reduce the stock of money.

As this analysis indicates, the proposed fiscal and monetary framework provides defense in depth against changes in aggregate demand. The first line of defense is the adjustment of transfer payments and tax receipts to changes in employment. This eases the shock while the defense is taken over by changes in prices. These raise or lower the real value of the community's assets and thereby raise or lower the fraction of income consumed. They also produce a government deficit or surplus in addition to the initial deficit or surplus resulting from the effect of changes in employment on transfer payments and tax receipts. The final line of defense is the cumulative effect of the deficits or surpluses on the stock of money. These changes in the stock of money tend to restore prices to their initial level. In some measure, of course, these defenses all operate simultaneously; yet their main effects are likely to occur in the temporal order suggested in the preceding discussion.

Even given flexible prices, the existence of the equilibrating mechanism described does not of course mean that the economy will in fact achieve relative stability. This depends in addition on the number and magnitude of the disturbances to which the economy is subject, the speed with which the equilibrating forces operate, and the importance of such disequilibrating forces as adverse price expectations. If the lags of response are minor, and initial perverse reactions unimportant, adjustments would be completed rapidly and there would be no opportunity for disequilibria to cumulate, so that relative stability would be attained. Even in this most favorable case, however, the equilibrating mechanism does not prevent disturbances from arising and does not counteract their effects instantaneously—as, indeed, no system can in the absence of ability to predict everything in advance with perfect accuracy. What the equilibrating mechanism does accomplish is, first, to keep governmental monetary and fiscal operations from themselves contributing disturbances and, second, to provide an automatic mechanism for adapting the system to the disturbances that occur.

Given flexible prices, there would be a tendency for automatic neutralization of any errors in the hypothetical income level assumed or in the calculations of the volume of expenditures and revenues at the hypothetical income level. Further, it would ultimately be of no great importance exactly what decision was reached about the relation to establish between expenditures and revenue at the hypothetical income level (i.e., whether exactly to balance, to strive for a deficit sufficient to provide a predetermined secular increase in the quantity of money, etc.). Suppose, for example that errors in the assumed income level, the calculated volume of expenditures and receipts, and the relation established between expenditures and receipts combined to produce a deficit larger than was consistent with stable prices. The resulting inflationary pressure would be analogous to that produced by an external disturbance and the same forces would come into play to counteract it. The result would be that prices would rise and the level of income tend to stabilize at a higher level than the hypothetical level initially assumed.

Similarly, the monetary and fiscal framework described above provides for adjustment not only to cyclical changes but also to secular changes. I do not put much credence in the doctrine of secular stagnation or economic maturity that is now so widely held. But let us assume for the sake of argument that this doctrine is correct, that there has been such a sharp secular decline in the demand for capital that, at the minimum rate of interest technically feasible, the volume of investment at a full-employment level of income would be very much less than the volume of savings that would be forthcoming at this level of income and at the current price.[21] The result would simply be that the equilibrium position would involve a recurrent deficit sufficient to provide the hoards being demanded by savers. Of course, this would not really be a long-run

equilibrium position, since the gradual increase in the quantity of money would increase the aggregate real value of the community's stock of money and thereby of assets, and this would tend to increase the fraction of any given level of real income consumed. As a result, there would tend to be a gradual rise in prices and the level of money income and a gradual reduction in the deficit.[22]

V. CONCLUSION

In conclusion, I should like to emphasize the modest aim of the proposal. It does not claim to provide full employment in the absence of successful measures to make prices of final goods and of factors of production flexible. It does not claim to eliminate entirely cyclical fluctuations in output and employment. Its claim to serious consideration is that it provides a stable framework of fiscal and monetary action, that it largely eliminates the uncertainty and undesirable political implications of discretionary action by governmental authorities, that it provides for adaptation of the governmental sector to changes occurring in other sectors of the economy of a kind designed to offset the effects of these changes, and that the proposed fiscal and monetary framework is consistent with the long-run considerations stated at the outset of this paper. It is not perhaps a proposal that one would consider at all optimum if our knowledge of the fundamental causes of cyclical fluctuations were considerably greater than I, for one, think it to be; it is a proposal that involves minimum reliance on uncertain and untested knowledge.

The proposal has of course its dangers. Explicit control of the quantity of money by government and explicit creation of money to meet actual government deficits may establish a climate favorable to irresponsible government action and to inflation. The principle of a balanced stable budget may not be strong enough to offset these tendencies. This danger may well be greater for this proposal than for some others, yet in some measure it is common to most proposals to mitigate cyclical fluctuations. It can probably be avoided only by moving in a completely different direction, namely, toward an entirely metallic currency, elimination of any government control of the quantity of money, and the re-enthronement of the principle of a balanced actual budget.

The proposal may not succeed in reducing cyclical fluctuations to tolerable proportions. The forces making for cyclical fluctuations may be so stubborn and strong that the kind of automatic adaptations contained in the proposal are insufficient to offset them to a tolerable degree. I do not see how it is possible to know now whether this is the case. But even if it should prove to be, the changes suggested are almost certain to be in the right direction and, in addition, to provide a more satisfactory framework on which to build further action.

A proposal like the present one, which is concerned not with short-run policy but with structural reform, should not be urged on the public unless and until it has withstood the test of professional criticism. It is in this spirit that the present paper is published.

NOTES

1. The reason for restricting the discussion to the federal government is simply that it alone has ultimate monetary powers, not any desire to minimize the role of smaller governmental units. Indeed, for the achievement of the long-run objectives stated above it is highly desirable that the maximum amount of government activity be in the hands of the smaller governmental units to achieve as much decentralization of political power as possible.

2. This proposal was advanced by Henry C. Simons. . . .

3. The adoption of 100 per cent reserves is essential if the proposed framework is to be entirely automatic. It should be noted, however, that the same results could, in principle, be achieved in a fractional reserve system through discretionary authority. In order to accomplish this, the monetary authorities would have to adopt the rule that the quantity of money should be increased only when the government has a deficit, and then by the amount of the deficit, and should be decreased only when the government has a surplus, and then by the amount of the surplus.

4. The volume of expenditures might remain stable either in money or real terms. The principle of determining the volume of expenditures by the community's objectives would lead to a stable real volume of expenditures on current goods and services. On the other hand, the usual legislative procedure in budget making is to grant fixed sums of money, which would lead to stability of money expenditures and provides a slight automatic contra-cyclical flexibility. If the volume of real expenditures were stabilized, money expenditures would vary directly with prices.

5. These transfer payments might perhaps more appropriately be regarded as negative revenue.

6. It may be hoped that the present complex structure of transfer payments will be integrated into a single scheme co-ordinated with the income tax and designed to provide a universal floor to personal incomes. But this is a separate issue.

7. These specifications about the hypothetical level of income to be used and the budget principle to be followed are more definite and dogmatic than is justified. In principle, the economic system could ultimately adjust to any tax structure and expenditure policy, no matter what level of income or what budget principle they were initially based on, provided that the tax structure and expenditure policy remained stable. That is, there corresponds some secular position appropriate to each possible tax structure and expenditure policy. The level of income and the best budget principle to choose depend therefore on short-run adjustment considerations: what choice would require the least difficult adjustment? Moreover, the level of income and budget principle must be chosen jointly: the same final result can obviously be obtained by combining a high hypothetical income with a surplus budget principle or a low hypothetical income with a deficit budget principle or

by any number of intermediate combinations. My own conjecture is that the particular level of income and budget principles suggested above are unlikely to lead to results that would require radical short-run adjustments to attain the corresponding secular position. Unfortunately, our knowledge about the relevant economic interrelationships is too meager to permit more than reasonably informed conjecture. See Section IV below, especially footnote . . . [20].

8. The principle of setting taxes so as to balance the budget at a high level of employment was suggested by Beardsley Ruml and H. Chr. Sonne, *Fiscal and Monetary Policy*, National Planning Pamphlet no. 24 (July, 1944).

Since the present paper was written, the Committee for economic Development has issued a policy statement in which it makes essentially the same tax and expenditure recommendations—that is, it calls for adoption of a stable tax structure capable of balancing the budget at a high level of employment, a stable expenditure policy, and primary reliance on automatic adjustments of absolute revenue and expenditures to provide cyclical stability. They call this policy the "stabilizing budget policy." The chief difference between the present proposal and the C.E.D. proposal is that the C.E.D. is silent on the monetary framework and almost silent on public debt policy, whereas the present proposal covers both. Presumably the C.E.D. plans to cover monetary and debt policy in separate statements still to be issued. . . .

9. For example, the tendency under the existing system of fractional reserve banking for the total volume of money to change when there is a change in the proportion of its total stock of money the community wishes to hold in the form of deposits; the tendency to reduce tax rates and increase government expenditures in booms and to do the reverse in depressions; and the tendency for the government to borrow from individuals at the same time as the Federal Reserve System is buying government bonds on the open market.

10. [*Reference deleted.*] This paragraph deliberately avoids the question of the payment of interest to banks on special issues of government bonds, as has been proposed in some versions of the 100 per cent reserve proposal. The fundamental issue involved in judging such proposals is whether government should subsidize the use of deposit money and a system of check clearance and if so, what form the subsidy should take.

The large volume of government bonds now outstanding raises one of the most serious problems in accomplishing the transition from the present framework. This problem would be eased somewhat by the monetization of bonds that would occur in the process of going over to 100 per cent reserves. But there would still remain a substantial volume. Two alternatives suggest themselves: (1) freeze the volume of debt at some figure, preferably by converting it into perpetuities ("consols"); (2) use the monetization of the debt as a means of providing a secular increase in the quantity of money. Under the second plan, which, on a first view, seems more attractive, the principle of balancing the stable budget would be adopted and the government would commit itself to retiring, through the issuance of new money, a predetermined amount of the public debt annually. The amount to be retired would be determined so as to achieve whatever secular increase in the quantity of money seems desirable. This problem, however, requires much additional study.

11. These statements refer, of course, to the ultimate operation of the proposal. Under the second of the alternatives suggested in the preceding footnote, the change in the quantity of money during the transitional period would equal the excess of government expenditures over receipts plus the predetermined amount of money issued to retire debt.

12. An example of the relevance of these two points is provided by the tendency during the 'thirties to recommend an increase in the progressiveness of the tax structure as a means of increasing the propensity to consume and hence, it was argued, employmnet. Applied to the postwar period, the same argument would call for a shift to regressive taxes, yet I wonder if many economists would wish to recommend regressive taxes on these grounds.

13. Though here presented as a byproduct of the proposed domestic framework, flexible exchange rates can be defended directly. Indeed, it would be equally appropriate to present the proposed domestic framework as a means of implementing flexible exchange rates. The heart of the matter is that domestic and international monetary and trade arrangements are part of one whole.

14. Reforms of other types, for example,

reforms increasing the flexibility of prices, might affect this lag.

15. The concept of flexible prices, though one we use continually and can hardly avoid using, is extremely difficult to define precisely. Fortunately, a precise definition is not required for the argument that follows. All that is necessary for the argument is that there there be a "substantial" range of prices that are not "rigid" because of long-term contracts or organized noncontractual agreements to maintain price and that these prices should react reasonably quickly to changes in long-run conditions of demand or supply. It is not necessary that there be "perfect" flexibility of prices, however that might be defined, or that contracts involving prices be subject to change at will, or that every change in long-run conditions of demand or supply be reflected instantaneously in market price.

16. The same analysis would apply to disturbances producing only a temporary decline. The reason for assuming a permanent decline is to trace through the entire process of adjustment to a new equilibrium position.

17. If the real value of other assets of the community should fall, this would simply mean that the price level would have to fall farther in order to raise the real value of the community's total stock of assets. Note that under the proposed framework, all money in the community is either a direct government obligation (nondeposit currency) or is backed one hundred per cent by a direct government obligation (deposits in the central bank). If this analysis were to be applied to a fractional reserve system, the assets whose aggregate real value could be guaranteed to rise with no directly offsetting fall in the real value of private assets would be the total amount of government obligations (currency and bonds) held outside the treasury and central bank. . . .

18. The effect of the lower price level on expenditures depends somewhat on the precise expenditure and transfer policy adopted. If, as is called for by the principle of determining the expenditure program by the community's objectives, the real volume of government expenditures on goods and services is kept cyclically stable and if the program of transfer payments is also stated in real terms, expenditures will decline proportionately. If government expenditures on goods and services are kept cyclically stable in dollar terms, or the program of transfer ex-

penditures is stated in dollar terms, expenditures will decline less than proportionately.

19. If the real volume of government expenditures on goods and services is kept cyclically stable and the transfer program is also stated in real terms, the aggregate expenditures of government under fixed expenditure and transfer programs would tend to be the same fraction of the full-employment income of society no matter what the price levels. This fraction would be the maximum net contribution the government could make to the income stream no matter how low prices, and with them money income and government receipts, fell. Consequently, this force alone would be limited in magnitude and might not, even in principle, be able to offset every disturbance. If either program is in absolute terms, there would be no limit to the fraction that the government contribution could constitute of the total income stream.

An alternative way to describe this effect is in terms of the relation between the expected expenditures and receipts of consumers, business, and government. It is a condition of equilibrium that the sum of the desired expenditures of these groups equal the sum of their receipts. If the government maintains a rigidly balanced budget, equilibrium requires that consumers and business together plan to spend what they receive (i.e., not seek to add to their money hoards). If the government runs a deficit, consumers and business together need not plan to spend all they receive; equilibrium requires that their planned expenditures fall short of their receipts by the amount of the deficit (i.e., that they seek to add to their hoards per period the amount of the deficit).

20. The limit to the possible effect of the surplus on the current income stream would be set by the character of the tax structure, since there would probably be some maximum percentage of the aggregate income that could be taken by taxes no matter how high the price level and the aggregate income.

21. Because of the effect discussed above of price changes on the real value of assets, and in this way on the average propensity to consume, it seems to me that such a state of affairs would not lead to secular unemployment even if the quantity of money were kept constant, provided that prices are flexible (which is the reason for including the qualifications "at the current price level" in the

sentence to which this footnote is attached). But I am for the moment accepting the point of view of those who deny the existence or importance of this equilibrating force. Moreover, if the quantity of money were constant, the adjustment would be made entirely through a secular decline in prices, admittedly a difficult adjustment. Once again changes in the government contribution to the income stream and through this in the quantity of money can reduce the extent of the required price change.

22. This and the preceding paragraph, in particular, and this entire section, in general, suggest a problem that deserves investigation and to which I have no satisfactory answer, namely, the characteristics of the system of equations implicit in the proposal and of their equilibrium solution. It is obvious that under strictly stationary conditions, including a stationary population, the equilibrium solution would involve constancy of prices, income per head, etc., and a balanced actual budget. The interesting question is whether there is any simple description of the equilibrium solution under specified dynamic situations. For example, are there circumstances, and if so what are they, under which the equilibrium solution will tend to involve constant money income per head with declining prices, or constant prices with rising money income per head, etc? It is obvious that no such simple description will suffice in general, but there may well be broad classes of circumstances under which one or another will.